DATABASE MANAGEMENT SYSTEMS (DBMS)

DATABASE MANAGEMENT SYSTEMS (DBMS)

[A Practical Approach]

• Concepts • Principles • Case Studies • Experiments (SQL)

For the Students of B.E./B.Tech., M.E./M.Tech. (CSE/IT) BCA and MCA

Dr. RAJIV CHOPRA

Ph.D. (Computer Science)

Assistant Professor (CSE/IT)

Guru Tegh Bahadur Institute of Technology (GTBIT), Delhi

(Affiliated to Guru Gobind Singh Indraprastha University, Delhi)

S Chand And Company Limited

(ISO 9001 Certified Company)

S Chand And Company Limited

(ISO 9001 Certified Company)

Head Office: D-92, Sector–2, Noida – 201301, U.P. (India), Ph. 91-120-4682700

Registered Office: A-27, 2nd Floor, Mohan Co-operative Industrial Estate, New Delhi – 110 044, Phone: 011-49731800

www.**schandpublishing.com;** e-mail: **info@schandpublishing.com**

Marketing Offices:

Chennai	:	Ph: 23632120; chennai@schandpublishing.com
Guwahati	:	Ph: 2738811, 2735640; guwahati@schandpublishing.com
Hyderabad	:	Ph: 40186018; hyderabad@schandpublishing.com
Jalandhar	:	Ph: 4645630; jalandhar@schandpublishing.com
Kolkata	:	Ph: 23357458, 23353914; kolkata@schandpublishing.com
Lucknow	:	Ph: 4003633; lucknow@schandpublishing.com
Mumbai	:	Ph: 25000297; mumbai@schandpublishing.com
Patna	:	Ph: 2260011; patna@schandpublishing.com

First Edition 2010
Subsequent Editions and Reprints 2011, 2012, 2013, 2014
Fifth Revised Edition 2016
Reprints 2018, 2019, 2020, 2021 (Twice), 2022 (Thrice), 2023, 2024 (Twice)

Reprint 2025

ISBN: 978-93-856-7634-5 **Product Code:** H3DMS50INFT10ENAE16O

PRINTED IN INDIA

By Vikas Publishing House Private Limited, Plot 20/4, Site-IV, Industrial Area Sahibabad, Ghaziabad – 201 010 and Published by S Chand And Company Limited, A-27, 2nd Floor, Mohan Co-operative Industrial Estate, New Delhi – 110 044.

PREFACE

It is indeed a matter of great pleasure to write this book entitled **Database Management Systems (DBMS)—A Practical Approach.** A DBMS forms the backbone of any software project. Without DBMS you risk building a system that is inefficient, slow and unreliable. This is so because DBMS is a second-tier in our multi-tier applications. It is a back-end tool available to us.

Without DBMS it is not possible to implement the client-server technology. The programmer must be aware of the methods and the techniques used by different database management systems. If GUI forms the front-end of any application, DBMS forms its back-end. It is desirable to put emphasis on the practical part of the subject rather than only the theory.

I am flattered that this book is one of the mandatory references on DBMS. Many books on DBMS are available in the market, they tend to be dry and formal. They are often difficult and boring for students. They lack freshness as they just give theories on DBMS and as such no practical knowledge is given. My approach is to make DBMS more interesting and concrete by giving practical examples, CASE studies and the experiments to be performed in the DBMS lab. The contents of this book can be used by practitioners to understand the state-of-the-practice in the software industry.

Unlike other books, I have written this book in such a simple and lucid style that makes the student feel as if the teacher is sitting behind him and guiding him. This book assimilates a comprehensive matter on the subject as it is bolstered with numerous examples. It covers the syllabi of GGSIPU, DU, UPTU, PTU, VTU, IGNOU, WBTU, KGTU, MGTU, SU and many other technical universities. It can be used as a textbook for B.E./B.Tech. (CSE/IT/EEE/ECE) and BCA courses of these universities. I have provided sufficient academic rigour to satisfy the contents of the syllabi of all the universities.

Last but not least, I would like to mention that no one is hundred percent accurate in this world, so any suggestions for further improvement of the book will be highly acknowledged.

Dr. Rajiv Chopra

(Email: raj_74chopra2004@yahoo.com)

ACKNOWLEDGEMENTS

A well-informed mind is the best security against the contagion of folly and of vice. The vacant mind is ever on the watch for relief, and ready to plunge into error, to escape from the languor of idleness.

First of all, I would like to thank the Almighty God for showering so many blessings on me. As no task is a single man's effort, various factors, situations and persons integrate to provide the background in the accomplishment of a task. I take this opportunity to express my deep sense of gratitude to all people who have been very cooperative during the preparation of this manuscript. I wish to acknowledge my Director, my colleagues and my students for motivating me to write this book.

I am thankful to the editorial team of S. Chand & Company Pvt. Ltd., New Delhi for their sincere cooperation and generous support in bringing out this book.

Finally, I am indebted to my parents Dr. J.R. Chopra and Mrs. Sushma Chopra for their motivation, encouragement and support in the preparation of this manuscript. I would also like to acknowledge my wife Mrs. Shakti Chopra and kids Arjeesh and Arshitha for their sincere cooperation.

Dr. Rajiv Chopra

DBMS—A Practical Approach

This book is useful for the following courses:

- B.Tech. (CSE)—4th Sem., GGSIPU, Delhi.
- B.Tech. (IT)—4th Sem., GGSIPU, Delhi.
- B.Tech. (ECE/EEE)—4th Sem., GGSIPU, Delhi.
- B.Tech. (CSE)—4th Sem., BPUT, Orissa.
- B.E. (CSE)—7th Sem., Nagpur University.
- B.Tech. (CSE/IT)—2nd Sem., JNTU, Hyderabad.
- B.E. (CSE)—8th Sem., DCE (DU).
- B.Tech. (CSE)—5th Sem., Singhania University.
- B.Tech. (CSE)—4th Sem., UPTU.
- MCA—3rd Sem., Delhi University (DU).
- M.Tech. (CSE/IT)—3rd Sem., GGSIPU, Delhi.
- M.Tech. (IT)—2nd Sem., VTU.
- M.Tech. (CSE)—1st Sem., VTU.
- M.Tech. (IS)—1st Sem., NSIT (DU), Delhi.
- MCA—3rd Sem., PTU.
- MCA—5th Sem., Pune University
- MBA—4th Sem., UPTU.

CONTENTS

UNIT–I

Chapter 1. Introduction to DBMS **1 – 86**

1.0 Basic Concepts 1
1.1 Conceptual Database Design 6
1.1.1 Database Administrator (DBA) 6
1.1.2 Database Users 7
1.1.3 Characteristics of Database Approach 7
1.1.4 Database Systems 7
1.1.5 Database Architecture 7
1.1.6 DBMS Components (Actors) 8
1.2 Data Models 10
1.2.1 Schemas and Instances 10
1.2.2 DBMS Architecture/3-tier Architecture/ANSI-SPARC Architecture 11
1.2.3 Data Independence 15
1.2.4 Database Languages 16
1.2.5 Procedure for Database Access 19
1.2.6 Database Structure 20
1.3 Overview of Hierarchical, Network and Relational DBMS 22
1.3.1 Comparison of the Three Models in Tabular Form 32
1.3.2 Comparison of the Three Models in Tabular Form (on the Basis of Operations) 33
1.3.3 Which Data Model to Select ? 33
1.4 Data Modeling Using ER-Model 33
1.4.1 Basic Terminology Related to ER-Model 34
1.4.2 Notations Used in ER-diagrams 37
1.4.3 Strong and Weak Entity Sets 39
1.5 Generalization, Specialization and Aggregation 40
1.6 Translating Your ER-Model into Relational Model 43
1.7 Some Solved Examples 44
- Summary 62
- Multiple Choice Questions [MCQs] 62
- Answers 64
- Conceptual Short Questions with Answers 64
- Exercise Questions 82

UNIT–II

Chapter 2. Relational Model, Languages and Systems **87 — 130**

2.0 Introduction 87
2.1 Terminologies Related to Relational Model 87
2.2 Types of Keys 88
2.3 Relational Integrity Rule 91
2.3.1 Entity Integrity Rule 91
2.3.2 Referential Integrity Rule 92
2.4 Codd's Rules 93
2.5 Views and their Purpose 95
2.6 Relational Algebra 95
2.7 Relational Calculus 107
2.8 Comparison of Relational Algebra and Relational Calculus in Tabular Form 108
2.9 QUEL and QBE 109
2.10 Solved Examples on QUEL and QBE 111
- Summary 112
- Multiple Choice Questions [MCQs] 112
- Answers 114
- Conceptual Short Questions with Answers 114
- Exercise Questions 126

Chapter 3. SQL **131 — 231**

3.0 Introduction 131
3.1 Features of SQL 131
3.2 Data Definition Language (DDL) 132
3.3 Data Manipulation Language (DML) 136
3.4 Views 142
3.5 Functions in SQL 144
3.6 RollBack, Commit and Savepoint 149
3.7 Indexes in SQL 149
3.8 SQL ODBC and JDBC 153
3.9. MS SQL Server 7 154
3.10 Solved Examples on SQL 158
3.11 Group By and Having Clauses 169
3.12 Subqueries 170
3.13 Reports Using SQL * Plus 172
3.14 PL/SQL 175
- Summary 201
- Multiple Choice Questions [MCQs] 201
- Answers 202
- Conceptual Short Questions with Answers 202
- Exercise Questions 227

UNIT–III

Chapter 4. Normaiization **232 – 299**

4.0 Introduction 232
4.1 Terminologies Related to Normalization 233
4.2 First Normal Form (1NF) 237
4.3 Second Normal Form (2NF) 241
4.4 Third Normal Form (3NF) and BCNF 242
4.5 Fourth Normal Form (4NF) and MVDs 251
4.6 Fifth Normal Form (5NF)/PJNF 255
4.7 Closure of A Set of FDs and MVDs 257
4.8 Minimal or Canonical Cover of FDs 261
4.9 Loss Less Join 264
4.10 Dependency Preserving Decomposition 264
4.11 Overall Flowchart of Normalization 264
4.11 Examples on Normalization Based on FDS and MVDS 269
4.13 Domain Key Normal Form (DKNF) 274
- Summary 275
- Multiple Choice Questions [MCQs] 275
- Answers 276
- Conceptual Short Questions with Answers 277
- Exercise Questions 295

Chapter 5. Oracle 8 Architecture **300 – 307**

5.0 Introduction 300
5.1 Oracle Software Structure 300
5.2 Database Storage 303
5.3 Shared Database Access Mechanism 303
5.4 Database Protection 304
- Summary 304
- Multiple Choice Questions [MCQs] 305
- Answers 305
- Conceptual Short Questions with Answers 305
- Exercise Questions 307

UNIT–IV

Chapter 6. Transaction Management **308 – 339**

6.0 Introduction 308
6.1 Transaction Concept and Properties 308
6.2 States of a Transaction 311

6.3 Concurrent Executions 311
6.4 Scheduling of transactions 312
6.5 Operations Conflicts 314
6.6 Testing for Serializability 317
6.7 Three Problems of Concurrency Control–Case Studies 321
- Summary 324
- Multiple choice Questions [MCQs] 325
- Answers 325
- Conceptual Short Questions with Answers 325
- Exercise Questions 338

Chapter 7. Concurrency Control Techniques 340 – 381

7.0 Introduction 340
7.1 Lock-based Protocols 340
7.2 Deadlock Handling 351
7.3 Recovery System 353
7.4 Failure Classification 353
7.5 Storage Structure 354
- Summary 355
- Multiple Choice Questions [MCQs] 355
- Answers 356
- Conceptual Short Questions with Answers 357
- Exercise Questions 379

Chapter 8. Recovery and Atomicity 382 – 409

8.0 Introduction 382
8.1 Categorization of Recovery Algorithms 382
8.2 Terminologies Used 383
8.3 Log-based Recovery 384
8.4 Shadow Paging 389
8.5 Recovery with Concurrent Transaction 397
8.6 Check Points/Syncpoints/Save Points 398
- Summary 400
- Multiple Choice Questions [MCQs] 400
- Answers 401
- Conceptual Short Questions with Answers 401
- Exercise Questions 408

UNIT–V

Chapter 9. Buffer Management 410 – 427

9.0 Introduction 410
9.1 Query Processing Overview 410

9.2 Measures of Query Cost 411
9.3 Evaluation of Expressions 412
9.4 Transformation Rules 413
9.5 Estimating Cardinalities 414
- Summary 419
- Multiple Choice Questios [MCQs] 419
- Answers 420
- Conceptual Short Questions with Answers 420
- Exercise Questions 427

Chapter 10. OODBMS — Object - Oriented DBMS 428 — 483

10.0 Introduction 428
10.1 Concepts of OODBMS 428
10.2 Distributed DBMS 446
10.3 Comparison of DBMS and DDBMS 456
10.4 Query Processing in Distributed Databases 456
10.5 Comparision of Parallel and Distributed Databases (DDB's) 458
10.6 Case Study on–DB2 458
- Summary 475
- Multiple Choice Questions [MCQs] 475
- Answers 476
- Conceptual Short Questions with Answers 476
- Exercise Questions 483

Chapter 11. Parallel Databases 484 — 498

11.1 Design of Parallel Databases 484
11.2 Parallel Query Evaluation 487
11.3 Advantages of Parallel Databases 487
11.4 Disadvantages of Parallel Databases 487
11.5 Elements of Parallel Database Processing 487
11.6 Parallelism in Query 488
- Summary 491
- Multiple Choice Questions [MCQs] 492
- Answers 492
- Conceptual Short Questions with Answers 492
- Exercise Questions 498

Chapter 12. Web Databases 499 — 525

12.0 Introduction 499
12.1 Accessing Database through the Web 499
12.2 Informix—Web Servers 500
12.3 XMl Database 501
12.4 Case Study on Internet History 502

12.4.1 Introduction 502
12.4.2 Goal 1 : Experimental Research for Advanced Network Technologies 504
12.4.3 Goal 2 : Next Generation Network Testbed 510
12.4.4 Goal 3 : Revolutionary Applications 515
12.4.5 NGI Initiative Accomplishments at DARPA 517
12.4.6 Conclusion 523
• Summary 523
• Multiple Choice Questions [MCQs] 523
• Answers 524
• Conceptual Short Questions with Answers 524
• Exercise Questions 525

Chapter 13. Advanced Topics in DBMS 526 – 534

13.0 Introduction 526
13.1 Deductive Databases 526
13.2 Multimedia Databases 526
13.3 Mobile Databases 527
13.4 Digital Databases 528
• Summary 529
• Multiple Choice Questions [MCQs] 529
• Answers 529
• Conceptual Short Questions with Answers 529
• Exercise Questions 534

Chapter 14. Case Study – Dataware Housing and Data Mining 535 – 567

Conceptual Short Questions with Answers **568**

Appendix-A : Examination Question Papers **573 – 580**
Appendix-B : Syllabus and Lecture Plan **583 – 584**
Appendix-C : Glossary of DBMS **587 – 599**
Appendix-D : Experiments in DBMS Lab **603 – 626**
Appendix-E : DBMS Project and Database Design Cycle **627 – 665**
Appendix-F : Bibliography **669**

UNIT-I

CHAPTER 1

Introduction to Database Management Systems

1.0 BASIC CONCEPTS

At a Conference in 1990, Silberschatz quoted on database systems—"The history of database system research is one of exceptional productivity and starting economic impact. Barely 20 years old as a basic science research field, database research has fueled an information services industry estimated at $10 billion per year in the U.S. alone. Achievements in database research underpin fundamental advances in the communication systems, transportation and logistics, financial management, knowledge-based systems (KBS), accessibility to scientific literature and a host of other civilian and defense applications. They also serve as the foundation for considerable progress in the basic science fields ranging from computing to biology."

The Database Management System (DBMS) is now the underlying framework of the information system. It has changed the way that many organizations operate. The database system remains a very active research area.

The roots of DBMS lie in file-based systems. Usually, we talk of three generations of DBMS. They are as follows :

1st Generation : The **hierarchical** and *CODASYL* systems represent the first generation of DBMS. The **hierarchical model** is typified by IMS (Information Management System) and the network or *CODASYL model* by IDS (Integrated Data Store). Both of these models were developed in mid-1960s.

2nd Generation : In 1970, Dr. E.F. Codd represented a research paper at an international conference where he proposed a **relational model**. It represents the second generation of DBMS. **Please note that today we have over hundred of relational DBMSs.**

3rd Generation : It is represented by the Object-Relational DBMS and the Object-Oriented DBMS.

Before we go further, we must define certain terms related to DBMS which have been used throughout this text :

1. *Data* : Data is the plural of datum, which means a single piece of information. Data is defined as a known fact that can be recorded and that have implicit meaning. Actually, data are raw or isolated facts from which the required information is produced. **Please note that data is the material on which computer programs work upon.** It can be numbers, letters of the alphabet, words, special symbols etc. **Also note that by themselves they have no meaning.**

For example, 651974 is meaningless by itself since it does not signify anything. So, it is our data and not information. Other example of data can be objects like documents, photographic images, video segments etc.

Thus, data items refer to an elementary description of things, events, activities and transactions that are recorded, classified and stored but they are not organized to convey any specific meaning.

2. *Information* : It is defined as collection of related data that when put together, communicate meaningful and useful message to a recipient who uses it, to make decision or to interpret the data to get the meaning. Actually, it is data that has been converted into a more useful or intelligible form. **For example,** marks obtained by students and their roll numbers form **data** where their marksheet is the **information.** Other examples of information can be pay-slips, schedules, reports, worksheet, bar charts, invoices etc.

Please note that the information may further be processed to form Knowledge. Information containing wisdom is known as **knowledge.** So, we can say that :

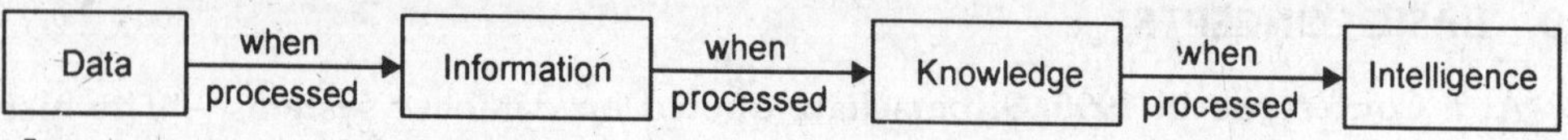

Let us compare data and information in a tabular form now.

S. No.	Data	Information
1.	Data is raw fact and figures *For example,* 89 is data.	Data when stored in some form like Marks: 89; then it becomes information.
2.	Data is not significant to a business.	Information is significant to a business.
3.	Data are atomic level pieces of the Information.	Information is a collection of data.
4.	Data does not help in decision-making.	Information helps in decision-making.
5.	Data is generally in unorganized form.	Information is in organized form.
6.	Data is collected from the source directly and hence is not dependent on information. **For example,** if we say that 89, 95, 90, 93, 98 are the numbers then it becomes data.	Information is dependent on the data that is gathered. **For example,** if we say 89, 95, 90, 93, 98 are the marks of 5 – Subjects then it becomes information whereas the marksheet of this student will be a meaningful information.

3. *Metadata* : A metadata/data dictionary is defined as the data about the data. It is also known as a **System Catalog.** The system catalog integrates the metadata. **Please note that the metadata is the data that describes the objects in the database.** So, it is easier to access those objects. It describes the database structure, constraints, applications, size of data types etc. **Also note that these are used as an integral tool for information resource management.** It is an important **deliverable** of the data integration process. It is found in documentation describing source systems. It is used by developers who depend on it to help them to develop their softwares, queries, controls and procedures to manage and manipulate the warehouse data. It is also used for report creations, change management and help in online system documentation.

4. *Database* : It is defined as the collection of logically interrelated data and a description of this data, designed to meet the information needs of an organization.

For example, a dictionary, a telephone directory student record register etc. They all store data in some particular arranged form *i.e.,* in some order.

Instead of having disconnected files with redundant data, here all data items are integrated with a minimum amount of duplication. **Please note that a database is a self-describing collection of integrated records. Also note that it is the self-describing nature of a database that provides program-data independence.** The data in a database should have the following features :

(*a*) **Shared :** Data in a database is shared among different users and applications.

(*b*) **Persistence :** Data in a database exists permanently *i.e.*, the data can live beyond the scope of the process that created it.

(*c*) **Validity :** Data should be correct with respect to the real world entity that they represent.

(*d*) **Security :** Data should be protected from unauthorized access.

(*e*) **Consistency :** Whenever more than one data element in a database represents related real world values, the values should be consistent with respect to the relationship.

(*f*) **Non-redundancy :** No two data items in a database should represent the same real world entity.

(*g*) **Independence :** Data should be abstract *i.e.*, it should be independent of each other at different levels. Changes at one level should not affect the other levels.

5. ***Database Management System (DBMS) :*** **It is defined as the software system that allows users to define, create, maintain and control access to the database.** Actually, we state an equation to understand this :

Database + DBMS software = Database system

DBMS is an intermediate layer between programs and data. **Please note that our programs access the DBMS, which then accesses the data. Also note that there are different types of DBMS ranging from small systems (running on PC) to huge systems that run on mainframes. For example**, ATMs, Airline Reservation systems etc. A DBMS is a piece of software that provides services for accessing a database but it maintains all required features of the data. **For example**, some commercial DBMS in market are dbase, Foxpro, MS-ACCESS, IMS, Oracle (9i/11i) Paradox, Sybase etc.

Please understand that :

(*a*) DBMS is basically a computerized record-keeping system.

(*b*) Database is the information to be stored whereas DBMS is the system used to manage the database.

The are two general modes for data use :

(*a*) Queries

(*b*) Transactions.

Both of these forms use the DBMS for processing. The *query* is processed for presentation in views and none of these processes are written to the database. The *transaction* is processed for updating values in the database variables. These updates are written to the database.

6. ***Application program :*** It is defined as a computer program that interacts with the database by issuing an appropriate request (like an SQL statement – to be discussed later) to the DBMS.

For example, Online applications written in some programming language or in some fourth-generation language like AI languages.

7. *Data warehouse and Data warehousing* : **It is defined as a subject-oriented, integrated, time-variant, non-updatable collection of data in support of management decision-making processes and business intelligence.** It is a **unique kind of database** which focuses on business intelligence, external data and time-variant data and not just current data. **And the process of extracting the meaning and making decisions from a dataware house is known as Data warehousing.**

8. *Data dictionary* : **It is defined as a repository of information about a database that documents the data elements of a database.** It is an integral part of DBMS which stores metadata or information about the database, attributes and definitions for each table in the database.

9. *Distributed database* : **It is defined as the collection of data under the different DBMS's running on different computers.** It is a central system connected to remote computers. We can access all data from each site and thus there is not so much load on a single central site. **Please note that these distributed databases can reside on network servers on WWW, on intranets or extranets also.**

10. *File-based system* : **It is defined as a collection of application programs that perform services for the end-users like Report production.** In such systems, each program defines and manages its own data. It's **main characteristics** are as follows :

(*a*) It is a group of files that stores the data of an organization.

(*b*) Each file is independent of one another.

(*c*) Each file is a flat file.

(*d*) Files are designed using programming languages like COBOL, C, C++ etc.

(*e*) Each file contains the processed information for one specific function.

COMPARISON OF DIFFERENT FILE ORGANIZATIONS

S.No.	Sequential	Indexed	Hashed/Direct
1.	Random retrieval on primary key is impractical.	Random retrieval of primary key is moderately fast.	Random retrieval of primary key is very fast
2.	There is no wasted space for data.	No wasted space for data but there is extra space for index.	Extra space for addition deletion of records.
3.	Sequential retrieval on primary key is very fast.	Sequential retrieval on primary key is moderately fast.	Sequential retrieval of primary key is impractical.
4.	Multiple key retrieval in sequential file organization is possible.	Multiple key retrieval is very fast with multiple indexes.	Multiple key retrieval is not possible.
5.	Updating of records generally requires rewriting the file.	Updating of records requires maintenance of indexes.	Updating of records is the easiest one.
6.	Addition of new records requires rewriting the file.	Addition of new records is easy and requires maintenance of indexes.	Addition of new records is very easy.
7.	Deletion of records can create wasted space.	Deletion of records is easy if space can be allocated dynamically.	Deletion of records is very easy.

FACTORS AFFECTING CHOICE OF FILE ORGANIZATION

(i) ***Access type*** : In order to search a record, whether random access or sequential access is required.

(ii) ***Access time*** : The total time taken by file organization to find a particular record.

(iii) ***File size*** : Choice is also dependent upon file size. If file size is large than choose direct access otherwise choose sequential access.

(iv) ***Overhead*** : Each technique has some overhead (it may be space overhead, time overhead etc.). Any technique giving fast access may waste more space then slower techniques.

(v) ***Updation time*** : Time required to add, delete and modify any record also plays important role in efficiency.

Advantages of File-based systems : Althougn no one uses files today yet they have not been eliminated completely from our literature. This is because of some of its advantages that are given below :

1. It helps in overall understanding of design complexity of database systems.
2. It provides a useful historical perspective on how we handle data.
3. It results in smooth transition from traditional file-based system to newer database systems. This is because we have already understood the problems inherent in file-based systems.

Disadvantages of File-oriented systems : Traditional (conventional) file-oriented system has the following disadvantages :

1. **Data redundancy :** Since these systems used a decentralized approach, so each department used its own application programs and files. This resulted in data redundancy or duplicacy of information in several files. **This is not required as it requires additional storage spaces, extra time and money. Also more effort is required to keep files up-to-date. Duplication can lead to loss of data integrity *i.e.,* data is no longer consistent.**
2. **Poor data control :** Since these systems are decentralized in nature, so there was no centralized control on the fields. This made field-names ambiguous-having many meanings. This results in poor data control.
3. **Poor data manipulation capabilities :** Since these systems do not provide strong connections between data in different files so it's data manipulation capability is quite low.
4. **Data dependence :** In these systems, files and records were described by specific physical formats that were coded into the application programs. If the format of a certain record was changed, the code in each file containing that format must be updated. Also, the instructions of data storage and access were written into the application's code. So, changes in storage structure or access methods could greatly affect the results of an application.
5. **Incompatible file formats :** As we know that the structure of files is embedded in the application programs, so the structures are dependent on the application programming language.

   For example, the structure of a file generated by a PASCAL program may be different from the structure of a file generated by a C/C ++ program. **Please note that the direct incompatibility of such files makes them difficult to process jointly.**

6. **Security problems :** Every user of the database system should not be allowed to access all data. Since application programs are added to the file-oriented systems in adhoc manner, it was difficult to enforce such security system.

Let us tabulate the differences between them now.

S. No.	File Management	Database Management
1.	These are small systems like a C++ or COBOL program.	These are large systems like Oracle or Sybase.
2.	They are relatively cheap.	They are relatively expensive.
3.	They have simple structure	They have complex structure.
4.	It needs very little preliminary design.	It needs vast preliminary design.
5.	They are not secure.	They are more secure.
6.	They are often single user oriented	They are multiple user oriented.
7.	They have isolated data.	They have shared data.
8.	They have simple, primitive backup/recovery mechanism.	They have complex and sophisticated backup/recovery.

1.1 CONCEPTUAL DATABASE DESIGN

1.1.1 Database Administrator (DBA)

A DBA is an individual person or a group of persons with an overview of one or more databases so that he/she can control the design and the use of these databases. A DBA is the highest salary paid person in an organization. A DBA provides the necessary technical support for implementing policy decisions of databases. **Please note that the DBA is the central controller of the database system who manages all resources like database, DBMS and related software.** A DBA is supported by a number of staff or a team of system programmers and other technical assistants. The main functions of a DBA are as follows :

1. **Defining conceptual schema :** A DBA creates the conceptual schema corresponding to the abstract level database design made by data administrator. **Please note that the DBA creates the original database schema and the structure of the database.**
2. **Physical database design :** A DBA decides how the data is to be represented in the stored database. This process is called as the **physical database design.**
3. **Security and integrity checks :** A DBA is responsible for providing the authorization and authentication checks so that no malicious users can access the database. DBA must ensure the integrity of the databases also.
4. **Give backup and recovery strategies :** A DBA must define and implement an appropriate periodical recovery strategy to recover the database from all types of failures.
5. **Granting access to users:** A DBA regulates the usage of specific parts of the database by various users. A DBA grants access to use the database to its users.

1.1.2 Database Users

The clients for the database are the end-users. End-users are classified as follows :

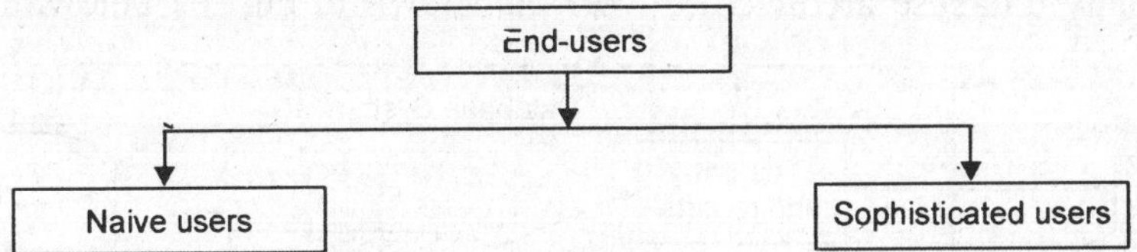

Fig. 1.1. *Database users*

Naive Users : They are usually unaware of the DBMS. They access the database by using specially written application programs. They invoke database operations by entering simple commands. **Please note that this means that they donot know anything about the database or DBMS.**

Sophisticated Users : The sophisticated end-user is familiar with the structure of the database and the facilities that DBMS provides. These type of users may use a high-level query language such as SQL to perform the required operations. Some sophisticated end-users may even write application programs for their own use.

1.1.3 Characteristics of Database Approach

The major characteristics of database approach are :

(*a*) Self-describing nature of a Database system.

(*b*) Insulation between programs, data and data abstraction.

(*c*) Support of multiple views of data.

(*d*) Sharing of Data and Multi-user Transaction Processing.

Data in the database has some characteristics that are discussed below :

1. **Shared :** Data in a database is shared among different users and applications.
2. **Persistence :** Data in a database exists permanently *i.e.*, the data can live beyond the scope of the process that created it.
3. **Integrity :** Data should be correct with respect to the real world entity that they represent.
4. **Security :** Data need to be protected from unauthorized access.
5. **Consistency :** Data must be consistent to the data-type that stores it. **For example,** an integer should store an integer only and not a character.

1.1.4 Database Systems

A database system is an integrated collection of related files along with the detail about their definition, interpretation, manipulation and maintenance. The data need for various applications in an organization could be satisfied with these systems. These systems removed the problem of duplication of data or redundancy also. **Please note that a database system is based on the data.** It can be run by using a software called as **Database Management System (DBMS).**

1.1.5 Database Architecture

To overcome the problems of file-oriented systems, database systems were developed. The file-oriented systems used many separate and unrelated files. On the other hand, the database approach uses a different way to show the change in which end-user data are stored, accessed and managed. **Please note that these systems emphasize the integration and sharing of data throughout the organization. Also note that these eliminate data**

redundancy with such a centralized data structure. Data are controlled via a central repository called as a data dictionary (DD) which is under the control of database administrators (DBA).

How actually database architecture works is shown in Fig. 1.2 below.

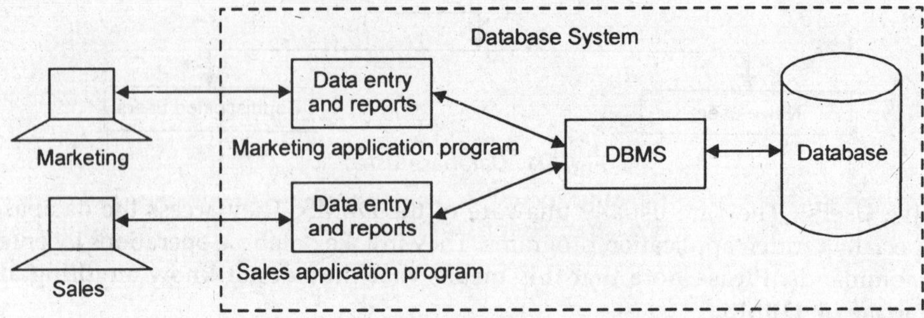

Fig. 1.2. *Database architecture working*

As shown in Fig. 1.2, the marketing and sales departments use their corresponding application programs to access the database through the DBMS. These are departmental application programs that handle data entry, data maintenance and the Report Generation.

1.1.6 DBMS Components (Actors)

A DBMS environment consists of five main components (or actors) and they are listed below :

(*a*) Hardware (*b*) Software
(*c*) Data (*d*) Users
(*e*) Procedures.

All these components are shown in Fig. 1.3.

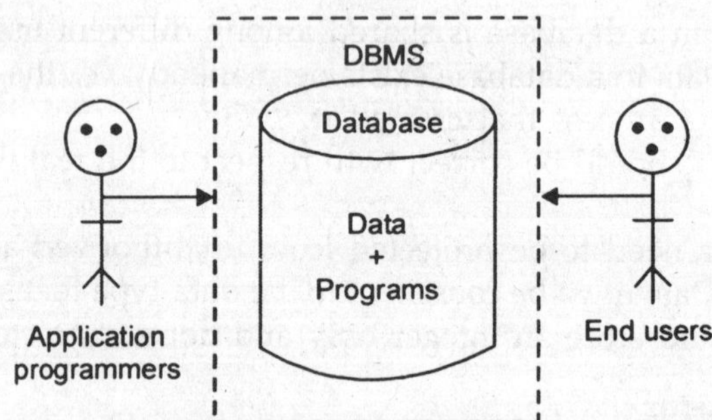

Fig. 1.3. *DBMS components*

Let us understand these components one by one now.

1. Hardware : The hardware of a DBMS consists of two components, namely :

(*a*) Processor and main memory.

(*b*) Secondary storage devices.

The processor and the MM are required to support the execution of DBMS.

The secondary or external or auxiliary storage devices like hard disk, CDs etc., that are used to store data.

Please note that the database will physically reside on the hard disks. A database system requires a minimum amount of MM and disk space to run. When number of users become large, a large amount of memory and disk is required to maintain this huge quantity of data. So, we now need high speed computers, networks and peripheral devices. Database run on variety of machines ranging from microcomputers, to a minicomputer, to a mainframe and to a network of computers depending on the organizational requirements. Other hardware issues for a DBMS includes database machines that refers to the hardware specifically designed to support DBMS.

2. Software : Software is the basic interface or layer between the physical database (*i.e.,* the data as actually stored) and the users of the system. It is most commonly known as the **Database Management System (DBMS). Please note that the software is the actual DBMS**. All user requests are handled by DBMS only. **Please note that DBMS provides one general function *i.e.,* of shielding of the database users from complex hardware-level detail.** Basically, this software component includes :

DBMS software + Application programs + O.S.

The application programs are written in 3GL or 4GL by the company employees to solve some specific problem. The operating system (O.S.) may include network software also if DBMS is being used over a network.

It is our O.S. only that manages all hardware components.

3. Data : From the end user's point of view, Data is the most important component of DBMS environment. This is shown in Fig. 1.4.

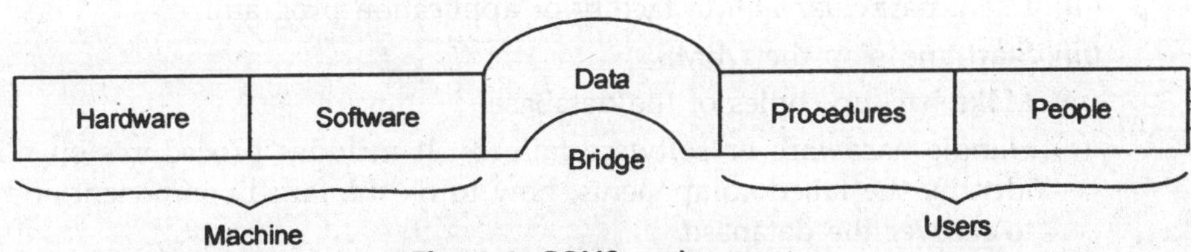

Fig. 1.4. *DBMS environment*

As shown in Fig. 1.4 above that **data acts as a bridge between the machine components and the user components.** The database contains both the operational data and the meta-data *i.e.,* 'data about data'. The database should contain all data needed by the organization. **Please remember that a database should always be designed, built and populated for a particular audience and for a specific purpose.**

4. Users : There are a number of users who can access or retrieve data on demand using the applications and interfaces provided by the DMBS. Each type of user needs different software capabilities. Database users can be classified as follows :

(*a*) Agile users/Naive users (*b*) Online users

(*c*) Application programmers (*d*) DBA.

Let us understand these various types of users.

(*a*) ***Agile users/Naive users :*** **Those users who need not be aware of the presence of the database system or any other system supporting their usage are called as Agile or Naive users. Please remember that these users are end users of the database who work through a menu driven application program where the type and the range of response is always indicated to the user.**

For example, an Automated Teller Machine (ATM) user. The operations that are performed by these users are very limited and affect only a precise portion of the database.

(*b*) ***Online users :*** **Those users who may communicate with the database directly via an online terminal or indirectly via a user interface and the application**

program are known as online users. These users are aware of the presence of the database system. They may have acquired a certain amount of expertise within the limited interaction permitted with a database.

(*c*) ***Application programmers :*** **Those programmers who write database applications programs in some programming language are known as application programmers or professional programmers.**

For example, programmers who write programs using general purpose programming language or the commands available to manipulate a database.

(*d*) ***Database Administrator :*** The database administrator (or DBA) is a person or a group incharge for implementing the database system within an organization. He/she is the highest salary paid person. The DBA has all the system privileges (rights) allowed by the DBMS. He can grant and remove access privileges to and from other users. **DBA is responsible for the evaluation selection and implementation of DBMS package.**

(*e*) ***Procedures :*** **They refer to the instructions and the rules that govern the design and the use of the database. Please note that the users of the system and the staff that manage the database require documented procedures on how to use or run the system.** These may consist of **instructions** on how to :

(*i*) Log on to the DBMS.

(*ii*) Use a particular DBMS facility or application program.

(*iii*) Start and stop the DBMS.

(*iv*) Make backup copies of the database.

(*v*) Handle hardware or software failures. It includes procedures on how to identify the failed components, how to fix the failed component and how to recover the database.

(*vi*) Change the structure of a table, reorganize the database across multiple disks improve performance or archive data to secondary storage.

1.2 DATA MODELS

1.2.1 Schemas and Instances

Schemas : The overall description of the database is called as the Database schema. Actually, DBMS has a three level architecture and accordingly there are three different types of schemas in the database. **A schema is defined as an outline or a plan that describes the records existing at a particular level.** The **schema diagram** is used to show the database schema. **For example,**

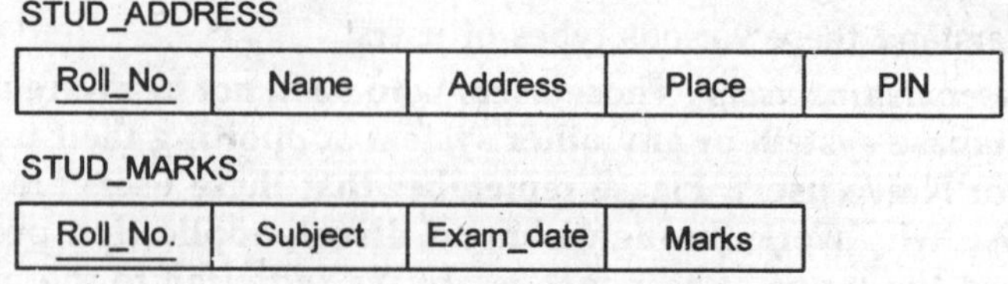

Fig. 1.5. *Schema diagram*

A schema diagram displays only some aspects of a schema like the names of record types and data items and some type of constraints. Other aspects are not specified in the schema diagram

Please note that it does not specify the data type of each data item and the relationships among the various files. So, we say that the description of the database is called as the database schema which is specified during database design and is not expected to change frequently. A displayed schema in Fig. 1.5 is called as a **schema diagram. Also note that there will be only one schema per level, per database.** The schema will describe the way in which data elements at one level can be mapped to the corresponding data elements in the next level. Schema establishes a sort of correspondence between the records at different levels. They are generally stored in a data dictionary.

Instance : Databases change over time when you insert or delete the information. **The collection of information stored in the database at a particular moment is called as an instance of the database.**

For example, the instances of our STUD_ADDRESS table are as shown below in Fig. 1.6.

Roll_No	Name	Addr	Place	Pin
10	Felix Simon	A-2/7, Janak Puri	Delhi	110038
20	Shilpa	B-5, Saket	Delhi	57601
30	Rajiv	G-8, Rajouri Garden	Delhi	110034

Fig. 1.6. *Instances of STUD_ADDRESS table*

Please note that the schema remains the same while the data stored in it changes from instant to instant. Also note that when the schema framework is filled in with data item values, it is referred to as an instance of the schema. The data in the database at a particular moment of time is called as a **database state or snapshot or current set of occurrences or instances in the database. Also remember that many database instances can correspond to the same database schema.**

> **NOTE :** The schema is sometimes called as the **intension** of the database while an instance is called as an **extension** (or state) of the database.

Subschema : A subschema is defined as an application programmer's or user's view of the data item types and record types, which he or she uses. It is a subset of the schema. It inherits the same property that a schema has. **The plan (or schema) for a view is many a times called as a subschema.** It gives the user (*s*) a window through which he/she can view the required part of the database. Therefore, different application programs can have different view of data.

1.2.2 DBMS Architecture/3-tier Architecture/ANSI-SPARC Architecture

In 1971, Conference on Data systems and Languages (CODASYL) appointed a Data Base Task Group (DBTG) who gave a standard terminology and general architecture for database systems. The DBTG said that there is a need for a **two level approach with a system view called as the schema and the user views called as a subschema.** However, in 1975, the **American National Standards Institute (ANSI)—Standards Planning and Requirements Committee (SPARC) produced a similar terminology and architecture.** *ANSI-SPARC* **recognized the need for a three-level approach** with a system catalog DBMS architecture has three levels :

(*a*) External or view level (*b*) Conceptual or logical level
(*c*) Internal or storage level.

The **main objective** of this three-level architecture is to separate each user's view of the database from the way the database is physically represented. This separation is required due to several reasons. Some of the reasons are given below :

1. Each user should be able to access the same data but should have a different customized view of the data. Each user should be able to change the way he or she views the data and this change should not affect other users.
2. A user's interaction with the database should be independent of storage considerations. That is, the users should not have to deal directly with physical database storage details like indexing or hashing.
3. The Database Administrator (DBA) should be able to change the database storage structures without affecting the user's views.
4. The internal structure of the database should be unaffected by the changes to the physical aspects of storage, such as the changeover to a new storage device
5. The DBA should be able to change the conceptual structure of the database without affecting all users.

This three-level or three-tier architecture is shown in Fig. 1.7. Let us explain these layers, one by one now.

Layer 1 : External or View Level. It is the user's of the database. It is the highest level of abstraction. It deals with the way in which data is viewed by the individual users. **Please note that any number of user views, even identical ones, may exist for a given conceptual or global view of the database. Also note that different views may have different representations of the same data.**

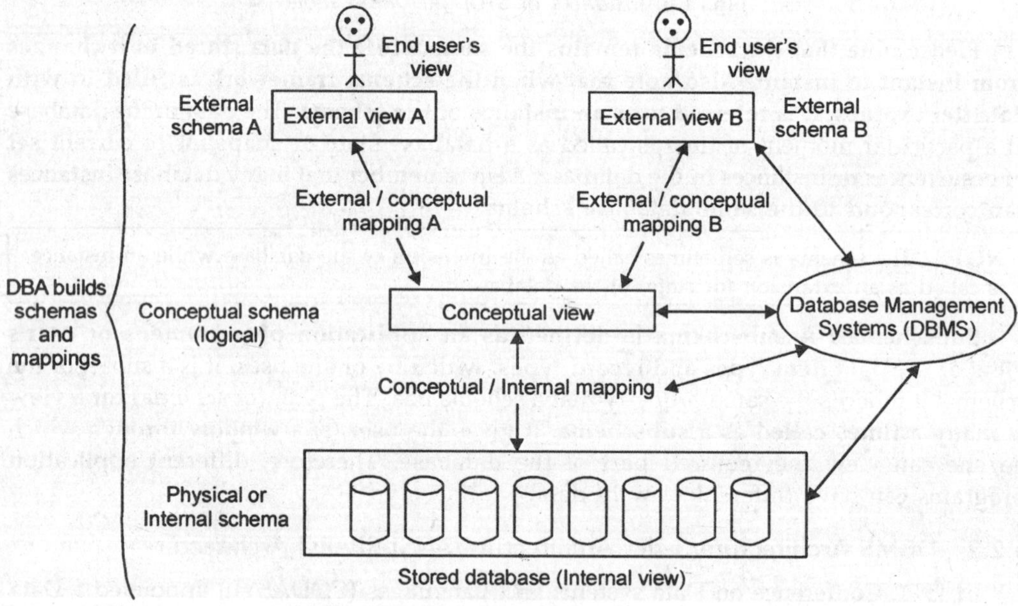

Fig. 1.7. *Three-tier DBMS architecture.*

The external view insulates users from the details of internal and conceptual levels.

For example, One user may view date as dd/mm/yyyy while another may view as yyyy/mm/dd. Some views may contain **derived or calculated data also.** Data that is not stored in the database but are created when needed are known as **derived or calculated data.**

The external view is described by means of a schema called as **external schema** that correspond to different views of the data. The external schema consists of the definition of the logical records and the relationships in the external view. **Please note that any given database has only one internal (or physical) schema and one conceptual schema because it has just one set of stored relations. But it may have several external schemas,**

each of which is created as per the user's need. Also note that the external schema is written using external data definition language.

Layer 2 : Conceptual or Logical Level. It is the global view of the database. This level describes **what** data is stored in the database and the relationships among the data. It is the middle level in this 3-tier architecture. This level contains the logical structure of the entire database as seen by the DBA. It is a complete view of the data requirements of the organization that is independent of any storage considerations. **Please note that one conceptual view represents the entire database. Also note that there is only one conceptual view per database.** This view is defined by the names, types, length of each data item. The **create table** command of oracle creates this view. We shall study these commands later on. It is independent of all hardware and software. The conceptual level represents :

(*a*) All entities, their attributes and their relationships. As we know that **entity is anything which exists and is distinguishable from one another. For example,** table, chair, ball, a student, light, fan, chalk, blackboard etc. are some examples of entities. **And an attribute is the property or the characteristic of an entity. For example,** a ball (entity) has attributes like its size, its diameter, its shape, its color and so on.

(*b*) The constraints on the data.

(*c*) Semantic information about the data.

(*d*) Security and integrity information.

Please remember that this level must not contain any storage dependent details. For example, the description of an entity should contain only data types of attributes (like integer, char, real and so on) and their length but not any storage details like the number of bytes occupied. The choice of tables (or relations) and the choice of fields (or attributes or data items) for each design is not always obvious. **The process of arriving at a good conceptual schema is called as conceptual database design. This conceptual schema is written using conceptual data definition language.**

Layer 3 : Internal Level or Storage Level. It is the physical representation of the database on the computer. This level describes how the data is stored in the database. It concerns with the way the data are physically stored on the hardware. **Please note that this internal level covers the physical implementation of the database to achieve optimal runtime performance and storage space utilization.** It covers the data structures and file organizations used to store data on storage devices. It interfaces with the operating system (OS) access methods to place the data on the storage devices, build the indexes, retrieve the data and so on. The level is concerned with the following :

(*a*) Storage space allocation for data and indexes.

(*b*) Record descriptions for storage with stored sizes for data items.

(*c*) Record placement.

(*d*) Data compression and data encryption techniques.

Please remember that there will be only one conceptual view consisting of the abstract representation of the database in its entirety. Similarly, there will be only one internal or physical view, representing the total database, as it is physically stored but there will be many external views.

The process of arriving at a good internal or physical schema is called as physical database design. The internal schema is written using SQL or internal data definition language. We will study SQL in detail later on.

Let us understand these three levels with one example.

Consider the following customer's database :

Cust_id	Cust_name	Cust_street	Cust_city	Cust_Bal

The Fig. 1.8 below shows the specific information actually available at each level regarding a particular user.

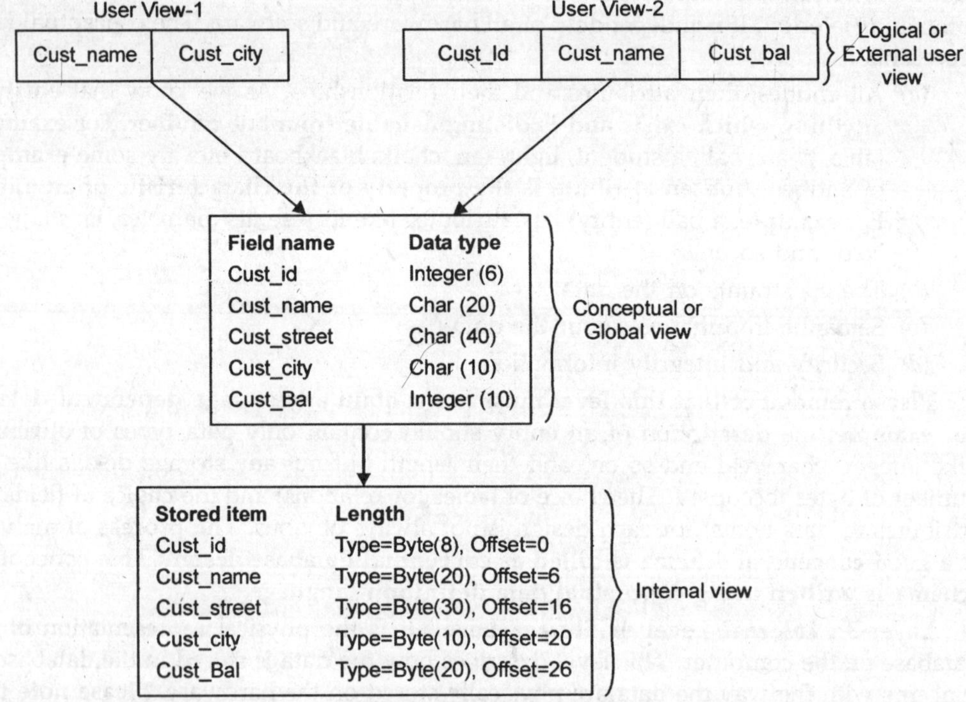

Fig. 1.8. *Three views of data*

Just note the following from the above Fig. 1.8 :

(*a*) **External view :** This view would depend upon the user who is accessing the database.

(*b*) **Conceptual view :** This view contains the logical view of the whole database. It represents the data type of each required field.

(*c*) **Internal view :** This view represents physical location of each element on the disk of the server as well as how many bytes of storage each element needs.

Also seen in Fig. 1.8 are the two types of mappings between three different views. It is our DBMS responsibility for mapping between these three tvpes of schema. They are discussed below :

I. External/Conceptual Mapping : Each external schema is related to the conceptual schema by the external/conceptual mapping. A mapping between the external and conceptual views gives the correspondence among the records and the relationships of the external and conceptual views. **Please note that the external view is an abstraction of the conceptual view, which in turn is an abstraction of the internal view.** It describes the contents of the database as perceived by the user or the application program of that view. The user of the external view sees and manipulates a record corresponding to the external view. **Also note that there is a mapping from a particular logical record in the external view to one (or more) conceptual records in the conceptual view.** There can be some differences between these External and Conceptual views.

For example, the names of fields and records may be different. A number of conceptual fields can be combined into a single external fields, like the fields last-name and first-name at the conceptual level but Name at the external level. Also remember that a given external record could be derived from a number of conceptual records.

II. Conceptual/Internal Mapping : Conceptual schema is related to the internal schema by the conceptual/internal mapping. This enables the DBMS to find the actual record or combination of records in physical storage that constitute a logical record in conceptual schema. **Please note that the mapping between the conceptual and the internal levels specifies the method of deriving the conceptual record from the physical database.** However, there can be some differences between the Conceptual and Internal views. These differences can be :

(*a*) Representation of numeric values could be different in the two views.

(*b*) Representation of string data can be considered by the two views to be coded differently.

(*c*) The value for a field in one view could be computed from the values in one or more fields of the other view.

Please remember that changing the storage structure of the record involves changing the conceptual view to internal view mapping so that the conceptual view does not require any alteration.

The information about the mapping requests among various schema levels are stored in the system catalog of DBMS. The DBMS uses additional software to accomplish the mappings by referring to the mapping information in the system catalog. **Please note that when schema is changed at some level, the schema at the next higher level remains unchanged. Also note that only the mapping between the two levels is changed.** Thus, data independence is accomplished. This ANSI-SPARC'S 3-tier architecture provides efficient mapping and more data independence.

1.2.3 Data Independence

The *major objective* of ANSI-SPARC's 3-level architecture is to provide **data independence which means that upper levels are unaffected by changes in lower levels.** There are two types of data independence :

(*a*) Physical data independence

(*b*) Logical data independence.

Let us discuss the two now.

Physical data independence : It indicates that the physical storage structures or devices could be changed without affecting the conceptual schema. The change would be absorbed by the mapping between the conceptual and internal levels. Physical data independence is achieved by the presence of the internal level of the database and the mapping or transformation from the conceptual level of the database to the internal level. So, conceptual level to internal level mapping provides a means to go from the conceptual view to the internal view and hence to store the data in the database.

If there is a need to change the file organization or the type of physical device used as a result of growth in the database or new technology, a change is required in the conceptual/internal mapping between the conceptual and internal levels. **Please understand that this change is necessary to maintain the conceptual level invariant. Also note that the physical data independence criterion requires that the conceptual level does not specify storage structures or the access methods (like indexing, hashing etc) used to retrieve the data from the physical storage medium.**

When we say that we should make the conceptual schema physically data independent, we mean that the external schema (which is defined on the conceptual schema) is in turn physically data independent.

Logical data independence : Logical data independence means that the conceptual schema (middle level) can be changed without affecting the existing external schemas. Herein, the users are shielded from changes in the logical structure of the data. The change would be absorbed by the mapping between the external and conceptual levels. It insulates application programs from operation such as combining two records into one or splitting an existing record into two or more records. This would require a change in the external/conceptual mapping so as to leave the external view unchanged. **Please note that it is difficult to achieve logical data independence than the physical data independence.** This is because logical data independence requires flexibility in the design of database and the programmer has to foresee the future requirements or modifications in the design.

Let us tabulate the differences between the two.

S. No.	Physical Data Independence	Logical Data Independence
1.	It is the ability to- modify the *physical schema* without causing application programs to be rewritten.	It is the ability to modify the *logical schema* without causing application programs to be rewritten.
2.	Modifications at the physical level are necessary to improve performance.	Modifications at the logical level are necessary whenever the logical structure of the database is altered.
3.	It is not difficult to be achieved.	It is more difficult to achieve as application programs are dependent on the logical structure of the data that they access.
4.	It provides immunity of conceptual or external schemas.	It provides immunity of external schemas or application programs.
5.	The conceptual schema insulates the users from changes in physical storage of data.	The users are shielded from changes in the logical structure of the data or changes in the choice of relations to be stored.

1.2.4 Database Languages

A DBMS must provide appropriate languages for each category of users to express database queries and updates. **Please note that these database languages are used to create and maintain database on computer. Also note that there are large number of database languages like dBase, MS-ACCESS, Foxpro, Oracle, MySQL, Sybase, Paradox etc.** These languages use structured query language (SQL) statements. We will discuss SQL in detail later on but now we categorize these SQL statements of DBMS.

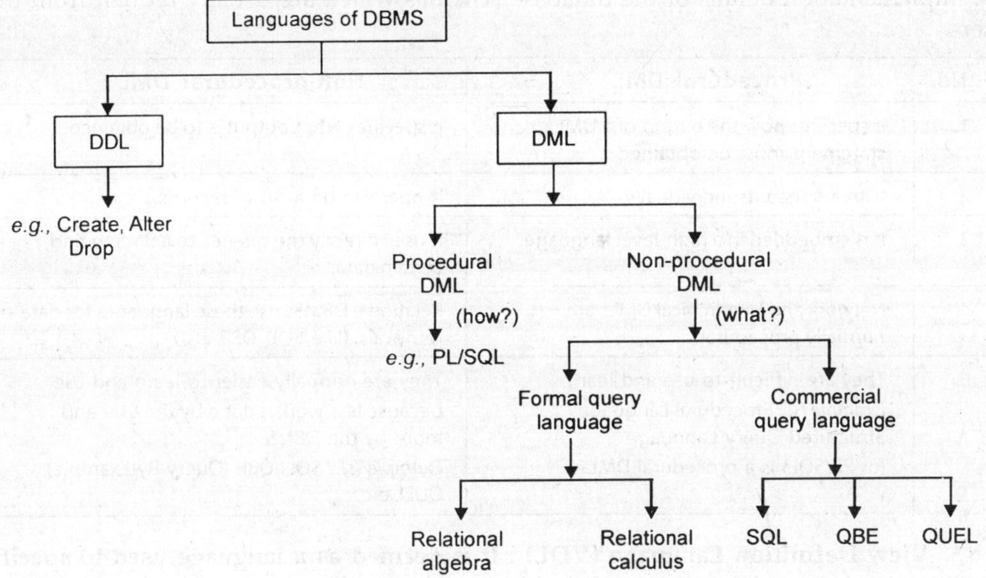

Fig. 1.9. *Categories of DBMS language*

DBMS provides the following languages to provide the facilities to its users :

1. Data Definition Language (DDL)/Data Description Language : It is a language that allows the users to define data and their relationships to other types of data. It is mainly used to create files, databases, data dictionary and tables within the databases. DDL can be used to define conceptual schema (Global). It is used to define a schema or to modify an existing one. **Please note that it cannot be used to manipulate data**.

After the compilation of the DDL statements, the result is a set of tables stored in special files collectively called as the **system catalog**. This system catalog integrates the **metadata** *i.e.,* data that describes objects in the database and makes it easier for those objects to be accessed or manipulated.

For example, CREATE, ALTER, DROP, RENAME are SQL, DDL statements.

2. Data Manipulation Language (DML) : It is defined as a language that provides a set of operations to support the basic data manipulation operations on the data held in the databases. It allows users to insert, update, delete and retrieve data from the database. Data manipulation applies to all the three levels but at the internal level we must define complex low-level procedures that allow efficient data access. At higher levels, we emphasize on efficient user interaction with the system. **The part of DML that involves data retrieval is called as a query language.**

As shown in Fig. 1.9 above, DML can be categorized as—**Procedural DML** and **non-procedural DML**.

Let us tabulate the differences between them (on next page).

3. Data Sub Languages (DSL) : It is the combination of both DML and DDL. So, we say that:

$$DSL = DDL + DML$$

4. Storage Definition Language (SDL) : It is defined as a language used to specify the internal schema in the database. In SDL, the storage structure and access methods used bv the database system is specified by a set of statements. These statements define the implementation details of the database schemas which are usually hidden from the users.

S. No.	Procedural DML	Non-procedural DML
1.	It specifies **how** the output of a DML statement must be obtained	It specifies **what** output is to be obtained.
2.	It treats records individually.	It operates on a set of records.
3.	It is embedded in a high-level language.	It uses directly the queries to DBMS to find certain data.
4.	Network and Hierarchical DMLs are normally procedural.	Relational DBMSs use these languages for data retrievals, (like SQL, QBE etc.)
5.	They are difficult to use and learn. *Example (s) :* Procedural Language / Structured Query Language (or PL/SQL) is a procedural DML.	They are normally easier to learn and use because less work is done by the user and more by the DBMS. *Example (s) :* SQL, QBE (Query-By-Example), QUEL etc.

5. View Definition Language (VDL) : It is defined as a language used to specify user's views (external schema) and their mappings to the conceptual schema. DDL is used to specify both the conceptual and external schemas. There are two views of data :

(*a*) ***Logical view of data :*** It is the form that the programmer perceives to be in.

(*b*) ***Physical view of data :*** It is the form in which the data is actually stored on auxiliary storage devices like disk.

6. Host Language : It is defined as a language in which DML commands are embedded. Many DBMS have a facility for *embedding* SQL queries in high-level programming languages like VB 6.0, VC ++ 6.0 etc.

NOTE : Most data sublanguages are non-embedded also. These commands can be input directly from a terminal.

7. Fourth-Generation Languages (4GL) : It is a compact, efficient and non-procedural programming that is used to improve the productivity of the DBMS. The following are the example of 4GLs :

(*a*) SQL
(*b*) Report Generators.
(*c*) Spreadsheets
(*d*) Code Generators
(*e*) Automated Generation of HTML.

8. Data Control Language (DCL) : DCL statements control access to data and the database using statements such as GRANT and REVOKE. A privilege can be granted to a user with the help of GRANT statement. The privileges assigned can be SELECT, ALTER, DELETE, EXECUTE, INSERT, INDEX etc. In addition to granting of privileges, you can also revoke (take back) these privileges by using REVOKE command.

The following are DCL commands in DBMS :

(*a*) ***GRANT :*** Given privileges to users.

(*b*) ***REVOKE :*** Take away privileges from users.

(*c*) ***COMMENT :*** Add a comment to the data dictionary.

Practically, DDL and DML are not different languages but are the part of SQL only.

1.2.5 Procedure for Database Access

Any access to the stored data is done by the data manager. The steps followed during database access are as follows :

1. A user's request for data is received by the **data manager** which determines the physical record required. The decision as to which physical record is needed may require some preliminary consultation of the database and /or the data dictionary prior to the access of the actual data ifself.
2. The data manager sends the request for a specific physical record to the **file manager**. The **file manager** decides which physical block of secondary storage devices contains the required record and sends the request for the appropriate block to the disk manager. **Please note that a block is a unit of physical I/O operations between primary and secondary storage.**
3. The disk manager retrieves the block and sends it to the file manager back which sends the required record to the data manager. This is shown in Fig. 1.10.

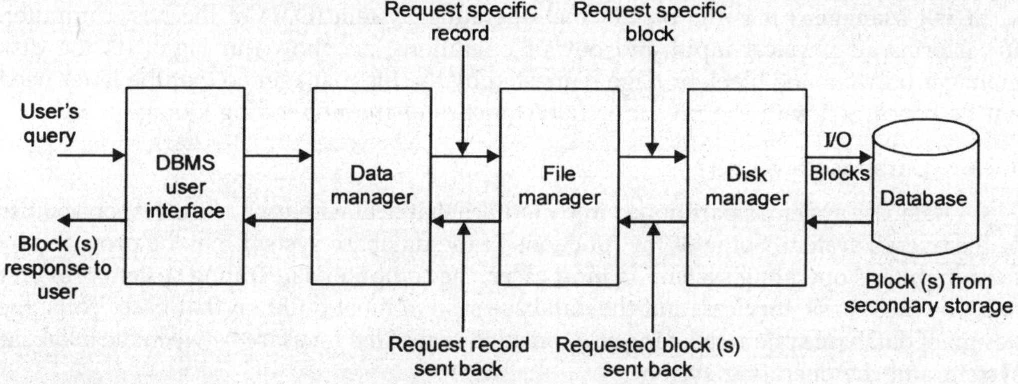

Fig. 1.10. *Database access procedure*

Working : As we have already discussed that DBMS acts as a bridge between the application program (that determines what data are needed and how they are processed) **and the operating system** (that is responsible) for placing data on magnetic storage devices). When a user issues a request to DBMS to retrieve data from the database then some basic, internal operations are performed. These operations are as follows :

(*a*) A user issues an access request. For this he/she uses some application program or DML.

(*b*) The application program determines what data are needed and communicates the need to the DBMS.

(*c*) The DBMS receives the request and interprets it.

(*d*) The DBMS then inspects the external schema, the external/conceptual mapping, the conceptual schema, the conceptual/internal mapping and storage structure definition.

(*e*) The DBMS instructs the O.S. to locate and retrieve the data from the specific location on the magnetic disk.

(*f*) A **copy** of data is given to the application program for processing.

Let us now see the main functions of the Data Manager, File Manager and Disk Manager one by one.

Data Manager : The data manager happens to be the **central** software component of DBMS. It is also called as the **database control system**. It's main functions are as follows :

1. It converts operations in the user's queries from the user's logical view to a physical file system.
2. It is responsible for interfacing with the file system (as shown in Fig. 1.10).
3. The tasks of enforcing constraints to maintain the consistency and integrity of data, as well as its security are also performed by the data manager.
4. It provides synchronization in the simultaneous operations performed by the concurrent users.
5. It maintains the backup and recovery operations.

File Manager : It is responsible for locating the block containing the required record, requesting this block from the disk manager and transmitting the required record to the data manager. This is shown in Fig. 1.10. It is responsible for managing the file structure and the file space also. The file manager can be implemented using an interface to the existing file subsystem provided by the O.S. of the host computer.

Disk Manager : It is the part of the Operating System (O.S.) of the host computer. It performs all physical input and output operations. As shown in Fig. 1.10, the disk manager transfers the block or page requested by the file manager so that the latter need not be concerned with the physical characteristics of the underlying storage media.

1.2.6 Database Structure

A database system is partitioned into modules that deal with each of the responsibilities of the overall system. Some of the functions of the database system may be provided by the computer's operating system. In most cases, the computer's operating system provides only the most basic services, and the database system must build on that base. Thus, the design of database system must include consideration of the interface between the database system and the operating system.

The functional components of a database system can be broadly divided into query processor components and storage manager components. The query processor components include.

I. Query Processor :

- **DML compiler,** which translates DML statements in a query language into low-level instruction that the query evaluation engine understands. In addition, the DML compiler attempts to transform a user's request into an equivalent but more efficient form, thus finding a good strategy for executing the query.
- **Embedded DML precompiler,** which converts DML Statements embedded in an application program to normal procedure calls in the host language. The precompiler must interact with the DML compiler to generate the appropriate code.
- **DDL interpreter,** which interprets DDL statements and records them in a set of tables containing **metadata**.
- **Query evaluation engine,** which executes low-level instructions generated by the DML compiler.

II. Storage Manager :

The *storage manager components* provides the interface between the low-level data stored in the database and the application programs and queries submitted to the system. The storage manager components include.

- **Authorization and Integrity Manager,** which tests for the satisfaction of integrity constraints and checks the authority of users to access data.

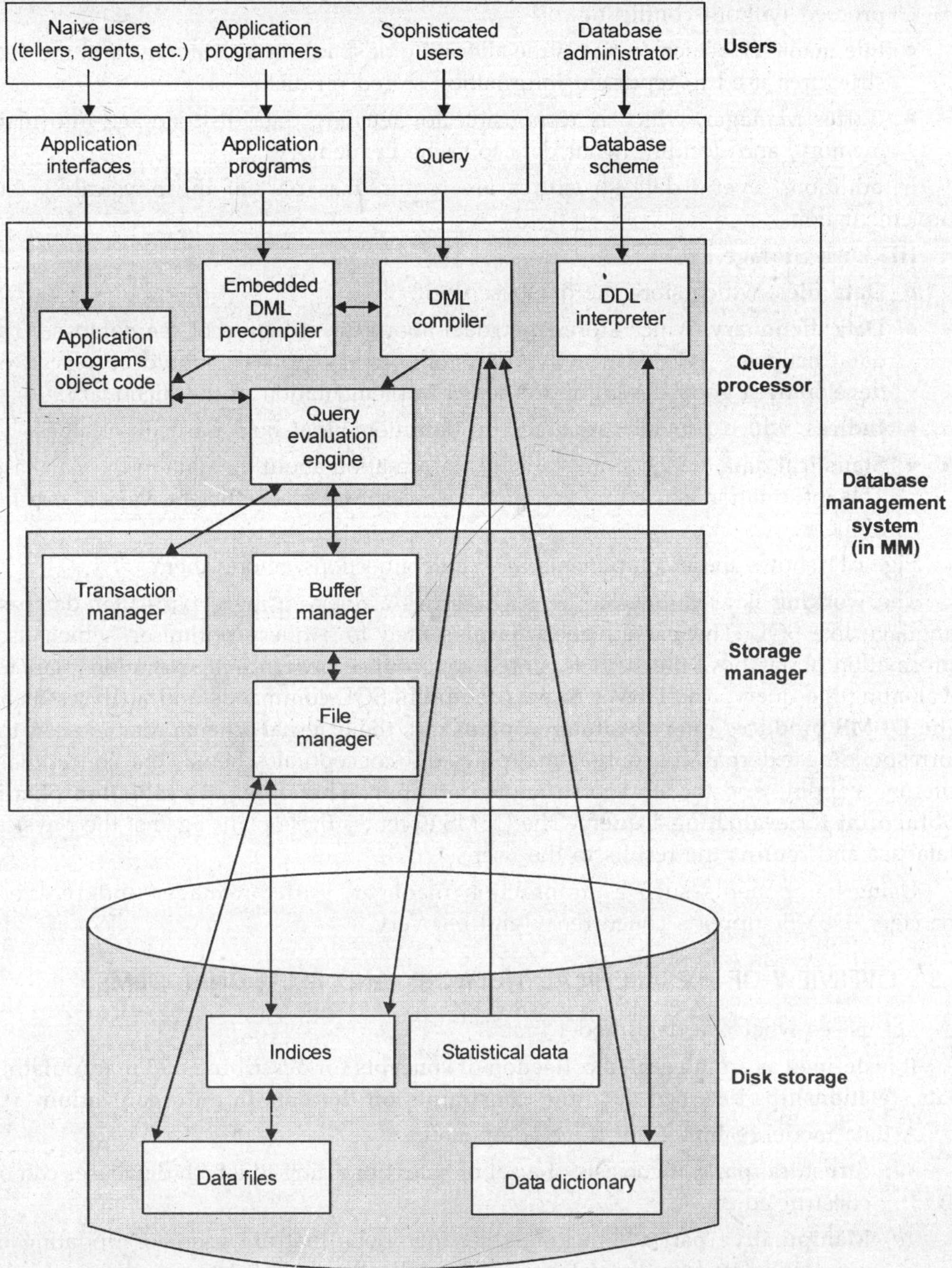

Fig. 1.11. *Disk structure*

- **Transaction manager,** which ensures that the database remains in a consistent (correct) state despite system failures, and that concurrent transaction executions proceed without conflicting.
- **File manager,** which manages the allocation of space on disk storage and the data structures used to represent information stored on disk.
- **Buffer Manager,** which is responsible for fetching data disk storage into main memory, and deciding what data to cache in memory.

In addition, several data structures are required as part of the physical system implementation :

III. Disk Storage :

- **Data files,** which store the database itself.
- **Data dictionary,** which stores metadata about the structure of the database. The data dictionary is used heavily. Therefore, great emphasis should be placed on developing a good design and efficient implementation of the dictionary.
- **Indices,** which provide fast access to data items that hold particular values.
- **Statistical data,** which store statistical information about the data in the database. This information is used by the query processor to select efficient ways to execute a query.

Fig. 1.11 shows these components and the connections among them.

The **working** is as follows : The users issues a query using a particular database language like SQL. The passed query is presented to a query optimiser, which uses information about how the data is stored to produce an efficient execution plan for evaluating the query. The DBMS accepts the users SQL commands and analyses them. **The DBMS produces query evaluation plans**, *i.e.,* the external schema for the user, the corresponding external/conceptual mapping, the conceptual schema, the conceptual/internal mapping and the storage structure definition. **Therefore, an evaluation plan is a blueprint for evaluating a query**. The DBMS executes these plans against the physical database and returns the results to the user.

Using components such as transaction manager, buffer manager and recovery manager, DBMS supports concurrency and recovery.

1.3 OVERVIEW OF HIERARCHICAL, NETWORK AND RELATIONAL DBMS

Let us see what is a data model first ?

It is defined as an integrated collection of concepts for describing and manipulating data, relationships between data and constraints on the data in an organization.

A data model comprises of three components :

(*a*) **Structural part :** It consists of a set of rules according to which databases can be constructed.

(*b*) **Manipulative part :** It includes the operations that are used for updating or retrieving data from the database and for changing the structure of the databases.

(*c*) **Integrity rules :** A set of rules which ensures that the data is accurate.

Basically, three types of models are there. They are as follows :

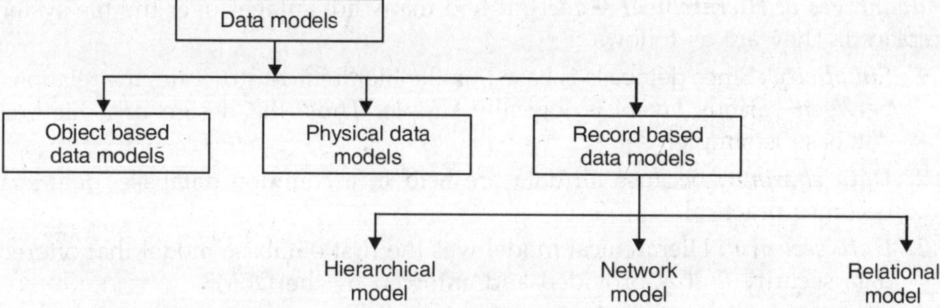

Fig. 1.12. *Categories of Data models*

The object-based and record-based data models are used to describe data at the conceptual and external levels, the physical data model is used to describe data at the internal level.

The **object-based data models** use the concepts of entities, attributes and relationships.

The **physical data models** describe how data is stored in the computer. It represents information like record structures, record ordering and access paths. **For example**, the Unifying model and the Frame memory model.

We are interested in the **Record-based Models**. These models are used in describing data at the logical and view levels. These models are so named because the database is structured in fixed format records of several types. Let us study the three record-based Models now.

I. Hierarchical Model : It the one of the oldest database models, dating from late 1950s. One of the first hierarchical databases Information Management System (IMS) was developed by IBM.

In hierarchical model, data are viewed as a collection of relations (also called as segments) that form a hierarchical relation.

A hierarchical relation is defined as a collection of relations that are connected together as a hierarchical tree by logical associations (*i.e.*, a fan structure)—**the hierarchical relation in a family tree. Each segment contains multiple instances**. Hence, even if the segments are connected as a **chain** by logical associations, the instance structure can be a fan structure with multiple branches. **Please note that these logical associations are directional associations. The segment pointed to by the logical association is referred to as the child segment and the other segment is called as the parent segment. Also note that these are referred to as a member-record type and the owner-record type respectively according to DBTG.**

In general, the segments themselves could form a tree with multiple levels and multiple branches at each level. **The segment without a parent is called the root. The segments that have no children are called as the leaves of the hierarchical model**.

Applications of Hierarchical :

1. These models are widely used as semantic models in practice because many real-world phenomenon are hierarchical in nature like administrative structures, biological structures, political and social structures.
2. These models are also widely used as a physical model because of the inherent hierarchical structure of the disk storage system like tracks, cylinders and so on.

Examples : (*a*) IMS by IBM, (*b*) IMB and system 2000, (*c*) NOMAD by NCSS.

Advantages of Hierarchical Model : It had many advantages over the file systems it has replaced. They are as follows :

1. ***Simplicity :*** Since database is based on the hierarchical structure, the relationships between various layers is logically simple. Thus, the design of a hierarchical database is simple.
2. ***Data sharing :*** Because all data are held in a common database, data sharing becomes practical.
3. ***Data security :*** Hierarchical model was the first database model that offered the data security that is provided and enforced by the DBMS.
4. ***Data integrity :*** Because this model is based on the parent/child relationship, there is always a link between the parent segment and the child segments under it. The child segments are always automatically referred by its parent, so this model promotes data integrity.
5. ***Efficiency :*** This model is very efficient when a database contains a large volume of data in one-to-many (1: N) relationships and when the users require large number of transactions, using data whose relationships are fixed over time.

Disadvantages of Hierarchical Data Model : The main disadvantages of this model are as follows :

1. ***Implementation complexity :*** Although this model is conceptually simple and easy to design, it is quite complex to implement. The database designers should have a very good knowledge of the physical data storage characteristics.
2. ***Inflexibility :*** A hierarchical database lacks flexibility. The changes in the new relations or segments often yield very complex system management tasks. A deletion of one segment may lead to the involuntary deletion of all the segments under it. Such an error could be very costly.
3. ***Database management problems :*** If you make any changes in the database structure of a hierarchical database, then you need to make the necessary changes in all the application programs that access the database. Thus, maintaining the database and the applications can become very difficult.
4. ***Operational anomalies :*** Hierarchical model suffers from the Insert, Update and Deletion anomalies. The retrieval operation is complex and asymmetric. So, this model is not suitable for all the cases.
5. ***No standards :*** The implementation of this model does not confirm to any specific standard.
6. ***Implementation limitation :*** Many of the common relationships do not conform to the 1:N format as required by the hierarchical model. **Please note that the many-to-many (M:N) relationships, which are more common in real life are very difficult to implement in a hierarchical model.**

We are in a position to solve some problems now.

Example 1. *Consider the two segments with student enrollment as the logical association. The faculty segment is the parent segment and the student segment is the child segment. Suppose that two students, Gurpreet and Mary are enrolled in courses taught by the faculty Rajiv. How will you represent the logical association between these instances in hierarchical model.*

Solution. Let the two segments be :

FACULTY : | Name, Department, Course taught |

STUDENT : | Name, Course Enrolled, Grade |

Then, an instance of hierarchical relation can be shown as follows :

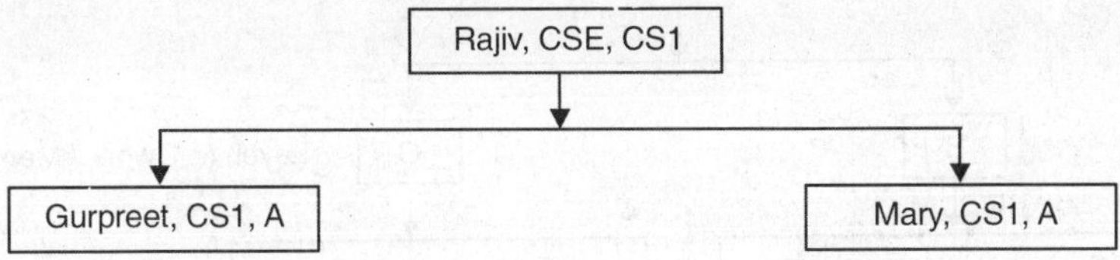

Example 2. *Consider a baseball database system. Draw its hierarchical scheme.*

Solution. For each player, there will be a set of positions he played, a set of homes and a set of birth date (s). This can be represented in hierarchical form as follows :

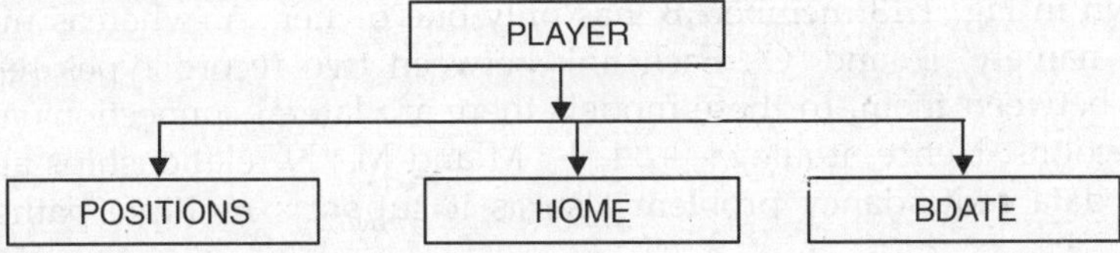

Here, each node represents a logical record type and is displayed by a list of its fields. The children of a node represent set of records that are associated with each record of the parent type. This is so because many-to-one relationship is from child to parent. **For example**, the tree above with root PLAYER tells us that for every player there will be a set of positions he played, a set of homes (naturally only one) and a set of birth dates (again only one).

Please note that the many one relationship from child-logical-record-type to parent type is from records to records and not values-to-values. Like in the figure above, there is a many-one relationship from POSITIONS to PLAYERS records meaning that each POSITIONS record is the child of only one PLAYERS record. **Also note that each position was played by only one player is not true**.

II. Network Model : In late 1960s, the Database Task Group formalized this model. A network model is the generalization of the hierarchical model. In this model, a segment can have multiple parent segments. In general, the segments are grouped as levels but logical associations can exist between segments belonging to any level. Although the logical associations are directional in nature, any two levels can have both types of directional associations. **Please note that in general, many-to-many logical associations can exist between any two segments and also their instances**. The diagrammatic representation of the different logical associations between the segments resembles a **graph**. Also remember that, in general, these logical associations between instances are implemented by pointers in the data set or by creating connecting relations that reflect the many-to-many associations between the instances.

Hence, the network model replaces the hierarchical tree with a graph thus allowing more general connections among the nodes. This model also handles many-to-many (M : N) relations *i.e.*, it allows a record to have more than one parent.

In network database terminology, a relationship is a set. Each set is made up of at least two types of records :

(*a*) An owner record (equivalent to parent in the hierarchical model)

(*b*) A member record (equivalent to child in the hierarchical model).

A network model will look like this (as shown in Fig. 1.13).

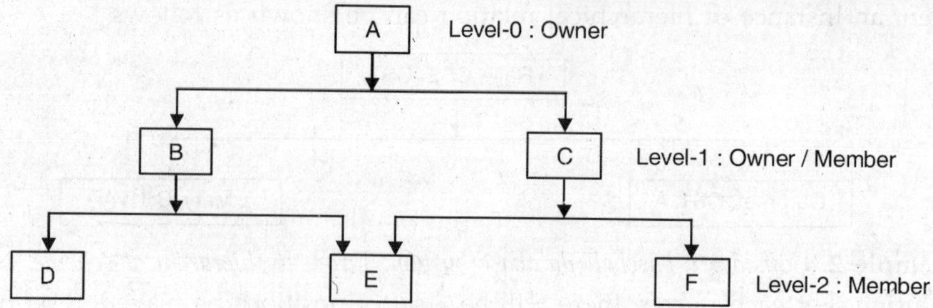

Fig. 1.13. *A network data model*

As shown in Fig. 1.13 member-'B' has only one owner 'A' whereas member-'E' has two owners namely 'B' and 'C'. Each link between two record types represents 1: M relationship between them. In these models there are lateral connections as well as top-down connections. Hence, it allows 1 : 1, 1 : M and M : N relationships among entities. This avoids data redundancy problem also as it supports multiple paths to the same record.

Examples:

(*a*) TOTAL by Cincom Systems Inc.

(*b*) IDMS by Cullinane corp.

(*c*) EDMS by Xerox corp.

Advantages of Network Model :

1. ***Simplicity :*** Network model is simple and easy to design just as our hierarchical data model.
2. ***Capable of handling more relationship types :*** The network model handles 1 : 1, 1 : N and M : N relationships which helps in modelling the real life applications.
3. ***Easier data access :*** The data access in this model is easier and superior. An application can access an owner record and all the members record within a set.
4. ***Data integrity :*** The network model does not allow a member to exist without an owner. Thus, a user must first define the owner record and then the member record. This ensures data integrity.
5. ***Data independence :*** The network model is better than the hierarchical model in isolating the programs from the complex physical storage details.
6. ***Database standards :*** The hierarchical model discussed earlier does not have any universal standards for the database design and modeling but the network model is based on the standards formulated by the DBTG. **Please note that all Network DBMS confirm to these standards, which also includes a DDL and DML.**

Disadvantages of Network Model : This model had some drawback also. Some of these drawbacks are discussed below.

1. ***System complexity :*** As all the records are maintained using pointers, so the whole database structure becomes very complex.
2. ***Operational anomalies :*** Since network model uses pointers for navigation so its implementation becomes quite complex.
3. ***Not user-friendly :*** The network model is not a design for user-friendly system and is a highly skill-oriented system.
4. ***Absence of structural independence :*** Since the data access method in the network database model is a **navigational system**, making structural changes to the database is very difficult in most cases and impossible in some cases. If changes

are made to the database structure then all the application programs need to be modified before they can access data. Thus, even though the network database model succeeds in achieving data independence, it still fails to achieve structural independence.

5. There is very little scope for automated query optimization.

We are in a position to solve some problems now.

Example 3. *Consider the two segments of faculty and student again. Suppose that the student Gurpreet takes courses both in Computer science and Electronics engineering departments. How many instances will be there?*

Solution. The student instance will have at least two parent instances. Thus, the relation between the instances of the student and faculty segments is no longer hierarchical but a network.

This network model becomes even more complex, if we include another segment, say 'Courses' and logical associations, like 'Students Enrolled in Courses' and 'Faculties Teaching Courses'. In this extended model, a student can be logically associated with multiple instances of Faculties and courses. The same type of association can exist between the instances of other segments.

Example 4. *Draw a Network Model for a sales organization.*

Solution. Say, for a sales organization- CUSTOMER, SALES-REPRESENTATIVE, INVOICE, INVOICE-LINE, PRODUCT and PAYMENT represent record types. So, we draw now :

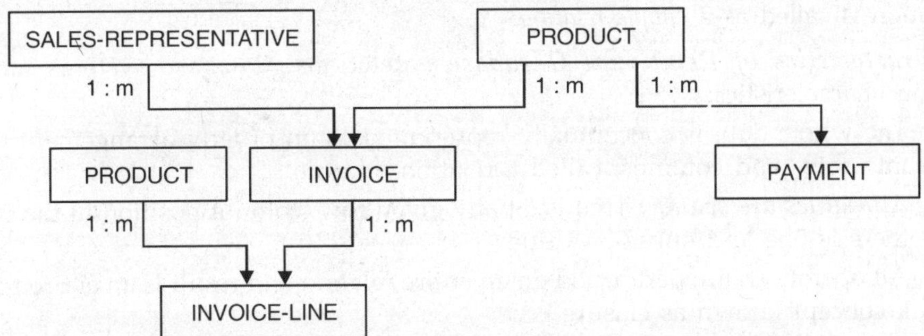

As shown in the figure, INVOICE-LINE is owned by both PRODUCT and INVOICE. Similarly, INVOICE has two owners namely SALES-REPRESENTATIVE and CUSTOMER. In network data model, each link between two record types represents a one-to-many (1 : N) relationship between them.

III. Relational Model : A relational model database is defined as a database that allows you to group its data items into one or more independent tables that can be related to one another by using fields common to each related table. In the relational model, the data are viewed as a collection of non-hierarchical time-varying relations. These are special constructs of mathematical relations and are different from the traditional data processing files and tables. **Please note that it is this view of data that enables the user to apply the powerful operations and expressions of relational algebra to data manipulations.** This model provides a means of describing data with its natural structure only, *i.e.,* without superimposing any additional structure for machine representation purposes. It provides a basis for a higher-level data language that yields maximal independence between the machine representation and organization of data. It also provides a sound basis of treating derivability, redundancy and consistency of relations.

In this model, relational algebra has been used to decompose a complex logical structure into a collection of simple relations so that complex relations of the real world can be expressed, also accessing and updating of data can be made simple and efficient.

Every relation has a unique name Relational model stores data inform of tables. This was proposed by Dr. E.F. Codd in 1971, at IBM. The relational model consists of three major components :

1. The set of relations and set of domains that define the way, data can be represented (data structures).
2. Integrity rules that define the procedure to protect data (data integrity).
3. The operations that can be performed on data (data manipulation).

In relational model, data are viewed as an **extension** or **intension** of a table. The **columns** of the table contain the values of the attributes and the **rows** are referred to as elements of the relation and correspond to values associated with individuals in the real world *i.e.,* **a row corresponds to a record**. The columns are assigned distinct names. Each column takes values from a collection of values known as **domain**. A domain may contain more values than present in the corresponding column of the relation. The same value may appear multiple times in a column of a relation but appears only once in a domain. The **degree** of a relation is the number of attributes it contains.

The rows of a relation are referred to as **tuples** and all rows of a relation are distinct. **Please note that in a relation there exists one or a collection of attributes that uniquely identify every tuple and no subset can do the same. These attributes are called identifiers or keys**. When every tuple of a relation is composed of single values from domains, then the relation is called as a *simple relation.*

Characteristics of Relational Database : Relational database systems have the following characteristics:

1. The whole data is conceptually represented as an orderly arrangement of data into rows and columns, called a relation or table.
2. ***All values are scalar :*** That is, at any given row/column position in the relation there is one and only one value.
3. All operations are performed on an entire relation and result is an entire relation, a concept known as closure.

Dr. E.F. Codd chose the term "relation" because it was comparatively free of connotations (unlike the word "table"). It is a **common misconception** that the relational model is so called because relationships are established between tables. Actually, the name is derived from the relations on whom it is based. **Please note that the model requires only that data can be conceptually represented as a relation, it does not specify how the data should be physically implemented. Also note that a relation is a relation provided that it is arranged in row and column format and its values are scalar.** Its existence is completely independent of any physical representation.

Before going further, let us define some basic terminologies that are used in Relational Model.

1. **Tuples : Each row of data is a tuple**—Actually, each row is an n-tuple but the 'n' is usually dropped.
2. **Cardinality : It is defined as the number of tuples in a relation. For example**, in Fig. 1.14 the cardinality of Relation (R) is 4.
3. **Degree of a relation :** Each column in the tuple is called as an **attribute**. The number of attributes in a relation is defined as its **degree. For example**, the relation in table 1.14 has a degree of 4.

4. **Domains : It is defined as a set of all possible values that an attribute may validly contain**. Domain is, however, different from a data type. **Data type is a physical concept while domain is a logical one. For example**, "Number" (data type) and "Age" (domain) are both of number type only but one is a data-type and the other is a domain. So, they belong to different domains.
5. **Body of a relation :** It consists of an unordered set of zero or more tuples. **Please note here that the relation is unordered**. Record numbers do not apply to relations. **Also note that a relation with no tuples still qualifies as a relation**. Also, a relation is a set. The items in a set are uniquely identifiable. **Therefore, for a table to qualify as a relation each record must be uniquely identifiable and the table must contain no duplicate records**.

   We draw a relation now in Fig. 1.14.

Attributes → (header row); Tuples → (rows S1–S4)

Emp_id	Ename	Salary	Age
S1	Rajiv	42,000	34
S2	Gurdeep	35,000	32
S3	Aman	40,000	30
S4	Kunal	30,000	28

Degree = 4
Tuples = 4
Cardinality = 4

Fig. 1.14. *A relation*

6. **Keys of a relation :** To understand the definition of a key, let us take an example of creating tables to store student data. Normally, all data related to students is not stored in a single table. **Data that is permanent** like data-of-birth, address, parent's name is stored in one table referred to as the *MASTER or PARENT table*. The MASTER table will contain only ONE record for every student.

The marks table, however, is the TRANSACTION table. It can have more than one record for every student *i.e.*, every time the student appears for an exam, a record will be added to the Marks table. This table will store data about the examinations only. So, the student-address file is the Master file of students containing **only one record for every student**. The marks-file is considered as a transaction file as they contain one or more rows for each student in the student-address file. That is,

ROLL_ NO	NAME	ADDR	PLACE	PIN
1.	SIMON	DELHI	DELHI	110009
2.	RAKSHIT	GOA	INDIA	110008
3.	RAHUL	KERALA	INDIA	57602

Student-address table

MASTER OR PARENT TABLE

Also, the student-marks table is a Transaction or child table

ROLL_NO	SUBJ	DATE	MARKS
1.	WIN-98	12-Dec-08	95
2.	WIN-NT	10-Jan-09	85
3.	WIN-NT	12-Dec-08	90
4.	Oracle	10-Jan-09	95

Student-marks table

TRANSACTION OR CHILD TABLE

Can the student-marks file contain a row for roll number 5? No, it cannot because roll number 5 does not exist in the PARENT TABLE. Can we delete the row of roll number = 2 from the student master? No, we cannot because roll number 2 has dependent rows in the student-marks table.

This is known as **referential integrity which states that "there are no rows in the transaction (child) table if there is no reference for it in the master (parent) table."** Now, the master table or the Parent table which contains the linking column must be a primary key. The linking column in the transaction table or child table references the parent table. **Please understand that the column in the child table which references a primary key of the parent table is called as a Foreign key**.

Examples :

1. DBASE
2. MS-ACCESS
3. VISUAL-FOXPRO
4. ORACLE
5. Sybase
6. MS-SQL Server
7. Paradox
8. System R by IBM
9. INGRES by University of California
10. MAGNUM by Tymshare

Advantages of Relational Model : The following are the advantages of the Relational Model :

1. ***Simple :*** It is a simpler model as it frees the designers from the actual physical data storage details. This allows them to concentrate on the logical view of the database.
2. ***No anomalies :*** Unlike hierarchical and network models, this relational model does not suffer from Insert, delete, update anomalies. The retrieval operation is very simple and symmetric.
3. ***Structural independence :*** Unlike hierarchical and network models, this relational model does not depend on the navigational data access system. So, changes in the database structure do not affect the data access.
4. ***Easier design, implementation, maintenance and usage :*** Both data as well as structural independence are provided by the relational model which makes database design, maintenance, administration and usage much easier than the other models.
5. ***Better query capability :*** The relational database model provides very powerful, flexible and easy-to-use query facilities. It uses fourth-generation languages like SQL that makes adhoc queries a reality.

Disadvantages of Relational Model : The following are the disadvantages of the Relational Model.

1. ***Hardware overheads :*** The relational data models need more powerful computing hardware and storage devices to perform RDMS-assigned tasks. RDMS hides the implementation complexities and the physical data storage details from the users. Because the processing power of modern computers is increasing at an exponential rate and now-a-days the need for more processing power is no longer a very big issue.
2. ***Easier to design :*** The relational database is easier to design and use. The users need not know the complex details of physical data storage. They need not know how the data is actually stored to access it. This ease of design and use can lead to the development and implementation of a poorly designed DBMS. **Please note that the database is efficient so these design inefficiencies will not be highlighted when the database is designed and when there is only a small**

amount of data. Also note that as the database grows, the poorly designed databases will slow the system and will result in performance degradation and data corruption.

3. ***Phenomenon of information island :*** Since relational database systems are easy to implement and use. This will create a situation where too many people or departments will create their own databases and applications. These are known as **information islands** which will prevent the information integration that is essential for the smooth and efficient functioning of the organization. These individual databases will also create problems like data inconistency, data duplication, data redundancy and so an.
4. SQL does not provide an efficient way to browse alphabetically through an index. Thus, some systems cannot provide a simple tittle A-Z browse.

We are in a position to solve some problems now.

Example 5. Consider the simple relation STUDENT (SN, SA, BK#) where

STUDENT = Name of the relation
SN = Student name
SA = Student age
BK# = Number of books belonging to a student.

What is the degree of this relation? How will you find an identifier for this relation? If we add two more domains to this STUDENT relation i.e., CO = Course and GR = Grade then what will be the repeating group?

Solution. Given a simple relation, STUDENT (SN, SA, BK#), the data for this relation can be :

SN	SA	BK#
Rajat	16	5
Rahul	17	8
Mayur	16	3

The degree of this relation is 3. In this relation, SN is an identifier.

If a value of a domain contains multiple types of values of a collection of domains, then the collection of domains is called as a repeating group. Thus, if the STUDENT relation also has the domains CO = Course and GR = Grade, then the tuple < CO, GR > forms a repeating group. **Please note that the repeating groups make tabular representation difficult and are a major source of access delays for instances within repeating groups.** In this relational model, this problem is eliminated by using operations of the relational calculus to create simple relational structures. **These relational structures with simple domains are called as first normal forms.** The above data of the STUDENT table is in 1 NF.

Example 6. Consider the following student-course (SC) data with a repeating group containing the domains (CO, GR, INS).

SC (SN, SA, BK#, CO, GR, INS)

SN	SA	BK#	CO	GR	INS
Rajat	16	3	CSI	A	Rajiv
			EEI	B	Kapil
			EE 2	A	Jim
Mary	18	8	EE 1	B	Ajay
			EE 4	A	Mayur
			CS 2	A	Ashish

Where INS = Instructor.

This table is in which normal form? Can you decompose it further?

Solution. The above table can be decomposed into two relations in 1NF using projection operations on domains (SN, SA, BK#) and (SN, CO, GR, INS) respectively. The data in the two normal forms are :

STU (SN, SA, BK#) is

Rajat	16	3
Mary	18	8

and COU (SN, CO, GR, INS) is

Rajat	CS1	A	Rajiv
Rajat	EE1	B	Kapil
Rajat	EE2	A	Jim
Mary	EE1	B	Ajay
Mary	EE4	A	Mayur
Mary	CS2	A	Ashish

The identifier for the relation COU is (SN, CO).

1.3.1 Comparison of the Three Models in Tabular Form

Let us compare the three models that we have discussed above in a tabular form now.

S. No.	Hierarchical Data Model	Network Data Model	Relational Data Model
1.	Relationship between records is of the **parent child type** (Trees).	Relation ship between records is expressed in the form of **pointers or links** (Graphs).	Relationship between records is represented by a relation that contains a key for each record involved in the relationship.
2.	Many to many relationship cannot be expressed in this model.	Many to many relationship can also be implemented.	Many to many relationship can be easily implemented.
3.	It is a simple, *straightforward* and natural method of implementing record relationships.	Record relationship implementation is very complex due to the use of **pointers**.	Relationship implementation is very easy through the use of a key or composite key field (s).
4.	This type of model is useful only when there is some hierarchical character in the database.	Network model is useful for representing such records which have many to many relationships.	Relational model is useful for representing most of the real world objects and relationship among them.
5.	In order to represent links among records, pointers are used. Thus relations among records are **physical**.	In Network model also the record relations are **physical**.	Relational model does not maintain physical connection among records. Data is organized **logically** in the form of rows and columns, and stored in table.
6.	Searching for a record is very difficult since one can retrieve a child only after going through its parent record.	Searching a record is easy since there are multiple access paths to a data elements.	A unique indexed key field is used to search for a data elements.

1.3.2 Comparison of the Three Models in Tabular Form (On the Basis of Operations)

Based on the operations performed, we compare the three models now :

Operation	Hierarchical Model	Network Model	Relational Model
1. *Insert operation*	We cannot insert the information of a child who does not have any parent.	It does not suffer from any insert anomaly.	It does not suffer from any Insert anomaly.
2. *Update operation*	There are multiple occurrences of child records, which lead to problem of inconsistency during the update operation.	This model is free from update anomalies because there is only a single occurrence for each record set.	This model is also free from update anomalies because it removes the redundancy of data by proper designing through normalization process.
3. *Delete operation*	It is based on parent-child relationship and deletion of parent results in deletion of child records also. This is known as a **cascading effect**.	It is based on many-to-many (M : N) relationship which make it free from delete anomalies.	It is also free from delete anomalies as the information is stored in different tables.
4. *Retrieve operation*	Retrieve algorithms are complex and asymmetric.	Retrieve algorithms are complex and symmetric.	Retrieve algorithms are simple and symmetric.

1.3.3 Which Data Model to Select ?

The data model that best suits an organization depends on the following factors :

1. The organization's primary goals and requirements.
2. The volume of daily transactions that will be done.
3. The estimated number of enquiries that will be made by the organization.

Out of the three models, the **relational data model is most widely used because it can be used for representing most of the real world objects and the relationships among them. Please note that the security and integrity are maintained easily by the relational data model. Also note that the use of relational model for database design increases the productivity of application programs since it eliminates the need to change the application programs when a change is made to the database**. Moreover, relational tables show only the logical relationship. End users need not know the exact physical structure of a table or relation.

Network model is also free from anomalies but due to its complex nature it is not a preferred model. Since hierarchical model suffers from lot of anomalies, it is useful only for those cases which are hierarchical in nature.

1.4 DATA MODELING USING ER-MODEL

An Entity Relationship (ER) model was introduced by P.P. Chen in 1976. **An ER model is defined as a conceptual data model that views the real world as entities and relationships**. An ER-model is useful to a database designer in the following ways :

1. An ER-model maps well to the relational model *i.e.*, the constructs used in the ER model can be easily transformed into relational tables.
2. An ER-model can be used by the database designer to communicate the design to the end user.

3. An ER-model can be used as a design plan by the database developer to implement a data model in specific DBMS software.

1.4.1 Basic Terminology Related to ER-Model

Before we go further, let us discuss some basic terminologies related to ER-model :

1. Entities : Anything which exists and is distinguishable from one another is known as an entity. For example, EMPLOYEES, TABLE, CHALK, BOARD, PEN etc. are some of the entities. **Please note that an entity is analogous to a table in the relational model.**

Entities are of two types : (*a*) Independent entity, (*b*) Dependent entity.

An **independent entity** is one that does not rely on another for identification. While a **dependent entity** is one that relies on another for identification. We shall be explaining these again in section 1.4.3 of this chapter. **But please note that an entity occurrence (or instance) is an individual occurrence of an entity. Also note that an occurrence is analogous to a row in the relational table.**

2. Entity Type (or Set) : It is defined as a set of entities of the same type that share the same properties of attributes. Associative entities (or intersection entities) are the entities used to associate two or more entities in order to reconcile a many-to-many relationship. **Please remember that the subtypes entities are used in generalization hierarchies to represent a subset of instances of their parent entity (or super type), but which have attributes or relationships that apply only to the subset.**

For example, an entity-set PROJECT with two entities P_1 and P_2 are shown below in Fig. 1.15.

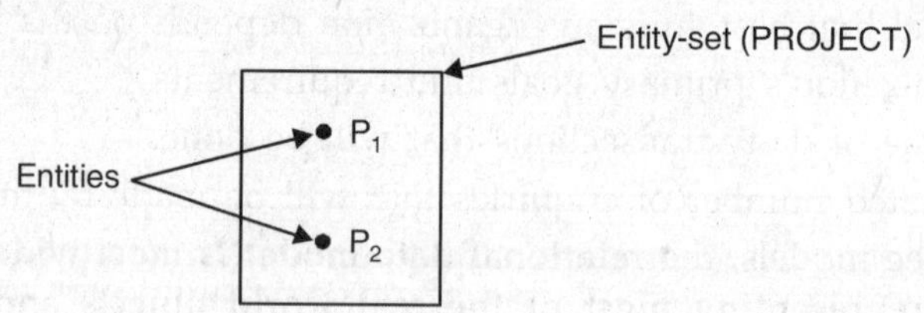

Fig. 1.15. *An entity-set PROJECT with entities P_1 and P_2*

Here, P_1 and P_2 are two entities (or relations) with some attributes (or fields), say, (PROJ-ID, START-DATE, END-DATE). Then, the data within this table will form a value whereas a combined values of P_1 and P_2 will form a **value-set.**

3. Relationships : A relationship represents an association between two or more entities. They are classified in terms of degree, connectivity, cardinality and existence. **For example,** ISA relationship, HASA relationship etc.

Please note that the relationship has no physical or conceptual existence other than that which depends upon their entity associations.

A particular occurrence of a relationship is called as a **relationship instance** or relational occurrence. In an ER-model similar relationships are grouped into relations sets called as the relationship type. It is a set of meaningful associations between one or more participating entity types. **Please remember that each relationship type is given a name that describes its function. Also note that the relationships with the same attributes fall into one relationship set.**

4. Degree of a Relationship : It is defined as the number of entities associated with the relationship.

There are three types of degrees of relationships :

(*a*) Unary or Recursive relationship

(*b*) Binary relationship

(*c*) Ternary relationship

Please remember that the *n*-ary relationship is the general form for degree, *n*.

Here, if $n = 1$, the relationship degree is 1, also called as Unary relationship. If $n = 2$, it is called as **binary relationship** and if $n = 3$, it is called as **ternary relationship.**

Recursive relationships are sometimes called as **unary relationships. It is defined as a relationship between the instances of a single entity type. This means that an entity relates only to another instance of its own type.**

For example, consider a recursive binary relationship "manages" that relates an entity PERSON to another PERSON by management. That is,

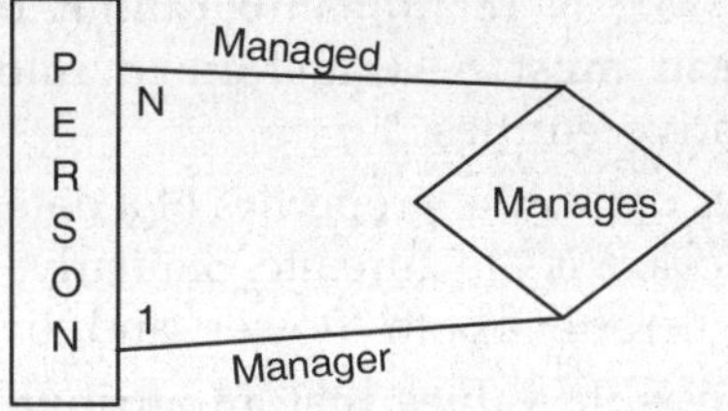

Fig. 1.16. *Recursive relationship*

Binary relationships are the association between the two entities. So, it's, degree = 2. **Please note that a recursive binary relationship occurs when an entity is related to itself. For example**, a binary relationship is shown in Fig. 1.17.

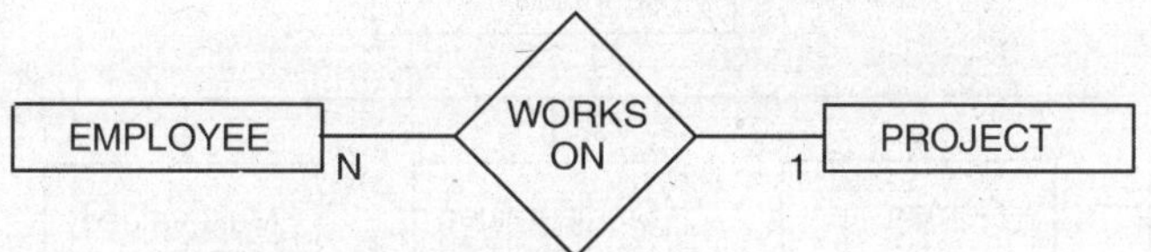

Fig. 1.17. *A binary relationship*

Ternary relationship is defined as an association among three entities and is used when binary relationship is not sufficient. **For example,**

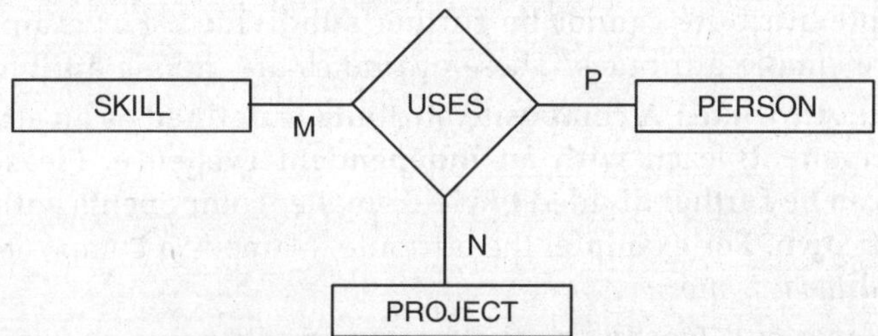

Fig. 1.18. *A ternary relationship*

Three entities are connected with a diamond (relationship) named USES. We can designate the connectivity of each entity as either 'one' or 'many'.

5. Connectivity or Cardinality : The connectivity of a relationship describes the mapping of associated entity instances in the relationship. The values of connectivity are "one" or "many". **While the actual count of elements associated with the connectivity is called as the cardinality of the relationship connectivity. Please note that the term**

cardinality is used much less frequently than the connectivity constraint because the actual values are usually variable across relationship instances.

There are three basic types of connectivity for relations and they are as follows :

(*a*) One-to-One (1 : 1)

(*b*) One-to-Many (1 : M)

(*c*) Many-to-Many (M : M).

A 1 : 1 relationship is when at most one instance of an entity (say, A) is associated with one instance of another entity (say, B). **For example,** one teacher teaches one student.

A 1 : N relationship is when for one instance of entity A there are zero, or many instances of entity B. **For example**, one teacher teaches many students.

A M : N relationship is when for one instance of entity A, there are zero, one or many instances of entity B. *For example,* many teachers teach many students.

Please remember that M : N relationship cannot be directly translated to the relational tables but instead must be transformed into two or more one-to-many relationships using associative entities.

6. Attributes : Attributes define the properties of a data object of entity. **For example**, attributes of flower are it's color, it's texture etc. Similarly, the attributes of a ball are its shape, color, size etc. Note here that both 'flower' and 'ball' are the data objects.

The collection of all possible values that an attributes can have is known as the domain of an attribute. For example, the date of birth attribute for both 'manager' and 'labourer' entities can share the same domain.

We shall now classify these attributes. (See Fig. 1.19).

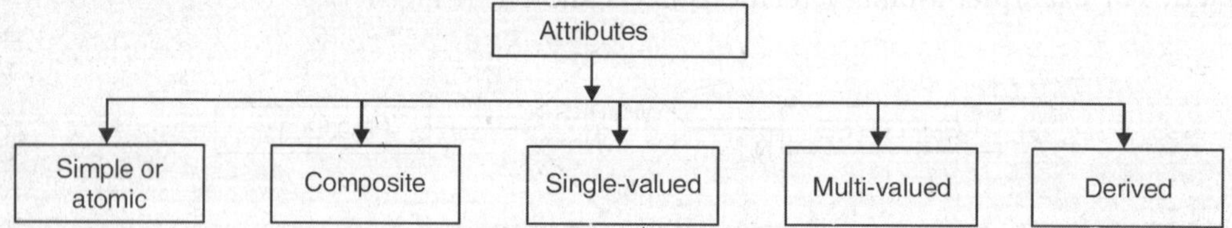

Fig. 1.19. *Types of attributes*

I. Simple (or atomic) Attributes : A simple or atomic attributes is defined as an attribute that is composed of a single component with an independent existence. Please note that a simple attribute cannot be further subdivided. For example, Age, Salary, Person-ID etc are simple attributes. These attributes are atomic attributes.

II. Composite Attribute : A composite attribute is defined as an attribute composed of multiple components each with an independent existence. Please note here that some attributes can be further divided to yield smaller components with an independent existence of their own. For example, the attribute, Name is a composite attribute which can be *further subdivided into*

—fname, mname and lname, *i.e.*, first-name, middle-name and last-name.

Also note that the decision of subdividing or modeling an attribute into simple or composite attributes depends on the user view of the data.

III. Single-Valued Attribute. It is defined as an attribute that holds a single value for a single entity. The majority of attributes are single-valued for a particular entity.

For example, the attribute (or property or characteristic or field) ROLL-NO is a single-valued attribute.

IV. Multi-valued Attribute : It is defined as an attribute that holds multiple values for a single entity. For example, for a 'student' entity, if one of the attributes is 'Hobby', then 'Hobby' can have multiple values like reading, dancing, gardening and so on.

Please note that a multi-valued attribute may have a set of numbers with upper and lower limits. Like, our Hobby attribute above a student may have a minimum of 1-hobby and a maximum of 3-hobbies where 1 is the lower-limit and 3 is the upper limit.

V. Derived Attribute : It is defined as an attribute that represents a value that is derivable from the value of related attribute or a set of attributes, not essentially in the same entity. So, the values held by some attributes are derived from two or more attribute values. For example, the age attribute can be derived from the date-of-birth attribute and so they are related.

VI. Direction : The direction of a relationship shows the originating entity of a relationship. The entity from which a relationship originates is the **parent entity** and the entity where the relationship terminates is the **child entity.**

Conventions used : The type of the relation is determined by the direction of the line connecting relationship component and the entity. We use a **directed line** or an **undirected line** between the relationship set and the entity set.

Directed line : Used to indicate one occurrence.

Undirected line : Used to indicate many occurrences.

As an example of one-to-one, consider that there is only one manager per department then we draw as shown :

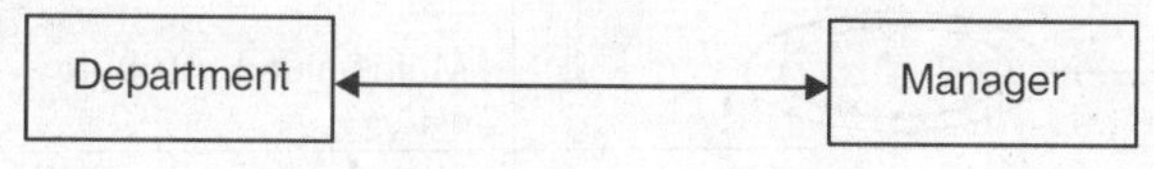

Fig. 1.20. *1 : 1 relationship*

Similarly, an example of 1 : M is as follows :

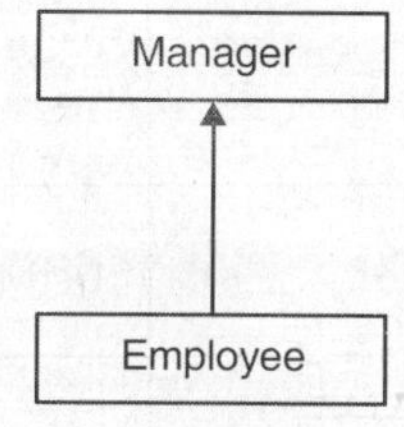

Fig. 1.21. *1 : M type*

And an example of M : N type is as follows :

Employee

Project

Fig. 1.22. *M : N type*

1.4.2 Notations Used in ER-diagrams

Let us draw a table and show the various notations used in drawing of an ER-diagrams :

S. No.	Symbol	Meaning
1.		Entity type
2.		Weak entity type
3.		Relationship
4.		Identifying relationship type
5.		Attribute
6.		Primary key attribute
7.		Multi-valued attribute
8.	...	Composite attribute
9.		Derived attribute
10.	E_1 R E_2	Total participation of E_2 in R
11.	E_1 1 R N E_2	Cardinality relation 1 : N for E_1 : E_2 in R

From the table it is clear that :

1. **Entities** are represented by labeled rectangles, where label is the name of the entity.
2. **Attributes** are represented by Ellipsis.
3. **Relationships** are represented by diamond.
4. **Primary key attributes** are underlined
5. **Multi-valued attributes** are represented by double ellipsis.
6. **Directed line** represents one occurrence while an **undirected line** represents many occurrences in a relation.

TIP : Developing of an ER-diagram requires an understanding of the system and its components.

1.4.3 Strong and Weak Entity Sets

Let us first of all understand what is a weak entity set ? **The entity set which does not have sufficient attributes to form a primary key is known as a weak entity set. On the other hand, an entity set that has a primary key is known as a strong entity set.**

For example, Consider an entity-set PAYMENT which has three attributes :

(*a*) payment-number

(*b*) payment-date and

(*c*) payment-amount.

Although each payment entity is distinct but payment for different loans may share the same payment number. Thus, this entity set does not have a primary key and it is a weak entity set. Each weak set must be a part of 1 : M relationship set. A member of a strong entity set is called **dominant entity** and a member of weak entity set is called as a **subordinate entity. Please note that a weak entity set does not have a primary key but we need a means of distinguishing among all those entries in the entity set that depend on one particular strong entity set. Also note that the discriminator of a weak entity set is a set of attributes that allows this distinction to be made.**

Let us consider an example to understand this. As shown in Fig. 1.23, the attribute payment-number acts as a **discriminator** for the payment entity set. It is also called as the **Partial key** of the entity set.

Then, **how to form the primary key of a weak entity set ?**.

The rule is—**"The primary key of a weak entity set is formed by the primary key of the strong entity set on which the weak entity set is existence dependent, plus the weak entity set's discriminator."**

So, we draw now.

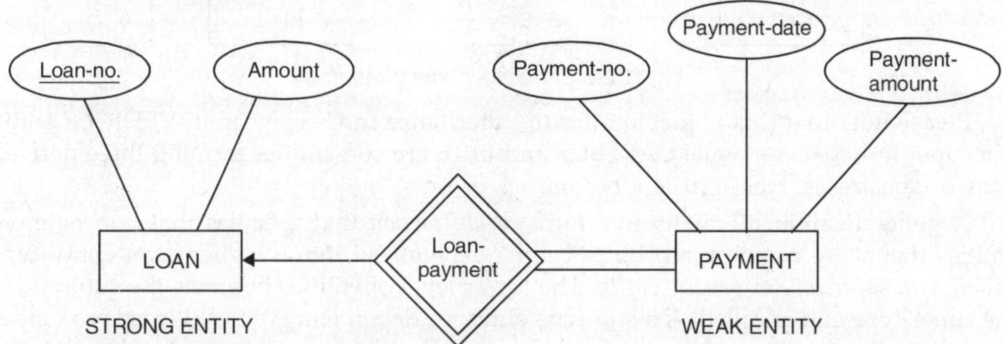

Fig. 1.23. *Relation between a strong and weak entity set*

In this example, (loan-no, payment-no) acts as a **primary key for payment entity set. The relationship between the weak entity and strong entity set is called as an 'Identifying Relationship'**. Like in our example above, loan-payment is the identifying relationship for the PAYMENT entity.

Notations Used :

(*a*) A weak entity set is represented by doubly outlined box and the corresponding identifying relation by a doubly outlined diamond.

(*b*) A double line indicates the total participation of weak entity in strong entity set. It means that, in our example, every payment must be related via loan-payment to some account.

(*c*) The arrow from loan-payment to loan indicates that each payment is for a single loan.

(*d*) The discriminator of a weak entity set is underlined with dashed lines rather than solid line.

1.5 GENERALIZATION, SPECIALIZATION AND AGGREGATION

Let us discuss these terms one by one.

Generalization : Generalization is defined as the process of identifying some common characteristics of a collection of entity sets and creating a new entity set that contains entities processing these common features. It can also be defined as **the process of minimizing the differences between entities by identifying their common characteristics**. Generalization is a **bottom up process** *i.e.,* say we have three sub-entities as Car, Bus, Bike. Now, these three sub-entities can be generalized into one general super class (or base class) named as VEHICLE. So, VEHICLE becomes an entity while Car, Bus and Bike are its sub-entities. That is,

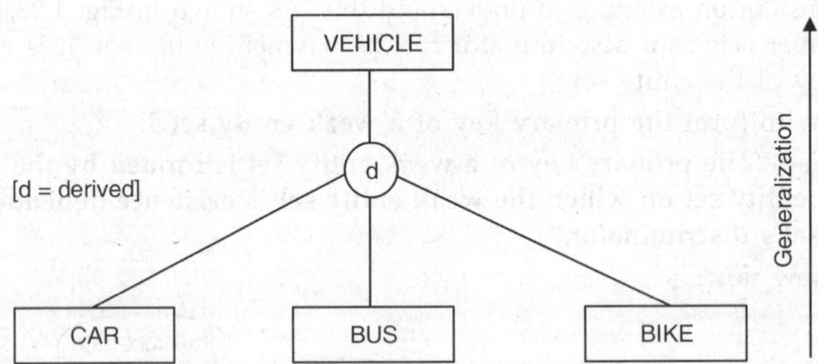

Fig. 1.24. *Showing generalization*

Please note that this is just similar to inheritance in C++, wherein VEHICLE entity is a super or base class while CAR, BUS and BIKE are sub-entities forming three derived class or subclasses. Hence, it is a bottom-up process.

A **generalization hierarchy** is a form of *abstraction* that specifies that two or more entities that share common attributes can be generalized into a higher level entity type called as a *super type or generic entity*. The lower level of entities becomes the sub-type to the super-type and is called as a sub-type entity or dependent entities. **Please remember that generalization is used to emphasize the similarities among lower-level entity sets and to hide differences.**

Specialization : Specialization is defined as the process of identifying subsets of an entity (super-class or super-type) that share some distinguishing characteristic. It is the process of taking subsets of a higher-level entity set to form lower level entity sets and is actually specialization. So, now we need to define a set of sub-classes of an entity type. The process of defining sub-class is based on the basis of some distinguishing characteristics of the entities in the super-class. **Please note that it is a top-down process of defining super-classes and their related sub-classes. Also note that we firstly define a super-class, then sub-classes and then their attributes and relationships. The advantage**

of doing generalizations or specializations is that now each of these entities or sub-entities can have the attributes of their own. Like in our example below, each sub-entity type has its own attributes/characteristics/features. This is shown in Fig. 1.25 below.

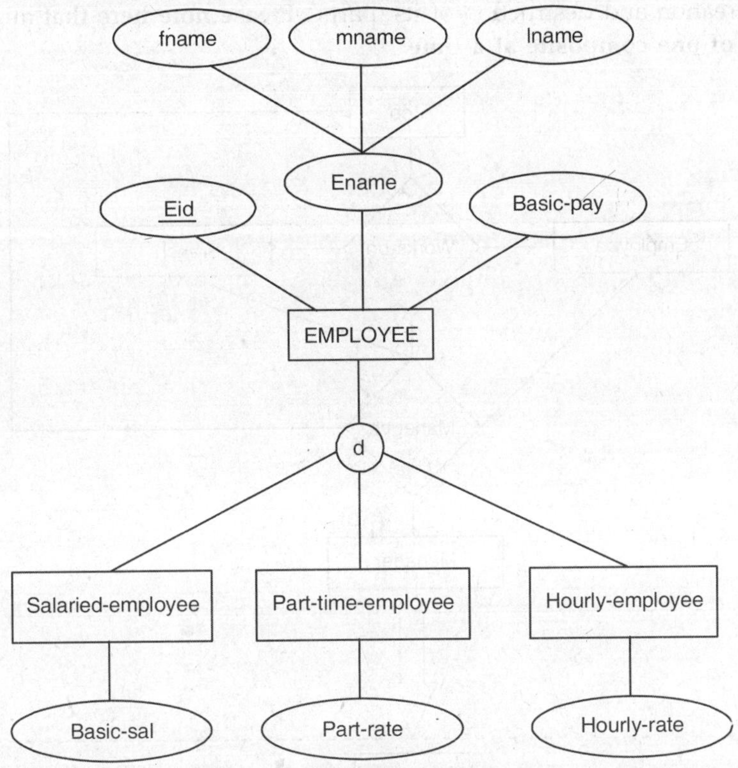

Fig. 1.25. *Showing specialization*

Aggregation : Aggregation is the process of compiling information on an object, thereby abstracting a higher-level object. One disadvantage of the ER-model is that it cannot express relationships among relationships. This problem is overcome here. So, aggregation shows a 'has-a' or 'is-part-of' relationship between entity types where one represents the 'whole' and the other the 'part'. A **relationship** represents an association between two entity types that are conceptually at the same level. **Please note that sometimes we want to model a 'has-a' or 'is part-of' relationship in which one entity represents a larger entity (the 'whole'), consisting of smaller entities (the 'parts'). This special kind of relationship is called as an aggregation** [BOOCH, 1998]. **Also note that this does not change the meaning of navigation across the relationship between the whole and its parts nor does it link the lifetimes of the whole and its parts**.

Let us consider an example shown in Fig. 1.26.

Consider a ternary relationship-'Work-on, between Employee, Branch and Manager as shown in Fig. 1.25. **The best way to model this situation is to use aggregation**. So, the relationship-set, work-on, is a higher-level entity-set. Such an entity-set is treated in the same manner as any other entity-set. We can then create a binary relationship, Manages, between work-on and manager to represent who manages what tasks.

However, there is a specific form of aggregation that represents an association between entities. There is a strong ownership and coincidental lifetime between the 'whole' and the 'part'. Actually, aggregation is totally a conceptual model and it does nothing more than just distinguish a 'whole' from a 'part'. In composition, however, the 'whole' is responsible for the disposition of the 'parts' which means that the composition must manage the creation and destruction of its 'parts'. **Please note here that an object may only be part of one composite at a time.**

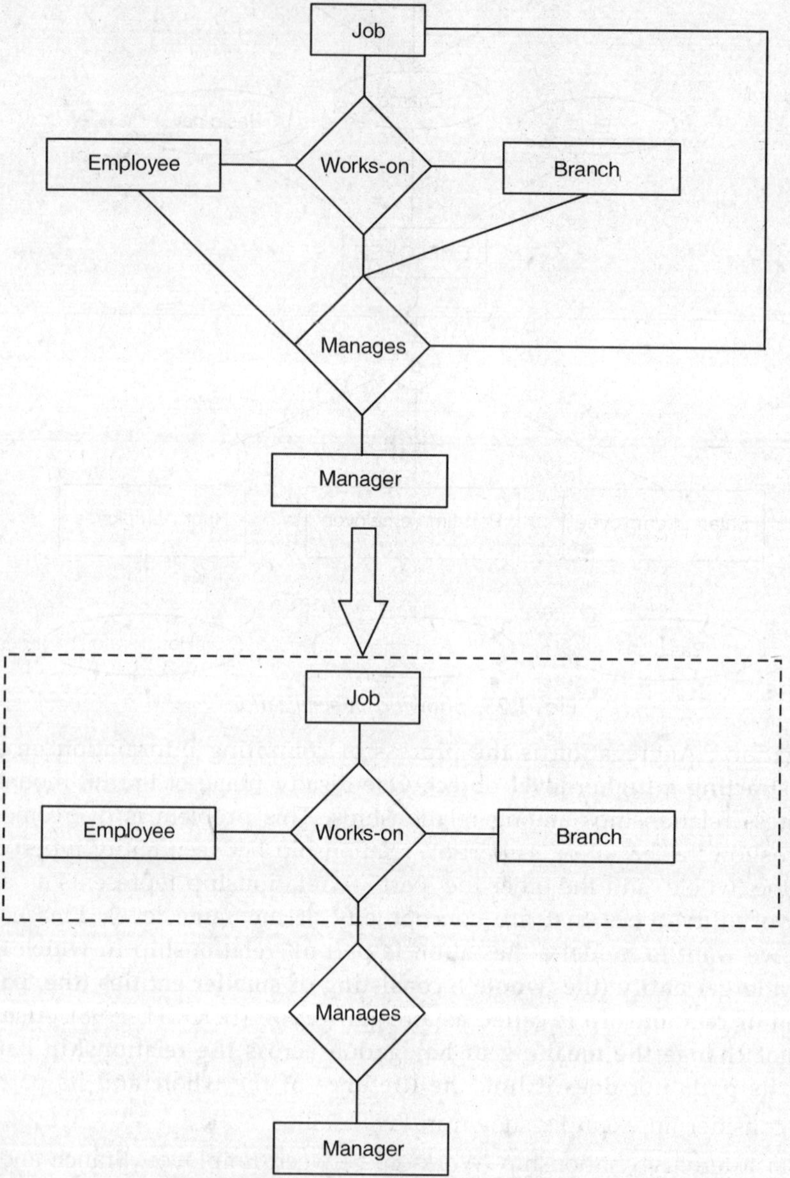

Fig. 1.26. *Shows aggregation concept*

For example, consider an entity Newspaper which has many advertisements. It can be represented as follows :

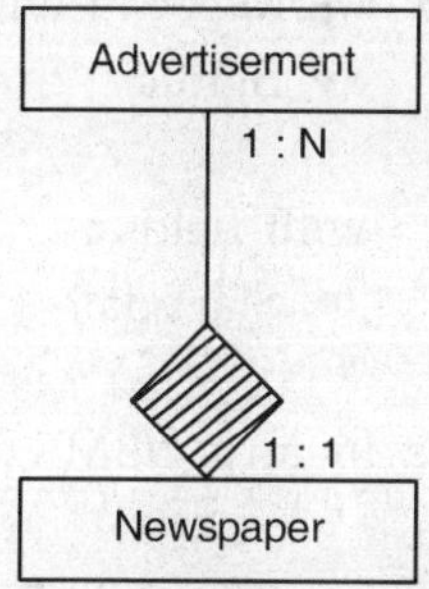

Fig. 1.27. *Shows composition concept*

Please note that these concepts should only be used when there is a requirement to stress on special relationships between entity types (like 'has-a' or 'is-part-of') **which has implications on the creation, update and deletion of these closely related entities.**

When the organization's data becomes very complex then we should use these concepts of aggregation and composition within our ER-model.

1.6 TRANSLATING YOUR ER-MODEL INTO RELATIONAL MODEL

A given (or drawn) ER-model can be converted to relations. Each entity-set and each relationship-set is converted to a relation. There is a direct mapping between the ER-model and the relational model. Consider the following snapshot of an ER-model :

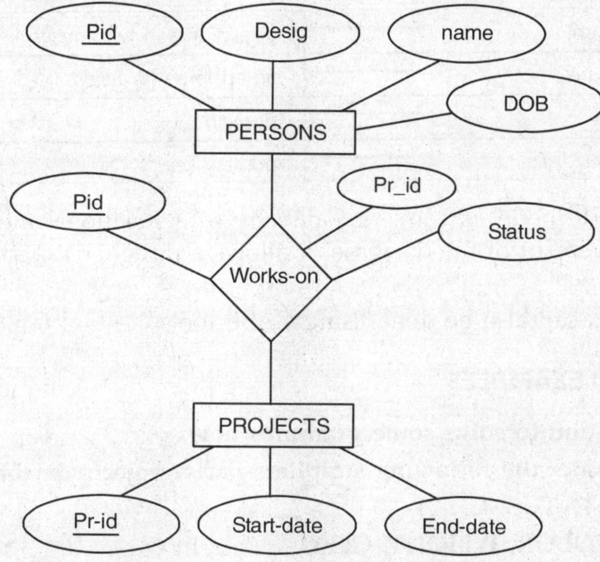

Fig. 1.28. *An Employee's ER-model*

Now, we can form 3 relations based on 3 entities above *i.e.,* PERSONS, WORKS-ON and PROJECTS.

Also, the attributes are directly transformed to the fields of these relations *i.e.,* PERSONS will have :

- Pid
- Desig
- Name
- DOB

as its fields.

Similarly, we can form a relation-WORKS-ON with the fields :

- *Pid*
- *Pr-id*
- Status

And the third relation-PROJECTS with fields :

- *Pid*
- End-date
- Start-date

It is now we can create tables in any DBMS. That is, overall transformation summary is :

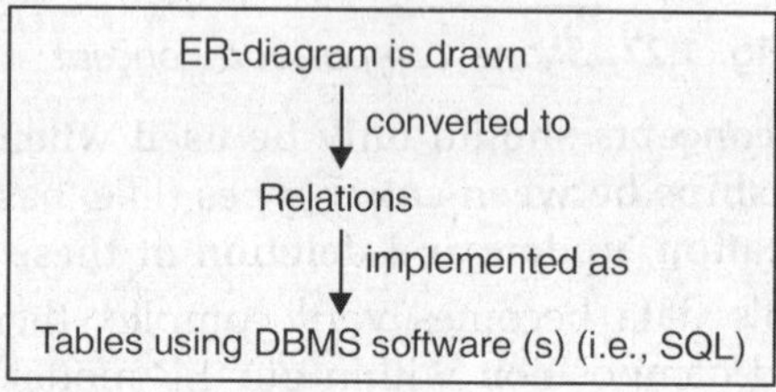

Thus, we can summarize the one-to-one mappings between ER-models and Relational models.

S. No.	ER-model		Relational Model
1.	Entity type is converted to	⟶	a relation (table)
2.	1 : 1 or 1 : N relationship type	⟶	to foreign key
3.	M : N relationship type	⟶	a relation and two foreign keys
4.	Simple attribute	⟶	an attribute (or fields)
5.	Value sets	⟶	domain
6.	Key attribute	⟶	primary key

This is how an ER-model is converted directly to a Relational model. So, an ER-diagram acts as a **blueprint** of the database. It allows a designer to communicate more precisely.

These conversions can also be done using CASE tools.

1.7 SOME SOLVED EXAMPLES

We are in a position to solve some examples now.

Example 1. Consider the following suppliers-parts-projects database:

S(S#, SNAME, STATUS, CITY)

P(P#, PNAME, COLOR, WEIGHT, CITY)

J(J#, JNAME, CITY)

SPJ(S#, P#, J#, QTY)

Where

S	**:**	**Information of suppliers**
P	**:**	**Parts**
J	**:**	**Projects**
SPJ	**:**	**Supplied quantity**

Draw it's ER-diagram?

Solution. Using our rules, listed earlier we get the following ER-diagrams :

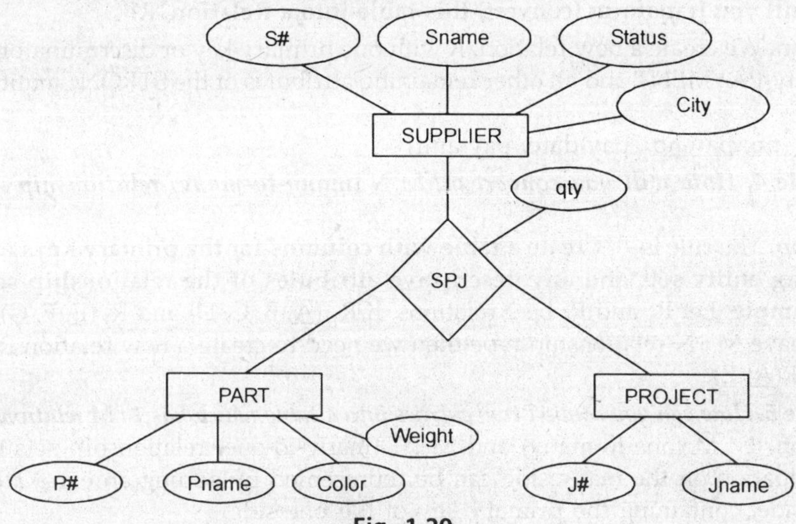

Fig. 1.29

Example 2. Consider the following CUSTOMER entity having composite attributes also. Convert it to a table (or relation).

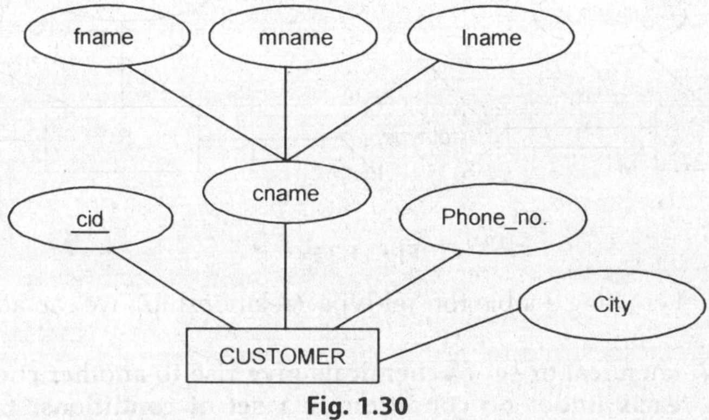

Fig. 1.30

Solution. Since CUSTOMER is an entity with composite attribute-cname. So, the rule followed is—**"The composite attributes are flattened out by creating a separate attribute for each component attribute."** So, in our table, we will have the following flattened attributes

CUSTOMER (Cid, fname, mname, lname, phone_no., city)

Thus, we can say that a multi-valued attribute, M, of an entity, E, is represented by a separate table EM. And that this table, EM, will have the attributes corresponding to the primary key of E and an attribute corresponding to multi-valued attribute, M.

Example 3. Consider an ER-diagram now that has a weak entity set-Payment as shown below:

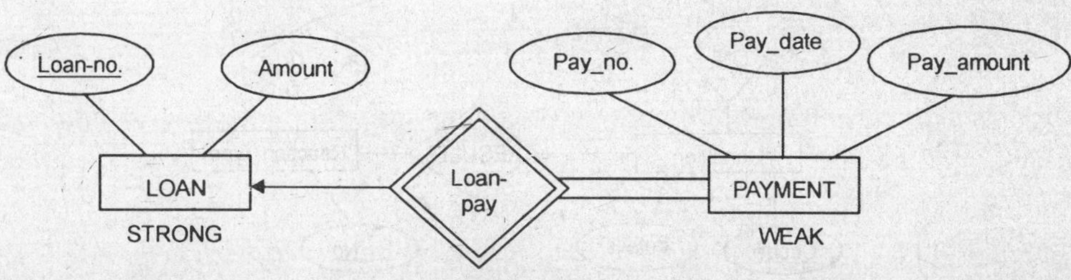

Fig. 1.31

How will you transform (convert) this table into a Relation, R?

Solution. We create a new relation, R with one primary key or discriminator from the WEAK entity-PAYMENT and all other remaining attributes of the STRONG entity-LOAN. That is,

R(loan –no, pay-no., pay-date, pay-amt)

Example 4. ***How will you convert a M : N (many-to-many) relationship set into a relation, R?***

Solution. The rule is—**"Create a table with columns for the primary keys of the two participating entity sets and any descriptive attributes of the relationship set."**

For example, Let R_1 and R_2 be 2 relations. If R_1 (A, B, C, D) and R_2 (E, F, G) and that R_1 and R_2 have M : N relationship type then we need to create a new relation R with the attributes, R(A, E).

Example 5. ***How can you convert two entities into a table which has 1 : M relationship type?***

Solution. 1 : M (one-to-many) and M : 1 (many-to-one) relationship sets that have total participation on the many side can be represented by adding an extra attribute to the many side, containing the primary key of the one side.

For example, say R_1 and R_2 are the two entities with M : 1 relationship type *i.e.,*

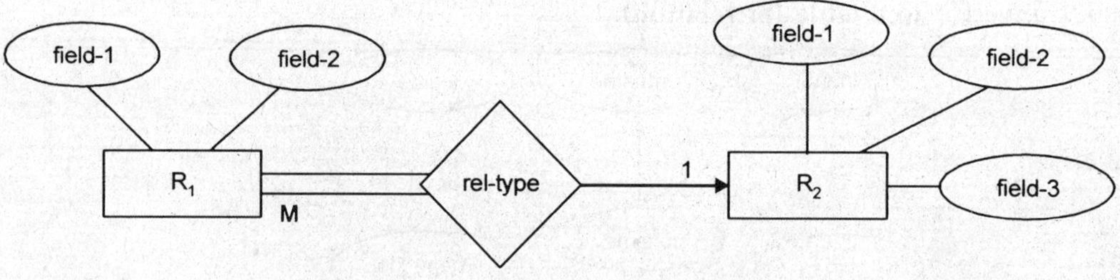

Fig. 1.32

Here, instead of creating a table for 'rel-type' (relationship), we can add an attribute/ field of R_2 to R_1.

Example 6. A chemical or set of chemicals give rise to another chemical or set of chemicals, when reacts under no condition or a set of conditions. Like, water and sodium react to give Sodium Hydroxide and Hydrogen and no condition is required. Whereas CH_4 and Cl_2 form chloromethane when exposed to light. There are numerous reactions possible and each reaction has to be given a reaction number. Each chemical and condition has to be given a code. Draw its ER-diagram.

Solution

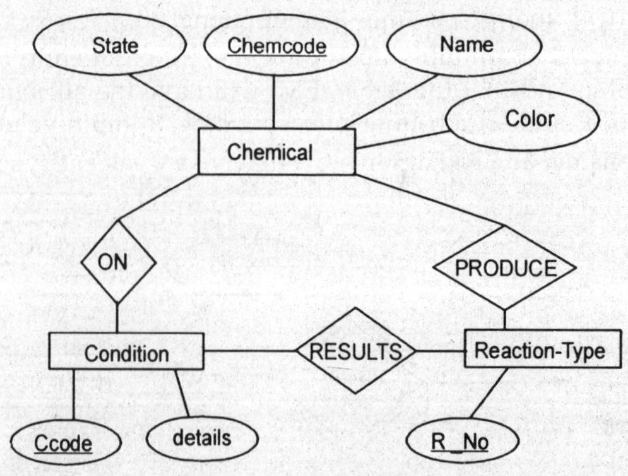

Example 7. An information system is to be designed for keeping the records of Universe cup cricket tournament. In all, there are teams from 10 countries participating in the tournament. Each country sends 15 players and 4 other members. For players, the runs he scores and the number of wickets taken (so far) are to be recorded. For non-players, the role (manager, coach etc.) and the number of years of experience in that capacity are to be recorded. There are matches scheduled amongst the teams on several grounds on fixed dates. Each ground has a fixed seating capacity and a size. For 38 matches, 11 referees have been assigned duties. Every match will have 3 referees working for it. The performance of every player in every match is to be recorded in terms of the runs he scored and the wickets he took. Draw an E-R model of the system.

Design table layouts from E-R model.

(Pune University, BE (CSE/IT) - 3rd yr., Dec. 98)

Solution.

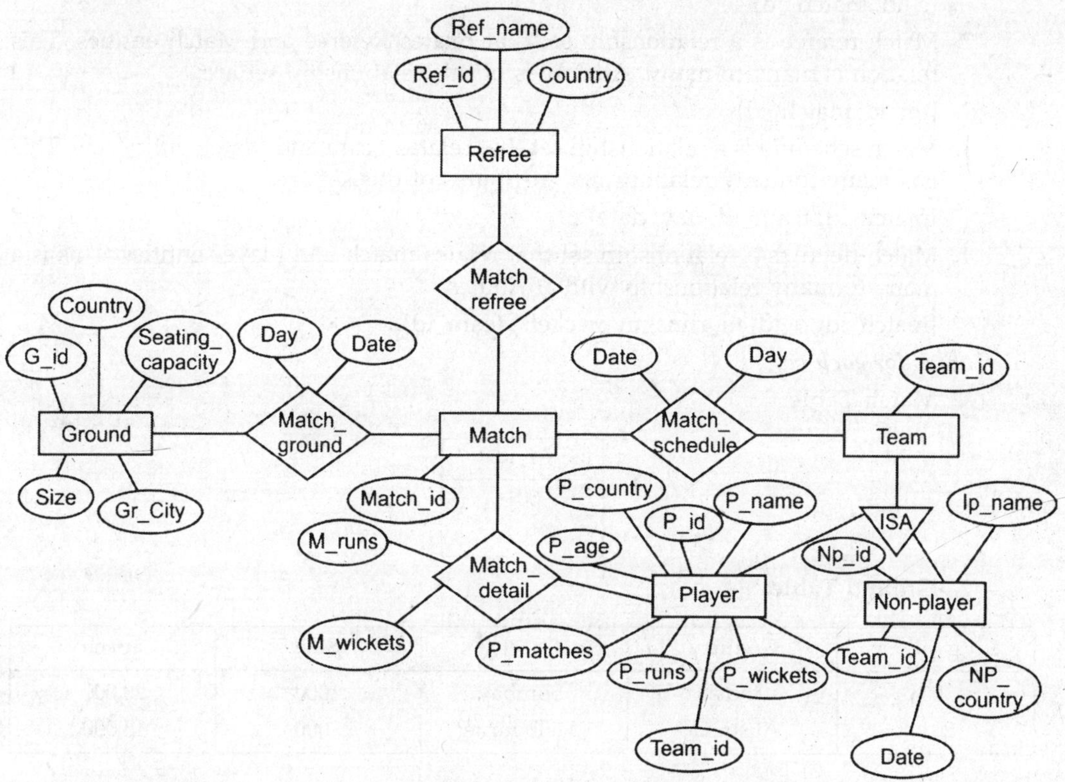

Fig. 1.34. E-R Diagram

Description of entities in E-R diagram:

1. Match – {match_id} primary key match_id.
2. Ground entity set with attributes:
   {g_id. country, city, size, seating_capacity}
   Primary key – g_id
3. Referee entity set with attributes:
   {ref_id, ref_name, country}
   Primary key – ref_id

4. Team entity set with attributes {Team_id}
   Primary key – Team_id
5. Player entity set with attributes:
   {P_id, Team_id, P_name, P_age, P_country,
   P_wickets, P_runs, P_matches:
   Primary key – {P_id, Team_id}
6. Non-player entity set with attributes:
   {Np_id, Team_id, Np_name, Np_country, role}
   Primary key – {Np_id, Team_id}.

Description of Relationship Sets in E-R Diagram:

1. Match-ground is a relationship set that relates Ground and Match entities. This relation is many-to-many. Attributes of this relationship set are:
   {g_id, match_id}
2. Match-referee is a relationship set that relates Referee and Match entities. This relation is many-to-many. Attributes of this relationship set are:
   {ref_id, match_id}
3. Match schedule is a relationship set that relates Team and Match entity sets. This is a many-to-many relationship. Attributes of this set are:
   {match_id, team_id, day, date}
4. Match-detail is a relationship set that relates match and player entities. This is a many-to-many relationship with attributes.
   {match_id, p_id, m_runs, m_wickets, team_id}.

Tables for each set.

1. Match Table:

M_id
001
002

2. Ground Table:

g_id	Country	Gr_city	Size	Capacity
101	India	Bombay	1000	20,000
201	Australia	Melbourne	2000	15,000

3. Referee Table:

Ref_id	Ref_name	Ref_country
011	XYZ	England
021	PQR	India

4. Player Relation:

Team_id	Player_id	Ply_age	Ply_name	Ply_runs	P_wick	Ply_match
1001	01	24	Sachin	8000	75	250
2001	01	34	Mark	6000	5	220

5. Non-player Table:

Team_id	NP_id	NP_name	NP country	NP exp	NP Role
1001	111	Gaikwad	India	2	Manage
2001	112	Kapil	India	1	Coach

6. Match Ground:

M_id	Gr_id	Day	Date
001	10L	Monday	12/2/2012
002	20L	Tuesday	13/3/2012

7. Match Referee:

m_id	Ref_id
001	011
001	021

8. Match Schedule:

m_id	team_id	m_day	m_date
001	1001	Monday	12/3/2012
001	2001	Monday	12/3/2012

9. Match Detail:

m_id	p_id	team_id	m_runs	m_wickets
001	01	1001	100	2
001	01	2001	57	0

Example 8. Assume you are to compose database requirements of a wholesale dealer for audio, video consumer equipment from different manufacturers (brands). Customers are the various retail outlets (retailers). Wholeseller extends credit to old customer and special discounts are offered to new customers (retailers). You have to generate an E-R model for the above DBMS application with the scope restricted to details (queries on) of customers (retailers), products stocked and their price discounts and credits offered etc. (Pune University BE (CSE/IT) Dec. 97)

Solution. ***Description of entities:***

1. Consumer-equipment with attributes {equip_id}
2. Audio-equipment with attributes {a_id, equip_id, brand}
3. Video equipment with attribute {V_id, equip_id, brand}
4. Wholesale-dealer with attributes {dealer_id}
5. Customer with attributes (c_id, c_name}
6. New with attributes {c_id, c_name, discount}
7. Old with attributes {c_id, c_name, credit}

Description of relationships:

Cons-whole with attributes {equip_id, dealer}

Equip-cost with attributes {equip_id, dealer, cust_id, cust_name}

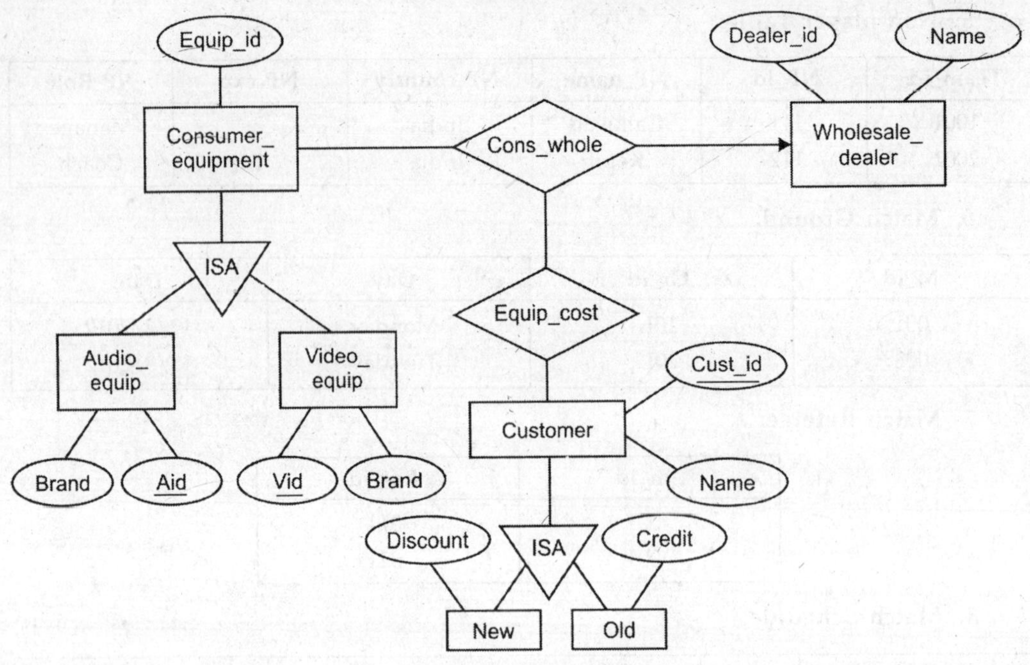

Fig. 1.35. E-R Diagram

Example 9. A movie studio wishes to institute a database to manage their files of movies, actors and directors. The following facts are relevant. Each actor has appeared in many movies.

- **Each director has directed many movies.**
- **Each movie has had one director and one or more actors.**
- **Each actor and director may have several addresses and telephone numbers.**

Identify the entities and attributes. Draw E-R diagram.

(Pune University BE (CSE/IT) May 1994)

Solution. Description of entities and relationships:

1. Actor is an entity with attributes {a_name, a_id}
2. Movie is an entity with attributes {m_id, a_name}
3. Director is an entity with attributes {d_id, name}
4. Act movie is a relationship with attributes {a_id, m_id}
5. Dir_Movie is a relationship with attributes {d_id, m_id}
6. Dir_add is a relationship with attributes {d_id, a_id}
7. Act_add is a relationship with attributes {a_id, add_id}
8. Act_address is an entity set with attributes {ad_id, city, street}
9. Dir_address is an entity set with attributes {add_id, city, street}

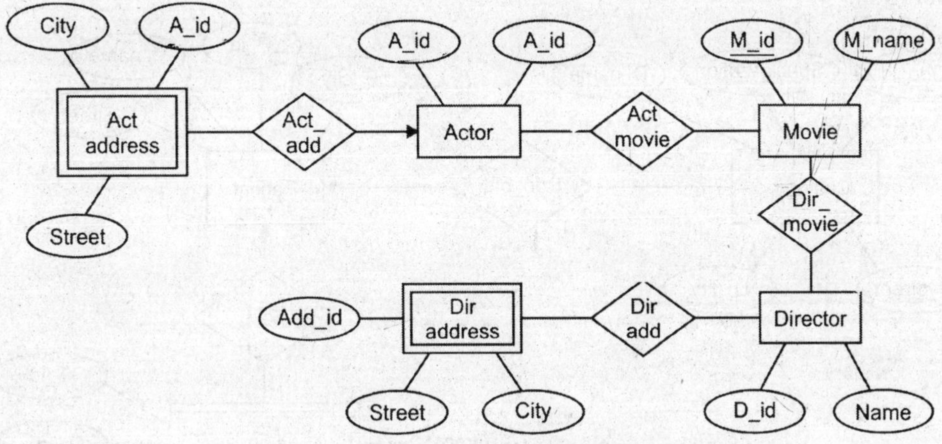

Fig. 1.36. E-R Diagram

Example 10. Construct an E-R diagram for a car-insurance company that has a set of customers, each of whom owns one or more cars. Each car has associated with it zero to any number of recorded accidents. (Pune University BE (CSE/IT); 3rd yr., Dec. 2002)

Solution.

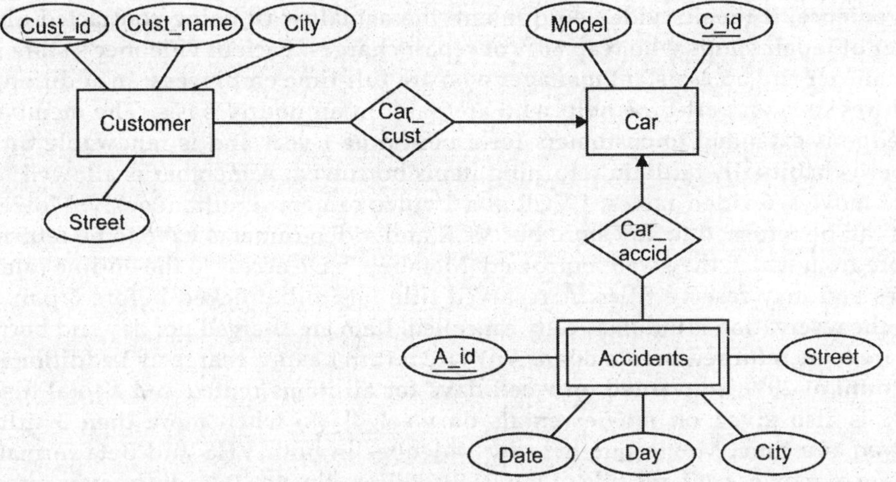

Fig. 1.37. E-R Diagram

Example 11. Construct an E-R diagram for a hospital with a set of patients and a set of medical doctors. Associate with each patient a log of the various tests and examination conducted. (Pune University BE (CSE/IT); 3rd yr., May 2001)

Solution.

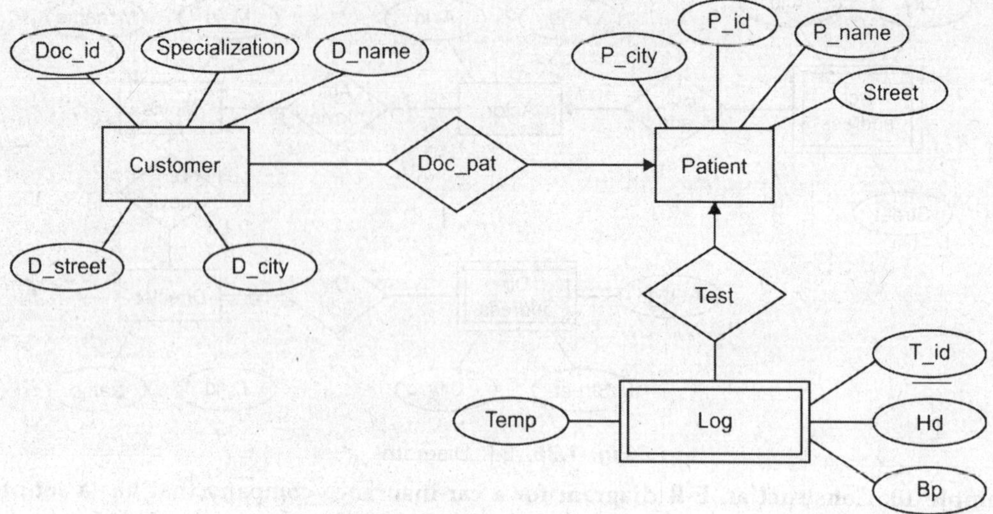

Fig. 1.38. E-R Diagram

Example 12. Videobec is the leading corporation in the growing video rental business. It has the largest number of stores and prides itself on having the most comprehensive list of video movies and games. It also rents VCR and video cameras to its members. As a convenience, it repairs video equipment, the actual work being contracted out to a number of repair shops who reap 80% of repair charges. Each of videobec's store is run by a manager and an assistant manager who are full-time employees. In addition, each store hires its own part-time help who are paid on an hourly basis. The membership priviledge is extended to customers for a period of 1 year and is renewable unless a member is habitually tardy in returning items borrowed. A member is allowed to rent upto 12 movies, 6 video games, 1 VCR and 1 video camera simultaneously. Movies and games can be returned to any store but VCR and video cameras have to be returned to the store from which they were borrowed. Members have access to the on-line catalogue of titles and may reserve titles. A reserved title has to be picked before 6 p.m., after which the reservation is automatically cancelled. Item are charged per day and borrowed items are to be returned before noon. Any late return bears a charge of 1 additional day. A discount of 20% is awarded on week days for all items rented and a total discount of 33% is also given on movie rentals on week days, when more than 3 titles are borrowed at a time. Movies are held by Videobec in both VHS and Beta format. The catalogue of movies contains title of movie, producer, director, 2 leading actors categories of movies, number of cassettes available and charge per day. The video games catalogue contains the name of the game, game system and charger per day. Videobec carries multiple copies of same title and a store would have been assigned any number of copies of each title. A store that has more copies will return these at the end of each week to Videobec's head office which redistributes them to appropriate stores. Draw E-R diagram.

Solution. Description of Entities:

1. Videobec is an entity with attributes name, address, e-mail, phone no., number of stores, number of movies, number of games, number of cameras, number of VCRs, number of members and number of repairs.
2. Store entity set with attributes store_id, number of games, number of movies, number of cameras, number of VCRs, number of employees.

   Primary key: store_id

3. Catalogue entity set with attributes catalogue_id, number of movies and number of games.
   Primary key: catalogue_id
4. The movies and games entity sets which we get as a result of generalization of catalogue entity set.
   Attributes of movie entity set are:
   movie_id, movie_title, movie_actor, movie_actress,
   movie_dir, number of copies, movie_type and charge-per-day.
   Primary key: catalogue_id, movie_id
   Attributes of game entity set are: game charge, game_id, game_system.
   Primary key: game_id, catalogue_id.
5. Equipment entity set attribute is equipment_id
   Primary key: equipment_id
6. VCR and Video Equipment are entity sets derived by generalization of Equipment entity set.
   Attributes of VCR are: VCR_id, VCR_company, and VCR_ent.
   Primary key: VCR_id, equipment_id
   Attributes of video equipment are
   V_id, V_company and V_rent

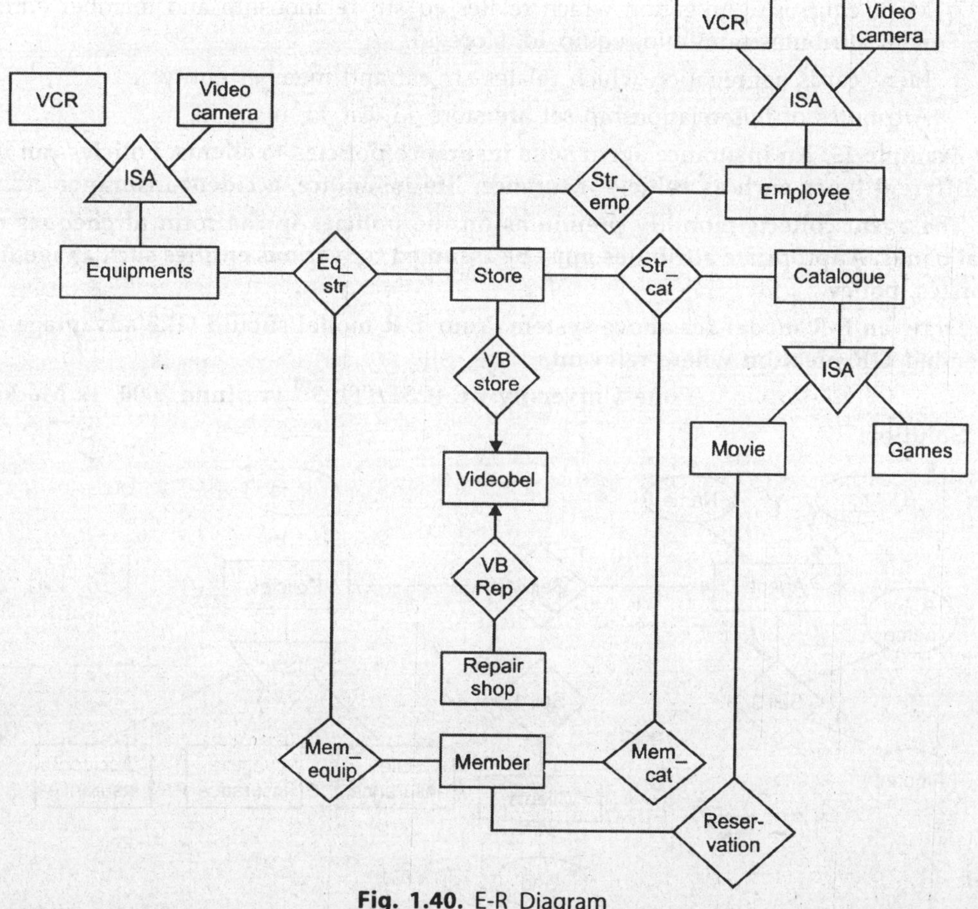

Fig. 1.40. E-R Diagram

7. Employee entity set attributes are emp_id
   Primary key: emp_id
8. Generalization of Employee set results in part-time and full-time.
   Attribute of these entity sets are id, name, salary, work.
9. Member entity set attributes are:
   member_id, name, date, rem.

Description of Relationship Sets:

1. Reservation entity set having attributes:
   movie_id, member_id
2. Vbstore – is one-to-many relationship between Videobec and store.
   Attributes are store_id.
3. Vbrep – is one-to-many relationship between Videobec and repair shop.
4. Eq_str is many-to-many relationship between Equipment and store with attributes equip_id, store_id.
5. Str_emp is many-to-many relationship between store and emplyee with attributes store_id and emp_id.
6. Str_cat is many-to-many relationship between store and catalogue with attributes store_id and cat_id.
7. Mem_equp is aggregation which relates eq_str, relationship and member entity with attributes num-mid, equip_id, store_id.
8. Mem_cat is aggregation which relates str_cat and member entity.
   Attributes of this relationship set are store_id, cat_id, mem_id.

Example 13. An insurance agent sells insurance policies to clients. Policies can be of different types such as vehicle insurance, life insurance, accident insurance etc.

The agent collects monthly premiums on the policies in the form of cheques of local banks. Appropriate attributes must be assumed for various entities such as agents, vehicles, policy.

Draw an E-R model for above system. Your E-R model should take advantage of extended E-R notation where relevant.

(Pune University BE (CSE/IT); 3rd yr., June 2000, 12 Marks)

Solution.

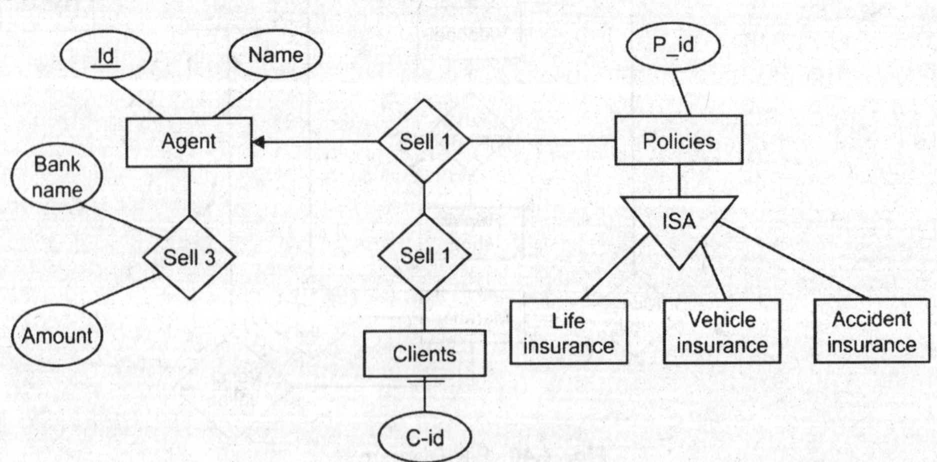

Fig. E-R Diagram for Ex. 13

Example 14. Following information is maintained manually in a library.

Books (Accession_number, name, authors, price, book_type, publisher)

Borrowers (membership_no, name, address, category, max_no of books that can be issued, Accession_number of books borrowed)

The following constraints are observed

(i) Each book has unique accession_number.

(ii) A book may have more than one author.

(iii) There may be more than one copy of a book.

(iv) The category of borrower determines the max. number of books that may be issued to borrower.

Identify the entities, relationship and draw E-R diagram.

Provide for issue and return of book, fine calculation and claiming of an issued book.

Solution.

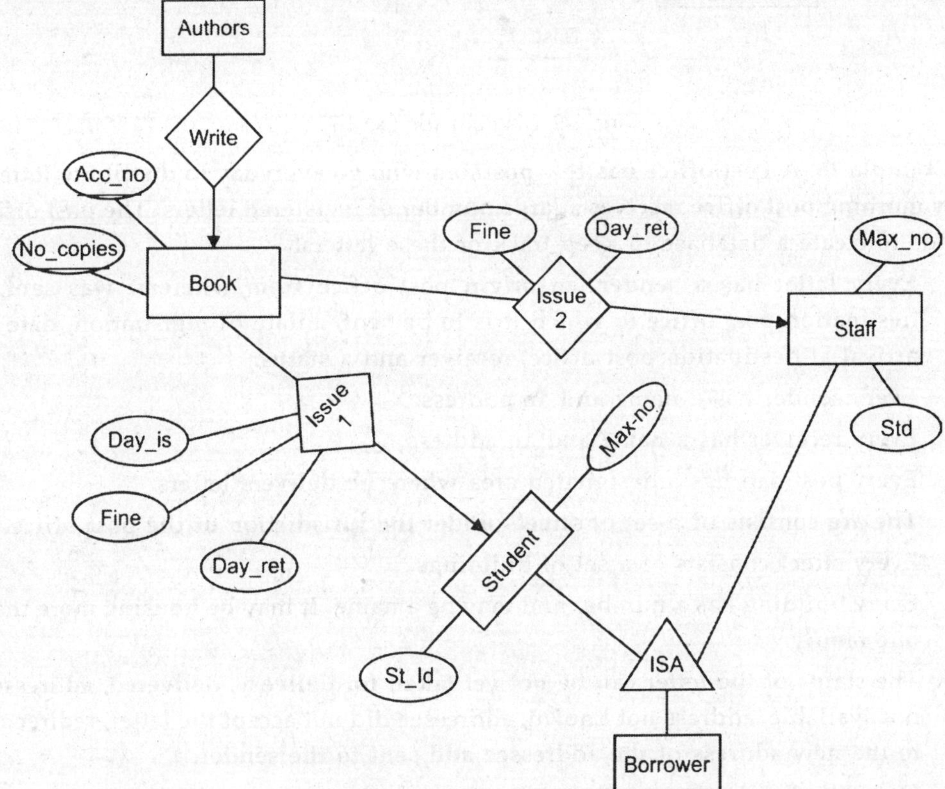

Fig. E-R Diagram for Ex. 14

Example 15. A is required to set-up medical record database system, given the following data

- **Patients identification number, name, address data of birth, blood group.**
- **Physician identification number, name, address and their specialties.**
- **Data about patients visit to physician like the date of visit, the medicine prescribed, the dose of each medicine, tests ordered at the visit, result of those tests, temperature, blood pressure.**

Give an E-R diagram for the database.

Solution.

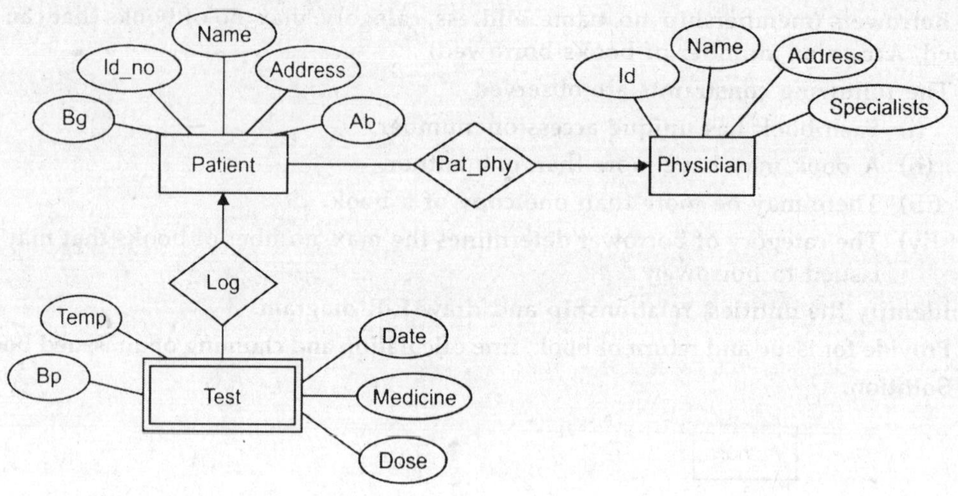

Fig. E-R Diagram for Ex. 15

Example 16. A Post office has few postmen who go everyday to distribute letters. Every morning post office receives a large number of registered letters. The post office intends to create a database to keep track of these letters.

- **Every letter has a sender, an origin post office from where it was sent, a destination post office to which it is to be sent, a date of registration, date of arrival at destination post office, receiver and a status.**
- **Every sender has a name and an address.**
- **Every receiver has a name and an address.**
- **Every postman has a designated area where he delivers letters.**
- **The are consists of a set of streets under the jurisdiction of the post office.**
- **Every street consists of a set of buildings.**
- **Every building has a number and may be a name. It may be housing more tnan one family.**
- **The status of the letter can be not yet taken for delivery, delivered, addressee not available, address not known, addressee did not accept the letter, redirected to the new address of the addressee and sent to the sender.**

Draw the E-R Diagram

Solution.

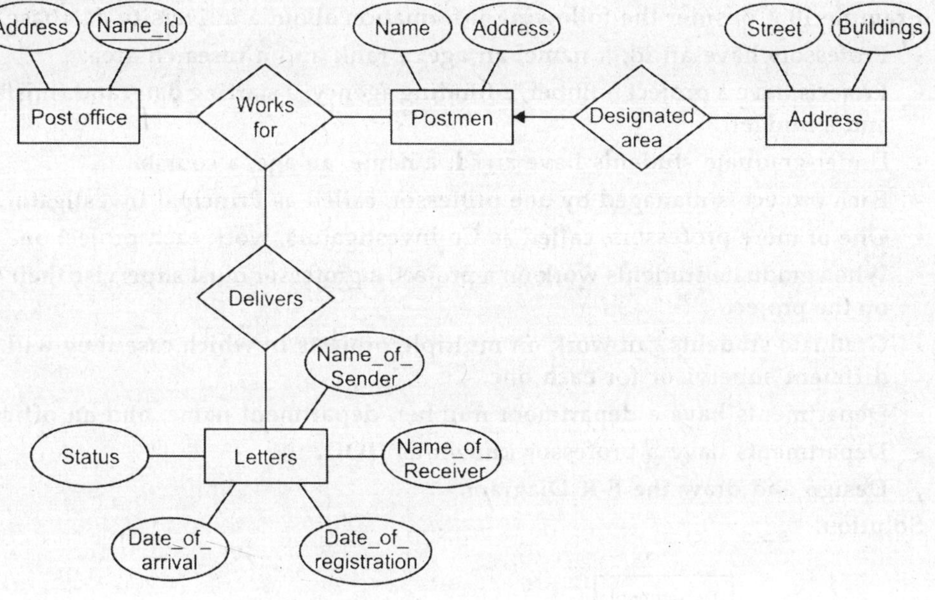

Fig. 1.44. E-R Diagram for Ex. 16

Example 17. A university database contains information about professors and courses. For each of the following situation draw an E-R diagram that describes it.

- **Professors can teach the same course in several semesters, and only the most recent such offerings need to be recorded.**
- **Professors can teach the same course in several semesters, and each offering is to be recorded.**
- **Every professor must teach some course.**
- **Every professor teaches exactly one course.**
- **Every professor teaches exactly one course and each course must be taught by one professor.**
- **Now suppose that team of professors can teach certain courses jointly, but it is possible that no one professor in a team can teach the course. Model this situation, introducing additional entity sets and relationship sets if necessary.**

Solution.

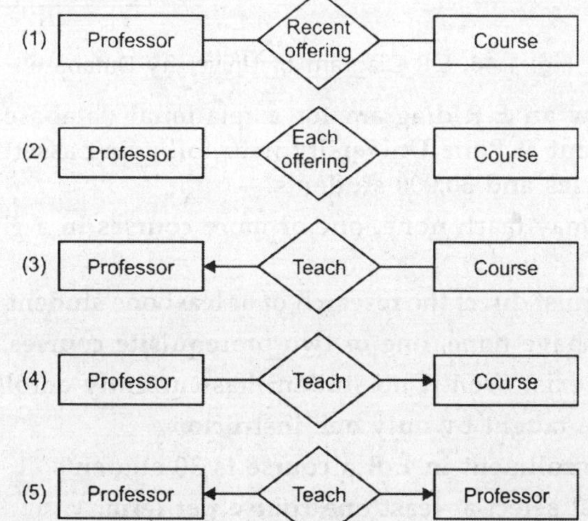

Fig. 1.45 University Database with Courses and Professors Information

Example 18. Consider the following information about a university database.

- **Professors have an id, a name, an age, a rank and a research area.**
- **Projects have a project number, a funding agency, a starting date, and finish data and a budget.**
- **Under-graduate students have an id, a name, an age, a course.**
- **Each project is managed by one professor, called as Principal Investigator.**
- **One or more professors, called as Co-investigators, work each project on.**
- **When graduate students work on a project, a professor must supervise their work on the project.**
- **Graduate students can work on multiple projects in which case they will have different supervisor for each one.**
- **Departments have a department number, department name, and an office.**
- **Departments have a professor known as HOD.**

Design and draw the E-R Diagram.

Solution.

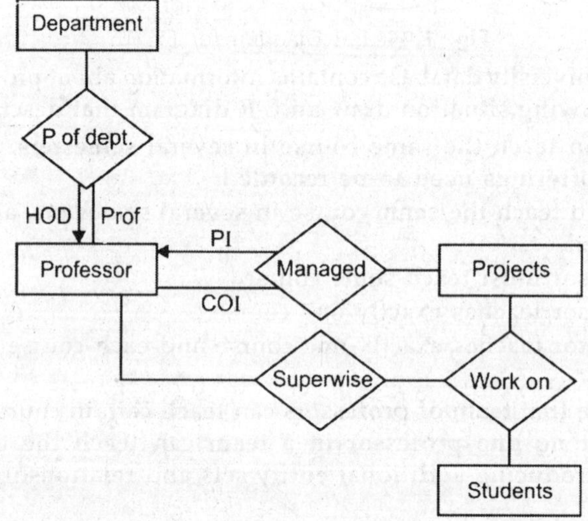

Fig. 1.46. E-R Diagram of University Database

Example 19. Draw an E-R diagram for a relational database that represents the current term enrollment at Pune University with following assertions. There are 2000 instructors, 4000 courses and 30,000 students.

- **An instructor may teach none, one or more courses in a given term (average 2 courses).**
- **An instructor must direct the research of at least one student (average 2 students).**
- **A course may have none, one or two prerequisite courses.**
- **A course may exist even if no student has currently enrolled for that.**
- **All courses are taught by only one instructor.**
- **The average enrollment in E-R a course is 30 students.**
- **A student must select at least one course per term.**

(Pune University BE (CSE/IT); 3rd yr., May 2002)

Solution.

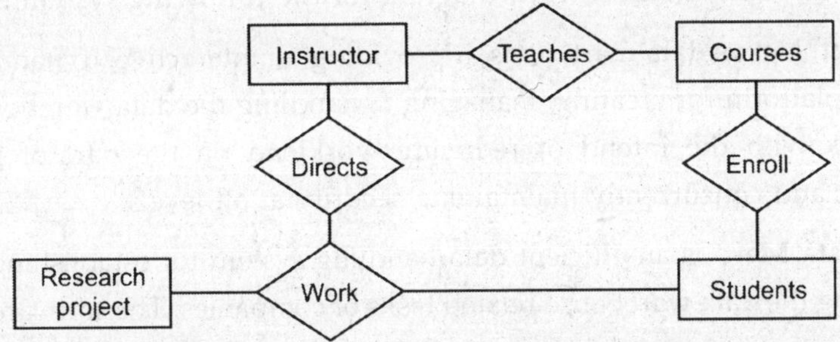

Fig. 1.47. E-R Diagram of Team Controller

Example 20. The people's bank offer five types of accounts: Loan, Checking, Premium savings, Daily interest saving and Money market. It operates a number of accounts. An account can be joint, i.e., more than one client may be able to operate a given account.

Identify entities and draw E-R Diagram.

(Pune University BE (CSE/IT); 3rd yr., Dec. 2004)

Solution.

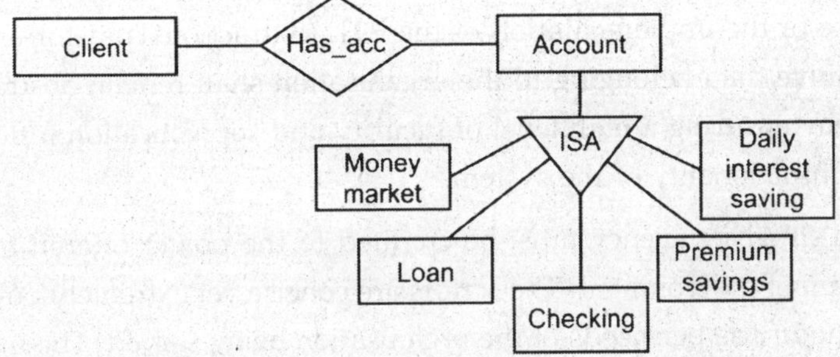

Fig. 1.48. E-R Diagram of Five Bank Accounts

Example 21. Design a generalization – specialization hierarchy for a motor – vehicle sales. The company sells motorcycles, passenger cars, vans and buses. Justify the placement of attributes at each level of hierarchy.

(Pune University BE (CSE/IT); 3rd yr., May 2003)

Solution.

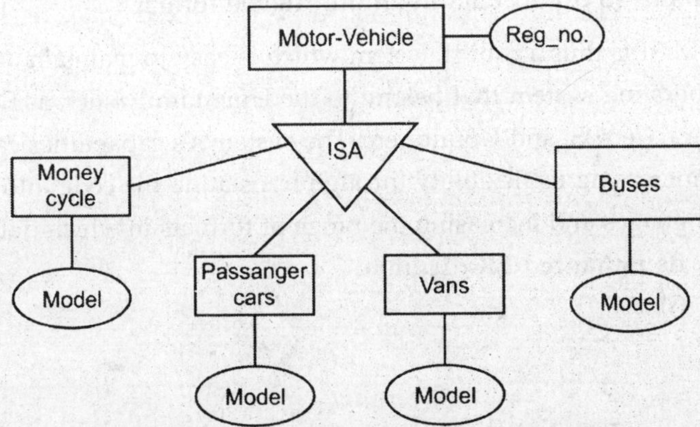

Fig. 1.49. E-R Diagram of Motor Vehicle

Example 22. Draw the EER (E^2R) diagram for the following system :

The project **'Nexus data mart'** aims at providing an interactive, dynamic, secure and user friendly platform for creating, managing & handling the data warehouse of Punjab National bank with the intend of reducing workload on the part of the Database Administrator and concurrently maintaining security at all levels.

'Nexus Data Mart' is an efficient data handling system for establishing, monitoring and automating the data warehouse related tasks of companies. The software components of the system are developed using the shell programming features of UNIX (operating system) and the hardware components adhere to the client-sever architecture.

A farewell has been established to enhanced the security of the whole system. The tasks performed by the system include extraction & transformation of data available in the form of raw data sheets, filtering of data to reduce the quantity or redundant information within the system, entertaining requests of communication from the end-user and establishing contact through a Mail Server and implementing an X-server to increase the ease of operability of the system.

At any state of the implementation of the ETL (Extraction-Transformation-Loading) processes, sensitive data belonging to the organisation shall remain abstracted from the End-User thereby ensuring a high level of security and sophistication for a naive user to get hold of the functionality of the system.

The system's high efficiency must be credited to the power offered by The Shell in UNIX programming environment. The scripts are concise yet extremely powerful, easy to maintain and modify as per needs of the organisation being served. The main advantage of programming within the UNIX environment is the security that is offered by the operating system at various levels. UNIX has three inherent provisions for protecting data. The first is provided by assigning password and login names to authorised users only. At the file level, high level of security is implemented through read, write and execute permissions that are assigned to users by the system administrator. Lastly, there is file encryption facility that allows us to export data in an unreadable format.

Nexus Data Mart is thus a robust system which is easy to maintain and modify. It is portable to all operating system that belong to the Unix family such as Solaris, Red Hat Linus, AIX, Fedora, CenOS, and Ubuntu etc. The system's's capabilities can be enhanced considerably by increasing its flexibility through translating the code into more than one programming languages and increasing the range of formats in which data sheets can be fed into it. **Draw its Enhanced ER diagram.**

Solution.

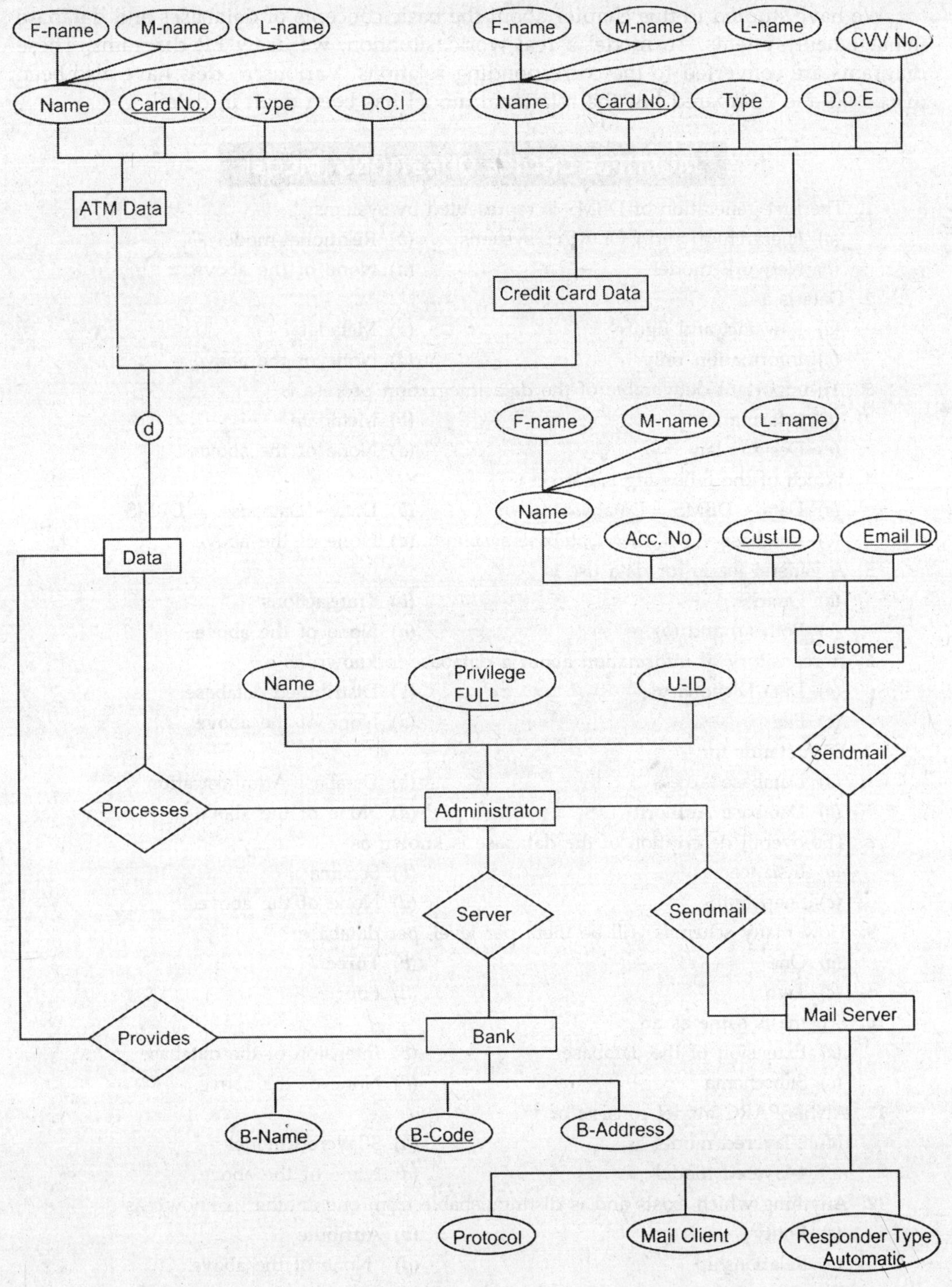

Fig. 1.50.

SUMMARY

We have studied in this chapter about the basic concepts of databases and database management systems. To model a real world situation, we draw ER diagrams. These diagrams are converted to the corresponding relations. Various models have also been discussed and compared but the relational model has been dealt in detail.

MULTIPLE CHOICE QUESTIONS [MCQs]

1. The first generation of DBMS is represented by systems
   (*a*) Hierarchical and CODASYL systems (*b*) Relational model
   (*c*) Network model (*d*) None of the above
2. Data is a
   (*a*) Raw fact and figure (*b*) Metadata.
   (*c*) Information only (*d*) None of the above
3. An important deliverable of the data integration process is
   (*a*) Information (*b*) Metadata
   (*c*) Design plan (*d*) None of the above.
4. Which of the following is correct
   (*a*) Data + DBMS = Databases (*b*) Data + Databases = DBMS
   (*c*) Database + DBMS = Database system (*d*) None of the above.
5. A general mode for data use is
   (*a*) Queries (*b*) Transactions
   (*c*) Both (*a*) and (*b*) (*d*) None of the above.
6. A repository of information about a database is known as a
   (*a*) Data Dictionary (*b*) Distributed database
   (*c*). File (*d*) None of the above.
7. DBA stands for –
   (*a*) Database Access (*b*) Database Administration
   (*c*) Database Authority (*d*) None of the above.
8. The overall description of the database is known as
   (*a*) Instance (*b*) Schema
   (*c*) Snapshot (*d*) None of the above.
9. How many schemas will be there per level, per database ?
   (*a*) One (*b*) Three
   (*c*) Two (*d*) Four.
10. Schema is same as an
    (*a*) Extension of the database (*b*) Intension of the database
    (*c*) Subschema (*d*) None of the above.
11. ANSI-SPARC model consists of
    (*a*) 2-layered model (*b*) 3-layered model
    (*c*) 4-layered model (*d*) None of the above.
12. Anything which exists and is distinguishable from one another is known as
    (*a*) Entity (*b*) Attribute
    (*c*) Relationship (*d*) None of the above.
13. The physical storage structures or devices could be changed without affecting the conceptual schema. This is known as

(*a*) Physical data independence (*b*) Logical data independence
(*c*) External data independence (*d*) None of the above.

14. DDL stands for
(*a*) Data domain language (*b*) Data definition law
(*c*) Data definition language (*d*) None of the above.

15. Create, Alter and Drop are the examples of
(*a*) DDL (*b*) DML
(*c*) VDL (*d*) SDL.

16. PL/SQL is a
(*a*) Non-procedural DML (*b*) Procedural DML
(*c*) Formal Query Language (*d*) None of the above.

17. SQL, QBE, QUEL are the examples of
(*a*) Formal Query language (*b*) Commercial query language.
(*c*) DDL (*d*) None of the above.

18. Which of the following is true for a Data Sub Language (DSL)
(*a*) DSL = DDL + DML (*b*) DSL = DDL – DML
(*c*) DSL = DDL + SDL (*d*) None of the above.

19. VDL stands for
(*a*) Very-small data language (*b*) View data language
(*c*) View definition language (*d*) None of the above.

20. SQL stands for
(*a*) Small Query Language (*b*) Structured Query Language
(*c*) Simple Query Language (*d*) None of the above.

21. SQL, Spreadsheets, Report Generators, Code Generators are the examples of
(*a*) 3GL (*b*) 4GL
(*c*) 5GL (*d*) None of the above.

22. GRANT and REVOKE are
(*a*) DDL (*b*) DML
(*c*) DCL (*d*) None of the above.

23. A compiler that converts embedded DML statements to normal procedure calls is known as
(*a*) C++ compiler (*b*) DML compiler
(*c*) Embedded DML precompiler (*d*) None of the above.

24. IMS, IMB, system 2000, NOMAD are the examples of
(*a*) Hierarchical model (*b*) Relational model
(*c*) Network model (*d*) None of the above.

25. The term 'relation' was chosen by
(*a*) Dr. Berry Boehm. (*b*) Dr. E.F. Codd.
(*c*) Dr. Jacobson (*d*) None of the above.

26. Each row of data is known as a
(*a*) Tuple (*b*) Cardinality
(*c*) Degree (*d*) None of the above.

27. The number of tuples in a relation is known as
(*a*) Cardinality (*b*) Degree
(*c*) Modality (*d*) None of the above.

28. An ER-model was introduced by
(*a*) E.F. Codd (*b*) P.P. Chen
(*c*) Constantine (*d*) None of the above.

29. The primary key of a weak entity needs to be formed. It is known as the
(*a*) Discriminator or partial key (*b*) Foreign key
(*c*) Weak key (*d*) None of the above.

30. The process of minimizing the differences between entities by identifying their common characteristics is known as
(*a*) Specialization (*b*) Generalization
(*c*) Multiplicity (*d*) None of the above.

31. The complement of Generalization is
(*a*) Specialization (*b*) Relation
(*c*) Distribution (*d*) None of the above.

32. The process of compiling information on an object, there by abstracting a higher level object is known as
(*a*) Specialization (*b*) Generalization
(*c*) Aggregation (*d*) None of the above.

33. The relationship between a weak entity-set is called as the
(*a*) Weak relationship (*b*) Identifying relationship
(*c*) Connecting relationship (*d*) Associative relationship.

34. An ER-diagram that shows the concepts of Specialization and Generalization are known as
(*a*) Extended ER-diagrams (*b*) Effective ER-diagrams
(*c*) Expanded ER-diagrams (*d*) Enhanced ER-diagrams.

35. The need of EER diagram arises depending upon the
(*a*) Nature of problem (*b*) Nature of entities
(*c*) Preferences of the database designer (*d*) All of the above.

ANSWERS

1. (*a*)	**2.** (*a*)	**3.** (*b*)	**4.** (*c*)	**5.** (*c*)	**6.** (*a*)	**7.** (*b*)	**8.** (*b*)
9. (*a*)	**10.** (*b*)	**11.** (*b*)	**12.** (*b*)	**13.** (*a*)	**14.** (*c*)	**15.** (*a*)	**16.** (*b*)
17. (*b*)	**18.** (*a*)	**19.** (*c*)	**20.** (*b*)	**21.** (*b*)	**22.** (*c*)	**23.** (*c*)	**24.** (*a*)
25. (*b*)	**26.** (*a*)	**27.** (*a*)	**28.** (*b*)	**29.** (*a*)	**30.** (*b*)	**31.** (*a*)	**32.** (*c*)
33. (*b*)	**34.** (*d*)	**35.** (*d*)					

CONCEPTUAL SHORT QUESTIONS WITH ANSWERS

Q.1. What is the difference between the Fact based and Heuristic knowledge?

Ans. Let us tabulate the differences between them.

S. No.	Fact Based Knowledge	Heuristic Knowledge
1.	The knowledge gained from the fundamentals and through experiments, is known as the fact based knowledge.	The Knowledge of good practice, experience and good judgement is known as the Heuristic knowledge.

2.	This knowledge is derived from the information contained in fundamental science derived from experiments, rules, regulations as agreed by experts.	It is the knowledge underlying "expertise", rules of thumb etc that usually achieve desired results.
3.	The results are guaranteed here.	The results are not guaranteed.

Q.2. What are different types of metadata?

Ans. Metadata is of three types :

(*a*) **Operational metadata :** It describes the data in the various operational systems that feed the enterprise data warehouse. They exist in various formats and are of poor quality.

(*b*) **Enterprise data ware house metadata :** They are derived from the enterprise data model. It describes the rules for transforming operational data to reconciled data.

(*c*) **Data mart metadata :** They describe the derived data and the rules for transforming the reconciled data to derived data.

Q.3. Give the differences between DBMS and RDBMS?

Ans. Let us tabulate the differences between DBMS and Relational DBMS :

S. No.	DBMS	RDBMS
1.	Storage, access paths and data structures can't be managed by DBMS.	Storage, access paths and data structures can be managed by RDBMS.
2.	Here, logical and physical view of database is considered.	Here, only logical view of database is considered.
3.	DBMS model cannot achieve the structural and data independence.	RDBMS model can achieve both the structural and data independence.
4.	Only single relationship exists in DBMS	One-to-one (1 : 1), one-to-many (1 : M) and many-to-many (M : N) relationships exists in RDBMS.
5.	System requirement is not so important as it can run with simple system configuration.	It requires very powerful and complicated hardware and operating system.

Q.4. List down the differences between an active and a passive data dictionary?

Ans. Let us tabulate the differences between the two :

S. No.	Active Data Dictionary	Passive Data Dictionary
1.	It is also known as an integrated data dictionary.	It is also known as a non-integrated data dictionary.
2.	It is managed automatically by the DBMS software.	It is managed by the users of the system.
3.	They are maintained by the system itself.	It is modified whenever the structure of database is changed.
4.	They are always consistent with the current structure and definition of the database.	Since, its, modification is a manual process, so it need not be current with the current structure of the database.

5.	Most of the RDBMS contain active data dictionaries that can be derived from their system catalog.	As they are maintained as separate database, so it allows developers to remain independent from using a particular RDBMS.

Q.5. What are pinned and unpinned records?

Ans. **Pinned records** are those which have pointers pointing to them somewhere in the database. Other records are known as **unpinned records.** This makes pinned records quite dangerous.

Q.6. Categorize various types of databases that may exist in an organization.

Ans. Various types of typical databases can be as follows :

1. **Operational databases/Transaction databases :** These databases store detailed data needed to support the operations of the entire organization. **For example,** customer databases, inventory databases etc.
2. **Distributed databases : A distributed database is a collection of data which belong logically to the same system but are spread over the sites of a computer network.** They can exist on WWW, intranets or extranets. Replication of databases is done to improve the performance and the security of Databases.
3. **External databases :** We have an external access to privately owned online databases which can be free or paid access. These are external databases like those available on internet.
4. **Hypermedia databases :** The set of interconnected multimedia pages at a website is a database of interrelated hypermedia page elements.

Q.7. Write a short history of databases.

Ans. Let us see the history of databases in a tabular form.

Year	Developments Made
1940s & 1950s	Calculators were used, stress on algorithms and military applications.
1960s	File-based systems were used for business uses.
1970s	Relational-model was given by E.F. Codd. *Examples :* Oracle DB2, Sybase etc.
1980s	Database programs like dbase, paradox, Ms-ACCESS were used to create small database
Late 1980s	LANS were used. Resource sharing (Like file sharing, printer sharing, emails) was done.
1990s	Centralized DBMS server used, clients (PCs) attached to this server.
After 1990s	Internet, WWW data warehousing and mining emerged.

Q.8. Classify DBMS on the basis of number of users, on the basis of the database site locations and on the basis of the type and extent of use.

Ans. We categorize DBMS as follows :

Category–I : On the basis of number of users

(*a*) single-user DBMS

(*b*) Multi-user DBMS

Category–II : On the basis of site location

(*a*) Centralized DBMS

(*b*) Parallel DBMS

(*c*) Distributed DBMS

(*d*) Client/Server DBMS

Category–III : On the basis of the type and the extent of use

(*a*) Transactional (or production) DBMS
(*b*) Decision support DBMS
(*c*) Data Warehouse.

Q.9. How is a single user DBMS different from Multi-user DBMS?

Ans. Depending upon the configuration of the hardware and the size of the organization we can classify DBMS as a single-user DBMS or Multi-user DBMS.

In an **single-user system,** the database resides on one computer and is accessed by one user at a time. This one user may design, maintain and write database programs.

In a **multi-user system,** data is both integrated and shared. We need these systems as there is large amount of data management. **Please remember that a database is integrated when the same information is not recorded in two places. For example,** both the library and the Accounts departments of a company may need student names and addresses. **Please note here that eventhough both departments may access different portions of the database, but the student's names and addresses should only reside at one place. Also note that it is the job of DBA to make sure that our DBMS makes the correct addresses available from one central storage area.**

Q.10. Explain the following DBMS :

(I) Centralized DBMS **(II) Parallel DBMS**
(III) Distributed DBMS **(IV) Client-server DBMS.**

Ans. Let us discuss them one by one.

(I) Centralized DBMS : This type of DBMS consists of a single processor together with its associated data storage devices and other peripherals. It is physically confined to a single location. **Please note that these systems offer data processing capabilities to users who are located either at the same site or through remote terminals at geographically dispersed sites. Also note that the management of the system and its data are controlled centrally from any one or central site.** This is shown in Fig. 1.33 below.

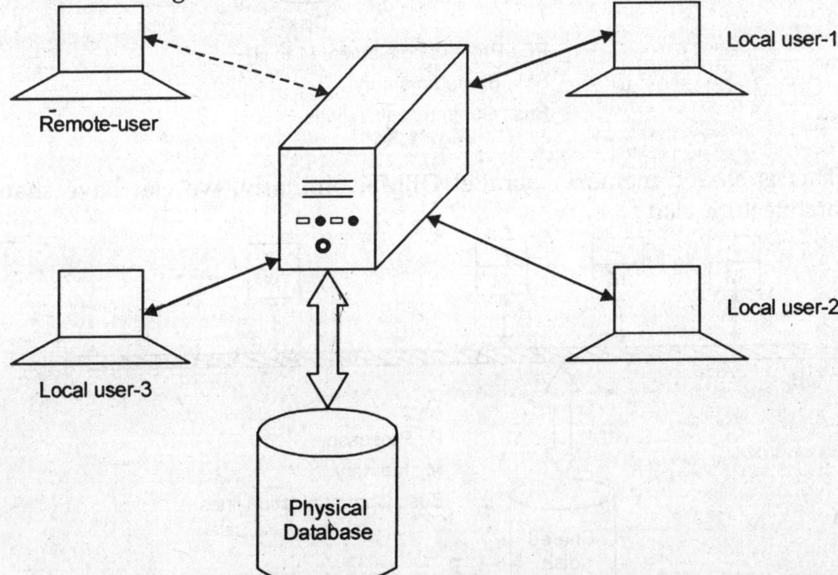

Fig. 1.33. *A centralized DBMS*

Let us discuss the advantages and the disadvantages of these centralized DBMS.

Advantages of Centralized DBMS : The following are the advantages of centralized DBMS :

(*i*) The basic functions of DBMS is easy updation, backup, query of relations. These functions are easier to accomplish in these centralized DBMSs.

(*ii*) The size of the database has no relation to the central location of a DBMS. **For example**, a small office with its database on one PC has a centralized database. On the other hand, a large company with many computers has database entirely controlled by a mainframe.

Disadvantages of Centralized DBMS : The following are the disadvantages of centralized DBMS :

(*i*) Imagine if this central computer goes down? All other local and remote users are not able to work until the central system comes to work again.

(*ii*) Practically speaking, the communication between these local and remote terminals is quite expensive.

(II) Parallel DBMS : Architecturally, these systems consist of multiple CPUs and multiple disk storages in parallel. So, the processing speeds increases manifold. Parallel database systems are used in the applications that have to query extremely large databases or that have to process a very large number of transactions-per-second (TPS). These systems may have shared-memory architecture or shared storage disk architecture or hierarchical architecture. These are shown below.

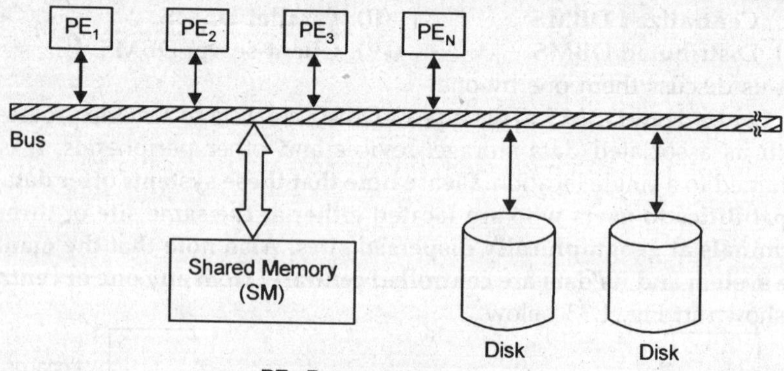

Fig. 1.34

This is shared-memory, parallel DBMS. Similarly, we can have shared disk architecture also.

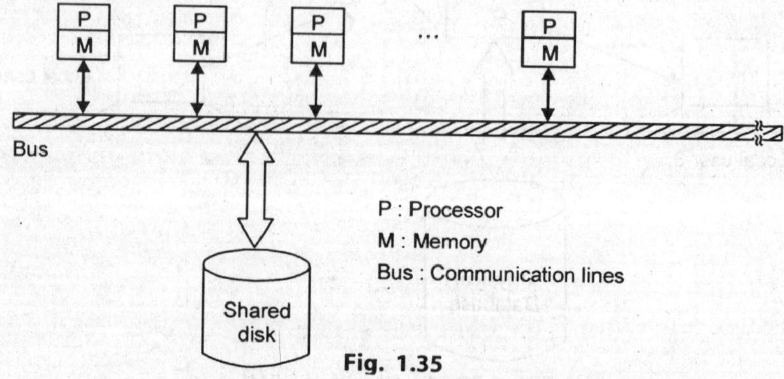

Fig. 1.35

Similarly, tree-like structure can be obtained. Let us now discuss the advantages and disadvantages of parallel DBMS.

Advantages of a Parallel DBMS : The following are the advantages of parallel DBMS :

(*i*) Parallel DBMS are very useful for the applications where :

(*a*) We have to query (through application) extremely large database, say of the order of terabytes or 10^{12} bytes.

(*b*) Or that have to process an extremely large number of transactions per second, say of the order of thousands of transactions per second.

(*ii*) As we already know that the number of tasks that can be completed in a given time interval is called as the **throughput**. And the time taken to complete a single task from the time it is submitted is known as the **response time. Please remember that in parallel systems, both throughput and the response time are very high.**

Disadvantages of Parallel DBMS : These systems have some disadvantages also. They are as follows :

(*i*) In these systems, there is a start up cost associated with initiating a single process. The startup-time may overshadow the actual processing time, affecting the speed adversely.

(*ii*) The processes executing in a parallel system access shared resources. This may result in slowdown from interference of each new process as it competes for common devices like shared disks, system bus etc.

(III) Distributed DBMS : It comprises of a large central computer to which a large number of remote terminals are attached. **It is defined as logically interrelated collection of shared data physically distributed over a computer network (is called as distributed database) and the software system that permits the management of the distributed database and makes the distribution transparent to the users is known as a Distributed DBMS**. So, it consists of single logical database that is split into a number of *fragments*. Each fragment is stored on one or more computers under the control of a separate DBMS.

Consider a bank having its branches throughout India and its head office is in Delhi. Also, we assume that this bank maintains the local data at the local branch and the copy of data of all branches at Delhi. Thus, we say that the data is distributed throughout India. This eases query processing for local customers of a branch and also of global customer.

A global customer is one who moves from one state to another. This is shown below :

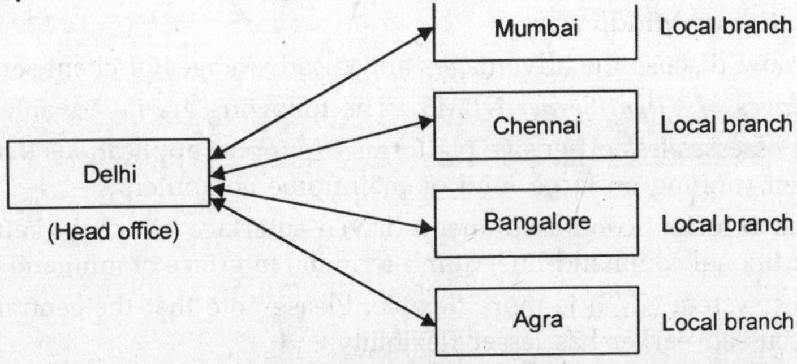

Fig. 1.36. *Bank using distributed processing*

Please note that it is a form of online processing that allows a single transaction to be composed of application programs that access one or more databases on one or more computers across a network. This type of transaction in which multiple application programs cooperate is called as a **distributed transaction. Also note that the computers here may be of different size and platforms.** They may include microprocessors, minicomputers etc. So, using this type of processing, we can **synchronize** the related data at these regional and branch locations, **up date** it simultaneously with sure results.

As shown in Fig. 1.36, in these systems data is spread across a variety of different databases. They are managed by a variety of different DBMS softwares running on a variety of different O.S. Let us see its advantages and disadvantages now.

Advantages of Distributed DBMS :

(*i*) These systems provides greater efficiency and better performance.

(*ii*) Response time and throughput is high

(*iii*) Resource sharing is possible.

(*iv*) Better failure-free operation (*i.e.,* Reliability)

(*v*) Easier communications, e-mails can be sent.

Disadvantages of Distributed DBMS : Recovery from failure is more complex in distributed DBMS than in centralized systems.

(IV) Client-server DBMS : Today, we prefer to work on client-server architecture of DBMS. It has two logical components : (*a*) client and (*b*) server.

(*a*) **Clients** are actually the PCs/nodes/workstations.

(*b*) **Server :** It is a large workstation, a minicomputer or a microcomputer.

The applications and tools of DBMS run on one or more client platforms while the DBMSs softwares reside on the server. The server computer is called as a **back-end** and the client's computer is called as a **front-end. Please note that these clients and server systems are connected through some network.** The applications and tools act as clients of DBMS, making requests for its services. DBMS processes these requests and returns the results to the client (s). Client/server architecture handles the graphical user interface (GUI). A two-tier client/server is shown below :

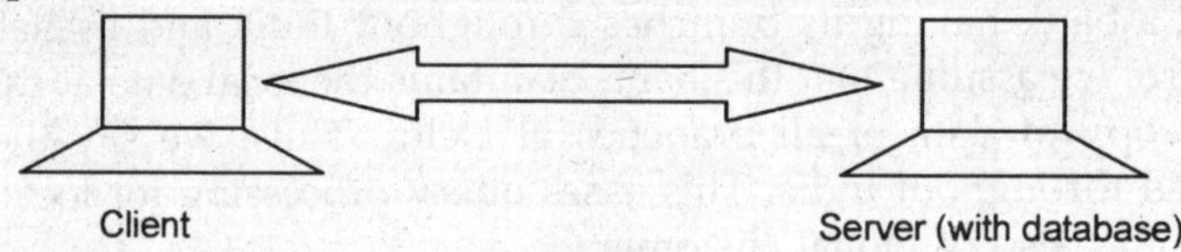

Fig. 1.37

In three-tier architecture, we have another middle layer also and is called as **Middle-tier** or **Middleware.**

Let us now discuss the advantages and disadvantages of client-server DBMS.

Advantages of Client/Server DBMS : The following are its advantages :

(*i*) It possesses less expensive platforms to support applications that had earlier been running on large mini or mainframe computers.

(*ii*) Clients offer icon-based menu-driven interface which is better than the traditional command-line, dumb-terminal interface of mini and mainframes.

(*iii*) This system (C/S) is more flexible. Please note that the centralized system discussed earlier has lesser flexibility.

(*iv*) Response time and throughput is high.

(*v*) The server (database) machine can be custom-built to the DBMS function. So, it can provide better DBMS performances.

Disadvantages of Client/Server DBMS : It has some disadvantages also. They are as follows :

(*i*) Programming cost is high in these systems, particularly in the initial phases.

(*ii*) There is a lack of management tools for diagnosis, performance monitoring, security control for DBMS, client and OS and networking environments.

Q.11. How DBMS provides users with a considerable degree of data independence?

Ans. DBMS actually, translates a DML statement into a procedure (or set of procedures) that manipulates the required set of records. This removes the concern of the user to know how data structure are internally implemented. This provides users with a considerable degree of data independence.

Q.12. The links in a network are bidirectional while in hierarchical model are unidirectional. How does that affect navigations?

Ans. In a hierarchical model, the basic operation is unidirectional *i.e.,* navigation is from parent to child only. Please note that this convention, however, causes certain relationships to be hard to extract from the database even if they may be implicit in the data.

Q.13. What are the steps of the implementation design phase of database design?

Ans. The following are the steps of the implementation design:

Step 1. Input the following

(*a*) DBMS independent schema/conceptual data model.

(*b*) Data volume and usage details.

(*c*) Characteristics of the selected DBMS data model.

Step 2. Map the conceptual data model into the desired logical data model. Use guidelines for mapping.

Step 3. Design sub-schemas of different users of the system.

Step 4. Prepare program design guidelines for each subschema.

Step 5. Perform design review and make corrections if required.

Q.14. Why can't a hierarchical model represent a many-to-many (M : N) relationships among records?

Ans. Please remember that different records present in the hierarchical tree structure have parent-child relationship. A parent element can have many children elements but a child element cannot have many parent elements. This implies that the hierarchical model cannot represent M : N relationships among records.

Q.15. What is a Fan trap and Chasm trap?

Ans. In an ER-model, due to the misinterpretation of the meaning of certain relationships, a problem known as **connection traps** results. It is of two types, namely : (*i*) Fan traps, (*ii*) Chasm traps.

In **Fan trap**, a model represents a relationship between entity types but the pathway between certain entity occurrences is ambiguous. **Please note that a fan trap may exist where two or more 1 : N relationships fan out from the same entity. For example,** consider the following ER-diagram.

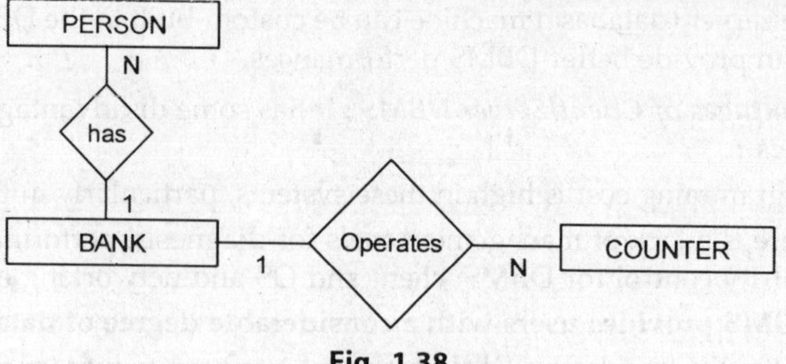

Fig. 1.38

Note here that there are two one-to-many (1 : N) relationships *i.e.,* 'has' and 'operates' which emanates from the same entity-BANK. **How to solve this problem?** We can solve fan trap problem by restructuring the original ER-Model to represent the correct association between these association. That is, we restructure the ER-model to eliminate fan trap *i.e.,*

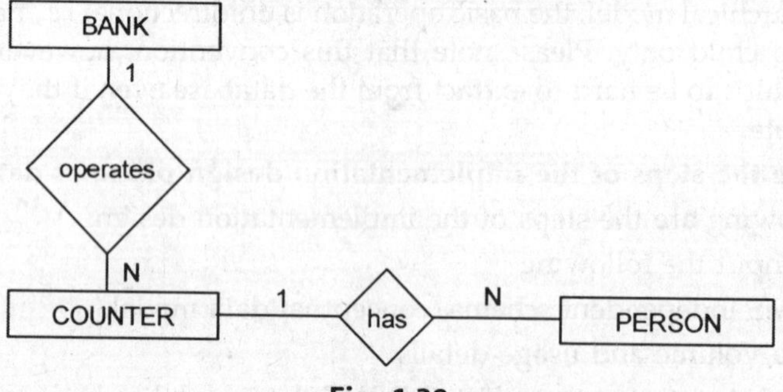

Fig. 1.39

In **chasm trap,** there are one or more relationships with a minimum multiplicity of zero forming part of the pathway between related entities. It shows the existence of a relationship between entity types but the pathway does not exist between certain entity occurrences. **For example**, consider the following ER-diagram.

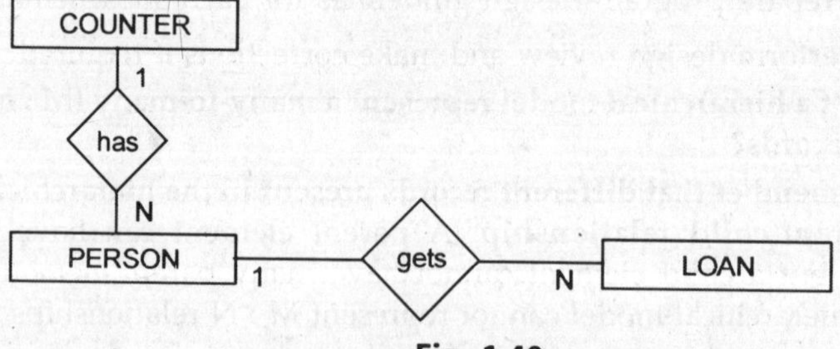

Fig. 1.40

Here, we find that a single counter has one or more person who oversees zero or more loan enquiries. **Please note that not all person oversees loan enquiries and not all loan enquires are overseen by a member person. A problem arises when we want to know which loan enquiries are available at each counter.** Also note that the multiplicity of both PERSON and LOAN entities in the "gets" relationship has a minimum value of zero. It means that some loans cannot be associated with a counter through a member of person. Thus, we need to identify the missing link to solve this problem.

How to solve this problem?

We need to identify the missing link. We find that the link "offers" relationship between the entities COUNTER and LOAN is a missing link. That is,

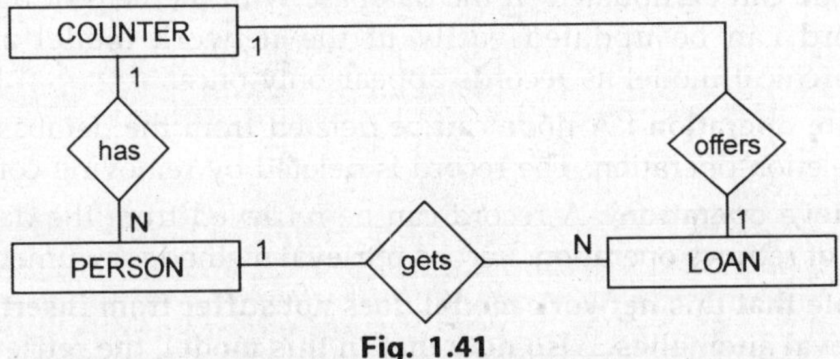

Fig. 1.41

So, by restructuring our ER-model, we have eliminated our problem of chasm trap.

Q.16 How insert, delete, update operations are done in a hierarchical model? How are they anomalies?

Ans. Let us understand all these operations one by one.

1. **Insert operation :** A node can be inserted into the database with the help of insertion operation. The newly entered record becomes the current node of the database. A new hierarchical tree is constructed if the record inserted is a root record. **The new record becomes the root of the tree. Please note that if the record to be inserted is not a root node then we must first insert the parent of the node and then insert the record. Also note that the insert anomaly exists for those children only which have no corresponding parents.**
2. **Delete operation :** A node can be deleted from the database with the help of deletion operation. The record to be deleted is first made as a **current node** and then deletion operation is performed. **If the record to be deleted does not have any child then we directly delete the record without any problem. But if the record to be deleted has many children then all will be deleted if the record is deleted.**
3. **Update operation :** A node can be updated in the database with the update operation. If we have to update root node in the hierarchical database then it can easily be done as there is only one root in the tree. If the record to be updated has multiple occurrences then we have to update each and every occurrence of the record otherwise it would lead to inconsistency in the database. This problem is called as **update anomaly**. So, we can say that update anomalies exist only for the children and not for parent because children may have multiple entries in the database.
4. **Retrieve operation :** A node can be retrieved from the database with the help of retrieve operation. The retrieval operation in hierarchical model is complex and asymmetric.

Please note that the hierarchical model suffers from the Insertion anomalies, update anomalies and delete anomalies. Also note that the retrieval operation is complex and asymmetric. Thus, this model is not suitable for all cases.

Q.17 Explain various operations that are to be performed on Network model?

Ans. Let us see the insert, update, delete and retrieval operations on Network Model.

1. **Insert operation :** A node can be inserted into the database with the help of insertion operation. The newly entered record is connected with the database with the help of connection record. There are no insert anomalies in network model as in hierarchical model.

2. **Update operation :** Unlike hierarchical model, where updation was carried out by search and had many inconsistency problems, in a network model updating a record is a much easier process.
   A node can be updated in the database with the help of update operation. Record can be updated easily in the network model as compared to hierarchical model as records appear only once.
3. **Delete operation :** A node can be deleted from the database with the help of deletion operation. The record is deleted by removing connection record.
4. **Retrieve operation :** A record can be retrieved from the database with the help of retrieve operation. Record retrieval method is symmetric but complex.

Please note that this network model does not suffer from insert, delete, update and retrieval anomalies. Also note that in this model, the retrieval operation is symmetric. But each of these operation is quite complex as it involves the modifications of pointers.

Q.18. Explain the various methods of converting ER-diagram containing specialization to tables?

Ans. There are 2-methods of converting ER-diagrams having specialization to tables. Let us discuss them one by one.

Method-I : Two rules are used here :

Rule 1. Form a table for higher-level entity.

Rule 2. Form a table for each lower level entity-set, include the primary key of higher-level entity-set and local attributes.

Let us consider an example to understand this. Say, the ER-diagram has this specialization as shown below :

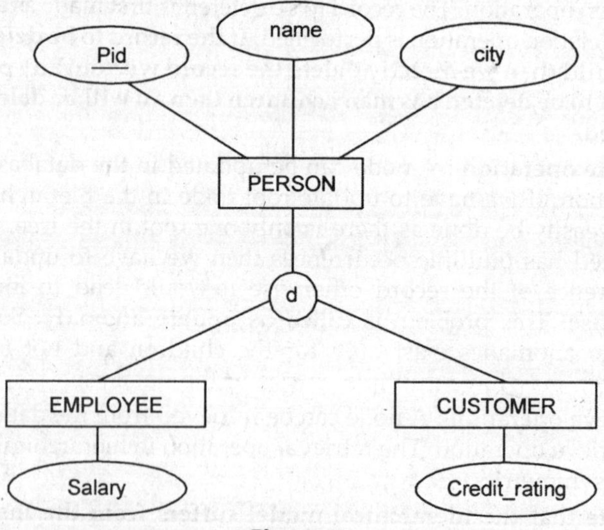

Fig. 1.42

Here, PERSON (entity) is specialized as Employee and Customer entity. To solve this problem we need to create 3 tables :

1. PERSON-table with attributes—(<u>Pid</u>, name city)
2. EMPLOYEE-table with attributes—(<u>Pid</u>, salary)
3. CUSTOMER-table with attributes—(<u>Pid</u>, credit-rating)

Please note here that we have created one-table for higher-level entity-set PERSON and two tables for each of the lower level entity set *i.e.,* EMPLOYEE and CUSTOMER. **We have used the above two Rule-1 and Rule-2 to get three resultant tables with each having a primary-key of higher-level entity-set and its own local attributes also.**

This method has a drawback also. Say, for getting information about the CUSTOMER requires accessing of two tables *i.e.,* CUSTOMER table and the PERSON table for retrieving his/her name and city.

Method-II : The **rule** used here is : **"Form a table for each entity-set with all local and inherited attributes. If specialization is total then there is no need to create table for generalized entity".**

Using this rule, for above example we will get the three tables as follows :

1. PERSON table with attributes—(Pid, name, city)
2. Employee table with attributes—(Pid, name, city, salary)
3. CUSTOMER table with attributes—(Pid, name, city, credit-rating).

This method also has a drawback. In this example, city may be stored redundantly for persons who are both customers and employees.

Q.19. Consider the following ER-diagram showing generalization also. How will you form tables from it?

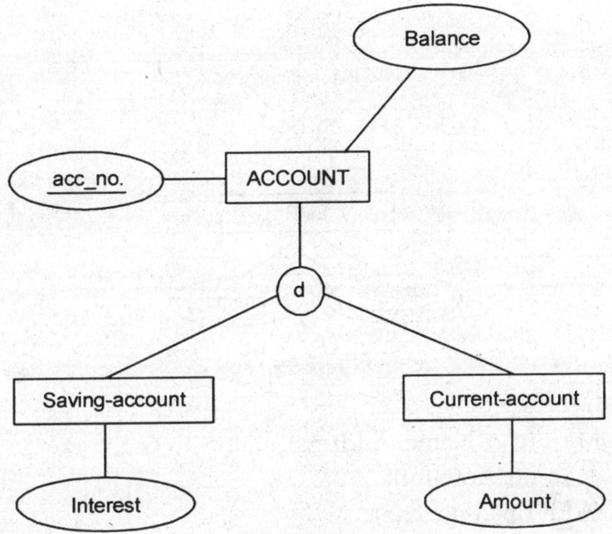

Fig. 1.43

Ans. There are 2-methods for generalizations also.

Method-I : Rule is : "Form the tables using the local attributes of all entities and the primary key of the base-entity." So, we get three tables now :

1. ACCOUNT (acc-no, Balance)
2. SAVING_ACCOUNT (acc-no, Interest)
3. CURRENT_ACCOUNT (acc-no, Amount)

Here, we need to join tables to extract say acc-no and interest attributes of the account holder.

Method-II : Or, we can create two tables as follows :

1. SAVING_ACCOUNT (acc-no, Balance, Interest)
2. CURRENT_ACCOUNT (acc-no, Balance, Amount)

But, here redundancy of balance field occurs.

Q.20. A certain ER-diagram shows the aggregation concept. How will you form tables out of it? Explain with an example.

Ans. The rule followed here is as follows : **"Create a table containing primary key of the aggregated relationship and the primary key of the associated entity set".**

For example, say our ER diagram is

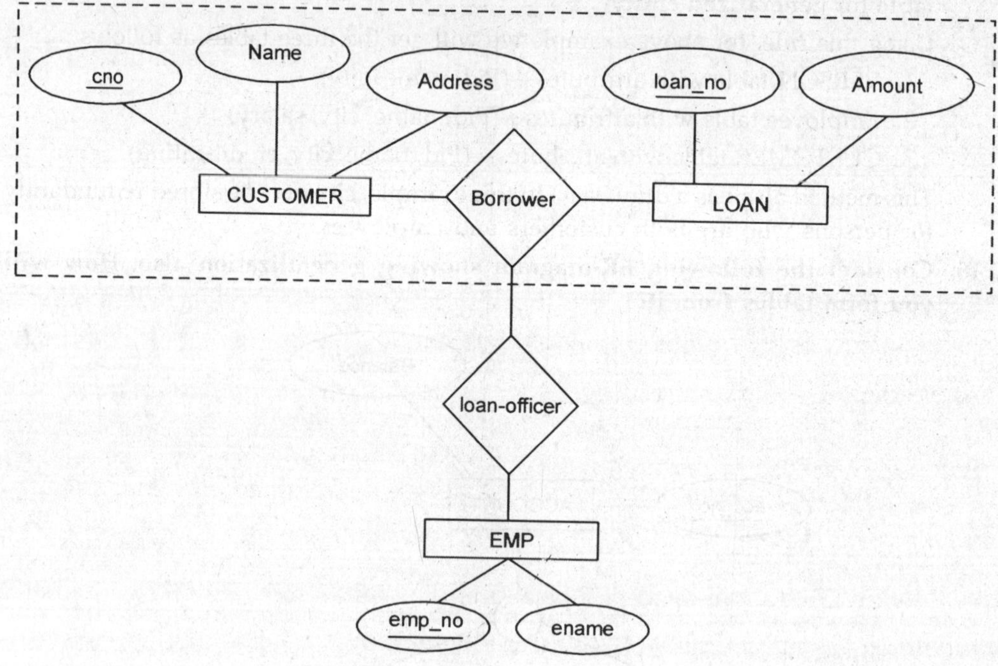

Fig. 1.44

Then, we can form 5-tables :

1. CUSTOMER (cno, Name, Address).
2. LOAN (loan-no, Amount).
3. BORROWER (loan-no, cno).
4. EMP (emp-no, ename).
5. LOAN-OFFICER (cno, loan-no, emp-no).

Thus, by applying our rule, for the aggregated relationship-LOAN-Officer, we form a table with the primary-key of aggregated relationship and the primary-key of the associated entity (*i.e.*, EMP).

Q.21. What is the difference between controlled and uncontrolled redundancy?

Ans. Redundancy occurs when the same fact is stored multiple times in several places in a database. It is controlled when the DBMS ensures that multiple copies of the same data are consistent. If DBMS has no control over this, we have uncontrolled redundancy.

Q.22. Composite and multi-valued attributes can be nested to any number of levels. Suppose we want to design an attribute for a STUDENT entity type to keep track of previous college education. Such an attribute will have one entry for each college previously attended, and this entry is composed of: college name, start and end dates, degree entries (degrees awarded at that college, if any), and transcript entries (courses completed at the college, if any). Each degree entry is formed of degree name and the month and year it was awarded, and each transcript entry is formed of a course name, semester, year, and grade. Design an attribute to hold this information.

Ans. {Previous Education (CollegeName, StartDate, EndDate,
{Degree (DegreeName, Month, Year)}
{Transcript (CourseName, Semester, Year, Grade)})}.

Q.23. A database is being constructed to keep track of the teams and games of a sports league. A team has a number of players, not all of whom participate in each game. It is desired to keep track of the players participating in each game for each team, the positions they played in that game, and the result of the game. Try to design an ER Schema diagram for this application, stating any assumptions you make. Choose your favorite sport (soccer, football, baseball, ...).

Ans. The following design may be used for a baseball league. Here, we assumed that each game in the schedule is identified by a unique Game#, and a game is also identified uniquely by the combination of Data, starting Time, and Field where it is played. The Performance attribute of PARTICIPATE is used to store information on the individual performance of each player in a game. This attribute can be designed to keep the information needed for statistics, and may be quite complex. One possible design for the Performance attribute may be the following.

Performance {Hitting(AtBat#, Inning#, HitType, Runs, RunsBattedIn, StolenBases)}, {Pitching (Inning#, Hits, Runs, EarnedRuns, StrikeOuts Walks, Outs, Balks, Wild Pitches)}, {Defense(Inning#, {Fielding Record(Position, PutOuts, Assists, Errors)})})

Here, Performance is a composite attribute made up of three multivalued components: Hitting, Pitching, and Defense. Hitting has a value for each AtBat of a player, and records the HitType (suitable coded; for exmple, 1 for single, 2 for double, 3 for triple, 4 for home run 0 for walk, –1 for strikeout, –2 for fly out,...) and other information concerning the AtBat. Pitching has a value for each inning during which the player pitched. Defense has a value for each inning a player played a fielding position. We can have a less detailed or a more detailed design for the performance of a player in each game, depending on how much information we need to keep in the database. Suitable variations of the ER-diagram shown below can be used for other sports.

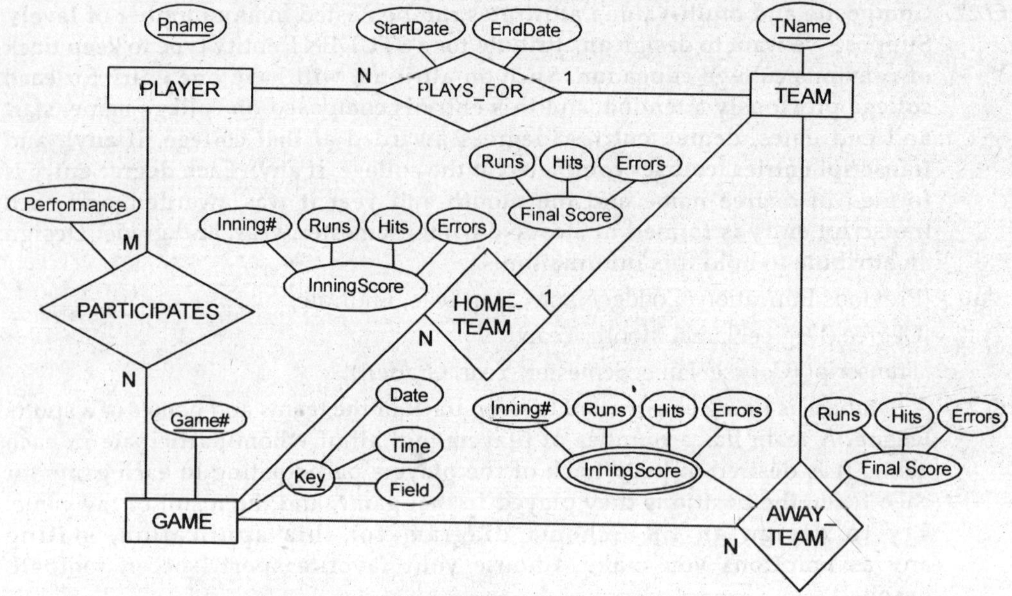

Fig. 1.45

Q.24. Consider the ER-diagram below. Assume that an employee may work in up to two departments or may not be assigned of any department. Assume that each department must have one and may have up to three phone numbers. Supply (min, max) constraints on this diagram. State clearly any additional assumptions you make. Under what conditions would the relationship HAS_PHONE be redundant in this example?

Ans. Assuming the following additional assumptions :

— Each department can have anywhere between 1 and 10 employees.

— Each phone is used by one, and only one, department.

— Each phone is assigned to at least one, and may be assigned to up to 10 employees.

— Each employee is assigned at least one, but no more than 6 phones.

The resulting ER-diagram will have the (min, max) constraints shown in Fig. 1.46.

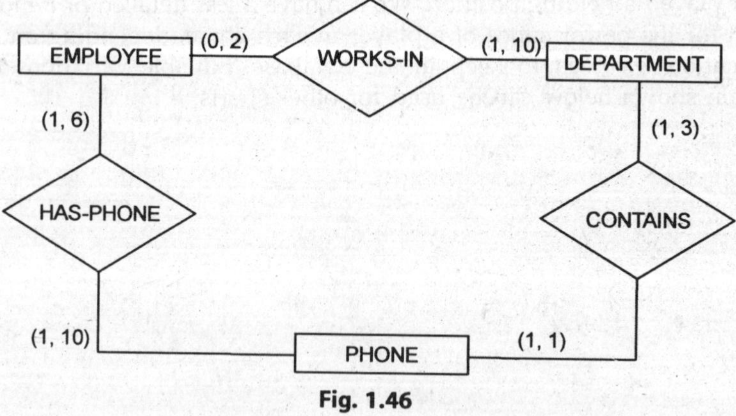

Fig. 1.46

Relationship HAS-PHONE would be redundant under the following conditions:

— Each employee is assigned all of the phones of each department that he/she works in.

— An employee cannot have any other phones outside the departments he/she works is

EMPLOYEE
PHONE
DEPARTMENT
HAS-PHONE CONTAINS
WORKS-IN
(0, 2)
(1, 3)
(1, 10)
(1, 10) (1, 1)
(1, 6)

Q.25. Consider the ER-diagram in Fig. 1.47 below. Assume that a course may or may not use a textbook, but that a text by definition is a book that is used in some course. A course may not use more than five books. Instructors teach from two to four courses. Supply (min, max) constraints on this diagram. State clearly any additional assumptions you make. If we add the relationship ADOPTS between INSTRUCTION and TEXT, what (min, max) constraints would you put on it? Why ? [Delhi University, B.Sc(G)—III year, 2007]

Ans. Assuming the following additional assumptions :

— Each course is taught by exactly one instructor.

— Each textbook is used by one and only one course.

— An instructor does not have to adopt a textbook for all courses.

— If a text exists :

— ___it is used in some course,

— ___hence it is adopted by some instructor who teaches that course.

— An instructor is considered to adopt a text if it is used in some course taught

— by that instructor.

The resulting ER-Diagram will have the (min, max) constraints shown in Fig. 1.46.

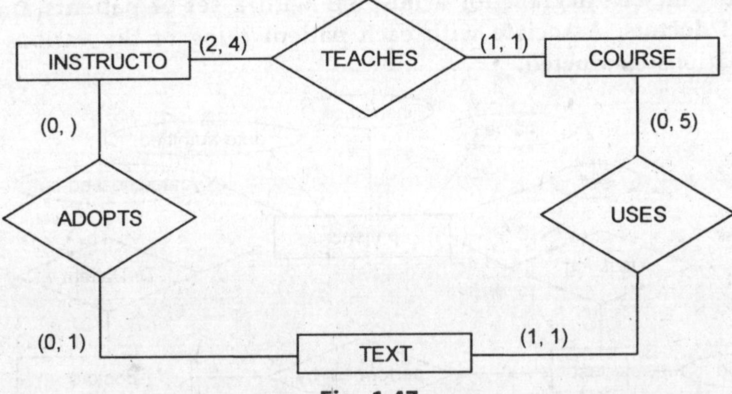

Fig. 1.47

Q.26. Consider the BANK ER schema and suppose that is necessary to keep track of different types of ACCOUNTS (SAVINGS_ACCTS, CHECKING_ACCTS,...) and

LOANS (CAR_LOANS, HOME_LOANS, ...) Suppose that is also desirable to keep track of each account's TRANSACTIONS (deposits, withdrawals, checks,...) and each loan's PAYMENTs; both of these include the amount, data, time.... Modify the BANK schema, ER and EER concepts of specialization and generalization. State any assumptions you make about the additional requirements.

Ans. The EER diagram is as follows :

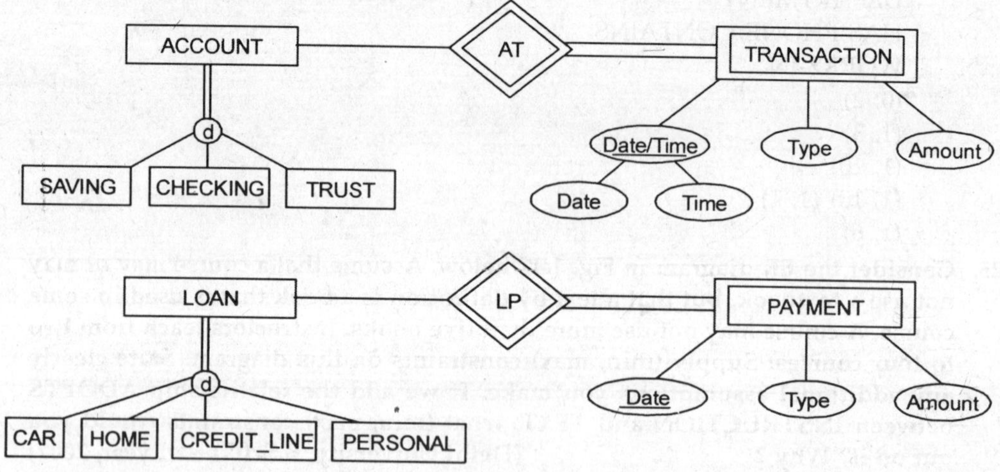

Fig. 1.48

Q.27. Explain the distinctions among the terms primary key, candidate key, and superkey. **[GGSIPU, B.Tech. (CSE)—5th Sem., Dec. 2007]**

Ans. A **superkey** is a set of one or more attributes that, taken collectively, allows us to identify uniquely an entity in the entity set. A superkey may contain extraneous attributes. If K is a superkey, then so is any superset of K. A superkey for which no proper subset is also a superkey is called a **candidate key**. It is possible that several distinct sets of attributes could serve as candidate keys. The **primary key** is one of the candidate keys that is chosen by the database designer as the principal means of identifying entities within an entity-set.

Q.28. Construct an ER-diagram for a hospital with a set of patients and a set of medical doctors. Associate with each patient a log of the various tests and examinations conducted.

Ans.

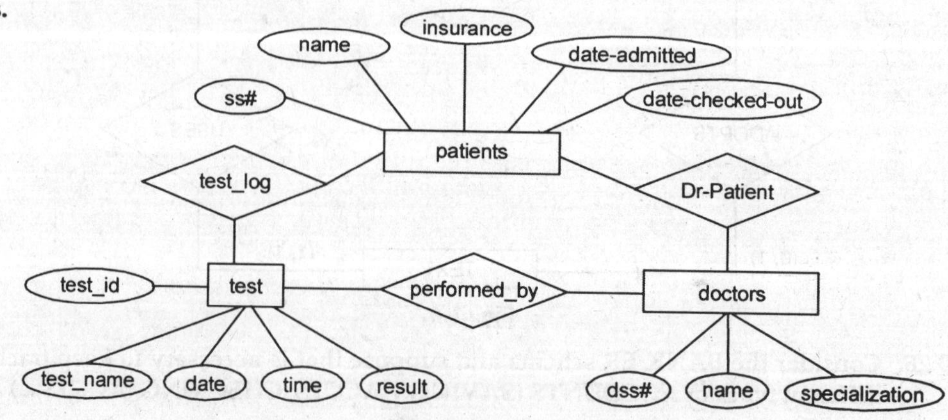

Fig. 1.49

Q.29. Draw a ER-diagram to show the cricket team statistics.

[GGSIPU, B.Tech (CS); 5th Sem., Dec. 2006]

Ans.

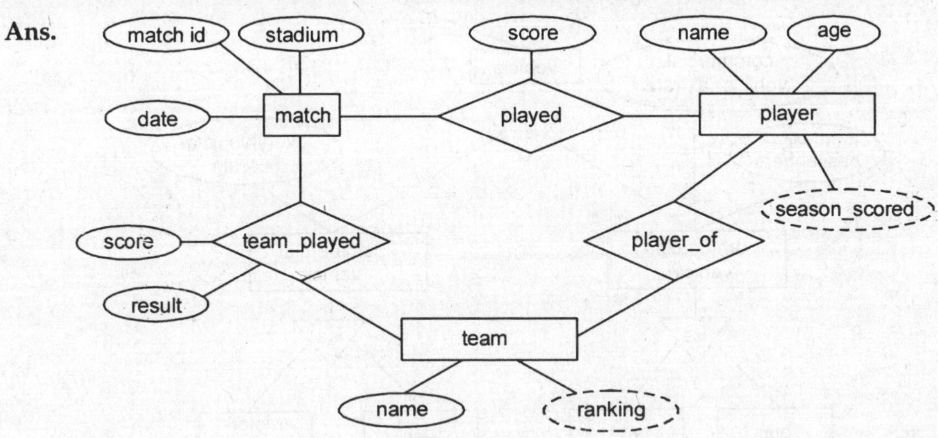

Fig. 1.50

Q.30. We can convert weak entity-set to a strong entity set by simply adding appropriate attributes. Why, then do we have weak entity sets?

[GGSIPU, B. Tech. (CSE/IT) 5th Sem., Dec. & Sep., 2007]

Ans. We have weak entities for several reasons :

- We want to avoid the data duplication and consequent possible inconsistencies caused by duplicating the key of the strong entity.
- Weak entities reflect the logical structure of an entity being dependent on another entity.
- Weak entities can be deleted automatically when their strong entity is deleted.
- Weak entities can be stored physically with their strong entities.

Q.31. Design a generalization–specialization hierarchy for a motor-vehicle sales company. The company sells motorcycles, passenger cars, vans, and buses. Justify your placement of attributes at each level of the hierarchy. Explain why they should not be placed at a higher or lower level.

Ans. Fig. 1.51 gives one possible hierarchy, there could be many different solutions. The generalization-specialization hierarchy for the motor-vehicle company is given in the figure. *Model, sales-tax-rate* and *sales-volume* are attributes necessary for all types of vehicles. Commercial vehicles attract commercial vehicle tax, and each kind of commercial vehicle has a passenger carrying capacity specified for it. Some kinds of non-commercial vehicles attract luxury vehicle tax. Cars alone can be of several types, such as sports-car, sedan, wagon etc., hence the attribute *type*. So, we draw now.

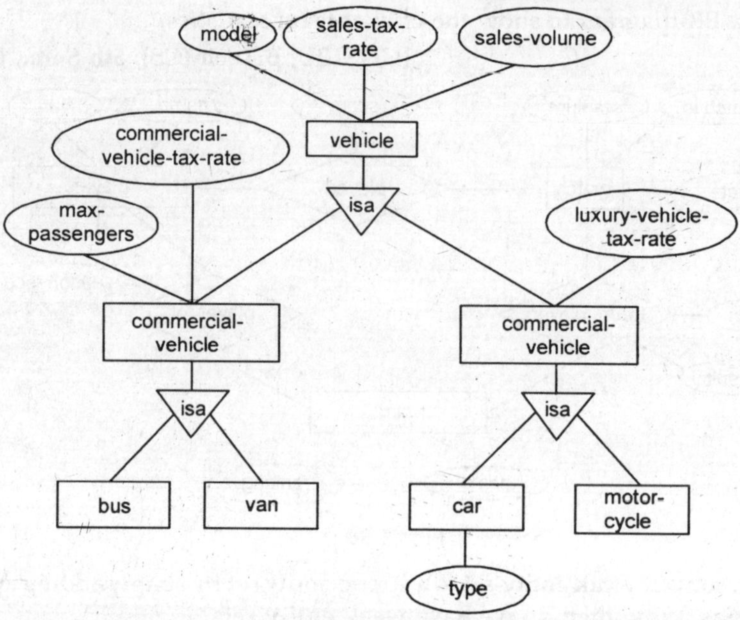

Fig. 1.51

Q.32. Explain the distinction between condition-defined and user-defined constraints. Which of these constraints can the system check automatically? Explain your answer.

Ans. In a generalization–specialization hierarchy, it must be possible to decide which entities are members of which lower level entity sets. In a condition-defined design constraint, membership in the lower level entity-sets is evaluated on the basis of whether or not an entity satisfies an explicit condition or predicate. User-defined lower-level entity sets are not constrained by a membership condition; rather, entities are assigned to a given entity-set by the database user.

Condition-defined constraints alone can be automatically handled by the system. Whenever any tuple is inserted into the database, its membership in the various lower level entity-sets can be automatically decided by evaluating the respective membership predicates. Similarly when a tuple is updated, its membership in the various entity sets can be reevaluated automatically.

Q.33. Explain the distinction between disjoint and overlapping constraints.

Ans. In a disjointness design constraint, an entity can belong to not more than one lower-level entity-set. In overlapping generalizations, the same entity may belong to more than one lower-level entity-sets. For example, in the employee-workteam example of the book, a manager may participate in more than one work-team.

Q.34. Explain the distinction between total and partial constraints.

Ans. In a total design constraint, each higher-level entity must belong to a lower-level entity-set. The same need not be true in a partial design constraint. For instance, some employees may belong to no work-team.

EXERCISE QUESTIONS

Q.1. (*a*) Differentiate between strong and weak entity-sets.

(*b*) Draw an ER-diagram using specialization and generalization hierarchy for a banking enterprise. Convert ER diagrams into tables.

[GGSIPU, B.Tech., (CSE); 5th Sem., Dec. 2006]

Q.2. (*a*) Define and explain the concept of data independence.

(*b*) What is the responsibility of DBA with respect to:

(*i*) Conceptual database design.

(*ii*) Data Integrity

(*iii*) Database System Performance.

[GGSIPU, B.Tech., (CS); 5th Sem., Dec. 2006]

Q.3. (*a*) What do you mean by set-membership in network model? Discuss the significance of set-membership status in detail.

(*b*) In which type of databases, hierarchical model will be best suitable? Give one example where hierarchical model will not be suitable. Give another example where the hierarchical model is suitable and justify.

[GGSIPU, B. Tech., (CS); 5th Sem., Dec. 2006]

Q.4. (*a*) What is a system-set ? Why was it introduced in the DBTG model?

(*b*) Compare hierarchical model with the relational model in terms of ease of learning and ease of use. **[GGSIPU, B. Tech., (CS); 5th Sem., Dec. 2007]**

Q.5. (*a*) Distinguish between weak and strong entity.

(*b*) What is the difference between physical and logical data independence?

[GGSIPU, B. Tech., (CS); 5th Sem., Dec. 2007]

Q.6. (*a*) Explain the responsibilities of these subsystems of database:

(*i*) Transaction manager

(*ii*) Query processor

(*iii*) Storage manager.

(*b*) With suitable example explain the physical, logical and view level of the database.

(*c*) What are the functions of DBA? **[GGSIPU, B. Tech., (CSE); 5th Sem., Dec. 2007]**

Q.7. (*a*) Explain the following concepts with an example of each: Unary relationship, generalization and aggregation.

(*b*) Draw an ER diagram for the Hospital Management System.

[GGSIPU, B. Tech., (CSE); 5th Sem., Dec. 2007]

Q.8. (*a*) Given below is a snapshot of data from the personal Diary of an Executive. Is it a database? Why/why not. Justify your answer.

Name	Phone-number
Rajiv saxena, IAS, DC	9210314258
Kamal Gandhi	9899125431 , 27392952
Priti kumari	55449321
Bhuvan kumar	9210315898, 27392521
9899125491	

(*b*) Consider a multiuser DBMS supporting thousands of end-users and preserving numerous integrity constraints. Suppose one integrity constraint is relaxed by the DBMS, what can you expect from such a DBMS. Explain with an example.

[GGSIPU, Ist Internal Test, B.Tech., (CSE/IT); 5th Sem., Sept. 2008]

Q.9. Suppose you create a DBMS for a UNIVERSITY in procedural languages like 'C' programming language and on the other side make the same DBMS in a non-procedural language like SQL. Which will be better and why? Compare both of above in terms of advantages in context of the DBMS for the UNIVERSITY.

[GGSIPU, Ist Internal Test, B.Tech., (CSE/IT/ECE); 5th Sem., Sept. 2008]

Q.10. What is the difference between a database schema and a database state. Which of them is liable to be changed frequently and why?

[GGSIPU, Ist Internal Test, B.Tech., (CSE/IT/ECT); 5th Sem., Sept. 2008]

Q.11. You opened a new database development firm. A local petty-shopkeeper approaches you for development of a DBMS for his business, his plea being that he also wants to be computer-savvy and wants to control his business through a DBMS, his annual turnover being Rs. 1,00,000/ per annum. What will be your decision and why? Elaborate briefly.

[GGSIPU, 1st Internal Test; B.Tech., (CSE/IT/ECE); 5th Sem., Sept. 2008]

Q.12. (*a*) Write down the functionalities of database manager module of DBMS.

(*b*) Explain how the data is organized in a Network DBMS? How it is different from Hierarchical DBMS? **[GGSIPU, B.Tech., (CSE/IT); 5th Sem., Dec. 2008]**

Q.13. (*a*) Explain generalization and specialization.

(*b*) Draw an ER-diagram for a garment manufacturing company. The entities include warehouses, production units, marketing wing, vendor and product types. Define the relationships between each of these entities. Take the attributes so that they can define a particular entity properly.

[GGSIPU, B.Tech. (CSE/IT); 5th Sem., Dec. 2008]

Q.14. What is data independence? What are the two forms of data independence? Explain the above with the help of one example each. **[IGNOU, MCA-3rd year, June 2004]**

Q.15. SQL is a very powerful DML and DDL. If so, what is the need of host languages in DBMS? Your explanation should include an example. Also describe static embedding of SQL with the help of an example. **[IGNOU, MCA-3rd year, June 2004]**

Q.16. (*a*) Explain three level architecture of databases with the help of a diagram.

(*b*) What do you understand by RDBMS? Distinguish between RDBMS and DBMS?

[Delhi University, B.Sc.(G); 3rd year]

Q.17. (*a*) Define the following terms: Weak Entity, Composite attributes, Data model, specialization.

(*b*) What is the difference between

(*i*) Database schema and database state.

(*ii*) Logical and physical data independence.

(*iii*) Primary and foreign key. **[Delhi University B.Sc., (G) -3rd year; 2006]**

Q.18. (*a*) Draw the overall structure of DBMS and explain its various components.

(*b*) Draw an ER-diagram for a hospital with a set of patients and a set of medical doctors, with each patient a log of the various conducted tests is also associated.

(*c*) Differentiate between database system and file system.

[UPTU, B.Tech. (CS) – 4th sem. 2006-07]

Q.19. (*a*) Define the following terms :

(*i*) Data model (*ii*) Referential integrity

(*iii*) External schema (*iv*) Internal schema

(*v*) Primary key

(*b*) When is the concept of weak entity used in data modeling? Define the terms owner entity, weak entity, identifying relationship, partial key.

[UPTU, MBA – 4th sem; 2006-07]

Q.20. (*a*) Comment on "the database management system is one of the most complex varieties of software in existence."

(*b*) Discuss different levels of abstraction present in database system.

[KUD, B.E. (CSE) – 5th sem; 1996]

Q.21. (*a*) Describe the three-schema architecture. Why do we need mappings between different schema levels?

(*b*) Discuss the capabilities that should be provided by a DBMS.
(*c*) What is a relational database? Explain different types of keys.
(*d*) Construct an ER-diagram for a car insurance company that has a set of customers, each of whom owns one or more car. Each car has associated with it, zero or more number of recorded accidents. Construct appropriate table from the diagram.
[GGSIPU, M.Tech. (IT)—3rd sem, 2005]

Q.22. Draw the ER diagram for a departmental shop. Take the entities to define different activities (*e.g.*, Sales etc), employees (different types *e.g.*, Manager), section (*e.g.*, Kids section), customers and other departments of the shop. Also take appropriate attributes to define the entities. Convert the ER-diagram to tables.
[GGSIPU, M. Tech (IT)-3rd sem; 2005]

Q.23. (*a*) What are the different tasks of database manager module of DBMS? Explain.
(*b*) Explain the differences between strong and weak entity-sets. Why sometimes weak entity-sets are needed in database design?
[GGSIPU, M.Tech (ITW); 3rd sem. Dec. 2004]

Q.24. (*a*) List the advantages of DBMS over file organization.
(*b*) What are the duties and responsibilities of a DBA?
(*c*) What do you understand by the degree of a relationship. Illustrate with examples.
(*d*) Construct an ER diagram for a author-publisher relation. An author can write for more than one publisher. The publisher publishes the work of many different authors. The database includes data about author, publisher and work the author has done. **[GGSIPU, BCA-3rd sem; Dec. 2002]**

Q.25. (*a*) Draw and explain with diagram the DBMS architecture?
(*b*) What is ER-modeling? What are it's drawbacks? What led to the development of enhanced ER-model?
(*c*) Draw an ER-diagram for a hospital system. **[GGSIPU, BCA – 3rd sem; Dec. 2003]**

Q.26. Differentiate between the following :
(*a*) Database and DBMS.
(*b*) Candidate and alternate key.
(*c*) Relational and Traditional file. **[GGSIPU, MCA – 2nd sem, May 2003]**

Q.27. (*a*) Describe the role of DDL compiler in the context of a general purpose DBMS.
(*b*) Differentiate among host language, data sublanguage and query language.
(*c*) How a "STUDENT" entity type is different from a "STUDENT" entity?
(*d*) Give one example and describe the concept of recursive relationship.
(*e*) Describe how the concept of relationship in ER-model can be represented in Hierarchical and Network model based systems.
[GGSIPU, MCA—2nd Sem., May 2004]

Q.28. (*a*) What is a relationship type? Explain the differences among a relationship instance, a relationship type and a relationship set.
(*b*) Design relational database for a university registrar office. The office maintains data about each class, including the instructor, the no of students enrolled and the time and place of the class meetings. For each student-class pair, a grade is recorded.
[GGSIPU, M.Tech (IT) -3rd Sem., Dec. 2004]

Q.29. (*a*) Differentiate between physical and logical data independence.
(*b*) What are the main functions of database manager module?
(*c*) Why sometimes weak entity-sets are needed in a database?
[GGSIPU, M.Tech. (ITW)-3rd Sem., Dec. 2005]

Q.30. (*a*) Define the concept of generalization and specialization.
(*b*) Construct an ER-diagram for a hospital with a set of patients and a set of medical doctors. A patient may be admitted to the hospital after a check up in OPD. Various tests may be conducted on patients. Rooms/Beds may be allocated to the patients on availability by the office. The patient may be released only after clearing all bills. Convert the ER-diagram into tables. **[GGSIPU, M. Tech. (ITW); Dec., 2005]**

Q.31. Describe the three levels of DBMS architecture ? Why do we need mapping between different levels ? **[GGSIPU, MCA – 3rd sem., 2010]**

Q.32. (*a*) Construct an ERD for railway reservation system keeping record of the following information :-

(*i*) Customer (*ii*) Train Schedules (*iii*) Booking (*iv*) Routes (*v*) Enquiry

(*b*) (*i*) Write the steps to convert any ERD in Relational Tables taking suitable example.

(*ii*) What are the shortcomings in handling a conventional database without using any DBMS ?

(*iii*) Explain generalization. **[GGSIPU, B. Tech. (CSE/IT)–5th Sem., Dec. 2010]**

Q.33. (*a*) How hierarchical and network data model differ from relational model ? Explain with an example.

(*b*) With proper example explain the following :-

(*i*) specialization (*ii*) Generalization (*iii*) Aggregation.

[GGSIPU, B. Tech. (CSE/IT)–5th Sem., Dec. 2010]

Q.34. (*a*) Differentiate between hierachical and Network model of a database taking suitable examples of each.

(*b*) What are different subsystems in DBMs architecture and what functionalities they provide? **[GGSIPU, B. Tech. (CSE/IT)–5th Sem., Dec. 2012]**

Q.35. Draw an ER diagram for a Prook store which maintains data of different books customers, suppliers and publishers. **[GGSIPU, B. Tech. (CSE/IT)–5th Sem., Dec. 2012]**

UNIT-II

CHAPTER

2

Relational Model, Languages and Systems

2.0 INTRODUCTION

In 1970, **Dr. Edgar F. Codd** of IBM presented a paper entitled as **"A Relational Model of Data for Large Shared Data Banks"**. He gave certain principles of database management which is called as **Relational model** now. In 1974, Chamberlain and Boyce from IBM only, presented a paper at database workshop at University of Michigan. They introduced the database language SEQUEL. The **first attempt** at a larger scale implementation of Codd's relational model was system R by IBM. The **second development** was of a relational DBMS INGRESS (Interactive Graphics Retrieval System) at the University of California at Berkeley, USA. This project involved the development of a prototype RDBMS.

At present there are many implementations of relational technology for both mainframes and microcomputers. IBM's DB2, Oracle, Sybase, MS-SQL Server, MS-ACCESS, Ingress etc are some RDBMS. These systems are based on Relational Models which is basically concerned with three things-Data Structure, Data Integrity and Data Manipulation

2.1 TERMINOLOGIES RELATED TO RELATIONAL MODEL

1. **Relation : A relation is defined as a table with columns and rows**. According to E.F. Codd, data can be stored in form of a two-dimensional (2D) table. In this table, rows will be the records and columns will be the attributes. **For example**, say a relation, R, is that of an employee-EMP. Then, it is shown as follows :

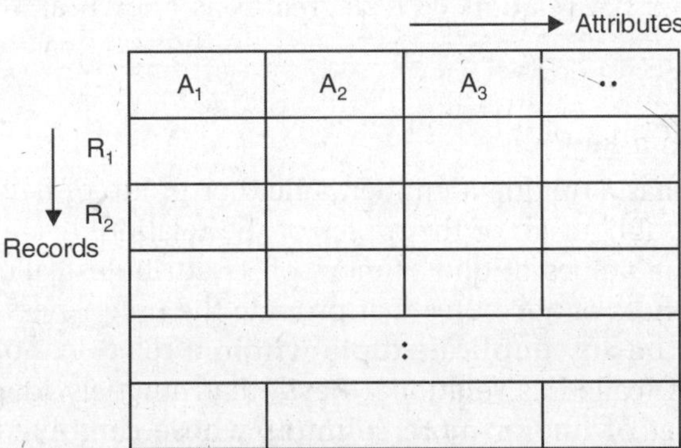

2. **Attribute : It is defined as a named column of a relation**. Recall that the entities are nothing else but relations and their attributes are nothing else but the columns of the relation. So, relations hold information about the objects to be represented

in the database. **Please note that attributes can appear in any order**. This will not change the meaning of a database.

3. **Domain : It is defined as a set of allowed values for one or more attributes.** Every attribute in a relation is defined on a domain. **Please note that at any given time, typically there will be values in a domain that do not currently appear as values in the corresponding attribute**. This domain concept is important. This is because it allows the user to define in a central place the meaning and source of values that attributes can hold. However, many RDBMS do not support them fully as it's implementation is not straight forward.
4. **Tuple : It is a row of a relation**. Tuples can appear in any order and the relation will still be the same relation.
5. **Extension (or state) of a relation : The extension of a Relation is defined as the set of tuples (or records) that appear in that relation at any given instant of time. Please note that it varies with time** *i.e.*, it changes as the tuples are created, destroyed or updated. **Also note that an extension is the same as the view of table.**
6. **Intension of a relation : It is a permanent part of the relation and is independent of time**. So, it corresponds to what is specified in the relational scheme. It remains fixed unless the meaning of a relation is changed to include additional attributes. It is actually a combination of a naming structure and a set of integrity constraints.
7. **Degree : The degree of a relation is defined as the number of attributes it contains. For example**, if a table has five attributes then it's degree is 5. **Please note that a relation with one attribute has a degree of one** (unary relation). Similarly if there are two attributes then degree is binary and if three then it is ternary. And after that N-ary term is used. **Also note that the degree of a relation is a property of the intension of the relation**.
8. **Cardinality : The cardinality of a Relation is defined as the number of tuples it contains**. So, it changes as we add new tuples (or records) or delete them. **Please note that the cardinality is a property of the extension of the relation**. It is determined from the particular instance of the relation at any given moment.
9. **Relational database : It is defined as the collection of normalized (or structured) relations with distinct relation names**. We will study normalization later on.
10. **N-ary relations** : A relation with degree, N is known as N-ary relations.

2.2 TYPES OF KEYS

Let us see what is a key?

A relation always has a unique identifier, a field or group of fields (attributes) whose values are unique throughout all of the tuples of the relation. Each tuple is distinct and can be identified by the values of one or more of its attributes called keys. So, keys are always minimal sequences of attributes that provide the uniqueness quality. **Please note that there should not be any duplicate tuple within a relation**. So, we should identify one or more attributes (called as **relational keys**) that uniquely identify each tuple in a relation. **A key is a set of one or more columns whose combined values are unique among all occurrences in a given table**. A key is the relational means of specifying uniqueness.

Based on the property of uniqueness, keys can be classified as :

(*a*) Candidate key, (*b*) Super key, and (*c*) Primary key.

(*a*) **Candidate Key (CK)** : When more than one or group of attributes serve as a unique identifier, they are each called as **candidate key**. CK are those attributes of a relation which posses the properties of **uniqueness** and **irreducibility**. The set of all attributes of relation, R, has the uniqueness property meaning that at any given time, no two tuples in the value of R, at that time are duplicates of one another.

Suppose that K is the set of attributes of relation, R. It represented as R(K). **Then K is candidate key for R if and only if it possesses both of the following properties** :

Property 1. Uniqueness property—It states that **"No legal value of R ever contains two distinct tuples with the same value for K".**

Property 2. Irreducibility property—It states that **"No proper subset of K has the uniqueness property".**

Please note that every relation does have at least one candidate key. The uniqueness property of such keys is self-explanatory. **There may be several candidate keys for a relation. When a key consists of more than one attribute, we call it as a composite key.** And the **irreducibility property means that if a candidate key is a composite key then no individual attribute of candidate key, which participate into it, is unique.**

For example, If (Name, Class) is unique then it can be identified as the candidate key if and only if Name and Class individually are not unique. That is,

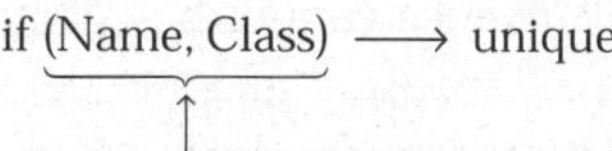

This will be a candidate key if and only if
Name ≠ unique and Class ≠ unique.

This is irreducibility property. Please note that since a null value is not guaranteed to be unique, no component of a candidate key is allowed to be null. Also note that there can be any number of candidate keys in a table. However, an instance of a relation cannot be used to prove that an attribute or combination of attributes is a candidate key.

(*b*) **Super Key : A Super key is defined as an attribute or a set of attributes that uniquely identifies a tuple within a relation.** A super key uniquely identifies each tuple within a relation. So, a super key has the uniqueness property but not necessarily the irreducibility property. A candidate key is a special case of a super key. All attributes in a relation taken together are a super key because only one row in a relation has a given value for all the relation attributes. **For example**, Consider the following relation-STUDENT

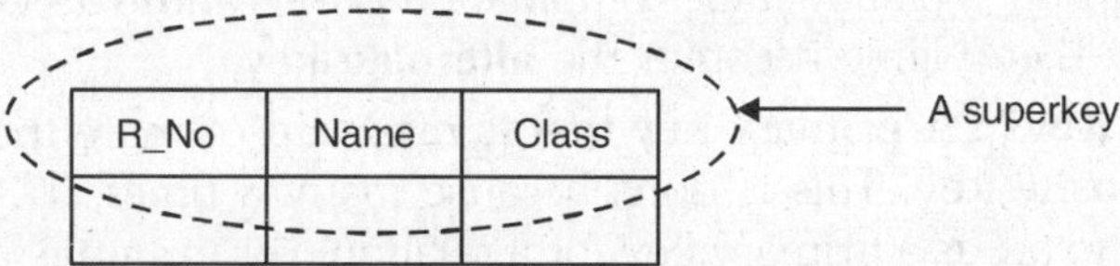

Here, if Roll_number is unique in relation STUDENT then the set of attributes (R_No, Name, Class) is a super key for this relation STUDENT. These set of attributes are also unique but this combination of keys (composite key) is not having the property of irreducibility because R-No which is one subset of the composite key is also unique itself. Thus, this composite key is called as super key because it has the property of uniqueness but not the irreducibility. So,

$$\text{Candidate key (CK)} = \text{Super key (SK)} - \text{Primary key (PK)}$$

or

$$\boxed{CK = SK - PK}$$

or

$$SK = PK + CK$$

So, we can say that – **"a superset of a candidate key is a super key"**.

(*c*) **Primary Key (PK) : It is defined as the candidate key that is selected to identify tuples uniquely within the relation**. The primary key is an attribute or a set of attributes that uniquely identify a specific instance of an entity. **Please note that the primary key cannot contain any NULL values because we cannot uniquely identify multiple NULL values.**

Properties of Primary Key : For any key, to qualify as a primary key for an entity, an attribute (key) must have the following four properties.

1. **Stable** : The value of a primary key must not change or should not become NULL throughout the life of an entity. A stable primary key helps keep the model stable. **For example**, the value of the primary key, say, Emp-number must not change with time as would happen with the age field of an employee.
2. **Minimal** : The primary key should be composed of the minimum number of fields that ensures the occurrences are unique.
3. **Definitive** : A value must exist for every record at the time of creation. This is so because an entity occurrence cannot be substantiated unless the primary key value also exists.
4. **Accessible** : Anyone who wants to create, read or delete a record must be able to see the primary key value.

The rule is—"once the candidate keys are identified, choose one and only one primary key for each entity. Candidate keys which are not chosen as the primary key to form super key are known as Alternate keys."

Please understand that the primary key of any table is any candidate key of that table which the database designer arbitrarily designates as "primary". This primary key may be selected for convenience, comprehension, performance and many other reasons.

(*d*) **Alternate Key (AK) : The alternate keys of any table are those candidate keys which are not currently selected as the primary key**. So, we can say that,

Alternate key (AK) = Candidate key (CK) – Primary key (PK)

or

$$AK = CK - PK$$

For example, if Roll_No and Name combination is the **candidate key**, then if Roll_No is the **primary key** then Name becomes the **alternate key**.

(*e*) **Composite Keys : A primary key that is made up of more than one attribute is known as a composite key**. This is done because many a times, it is required to have more than one key to act as a primary key for a relation. **For example**, consider a relation, PROJECT as follows :

PROJECT (<u>Eid</u>, <u>Pid</u>, Hours_worked)

Here, (<u>Eid</u>, + <u>Pid</u>) is a composite key meaning that each instance of the entity (or relation) PROJECT can be uniquely identified only by a composite key that is composed of <u>Eid</u> and <u>Pid</u>, here.

(*f*) **Artificial keys** : An artificial key is created when **no attribute has all primary key properties or when the primary key is large and complex**. This key has no meaning to the business or organization.

For example, the Enrollment table below from a business point of view has (student, class) combination as primary key. But this primary key is large and complex. So DBA decides to add row-id column as the primary key. That is,

Student	Class	row_id

← Artificial key added by DBA

(*g*) **Foreign Keys :** As we have already studied the concept of Master or Parent tables and that of the child tables or Transaction tables. **We now say that the column in the child table that references a Primary key of the Parent table is called as a Foreign key**. They are used to link together two or more different tables which have some form of relationship with each other. **For example**, consider the following Parent/Master table–STD ADD with the following attributes.

STD_ADD (Roll_no, Name, Addr, Place, Pin)

Now consider another transaction/child table : STD_MARKS with the following attributes :

STD_MARKS (Roll_no, Subject, Marks, Date)

Then, Roll_no column of STD_ADD table is the **primary key** whereas the Roll_No column of STD_MARKS table is **Foreign key**.

Please note that Foreign keys provide a method for maintaining integrity in the data and for navigation between different instances of an entity. Also note that the Foreign keys values must be matched by the corresponding primary key values.

Foreign key attributes are not considered to be owned by the entities to which they migrate because they are reflections of attributes in the parent entities. If the primary key of a child entity contains all attributes in a foreign key, the child entity is said to be **"identifier dependent"** on the parent entity and the relationship is called as an **"identifying relationship"**. If any attributes in a foreign key do not belong to the child's primary key, the child is not identifier dependent on the parent and the relationship is called as **"non-identifying"**.

2.3 RELATIONAL INTEGRITY RULE

There are two important integrity rules. These rules are basically the constraints or restrictions that apply to all instances of the database. These two rules are named as follows :

(*a*) Entity integrity rule.
(*b*) Referential integrity rule.

Let us discuss these 2-rules first.

2.3.1 Entity Integrity Rule

This rule states that "In a base relation, the value of attribute of a primary key cannot be null". By **base relation**, I mean a relation that corresponds to an entity in the conceptual scheme. A **primary key** is a minimal identifier that is used to identify tuples uniquely. This means that no subset of the primary key is sufficient to provide unique identification to tuples. If we allow a **null** for any part of a primary key, we are implying that not all the attributes are needed to distinguish between tuples, which contradicts the definition of the primary key.

For example, in a STUDENT relation as given below :

STUDENT (R_no , Name, Addr, Age, Sex) if R_no of the student is the primary key of this table then we should not be able to insert a tuple into this STUDENT relation with a NULL for the R_No attribute. If a user tries to do so then RDBMS reports an error message.

But the question is **what are these NULLS or unknown values?**

A Null represents a value for an attribute that is currently unknown or is not applicable for this tuple. A null can be taken to mean the logical value **'unknown'. Please note that it can mean that a value is not applicable to a particular tuple or it could merely mean that no value has yet been supplied**. Nulls are a way to deal with incomplete or exceptional data. **Also note that a null is not the same as a zero numeric value or a text string filled with spaces as zeros and spaces are values but a null represents the absence of a value**. Hence, nulls should be treated differently from other values.

Nulls can cause implementation problems also. This is because the relational model is based on FOPL (First Order Predicate Logic) which is a Boolean logic (T or F allowed) and Nulls means we have to work with higher order logic like three or four-valued logic, [Codd 1990].

Usually, RDBMS displays **blanks** if the data in a particular row and column is missing. This is not proper. Can't we use terms like **'Not applicable'** here? No, because then some where we will have **'nulls'** and somewhere **'Not applicable**' which results in **semantic** and **syntactic incompatibility**. This leads to practical problems.

But we must remember that Null is not some value. It implies that we cannot say that one null equals another one or is greater or lesser than the other null.

Let us discuss the Second Rule now.

2.3.2 Referential Integrity Rule

This rule states that "if a foreign key exists in a relation, either the foreign key value must match a candidate key value of some tuple in its home relation or the foreign key value must be wholly null." So, it is a property that guarantees that values from one column depend on values in another column. This property can be enforced through this rule.

For example, we try to create tables to store student data. Normally, all data related to students is not stored in a single table. Data that is permanent like his/her date-of-birth, address, name can be stored in one table referred to as the MASTER table or the PARENT table. **This table will contain only one record for every student. On the other hand, the marks table can be a transaction table or child table**. It can have more than one record for every student, *i.e.*, every time the student appears for an exam, a record will be added to the Marks table. So, this table will store that data about the examinations only. That is, if

STUD_ADDR is a MASTER/Parent table

STUD_MARK is a TRANSACTION/Child table

With the following attributes and records :

STUD_ADDR

R_no	Name	Address	Place	Pin
1.	Rakshit	Greater kailash	Delhi	90
2.	Shilpa	South Ex.	Delhi	81
3.	Rajan	Mahe	Karnataka	101
4.	Rajat	Rajouri Garden	Delhi	34

While STUD_MARKS table is :

STUD_MARKS

R_no	Subject	Exam_date	Marks
1.	WIN-98	12-Feb-09	95
2.	WIN-98	12-Feb-09	80
2.	C++	15-Mar-10	95
3.	Oracle 8i	15-Mar-10	90

Now, **can the student marks table contain a row for roll number = 5?**

No, certainly not. This is because roll number 5, does not exist in the PARENT table (STUD_ADDR). This is **referential integrity** which ensures that there are no rows in the transaction/child table if there is no reference for it in the master/parent table. Another question is, **can we delete the row of Roll number = 2 from the student address master table?**

No, certainly not. This is because Roll number = 2 has dependent rows in the child table (STUD_MARKS). **But please note that we can delete the row of Roll-number = 4 from the student master as there are no dependent rows in the child table (STUD_MARKS).**

Practically speaking, to maintain or implement this rule, we follow certain methods like :

1. The master table or the parent table which contains **the linking column must be a primary key**.
2. The linking column in the transaction table or the child table references the parent table. **This column in the child table which references a primary key of the parent table is called as a Foreign key.**

For example, in the above STUDENT database, R_No column of STUD_ADDR is the **primary key** whereas R_No column of STUD_MARKS table is the **foreign key.**

The referential integrity rule which allows the user to delete rows from the master and at the same time it will delete the dependent rows in all the child tables is actually known as ON DELETE CASCADING.

For example, if row with R_No = 2 is deleted from STUD_ADDR file then automatically two rows will be deleted from the STUD_MARKS file.

2.4 CODD'S RULES

E.F. Codd formulated thirteen rules including zero rule for RDBMS. Based upon these r ules we can decide a DBMS, to be an RDBMS or not. This is a theoretical evaluation of any product claiming to be a RDBMS.

0-Single foundation rule : RDBMS must manage every aspect of the database entirely through itself using its relational capabilities without using any external language. The processing should not be done with external storage. If any package needs help of external medium, the package cannot be taken as RDBMS.

1. **Information rule :** The information can be represented in one and only one way i.e. tables also known as **relations**. This rule emphasizes the fact that the information can be stored in rows and columns, whenever the data has to be stored or represented, it has to be in tabular form only, as it gives ease and flexibility.

2. **Guaranteed access** : The access to table follows the sequence of table name, tuple, attribute. This also states that at the intersection of each column and a row there should be one and only one value of data. The value of data must be logically addressable by using combination of table name, column name and value. Every step of data access is identified where the access to work area involves qualifying the user name and password.
3. **Systematic treatment of null** : One should be able to operate with null values. The operations with null values should be performed using single command. The treatment of null should be independent of data type. Not null value should be provided. If these null values are included, they should pose no problems, for application using and manipulating them.
4. **Active on-line catalogue** : RDBMS should maintain data dictionary tables to keep track of current state of the database. These are special tables, which keep track of the current state of the database. These tables contain information about table definitions, views, column definitions, synonyms and every other type of database object updated automatically, when changes are made to database.
5. **Comprehensive data sublanguage (DSL)** : RDBMS should have comprehensive transactional data definition language, Data Manipulation Language and Data Control Language. All the operations on database should be supported by the data language which is a part and parcel of the package.
6. **View updation rule** : One can feel that any view can be updated, but in real practice, one cannot update all the views, as some views are based on aggregating and virtual columns.
7. **High level global insert, update and delete** : RDBMS must be capable of doing more than just retrieving the relational data. It should be able to do insert, update and delete data items with the use of single command for each operation. It should be able to do these operations on more than one row also.
8. **Physical data independence** : The recording on the database should be left to the discretion of the type of system used i.e. whenever data is retrieved it should be independent of the storage structures and representation. A change in the storage strategy should not effect the performance of data.
9. **Logical data independence** : The data should be independent of logic involved in programming, in case the database design is changed then the programs should be independent of these changes *i.e.,* once the programs are written, the effort should not be wasted as to changing logic, depending on storage style.
10. **Integrity independence** : The data available should pose no limitations in terms of integration. The limits of system used should only be taken into consideration. The integrity constraints specific to a particular relational database must be definable in relational data sublanguage and storable in the data dictionary, not in application programs.
11. **Distribution independence:** This is one of the most important aspect for any RDBMS. This emphasizes the fact that the system should look like a centralized system to the user, even if it is distributed across. It is important as the user should not face difficulties, while accessing data, if it is at remote server, the RDBMS should take care of it, posing no problems to the user.
12. **Non subversion rule:** In case, if RDBMS takes help of any low language, it must not bypass any integrity rules or constraints of the relational language. Thus, any operation must be governed by the relational rules.

2.5 VIEWS AND THEIR PURPOSE

Views are defined as the logical tables of data extracted from existing tables. It can be queried just like a table but does not require any disk space. So, it is also known as a **virtual relation**. The contents of the view are defined as a query on one or more base relations. Any operations on the view are automatically translated into operations on the relations from which it is derived. **Please note that views are dynamic meaning that changes made to the base relations that affect the view are immediately reflected in the view. Also note that when users make permitted changes to the view, these changes are made to the underlying relations.**

Purpose of Views : Views are required for several reasons. Some of them are as follows :

1. It can be used to **hide sensitive columns**. To do this the owner of the view must grant the SELECT privilege on the view and revoke the privileges on the underlying tables.
2. It can be used *to* **hide complex queries** involving multiple tables. Users need not concern with the syntax of complex queries.
3. Views created with a check option, prevents the updating of other rows and columns.
4. It allows the users to see the same data in different ways, at the same time.
5. It can simplify complex operations on the base relations.

Views allow a more significant type of **logical data independence** that supports the reorganization of the conceptual scheme. **For instance**, say if a new attribute is added to a relation, existing users can be unaware of its existence if their views are defined to exclude it. **Please note here that if an existing relation is rearranged or split up, a view may be defined so that users can continue to see their original views.**

Updating Views : All updates to a base relation should be immediately reflected in all views that reference that base relation. **Also note that if a view is updated then the underlying base relation should reflect the change**. Rules that govern whether an update is allowed through a view or not are discussed below.

Rule 1. Updates are allowed through a view defined using a simple query involving a single base relation and containing the primary key or a candidate key of the base relation.

Rule 2. Updates are not allowed through views involving multiple base relations.

Rule 3. Updates are not allowed through views involving aggregation or grouping operations

So, views allows a designer to customize a user's model. But all views are not updatable.

2.6 RELATIONAL ALGEBRA

It is a procedural language with operations that is performed on one or more existing relation to derive result (another) relations without changing the original relations. So, it defines a complete scheme for each of the result relations. It consists of a set of relational operators. **Please note that each operator has one or more relations as its input and produces a relation as its output**. So, both operands and results are relations. Thus, **the output from one operation can become the input to another operation**. This allows expressions to be nested in the relational algebra, just as we can nest arithematic operations. This property is called as **closure**. That is, relations are closed under the algebra (just as numbers are closed under arithematic operations).

We also say that the relational algebra is a relation-at-a-time language in which all tuples from several relations are manipulated in one statement without looping. In 1972, Dr. E.F. Codd proposed eight operations to be included in relational algebra. Relational operators are put under two categories :

(*a*) Common set operations.

(*b*) Native relational operations.

Let us tabulate common set operations now.

Table. Common Set Operations

S. No.	Operations	Symbol	Keyboard Symbol	Example
1.	Union	∪	UNION	$R_1 \cup R_2$
2.	Intersection	∩	INTERSECT	$R_1 \cap R_2$
3.	Difference	–	MINUS	$R_1 - R_2$
4.	Product	X	TIMES	$R_1 * R_2$

These operations make use of the fact that tables are essentially sets of rows. Let us explain these operations with an example of each.

UNION : Say there are two tables, R and S with the following tuples at some instant of time :

R

cname	cstatus
Rajat	Good
Rahul	Excellent

S

cname	cstatus
Karan	Bad
Rajat	Good

Then RUS yields :

R ∪ S

cname	cstatus
Rajat	Good
Rahul	Excellent
Karan	Bad

Please note that in order to perform Union operation on two relations, both operand and relations must be union-compatible which means that they must have same number of columns drawn from the same domain (*i.e.*, must be of same data type).

INTERSECTION : An intersect operator is used to get common record (s) from the two relations. **For example**, consider the above two relations again, *i.e.*, R and S, then R and S yields :

R ∩ S

cname	cstatus
Rajat	Good

NOTE : This operation is just like AND function.

DIFFERENCE : A difference operator can be applied only when the tables are union-compatible **For example**, consider again the above two relations R and S, then (R – S) yields :

cname	cstatus
Rahul	Excellent

and (S – R) yields :

cname	cstatus
Karan	Bad

NOTE : It behaves like a NOT function.

Also note that minus is not associative

i.e., $(A - B) - C \neq A - (B - C)$

where, A, B and C are 3 relations.

And minus is not commutative *i.e.,*

$$(A - B) \neq (B - A)$$

where A, B and C are 3 relations

CARTESIAN PRODUCT : It means a set of all possible records. **For example**, consider two relations as Female and Male below :

Female (F)

F_name	F_job
Kajal	Clerk
Anamika	Sales

Male (M)

M_name	M_job
Rahul	Clerk
Rakesh	Sales

Then (F × S) yields –

F × S

F_name	F_Job	M_name	M_Job
Kajal	Clerk	Rahul	Clerk
Kajal	Clerk	Rakesh	Sales
Anamika	Sales	Rahul	Clerk
Anamika	Sales	Rakesh	Sales

Also we have some native relational operations :

(*a*) Selection (*b*) Projection

(*c*) Join (*d*) Division.

Let us tabulate them with their symbols :

S. No.	Operations	Symbol	Keyboard Symbol	Example
1.	Selection	R_1 where condition	R_1 where condition	R_1 where $A_1 = 10$
2.	Projection	$R_1[\ ]$	$R_1[\ ]$	R_1
3.	JOIN	$\bowtie$	JOIN	$R_1 \bowtie R_2$
4.	DIVISION	$\div$	DIVIDE BY	$R_1 \div R_2$

Let us understand them in relational algebra how are they written?

SELECTION (σ) : We can use a lowercase Greek letter sigma (σ) to denote selection.

For example, Consider the following relation, R.

#P_no	P_name	Color	Weight	City
P1	Nut	Red	15	Delhi
P4	Screws	Red	12	Dharwad

If we find out all those parts which have weight less than 15, then I would write

: $\sigma_{weight<15}$ (R)

in Relational algebra. This query then yields

#Pno	Pname	Color	Weight	City
P4	Screws	Red	12	Dharwad

PROJECTION (Π) : This operation works on a table to create another table by copying specified columns from the original table, eliminating, any duplicated rows.

For example, consider the following relation.

emp

emp_id	ename	Age	Salary
1.	Rajat	22	8000
2.	Mayur	43	10,000
3.	Rahul	22	5,000

then π_{age} (emp) yields

Age
22
43

Please note here that Age = 22 has been listed only once as it is redundant in that column. Also note that projection works column wise only.

Similarly, $\pi_{ename,salary}$ (emp) yields.

ename	Salary
Rajat	8000
Mayur	10000
Rahul	5000

JOIN : The most general from of join operation is called as a **theta join**. Theta (θ) here has the same meaning as 'compares with' *i.e.*, it stands for some comparison operator like =, <=, <, >=, >, ≠. This type of join is performed on two tables which have one or more columns in common that are domain compatible. If the θ-operator is "equals" then it is called as **equi-join. Please note that an equi-join must always result in a table which contains identical list of attribute values.**

Another type of join is **'Natural join'** in which this duplication of column values is eliminated by taking a projection of the table which includes only one of the duplicated columns.

The join is actually a composite operator. The θ-join (or theta join) is a cartesian product operation on the two tables followed by a restriction operation on the resultant table. The join operator is a combination of Cartesian Product, Selection and Projection Operator. JOIN is commutative *i.e.*, A JOIN B = B JOIN A.

All these are actually **inner joins. Outer join** is also used. It is a join in which tuples from R that do not have matching values in the common attributes of S are also included in the result relation. The missing values in the second relation are set to null. JOIN is an associative operator *i.e.*, (A JOIN B) JOIN C = A JOIN (B JOIN C). **To know more about joins, refer to Conceptual Short Questions of this chapter.**

DIVISION : The division operator divides a dividend relation, A, of degree ($m + n$) by a divisor relation, B, of degree, n, and produces a resultant relation of degree, m.

Consider the following relations :

Relation A has 1-table, as follows :

Sno	Pno
S1	P1
S1	P2
S1	P3
S1	P4
S1	P5
S1	P6
S2	P1
S2	P2
S3	P2
S4	P2
S4	P4
S4	P5

Relation B has 3-tables, as follows :

Case 1

Pno
P1

Case 2

Pno
P2
P4

Case 3

Pno
P1
P2
P3
P4
P5
P6

Then, A DIVIDE BY B gives the following resultant tables for all the three, cases, as follows :

Case 1

Sno
S1
S2

Case 2

Sno
S1
S4

Case 3

Sno
S1

Please note that, here the relation A has two attributes of (Sno, Pno) of degree 2 and divisor relation B has only one attribute Pno of degree 1. Thus, A divide by B gives a resultant relation of degree 1. This means that it has only one attribute of Sno. That is,

$$\frac{A}{B} = \frac{(\text{S no*P no})}{\text{Pno}} = \text{S no}$$

That is , the resultant relation has those tuples that are common values of those attributes which appear in the resultant attribute, S no.

For example, in Case 2, above

P2 has S no as (S1, S2, S3, S4)

and P4 has S no as (S1, S4).

Please note here that (S1, S4) are the common suppliers who supply both P2 and P4. So, the resultant relation has tuples S1 and S4. Similarly in case -3, there is only one supplier S1, who supply all the parts from P1 to P6.

We are in a position to solve some problems now.

Example 1. *Consider the following schema :*

SUPPLIER (Sid, S name, S addr)

PARTS (Pid, p name, color)

CATALOG (sid, pid, cost)

Now, answer the following queries in Relational Algebra:

(*a*) *Find the name of all the Suppliers who supply yellow parts.*

(*b*) *Find the name of suppliers who supply both Blue and Black parts.*

(*c*) *Find the name of suppliers who supply all parts.*

Solution. (*a*) π_{sname} (SUPPLIER) ⋈ CATALOG ⋈ ($\sigma_{\text{color = 'yellow'}}$ (PARTS));

(*b*) $\pi_{\text{sname.color}}$ (SUPPLIER) ⋈ (CATALOG ⋈ PARTS) ÷ π_{color}($\sigma_{\text{color='Blue' or color = 'Black')}}$ PARTS));

(*c*) $\pi_{\text{sname, color}}$ (SUPPLIER) ⋈ (CATALOG ⋈ PARTS) ÷ π_{color} (PARTS).

Example 2. *Consider the following relational schema and answer the following queries in Relational algebra:*

Employee (person-name, street, city)

Works (person-name, company-name, salary)

Company (Company-name, city)

Manages (person-name, manager-name)

(*a*) *Find the names of all employees who work for First bank corporation.*

(*b*) *Find the names and cities of residence of all employees who work for first bank Corporation.*

(*c*) *Find the names, street address and cities of residence of all employees who work for First bank corporation and earn more than $10,000 per annum.*

(*d*) *Find the names of all employees in this database who live in the same city as the company for which they work.*

(*e*) *Assume the companies may be located in several cities. Find all companies located in every city in which Small bank corp. is located.*

(*f*) *Give all employees of first bank corporation a 10 percent salary raise.*

(*g*) *Give all managers in this data base a 10 percent salary raise, unless the salary would be greater than $100,000. In such cases, give only, a 3 percent raise.*

(*h*) *Delete all tuples in the works relation for employees of small bank corporation.*

(*i*) *Find the company with the most employees.*

(*j*) *Find the company with the smallest payroll.*

(*k*) *Find those companies whose employees earn a higher salary, on average, than the average salary at first bank corporation.*

Solution. (*a*) $\pi_{\text{person-name}}$ ($\sigma_{\text{company-name = "First bank corporation"}}$ (Works))

(*b*) $\pi_{\text{person-name, city}}$ (employee ⋈ ($\sigma_{\text{company-name}}$ = "First Bank Corporation" (works)))

(*c*) $\pi_{\text{person-name, street, city}}$ (σ $_{\text{(company -name}}$ = "First Bank Corporation" $_{\wedge \text{ salary > 10000)}}$ works ⋈ employes) (*d*) $\Pi_{person\text{-}name}$ (employee ⋈ works ⋈ company)

(*e*) **NOTE:** Small Bank Corporation will be included in each answer.

$\Pi_{company\text{-}name}$ (company ÷

(Π_{city} (σ $_{company\text{-}name}$ = "Small Bank Corporation" $^{(company))))}$

(*f*) Works ← $\Pi_{person.name\ company\text{-}name,\ 1.1*salary}$

$\sigma_{(company\text{-}name=}$"First Bank Corporation"$_{)}$ (works))

U(works – $\sigma_{company\text{-}name}$= "First Bank Corporation" (works))))

(*g*) The same situation arises here. As before, t_1, holds the tuples to be updated and t_2 holds these tuples in their updated form.

$t_1 \leftarrow \pi_{works,\ person\text{-}name,\ company\text{-}name,\ salary}$

($\sigma_{works.person\text{-}name=manager\text{-}name}$ (works × manages))

$t_2 \leftarrow \pi_{works.person\text{-}name,company\text{-}name,salary*1.03}$

(σ t_1 salary * 1.1 > 100000 (t_1)

$t_2 \leftarrow t_2$ U ($\Pi_{works.person\text{-}name,company\text{-}name,salary*1.1}$

(σ $t_1$salary * 1.1 < 100000 (t_1)))

Works ← (works – t_1) U t_2

(*h*) *Works* ← *works* – σ $_{company\text{-}name}$ = "Small Bank Corporation" (works)

(*i*) $t_1 \leftarrow$ $_{company\text{-}name}$ *g* count-distinct$_{person\text{-}name}$ (works)

$t_2 \leftarrow$ Max $_{num\text{-}employees}$ (P $_{company\text{-}strength(company\text{-}name,\ num\text{-}employees)}$ (t_1))

$\Pi_{company\text{-}name}$ (P$t_{3(company\text{-}name\text{-}num\text{-}employees)}$($t_1$) ⋈ P$t_4$ $_{(num\text{-}employees)}$($t_2$)

(*j*) $t_1 \leftarrow$ $_{company\text{-}name}$ ***Gsum*** $_{salary}$ (works)

$t_2 \leftarrow$ **min**$_{payrol\ (P\ company\text{-}payroll(company\text{-}name,payroll)}$ (t_1))

$\Pi_{company\text{-}name}$ ($\rho t_{3(company\text{-}name,payroll)}$($t_1$) ⋈ ρt_4 (payroll) (t_2))

(*k*) $t_1 \leftarrow$ $_{company\text{-}name}$ Gnavg $_{salary}$ (works)

$t_2 \leftarrow \sigma_{company\text{-}name}$ = "First Bank Corporation" (t_1)

$\Pi_{t_3.company\text{-}name}$ ((ρt_3(company-name,avg-salary) (t_1))

$⋈_{t_3.avg\text{-}salary\ >\ first\text{-}bank.avg\text{-}salary}$ (ρ $_{first\text{-}bank(company\text{-}name,,avg\text{-}salary)}$ (t_2)))

Example 3. *Consider the following relations for a database that keeps track of student enrollment in courses and the books adopted for each course:*

STUDENT (SSN, Name, Major, Bdate)

COURSE (Course#, Quarter, Grade)

ENROLL (SSN, Course #, Quarter, Grade)

BOOK_ADOPTION (Course#, Quarter, Book-ISBN)

TEXT (Book-ISBN, Book-Tittle, Publisher, Author)

Specify the foreign keys for this schema, stating any asumptions you make. Write the queries in Relational Algebra.

(*a*) *List the number of courses taken by all students named 'John Smith' in winter 1999 (i.e., Quarter = 'W99').*

(*b*) *Produce a list of textbooks for the courses offered by the 'CS' department that have used more than two books.*

(*c*) *List any department that has all its adopted books published by 'BC Publishing'.*

Solution. The schema of this question has the following **four** foreign keys:

1. The attribute SSN of relation ENROLL that references relation STUDENT,
2. The attribute Course# in relation ENROLL that references relation COURSE,

3. The attribute Course# in relation BOOK_ADOPTION that references relation COURSE, and
4. The attribute Book_ISBN of relation BOOK_ADOPTION that references relation TEXT.

We now give the queries in relational algebra:

(*a*) COURSES_JS_W99_$_{\text{Name = 'John Smith'}}$ (STUDENT)* $_{\text{Quarter = 'W99'}}$ (ENROLL)
RESULT _ F COUNT course# (COURSES_JS_W99)

(*b*) CS_ADOPTIONS_$\pi_{\text{Course\#,Book_ISBN}}$ (_Dept = $_{\text{'CS'}}$ (COURSE)* BOOK_ADOPTION)
BOOK_COUNT-Course# F COUNT Book_ISBN (CS_ADOPTIONS)
COURSES_NEEDED_$\pi_{\text{Course\#}}$ ($_{\text{COUNT\_Book\_ISBN > 2}}$ (BOOK_COUNT))
RESULT_$\pi_{\text{Course\#, BOOK_ISBN, Book_title}}$ (COURSES_NEEDED*BOOK_ADOPTION * TEXT)

(*c*) DEPT_PUBS_$\pi_{\text{Dept,Publisher}}$ (COURSE * BOOK ADOPTION * TEXT)
RESULT_π_{Dept} (COURSE)_π_{Dept} ($_{\text{Publisher} \neq \text{'BC Publishing'}}$ (DEPT_PUBS)

It is interesting to observe that, contrary to intuition, the above expression does not employ the DIVISION operation, despite the fact that the query involves the word *all.* If, however, the query to list any department that has adopted *all* books published by 'BC publishing', then the solution would be the following expression involving DIVISION:

DEPT_BOOKS_$\pi_{\text{Dept, Book_ISBN}}$ (COURSE*BOOK_ADOPTION)
BOOKS_BY_BC$\pi_{\text{Book_ISBN}}$ ($_{\text{Publisher = 'BC publishing}}$ (TEXT))
RESULT_DEPT_BOOKS BOOKS_BY_BC

Example 4. *Consider the following relations for a database that keeps track of business trips of salespersons in a sales office :*

SALESPERSON (SSN, Name, Start-year, Dept-No)

TRIP (SSN, From_city, To_city,Departure_Date,

Return_Date, Trip – ID)

EXPENSE (Trip–ID, Account #, Amount)

Specify the foreign keys for the above schema, stating any assumptions you make. And Solve the following queries in relational algebra:

(*a*) *Give the details (all attributes of TRIP relation) for trips that exceeded $ 2000 in expenses.*

(*b*) *Print the SSN of salesman who took trips to 'Honolulu'.*

(*c*) *Print the total trip expenses incurred by the salesman with SSN= '234-56-7890'.*

Solution. The schema of this question has the following two foreign keys:

1. The attribute SSN of relation TRIP that references relation SALESPERSON, and
2. The attribute Trip_ID of relation EXPENSE that references relation TRIP.

In addition, the attributes Dept_No of relation SALESPERSON normal Account# of relation EXPENSE are probably also foreign keys referencing other relations of the database not mentioned in the question. We now give the queries in relational algebra :

(*a*) COSTLY_TRIPS__SUM_$_{\text{Amount > 2000}}$ ($_{\text{Trip\_Id}}$ F $_{\text{SUM Amount}}$ (EXPENSE)
RESULT_TRIP* $\pi_{\text{Trip\_Id}}$ (COSTLY_TRIPS)

(*b*) RESULT_ π_{SSN} ($_{\text{To\_City = 'Honolulu'}}$ (TRIP))

(*c*) RESULT _ F_{SUM} Amount ($_{\text{SSN = '234-56-7890'}}$ (TRIP)* EXPENSE)

Example 5. *Consider the following six relations for an order-processing database application in a company :*

CUSTOMER (<u>Cust#</u>, Cname, City)

ORDER (<u>Order#</u>, Odate, Cust#, Ord_Amt)

ORDER_ITEM (<u>Order#</u>, <u>Item#</u>, Qty)

ITEM (<u>Item#</u>, Unit_price)

SHIPMENT (<u>Order#</u>, <u>Warehouse#</u>, Ship_date)

WAREHOUSE (<u>Warehouse#</u>, City)

Here, Ord_Amt refers to total dollar amount of an order; Odate is the data the order was placed. Ship_date is the date an order is shipped from the warehouse. Assume that an order can be shipped from several warehouses. Specify foreign keys for this schema, stating any assumptions you make.

Now, answer the following queries in Relational Algebra :

(*a*) *List the order# and ship_data for all orders shipped from warehouse number 'W2'.*

(*b*) *List the Warehouse information from which the customer named 'Jose Lopez' was supplied his orders. Produce a listing. Order#, Warehouse#.*

(*c*) *Produce a listing: CUSTNAME,#OFORDERS, AVG_ORDER_AMT, where the middle column is the total number of orders by the customer and the last column is the average order amount for that customer.*

(*d*) *List the orders that were not shipped within 30 days of ordering.*

(*e*) *List the order# for orders that were shipped from all warehouses that the company has in Newyork.*

Solution. Strictly speaking, a foreign key is a set of attributes, but when that set contains only one attribute, then the attribute itself is often informally called a foreign key. The schema of this question has the following five foreign keys.

1. the attribute Cust# of relation ORDER that references relation CUSTOMER,
2. the attribute Order# of relation ORDER_ITEM that references relation ORDER,
3. the attribute Item# of relation ORDER_ITEM that references relation ITEM,
4. the attribute Order# of relation SHIPMENT that references relation ORDER, and
5. the attribute Warehouse# of relation SHIPMENT that references relation WAREHOUSE.

We now give the queries in relational algebra :

(*a*) SHIP_W2_ – $_{\text{Warehouse\#='W2'}}$ (SHIPMENT)

RESULT_ $\pi_{\text{Order\#, Ship\_date}}$ (SHIP_W2)

(*b*) ORDERS_JL_ORDER* – $_{\text{Cname = 'Jose Lopez'}}$ (CUSTOMER)

RESULT_ $\pi_{\text{Order\#, Warehouse\#}}$ (ORDERS_JL* SHIPMENT)

(*c*) BY_CUSTNUM_Cust# $\mathbf{F}_{\text{COUNT Order\#, AVERAGE Ord\_Amt}}$ (ORDER)

RESULT (CUSTNAME, #OFORDERS, AVG_ORDER_AMT)-

$\pi_{\text{Cname, COUNT\_Order\#, AVERAGE\_Ord\_Amt}}$ (BY_CUSTNUM* CUSTOMER)

(*d*) TIMELY_SHIPPED – – $_{\text{Ship\_date}}$ ≤ Odate + 30 (ORDER* SHIPMENT)

RESULT_$\pi_{\text{Order\#}}$ (ORDER– $\pi_{\text{Order\#}}$ (TIMELY_SHIPPED)

The above query lists all orders for which no"timely" shipment was made, including orders for which no shipment was ever made. It is instructive to compare the above query with the one below that lists those orders for which at least one "late" shipment was made.

LATE_SHIPPED $\leftarrow \sigma_{Ship\_date > Odate + 30}$ (ORDER* SHIPMENT)
RESULT_$\pi_{Order\#}$ (LATE_SHIPPED)

(*e*) NEW_YORK_ $\pi_{Warehouse\#}$ ($_{City\ 'New\ York'}$(WAREHOUSE))
RESULT_$\pi_{Order\#,\ Warehouse\#}$ (SHIPMENT) ÷ NEW_YORK

Example 6. *Consider the following database :*

Emp_id	*Name*
101	Rahul
103	Sachin
104	Ashish
106	Sumit
107	Anil
110	Kapil
112	Omkar

Assigned to

Emp_id	*Project_id*
101	C-453
103	C-354
104	C-343
104	C-354
106	C-231
106	C-278
106	C-353
106	C-354
106	C-453
107	C-231
107	C-353
110	C-278
112	C-353
112	C-354

Project

Project_id	*Project_Name*	*Chief_arch*
C-231	Oracle	107
C-278	Java	110
C-353	Operating system	107
C-354	C	104
C-453	VB	10L

Write relational algebra queries for the following :-

Get Emp_id of employees working on project C-353.

Solution.

1. Find all the tuples of relation assigned_To such that the value of project_id = C-353,

$\sigma_{project\_id\ =\ C\text{-}353}$ (Assigned_To).

2. Project Emp_id from this relation,

Query = π_{emp_id} ($\sigma_{sproject\_id\ =\ C\text{-}353}$ (Assigned_To))

Emp_id
106
107
112

Example 7. *Get details of employees (both number and name) working on project C-353.*

Solution.

1. Select all the tuples from assigned_To relation for which project_id is C-353. $\sigma_{project\text{-}id\ =\ C\text{-}353}$(Assigned_To)

2. Projet emp_id from this reult relaton.

$\pi_{emp\_id\ (project\_id\ =\ C\text{-}353}$ (Assigned_To))

3. To find names corresponding to emp_ids in result relation, use natural join with employee relation.

Employee ⋈ ($\pi_{project\_id}$ = ($\sigma_{project\_id\ =\ 'C\text{-}353'}$(C-353 (Assigned_To))

Result:

Emp-id	*Name*
106	Sumit
107	Anil
112	Omkar

Example 8. *Obtain details of employees working on operating system project.*

Solution.

1. Find the project_id of operating system project from project relation

   $\pi_{project\_id}$ ($\sigma_{project\_name\ =\ 'operating\ system'}$ (Project))

2. Find employee_ids of employees working on that project from Assigned_To relation.

   π_{emp_id}(Assigned_To ⋈ ($\pi_{project\_id}$($\sigma_{project\ name\ =\ 'operatingsystem'}$ (Project)))

3. Find details of employees using employee relation.

   Employee ⋈ π_{emp_id} (Assigned To ⋈ ($\pi_{project\_id}$ ($\sigma_{project\_name\ =\ 'Operating\ system'}$ (Project))))

Emp_id	*Name*
101	Rahul
106	Sumit
107	Anil
112	Omkar

Example 9. *Gather details of employees working on both C-353 and C-354.*

Solution.

1. Select those tuples of Assigned-To where the project id is C-353 or C-354 and then project the result on project_id.

   $q_1 \longleftarrow \pi_{project\_id}$ ($\sigma_{project\_id\ =\ 'C\text{-}353'\ v\ project\_id\ =\ 'C\text{-}354'}$) (Assigned_To)

2. Find emp_id of employees working on both projects from Assigned_To using ÷ operation.

   $q_2 \longleftarrow$ Assigned_To ÷ q_1

3. Find details of employees working on both projects using employee relation and ⋈ operator.

   Employee ⋈ (Assigned_To ÷ $P_{project\_id}$ ($S_{(project\_id\ =\ 'C\text{-}345'}$)

   ($\Delta_{project\_id\ =\ 'C\text{-}354'}$) (Assigned_To)))

Emp_id	*Name*
106	Sumit
112	Omkar

Example 10. *Find the employee numbers of the employees who work on at least all of the projects that employee 107 works on.*

Solution.

1. Find all the project_ids on which employee 107 works using Assigned_To relation.

   $\pi_{project\_id}$ (σ_{emp_id} = 107 (Assigned_To))

2. Find the employees working on all the projects that 107 works on using Assigned_To relation and ÷ operation.

   Assigned_To ÷ $\pi_{project\_id}$ ($\sigma_{emp\_id\ =\ 107}$ (Assigned_To))

3. Result of above query includes 107 employees. Remove that value to get final result.

   (Assigned_To ÷ $\pi_{project\_id\ (\sigma emp\_id\ =\ 107}$ (Assigned_To))) – 107

Result:

Emp_id
106

Example 11. *Find the employee numbers of the employees who do not work on project C-453.*

Solution.

1. Find employees working on 'C-453'

   π_{emp_id} ($\sigma_{project\_id\ =\ 'C-453'}$ (Assigned_To))

2. Subtract this result from Assigned_To relation,

   π_{emp_id} (Assigned_To) - π_{emp_id}($\sigma_{project\_id\ =\ 'C-453'}$ (Assigned_To))

Emp_id
103
104
107
110
112

Example 12. *Get the employee numbers of the employees who work on all projects.*

Solution. Find the projectids of all projects

1. Find the projectids of all projects

   $\pi_{project\_id}$ (Project)

2. Find the employees working on all projects using ÷ operator

   Assigned_To ÷ $\pi_{project\_id}$ (Project)

Example 13. *List the employee number of the employees other than 107 who work on at least one project that employee 107 works on.*

Solution.

1. Find the projects on which 107 works.

   $\pi_{project\_id}$ ($\sigma_{emp\_id\ =\ 107}$ (Assigned_To))

2. Find empids of employees working on at least one project using $\bowtie$ operator, and subtract 107 empoloyee.

π_{emp_id} (Assigned_To $\bowtie_{project\_id}$ ($\sigma_{emp\_id\ =\ 107}$ (Assigned_To)))–107

Emp_id
106
112

2.7 RELATIONAL CALCULUS

In relational calculus, a query is expressed as a formula consisting of a number of variables and an expression involving these variables. It is up to the DBMS then to transform these nonprocedural queries into equivalent, efficient, procedural queries. This concept was first proposed by E.F. Codd only. **Please note that the relational is used to measure the selective power of relational language. Also note that the language that can be used to produce any relation that can be derived using the relational calculus is said to be relationally complete**. This calculus is based on predicate calculus—a formal language used to symbolize logical arguments in mathematics.

Types of Relational Calculus : Relational calculus is of two types:

(*a*) Tuple Oriented Relational Calculus.
(*b*) Domain Oriented Relational Calculus.

Let us discuss these one by one now.

I. Tuple Oriented Relational Calculus (TRC) : It is a non-procedural query language. It gives the desired information without giving a specific procedure for obtaining that information.

A query in TRC is expressed as :

$$[t \mid P(t)\}$$

i.e., is the set of all tuples,t such that predicate P is true for *t*.

Also, *t*[A] is used to denote the value of tuple *t* on attribute, A.

We can use ∧ (AND), ∨ (OR) and ¬(NOT) connectives also.

For example, if the query is—'Find the information about all the employees' from the relation, emp, then in TRC, we can write –

$$\{t \mid t \in \text{emp}\}$$

Another query can be—'Find all those employees whose salary is greater than 5000'. Then, in TRC, one can write —

$$\{t \mid t \in \text{emp} \wedge t\,[\text{sal}] > 5000\}$$

Let us take another query now –

"Find all the employees working in systems department'. It's TRC can be

$$\{t \mid \exists\ s \in \text{emp} \mid (t\ [\text{dno}] = s[\text{dno}])$$
$$\wedge \exists\ u \in \text{dept} \mid (t[\text{dno}] = u[\text{dno}])$$
$$\wedge(u[\text{dname}] = \text{'Systems'})\}$$

Please note here that we have used an existential quantifier (∃) meaning that there exists some value that is true for at least one instance. Also note that we have another quantifier ∀ (read as for all), used in statements many a times, about every instance. Tuple variables that are quantified by ∃ or ∀ are called as bound-variables, otherwise, they are called as free variables.

II. Domain Oriented Relational Calculus (DRC) : Domain Oriented Relational Calculus was proposed by Lacroix and Pirotte in 1977. Herein, the variables take their values from domains of attributes rather than tuples of relations. **Please note that to form a relation of degree *'n'* for a query result, we must have *'n'* of these domain**

variables (*i.e.*, one for each attribute). In general, a DRC expression is expressed as $\{d_1, d_2 .... d_n \mid P(d_1,d_2,..... d_m)\}$ where $m \geq n$ Here, $d_1, d_2, ... d_n$ represent domain variables and $P(d_1,d_2, ... d_m)$ represent a formula composed of atoms.

Each atom has one of the following forms :

(*a*) $R(d_1, d_2 -- d_n)$, where R is a relation of degree '*n*' and each d_i is a domain variable.

(*b*) $d_i \ \theta \ d_j$ where d_i and d_j are domain variables and θ is one of the comparison operators ($<, \leq, >, \geq, =, \neq$).

(*c*) $d_i \ \theta \ c$ where d_i is a domain variable, c is a constant from the domain of d_i and θ is one of the comparison operators.

We **recursively** build up formula from atoms using the following rules :

1. An atom is a formula.
2. If F_1 and F_2 are formula, so are
   - $F_1 \wedge F_2$ (conjunction)
   - $F_1 \vee F_2$ (disjunction)
   - $\neg F_1$ (Negation)
3. If $P(x)$ is a formula with x as a domain variable, then $(\exists x)\ (P(x))$ and $(\forall x)\ (P(x))$ are also the formulas.

For example, say, if the query is to - "Find eno, ename, sal, dno for employees having sal > 10000". Then in DRC, its solution is -

$$\{< e, en, s, d > \mid <e, en, s, d > \in \text{emp} \wedge s > 1000\}$$

Also remember that the rules regarding free and bound variables given for TRC are same for DRC also.

2.8 COMPARISON OF RELATIONAL ALGEBRA AND RELATIONAL CALCULUS IN TABULAR FORM

Let us tabulate the differences between Relational Algebra and Relational Calculus as given by Dr. E.F. Codd.

S. No.	Relational Algebra	Relational Calculus
1.	It describes about 'how' to evaluate a query.	It describes about 'what' is to be retrieved.
2.	It is a procedural method of solving the queries.	It is a non-procedural method of solving the queries.
3.	Here, the solution to the database access problem is obtained by stating what is required and what are the steps to obtain that information.	Here, the solution to the database access problem problem is obtaied by simply stating what is required and letting the system find the answer.
4.	It is used as a driver of Relational Calculus.	Relational calculus queries are converted into equivalent relational algebra format by using *Codd's Reduction Algorithm* and then it is implemented using some relational algebra operators.
5.	Relational algebra operators are used as a yardstick for measuring the expressive power of any given language.	A language is said-to-be complete if it is atleast as powerful as the calculus *i.e.*, if any relation definable by some expression of the calculus is also definable by some expression of the language in question.

Please note that any calculus expression can be reduced to an equivalent algebraic expression. Thus, we can say that **the algebra is atleast as powerful as the calculus.** And **the converse is also true.** That is, **it is possible to show that any algebra expression can be reduced to a calculus equivalent and hence that the calculus is atleast as powerful as algebra.**

2.9 QUEL AND QBE

QUEL : It is a TRC language of a relational database system-INGRESS (Interactive Graphics and Retrieval System) INGRESS runs under UNIX O.S and is implemented using C language. Commands are written to QUEL processor or embedded in C language. If embedded in C, then QUEL statements are preceded by hash symbol (*i.e.*, #) and are handled by a processor. **Please note here that INGRESS statements are used for implementing QUEL**. QUEL uses 3 clauses :

- range of
- retrieve
- where

It's syntax is :

range of t_1 is r_1
range of t_2 is r_2
⋮
range of t_n is r_n
retrieve $(t_{i1}.A_{j1}, t_{i2}.A_{j2}, \ldots t_{in}.A_{jn})$
Where P

Please note that when we say that "range of *t* is *r*" then we mean that any subsequent operations until *t* is redeclared by another range statement, are to be carried out once for each tuple in *r*, with *t* equal to each of these tuples in turn.

For example, if we want to retrieve all those employee names whose employee number is 'e1' then we may write in QUEL as follows :

range of *t* is emp
retrieve (*t*.ename)
where (*t*.eno = 'e1')

Note the following things here :

1. range of, retrieve and where are the reserved keywords of QUEL.
2. 'emp' is the name of relation from where records are to be retrieved and displayed.
3. dot (.) operator is used along with the fields (or attributes), preceded by the range variable, *t*, in our case.

However, if we want to implement a **join** operation then we may want to display dname also from dept table as follows :

range of *t* is emp
range of *u* is dept
retrieve (*t*.ename, *u*.dname)
where (*t*.dno = *u*.dno)

Here, '=' is an equi-join only.

We can use **aggregate functions** also in TRC like count, sum, avg, max, min, countu, sumu, argu etc.

For modifications to the database—*i.e.*, Insertion, Deletion and Updation operations, in QUEL TRC, one may write —

For **Insertion of a record** in the emp' table with eno = 'e5', ename = 'Rajiv', sal = 42,000 and dno = 'd1' one may write —

append to emp (eno = 'e5',
ename = 'Rajiv',
Sal = 42,000,
dno= 'd1')

For **deletion of record** from emp table with eno = 'e1', one may write

range of t is emp
delete *t*
where *t*.eno = 'e1'

For updation of records, **replace command** is used. **For example,**

range of *t* is emp
replace *t* (sal = sal*1.5)
where *t*.sal > 42000.

Let us discuss about QBE now.

QBE (Query By Example) : QBE is a name of both a database system and data manipulation language. QBE database system was developed at IBM in 1970's. QBE DML has a 2–D syntax *i.e.*, like a **table.** Queries are expressed by example.

For example,

emp	eno	ename	Sal	dno
	P.		>42000	

It means that print (P.) all enos where salary > 42000. **Please note here that all operators in QBE end with a dot (.) and the dot is not ifself an operator.** When a tuple or combination of tuples matching the conditions specified by the query are found, the components for those attributes preceded by P. are printed.

Also, we can use :

P._*x* = 42000

The underscore (_) here means it is a sample value taken.

Let us draw a table for various QBE statements.

emp	eno	ename	Sal	dno	Meaning
	P.	P._x = 'Ajay'	>1000		Print e-name where sal> 1000
I.	'e5'	'ADE'	20000	'd2'	Insert eno as e5, name as ADE, sal as 20000 and dno as d2
D.	'el'				Delete record for eno='el'
U.			_x *. 15	'd1'	Update salary by 15% or 0.15 where dept-no = dl

Also, the multiple conditions are given in a Condition Box, as shown below –

Condition
Sal > 10000 AND dno = '*d*1'

QBE also has 5 aggregate operators SUM., AVG., MAX., MIN. and CNT. (count). Also, All and UN (unique) are used in conjunction with aggregate operators. When All is applied to a domain variable then it produces the multiset of values that the variable takes on as we run through all the tuples in the relevant relation. **Please note that a multiset is a set with repetitions allowed while most other QBE operations will eliminate duplicates.**

We are in a position to solve some example on QUEL and QBE now.

2.10 SOLVED EXAMPLES ON QUEL AND QBE

Example 1. Solve the following with QUEL tuple calculus:

Consider the following database-EMP (emp no, ename, job, mgr, hiredate, sal, comm, deptno)

DEPT (deptno, dname, loc)

(a) Get the name of all employees working for the 'Sales' department.

(b) Get the name, location of department of all employees whose pay is less than 5000.

(c) Get the name of all departments who have more than five employees.

Solution.

(*a*) *range of t* is emp
range of d is dept
retrieve (*t*.ename)
where (*t*.dname ='sales') and
(*t*.dept no = *d*.dept no)

(*b*) *range of t* is emp
range of d is dept
retrieve (*t*.ename, *d*.dept, *d*.loc)
where (*t*. dept no = *d*.dept no) and (sal < 5000)

(*c*) *range of t* is emp
range of d is dept
retrieve (*d*. dname)
where (*t*.dept no = *d*.dept no) and (count > 5)

Example 2. Consider the following relations :

CUSTOMERS (cname, caddr, balance)

ORDERS (order_no, cname, item, qty)

SUPPLIERS (sname, saddr, item, price)

Write the following QUEL queries :

(a) Print the names of customers with negative balances.

(b) Print the supplier names, items and prices of all suppliers that supply atleast one item ordered by HCL.

Solution. QUEL queries are as follows :

(*a*) *range of t* is CUSTOMERS

retrieve (*t*.cname)
where *t*.balance < 0.

(*b*) *range of t* is ORDERS
range of s is SUPPLIERS
retrieve (*s*.sname, *s*.item, *s*.price)
where *t*.cname = "HCL" and *t*.item = *s*.item.

SUMMARY

In this chapter we have studied the important terminologies related to the most common and popular model—Relational Model. We have studied various Relational Integrity Rules. Dr. E.F. Codd (in 1970s) gave certain rules called as Codd Rules. A good RDBMS must satisfy some or all of these rules. We now know the purpose of views also. Relational algebra and calculus have been dealt completely with many solved examples.

MULTIPLE CHOICE QUESTIONS [MCQs]

1. A table with columns and rows is called as a
   (*a*) Table (*b*) Relation
   (*c*) Key (*d*) None of the above.
2. Entities are nothing else but
   (*a*) Relations (*b*) DBMS
   (*c*) Attributes (*d*) None of the above.
3. Attributes correspond to
   (*a*) Rows of a table (*b*) Columns of a table
   (*c*) Degree of a table (*d*) None of the above.
4. A row of a relation is called as a
   (*a*) Domain (*b*) Tuple
   (*c*) Relation (*d*) None of the above.
5. A set of tuples at any given instant of time is called as
   (*a*) Table (*b*) Relation
   (*c*) Extension (*d*) None of the above.
6. The number of tuples of a relation is its
   (*a*) Degree (*b*) Intension
   (*c*) Cardinality. (*d*) None of the above.
7. A relation with degree, N, is known as
   (*a*) N-ary relation. (*b*) 1-ary relation
   (*c*) 2-ary relation (*d*) None of the above.
8. Which of the following is a correct form of the equation
   (*a*) CK = SK + PK. (*b*) CK = SK – PK
   (*c*) CK = SK * PK (*d*) None of the above.
9. Those candidate keys which are not currently selected as the primary key are called as
   (*a*) Super keys (*b*) Candidate key
   (*c*) Alternate key (*d*) None of the above.
10. Which of the following is correct if AK = Alternate key, CK = Candidate key and PK = Primary key
    (*a*) AK = CK – PK (*b*) AK = CK + PK
    (*c*) AK = SK – PK (*d*) None of the above.

11. A key that has no meaning to the business or organization is
    (*a*) Candidate key (*b*) Alternate key
    (*c*) Artificial key (*d*) None of the above.
12. The column in the child table that references a primary key of the parent table is called as
    (*a*) Candidate key (*b*) Foreign key
    (*c*) Composite key (*d*) None of the above.
13. A rule that states that in a base relation, the value of attribute of a primary key cannot be null is called as
    (*a*) Entity integrity rule (*b*) Referential integrity rule
    (*c*) Security integrity rule (*d*) None of the above.
14. A NULL means
    (*a*) Unknown (*b*) Known
    (*c*) known partially (*d*) None of the above.
15. Dr. E.F. Codd gave
    (*a*) 10-rules (*b*) 11-rules
    (*c*) 12-rules (*d*) 13-rules.
16. A virtual relation is also known as a
    (*a*) View (*b*) Table
    (*c*) Snapshot (*d*) None of the above.
17. In order to perform Union operation on two relations, both operand and relations must be
    (*a*) Union-compatible (*b*) Set-compatible
    (*c*) Difference-compatible (*d*) None of the above.
18. Which is true out of the following
    (*a*) (A – B) = (B – A) (*b*) (A – B) ≠ (B – A)
    (*c*) (B – A) = (B – C) (*d*) None of the above.
19. Select-operator (σ) works row wise whereas project-operator (π) works
    (*a*) Row-wise only (*b*) Column wise
    (*c*) Both '*a*' and '*b*' (*d*) None of the above.
20. When we want to display records with attributes from many relations then we use-
    (*a*) SELECT operation (*b*) PROJECT operation
    (*c*) JOIN operation (*d*) None of the above.
21. Relational calculus describes about
    (*a*) 'How' to evaluate a query (*b*) 'What' is to be retrieved
    (*c*) 'When' to evaluate a query (*d*) None of the above
22. QUEL is a TRC language of which RDBMS –
    (*a*) INGRESS (*b*) DB2
    (*c*) Oracle 8i (*d*) None of the above.
23. How many tables can be joined to create a view
    (*a*) 1 (*b*) 2
    (*c*) Depends on DBMS (*d*) None of the above.
24. What is the *cardinality* of a table with 50 rows and 5 columns?
    (*a*) 50 (*b*) 5
    (*c*) 250 (*d*) None of the above.
25. What is the *degree* of a table with 50 rows and 5 columns?
    (*a*) 50 (*b*) 5
    (*c*) 250 (*d*) None of the above.

ANSWERS

1. (*b*)	**2.** (*a*)	**3.** (*b*)	**4.** (*b*)	**5.** (*c*)	**6.** (*c*)	**7.** (*a*)	**8.** (*b*)
9. (*c*)	**10.** (*a*)	**11.** (*c*)	**12.** (*b*)	**13.** (*a*)	**14.** (*a*)	**15.** (*c*)	**16.** (*a*)
17. (*a*)	**18.** (*b*)	**19.** (*b*)	**20.** (*c*)	**21.** (*b*)	**22.** (*a*)	**23.** (*d*)	**24.** (*a*)
25. (*b*)							

CONCEPTUAL SHORT QUESTIONS WITH ANSWERS

Q.1. Give some properties of Relations?

Ans. A relation has the following properties :

1. A relation has a name that is distinct from all other relation names in the relational schema.
2. Each cell of the relation contains exactly one atomic (single) value.
3. Each attribute has a distinct name.
4. The values of an attribute are all from the same domain.
5. Each tuple is distinct. There are no duplicate tuples.
6. The order of attributes has no significance.
7. Theoretically, the order of tuples has no significance.

Q.2. Write down the differences between the select and project operator?

Ans.

S. No.	Select	Project
1.	It is represented by a Greek letter, σ (sigma)	It is represented by a Greek letter, π (pi)
2.	It selects entire row that satisfies the given condition.	It selects one or more than one column out of the rows that satisfies the given condition.
3.	It does not eliminate duplicated rows.	It eliminates any duplicated rows.

Q.3. Records in a file can be either of fixed length or of variable length. How are they different?

Ans. In a file with **fixed-length records**, all records on the page are of same slot length. The record slots are uniform and records are arranged consecutively within a page. Herein, insertion and deletion for files are simple to implement.

On the other hand, a file with variable-length record has all records that are not of the same length. So, different records in the file have different sizes.

In file header method, pointers are used to chain together only deleted records whereas in list representation, pointers of all records are chained together.

Q.4. What is chaining ? Why are chains so popular?

Ans. Chaining means including pointers with the data to indicate where to go next. In practice, chaining is used broadly. Almost all DBMS employ chains in one way or another. **For example**, IMS, system R, system 2000 and many other DBMS use pointers to create chains.

Why are chains so popular?

The basic reason is that records can only be stored physically in a sequential manner with respect to only one field. Chaining is a mechanism that makes possible another sequence of search with respect to another field. **For example,** chaining occurs in DBTG systems where rings or networks are created.

Q.5. What is B⁺ tree indexing?

Ans. B⁺ tree index is a balanced tree in which the internal nodes direct the search operation and the leaf (or terminal) nodes contain the data entries. Every path from the root to the leaf node is of the same length. **Please note that the tree structure grows and shrinks dynamically, so it is not feasible to allocate the leaf pages sequentially.** Actually, a B⁺ tree index is a regular B–tree plus a linked list of data. In a B⁺ tree index, references to data are made only from the leaves. The internal nodes of the B⁺ tree are indexed for fast access of data, which is called an index set. The leaves are linked sequentially to form a sequence set so the scanning this list of leaves results in data given in ascending order. **We give some characteristics of a B⁺ tree now** :

(*i*) It is a balanced tree.

(*ii*) A minimum occupancy of 50% is guaranteed for each node except the root.

(*iii*) Searching for a record requires just a traversal from the root to the appropriate leaf.

Q.6. Describe the differences in meaning between the terms *relation and relation schema*.

Ans. A relation schema is type definition, and a relation is an instance of that schema. For example, *student* (*ss#, name*) is a relation schema and

ss#	name
123-45-6789	Tom Jones
456-78-9123	Joe Brown

is a relation based on that schema.

Q.7. Consider the following table :

Customer_name	Loan_number	Amount
Rajiv	L-15	800
Rahul	L-11	900
Mayur	L-17	1000
Rajat	L-18	2000
Rajat	L-10	900

Now, write relational algebra queries to find the accounts held by more than two customers in the following ways :

(*a*) Using an aggregate function.

(*b*) Without using any aggregate function ?

Ans. (*a*) $t_1 \leftarrow {}_{\text{account-number}}\ \mathbf{G}\text{count}_{\text{customer-name}}$ (depositor)

$\Pi_{\text{account-number}}(\sigma_{\text{num-holders} > 2}(\rho_{\text{account-holders(account-number,num-holders)}}(t_1)))$

(*b*) $t_1 \leftarrow (\rho_{d1}(\text{depositor}) \times \rho_{d2}(\text{depositor}) \times \rho_{d3}(\text{depositor}))$

$t_2 \leftarrow \sigma_{(\text{d1.account-number=d2.account-number=d3.account-number})}(t_1)$

$\Pi_{\text{d1.account-number}}(\sigma_{(d1.\text{customer-name} \neq d2.\text{customer-name} \wedge d2.\text{customer-name} \neq \text{d3.customer-name} \wedge d3.\text{customer-name} \neq d1.\text{customer-name})}(t_2)$

Q.8. List two reasons why null values might be introduced into the database.

[GGSIPU, B.Tech. CSE, 5th Sem. Sept. 2007]

Ans. Nulls may be introduced into the database because the actual value is either unknown or does not exist. **For example**, an employee whose address has changed and whose new address is not yet known should be retained with a null address. If employee tuples have a composite attribute **dependents**, and a particular employee has no dependents, then that tuple's **dependents** attribute should be given a null value.

Q.9. Consider the employee database of Fig. 2.1 below. Give expressions in tuple relational calculus and domain relational calculus for each of the following queries:

(*a*) Find the names of all employees who work for First Bank Corporation.

(*b*) Find the names and cities of residence of all employees who work for First Bank Corporation.

(*c*) Find the names,street addresses, and cities of residence of all employees who work for first Bank Corporation and earn more than $10,000 per annum.

(*d*) Find all employees who live in the same city as that in which the company for which they work is located.

(*e*) Find all employees who live in the same city and on the same street as their managers.

(*f*) Find all employees in the database who do not work for First Bank Corporation.

(*g*) Find all employees who earn more than every employee of Small Bank Corporation.

(*h*) Assume that the companies may be located in several cities. Find all companies located in every city in which Small Bank Corporation is located.

employee (person-name, street, city)
works (person-name, company-name salary)
company (company-name, city)
manages (person-name, manager-name)

Fig. 2.1

Ans. (*a*) Find the names of all employees who work for First Bank Corporation :

(*i*) {t | ∃ s ∈ *works* (*t[person_name]* = *s[person_name]*
∧ *s[company-name]*="First Bank Corporation")}

(*ii*) {< *p* > | ∃*c*, *s* (< *p*, *c*, *s* > ∈ *works* ∧ *c* = 'First Bank Corporation")}

(*b*) Find the names and cities of residence of all employees who work for First Bank Corporation :

(*i*) {t | ∃ s ∈ *employee* ∃ s ∈ *works* (*t[person_name]* = *r[person_name]*
∧ *t[city]* = *r[city]* ∧ *r[person_name}* = *s[person_name]*
∧ *s[company_name]* = 'First Bank Corporation' |]}

(*ii*) {< *p*, *c* > | ∃ *co*, *sa*, *st* (< *p*, *co*, *sa* > ∈ *works*
∧ < *p*, *st*, *c* >∈ employee ∧ *co* = "First Bank Corporation")}

(*c*) Find the names, street address, and cities of residence of all employees who work for First Bank Corporation and earn more than $10,000 per annum :

(*i*) {*t* | *t* ∈ *employee* ∧ (∃ s ∈ *works* (*s[person_name]* = *t[person_name]*
∧ *s[company_name]* = "First Bank Corporation" ∧ *s[salary]* > 10000))}

(ii) $\{ < p, s, c > \mid < p, s, c > \in$ employee $\wedge \exists\, co, sa\ (< p, co, sa > \in works$
$\wedge\ co =$ 'First Bank Corporation' $\wedge\ sa > 10000)\}$

(d) Find the names of all employees in this database who live in the same city as the company for which they work:

(i) $\{t \mid \exists\, e \in employee\ \exists\, w \in works\ \exists\, c \in company$
$(t[person\_name] = e[person\_name]$
$\wedge\ e[person\_name] = w[person\_name]$
$\wedge\ w[company\_name] = c[company\_name] \wedge e[city] = c[city])\}$

(ii) $\{ < p > \mid \exists\, st, c, co, sa\ (< p, st, c > \in$ employee
$\wedge < p, co, sa > \in works \wedge < co, c > \in company)\}$

(e) Find the names of all employees who live in the same city and on the same street as do their managers :

(i) $\{ t \mid \exists\, l \in employee\ \exists m \in manages\ \exists r \in company$
$(l\,[person\_name] = m[person\_name] \wedge m[manager\_name] = r[person\_name]$
$\wedge\ l[street] \doteq r[street] \wedge l[city] \wedge l[person\_name] = l[person\_name])\}$

(ii) $\{ < t > \mid \exists\, s, c, m\ (< t, s, c > \in$ employee $\wedge < t, m > \in manages \wedge < m, s, c > \in employee)\}$

(f) Find the names of all employees in this database who do not work for First Bank Corporation :

If one allows people to appear in the database (e.g. in *employee*) but not appear in *works*, the problem is more complicated. We give solutions for this more realistic case later.

(i) $\{ t \mid \exists\, w \in works\ (w[company\_name] \neq$ "First Bank Corporation"
$\wedge\ t[person\_name\} = w[person\_name])\}$

(ii) $\{ < p > \mid \exists\, c, s\ (< p, c, s > \in works \wedge c \neq$ "First Bank Corporation")}

If people may not work for any company :

(i) $\{ t \mid \exists\, e \in employee\ (t[person\_name] = e[person\_name] \wedge \neg \exists\, w \in works.$
$(w[company\_name] =$ "First Bank Corporation"
$\wedge\ w[person\_name] = t[person\_name]))\}$

(ii) $\{ < p > \mid \exists\, s, c\ (< p, s, c > \in employee) \wedge \neg \exists\, x, y$
$(y =$ "First Bank Corporation" $\wedge <p, y, x > \in works)\}$

(g) Find the names of all employees who earn more than every employee of Small Bank Corporation :

(i) $\{t \mid \exists\, w \in works\ (t[person\_name] = w[person\_name] \wedge \forall\, s \in works$
$(s[company\_name] =$ "Small Bank Corporation" $\Rightarrow w[salary] > s[salary]))\}$

(ii) $\{< p > \mid \exists\, c, s\ (< p, c, s > \in works \wedge \forall\, p_2, c_2, s_2,$
$(<p_2, c_2, s_2 > \notin works \vee c_2 \neq$ "Small Bank Corporation" $\vee\ s > s_2))\}$

(h) Assume the companies may be located in several cities. Find all companies located in every city in which Small Bank Corporation is located.

NOTE: Small Bank Corporation will be included in each answer.

(i) $\{t \mid \forall\, s \in company\ (s[company\_name] =$ "Small Bank Corporation" $\Rightarrow$
$\exists r \in company\ (t[company\_name] = r[company\_name] \wedge r[city] = s[city]))]$

(ii) $\{ < co > \mid \forall\, co_2, ci_2\ (< co_2, ci_2 > \notin company$
$\vee\ co_2 \neq$ "Small Bank Corporation" $\vee < co, ci_2 > \in company)\}$

Q.10. Let $R = (A, B)$, and $S = (A, C)$, and let $r(R)$ and $s(S)$ be relations. Write relational-algebra expressions equivalent to the following domain-relational-calculus expressions.

(a) $\{< a > \mid \exists\, b\, (< a, b > \in r \wedge b = 17)\}$

(b) $\{< a, b, c > \mid < a, b > \in r \wedge < a, c > \in s\}$

(c) $\{< a > \mid \exists\, b\, (< a, b > \in r) \wedge \forall\, c\, (\exists\, d\, (< d, c > \in s) \Rightarrow < a, c > \in s)\}$

(d) $\{< a > \mid \exists\, c\, (< a, c > \in s \wedge \exists\, b_1, b_2\, (< a, b_1 > \in r \wedge < c, b_2 > \in r \wedge > b_1 > b_2))\}$

Ans. (a) $\Pi_A\ (\sigma_{B = 17}\ (r))$

(b) $r \bowtie s$

(c) $\Pi_A\ (r)\ U\ (r \div \sigma_B\ (\Pi_C(s)))$

(d) $\Pi_{r.A}\ ((r \bowtie s) \bowtie_{c\, =\, r2.A\, \wedge r.B\, >\, r2.B(\rho r_2}(r)))$.

Q.11. Let R = (A, B) and S = (A, C), and let $r(R)$ and $s(S)$ be relations. Using the special constant *null*, write tuple-relational-calculus expressions equivalent to each of the following :

(a) $r ⟕ s$

(b) $r ⟗ s$

(c) $r ⟖ s$

Ans. (a) $\{t \mid \exists r \in \exists s \in S(r[A] = s[A] \wedge t[A] = r[A] \wedge t[B] = r[B] \wedge t[C] = s[C]) \vee \exists s \in S(\neg\exists r \in R(r[A] = s[A] \wedge t[A] = s[A] \wedge t[C] = s[C] \wedge t[B] = null)\}$

(b) $\{t \mid \exists r \in R \exists s \in S\ (r[A] = s[A] \wedge t[A] = r[A] \wedge t[B] = r[B] \wedge t[C] = s[C]) \vee \exists r \in r(\neg\exists s \in S(r[A] = s[A] \wedge t[A] = r[A] \wedge t[B] = r[B] \wedge t[C] = null)\} \vee \exists s \in S(\neg\exists r \in R(r[A] = s[A] \wedge t[A] = s[A] \wedge t[C] = s[C] \wedge t[B] = null)\}$

(c) $\{t \mid \exists r \in \exists s \in S(r[A] = s[A] \wedge t[A] = r[A] \wedge t[B] = r[B] \wedge t[C] = s[C]) \vee \exists r \in R(\neg\exists s \in S(r[A] = s[A] \wedge t[A] = r[A] \wedge t[B] = r[B] \wedge t[C] = null)\}$

Q.12. Repeat Exercise 9 using QBE.

Ans. (a) Find the names of all employees who work for First Bank Corporation.

works	person_name	company_name	salary
	P._x	First Bank Co	

(b) Find the names and cities of residence of all employees who work for First Bank Corporation.

employee	person_name	street	city
	P._x		P._y

works	person_name	company_name	salary
	_x	First Bank Corporation	

(c) Find the names, street addresses, and cities of residence of all employees who work for First Bank Corporation and earn more than $10,000 per annum. If people may work for several companies, the following solution will only list those who earn more than $10,000 per annum from "First Bank Corporation" alone.

employee	person_name	street	city
	P._x	P._y	P._z

works	person_name	company_name	salary
	_x	First Bank Corporation	>10000

(*d*) Find all employees who live in the city where the company for which they work is located.

employee	person_name	street	city
	P._x		_y

works	person_name	company_name	salary
	_x	_c	

company	company_name	city
	_c	_y

(*e*) Find all employees who live in the same city and on the same street as their managers.

employee	person_name	street	city
	P._x	_s	_c
	_y	_s	_c

manages	person_name	manager_name
	_x	_y

(*f*) Find all employees in the database who do not work for First Bank Corporation.
The following solution assume that all people work for exactly one company.

works	person_name	company_name	salary
	P._x	First Bank Co.	

If one allows people to appear in the database (*e.g.*, in *employee*) but not appear in *works*, or if people may have jobs with more than one company, the solutions are slightly more complicated. They are given below :

employee	person_name	street	city
	P._x		

works	person_name	company_name	salary
¬	_x	First Bank Corporation	

(*g*) Find all employees who earn more than every employee of Small Bank Corporation.

The following solutions assume that all people work for at most one company.

works	person_name	company_name	salary
	P._x	Small Bank Corporation	_y MAX.All._y

or

works	person_name	company_name	salary
 ¬	P._x	 Small Bank Corporation	_y >_y

(*h*) Assume that the companies may be located in several cities. Find all companies located in every city in which Small Bank Corporation is located.

NOTE : Small Bank Corporation will be included in each answer.

located_in	lompany_name	salary
	Small Bank Corporation P._c Small Bank Corporation	_x _y _y

condition
CNT.ALL._y= CNT.ALL._x=

Q.13. Let R = (A, B, C) and let r1 and r2 both be relations on schema R. Give expressions in QBE, to each of the following queries :

(*a*) $r_1 \cup r_2$

(*b*) $r_1 \cap r_2$

(*c*) $r_1 - r_2$

(*d*) $\Pi_{AB}(r_1) \bowtie \Pi_{BC}(r_2)$ **[GGSIPU, M.Tech (IT); 3rd Sem., Dec. 2005]**

Ans. (*a*) $r_1 \cup r_2$

result	A	B	C
P.	_a	_b	_c
P.	_d	_e	_f

r1	A	B	C
	_a	_b	_c

r2	A	B	C
	_d	_e	_f

(*b*) $r_1 \cap r_2$

r1	A	B	C
	_a	_b	_c

r2	A	B	C
	_d	_e	_f

(c) $r_1 - r_2$

r1	A	B	C
	_a	_b	_c

r2	A	B	C
	_d	_e	_f

(d) $\Pi_{AB}(r_1) \bowtie \Pi_{BC}(r_2)$

result	B	C
P.	_a	_b	_c

r1	A	B	C
	_a	_b	

r2	A	B	C
		_b	_c

Q.14. In a TRC query with *n* tuple variables, what would be the typical minimum number of join conditions? Why? What is the effect of having a smaller number of join conditions?

Ans. Typically, there should be atleast (n – 1) join conditions. Otherwise, a cartesian product with one of the range relations would be taken, which usually does not make sense.

Q.15. Show how you may specify the following relational algebra operations in both tuple and domain relational calculus.

(*a*) SELECT A = *c* (R(A, B, C)):

(*b*) PROJECT <A, B> (R(A, B, C)

(*c*) R(A, B, C) NATURAL JOIN S(C, D, E):

(*d*) R(A, B, C) UNION S(A, B, C)

(*e*) R(A, B, C) INTERSECT S(A, B, C)

(*f*) R(A, B, C) MINUS S(A, B, C)

(*g*) R(A, B, C) CARTESIAN PRODUCT S(D, E, F)

(*h*) R(A, B) DIVIDE S(A):

Ans. For each operation, we give the tuple calculus expression followed by the domain calculus expression.

(*a*) {*t* | R(*t*) AND *t*.A = *c*} {*xyz* | R(*xyz*) AND *x* = *c*}

(*b*) {*t*.A, *t*.B | R(*t*)} {(*xy* | R(xyz)}

(*c*) {*t*.A, *t*.B, *t*.C, *q*.D, *q*.E | R(*t*) AND S(*q*) AND *t*.C = *q*.C},
{*xyzvw* | R(*xyz*) AND (exists *u*) (S(*uvw*) AND *z* = *u*)}

(*d*) {*t* | R (*t*) OR S(*t*)},
{*xyz* | R(*xyz*) OR S(*xyz*)

(*e*) {*t* | R (*t*) AND S(*t*)},
{*xyz* | R(*xyz*) AND S(*xyz*)
(*f*) {*t* | R (*t*) AND NOT S(*t*)},
{*xyz* | R(*xyz*) AND NOT S(*xyz*))}
(*g*) {*t*.A, *t*.B, *t*.C, *q*.D, *q*.E, *q*.F, | R (*t*) AND S(*q*)},
(*xyzuvw* | R(*xyz*) AND S(*uvw*)}
(*h*) {*t*.B | R(*t*) AND (FORALL *s*)
(NOT (S(*s*)) OR (EXISTS *q*)(R(*q*) AND *s*.A = *q*.A AND *q*.B = *t*.B))},
{*y* | R(*xy*) AND (FORALL *z*) (NOT (S(*z*)) OR (EXISTS *u*) (R(*uy*) AND *z* = *u*)}

Q.16. Consider the relation CLASS (Course#, Univ_Section#, InstructorNAME, Semester, Building Code, Room#, Time Period, Weekdays, CreditHours). This represents classes taught in a university with unique Univ_Section#. Give what you think should be various candidate Keys and write in your own words under what constraints each candidate key would be valid.

Ans. Possible candidate keys include the following (**NOTE:** We assume that the values of the Semester attribute include the year; for example "Spring/94" or Fall/93" could be values for Semester):

1. {Semester, Building Code, Room#, Time Period, Weekdays} if the same room cannot be used at the same time by more than one course during a particular semester.
2. {Univ_Section#} if it is unique across all semesters.
3. {Instructor Name, Semester} if an instructor can teach at most one course during each semester.
4. If Univ_Section# is not unique, which is the case in many universities, we have to examine the rules that the university uses for section numbering. For example, if the sections of a particular course during a particular semester are numbered 1,2,3,..., then a candidate key would be {Course#, Univ_Section#, Semester}. If, on the other hand, all sections (of any course) have unique numbers during a particular semester only, then the candidate key would be {Univ_Section#, Semester}.

Q.17. Consider the following schema of a relational data base
employee (emp_no, name, address)
project (*p*_no, *p*_name)
work_no (emp_no, *p*_no)
part (part_no, part_name, qty_on_hand, size)
use (emp_no, *p*_no, part_no, number)
Let us try answer the following queries:

1. **Print the names of the employees who are working on a project named "DBMS"**
2. **Print the names of the employees who are not working in any project.**
3. **List the names of the employees and the projects with which the employees are associated with and for which they have used no part so far.**
4. **List the names of the projects such that every employee working on these projects has used a part "bolts" with size 6.**
5. **List the part numbers and names of the parts used in both the projects "DBMS" and "MIS".**

6. List the names of the employees who are working in both the projects "DBMS" and "MIS".

Ans. 1. π_{name}(employee) ⋈($\sigma_{p\_name\ =\ "DBMS"}$ (project))⋈ work_no)

2. π_{name} (employee) – π_{name} (employee ⋈ work _no)

3. π_{name}, ρ_{-name} ((work_on $\pi_{1.2}$ (*use*)) ⋈ project ⋈ employee)

4. A = $\pi_{emp\_no,\ p\text{-}no}$ ($\sigma_{part\_name\ =\ "bolts"size\ =\ 6}$ (part) ⋈ use)

{(emp_no, proj_no) pairs related to the part "bolts" with size "6"}

B = work_on ⋈ π_{p_no} (A)

{(emp_no, p_no) pairs such that at least one employees who is associated with the project has used the part "bolts" with size "6" for the project)}

C = B – A

{(emp_no, p_no) pairs not related to "bolts"}

D = π_{p_no} (A) – π_{p_no} (C)

{project nos of the projects such that every one working there has used "bolts")

N = π_{p_name} (project ⋈ D)

5. $\pi_{part\_no,\ part\_name}$ (part, ⋈ (π_{part_no}

($\sigma_{p\_name\ =\ "DBMS}$ (project) ⋈ use)

∩ π_{part_no} ($\sigma_{p\_name\ =\ "MIS"}$(project) ⋈ use)))

6. A = π_{p_no} ($\sigma_{p\_name\ =\ "MIS"\ |\ p\_name\ =\ "DBMS"}$ (project)

B = π_{emp_no} (work_on) – π_{e_no} ((π_{emp_no} (work_on) × A) – work_on)

C = π_{name} (employee ⋈ B)

Also answer these queries for this example now.

1. List the names of the employees who are working in both the projects "DBMS" and "MIS".
2. List the names of the employees who are participating in every project and have used every part.

Answer to these queries are given below by using quotient operator :

1. π_{name} (employee ⋈ (work_on ÷ π_{p_no} ($\sigma_{p\_name\ =\ "MIS"\ |\ p\_name\ =\ "DBMS"}$ (project)))
2. π_{name} (employee ⋈ (((work_on) ÷ π_{p_no} (project))

∩($\pi_{emp\_no,\ part\_no}$ (use) ÷ π_{part_no} (part))))

Q.18. Theorem : If E is a relational algebraic expression then, there is a safe expression in tuple relational calculus, which is equivalent to E.

[KUD, B.E.-CSE; 6th Sem., 1995]

Ans. Proof : Assume that no relational algebraic operation symbol appears in E. Hence, E is either

Case I a relation symbol or

Case II a tuple of a relation E.

CASE I : In this case, E is equivalent to the tuple calculus expression {t/R(t)} which is a safe expression.

CASE II : Here, E is equivalent to the safe expression

$$\{t/t = t_1 \vee t = t_2 \vee t = t_3 \vee .\ \ \vee t = t_k\}$$

Induction : Assume that E has within it at least one relational algebraic operation symbol. Also, assume that the theorem is true for expression having a lesser number of relational algebraic operation symbols than what E has.

CASE I : $E = E_1 \cup E_2$, where E_1, E_2 each has a fewer occurrences of relational operation symbols symbols than what E has.

Hence, according to the inductive hypothesis, there are safe expressions $\{t/\psi_1(t)\}$ and $(s/\psi_2(s))\}$ equivalent to E_1 and E_2, respectively. Finally, E is equivalent to the safe expression $\{t/\psi_1(t) \vee \psi_2(t)\}$.

CASE II : $E = E_1 - E_2$.

Likewise as in case I, the safe expression $(t/\psi_1(t) \wedge \neg \psi_2(t)\}$ equivalent to E can be obtained.

CASE III : $E = E_1 \times E_2$.

The following expression in tuple calculus

$\{t^{(r+s)}/\{\exists u^{(r)}\}\{\exists v^{(s)}\}(\psi_1(u) \wedge \psi_2(v) \wedge t[1] = u[1] \wedge \ldots$

$\wedge\ t[r] = u[r] \wedge t[r+1] = v[1] \wedge \ldots \wedge t[r+s] = v[s])\}$

This is a safe expression.

CASE IV : $E = \pi_{i1,\, i2,\, \ldots\, im}(E_1)$

The following tuple calcules expression is equivalent to E

$$\{t^{(m)}/(\exists u)\ (\psi_1(u) \wedge t[1] = u[i_1] \wedge \ldots \wedge t[m] = u[i_m])\},$$

Where $\{s/\psi_1(s)\}$ is a safe expression equivalent to E_1.

The above expression is clearly a safe expression because the set of all t's which is denoted by the expression are composed of the components of those u's which satisfy the quasi-formula specified in the expression. Since ψ_1 is already a safe expression, all the u's that satisfy ψ_1 are indeed in DOM (ψ_1).

CASE V : $E = \sigma_F(E_1)$.

The expression in tuple calculus which is equivalent to E is follows.

$\{t/\psi_1(t) \wedge F\}$, where F' is obtained from F by replacing each operand denoting the ith component of t by $t[i]$; $\{s/\psi_1(s)\}$ is a safe expression equivalent to E_1.

The above expression equivalent to E is clearly a safe expression because ψ_1 is already a safe expression.

Q.19. Explain outer join with examples. [GGSIPU, B.Tech (CSE / IT); 5th Sem., 2012]

Ans. It is an extension of the join operation to deal with missing information. There are three forms of outer join:

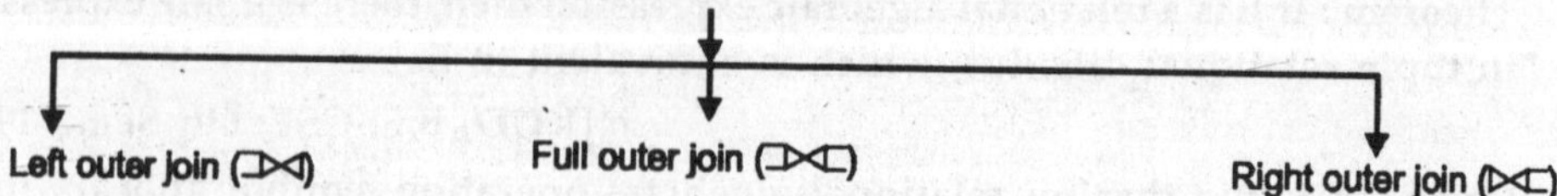

1. **Left outer join (⟕):**

   It takes all tuples in the left relation that did not match with any tuples in the right relation pads these tuples with null values for all other attributes from right relation and adds them to the result of natural join.

2. **Right outer join (⟖):**

   It takes all tuples in the right relation that did not match with any tuples in the left relation., pads these tuples with null values for all other attributes from left relation and adds them to the result of natural join.

3. **Full outer join (⟗) :**

It does both of those operations: padding tuples from left relation did not match with any tuples from the right relation and adding them to result of natural join. Padding tuples from right relation that did not match with any tuples from the left relation and adding them to the result of natural join.

Consider the following two relations :

Employee_Scheme (emp_name, street, city)

Pt works (emp_name, branch_name, salary)

Employee :

Emp_name	Street	City
Rohit	Linking Road	Mumbai
Rahul	Nephancy Road	Nephancy
Sachin	K. Khade Marg	Mumbai
Anil	Paud Road	Pune

Ft Employee

Emp_name	Branch_name	Salary
Sachin	ICICI Mumbai	20,000
Rahul	SBI Nephancy	30,000
Ashish	City Bank Pune	10,000
Rohit	HDFC Mumbai	15,000

1. Result of Employee ⋈ Ft_Employee (Natural Join) is :

Emp_name	Street	City	Branch_name	Salary
Rohit	Linking Road	Mumbai	HDFC Mumbai	15,000
Sachin	K. Khade Marg	Mumbai	ICICI Mumbai	20,000
Rahul	Nephancy Road	Nephancy	SBI Nephancy	30,000

Natural join (⋈) eliminates tuple Ashish of Ft-employee relation and tuple Anil of Employee relation.

2. Result of Employee ⟕ Ft_employee (left outer join) is shown in :

⟕ operation will eliminate tuple Ashish of Ft_employee (right) relation.

Employee ⟕ ft_employee

Emp_name	Street	City	Brnach name	Salary
Rohit	Linking Road	Mumbai	HDFC Mumbai	15,000
Sachin	K. Khade Marg	Mumbai	ICICI Mumbai	20,000
Rahul	Nephancy Road	Nephancy	SBI Nephancy	30,000
Anil	Paud Road	Pune	NULL	NULL

3. Result of employee ⟖ Ft_employee right outer join is given below.

It eliminates Anil tuple of employee relation (left relation).

Employee ⟕ Ft_employee

Emp_name	Street	City	Brnach name	salary
Rohit	Linking Road	Mumbai	HDFC Mumbai	15,000
Sachin	K. Khade Marg	Mumbai	ICICI Mumbai	20,000
Rahul	Nephancy Road	Nephancy	SBI Nephancy	30,000
Ashish	NULL	NULL	City Bank Pune	10,000

The result of employee ⟕ Ft_employee is given below.

Employee ⟗ Ft_employee

Emp_name	Street	City	Brnach name	salary
Rohit	Linking Road	Mumbai	HDC Mumbai	15,000
Sachin	K.Khade Marg	Mumbai	ICICI Mumbai	20,000
Rahul	Nephancy Road	Nephancy	SBI Nephancy	30,000
Anil	Paud Road	Pune	NULL	NULL
Ashish	NULL	NULL	City Bank Pune	10,000

Pt_employee Relation

Emp_name	Branch_name	Salary
Raj	ICICI Pune	1000
Ajay	HDFC Mumbai	2000
Sachin	City Bank Pune	3000
Rahul	ICICI Pune	1500
Ashish	HDFC Mumbai	1000

EXERCISE QUESTIONS

Q.1. Let the following relatational schema be given

EMPLOYEE (SSN, Name, Age, Dno)

SALARY (SSN, Salary)

WORK_ON (Project#, SSN)

PROJECT (Project#, project_name, plocation)

For each of the following queries, give an expression in QUEL and QBE.

(*i*) Display the names of projects at "Delhi'.

(*ii*) Find the salaries of employees by Name.

(*iii*) Retrieve the name and SSN of employees working on project #A100.

[GGSIPU, B.Tech.(CS); 5th Sem., 2nd Internal Test]

Q.2. Consider the following DreamHome rental database and answer the queries in relational algebra expression :

Branch (branch No, street, city, post code)

Staff (Staff No, Name, Position, Sex, DOB, Salary, Branch No)

Property-for-Rent (Property No, Strect, City, Postcode, Type, Rooms, Rent, Owner No, Staff No, Branch No)

Client (Client No, Name, Tel No, Preftype, MaxRent)

Private owner (Owner No, Name, Address, Telno)

Viewing (Client No, Property No, Viewdate, Comment)

Registration (Client No, Branch No, Staff No, Date joined)

(*a*) List all cities where there is a branch office but no properties for rent.

(*b*) Produce a status report on property viewings.

(*c*) Identify all clients who have viewed all properties with three rooms.

(*d*) List all cities where there is either a branch office or a property for rent.

(*e*) List the names and comments of all clients who have viewed a property.

[GGSIPU, B.Tech. (CSE); 5th Sem., Dec 2006]

Q.3. (*a*) What do you mean by integrity constraints?

(b) Discuss the different relationship algebra operator? Explain with suitable examples. How data modifications can be done using relational algebra operations?

[GGSIPU, B.Tech. (CSE); 5th sem., Dec. 2006]

Q.4. (*a*) List two reasons why you may choose to define a view.

(*b*) Explain the terms referential integrity, with examples.

[GGSIPU, B.Tech. (CSE); 5th Sem. Sept. 2007]

Q.5. Define the following terms:

(*i*) Superkey (*ii*) Candidate key

(*iii*) Primary key (*iv*) Foreign key

Now, consider the following two relations from the RDBMS of a University System.

TEACHER (Name, Id, Sex, Address)

DEPARTMENT (D Name, Dnumber)

(you may assume any other attribute in the above relations. It is given that each teacher works in a unique department.

Now using the definitions given by you earlier, identify each of the above four keys in the two relations (wherever they exist) and show that the keys identified by you satisfy your definition. **[GGSIPU, B.Tech (CS); 5th Sem., 2nd term, Exam., 2008]**

Q.6. (*a*) Describe the differences in meaning between the terms relation and relation schema.

(*b*) What is a view? What are its advantages? Explain the syntax for creating views.

(*c*) What are integrity constraints? Explain each of them.

[GGSIPU, B.Tech (CS); 5th Sem., Dec. 2008]

Q.7. Describe the following relational algebraic operations giving one example each-

(*i*) Natural join

(*ii*) Semi join

(*iii*) Division operation. **[IGNOU, MCA; 3rd year, June 2004]**

Q.8. Consider the following table structrue :

S_PERSON (S_NO, S_NAME, COMMISION)

PRODUCT (P_ID, DESCRIPTION)

SALE (DATE, CUSTOMERS_NO, S_NO, P_ID, QTY)

CUSTOMER (CUSTOMER_NO, C_NAME, C_ADDRESS)

Basea on table, write queries in relational algebra meet the following needs:

(*i*) Get names of the salesman who sold product 48.

(*ii*) Get the names of those customers who bought table lamps (in addition to other products). **[Delhi University, Internal Test, 3rd year; 2009]**

Q.9. Discuss the candidate key, primary key, superkey, composite key, and alternate key.

[UPTU, B. Tech. (CSE) 4th Sem, 2006–07]

Q.10. Given the relational schema :

ENROLL (S#, C#, Section)

TEACH (Prof, C#, Section)

ADVISE (Prof, S#)

PRE_REQ (C#, Pre_C#)

GRADE (S#, C#, grade, year)

STUDENT (S#, Sname)

Give queries expressed in tuple calculus :

(*i*) List of students taking courses with Smith or Jones.

(*ii*) List all students taking atleast one course that their advisor teaches.

(*iii*) List those professors who teach more than one section of the same course.

(*iv*) List all students number and course number.

(*v*) List the student number and course number who got grade A.

[UPTU, B.Tech. (CSE) 4th Sem., 2006–07]

Q.11. (*a*) Specify the following queries in relational algebra–

Supplier (<u>sid</u>, sname, address)

Part (<u>sid</u>, pname, color)

Catatog (<u>sid</u>, pid, cost)

(*i*) Find names of suppliers who supply some red or green part.

(*ii*) Find the sids of suppliers who supply every part.

(*iii*) Find the sids of suppliers who supply red and green parts.

(*b*) List the operations of relational algebra and the purpose of each.

[UPTU, MBA; 4th Sem., 2006–07]

Q.12. If R and S are two relations, how is the quotient operation R ÷ S defined? Develop a relational algebra expression for R ÷ S using basic relational algebraic operators.

[KUD, B.E. (CSE); 6th Sem., 1995]

Q.13. Explain the concept of Relational algebra and discuss various operations that serve to define relational algebra. **[KUD, BE(CSE); 6th Sem., 1996]**

Q.14. (*a*) What are unions? When two tables are said to be union compatible. How are the results ordered in a union compatible.

(*b*) State and explain integrity and referential integrity.

[GGSIPU, BCA—3rd, Sem., Dec. 2002]

Q.15. Give relational schema for SUPPLIER-PART database where different suppliers supplying various parts at different rates and each part is supplied by a number of suppliers. Assuming that the following are meaningful, state the semantic and integrity constraints; additional assumptions may be made for the job at hand :

(*i*) Retrieve names of cities from which part P2 may be supplied.

(*ii*) Retrieve supplier numbers of suppliers who are capable of supplying all parts.

[GGSIPU, MCA-2nd Sem., May 2003]

Q.16. Within the context of manipulating database, differentiate among host language data sub language and query language. **[GGSIPU, MCA 2nd; Sem., May 2004]**

Q.17. Consider the following relations and write the queries in Relational Algebra and Tuple Relational Calculus :

Supplier (sno, sname, status, city)

Parts (pno, pname, color, weight, city)

Project (Jno , jname, city)

SPJ (sno, pno, Jno , qty)

(*a*) Get Sname values for suppliers who supply project *j*1.

(*b*) Get Sno values for suppliers who supply project *j*1 with part *p*1.

(*c*) Get jname values for projects supplied by supplier *s*1.

(*d*) Get color values for parts supplied by supplier ABC.

(*e*) Get jnames for those project which are supplied by supplier XYZ.

[GGSIPU, M.Tech (IT) - 3rd Sem., Dec. 2005]

Q.18. List the reasons why the null values might be introduced into the database.

[GGSIPU, M.Tech. (IT); 3rd Sem., Dec. 2005]

Q.19. Consider the following relations –

Employee (emp_name, street, city)

Works (emp_name, company_name, salary)

Company (company_name, city)

Manages (emp_name, manager_name)

Write the following queries in relational algebra :

(*a*) Find the names of all employees who live in the same city as the company for which they work for.

(*b*) Find the names of all employees who live in the same city as do their managers.

(*c*) Find the names and cities of residence for all employees who work for company "XYZ".

(*d*) Find the name of the city where employee "X" works.

[GGSIPU, M.Tech (IT); 3rd, Sem., Dec. 2004]

Q.20. (*a*) Explain the differences between a primary key, candidate key and super key.

(*b*) What are the restrictions that are put on update operations using a view?

[GGSIPU, M. Tech. (IT); 3rd Sem., Dec. 2005]

Q.21. Identify two entities that might be important for a theater. List atleast three attributes for each entity. Then show what the entities and attributes would look like in an ER diagram.

[GGSIPU, MCA 3rd sem., Dec. 2010]

Q.22. Consider the following relationes for a database of business trip of sales persons in a sales office :-

Sales-person (ssn, name, start-year, dept_no)

Trip (ssn, from_city, to_city, deparature-date, return_date, trip_id)

Expense (Trip_id, account_no, amount)

Specify the following queries in relational algebra :-

(i) Find the most expensive and least expensive trips.

(*ii*) Find the average expenditure of trips involving amount more than 2000.

(*iii*) Find the department of person spending maximum amount on a trip.

(*iv*) Find the person going maximum number of times on trips.

(*v*) Find the person with maximum number of trips in the last 5 years.

[GGSIPU, B.Tech. (CSE/IT) 5th Sem., Dec. 2010]

Q.23. (*a*) What are integrity constraints ? Explain.

(*b*) Consider the following relational algebra expressions on relations R(*a*, *b*, *c*) and S(d, e, f).

(*i*) $\pi_{a, e}(R \bowtie S)$ (*ii*) $\sigma_{b=20 \text{ and } f=5}(R \bowtie S)$

(*iii*) $\pi_{c, a\ (\sigma b\ =\ 20 \text{ and } c\ =\ 5}(R))$

Wirte down the equivalent SQL statements.

[GGSIPU, B.Tech. (CSE/IT) 5th Sem., Dec. 2011]

CHAPTER

3

SQL

3.0 INTRODUCTION

Structured Query Language (SQL) is both data definition language and data manipulation language of a number of relational database systems such as DB2 of IBM, ORACLE of Oracle Corporation, INGRESS of Relational Technologies and so on. ORACLE was the first commercial RDBMS developed in 1979, that supported SQL.

Today, we have many software packages like SQL generators, CASE tools like Designer-2000, IEF (Information Engineering Facility) can be used to generate the entire application alongwith SQL. **Please note that SQL is the main interface for communicating between the users and RDBMS.**

Table 3.1. Difference between Filter and Query

Filter	Query
1. Filter is saved with a table.	1. Query is a separate database object which appears in the navigation pane.
2. To view the result of a filter, we must open the table first.	2. There is no need to open a table first to view the result because a query is an independent object.
3. We can apply on a single table.	3. We can create a query using multiple tables.
4. We cannot perform operations (insert, update, delete) on data using a filter.	4. We can perform operations (insert, update, delete) on fields using a query.

3.1 FEATURES OF SQL

1. SQL is a **high level language**.
2. SQL is a **free-format syntax** which gives users the ability to structure SQL statements on any part of the screen.
3. SQL is very **flexible**.
4. SQL can be **embedded** also in Front end application code like of V.B. 6.0, JAVA 2, VC++ 6.0 and so on.
5. SQL based applications are **portable** *i.e.,* they can be run on any system.

Basic Data Types

The SQL supports a variety of data types as shown in the Table 3.2.

Table 3.2

Datatype	Description	Size
Number (p, s)	It is used to store numeric data types. p stands for precision (total number of decimal digits) and s stands for scale (total number of digits after decimal point).	Range of p is from 1 to 38. And s is from –84 to 127.
Date	It is used to store date and time values	Range of date is from Jan 1, 47 B.C. to Dec. 31, 9999 A.D.
Char(size)	It is used to store fixed size character data	Range of char is 1 (By default) to 2000 bytes.
Varchar2(size)	It is used to store variable size character data.	Range of varchar2 is 1 (By default) to 4000 bytes.
Long	It is used to store variable size character data.	Range of long is upto 2 GB.
Clob	It is used to store variable size character data.	Range of clob is upto 4 GB.
Raw(size)	It is used to store fixed binary data.	Maximum size is upto 2000 bytes.
Long raw	It is used to store variable binary data.	Maximum size is upto 2 GB.

3.2 DATA DEFINITION LANGUAGE (DDL)

DDL is used to create and remove database objects. **For example**, Create, Alter, Drop. We have already discussed DDL in chapter 1. Let us now study these DDL commands of SQL.

Creating a table using SQL

In order to create a table, the DDL, CREATE command is used and the columns of the table along with the datatypes and the width are to be specified. **Please note that when a table is created, Oracle puts the table definition into the data dictionary**. We follow **certain rules for table and column names**. These rules are given below :

1. Names can be upto 30 characters.
2. Names must begin with an alphabet.
3. Names are not case sensitive.
4. Names can contain characters like *a-z*, 0-9, _ (underscore), – (hyphens), $ and #.
5. Database names can be upto 8 characters.
6. Names cannot be reserved words.

Also note that the above rules can be bypassed by using double quotes.

Syntax :

```
CREATE TABLE <table_name>
(
    Field_name 1 Field_type (width),
    Field_name 2 Field_type (width),
                :
    Field_name_N Field_type (width)
```

Example. Let us create a table to store student's data-Roll number, name and date of birth. So, we write now-

```
SQL > CREATE TABLE student
      (roll_no number (5),
      name char (30),
      birth_date date);
```

Please note here that for the date type of data, width must not be specified. SQL responds by displaying the message 'Table Created".

How to add data to tuples (or rows) of this table?

The **syntax** used here is

INSERT INTO <table_name>
VALUES (V_1, V_2, V_3,......);

For example,

INSERT INTO STUDENT
VALUES (1, 'GGSIPU', '20-FEB-09');

Also note that we can add certain constraints also, as the fields are named. **These constraints are the rules to control the data in a column.**

There are three common constraints :

- Primary Key
- Not Null
- Check constraint.

Primary key is a constraint for the column of a table. **This constraint ensures that the column cannot be null and that the values in the column will be unique.**

Not Null constraint ensures that the user always type the data for that column.

Check Constraint ensures that when data is entered, the data in the column is limited to specific values like *a*, *b* or *c*.

Let us apply these constraints to our table but we will see it's syntax first.

Syntax :

```
CREATE TABLE <table_name>
(
    Field_name 1 Field_type (width) PRIMARY KEY,
    Field_name 2 Field_type (width) NOT NULL,
                :
    Field_name N Field_type (width), CHECK
    field_name in (a', 'b', 'c',))
);
```

We are in a position to solve a problem now.

Example 1. *Create a table_customer with the following fields:*

Cust_no	*NUMBER (4)*	*Primary key.*
Lname	*VARCHAR2(10)*	
Fname	*VARCHAR2(15)*	*Not null.*
Addr	*VARCHAR2(20)*	
City	*VARCHAR2(5)*	
Sate	*VARCHAR2(10)*	
Pin	*VARCHAR2(5)*	
Birth_date	*DATE*	
Status	*VARCHAR2(1)*	*Check status in 'V' or 'I'*

Also write another SQL query to insert a record into your customer table. How will you view the structure of the table?

Solution. A SQL query to create the customer table is as follows :

```
CREATE TABLE CUSTOMER
    CUST_NO       NUMBER (4)        PRIMARY KEY,
    LNAME         VARCHAR2 (10),
    FNAME         VARCHAR2 (15)     NOT NULL,
    ADDR          VARCHAR2 (20),
    CITY          VARCHAR2 (5)
    STATE         VARCHAR2 (10),
    PIN           VARCHAR 2(5),
    BIRTH_DATE    DATE,
```

```
    STATUS        VARCHAR2 (1),     CHECK (STATUS IN ('V', 'I'))
);
```

Now, we write an SQL query to add data *i.e.*, rows (or tuples) into this table_

```
INSERT INTO CUSTOMER
VALUES (98,'CHOPRA' 'RAJIV', 'OUTRAM LINES', 'CAMP', 'DELHI',
    '110009', '06-MAY-74', 'V');
```

Please remember the following points now.

1. The values are specified in the **same order** as was used during table creation.
2. The **character values** are typed within single quotes.
3. The **Data values** are typed within single quotes.
4. The numeric values are typed as it is.

To view the structure of this table we have another command in SQL, as follows :

```
DESCRIBE CUSTOMER;
OR
DESC CUSTOMER;
```

Other DDL Commands : We have seen how, DDL's create works. Now, let us discuss other two DDL commands—ALTER and DROP.

ALTER command (DDL) of SQL : The DDL, ALTER command can be used to make the following changes to any table

1. To add new columns.
2. To add new integrity constraints.
3. To modify existing columns, *i.e.,*
   - to expand length.
   - to change default.
   - to decrease length but all values in the column must be NULL.
   - to change data type but all values in the column must be NULL.
4. To drop integrity constraints.

Please note that you cannot drop or rename columns. We need to rebuilt the table for this. Also note that you must have one of the following privileges to alter a table

(*a*) Ownership of the table.
(*b*) ALTER privilege on the table.
(*c*) ALTER any table, even outside your schema.

Let us see the syntax of ALTER command of SQL now.

Syntax 1 : To add a column :

```
ALTER TABLE <TABLE NAME>
ADD (COLUMN 1 TYPE WIDTH);
```

Syntax 2 : To modify a column :

```
ALTER TABLE <TABLE NAME>
MODIFY (COLUMN 1 TYPE WIDTH);
```

Also, we can specify constraints here. The constraints given for a table can be given names. These names can be given during table creation or can be given after creation of the table by using this ALTER command.

We are in a position to solve a problem now.

Example 1. Create a table–SUPPLIER with the following structure :

id	**number**	**3**
name	**varchar2**	**20**
S_code	**number**	**4**

deposit number 6.

Now, write the following SQL queries :

1. **Add new columns pincode and city to table–supplier.**
2. **Change the width of pincode to 5.**
3. **Add a primary key (after table creation).**
4. **Remove a primary key.**
5. **Add a NOT NULL constraint.**
6. **Drop a NOT NULL constraint.**
7. **Add constraint–check to the deposit column.**
8. **To drop this check constraint.**
9. **To add a primary key constraint.**
10. **Drop the primary key constraint.**

Solution. We create the table –SUPPLIER as explained earlier. We now write the SQL queries one by one :

1. ALTER TABLE SUPPLIER
   ADD (PINCODE VARCHAR2 (3));
   CITY VARCHAR2 (5));
2. ALTER TABLE SUPPLIER
   MODIFY (PINCODE VARCHAR2 (5));
3. ALTER TABLE SUPPLIER
   ADD PRIMARY KEY(ID);
4. ALTER TABLE SUPPLIER
   DROP PRIMARY KEY;
5. ALTER TABLE SUPPLIER
   MODIFY NAME NOT NULL;
6. ALTER TABLE SUPPLIER
   MODIFY NAME NULL;
7. ALTER TABLE SUPPLIER
   ADD CONSTRAINT CKDEP
   CHECK (deposit between 40000 and 50000);
8. ALTER TABLE SUPPLIER
   DROP CONSTRAINT ckdep;

   NOTE : ckdep is the name of the constraint.

9. ALTER TABLE SUPPLIER
   ADD CONSTRAINT PID PRIMARY KEY(ID);
10. ALTER TABLE SUPPLIER
    DROP CONSTRAINT PID;

    NOTE : PID is the name of the constraint.

DROP Command DDL : We have already seen above, how DROP is used to remove constraints. It can be used to delete tables from the schema. It's syntax is –

Drop table <table-name>;

Example. DROP TABLE SUPPLIER:

Please note that you cannot drop or rename columns. The table must be rebuilt for this.

3.3 DATA MANIPULATION LANGUAGE (DML)

As discussed earlier also, DML is used to manipulate data in the database. Some commands are—INSERT, DELETE UPDATE and SELECT. Let us discuss them now.

We have already discussed how to INSERT records (data) into a table. Let us now see, **how to add records through keyboard *i.e.,* interactively?**

Consider the database of Example 1 again. To add data to the fields **interactively** we write an SQL as follows :

```
INSERT INTO CUSTOMER VALUES
(& CUST_NO, '&LNAME', '&FNAME', '& ADDR', '& CITY', '&STATE',
   '&PIN', '&BIRTH_DATE', '& STATUS');
```

Please note here that the names need not match the column names but the type and order is important.

Also note that it is possible to add only specific data into specific fields. The syntax is as follows:

Syntax :

```
INSERT INTO  <table-name> (columns to insert)
VALUES (values to insert);
```

Example.

```
INSERT INTO CUSTOMER
(CUST_NO, LNAME, FNAME, STATUS)
VALUES (99, 'Sharma', Ashish', 'I');
```

How can we view these rows in a table?

We use another DML statement *i.e.,* SELECT here. It's syntax is

```
SELECT    <column_name>
FROM      <table_name>;
        or
SELECT    <column_name>
FROM      <table_name>
WHERE     <condition>;
```

For example, to list all fields from the table of Example 1, CUSTOMER, we can write –

```
SELECT * FROM CUSTOMER;
```

This command will display all data from the table.

However, if we want to select all records from the customer table where state = 'Delhi' then I will write –

```
SELECT *
FROM CUSTOMER
WHERE STATE = 'DELHI';
```

Now, to list the firstname and lastname from the customer table, I can write –

```
SELECT FNAME, LNAME
FROM CUSTOMER;
```

Note here that two columns (fields) are selected for display. **This is called as SQL Projection**.

However, when a condition has been specified, only rows that meet the condition are displayed. **This is called as SQL selection.**

We can also do concatenation. **Concatenation is the process of joining of multiple strings.** We use ¦¦ (vertical bar typed twice) as a concatenation operator.

For example,

```
SELECT FNAME ¦¦' '¦¦ LNAME ¦¦ " ¦¦ STATE
FROM CUSTOMER;
```

Please note that we have inserted 1-blank between the first name and last names of the customers.

If our query is—To select records where the pincode has not been entered, we may write—

```
SELECT *
FROM CUSTOMER
WHERE PIN IS NULL;
```

If, however, we have multiple records for Delhi, Karnataka, UP etc. Then the following command will display a **single record** for each of these states –

```
SELECT DISTINCT STATE
FROM CUSTOMER;
```

Now if the query is to select rows of valid customers from Delhi, we will write

```
SELECT *
FROM CUSTOMER
WHERE STATE = "DELHI' AND STATUS = 'V';
```

But if we want to select rows of customers from Delhi or karnataka, then we write

```
SELECT  *
FROM CUSTOMER
WHERE STATE = "DELHI' OR
        STATE = 'KARNATAKA';
```

How to sort these records?

To sort the data (*i.e.,* arrange the data) on any key field, we use another clause *i.e,* **ORDER BY clause. Here, by default the data is sorted in the ascending order of the key field.**

For example, to sort the customer data, in sorted order of state, we write.

```
SELECT LNAME, FNAME, PIN, STATE
FROM CUSTOMER
ORDER BY STATE;
```

So, here records are sorted (by default) in ascending order. However, to display these records in descending order, we write –

```
SELECT FNAME, LNAME, PIN, STATE
FROM CUSTOMER
ORDER BY STATE DESC;
```

But if the query is—To sort the customer data, statewise and within state by the last name, then we may write –

```
SELECT LNAME, FNAME, PIN, STATE
FROM CUSTOMER
ORDER BY STATE, LNAME;
```

Can we use operators in our SQL?

Yes, we can use = , >, > = <, < = and <> (not equal to). We can even use AND, OR, NOT for complex conditions.

Say, the query is to retrieve records of Delhi customers who are VALID, then we can write –

```
SELECT    * FROM CUSTOMER
WHERE     UPPER(STATE) = 'DELHI' AND
          UPPER (STATUS) = 'V';
```

Please note here that AND ensures that rows satisfying both the conditions are selected. But if the query is to display the records of karnataka or Delhi customers, then I write

```
SELECT    * FROM CUSTOMER
WHERE     UPPER(STATE) = 'KARNATAKA' OR
          UPPER (STATE) = 'DELHI';
```

Also note here that OR ensures that rows satisfying any one of the conditions is retrieved. Please note that the UPPER function will convert the data in the STATE and STATUS columns to uppercase. Similarly, LOWER function will convert the data in the STATE column to lowercase.

Now consider another query-Retrieve all rows from the table except customer number = 98. We can write now –

```
SELECT * FROM CUSTOMER
WHERE NOT CUST_NO = 98;
```

LIKE Operators : We use LIKE 'pattern' where the pattern can contain wildcard characters like

1. % (percentage)
2. – (underscore).

Here, % is used to denote any number of unknown characters and_denotes one unknown character. If we want to denote more than one unknown character using _, then the number of_must be equal to the number of unknown characters.

For example, If we want to retrieve rows where the state name begins with 'D', followed by any other character then I can write –

```
SELECT    FNAME, LNAME,STATE
FROM      CUSTOMER
WHERE     STATE LIKE 'D%';
```

Query 2. *To retrieve all rows where the first name contains the word 'RAJ' embedded in it.*

Solution.

```
SELECT    FNAME
FROM      CUSTOMER
WHERE     FNAME LIKE '%RAJ%';
```

Query 3. *To retrieve rows where ADDR field contains the word—UDUPI or UDIPI in which the 3rd character may be anything.*

This is done using **underscore**. That is,

```
SELECT    FNAME, LNAME, STATE
FROM      CUSTOMER
WHERE     ADDR LIKE 'UD_PI' ;
```

Now, if we want to retrieve all rows which fall within a range then we use another SQL operator *i.e.,* BETWEEN operator.

For example, Retrieve all rows where cust_no is between 98 and 100, both numbers included, we write as follows :

```
SELECT    *
FROM      CUSTOMER
WHERE     CUST_NO BETWEEN 98 AND 100;
```

Alternate Method : We can write the above query in another way –

```
SELECT * FROM CUSTOMER
WHERE CUST_NO > = 98 AND CUST_NO < = 100;
```

This BETWEEN operator is used on dates also. Like, to retrieve customer data if there birth dates are between '10-JAN-2009' and '10-FEB-2009', we can write-

```
SELECT *
  FROM CUSTOMER
  WHERE BIRTH_DATE BETWEEN '10-JAN-2009'
    AND '10-FEB-2009';
```

IN Operator : It is used to specify a list of possible values for a column.

For example, to retrieve rows where the city column has data which is equal to DEL or KAR or BNG, one can write –

```
SELECT * FROM CUSTOMER
WHERE CITY IN ('DEL', 'KAR', BNG');
```

Alternate Method : The above query can also be coded as follows –

```
SELECT * FROM CUSTOMER
WHERE CITY = 'DEL' OR CITY = 'BNG'
      OR CITY = 'KAR';
```

Special DMLs : Say, if we want to rename our old table name to a new table name then one can write –

Syntax :

```
RENAME < OLD TABLE NAME> TO <NEW TABLE NAME >;
```

For example, we can rename our customer table to cust, as follows –

```
RENAME CUSTOMER TO CUST;
```

Also, say if we want to list all tablenames that we have created in all, then I write–

```
SELECT * FROM tab;
```

How to implement primary key and foreign key concept in SQL now?

Firstly, we create a base/Master table → STD_ADD as follows :

```
Create table STD_ADD
   (Roll_no    number (4) Primary key,
    Name       varchar 2 (10),
    Addr       varchar 2 (10),
    place      varchar 2 (5),
    pin        varchar 2 (5));
```

Secondly, we create a child/transaction table → STD_MARKS as follows :

```
Create table STD_MARKS
   ( Roll_no number (4) References STD_ADD,
    Subject varchar 2 (8),
    Exam–date date,
    Marks number (3));
```

Here, Roll_no is the PK of STD_ADD table and Roll_no is the FK of STD_MARKS table.

If say, we delete rows from the Master then at the sametime it will delete the dependent rows in all the child tables, this can be implemented in SQL using ON DELETE CASCADE as follows :

```
Create table STD_MARKS
    (Roll_no number (4) References STD_ADD ON DELETE CASCADE,
    Subject varchar 2 (8),
    Exam_date date,
    Marks number (3));
```

JOIN Operation (s) in SQL : When we want to retrieve data from two or more tables, a join operation is used. It involves that the two (or more) tables must be joined with a where clause in which the **common key field** must be specified.

When matching records are only displayed from both the tables, it is called as an **Equi Join**.

For example, Consider the following MASTER and TRANSACTION tables respectively–

MASTER TABLE : PLAYER

ROLL NO #	NAME
10	AJAY
20	VIJAY
30	SANJAY
40	SANJEEV

PK : ROLLNO#

TRANSACTION Table : MATCH

MATCH NO	ROLLNO	MATCH_DATE	OPPONENT
1	20	10-JAN-2009	RAJIV
2	30	10-FEB-2009	RAHUL
3	20	12-FEB-2009	RAJAT
4	30	10-JAN-2009	MAYUR

FK:ROLLNO#

Now, to retrieve data from both the tables, a join operation is required *i.e.,*

```
SELECT PLAYER. ROLLNO, NAME, MATCH_DATE,
    OPPONENT
FROM PLAYER, MATCH
WHERE PLAYER. ROLLNO = MATCH. ROLLNO;
```

This will display these results

ROLL NO	NAME	MATCH_DATE	OPPONENT
20	VIJAY	10-JAN-2009	RAJIV
20	VIJAY	12-FEB-2009	RAJAT
30	SANJAY	10-FEB-2009	RAHUL
30	SANJAY	15-FEB-2009	MAYUR

This is called as INNER JOIN. Please note that since ROLLNO field is same in both the tables, so we need to specify the name of the table also like PLAYER.ROLL NO means the ROLL NO column of the PLAYER relation. Also note that the dot-operator is being used.

Please understand this that as seen in above inner-join, if the matching records are not present in the second file, then certain names from the first file are not listed at all, like roll numbers 10 and 40 are not displayed at all. Now, to retrieve these records also, we have to perform an OUTER-JOIN operation using the outer-join operator (+). And the data which is not available in the second table, will be presented as NULL values. So, an

OUTER-JOIN query is as follows :

```
SELECT PLAYER.ROLLNO,NAME, MATCH_DATE,
       OPPONENT
  FROM PLAYER, MATCH
WHERE PLAYER. ROLLNO = MATCH. ROLLNO (+);
```

Please note here that the MATCH table is deficient, so '+' is used with match table.

So, the above query will give the output as shown below.

ROLL NO	NAME	MATCH_DATE	OPPONENT
10	AJAY		
20	VIJAY	10-JAN-2009	RAJIV
20	VIJAY	12-FEB-2009	RAJAT
30	SANJAY	10-FEB-2009	RAHUL
30	SANJAY	15-FEB-2009	MAYUR
40	SANJEEV		

We can make our first query of INNER-JOIN also quite simple–

```
SELECT P. ROLL NO, NAME, MATCH_DATE, OPPONENT
  FROM PLAYER P, MATCH M
WHERE P. ROLL NO = M. ROLLNO;
```

Here, P is an **alias** (another name) for the PLAYER table.

M is an **alias** for the MATCH table.

TIP : Oracle allows an unlimited number of tables to be joined in a single query using this JOIN operation.

If we want to clear our screen then we can write –

```
SQL > CLEAR SCREEN
```

Also, we can give aliases (another name) to our columns of a table.

For example, the following query will display two columns from the table Employee with the two headings–NUMBER and NAME as follows –

```
SELECT EMP_NO "NUMBER", EMP_NAME "NAME"
  FROM EMPLOYEE;
```

We can even do computations in our SQL –

```
SELECT EMP_NO "NUMBER", BASIC "BASIC SALARY",
       BASIC + COMMISSION–DEDUCTION
       "NET SALARY" FROM SALARY;
```

We can also format our columns.

For example, to display basic salary as follows : 9,99,999.99 *i.e.*, with commas as shown and two decimal places, we can write –

```
COLUMN BASIC FORMAT 9,99,999.99;
SELECT EMP_NO, BASIC FROM EMP;
```

Similarly, if we want to display name upto 10 characters only and to truncate it, if is more than 10 characters, then I can write –

```
COLUMN FNAME FORMAT A10 TRUNC;
```

NOTE : CLEAR COLUMN command is used to release formatting.

Delete Command (DML) of SQL : To delete rows from a table, we use the delete command as follows :

Syntax 1 : DELETE FROM <table_name> ;

Syntax 2 : DELETE FROM <table_name> WHERE < condition > ;

For example 1, DELETE FROM STD_ADDR ; This command will delete all rows from the STD_ADDR table.

Example 2, DELETE FROM CUSTOMER
WHERE PIN = '1001'

It will delete only those rows which contain '1001' in the PIN column.

Update Command (DML) of SQL : To update rows in the table, we use update command as follows :

Syntax 1 :
```
UPDATE <table name>
      SET <field name> = value;
```

Syntax 2 :
```
UPDATE <table name>
      SET <field name> = value
 WHERE <field name> = value;
```

For example 1,
```
UPDATE CUSTO
      SET PIN = '110001';
```

This command will update the PIN column (all pincodes) to 110001.

Example 2,
```
UPDATE CUSTO
      SET PIN = '110001'
 WHERE CUST_NO = 100;
```

This command will update the PIN column for the row where CUST_NO is 100.

NOTE : Multiple columns can also be used above in SET statement but seperate them with commas.

Please note that if the WHERE clause is not given, then all rows in the table will be updated.

3.4 VIEWS

As already explained, views are the logical tables of data extracted from existing tables. It can be queried just like a table but does not require any disk space.

Uses of Views :

1. It can be used to hide sensitive columns. To do this the owner of the view must grant the SELECT privilege on the view and revoke the privileges on the underlying tables.
2. It can be used to hide complex queries involving multiple tables. Users need not be concerned with the syntax of complex queries.
3. Views that are created with a check option, prevents the updating of other rows and columns.

Let us now see how to create a view?

The **syntax** is as follows :

CREATE or REPLACE VIEW < view_name> AS < query >;

For example,

```
CREATE VIEW EVIEW AS
SELECT emp_no, e_name, d_name
FROM emp, dept
WHERE emp.dept_no = dept.dept_no;
```

Please understand that depending upon the requirements of different users, different views are created based upon one or more than one base tables. Also note that we can manipulate the contents of the base (or original) table through these views. Once a view is created it can be treated just like any other table. **Views can also be joined to other views or table.**

How to display the view ?

Syntax : SELECT * FROM < view_name > ;

Example. SELECT * FROM EVIEW;

How to view the columns in a view?

Syntax : DESC < view_name > ;

Example. DESC EVIEW;

How to delete a view?

Syntax : DROP VIEW < view_name >;

Example. DROP VIEW EVIEW;

Please note that the ORDER BY clause cannot be used in this Create View Statement. Also note that a view cannot be updated if it contains –

(*a*) Joins,

(*b*) Set operators (like Union, Intersect, Minus etc),

(*c*) GROUP function,

(*d*) GROUP BY clause,

(*e*) DISTINCT

What is the check option?

The CHECK OPTION will validate the data during an INSERT or UPDATE into a view.

For example,

```
CREATE OR REPLACE VIEW EVIEW AS
SELECT * FROM CUSTOMER
WHERE CITY = 'DEL' WITH CHECK OPTION,
```

Here, the CHECK option will validate data during input or update based on the constraint *i.e.,* CITY = 'DEL'. When a row is inserted into view EVIEW, CITY has to be 'DEL'. Similarly, when a row is updated, the value in column CITY has to be 'DEL'.

INSERT on a VIEW is allowed. If the view does not contain all the columns in the base table, then the missing columns can be specified as NULL,unless it is a primary key. **For example**, the following command will list the text of the views created by the user –

```
SQL > SELECT * FROM USER_VIEWS;
```

Here,USER_VIEWS is a data dictionary table.

Views, consumes very little storage space. However, because its contents must be calculated again and again, so they are very costly.

Please note that views are dynamic which means that changes made to the base relation that affect the view are immediately reflected in the view. Also note that when users make permitted changes to the view, these changes are made to the underlying relations.

3.5 FUNCTIONS IN SQL

Oracle supports a number of functions. These functions fall into five different categories :

(*a*) Number function (*b*) Aggregate function

(*c*) Character function (*d*) Conversion function

(*e*) Date functions.

Let us discuss these functions one by one.

Number Function

1. **Absolute function :** It returns the absolute value of data *i.e.,* a positive value.
   Syntax : ABS (data)
   Example. SQL>SELECT ABS (–200) FROM DUAL; It returns 200 as output.

NOTE : Oracle provides a special table named DUAL, which can be used to test any function.

2. **CEIL function :** It returns the smallest integer greater than or equal to data.
   Syntax : CEIL (data)
   Example. SQL > SELECT (74.55) FROM DUAL ;
   = 75
3. **FLOOR function :** It returns the largest integer less than or equal to data.
   Syntax : FLOOR (data)
   Example. SQL > SELECT FLOOR (74.5) FROM DUAL;
   = 74
4. **MOD function :** It returns the modulus or remainder.
   Syntax : MOD (data, *y*)
   Example. SQL > SELECT MOD (11,2) FROM DUAL;
   = 1
5. **POWER function :** It returns the data raised to the power of y as given below.
   Syntax : POWER (data, Y)
   Example. SQL > SELECT POWER (3,2) FROM DUAL;
   = 9
6. **ROUND function :** It rounds up the data to the specified number of decimal places.
   Syntax : ROUND (data, *n*)
   Example . SQL > SELECT ROUND (123.5,0) FROM DUAL;
   = 124
   SQL > SELECT ROUND (123.55,1) FROM DUAL;
   = 123.6
7. **SQRT function :** It returns the square root of data.
   Syntax : SQRT (data)
   Example. SQL > SELECT SQRT (81) FROM DUAL;
   = 9
8. **TRUNC function :** It truncates the data to the specified number of decimal places.
   Syntax : TRUNC (data, *n*)
   Example. SQL > SELECT TRUNC (123.55,1) FROM DUAL;
   = 123.5

Similarly, we have some more mathematical functions like :

1. COS (x)—Returns the cosine value of x.
2. COSH (x)—Returns the hyperbolic cosine of x.
3. SIN(x)—Returns the sine of x.
4. SINH (x)—Returns the hyperbolic sine of x.
5. TAN (x)— Returns the tangent of x.
6. TANH(x)—Returns the hyperbolic tangent of x.
7. LN (data)—Returns the natural logarithm of data.
8. LOG (b, data)—Returns the base 'b' logarithm of data.

Aggregate Functions

They are also known as *group functions*. These functions are as follows :

1. **AVG function :** It can be used on numeric data or character data that contains only numerics.

   For example,
   ```
   SELECT AVG (BASIC)
     FROM SALARY;
   ```
2. **COUNT function :** It returns the number of rows in the result. It doesn't count the null values.

   For example,
   ```
   SELECT COUNT (BASIC)
     FROM SALARY;
   ```
3. **MAX function :** It is used to find the maximum value of x. It can be used on any type of data.

   For example,
   ```
   SELECT MAX (BASIC)
     FROM SALARY;
   ```
4. **MIN function :** It is used to find the minimum value of x.

   For example,
   ```
   SELECT MIN (BASIC), MIN (COMMISSION)
     FROM SALARY;
   ```
5. **SUM function :** It sums the values and can be used on numeric data also.

   For example,
   ```
   SELECT SUM (BASIC)
     FROM SALARY;
   ```
6. **STDDEV function :** It is used to find the standard deviation of the value specified as argument.

   For example,
   ```
   SELECT STDDEV (BASIC)
     FROM SALARY;
   ```
7. **VARIANCE function :** It finds the variance of the argument specified.

   For example,
   ```
   SELECT VARIANCE (BASIC)
     FROM SALARY;
   ```

Actually, the COUNT function has three forms :

1. **COUNT (*) :** It counts the number of rows in the table or the number of rows in the group including NULL.
2. **COUNT (column_name) :** It counts the number of non-null values in the column.
3. **COUNT (DISTINCT column_name) :** It counts the number of different values in the column.

Character Functions

The following are the most commonly used character functions in Oracle.

1. **INITCAP (data) :** It will convert the first letter of the string to the uppercase.

   For example, SELECT INITCAP ('RAJIV')
   FROM DUAL;

   This will give—Rajiv as output.

2. **LENGTH (data) :** It will return the length of the string.

   For example, SELECT LENGTH ('RAJIV')
   FROM DUAL;

   This will return 5.

3. **SUBSTR (data *x, y*) :** This function will extract *y* characters starting from the xth character of data.

   For example, SELECT SUBSTR ('Delhi-University' 5,3)
   FROM DUAL;

   This query will return *i* – U from the above string.

4. **INSTR (data, X) :** It will find the location of string X in the string data.

   For example, SELECT INSTR ('GGSIPU,Delhi','IPU')
   FROM DUAL;

   This query will return 4 *i.e.,* the position at which the string 'IPU' begins.

5. **INSTR (data X, S, N) :** It will find the location of the nth occurrence string X in the string data starting from the position, S.

   For example, SELECT INSTER (''GGSIPU,Delhi','I' 1, 2)
   FROM DUAL;

   It will return 12 *i.e.,* position at which the 2nd occurrence of 'I' begins.

6. **GREATEST (expr1, expr2, ... exprn) :** It displays the greatest value from a group of expressions.

   For example, SELECT GREATEST (85, 95.5, 74.4)
   FROM DUAL;

   This query will return 95.5 Consider another data example –

   SELECT GREATEST (TO_DATE ('26-JAN –99')
   TO_DATE (26-AUG-02'))
   FROM DUAL;

   It will return 26-AUG-02.

7. **LEAST (*expr*1, *expr*2, *expr*3, ...)**

   It displays the least value from a group of expressions.

   For example, SELECT LEAST (85, 95.5, 74.4)
   FROM DUAL;

   It returns 74.4

Conversion Functions

In addition to this, we also have some conversion functions in Oracle. Let us discuss them one by one.

1. **TO_CHAR function :** This function can be used to convert a date or a number to a character string. It formats the date field in many ways. The format must be enclosed within single quotes.

   SELECT TO_CHAR (SYSDATE, 'MONTH') FROM DUAL;

   This query will return March, Consider another query now.

   For example, SELECT TO_CHAR (SYSDATE, 'dd/mm/yyyy')
   FROM DUAL;

   This query will return 04/03/2009 But if I write –

   SELECT *
   FROM SALARY
   WHERE TO_CHAR (SALARY_DATE, 'MM') = '03'

   Then, this query will return the rows of the March salary.

2. **NVL function :** The NVL function is used to substitute any NULL value with a user specified value.

   For example, Say our query is –

   UPDATE SALARY
   SET COMMISSION = NULL
   WHERE EMP_NO = 101;

   This command will set the COMMISSION data for 101 as NULL.
   Consider another query now –

   SELECT ENO, BASIC, NVL (COMMISSION, 5000)
   FROM SAL;

   Here, NVL (COMMISSION, 5000) means that if there is no value in the COMMISSION field then it should be displayed as 5000.

NOTE : Null values can also be substituted with 0 : NVL (COMMISSION, 0)

3. **DECODE function :** This function can be used to expand any abbreviations used in the table.

   For example, SELECT CITY, DECODE(CITY, 'UDP', 'UDUPI' 'BNG', BANGALORE') "CITY NAME"
   FROM CUSTOMER;

   This query will display—

CITY	**CITY NAME**
UDP	UDUPI
BNG	BANGALORE

DATE Function

We can also use some date functions as given below :

1. **ADD_MONTHS (date, count) :** This function will add 'count' months to 'date'.

   For example, SELECT ADD_MONTHS ('4-MAR-2009',2)
   FROM DUAL;

   This query will return, 4-MAY-2009

2. **LAST_DAY (date) :** This function gives **date** of the last day of the specified month in the date.

   For example, SELECT LAST_DAY ('4–MAR-2009')
   FROM DUAL;

   Will return, 31-MAR-2009.

3. **MONTHS_BETWEEN (date2, date1) :** This function gives (date2, date1) in months.

   For example, SELECT MONTHS_BETWEEN ('15-JAN-99', '20-MAR-99')
   FROM DUAL;

   It will return, –2.16129.

4. **NEXT_DAY (date, day) :** This function gives **date** of the next day after specified date where 'day' is Mon, Tue, Wed and so on.

   For example, SELECT NEXT_DAY ('12–JAN-2009' 'MON')
   FROM DUAL;

   This gives 19-JAN-2009 which is the next, Monday after 12-JAN-2009.

5. **NEW_TIME (date, 'this, 'other') :** It gives the date (and time) in this time zone *i.e.*, **'this'** will be replaced by 3-letter abbreviation for the current time zone.

   'other' will be replaced by a 3-letter abbreviation for the othertime zone for which you would like to know the time and date.

   For example, NEW_TIME (*d*, *z*1, *z*2).

   This function returns the date and time in time zone, *z*2, when, date and time in time zone, *z*1 are *d*.

   Here, the arguments *z*1 and *z*2 can be any of these text strings

Arguments	Meaning
'AST'	Atlantic Standard
'BST'	Bering Standard
'CST'	Central Standard
'EST'	Eastern Standard
'GMT'	Greenwich Mean Time
'HST'	Alaska_Hawaii Standard Time
'MST'	Mountain Standard
'NST'	New Foundland Standard Time
'PST'	Pacific Standard
'YST'	Yukon Standard

6. **TO_DATE (string) :** It converts a string into an oracle date. It will also accept a number instead of a string with certain limit.

   For example, INSERT INTO SALARY VALUES (10,20,30,40, TO_DATE ('01-JAN-2001', 'DD-MM-YYYY'));

3.6 ROLLBACK, COMMIT AND SAVEPOINT

ROLLBACK, COMMIT and SAVEPOINT are collectively considered as Transaction Control commands.

Please note that a transaction is a sequence of SQL statements that Oracle treats as a single (or atomic) unity. It means that this group of SQL statements will be executed either in its entirety or will not be executed at all. **Also note that to make the set of**

changes permanent, COMMIT must be issued. However, a part or all of transaction can be undone with the ROLLBACK statement.

A transaction begins with the execution of the first SQL statement in the transaction and ends with either the Rollback statement or the commit statement. Let us consider an example now.

Consider the following query –

```
DELETE FROM CUSTOMER
WHERE STATE = 'DELHI';
COMMIT;
```

This will delete records permanently. If a COMMIT is not issued, it is possible **to undo the delete operation** by issuing a ROLLBACK. **For example,**

```
DELETE FROM CUSTOMER
WHERE STATE = 'DELHI';
ROLLBACK;
```

Now, if we want to ROLLBACK to a certain point, a SAVE POINT may be issued. **For example,**

```
SAVEPOINT D1;
DELETE FROM CUSTOMER WHERE STATE 'DELHI'
SAVE POINT D2;
DELETE FROM CUSTOMER WHERE STATE = 'KERELA',
ROLLBACK TO D2;
COMMIT;
```

This will undo the second delete operation. COMMIT will also release the exclusive ROW lock that is held on the updated data, so that other users can see and use the data. Data is stored in special files called **Redo log files** until commit statement is executed.

3.7 INDEXES IN SQL

An index is defined as a table or a data structure that is maintained to determine the location of rows or records in a file that satisfy some condition. Such a table is known as an **index table** which consists of a key field and a pointer to the location where the record is stored. **Please note that each index entry corresponds to a data record on the secondary storage disk device**. Firstly, this index table is searched for the address of the record in it and then reading of the record from this address.

For example, the index of this book works in the same way as that of an index for a file in a database system. Another example could be a library catalogue.

Indexing is of two types :

(*a*) Ordered indexing

(*b*) Hashed indexing

(*a*) **Ordered indexing** is based on a sorted orderings of the values of records.

(*b*) **Hashed indexing** is based on the values of record being uniformly distributed using a fast mathematical function called as a hashed function.

How many index files to create ?

One may create a large number of index files or very few index files. To understand about an insight in the selection of levels consider the following analysis—Let us consider that these files are stored on disks. Disk search generally requires a position seek time to move the arm, latency time to position the head at the right spot on a track and the time to transfer the data. Thus even though a pointer indicates the exact location where the desired data are stored, the time to get to that data can be substantial. **Please note that it is generally true that data transfer time is much less than seek time. Also note that if one builds an extra level of index, one must be sure that the gain out-weighs the cost. A rule of thumb is to check if the time required to transfer the data in the nth level index file is much less than the seek and latency time of the device.**

Another factor to be considered is **the size of an index file**. If at any time an entire index file can be read into a buffer without significant impact on the available buffer space, then one should not consider having another level of an index. **Please note that, in general, there should be very few index levels since each index block can store a large number of index–pointer pairs.**

Also note that a two level index structure can handle millions of records readily.

A file may have several indices on different search keys. We have two types of indices :

(*i*) Primary or Clustering Index : Primary index associates a primary key with the physical location in which a record is stored. When a user requests a record, the O.S. firstly loads the primary index into the Main Memory (MM) and searches the index sequentially for the primary key. When it finds the entry for the primary key, it then reads the address in which record is stored. The system then proceeds to this address and reads the contents of the desired record. **Please note that in the primary index, the file containing the records is sequentially ordered. For example**, an Indexed–sequential file organization is an example of primary index.

Also note that a primary index contains 2 things :

(*a*) the primary key (PK) of the record.

(*b*) the physical address of the record.

So, the search operation is very fast.

(*b*) Secondary or Non-clustering Index : It is not always necessary to have PK as a search key. **Such indices whose search key specifies an order different from the sequential order of the file are called as non-clustering or secondary indices.** A secondary index is also an ordered file with two fields :

(*a*) An indexing field,

(*b*) A block pointer or a record pointer. A secondary index is used to search a file on the basis of secondary keys.

There are two types of ordered indices that we can use –

(*a*) Dense index.

(*b*) Sparse index.

In **dense indexing**, an index record appears for every search-key value in the file. In a dense clustering index, the index record contains the search-key value and a pointer to the first data record with that search key value. The rest of the records with the same search-key value would be stored sequentially after the first record, since, because the index is a clustering one, records are sorted on the same search key. **Please note that dense index implementations may store a list of pointers to all records with the same search-key value. Also note that doing so is not essential for clustering indices.**

In **sparse index**, an index record appears for only some of the search-key values. As discussed above in dense indices, each index record contains a search-key value and a pointer to the first data record with that search-key value. To locate a record, we find the index entry with the largest search-key values that is less than or equal to the search-key value for which we are looking. We start at the record pointed to by that index entry and follow the pointers in the file until we find the desired record.

Which one to select ?

Generally speaking, locating a record if we have a dense index is faster than a sparse index. However, sparse indices have advantages over dense indices in that they require less space and they impose less maintenance overhead for insertions and deletions.

Actually, a trade-off exists. A system designer must decide upon the access time and space overhead. This decision will depend upon the specific application. **A good choice is to have a sparse index with one index entry per block**. Why? This is because the dominant cost in processing a database request is the time that it takes to bring a block from disk into main memory once we have brought in the block, the time to scan the entire block is negligible. Using this sparse index, we locate the block containing the record that we are seeking.

Consider an example to understand this. Consider a student file with this schema–

STUDENT (**SID**, CITY, TOTAL).

and an index file with CITY field and a pointer field as shown in Fig. 3.1 below.

Two cases arise

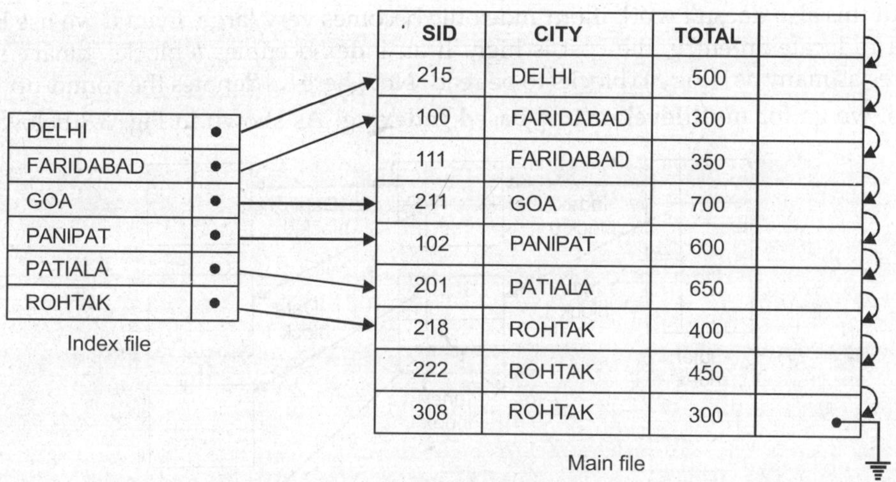

Fig. 3.1. *Dense index*

Case 1 : Using Dense Indexing. Herein, if we use the dense indexing (as shown in Fig. 3.1), we follow the pointer directly. Say, we want to search for Faridabad record then firstly we go to our index file and then follow the pointer to the first FARIDABAD record, in that order. We continue processing records until we encounter a record for a city other than Faridabad.

Case 2 : Using Sparse Indexing. But what happens in a *sparse indexing*?

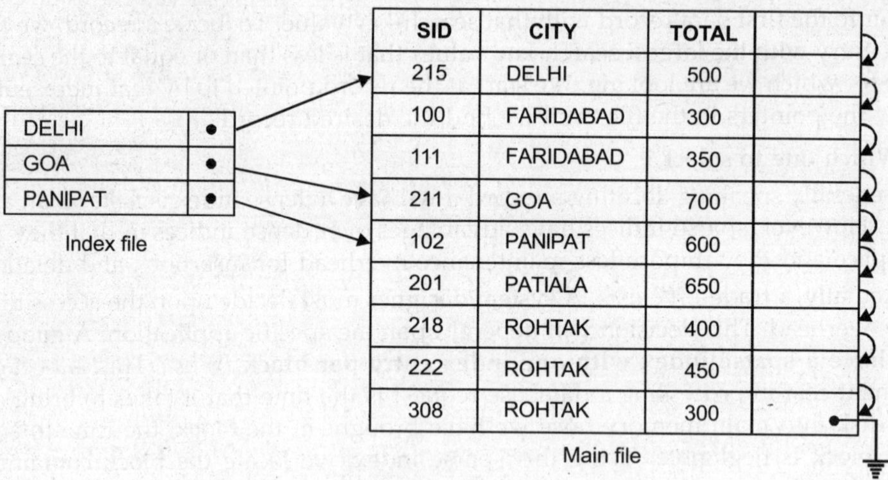

Fig. 3.2. *Sparse index*

Herein, we find that there is no index entry for FARIDABAD. Since the last entry in alphabetic order before FARIDABAD is DELHI, so we follow that pointer. We then read the Main file in sequential order until we find the first FARIDABAD record and begin processing at that point.

But this also doesn't work if our index file becomes very large. Even if we use Binary search to locate an entry, the cost is high. If an index occupies b blocks, binary search requires as many as $\lceil(\log_2 b)\rceil$ blocks to be read. Note here $\lceil\ \rceil$ denotes the round-up value.

So, we go for **multilevel or tree-based indexing**. As shown in Fig. 3.3 below.

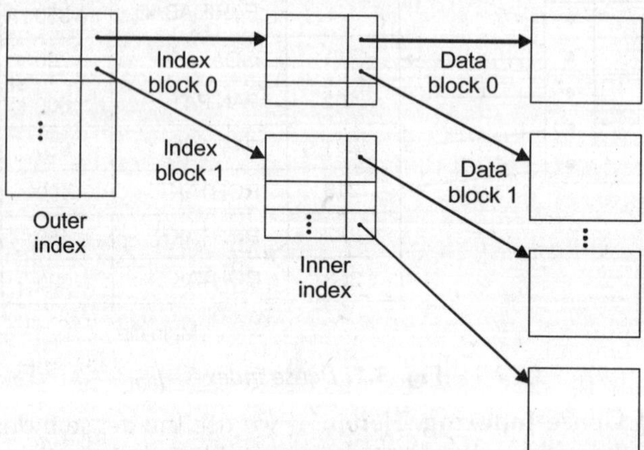

Fig. 3.3. *Two level indexing*

How searching is done here?

To locate a record, we firstly apply our binary search algorithm on the **outer index**. We try to find the record for the largest search-key value less than or equal to the one that we desire. **The pointer points to a block of the inner index**. We scan this block until we find the record that has the largest search-key value less than or equal to the one that we desire. It is the pointer in this record that points to the block of the file that contains the record for which we are looking.

When the outer index becomes a large file then we can create another level of index. **Please note that we can repeat this process as many times as required**. This results in multilevel indexing which requires fewer I/O operations. **Also note that each level of index could correspond to a unit of physical storage**. We may have indices at the track, cylinder and disk levels.

For example, a dictionary is an example of a multilevel index.

Next we discuss about B and B^+-tree indexing.

B-tree indexing : B-tree indexing operates closely with the secondary storage. The size of each node of B-tree is as large as the size of a block. The number of keys in one node can vary depending on the sizes of the keys, data organisation and block size. **Block size** is the size of each node of a B-tree. The **order** of a B-tree specifies the maximum number of children.

B-tree provides fast sequential access, random access, dynamic maintenance to overcome overflow problems that occur in the indexed sequential and hashing methods. The B-tree index has some characteristics that are discussed below :

1. The root has atleast two sub-trees unless it is a leaf.
2. Each non-root and each non-leaf node holds $(k - 1)$ keys and k references to sub-trees where $k \leq m$.
3. Each leaf node holds $(k - 1)$ keys where
$$(m/2) \leq k \leq m.$$
4. All leaf nodes are on the same level.

Let us now discuss B^+-tree indexing.

A B^+-tree index is a balanced tree in which the **internal nodes** direct the search operation and the *leaf nodes* contain the data entries. **Also note that here every path from the root to the tree leaf is of the same length**. It is not possible and feasible to allocate the leaf pages sequentially because the tree structure grows and shrinks dynamically. All pages are linked using page pointers.

In this indexing technique, references to data are made from the leaves only. The internal nodes of the B^+-tree are indexed for fast access of data and is called as an **index set**. Actually, we say that a B^+-tree index is a regular B-tree plus a linked list of data *i.e.*,

$$B^+ \text{ tree index} = \text{B-tree} + \text{Linked list of data.}$$

We now discuss some of the **characteristics of a B^+-tree index** :

1. It is a balanced tree.
2. Except the root node, a minimum occupancy of 50% is guaranteed.
3. We locate the data entry, remove it without any tree adjustment. This is how deletion is done. This is because the file grows rather than shrink.
4. Searching for a record requires just a traversal from the root to the appropriate leaf.

3.8 SQL ODBC AND JDBC

A way for the Java programs to communicate with different database engines is through the *jdbc-odbc* bridge. Microsoft established a common standard for communicating with databases called as Open Database Connectivity (ODBC). Until ODBC, most database clients were server specific. ODBC drivers abstract away vendor-specific protocols, providing a common application programming interface (API) to the database clients. **Please note that by writing your database clients to the ODBC API, you enable your programs to access more database servers**. So, your program interaction with different databases through *jdbc-odbc* bridge might look something as shown below.

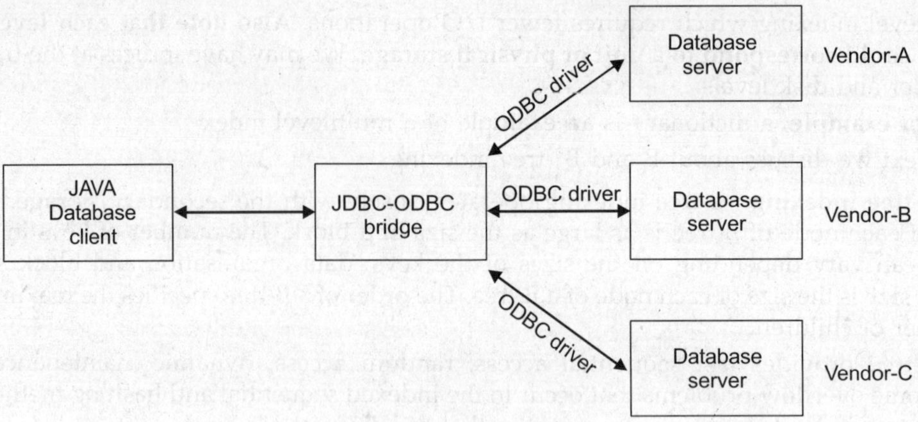

Fig. 3.4. *JDBC-ODBC bridge*

When all preparations are over, we are in position to actually execute an SQL statement. The method used to execute a simple query is –

Statement.execute Query().

For example, Result set rs = stmtl. execute Query ("Select * from student");

Please note here that the execute–Query () method takes an SQL query string as an argument and returns the results of the query as a Result Set object. Also note that the ResultSet object contains both the data returned by the query and methods for retrieving the data.

We also have several **variations** on execution methods. Like, the execute update() method is used to update the results and the execute () method is used for SQL statements that return multiple results.

3.9 MS-SQL SERVER 7

Tables

Tables are the heart of the database knowing how to create and maintain tables is among the most important pieces of knowledge for database users. In order to create a table, you must know the concepts and characteristics of the database used.

The process of creating a table must begin only the database has been carefully defined. Many developers have the bad habit of defining the database "online", i.e., they open the module that create the tables and then start thinking about the database. This can cause many problems.

Characteristics of Tables

The SQL server 7 allows the creation of temporary and permanent tables. Temporary tables are those created in memory while permanent tables are those that are written to disk.

A SQL Server 7 table can contain upto 1, 024 columns. Each column must be created through the specification of basic information such as its name, the data type it will store, and the optional specification of default values and constraints imposed on the contents.

The name of a column must be enclusive inside a database. There cannot be two columns called state inside the same table. However, different tables inside a database can contain columns with the same name. For example, two tables called clients and suppliers can each contain address information data in columns called street address, city and state.

The name of a table must be enclusive among the tables created by an owner. However, inside a database there can be tables with the same pertaining to different users.

Filegroups

When a table is created, it is automatically put in the default filegroup. However, if the table contains fields of type text, Ntext, or image, then can be put in a filegroup different from the rest of the table.

Data Types

Each column in a table must have a data type specified to it. In other words, one must indicate that the column will store a particular type of data such as text, number, data, or image. The SQL Server 7 can use several types of data and also allows the user to create his or her own data types.

Data stored in a SQL Server 7 table can be of these types:

(i) Integer

Bit : Integer with 0 or 1 value

Int : Integer number with values between

2^31(–2,147,483,648) upto

2^31–1(2,147,483,647)

Smallint : 2^15(–32,768) upto 2^15–1(32,767)

Tinyint : Integer between 0 and 255

Decimal or : Number with fixed accuracy

Numeric: Between–10^38–1 upto 10^38–1

Money: Monetary data values from –2^63–(–922,337,203,685,477.5808) through 2^63–1(922,337,203,685,477,5807), with accuracy to a ten-thousandth of a monetary unit.

Smallmoney:–214,748.3648 through 214,748.3647) with accuracy to a ten-thousandth of a monetary unit.

Float: –1.79E + 308 through 1.79E + 308

Real : –3.40E + 38 through 3.40E + 38

Datetime: January 1,1753, upto December 31, 1999, with accuracy upto the 3.33th millisecond.

Smalldatetime: January 1, 1900, upto June 6, 2079, with precision of upto 1 minute.

Miscellaneous

Cursor: A reference to a cursor

Time stamp: An exclusive number recognized by the database

Uniqueidentifier: An exclusive global identifier.

Strings

Char : A fixed field with maximum size of 8,000 bytes

Varchar : A fixed field with maximum size of 8,000 bytes

Text : Variable with size upto 2^31–1(2, 147, 483, 647) bytes.

(iv) Unicode Strings

Nchar : Unicode character with fixed size of upto 4,000 bytes

Nvarchar : Unicode character with variable size of upto 4,000 bytes

Ntext : Variable with size upto 2^30–1(1,073, 741,823) bytes.

(v) Binary Strings

Binary : Fixed size of upto 8,000 bytes.

varbinary : Variable size of upto 8,000 bytes.

Image: Variable size with upto 2^31–1 (2,147,483,647) bytes.

(v) Synonyms

Some synonyms were created for compatibility with the SQL–92 language.

Synonym	Equivalent to
binary varying	varbinary
char varying	varchar
character	char
character	char(1)
character(*n*)	char(*n*)
character varying(*n*)	varchar(*n*)
dec	decimal
double precision	float
float(*n*)for *n*=1–7	real
float[(*n*)]for *n*=8–15	float
integer	int
notional character(*n*)	nchar(*n*)
notional char (*n*)	nchar(*n*)
notional character varying(*n*)	nvarchar(*n*)
notional char varying(*n*)	nvarchar(*n*)
notional text	ntext
numeric	decimal

Constraints

Constraints are to ensure the integrity of a database through the filtering of information inserted in a table's column. Constraints are the basic mechanism to ensure the integrity of a field. They have priority over triggers, rules, and default values. There are five types of constraints.

NOT NULL specifies that a column cannot accept the value Null. CHECK limit the values that can be put in the column by testing for a condition. Boolean is based on the contents that are attributed to the column. If a tested condition returns TRUE, the entered value is attributed to the column.

UNIQUE forces the columns to have enclusive values, in other words, in a column that is designated UNIQUE, there cannot be two records with the same contents. For example, a product code or social security number must be enclusive. On the other hand, the contents of a state or city field can be duplicated.

PRIMARY KEY creates the primary key to the table, a column, or combination of columns with values that must be exclusive inside the table in order to identify a row. A column with a primary key constraints cannot more than one column, just one of them will be considered the primary key. The other columns that form the key are called candidate keys.

FOREIGN KEY identifies the relationship between the tables. This is a field in the current table that point to a key field in another table. The use of a foreign key prevents the deletion of rows in the current table when there are references to key fields of external tables. This kind of constraints prevents a value form being introduced in the current table that is not found in the key fields of the external table that was joined.

Sample Tables

In this chapter, we will create one table with author data, another with book data, and a third that will be used to join the author and book table. Those tables will be created in the Newpub database. The Authors table must have the structure shown on the next page, with the au-id column as the primary key with an exclusive value defined by ID.

Column	Name	Type	Size	Null ?	Default
1.	au-id	int	10	no	
2.	au-name	varchar	30	no	
3.	au-phone	varchar	18	yes	
4.	au-e-mail	varchar	25	yes	
5.	au-addn	varchar	40	yes	
6.	au-city	varchar	30	yes	
7.	au-state	char	2	yes	
8.	au-zip	char	8	yes	
9.	au-country	char	15	yes	'Brazil'
10.	active	bit	1		

The active field indicates wheather the author has had a book published.

The Books table must contain the following fields. The book_id column must be the primary key with an exclusive value defined by ID.

Column	Name	Type	Size	Null ?	Default value
1	book_id	ID	4	no	
2	title	varchar	50	no	
3	Price	Money	8	no	
4	Category	Char	10	no	
5	Comments	Varchar	100	yes	
6	Publidate	datetime	8	yes	'not available'

The autbook table must contain the following structure, and the book_id column must be the primary key:

Column	Name	Type	Size	Null ?
1	book_id	ID	4	no
2	au_id	ID	10	no

Expressions and Operators

SQL Server 7 supports all of the most common operators found in most languages. The operators act on the operands, i.ey., the elements that are analyzed by the operator. There are two classes of operators: unary operators that act on only one operand and binary operators that act on two or more operands.

Operator Precedence

There are several types of operators. When more than one type of operator is present in an expression, they are evaluated according to the following precedence order:

- +(positive),–(negative),~(bitwise NOT)
- *(multiplication),/(division),% (Module)
- +(addition),+(concatenation),– (subtraction)
- =, >,<, >=,<=,<>,!=,!>,!< (comparison)
- ^(bitwise Exclusive OR), & (bitwiseAND),| (bitwise OR)
- NOT

- AND
- ALL, ANY, BETWEEN, IN, LIKE, OR, SOME
- =(assignment)

Operators

Following are the types of operators by SQL Server 7:

Arithmetic

Multiplication *
Division /
Subtraction –
Addition +
Modulo %

Character

Concatenation ||

Comparison

Equal =
Not equal <>
Greater than >
Less than <
Greater than or equal to >=
Less than or equal to <=
Not less than !<
Not more than !>
Not equal to !=

Logic

NOT Inverts the boolean value
AND True when both expressions are true
OR True when one expression is true
BETWEEN True when the operand is inside the range
LIKE True when the operand finds a standard
IN True when some item is true
SOME True when any item is true
ANY True when some item is true
ALL True when all the set is true

Bitwise

realise operations of bit manipulation between two integer expressions
& (Bitwise AND)
| (Bitwise OR)
^ (Bitwise Exclusive OR)

Unary

+ (Positive): The numeric value is positive.
– (Negative): The numeric value is negative.
– (Bitwise NOT): Returns the complement of the number.

3.10 SOLVED EXAMPLES ON SQL

We are in a position to solve some queries based on SQL now :

Example 1. Create the following relations:

1. **Course (course_no char(4), course_name varchar (20))**
2. **Course_fee (course_no char(4), full_part char(1) (F/P), fees number (10))**
   [course_no and full-part should be unique]

3. **Student (prospectus_no number (10), name varchar (20), address varchar (30), phone_no number (11), D_O_B date, total_amt number (10,2), amt_paid number (10,2) installment char(1) (I/F))**
4. **Installment (prospectus_no number (10) FK on delete cascade, installment_amt number (10,2), due_dt date, paid char(1) (P,U))**
   [prospectus_no and due_dt should be unique]
5. **Course_taken (prospectus_no number (10) FK, course_no char(4), start_dt date, full_part char (1) (F/P), time_slot char (2), performance varchar2 (20))**

And now answer these queries :

1. **Retrieve name and course no of all students.**
2. **List the names of students who have paid the full amount at the time of admission.**
3. **Find the names of students starting with A.**
4. **Print the names of students whose total amount is not equal to amount due.**
5. **Count the number of students who have joined in current year current month.**
6. **Determine the maximum and minimum course fees.**
7. **Increase the fee of oracle by 50%.**
8. **Print the details of courses whose fees are between 5000 and 10000.**
9. **Display the admission date in Date. Month. Year format.**
10. **Find out in which course maximum number of students have taken admission.**
11. **Change the course_name from Unix to Unix Operating System.**
12. **Display the admission date in DD-MONTH-YYYY format.**
13. **Get the sum of amount to be collected from students in this month.**
14. **Find out in which course the maximum number of students have taken admission in the current month.**
15. **Select the students who have not yet paid full amount of fees.**

Solution.

1. Select student_1. name, course-taken. Course_no from student_1, course_taken where student_1. prospectus_no = course_taken. prospectus_no;
2. Select name from student_1 where installment = 'f';
3. Select name from student_1s where s.name like 'A%';
4. Select name from student_1 where s.total-amt <> s.amt_paid;
5. Select count (prospectus_no), start_dt from course_taken group by start_dt;
6. Select max (fees), min (fees) from course_fee;
7. Update course_fee set fees=fees+fees* 50/100 where course_no in (select course_no from course where course_name='oracle');
8. Select c.course_name, f.course.no f.fees from course c,course_fee f where ((c. course_no = f.course_no) and (f.fees between 5000 and 10000))
9. Select to_char(start_dt, 'dd-month-yyyy') from course_taken;
10. Select max (count(course_no)) from course group by course_no;
11. Update course set course-name=' os system' where course-name='os';
12. Select to_char(start_dt,'dd-month-yyyy') from course _taken;

    Or

    Select to_char(start_dt, 'DD-MONTH-YYYY')from course_taken;

13. Select sum (installment_amt) from installment where due_dt >=' 01-feb-07' and due_dt <=' 28-feb-07';
14. Select max (count (course_no)) from course_taken group by start-dt;
15. Select name from student1 where prospectus_no in (select prospectus_no from installment where paid= 'n');

Example 2. Assume an Employee database and answer these queries –

1. **Display each employee name and hiredate of systems department.**
2. **Write query to calculate length of service of each employee.**
3. **Find the second maximum salary of all employees.**
4. **Display all employee name and department name in department name order.**
5. **Find the name of lowest paid employee for each manager.**
6. **Display the department that has no employee.**
7. **Find the employees who earn the maximum salary in each job type. Sort in descending order of salary.**
8. **In which year did most people joined the company? Display the year and number of employees.**
9. **Display the details of those employees who earn greater than average of their department.**
10. **List the employees having salary between 10000 and 20000**
11. **Display all employees hired during 1983.**
12. **Update the salaries of all employees in marketing department & hike it by 15%**
13. **Get the gross salaries of all the employess.**
14. **Get the names of employees and their managers name.**
15. **Display the name, location and department name of all the employees earning more than 1500.**
16. **Show all the employees in Dallas.**
17. **List the employees name, job, salary, grade, and department for employees in the company except clerks. Sort on employee names.**
18. **Find the employees who earns the minimum salary for their job. Sort in descending order of salary.**
19. **Find the most recently hired employees in the department order by hiredate.**
20. **Find out the difference between highest and lowest salaries.**

Solution

1. Select ename, hiredate from emp, dept where upper (dname) = 'SYSTEMS';
2. Select ename, (sysdate-hiredate) LOS from emp;
3. Select max (sal) from emp where sal not in (select max (sal) from emp);
4. Select ename, dname from emp, dept where emp. deptno=dept.deptno order by dname;
5. Select ename, sal from emp where sal in (select min (sal) from emp group by mgr);
6. Select dname from dept where deptno not in (select deptno from emp);
7. Select ename, job, sal from emp where sal in (select max (sal) from emp group by job) order by sal desc;
8. Select to_char(hiredate,'yyyy') year, count (empno) from emp group by to_char

(hiredate, 'yyyy') order by count (empno);

9. Select * from emp a where sal > (select avg (sal) from emp b where a.deptno = b.deptno) order by deptno;
10. Select * from emp where sal between 10000 and 20000;
11. Select * from emp where to_char (HIREDATE, 'yyyy') = 1983;
12. Update emp set=sal + (sal*15/100) where deptno = 30;
13. Select ename, sal+nvl (comm, 0) gross from emp;
14. Select a.ename, b.ename manager from emp a, emp b where a. mgr = b.empno (+);
15. Select ENAME, LOC, DNAME from emp a, dept d where a.deptno = d.deptno and sal > 1500;
16. Select a.* from emp a,dept d where a.deptno = d.deptno and loc = 'DALLAS';
17. Select ename, job, sal, grade, dname from emp a, salgrade, dept d where sal between losal and hisal and upper (job) <>' CLERK' and a.deptno = d.deptno order by ename;
18. Select * from emp where sal in (select min(sal) from emp group by job) order by sal desc;
19. Select * from emp order by HIREDATE desc;
20. Select max (sal), min (sal), max (sal) – min (sal) from emp;

Example 3. Consider the following three relations–

Employee (Emp#, Name)

Assigned_to (Project#, Emp#)

Project (<u>Project#</u>, Project_Name, Chief-Architect) Now, answer the following queries-

(a) Print the Emp# of the employees working on project 'AAA'.

(b) Print the details of employees working on project 'AAA'.

(c) Print details of employees working on the Data Mining project.

(d) Print the details of all employees working on both projects 'AAA' and 'BBB'.

(e) Print the employees numbers of employee who do not work on project 'AAA'.

(f) Print the employee number of employees who work on all projects.

(g) Print the Emp# of employees other than employee 39 who work on atleast one project that employee 39 works on.

Solution. Let us solve these queries in SQL.

(*a*) $\Pi_{\text{Emp\#}} (\sigma_{\text{Project\#} = \text{'AAA'}} (\text{ASSIGNED\_TO}))$

(*b*) $\text{EMPLOYEE} \bowtie_{\Pi \text{Emp\#}} (\sigma_{\text{Project\#} = \text{'AAA'}} (\text{ASSIGNED\_TO}))$

(*c*) $\text{EMPLOYEE} \bowtie_{\Pi \text{Emp\#}} (\text{ASSIGNED\_TO} \bowtie (\pi_{\text{Project\#}} (\sigma_{\text{Project\_Name} = \text{'Data mining'}} (\text{PROJECT})))$

> **NOTE :** Firstly we find the number of projects named Data Mining. So, we do selection of the RELATION PROJECT, which is followed by projection on the attribute Project#. The result of this projection is joined with the ASSIGNED_TO relation to give tuples of the ASSIGNED_TO involving Data Mining. This is then projected on Emp# and then joined with EMPLOYEE relation to get the required employee datails.

(*d*) $\text{EMPLOYEE} \bowtie (\text{ASSIGNED-TO} \div \Pi_{\text{Project\#}}(\sigma_{(\text{project\#='AAA'} \vee \text{Project\# 'BBB'}} (\text{ASSIGNED\_TO})))$

(*e*) $\Pi_{\text{Emp\#}} (\text{ASSIGNED\_TO}) - \Pi_{\text{Emp\#}} (\sigma_{\text{Project\#} = \text{'AAA'}} (\text{ASSIGNED\_TO})))$

NOTE : This is just as R-S which gives a set of tuples that are in R.

(*f*) ASSIGNED_TO $\div \Pi_{Project\#}$ (PROJECT)

(*g*) $\Pi_{Emp\#}$ (ASSIGNED_TO $\bowtie \Pi_{Project\#}$ ($\sigma_{Emp\# = 39}$ (ASSIGNED_TO)))

Example 4. Consider the following scheme –

SUPPLIER (<u>SUPPLIER_ID</u>, SUPPLIER_NAME, SUPPLIER_ADDRESS)

PARTS (<u>PART_ID</u>, PART_NAME, COLOR)

CATALOG (<u>SUPPLIER_ID</u>, <u>PART_ID</u>, COST)

Answer the following in SQL :

(a) Find the name of the suppliers who supply 'Green' parts.

(b) Find the name of suppliers who supply both Blue and Green parts.

(c) Find the name of suppliers who supply all parts.

Solution. (*a*)

```
SELECT SUPPLIER_NAME
  FROM SUPPLIER, PARTS, CATALOG
WHERE SUPPLIER. SUPPLIER_ID
         = CATALOG. SUPPLIER_ID
   AND PARTS. PART_ID = CATALOG. PART_ID
   AND PARTS. COLOR = 'GREEN';
```

(*b*)

```
SELECT SUPPLIER_NAME
  FROM SUPPLIER, PARTS, CATALOG
WHERE SUPPLIER. SUPPLIER_ID = CATALOG. PART_ID
   AND PART. COLOR = 'BLUE';
INTERSECT
SELECT SUPPLIER_NAME
  FROM SUPPLIER, PARTS, CATALOG
WHERE SUPPLIER. SUPPLIER_ID = CATALOG. SUPPLIER_ID
   AND PARTS. PART_ID = CATALOG. PART_ID
   AND PART. COLOR = 'GREEN';
```

(*c*)

```
SELECT SUPPLIER_NAME, COLOR
  FROM SUPPLIER, CATALOG, PARTS
WHERE SUPPLIER. SUPP_ID = CATALOG. SUPP_ID
   AND PARTS. PART_ID = CATALOG. PART_ID
   AND PARTS. COLOR IN (SELECT COLOR FROM PARTS);
```

Example 5. Consider the following database

Employee (emp_no, name, skill, pay_rate)

Position (posting_no, skill)

Duty-allocation (posting_no, emp_no, day, shift)

Find SQL queries for the following :

(GGSIPU, B. Tech (CSE/IT) 5th Sem., Ist Internal Test 2012)

1. Get complete details from Duty_allocation:

Select*
from Duty_allocation:

2. **Get duty allocation details for Emp_no 123461 for the month of April 1986.**

```
select posting_no., shift, day
from Duty_allocation
where emp_no.=123461 and
Daye≥19860401 and Day ≤19860430 ;
```

3. **Find the shift details for employee 'XYZ'.**

```
select posting_no., shift, day
from Duty_allocation, Employee
where Duty allocation.emp_no.=Employee.emp_no and
        Name = 'XYZ';
```

4. **Get employees whose rate of pay is more than or equal to the rate of pay of employee 'XYZ'**

```
select S. name, S. pay_rate
from Employee as S, Employee as T
where S.pay_rate>T. Pay_rate
and T.name='XYZ';
```

5. **Compile all pairs of posting_nos requiring the same skill**

```
select S. posting_no., T.posting_no.
from Position S, Position T
where S. skill=T.skill
and S. posting_no.<T. posting_no.;
```

6. **Find the employees eligible to fill a position.**

```
select Employee.emp_no, position.posting_no, position.skill
from Employee, Position
where employee.skill = position.skill;
```

7. **Get the names and pay rates of employees with emp_no less than 123460 whose rate of pay is more than the rate of pay of at least one employee with emp_no greater than or equal to 123460.**

```
select name, pay_rate
from Employee
where emp_no<123460   and
      pay_rate>some
      (select pay_rate
             from Employee
             where emp_no≥123460);
```

8. **Get employees who are working either on the date 19860419 or 19860420**

```
select emp_no
from Duty_allocation
where Day in (19860419, 19860420);
select emp_no
from Duty_allocation
where Day = 19860419  or  Day = 19860420;
```

9. **Find the names of all employees who are assigned to all positions that require a Chief's skill.**

```
(select s_Name
from Employees
where
    (select posting_no
    from Duty_allocation_D
    where S.emp_no=D.emp_no)
    contains
    (select p.posting_no
    from position P
    where P.skill='chef';
```

10. Find the employees with the lowest pay rate

```
select emp_no, Name, Pay_rate
from Employee
where pay_rate≤all
(select pay_rate
from Employee)
```

11. Get the names of Chef's paid at the minimum pay_rate.

```
select name
from Employee
where skills 'Chef' and
pay_rates
(select pay_rate
from Employee)
where skill='Chef' ;
```

12. Find the names and the rate of pay of all employees who are allocated a duty.

```
select name, pay_rate
from Employee
where EXISTS
(select*
from Duty_allocation
where Employee.emp=no+duty_allocation.emp_no);
```

13. Find the names and the rate of pay of all employees who are not allocated a duty.

```
select name, pay_rate
from Employee
where NOT EXISTS
(select *
from Duty_allocation
where Employee.emp_no
   =Duty_allocation.emp_no);
```

14. Get employees who are waiters or work at posting_no 321.

```
(select emp_no
from Employee
where skill='waiter')
Union
```

```
(select emp_no
from Duty_allocation
where posting_no=321);
```

15. Get employee numbers of persons who work at posting_no 321 but don't have the skill of waiter.

```
(select emp_no
from Duty_allocation
where posting_no=321)
minus
(select emp_nofrom Employee where skill='waiter')
```

16. Get a list of employees not assigned a duty

```
(select emp_no
from Employee)
minus
(select emp_no
    from Duty_allocation);
```

17. Get a list of names of employees with the skill of Chef who are assigned a duty.

```
select Name
from Employee
where emp_no in
((select emp_no
from Employee
where skill='Chef')
interesect
(select emp_no
from Duty_allocation));
```

18. Get a count of different employees on each shift.

```
select shift, count (distinct emp_no)
from Duty_allocation
group by shift;
```

19. Get the employee numbers of all employees working on at least two dates.

```
select emp_no
from Duty_allocation
group by emp_no
having (count*)>1;
```

(II) Consider the given database;

Project (project_id, proj_name, chief_arch)
Employee (Emp_id, Emp_name)
Assigned_To (Project_id, emp_id)

Find the SQL queries for the following statements:

1. Get employee number of employees working on project C353.

```
select emp_id
from Assigned _To
```

```
where=project_id='C353';
```

2. **Get details of employees working on project C353.**

```
select A.emp_id, emp_name
from A.Assigned_To A, Employee
where project_id='C353';
```

3. **Obtained details of employees working on Database project.**

```
select Emp_name, A. Emp_id
from A. Assigned_To A, Employee
where project_id in (select P. Project_id
        from P. Project
    where P. project_name='Database';
```

4. **Get details of employees working on both C353 and C354**

```
(select Emp_name, A. emp_id
from Assigned_to A, Employee
where A. Project_id=C354)
intersect
(select emp_name, A. emp_id
from A.Assigned_To A, Employee
where project_id=='C354');
```

5. **Get employee numbers of employees who do not work on project C-453**

```
(select emp_id)
from Employee)
minus
(select emp_id
from Assigned_to
where project_id='C453');
```

6. **Get the employee, numbersof employees who work on all projects.**

```
select emp_id
from Assigned_To
where project_id=all
(select project_id
from project);
```

7. **Get employee number of employees who work on at least all those projects that employee 107 works on**

```
((select emp_id
from Assigned_To
    where project_id=all
     (select project_id
     from Assigned_To
     where emp_id=107))
minus  1017);
```

8. **Get employee numbers who work on at least one project that employee 107 works on.**

```
((select emp_id
from Assigned_To
```

```
where project_id in
        (select project_id
        from Assigned_To
        where emp_id=107)
minus 107);
```

III. Consider the employee database:

employee (employee_name, street, city)
works (employee_name, company_name, salary)
company (company name, city)
manages (employee_name, manager_name).

Give an expression in SQL for each of the following:

1. Find the names of all employees who work for FBC.

```
select employee_name
from works
where company_name = 'FBC';
```

2. Find the names and cities of all employees who work for FBC.

```
select employee.employee_name, city
from works, employee
where  employee.employee_name  = works.employee_name and
company_name = 'FBC';
```

3. Find the names, street address, and cities of residence of all employees who work for FBC and earn more than $ 10,000.

```
select employee.employee_name, street, city from works employee
where employee.employee_name=works.employee_name and
company_name = 'FBC' and salary > 10000;
```

4. Find all employees in the database who live in the same cities as the companies for which they work

```
select w.employee_name
from work w, emple, comp c
where e.emp_name=w.emp_name and
C. company_name.w.company_name and e.city = city;
```

5. Find all employees in the database who live in the same cities and on the same street as do their managers.

```
select E. employee_name
from employee E.employee T, manages
where E.employee_name=manages.employee_name
and E.street=T.street and E.city=T.city and
T.employee_name=manages.manager_name;
```

6. Find all employees in the database who do not work for FBC.

```
(select employee_name
from employee)
minus
(select employee_name
from works
where company_name='FBC');
```

7. **Find all employees in the database who earn more than every employee of small bank corporation.**

```
select employee_name
from works
where salary>(select max (salary)
from works
where company-name='FBC');
```

8. **Find all employees who earn more than the average salary of all employees of their company.**

```
select T.employee_name
from works T.
where salary>(select avg (S.salary)
from works S
where T. company_name=S. company_name);
```

9. **Find the company that has the smallest payroll.**

```
SQL>  create view payroll (compname, smallpay)
      as
      select company_name, min (salary)
      from works
      group by company_name;
SQL>  select company_name
      from payroll
      where small_pay=(select min (small_pay) from payroll);
```

10. **Find those companies whose employees earn a higher salary, on average than the average salary at FBC**

```
SQL>  create view avg_salary (comp_name, av_sal)
      as
      select companyname, avg (salary)
      from works
      group by company_name;
SQL>  select T. comp_name
      from avg_salary T. avg_salary S.
      where s. company_name='FBC'
      and T.av_sal>S.av_sal;
```

11. **Find the company that has must employees.**

```
SQL>  create view no_emp (compname, no_employee)
      as
      select company_name, count (employee_name)
      from works
      group by company_name;
SQL>  select company_name
      from no_emp
      where no_employee=(select max no_employee)
      from no_emp);
```

3.11 GROUP BY AND HAVING CLAUSES

The **GROUP by clause** is used to produce summary information for a subset of the table. This clause will produce a single row for all the rows that meet a particular condition.

For example, consider a relation, SAL as shown below.

EMP_NO	BASIC	COMM	DEDUCT	SALARY_DATE
1001	3000	200	200	1-MAR-09
1002	2500	100	150	1-MAR-09
1003	2000	180	100	1-MAR-09
1001	3000	200	250	1-APR-09
1002	2500	120	200	1-APR-09
1003	3000	100	280	1-APR-09

Now, if our query is to sum the salary of each employee then I may write –

```
SQL > SELECT EMP_NO, SUM (BASIC)
      FROM SALARY
      GROUP BY EMP_NO;
```

This query will give us the output as –

EMP_NO	SUM (BASIC)
1001	6000
1002	5000
1003	5000

However, if our query is to sum the salary of each employee and sort it on the sum of basic, then I will write

```
SQL > SELECT EMP_NO, SUM (BASIC)
      FROM SALARY
      GROUP BY EMP_NO
      ORDER BY SUM (BASIC);
```

This query will result as –

EMP_NO	SUM (BASIC)
1002	5000
1003	5000
1001	6000

But if we want to sum the salary of each employee and sort it in the decending order of the sum of basic, then I may write –

```
SQL > SELECT EMP_NO, SUM (BASIC)
      FROM SALARY
      GROUP BY EMP_NO
      ORDER BY SUM (BASIC) DESC;
```

Please note that the GROUP BY clause does not sort the data. It only groups together data which are alike. To sort data, ORDER BY clause is used.

Let us discuss HAVING clause now.

HAVING Clause : The HAVING clause can also be used with a join query that includes a GROUP BY clause. **The HAVING clause is useful for specifying a condition for the group**. The WHERE clause is used to specify conditions to retrieve rows of a table and the **HAVING clause is used to specify a condition to retrieve group data**.

For example,

```
SQL > SELECT S.EMP_NO, EMP_NAME, AVG (BASIC)
      FROM SALARY S, EMP
      WHERE S.EMP_NO = EMP. EMP_NO
      GROUP BY S.EMP_NO, EMP_NAME
      HAVING AVG(BASIC) > = 5500
      ORDER BY  AVG (BASIC);
```

Please note here that the Group function—AVG cannot be used in the WHERE clause.

3.12 SUBQUERIES

What is a subquery?

A subquery is a query within a query *i.e.*, a SELECT statement is used as a part of another SQL statement. The outer statement is called as the **parent** and the nested query passes a value to the outer query. **Please note here that the nested query executes first.**

Before we go further, let us see some important points to remember :

1. The nested query must return a single column.
2. The result can only contain columns from the tables referenced in the outer most query.
3. The nested query must return a single row when a standard operator such as =, <, > is used.
4. The BETWEEN operator cannot be used with a subquery.
5. Subqueries can also be used in INSERT, UPDATE and DELETE statements.

Need of Subqueries : Say, we want to display the employees who earn less than the average salary in the organization. Then, a group function AVG must be used to calculate the average salary. **But please remember that the group function cannot be used in the WHERE clause**. In such a case, we need sub-queries. So, I write –

```
SELECT *
  FROM SALARY
WHERE BASIC < (SELECT AVG (BASIC)
  FROM SALARY);
```

However, sub-queries are also used to retrieve data in a join operation with a negativ condition. **For example**, if we want to list the names of employees who do not work in th marketing department, then I may write –

```
SELECT EMP_NO, EMP_NAME
  FROM EMP
WHERE EMP_NO NOT IN
(SELECT EMP_NO FROM SALARY WHERE
        DEPARTMENT = 'MKT');
```

Please note that this query cannot be rewritten as a join as joins should not b negated. Can a subquery return a single value?

Yes, a subquery can return a single value also. **For example,**

```
SELECT * FROM EMP WHERE EMP_NO <
(SELECT EMP_NO FROM SALARY WHERE
        DEDUCTION = 5000);
```

This sub query returns a single value as there is only one row in SALARY where DEDUCTION = Rs 5000/-

What if a subquery returns more than one value?

If the subquery returns more than one value then the IN-operator is used. **For example**, to select names of employees where deduction < 500, we may write

```
SELECT * FROM EMP WHERE EMP_NO IN
(SELECT EMP_NO FROM SALARY WHERE
        DEDUCTION< 500);
```

Example 2. Select the names of employees who are in CSE department, then we can write

```
SELECT EMP_NAME FROM EMP
WHERE EMP_NO    IN
(SELECT EMP_NO FROM SALARY
WHERE DEPARTMENT = 'CSE');
```

Example 3. Select the salary rows where basic is less than the average salary. Then, we can write

```
SELECT * FROM SALARY WHERE BASIC <
(SELECT AVG (BASIC) FROM SALARY);
```

Please note that the group function, AVG, cannot be used in the WHERE clause and hence must be coded as a subquery. So, we need subqueries.

Example 4. Select all the fields of the first table –SALARY and the names of employees from the second table–EMP for those employees who had basic less than the average salary. Now, to write its query we need a join operation.

```
SELECT SALARY. *, EMP_NAME
  FROM SALARY, EMP
WHERE EMP. EMP_NO = SALARY.EMP_NO AND
        BASIC < (SELECT AVG (BASIC) FROM SALARY);
```

EXIST operator is also used many a times to test for existence. It does not match a column or columns. **For example**, to display the names of the employees who belong to CSE department, we can write.

```
SELECT EMP_NAME
  FROM EMP
WHERE EXISTS
(SELECT * FROM SALARY WHERE
        EMP.EMP_NO = SALARY. EMP_NO
    AND DEPARTMENT = 'CSE');
```

We can also use a subquery to insert data. **For example**,

```
CREATE TABLE EMP DUP
AS SELECT * FROM EMP;
```

This query will create a new table EMPDUP which is a copy (duplicate) of the table EMP.

We can also use subqueries to delete rows.

For example, delete rows from EMPDUP (depending on the rows in EMPDUP) where basic < 200.

Then, we can write –

```
DELETE FROM EMPDUP
WHERE BASIC <
(SELECT BASIC FROM EMPDUP WHERE BASIC < 200);
```

Similarly, we can use a **subquery to update data** also. **For example,**

```
UPDATE SALDUP SET (BASIC, COMMISSION) =
(SELECT SUM BASIC), SUM (COMMISSION)
  FROM SALARY WHERE EMP_NO = 1010)
WHERE DEPARTMENT = 'CSE';
```

Please remember that when we use subqueries with UPDATE, we must be certain that the sub-query will return no more than one record for each of the updated records.

3.13 REPORTS USING SQL * PLUS

Formatted Reports can be generated by storing the SQL * Plus commands in a file. The commands are typed in a file using any editor, \. For *e.g.*, Notepad.

To execute the file, we use

SQL > START <filename>;

Various commands that can be used in Report Generation are as follows :

S. No.	Commands Used	Meaning & Purpose of these Commands
1.	Remark	It tells SQL *PLUS that the words to follow are to be treated as comments and not as instructions.
2.	--	It marks the beginning and end of an inline comment within a SQL query. This is similar to remark only.
3.	Ttitle	Sets the top title for each page of a report.
4.	Btitle	Sets the bottom title for each page of a report.
5.	Column	Gives SQL *PLUS a variety of instructions in the heading, format and treatment of a column.
6.	Break on	Tells SQL * PLUS where to put spaces between sections of a report or where to break for subtotals and totals.
7.	Compute sum	Makes SQL * PLUS calculate subtotals.
8.	Set linesize	Sets the maximum number of characters allowed on any line of the report.
9.	Set pagesize	Sets the maximum no. of lines per page.
10.	Set newpage	Sets the no. of blank lines between pages.
11.	Set headsep	The heading separator identifies the single character that tells SQL* PLUS to split a title onto two or more lines.
12	Spool	It moves a report into a file which can be printed later.
13.	Save	It saves the SQL query you have created into the file of your choice.
14.	Host	It sends any commnad to the host O.S.
15.	Start	It tells SQL*PLUS to execute instructions saved in a file.
16.	Edit	Moves you out of SQL*PLUS and into an editor of your choice.
17.	Define_editor	It tells SQL * PLUS the name of the editor of your choice.

For example, the following commands can be used :

SET PAGESIZE 50

Here, default pagesize is 14 *i.e.,* if you will not set your pagesize with the above command then by default, the pagesize taken is 14.

Similarly, we have other commands like

```
SET   LINESIZE     (default is 80)
SET   NULL 'N/S'   (default is BLANK)
SET   SPACE 10     (default is 1)
SET   TERM OFF     (default is ON)
SET   WRAP OFF     (default is ON)
SET   PAUSE ON     (Sets system to pause after each page).
```

We are in a position to write some code to generate reports in SQL*PLUS.

Example 1. Write the set of commands/Program to generate a salary Report in SQL* PLUS.

Solution. Firstly, type EDIT SALREP, to type the commands in the program. Here, SALREP is the filename. EDIT is to invoke the notepad editor to SQL * PLUS.

Next, we write our program—Program to print the salary Report.

```
SET       PAGESIZE 30
SET       LINESIZE 75
TTITLE    CENTER 'SALARY REPORT'
BTITLE    'END OF SALARY REPORT'
COLUMN    EMP_NAME FORMAT A10 TRUNC
COLUMN    "NET SALARY" FORMAT 9,999.000
SELECT    S.EMP_NO, EMP_NAME, BASIC, COMMISSION,
          DEDUCTION, BASIC + COMMISSION –
          DEDUCTION " NET SALARY"
    FROM SALARY S,EMP
    WHERE S. EMP_NO = EMP. EMP_NO;
TTITLE OFF
BTITLE OFF
CLEAR COLUMN
--END OF PROGRAM
```

Now, to execute this file, just type SQL > START SALREP

The output so obtained is

SALARY REPORT

EMP_NO	EMP_NAME	BASIC	COMM	DEDUCT	NETSAL
100	Ajay	1800	100	250	1,650.00
101	Rajat Gupta	2000	200	250	1,950.00
102	Rajiv Gupta	2300	20	200	2,220.00
103	Vijay Chauhan	1500	500	290	1,710.00
104	MC Cabe	2000	200	300	1,900.00

END OF REPORT

5 rows selected.

But if we want to suppress this last message—'5 rows selected' then we use another command *i..e*,

SET FEEDBACK OFF

It is typed at the beginning of the report and SET FEEDBACK ON is typed at the end of the program.

Please note here that by default TTITLE is left aligned and BTITLE is centered.

Example 2. Write an SQL * PLUS program to generate a summary salary Report now.

Solution. We need to save the commands given below in a file, SALSUM.

```
SET      FEEDBACK OFF
SET      PAGESIZE 30
SET      LINESIZE 60
COLUMN   EMP_NO          FORMAT 9999
COLUMN   BASIC           FORMAT 99999.99
COLUMN   COMMISSION      FORMAT 99999.99
COLUMN   DEDUCTION       FORMAT 99999.99
COLUMN   EMP_NAME        FORMAT A15 TRUNC
COLUMN   EMP_NO          HEADING "EMPLOYEE ¦ NUMBER"
COLUMN   EMP_NAME        HEADING "EMPLOYEE ¦ NAME"
COLUMN   BASIC           HEADING "TOTAL ¦ BASIC"
COLUMN   COMMISSION      HEADING "TOTAL ¦ COMMISSION"
COLUMN   DEDUCTION       HEADING "TOTAL ¦ DEDUCTION"
TTITLE   CENTER 'SALARY REPORT' SKIP 1- RIGHT 'PAGE' FORMAT 99
         SQL. PNO SKIP 2.
SELECT   S. EMP_NO, INITCAP (EMP_NAME)
         "EMP_NAME', SUM (BASIC) "BASIC",
         SUM (COMMISSION) "COMMISSION",
         SUM (DEDUCTION) "DEDUCTION"
         FROM SALARY S, EMP
         WHERE S.EMP_NO=EMP.EMP_NO
         GROUP BY S.EMP_NO, EMP_NAME;
CLEAR    COLUMN
TTITLE   OFF
SET      FEEDBACK ON
         END
```

Now, to execute this program, just type –

SQL > START SALSUM

The output so obtained is as follows –

SALARY REPORT

PAGE 1

EMPLOYEE NUMBER	EMPLOYEE NAME	TOTAL BASIC	TOTAL COMMISSION	TOTAL DEDUCTION
100	Ajay Gupta	6000.00	500.00	500.00
101	Rajiv Gupta	5000.00	550.00	420.00
102	Yogesh Sharma	6000.00	1000.00	300.00

3.14 PL/SQL

PL/SQL is Oracle's procedural language (PL), superset of structural Query language (SQL). We can use PL/SQL to codify our business rules through the creation of stored procedures and packages, to trigger database events to occur, or to add programming logic to the execution of SQL commands. PL/SQL code is grouped into structures called **blocks**.

In a PL/SQL program, there is an exception handling section. It provides customized handling of error conditions. When the PL/SQL block encounters an error, the control of PL/SQL block shifts to the exception handling section. PL/SQL provides a set of system-defined exceptions. Also, you can add your own exceptions.

Please note that if we use a SELECT statement in a PL/SQL program, then only one row can be retrieved. Also note that in oracle, cursors are used to retrieve an arbitrary number of rows with a SELECT statement.

PL/SQL supports the use of subprograms named procedures and functions. A PL/SQL procedure performs some action and accepts optional parameters. On the other hand, a PL/SQL function returns a value of some specified datatype.

What is PL/SQL?

PL/SQL is a procedural language for the oracle server and its clients. It provides for variable definition, assignment, selection and looping constructs for programming.

When we write a PL/SQL program, SQL statements are used for data manipulation and transaction processing. PL/SQL is a block structured language. A PL/SQL block is made up of three parts.

(*a*) Declaration part

(*b*) Executable part.

(*c*) Exception handling part.

That is,

DECLARE PART	—	Where all declarations of variables and constants is done.
BEGIN PART	—	Here, PL/SQL statements and DML statements are used.
EXCEPTION	—	Statements to be executed in case of errors.
END;		
/		

Please note here that we terminate the PL/SQL block with a / on a line and press the Enter key. Also note that SQL * PLUS commands may be added but outside the PL/SQL block.

> **NOTE :** PL/SQL block can be created using any editor like NOTEPAD.

We are in a position to solve a problem.

Example 1. Write a PL/SQL code to retrieve the employee name, join-basic, and designation of an employee whose number is input by the user.

Solution. Firstly, at the SQL prompt, type ED EMP to open the NOTEPAD editor. Now, type the following program.

– – PL/SQL code to display the name, basic, designation of employee

```
SET       SERVER OUTPUT ON
PROMPT    Enter the employee number
ACCEPT    N
DECLARE
DNAME     EMP. EMP_NAME % TYPE;
DBASIC    EMP. JOIN_BASIC % TYPE ;
DDESIG    EMP. DESIG% TYPE;
BEGIN
SELECT    EMP_NAME, JOIN_BASIC, DESIG
INTO      DNAME, DBASIC, DDESIG
FROM      EMP
WHERE     EMP_NO = & N;
DBMS_OUTPUT. PUT_LINE ('NAME:' ¦¦ DNAME);
DBMS_OUTPUT. PUT_LINE ('Salary:' ¦¦ DBASIC);
DBMS_OUTPUT. PUT_LINE ('Designation:' ¦¦ DDESIG);
END;
/
SET SERVEROUTPUT OFF
```

Save this file. Close the editor. At SQL prompt, we execute this program now

SQL > START EMP

or

SQL > @ EMP

This code will be executed if there are no errors in the program. If an error is found then we switch back to Notepad, correct the errors and save the file and execute again.

What is DBMS_OUTPUT. PUT_LINE for?

To output data from a PL/SQL block, we make use of procedure named, PUT_LINE which is part of a system package called, DBMS_OUTPUT. **Please note that to use this procedure, we must also use another option**, SET SERVEROUPUT ON.

CONSTRUCTS of PL/SQL

1. IF-command : The IF command is used for selection or decision. It can be used in various forms :

(*a*) If <condition > THEN
```
< action> (Statements)
END IF;
```

(*b*) IF < condition > THEN
```
<action>
ELSE
< action>
END IF;
```

(*c*) IF < condition> THEN
```
<action>
ELSIF < condition> THEN
```

```
<action>
ELSIF
(condition> THEN
< action >
END IF;
```

Please note that END IF can be written as one word also, *i.e.,* ELSIF.

2. For-loop : It is used to repeatedly execute a set of statements for a certain number of times specified by a starting number and an ending number. A variable is defined which starts from the starting number and increments itself for every iteration of the loop and exits when the ending number has been exceeded.

Syntax of FOR-loop :

```
FOR <var> IN <STARTNUM> .. <ENDNUM> Loop
<Statements>
END LOOP;
```

Example. FOR *i* in 1.. 10 LOOP

```
        .............
        ............,
    END LOOP;
```

Can we run a FOR-loop in reverse direction also ?

Yes, we can. It's syntax is –

```
FOR <var> IN REVERSE < STARTNUM>...<ENDNUM > Loop
<Statements>
END LOOP;
```

CASE Function

Syntax : CASE expression

```
CASE expression     WHEN expr1 THEN result1
                    WHEN expr2 THEN result 2
                         |
                         |
                    When exprN THEN RESULTN
        END         ELSE default
```

Example :

```
SELECT EID,   CASE job
              WHEN  'Analyst' THEN Salary  + 10000
              WHEN 'Manager' THEN Salary + 20000
              ELSE Salary
              END
      FROM Emp;
```

We are in a position to solve some problems now.

Example 1. ***Write a PL/SQL program to display the value of the index of the FOR–LOOP?***

Solution.

```
SET SERVEROUTPUT ON
BEGIN
DBMS_OUTPUT. PUT_LINE ('FOR_loop demo')
```

```
FOR i IN 1. .5 LOOP
    DBMS_OUTPUT. PUT_LINE ('Index' ¦¦i);
END LOOP;
END;
/
SET SERVEROUTPUT OFF
```

Example 2. ***Write a PL/SQL code to show the changing of the loop increment.***

Solution.

```
SET SERVEROUTPUT ON
BEGIN
FOR I IN 1. .6 LOOP
    IF MOD (I, 2) = 0 THEN
DBMS_OUTPUT. PUT_LINE (; 'LOOP COUNTER IS :' ¦¦ I);
END IF;
END LOOP;
END ;
/
```

Example 3. ***Write a PL/SQL code to run a FOR loop in reverse.***

Solution.

```
SET SERVEROUTPUT ON
    BEGIN
        DBMS_OUTPUT. PUT_LINE ('FOR-loop: ...')
    FOR I IN REVERSE 1. .10 LOOP
        DBMS_OUTPUT. PUT_LINE ('LOOPINDEX' ¦¦I);
END LOOP;
END;
/
SET SERVEROUTPUT OFF.
```

3. LOOP Structure : The Loop structure is used to execute certain statements repeatedly. **Please note that the syntax of this loop structure is such that there is no exit from the loop**. So, we add an EXIT statement also. It's syntax is as follows :

```
LOOP
<Statements>
END LOOP;
```

We are in a position to solve an example now.

Example 1. ***Write a PL/SQL program to show the working of the LOOP Structure.***

Solution. To show working of LOOP structure

```
SET SERVEROUTPUT ON
DECLARE
    CTR NUMBER (2): = 0;
BEGIN
DBMS_OUTPUT. PUT_LINE ('The loop starts here ...');
LOOP
```

```
        CTR : = CTR + 1;
        EXIT WHEN CTR > 10;
        DBMS_OUTPUT. PUT_LINE ('LOOP INDEX:' ¦¦CTR);
    END LOOP,
    END;
    /
    SET SERVEROUTPUT OFF
```

4. WHILE Loop : In while-loop of PL/SQL, the condition is checked at the beginning. It's **syntax** is

```
    WHILE <Condition> LOOP
            <Statements>
    END LOOP;
```

Before we go further, let us solve an example.

Example 1. *Write a PL/SQL code to show the working of a while loop.*

Solution.

```
    SET SERVEROUTPUT ON
    DECLARE
        CTR NUMBER (2) : = 1;
    BEGIN
    DBMS_OUTPUT. PUT_LINE ('The while-loop starts here ...');
    WHILE CTR <= 8 LOOP
        DBMS_OUTPUT. PUT_LINE('LOOP INDEX:' ¦¦TO_CHAR (CTR,'999');
            CTR := CTR + 1;
    END LOOP,
    END;
    /
    SET SERVEROUTPUT OFF
```

PL/SQL TABLES : We define PL/SQL tables as the objects of type TABLE. They are modeled on database tables. **Please note that these PL/SQL tables use a primary key to give you array-like access to rows. Also note that the size of a PL/SQL table is unconstrained *i.e.,* the number of rows in a PL/SQL table can increase dynamically**, PL/SQL tables can have one column and a primary key, neither of which can be named. The column can belong to any scalar type but the primary key must be of the BINARY_INTEGER type.

How to declare these PL/SQL tables?

Declaration of PL/SQL tables is done in two steps :

Step 1. Define a TABLE type.

Step 2. Declare PL/SQL tables of that type.

We can declare it in the declarative part of any block, subprogram or package using the following **syntax**.

```
    TYPE type_name IS TABLE OF
        {column_type ¦ variable % TYPE ¦table. column % TYPE [NOT NULL]
    INDEX BY BINARY_INTEGER;
```

Where 'type_name' is a type specifier used in subsequent declarations of PL/SQL tables 'Column_type' is any scalar datatype such as CHAR, DATE or NUMBER.

We can use the % TYPE attribute to specify a column datatype.

We are in a position to solve an example now.

Example 1. *Write a PL/SQL code to show TABLE type of data* **(***Array***).**

Solution.

```
SET SERVEROUTPUT ON
DECLARE
TYPE NAME_TABLE IS TABLE OF
    EMP. EMP_NAME % TYPE
INDEX BY BINARY_INTEGER;
TYPE JBASIC_TABLE IS TABLE OF
    EMP.JOIN_BASIC% TYPE
INDEX BY BINARY_INTEGER;
D_NAME NAME_TABLE;
_ _ D_NAME is table type.
R BINARY_INTEGER := 0;
D-JBASIC JBASIC-TABLE;
BEGIN
FOR EMPREC IN (SELECT * FROM EMP) LOOP
    R : = R + 1;
    D_NAME (R) : = EMPREC. EMP_NAME;
    D_JBASIC (R) : = EMPREC. JOIN_BASIC;
END LOOP;
FOR I IN 1...R LOOP
    DBMS_OUTPUT. PUT_LINE ('NAME:' ¦¦ D_NAME (I));
    DBMS_OUTPUT. PUT_LINE ('SALARY:' ¦¦ D_JBASIC (I));
    DBMS_OUTPUT. PUT_LINE ('- - - - -- - - - - );
END LOOP;
        DBMS_OUTPUT. PUT LINE ('TOTAL EMPLOYEES:' ¦¦ R);
END;
```

Please note that we cannot reference. PL/SQL tables in the INTO clause. For example, the following SELECT statement is illegal.

```
SELECT ENAME. JOIN_BASIC
INTO D_NAME, D_JBASIC
FROM EMP;
```

Also note that you cannot simply delete individual rows from a PL/SQL table because the DELETE statement cannot specify PL/SQL tables. Then how to delete ? When we want to delete a PL/SQL table, we assign a NULL to it.

For example, D_NAMES: = NULL;
where D_NAMES is a table of names.

Exceptions Handling : Exceptions are the error conditions. Errors may be user-defined or system exceptions which are automatically raised by PL/SQL.

Let us now discuss some system exceptions and understand their meanings.

S. No.	Exceptions	Meanings
1.	DUP_VAL_ON_INDEX	When a user tries to insert a duplicate value into a unique column.
2.	LOGIN_DENIED	When the user's request for the connection has been denied.
3.	NO_DATA_FOUND	This flag becomes TRUE when SQL's SELECT fails to retrieve any rows.

4.	PROGRAM_ERROR	When a user hits a PL/SQL internal error.
5.	STORAGE_ERROR	When a user hits a PL/SQL memory error.
6.	TOO_MANY_ROWS	This flag becomes TRUE when SQL's select statement retrieves more than one row and it was supposed to retrieve only one row.
7.	VALUE_ERROR	When user encounters an arithematic, conversion, truncation or constraint error.
8.	ZERO_DIVIDE	This flag becomes TRUE when SQL select statement tries to divide a number by zero.
9.	OTHERS	This flag is used to catch any error situations not coded by the programmer in the EXCEPTION section. So, it must appear last in the EXCEPTION section.

We are in a position to solve some examples now.

Example 1. ***Write a PL/SQL code to insert rows into a new table.***

Solution. We follow certain steps and conventions here.

Step 1. Create a new table-NEWEMP

Step 2. Read the record from the old table say EMP and move them to some variables defined by you.

Step 3. Move the data in these variables into the NEWEMP table now.

To follow these steps, open any editor and type the following code :

```
—Program to insert rows into a new table.
    PROMPT ENTER EMPLOYEE NUMBER:
    ACCEPT USER NO NUMBER
    DECLARE
        DNO NUMBER (4);
        DNAME VARCHAR 2 (30);
        DDATE DATE;
    BEGIN
        SELECT EMP_NO, EMP_NAME, JOIN_DATE
        INTO D NO, DNAME, DDATE
        FROM EMP WHERE EMP_NO = & USER NO;
    IF SQL % ROW COUNT > 0 THEN
        INSERT INTO NEWEMP VALUES (D NO, DNAME, DDATE);
    END IF;
    END;
    /
```

Save this file and execute. **Please note here that the statement SQL%ROW COUNT returns the number of rows retrieved after an insert, update, delete or a single row select statement.**

If, say, we want to modify the above code to handle error conditions like the user entering a number which does not exist in the EMP table. Then, we write another set of statements to handle exceptions. –

```
    EXCEPTION
    WHEN NO_DATA_FOUND THEN
        DBMS_OUTPUT PUT_LINE
        ('RECORDS' ¦ ¦ & USERNO ¦ ¦ 'DOES NOT EXIST');
```

Example 2. *Write a PL/SQL code to calculate tax for an employee of an organization–XYZ and to display his/her name and tax.*

Solution. PL/SQL code for tax calculation

```
SET SERVEROUTPUT ON
DECLARE
TOT_BASIC NUMBER (10, 2);
TAX NUMBER (10,2);
NAME VARCHAR 2 (30);
BEGIN
SELECT EMP_NAME, SUM (BASIC)
INTO NAME, TOT_BASIC
FROM SALARY, EMP
WHERE SALARY. EMP_NO = EMP.EMP_NO
    AND SALARY. EMP_NO = 1104
GROUP BY EMP_NAME;
IF TOT_BASIC = 0 OR TOT_BASIC IS NULL THEN
    DBMS_OUTPUT. PUT_LINE ('NO BASIC');
    ELSIF TOT_BASIC < = 3000 THEN
        TAX: = TOT_BASIC * 0.02;
    DBMS_OUTPUT. PUT_LINE (NAME ¦ ¦ 'TOTAL BASIC': ¦ ¦ TOT_BASIC);
    DBMS_OUTPUT. PUT_LINE (NAME ¦ ¦ 'TOTAL TAX': ¦ ¦ TAX);
ELSE
    TAX : = TOT_BASIC * 0.04;
    DBMS_OUTPUT. PUT_LINE (NAME ¦ ¦ 'TOTAL BASIC:' ¦ ¦ TOT_BASIC);
    DBMS_OUTPUT. PUT_LINE (NAME ¦ ¦ 'TOTAL TAX:' ¦ ¦ TAX);
END IF ;
END;
/
SET SERVEROUTPUT OFF
```

CURSORS in PL/SQL : When the SQL's select statement is expected to return **more than one row** then cursors are used. **Cursor is a buffer which will store the results of the recent query**. We must declare a cursor and its definition contains the query. CURSOR is defined in the DECLARE section of the program. A cursor must be opened before processing and closed after processing. It's **syntax** is –

```
CURSOR <CURSOR_NAME>
IS <SELECT statement >
```

To open the cursor, the **syntax** is –

```
OPEN < CURSOR_NAME>
```

To store data in the cursor, the **syntax** is –

```
FETCH < CURSOR _NAME > INTO < VAR1 >,<VAR2> ...
```

OR

```
FETCH< CURSOR_NAME> INTO <RECORD_NAME>
```

We must close the cursor also. It's **syntax** is –

```
CLOSE <CURSOR_NAME>
```

Cursor have four attributes that provide information on the status of a cursor.

They are as follows :

S. No.	Exceptions	Meanings
1.	%NOT FOUND	Is used to determine if a row was retrieved. Is used after FETCH. NOT FOUND is TRUE if a row was not retrieved and is FALSE if a row was retrieved.
2.	% FOUND	Is used to determine if a row was retrieved. Used after FETCH.
3.	% ROW COUNT	ROW COUNT is zero when the cursor is opened. It returns the number of rows retrieved.
4.	% IS OPEN	Is used to determine if a cursor is open. IS OPEN is TRUE if a cursor is open else it is FALSE.

We are in a position to solve some example now.

Example 1. ***Write a PL/SQL code to calculate the total and the percentage of marks of the students in four subjects from the table–STUDENT with the schema given below.***

STUDENT (RNO,S1, S2, S3, S4, total, percentage)

The roll numbers and the marks in each subject are stored in the database. Also update your database.

Solution. —PL/SQL code using CURSORS

```
DECLARE
    T NUMBER;
    PER NUMBER;
    CURSOR C1 IS
    SELECT * FROM STUDENT;
    REC C1 % ROWTYPE;
BEGIN
    OPEN C1;
    LOOP
        FETCH C1 INTO REC;
        EXIT WHEN C1% NOT FOUND;
        T: = REC. S1 + REC. S2 + REC. S3 + REC . S4;
        PER : = T/4;
        UPDATE STUDENT
        SET TOTAL = T, PERCENTAGE = PER
        WHERE RNO = REC. RNO;
    END LOOP;
    CLOSE C1;
    END;
```

Example 2. ***Write a PL/SQL code to display employee number, name and basic of 5 highest paid employees.***

Solution.

```
SET SERVEROUTPUT ON
DECLARE
ENO SALARY. EMP_NO% TYPE;
ENAME EMP.EMP_NAME % TYPE;
```

```
EBASIC SALARY. BASIC % TYPE;
CURSOR CUR_SAL IS
SELECT DISTINCT SALARY. EMP_NO,
EMP. EMP_NAME, BASIC
FROM SALARY, EMP
WHERE SALARY. EMP_NO = EMP. EMP_NO
ORDER BY BASIC DESC;
BEGIN
OPEN CUR_SAL;
LOOP
    FETCH CUR_SAL INTO ENO, ENAME, EBASIC;
    EXIT WHEN CUR-SAL% NOT FOUND;
    EXIT WHEN (CUR_SAL%ROW COUNT > 5);
        DBMS_OUTPUT. PUT_LINE (ENO) ¦¦' '¦¦ ENAME ¦¦' '¦¦ EBASIC);
    END LOOP;
CLOSE CUR_SAL;
END;
/
```

Deletion/Updation using CURSORS : To delete or update rows, the cursor must be defined with the FOR UPDATE clause. Say, we want to delete records from the table SALARY where BASIC > 10,000. Then, we may write the PL/SQL code as follows :

```
DECLARE
    REC_SAL SALARY% ROW TYPE;
    CURSOR CUR_SAL IS
    SELECT * FROM SALARY
    WHERE BASIC > 10000 FOR UPDATE;
BEGIN
    OPEN CUR_SAL;
    LOOP
        FETCH CUR_SAL INTO REC_SAL;
        EXIT WHEN CUR_SAL%NOT FOUND;
        DELETE FROM SALARY
        WHERE CURRENT  OF CUR_SAL;
    END LOOP;
CLOSE CUR_SAL;
END;
/
```

NOTE : To update the table, we replace the delete statement with update in the above code, *i.e.*,

```
UPDATE SALARY
    SET BASIC = 10000 WHERE CURRENT OF CUR_SAL;
```

Please note that the FOR UPDATE must be used in the CURSOR declaration as CURRENT OF clause is used in the procedure. The FOR UPDATE statement will lock the rows of that table so that another user cannot change the row before the update. Unless the application locks all the rows on the cursor's return set, when the cursor is opened, there is a chance that another transaction will lock one of the rows of the cursor's return set. Then this application has to wait until the other transaction completes and releases the lock so that this application can update.

Also note that when multiple tables are used in the SELECT statement of the CURSOR then we can lock only one table which contains the column to be updated. This is done as follows.

```
Cursor CUR_SAL is SELECT ....
....... FOR UPDATE OF BASIC;
```

i.e., FOR UPDATE OF <column name> can be used.

FOR_loop in CURSORS : The cursor FOR_loop can be used to process multiple records. The advantage of this loop is that it will itself open the cursor, read records into the cursor from the table until end of file and close the cursor.

Syntax is –

```
FOR <variable> IN < CURSOR_NAME> LOOP
<Statement>
END LOOP;
```

Please note here that the variable used in the cursor FOR loop is not declared as it is automatically created.

We can even have **parameterized cursors**. Parameters allow values to be passed to a cursor when it is opened and used within a query when it executes. The parameters can be either a constant or a variable. It's **syntax** is as follows :

```
CURSOR cursor_name (variable_name datatype) IS <SELECT statement....>
```

To open a parameterized cursor and passing values to the cursor:

```
OPEN cursor_name (value/variable/expression);
```

Please note that the scope of cursor parameters is local to that cursor. It means that they can be referenced only within the query declared in the cursor declaration. Also note that each parameter in the declaration must have a corresponding value in the open statement.

We are in a position to solve some problems now.

Example 1. ***Write a PL/SQL code to calculate the total salary of first n records of emp table. The value of n is passed to cursor as parameter.***

Solution.

```
DECLARE
    E NUMBER (5);
    S NUMBER (5): = 0;
    CURSOR C1 (N NUMBER) IS
    SELECT SAL FROM EMP
    WHERE ROWNUM < = N;
BEGIN
    OPEN C1 (&N);
    LOOP
```

```
        FETCH C1 INTO E;
        EXIT WHEN C1% NOTFOUND;
        S : = S+ E;
    END LOOP;
    DBMS_OUTPUT. PUT_LINE (S);
    CLOSE C1;
END;
```

Example 2. ***Write a PL/SQL code to update the salary of employees who earn less than the average salary.***

Solution.

```
    DECLARE
        AVG_SAL NUMBER (8, 2);
        CURSOR CUR_AVG IS
            SELECT * FROM SALARY
            FOR UPDATE;
        BEGIN
            SELECT AVG (BASIC) INTO AVG_SAL
            FROM SALARY;
            FOR REC_AVG IN CUR_AVG LOOP
    IF REC_AVG. BASIC< AVG-SAL THEN
        REC_AVG. BASIC: = AVG_SAL;
        UPDATE SALARY SET BASIC = REC_AVG. BASIC
        WHERE CURRENT OF CUR_AVG;
        DBMS_OUTPUT. PUT_LINE (REC_AVG. EMP_NO ¦¦' UPDATED');
    END IF ;
        END LOOP;
    END;
    /
```

TRIGGERS in PL/SQL : A trigger consists of PL/SQL code which defines some action that the database should take when some database-related event occurs. Triggers are executed when a data manipulation command (DML) is performed on a table for which the trigger has been written.

Please note that triggers are executed automatically and are transparent to the user. Also note that in order to create a trigger, the user must have the CREATE TRIGGER privilege. This privilege is the part of the RESOURCE role.

Triggers are required

(*a*) To enforce rules that cannot be coded through referential integrity.
(*b*) To enforce certain business rules (validation) in an application.
(*c*) To maintain an audit of changes made to data.
(*d*) To derive column values.

Syntax to create trigger

```
Create [or replace] trigger < trigger name >
    [before/after]
    [delete/insert/update] [of column]
```

```
on [user]. table
[for each row]
[when condition ]
[PL/SQL block].
```

Explanation : Here, if 'before' is used then trigger fires before the DML else if 'after' is used then trigger fires after the DML.

Triggering event is like DELETE, UPDATE or INSERT issued against the table.

Trigger type : FOR EACH ROW option creates a trigger which will be fired once for each row that is updated. Such a trigger is called as a **row-level trigger**. If the clause FOR EACH ROW is not coded then the trigger is executed once for that statement. This is called as a **statement level trigger**.

When condition : We can even specify a condition apart from the triggering event. This condition is specified with the use of the *WHEN clause*. When the FOR EACH ROW clause is used, the trigger will be a **row-level trigger**, otherwise it will be a **statement-level trigger**. WHEN clause is used to further restrict when the trigger is executed. The restrictions enforced in the WHEN clause may include checks of old and new data values. The WHEN clause adds further criteria to the triggering condition.

Please note the following points and remember them

1. Triggers are associated with a table and are automatically fired when the user performs any DML like insert, update or delete on the table.
2. There can be many triggers for one table.
3. There can be only one trigger of a particular type *i.e.,* update, insert or delete.
4. Only one table can be specified in the triggering statement.
5. Triggers cannot include COMMIT, ROLLBACK and SAVEPOINT.
6. Trigger code can be typed at SQL * Plus command live or any editor like Notepad.
7. Inside the triggers, the correlation names, : new and : old can be made use of , to refer to data on the command line and data in the table respectively.

We are in a position to solve some examples now.

Example 1. ***Write a row trigger to insert the existing values of the salary table into a new table when the salary table is updated.***

Solution. We follow certain steps when we create triggers. The steps to be followed are :

Open the editor and type the code given below in a file (say, RAJTR)

```
Create trigger UPDSAL
before update on salary
for each row
begin
insert into salaryaud values
    (: old. emp_no, : old. basic,
    : old. commission, : old. deduction,
    : old. salary_date, : old. department);
end;
/
```

Now, save the file. To execute this file, just type –

SQL > START RAJTR

'Trigger created' is displayed. Thus, we have created a trigger that is stored in the database and is available for execution. The name of the trigger is UPDSAL.

How to execute trigger?

Once a trigger is created, it is associated with the table on which it is created. This trigger will be executed when the user executes an UPDATE statement on the table. Create the table, SALARYAUD into which data must be inserted when the trigger is fired.

For example, a trigger named, UPDSAL has been created and it is associated with the table–SALARY. This will be executed when the user types the following :

```
SQL > UPDATE SALARY
      SET BASIC = 10000
      WHERE ENO = '1A2B';
```

Now, data will be updated in SALARY and the old data will be added to the table, SALARYAUD. This can be viewed by executing the SELECT statement.

SQL > SELECT * FROM SALARYAUD;

How to modify a trigger?

If a trigger has to be modified, change the CREATE TRIGGER header to, CREATE OR REPLACE trigger updsal.

Since the same trigger is replaced, the privileges granted to the original trigger is retained. What we do is, in the NOTEPAD, open the file containing the commands to create the trigger and make the changes. Save the file. Return to SQL * Plus and execute the file. The new trigger will replace the old trigger in the database.

How to Drop the trigger?

The trigger can be removed by using the drop statement, as given below :

SQL > DROP TRIGGER UPDSAL;

Once a trigger is dropped, the trigger must be created again to use it again,

SQL > START RAJTR;

How to disable the trigger ?

A trigger can be disabled during a large data load by executing the command –

ALTER TRIGGER UPDSAL DISABLE;

We can also use an ALTER table statement to disable the trigger –

```
ALTER TABLE SALARY
DISABLE ALL TRIGGERS;
```

How to enable the trigger?

The trigger can be made operational again by using the command,

ALTER TRIGGER UPDSAL ENABLE;

We can also use an ALTER table statement to enable the trigger –

ALTER TABLE SALARY ENABLE ALL TRIGGERS ;

Trigger for Multiple Operations : The trigger can be written to handle multiple situations like UPDATE, INSERT or DELETE and to enable the trigger to be fired for each situation by making use of three conditional predicates-Inserting, updating or deleting.

Please note, however that two triggers for the same event cannot be created for a table.

What are the correlation names?

Within the body of a row trigger, the old and new column values of the current row can be accessed using the correlation names OLD and NEW.

For example, old.desig and : new.desig

Please remember the following points :

1. During updation, both 'old' and'new' are available.
2. During insert only 'new' has meaning.
3. The : new and : old cannot be used with long and long row data type columns.

We are in a position to solve some example now.

Example 1. ***Write a trigger on the emp table which shows the old values and new value of ename after any updation on ename of emp table.***

Solution.

```
CREATE OR REPLACE TRIGGER EMP_UPDATE
AFTER UPDATE OF ENAME ON EMP FOR EACH ROW
BEGIN
    DBMS_OUTPUT.PUT_LINE ('OLD NAME:' ¦¦: OLD. ENAME);
    DBMS_OUTPUT.PUT_LINE ('NEW NAME:' ¦¦: NEW. ENAME);
END;
```

Example 2. ***Write a code to create a trigger so that no operation can be performed on emp table on Tuesday.***

Solution. The oracle engine provides a procedure named as raise_application_error that allows programmers to issue user_defined error messages. It's *syntax* is –

```
RAISE_APPLICATION_ERROR (error_number, message);
```

Where, error_number : is a –ve integer in the range –20000 to – 20999 and 'message' is a character string upto 2048 bytes in length.

So, we write a trigger now.

```
CREATE OR REPLACE TRIGGER EMP_TUE
BEFORE INSERT OR UPDATE OR DELETE ON EMP
BEGIN
    IF RTRIM (UPPER (TO_CHAR (SYSDATE,' DAY'))
        = 'TUESDAY' THEN
    RAISE_APPLICATION_ERROR
            (–20101, 'Cannot use table on Tuesday');
END IF;
END;
```

Please note that the procedure RAISE_APPLICATION_ERROR, terminates procedure execution, rolls back any effects of the procedure and returns a user specified error number and message.

Also note here that the procedure

(*a*) to_char (sysdate, 'DAY') will return the day in upper case.

(*b*) to_char (sysdate, 'Day') will return the day in lower case.

(*c*) to_char (sysdate, 'Day') will return the day in proper case.

Procedures and Functions in PL/SQL : Groups of SQL and PL/SQL statements can be stored in the database. The code stored once in the database can be used by multiple applications. Since the code is in the database (*i.e.,* in server), so processing is faster. Both procedures and functions are also referred to as subprograms because they can take parameters and can be invoked.

Actually, there are three types of procedural objects :

(*a*) Procedures

(*b*) Functions.

(*c*) Packages

Procedures are the subprograms which will perform an action.

Functions are subprograms that are generally coded to compute some value.

Please understand that the clients execute the procedure or function and the processing is done in the server. So, the network traffic is reduced to the procedure or function call. **Also note that the stored procedures are callable subprograms** *which are* compiled and stored permanently in a oracle database or a tool like oracle's FORMS.

To **execute** a procedure, we write :

SQL > EXECUTE < procedure_name>;

To **pass** parameter for execution, we write –

SQL > EXECUTE < procedure name > (parameter);

Can we execute a procedure from a trigger also?

Yes, we can. To execute the procedure named as RAJ by passing a parameter *i.e.,*

RAJ (: NEW. BASIC);

Parameter Passing in Procedures : Communication is passed to a procedure through a parameter and communication is passed out of a procedure through a parameter. When we call a procedure, the parameters passed, also known as **actual parameters**, can be **positional or named notation. For example**, in this procedure given below.

BONUS (PERIOD NUMBER, AMOUNT NUMBER)

Then, it's positional notation will be

BONUS (PRD, AMT);

And it's named notation will be

BONUS (AMOUNT ⇒ AMT, PERIOD ⇒ PRD);

The parameters, depending on its use, can be declared to be IN, OUT or IN OUT.

The **IN parameter** is used to pass values to the procedure being called. It behaves like a **constant** inside the procedure.

The **OUT parameter** is used to pass values out of a procedure to the caller of the procedure. It behaves like a **uninitialised variable** inside the procedure.

The IN OUT parameter is used to pass values to the procedure being called and it is also used to pass values out to the caller of the procedure. This parameter behaves like a **regular variable** inside the procedure.

We are in a position to write some procedures now.

Example 1. ***Write a PL/SQL procedure to calculate the sales made to a particular customer. The customer_id in the transaction file must be selected, the quantity sold must be multiplied by the price which is in the ITEM master. This value must be accumulated for all records of that customer in the transaction file.***

Solution. In the Notepad editor, type the code given below.

```
CREATE OR REPLACE PROCEDURE TOTSALES
(CID IN CSTMAST. CSTID%TYPE, SAL OUT NUMBER)
IS
ID TRN. ITMID%TYPE;
QTY TRN.TRNQTY%TYPE;
PRICE ITMMAST. ITMPRICE% TYPE;
SALES NUMBER (10,2) : = 0;
CURSOR CUR-TR IS
SELECT TRN. ITMID, TRNQTY, ITMPRICE
FROM TRN, ITMMAST
    WHERE TRN. CSTID = CID AND
        TRN. ITMID = ITMMAST.ITMID;
BEGIN
OPEN CUR_TR;
LOOP
    FETCH CUR_TR INTO ID, QTY, PRICE;
    IF CUR_TR% ROWCOUNT = 0 THEN RAISE_APPLICATION_ERROR
        (-20020, 'There is no data');
    END IF;
    EXIT WHEN CUR_TR% NOT FOUND;
    SALES : = SALES + QTY * PRICE;
END LOOP;
CLOSE CUR_TR;
SAL:= SALES;
END TOTSALES;
/
```

Save the file, say as RAJ. SQL Return to SQL * PLUS and execute it –

```
SQL> START RAJ;
```

OUTPUT : Either the message 'Procedure created' is displayed or the compilation error message is displayed. If an error message is received then type –

```
SQL > SHOW ERRORS.
```

This will display the line number and error of the most recent compilation errors. At the SQL prompt, type show errors and the lines at which errors were detected is displayed.

How to execute the procedure?

```
SQL > VARIABLE SL NUMBER
SQL > EXECUTE TOTSALES (2009,: SL)
SQL > PRINT SL.
```

Here, 2009 is the customer_id.

Example 2. ***Write a procedure to increase the salary of all employees who work in the department given by the procedure as parameter. Also, the percentage of the salary increase is given as a second parameter.***

Solution.

```
Create procedure raise_salary (dno number, percentage number
        DEFAULT 2.2)
is
    cursor emp_cur (dept_no number) is
        select SAL from EMP
        where DEPTNO = dept_no
        for update of SAL;
    empsal number (10);
begin
    open emp-cur (dno); --- Assign dno to dept_no
    loop
    fetch emp-cur into empsal;
    exit when emp-cur% NOT FOUND;
    update EMP set SAL = empsal * (( 100 + percentage)100)
    Where current of emp-cur;
end loop;
close emp_cur;
commit;
end raise_salary;
```

To call the procedure from SQL* PLUS, we type –

```
execute raise_salary (8, 2);
```

If the 2nd parameter is not specified then it will be taken by default as 2.2.

To call the procedure from a PL/SQL block, the keyword execute is omitted.

Example 3. ***Write a stored procedure del_employee to delete an employee on the basis of the employee number. Also, write a code to call this procedure.***

Solution.

```
CREATE PROCEDURE del_employee (emp_id Number) AS
BEGIN
    DELETE FROM emp
    WHERE emp no = emp_id;
END;
DECLARE—calling procedure
e number;
BEGIN
    e := & emp no;
    del_employee (e) ;
END;
```

Functions in PL/SQL : Functions can return a single value to the caller.They do not allow the OUT, IN OUT arguments. The value is returned using the RETURN keyword within the function. Actually, a function is a subprogram that computes a value. **Please note that we cannot impose the NOT NULL constraint on a parameter and we cannot specify a constraint on the datatype.**

The RETURN statement has 2 forms –

(*a*) return datatype.

(*b*) return.

The first option specifies the datatype of the result value. The second option, the RETURN statement immediately completes the execution of a subprogram and returns control to the caller. **Please note that a subprogram can contain several RETURN statements**. Executing any of them completes the subprogram, immediately in procedures a return statement cannot contain an expression but in functions, a return statement must contain an expression, which is evaluated when the RETURN statement is executed. Let us tabulate the differences between a procedure and Function now.

S. No.	Procedure	Function
1.	A Procedure is a subprogram that can accept parameters, perform an action and return parameters.	A Function is a subprogram that can accept parameters, compute a value and return that value to caller.
2.	A procedure may return no value.	A function must return only one value.
3.	A procedure cannot return a value.	A function can return a value.
4.	We use procedures to perform an action.	We use a function to compute a value.

Inspite of these differences, both have some similarities too. Both have a declarative part, an executable part and an exception-handling part. **We are in a position to solve some examples now.**

Example 1. ***Write a PL/SQL function to return the square of a given number.***

Solution.

```
CREATE OR REPLACE FUNCTION SQR (N NUMBER)
RETURN NUMBER
IS
BEGIN
    RETURN N*N;
END;
/
```

RUN : In the editor, type the following :

```
SET SERVEROUTPUT ON
    BEGIN
        DBMS_OUTPUT. PUT_LINE ('5 Square is' ¦ ¦ SQR (5));
    END;
/
SET SERVEROUTPUT OFF
```

Example 2. ***Create a stored function that accepts two numbers and returns the addition of passed values. Also, write the code to call your function.***

Solution.

```
CREATE OR REPLACE FUNCTION ADDN (A IN NUMBER, B IN NUMBER)
    RETURN NUMBER IS
    C NUMBER;
BEGIN
```

```
        C := A + B
        RETURN (C);
    END;
    DECLARE --- function call code
        A NUMBER;
        B NUMBER;
        C NUMBER;
    BEGIN
        A : = & FIRST NUMBER;
        B : = & SECOND NUMBER;
        C : = ADDN (A, B);
    DBMS_OUTPUT. PUT_LINE ('ADDITION IS' ¦¦ C);
    END;
```

Example 3. ***Write a PL/SQL function that accepts department number and returns the total salary of that department. Also, write a function to call the function.***

Solution.

```
    CREATE OR REPLACE FUNCTION SALARY (dept NUMBER)
    RETURN NUMBER IS
    S NUMBER;
    BEGIN
        Select sum (sal) into S
        from emp
        where deptno = dept;
        RETURN (S);
    END;
    DECLARE ---function call code
    D NUMBER
    BEGIN
        D : = & DEPTNO ;
        SAL : = SALARY (D);
        DBMS_OUTPUT. PUT_LINE ('Salary of department number'
                ¦¦ d ¦¦ 'is' ¦¦ sal);
    END;
```

Example 4. ***Write a PL/SQL function to return the netsalary given the employee number.***

Solution.

```
    CREATE OR REPLACE FUNCTION NETSALARY
        ( ID IN SALARY. EMP_NO % TYPE)
        RETURN NUMBER
        IS
        NETSAL SALARY. BASIC% TYPE;
        BEGIN
        SELECT SUM (BASIC) + SUM (COMMISSION)-SUM(DEDUCTION)
        INTO NETSAL
```

```
        FROM SALARY
        WHERE emp_no = id;
        RETURN (NET SAL);
    END;
    /
```

To run this function just type –

```
    SQL > SELECT NET SALARY (2002) FROM DUAL;
```

Where '2002' is the employee number.

or

```
    SQL > VARIABLE NET NUMBER
    SQL > EXECUTE : NET : = NETSALARY (2002)
    SQL > PRINT NET.
```

Example 5. ***Write a PL/SQL function to return the balance-amount of the account number for which the balance is desired.***

Solution.

```
    DECLARE
        acc_no NUMBER;
        bal NUMBER;
            FUNCTION balance (acct_id NUMBER)
            RETURN NUMBER IS
            acct_bal NUMBER;
            BEGIN
            SELECT bal INTO acct_bal
            FROM accts
            WHERE acct_no_acct_id;
            RETURN acct_bal;
            END balance;
    BEGIN
        acc_no : = & acc_no;
        bal : = balance (acc_no);
        DBMS_OUTPUT. PUT_LINE ('Balance is:' ¦ ¦ bal);
    END ;
```

Packages in PL/SQL : Packages are defined as groups of procedures, functions, variables, constants, cursors, exceptions and SQL statements that are grouped together into a single unit. They are created using a tool– SQL*PLUS. A package once written and debugged is compiled and stored in Oracle's system tables held in an oracle database. **Please note that unlike the stored programs, the package itself cannot be called**. A package has usually two components.

(*a*) Package specification

(*b*) Package body.

Package Specification: It declares the memory variables, constants, exceptions, cursors and subprograms that are available for use. It's **syntax** is –

```
    CREATE OR REPLACE PACKAGE < package_name> AS
    FUNCTION < function_name> (list of arguments)
```

```
RETURN data type,
PROCEDURE < procedure_name> (list of arguments)
END < package_name> ;
```

Package Body : It contains the definition of public objects that are declared in the specification. It implements the specifications. It can contain subprogram bodies also. It may include objects that are not listed in the package specification. Such objects are said to be private and are not available to the users of the package. Private objects may only be called by other objects within the same package body. **Please note that a package body may also include code that is run every time the package is invoked, regardless of the part of the package that is executed**. It's **syntax** is –

```
CREATE OR REPLACE PACKAGE BODY < NAME>
{ IS/AS}
PL/SQL package body;
```

Also note that the name of the package body should be the same as the name of the package specification.

How to create packages ?

The **first step** to create a package is to create its specification. The specification declares the objects that are contained in the body of the package. A package is created using oracle's SQL*PLUS interactive tool.

The **second step** is to create the body of the package. This body of the package is a collection of detailed definitions of the objects that were declared in the specification.

How to refer to the package contents?

The package contents can be referenced from database triggers, stored programs or PL/SQL blocks. To refer to a package'subprogram and objects,

We follow a syntax –

```
Package_name. type_name
```

For example,

```
Package_name.object_name
Package_name.subprogram_name
```

Here,

Package_name is the name of the declared package.

Type_name is the name of the type that is user defined (like record).

Object_name is the name of the constant or variable that is declared by the user.

Subprogram is the name of the procedure or function contained in the package body.

For example, to refer to a procedure add in the package – CALC, we can write –

```
CALC. add (list–of-arguments);
```

Comparison of Procedures and Packages : Packages allow multiple procedures to use the same variables and cursors. Procedures within packages may be public or private. Private means they are only accessible via commands from within the package such as calls from other procedures.

How to delete a package ?

The **syntax** used is—

```
DROP PACKAGE < package_name>;
```

This will delete both the package specification and the package body that was created. If we want to use the package again, we must create the package specification and the package body.

> **NOTE :** The source code for existing procedures, functions, packages and package bodies can be queried from the data dictionary view named as, USER_SOURCE. For this just type—
> SQL > SELECT*from USER_SOURCE;

Advantages of Packages : Packages have some advantages also which are discussed below :

1. **Better productivity :** The application design becomes easier as a package specification can be coded and compiled without its body. This increases the designer's productivity.
2. **Better modularity :** Packages encapsulates objects, procedures, functions, variables, constants, cursors and exceptions into a single, named PL/SQL module.
3. **Better functionality :** The package's public variables and cursors persist for the duration of the session. So, all cursors and procedures that execute in this environment can share them.
4. **Better performance :** Packages improve performance by loading multiple objects into memory at once. Hence, subsequent calls to related subprograms in the package require no Input/Output.
5. **Better security :** Packages hide implementation details in its body. So, better security is provided to the system.

Let us now see, **how to make alterations to an existing package?**

In order to recompile a package, we use the Alter package command.

It uses the compile keyword. It eliminates the need for any implicit run time recompilation and prevents any associated runtime compilation errors and performance overhead. We explicitly recompile a package after modifications are done to it. **Please understand that recompiling a package recompiles all objects defined within the package. Also note that recompiling does not change the definition of the package or any of its objects.**

The **syntax** used is as follows :

```
ALTER PACKAGE < package_name> COMPILE PACKAGE;
```

Whereas to recompile the body of the package, the **syntax** is –

```
ALTER PACKAGE <package_name > COMPILE BODY;
```

We are in a position to solve some problems based on packages now.

Example 1. *Write a PL/SQL code to create*

(a) package specification

(b) package body, to do all tax calculation of the employees, total sales.

Solution. (*a*) **To create package specification :** We create a file named RAJPACK and type these commands :

```
CREATE OR REPLACE PACKAGE RAJIVPACK AS
FUNCTION NET SALARY
(ID IN SALARY.EMP_NO% TYPE)
RETURN NUMBER;
PROCEDURE TAX
(ID IN SALARY.EMP_NO% TYPE, TAX OUT NUMBER);
PROCEDURE TOTSALES
```

```
(CID IN CSTMAST.CSTID%TYPE, SAL OUT NUMBER);
END;
/
```

Here, two procedures and a function will comprise the package named RAJIVPACK. This will create the package specification. The actual code for the procedures and functions will be stored in the body of the package, which is created below.

(*b*) **To create package body :** Create another file named RPACKB and type the following code.

```
CREATE OR REPLACE PACKAGE BODY RAJIVPACK AS
FUNCTION NETSALARY (ID IN SALARY.EMP_NO% TYPE)
RETURN NUMBER
IS
NETSAL
SALARY.BASIC% TYPE;
BEGIN
    SELECT SUM (BASIC) + SUM (COMMISSION) – SUM(DEDUCTION)
    INTO NETSAL FROM SALARY
    WHERE EMP_NO = ID;
RETURN (NETSAL);
END;
PROCEDURE TOTSALES (CID IN CSTMAST.CSTID% TYPE,
    SALOUT NUMBER)
IS
ID          TRN.ITMID% TYPE;
QTY         TRN.TRNQTY% TYPE;
PRICE       ITMMAST.ITMPRICE% TYPE;
SALES       NUMBER(10, 2);
CURSOR      CUR_TR IS SELECT TRN.ITMID,
TRNQTY, ITMPRICE FROM TRN, ITMMAST
WHERE TRN.CSTID = CID AND TRN.ITMID = ITMMAST.ITMID;
BEGIN
    SALES := 0;
    OPEN CUR_TR;
LOOP
    FETCH CUR_TR INTO ID, QTY, PRICE;
    IF CUR_TR% ROWCOUNT=0 THEN
        RAISE_APPLICATION_ERROR (–20020, 'There is no data');
    END IF;
    EXIT WHEN CUR_TR% NOT FOUND;
    SALES := SALES + QTY * PRICE;
END LOOP;
CLOSE CUR_TR;
SAL := SALES;
```

```
END TOTSALES;
- - Tax calculations
PROCEDURE TAX (ID SALARY.EMP_NO% TYPE, TAX OUT NUMBER)
IS
    NETSAL NUMBER (10, 2);
BEGIN
NETSAL := NETSALARY (ID);
IF NETSAL <2000 THEN
    TAX := NETSAL * 0.02;
ELSIF NETSAL <4000 THEN
    TAX := NETSAL * 0.04;
ELSE
    TAX := NETSAL * 0.01;
END IF ;
END TAX;
END RAJPACK;
/
```

Save the file.

To create the package specification, we type

```
SQL > START RAJPACK
```

Correct the errors if any and again start the specification file till a message—**'Package Created'** is obtained.

Now, to create the package body, just type

```
SQL > START RPACKB
```

Please understand that once a package is created, the functions or procedures included in it can be executed anytime until it is deleted.

How to execute a procedure from a package?

```
SQL > VARIABLE TX NUMBER
SQL > EXECUTE RAJIVPACK.TAX(1010, : TX);
SQL > PRINT TX
```

How to execute a function from a package ?

```
SQL > VARIABLE NSAL NUMBER
SQL > EXECUTE : NSAL := RAJIVPACK.NETSALARY (1010);
SQL > PRINT NSAL
```

Example 2. *Write a PL/SQL code to create*

(*a*) *a package specification.*

(*b*) *a package body.*

for the insert, retrieve, update and delete operation on a employee table.

Solution. (*a*) We write the **package specification first**.

```
CREATE OR REPLACE PACKAGE OPERATION AS
    PROCEDURE INSERT (ENO NUMBER, NAME VARCHAR,
        JOB VARCHAR, SAL NUMBER, DNO NUMBER);
    PROCEDURE RETRIEVE (ENO IN NUMBER, NAME OUT VARCHAR,
        SAL OUT NUMBER);
```

```
    FUNCTION UPDATE (DNO NUMBER, AMOUNT NUMBER)
    RETURN NUMBER;
    FUNCTION DELETE (ENO NUMBER) RETURN CHAR;
END;
```

(*b*) Now, we create its **package body**

```
CREATE OR REPLACE PACKAGE BODY OPERATION IS
    PROCEDURE INSERT (ENO NUMBER, NAME VARCHAR,
        JOB VARCHAR, SAL NUMBER, DNO NUMBER) AS
    BEGIN
        INSERT INTO EMP (EMP NO, ENAME, JOB, SAL, DEPT NO)
        VALUES (ENO, NAME, JOB, SAL, DNO);
    END INSERT;
    PROCEDURE RETRIEVE (ENO IN NUMBER, NAME OUT VARCHAR,
        SAL OUT NUMBER) IS
    BEGIN
        SELECT ENAME, SAL
        INTO NAME, SAL
        FROM EMP
        WHERE EMPNO = ENO;
    END RETRIEVE;
    FUNCTION UPDATE (DNO NUMBER, AMOUNT NUMBER)
    RETURN NUMBER IS
        N NUMBER;
    BEGIN
        UPDATE EMP SET SAL = SAL + AMOUNT
        WHERE DEPTNO = DNO;
        N := SQL% ROWCOUNT;
        RETURN (N);
    END UPDATE ;
    FUNCTION DELETE (ENO NUMBER)
    RETURN CHAR IS
    BEGIN
        DELETE EMP WHERE EMP NO = ENO;
        IF SQL% FOUND THEN
        RETURN ('Y');
    ELSE
        RETURN ('N');
    END IF;
END DELETE ;
END OPERATION;
```

SUMMARY

Oracle is an RDBMS.SQL*PLUS is an extension to the standard SQL. It has an on line command interpreter. Users can create program files and generate formatted reports. It is an interactive tool. PL/SQL stands for Procedural Language/Structured Query Language. It is an extension of SQL. PL/SQL is the superset of SQL. With PL/SQL, a mechanism called exception handling will **'bullet proof'** our program so that it can continue operating in the presence of errors.

The Oracle engine uses a work area to execute SQL statements and store information. A cursor is a PL/SQL construct that allows us to name these work areas and access stored data. This data that is stored in the cursor is called as an **active data-set**. Subprograms are named PL/SQL blocks that allow parameter passing and calling them anywhere. We can even group these functions, procedures, variables, constants, cursors, exceptions and SQL as a package.

MULTIPLE CHOICE QUESTIONS [MCQs]

1. SQL stands for
(*a*) Structured Questioning Language (*b*) Structured Query Language
(*c*) Simple Query Language (*d*) None of the above.

2. DDL stands for
(*a*) Data Definition Language (*b*) Data Design Language
(*c*) Data Development Language (*d*) None of the above.

3. INSERT, DELETE, UPDATE and SELECT are put under
(*a*) DDLs (*b*) TCLs
(*c*) DMLs (*d*) VDLs.

4. The process of joining of multiple strings is known as
(*a*) Selection (*b*) Projection
(*c*) Concatenation (*d*) None of the above.

5. To sort records we use
(*a*) ORDER BY clause (*b*) HAVING clause
(*c*) GROUP clause (*d*) None of the above.

6. % and _(underscore) are
(*a*) Relational operators (*b*) Arithematic operators
(*c*) Like operators (*d*) None of the above

7. The logical tables of data extracted from existing tables are known as
(*a*) Records (*b*) Views
(*c*) Queries (*d*) None of the above.

8. Oracle provides a special table that can be used to test any function. This table is
(*a*) DUAL table (*b*) EMPLOYEE table
(*c*) SALARY table (*d*) None of the above.

9. To substitute any NULL value with a user specified value, we use
(*a*) TO_CHAR function (*b*) NVL function
(*c*) DATE function (*d*) None of the above.

10. ROLLBACK, COMMIT and SAVEPOINT are
(*a*) DMLs (*b*) DDLs
(*c*) VDLs (*d*) TCLs

11. Hash functions are used in which of these indexing methods
(*a*) Ordered indexing (*b*) Hashed indexing
(*c*) Pinned indexing (*d*) None of the above.

12. Primary indexing is also known as
(*a*) Clustering index (*b*) Non-clustering index
(*c*) Hashed index (*d*) None of the above.

13. ODBC stands for
(*a*) Open Database Connectivity (*b*) Open Data Connection
(*c*) Online Database Connection (*d*) None of the above.

14. A query within a query is called as
(*a*) Subquery (*b*) New query
(*c*) Parent query (*d*) None of the above.

15. The command used to set the top title for each page of a report is
(*a*) BTITLE (*b*) CTITLE
(*c*) TTITLE (*d*) None of the above.

16. PL/SQL stands for
(*a*) Procedural Language/Structured Query Language
(*b*) Primary Language/Simple Query Language
(*c*) Parallel Language/Simple Query List
(*d*) None of the above.

17. A buffer use to store results of the recent query
(*a*) Cursor (*b*) Triggers
(*c*) Packages (*d*) Exceptions.

18. The OUT parameter behaves like a
(*a*) Constant (*b*) Uninitialized variable
(*c*) Regular variable (*d*) None of the above.

19. Functions return value and they use which of these statements for the same
(*a*) Call (*b*) Return
(*c*) Return <datatype> <function_name> (*d*) None of the above.

20. Group of procedures, functions, variables, constants, cursors, exceptions and SQL statements are put in a single unit called as
(*a*) Class (*b*) Package
(*c*) PL/SQL (*d*) None of the above.

ANSWERS

1. (*b*)	**2.** (*a*)	**3.** (*c*)	**4.** (*c*)	**5.** (*a*)	**6.** (*c*)	**7.** (*b*)	**8.** (*a*)
9. (*b*)	**10.** (*d*)	**11.** (*b*)	**12.** (*a*)	**13.** (*a*)	**14.** (*a*)	**15.** (*c*)	**16.** (*a*)
17. (*a*)	**18.** (*b*)	**19.** (*b*)	**20.** (*b*)				

CONCEPTUAL SHORT QUESTIONS WITH ANSWERS

Q.1. Consider the following Employee database

employee (<u>employee_name</u>, street, city)

works (<u>employee_name</u>, company_name, salary)

company (<u>company_name</u>, city)

manages (<u>employee_name</u>, manager_name)

NOTE : Primary keys are underlined.

Write SQL queries for the following :

(*a*) Find the names of all employee who work for First Bank Corporation.

(*b*) Find all employees in the database who live in the same cities as the companies for which they work.

(*c*) Find all employees in the database who live in the same cities and on the same streets as do their managers.

(*d*) Find all employees who earn more than the average salary of all employees of their company.

(*e*) Find the company that has the smallest payroll.

(*f*) Give all employees of First Bank Corporation a 10% raise.

(*g*) Give all managers of First Bank Corporation a 10% raise.

(*h*) Delete all tuples in the works relation for employees of Small Bank Corporation.

Ans. We write their SQL queries now.

(*a*)
```
SELECT employee_name
  FROM works
WHERE company_name = 'First Bank Corporation';
```

(*b*)
```
SELECT e.employee_name
  FROM employee e, works w, company c
WHERE e.employee_name = w.employee_name and
          e.city = c.city and w.company_name = c.company_name;
```

(*c*)
```
SELECT P.employee_name
  FROM employee P, employee R, manages M
WHERE P.employee_name = M.employee_name
          and M.manager_name = R.employee_name
          and P.street = R.street and P.city = R.city;
```

(*d*) Assume that all people work for at most one company. So, we write
```
SELECT employee_name
  FROM works T
WHERE salary > (select avg (salary) from works S
          where T.company_name = S.company_name);
```

(*e*)
```
SELECT company_name
  FROM works
GROUP BY company_name
  HAVING SUM (salary) <= all (SELECT SUM (salary)
  FROM works
GROUP BY company_name);
```

(*f*)
```
Update works
    Set salary = salary * 1.1
  Where company_name = 'First Bank Corporation';
```

(*g*)
```
Update works
    Set salary = salary * 1.1
  Where employee_name in (select manager_name from manages)
```

and company_name = 'First Bank Corporation';

(*h*) Delete works
Where company_namc = 'Small Bank Corporation';

Q.2. Show that, in SQL <> all is identical to not in.

Ans. Let the set S denote the result of an SQL subquery. We compare (x <> **all** S) with (x **not in** S). If a particular value x_1 satisfies (x_1 <> **all** S) then for all elements y of S $x_1 \neq y$. Thus x_1 is not a member of S and must satisfy (x_1 **not in** S). Similary, suppose there is a particular value x_2 which satisfies (x_2 **not in** S). It cannot be equal to any element w belonging to S, and hence (x_2 <> **all** S) will be satisfied. Therefore the two expressions are equivalent.

Q.3. Write an SQL query, without using a with clause, to find all branches where the total account deposit is less than the average total account deposit at all branches,

(*a*) Using a nested query in the FROM clause.

(*b*) Using a nested query in the HAVING clause.

Ans. We output the branch names along with the total account deposit at the branch.

(*a*) Using a nested query in the **from** clause.

```
SELECT branch_name, tot_balance
  FROM (select branch_name, sum (balance)
        from account
        group by branch_name) as branch_total
        (branch_name, tot_balance)
 WHERE tot_balance !
        ( select avg (tot_balance)
        from (select branch_name, sum (balance)
        from account
        group by branch_name) as branch_total (branch_name,
          tot_balance)
```

(*b*) Using a nested query in a **having** clause.

```
       SELECT branch_name, sum (balance)
         FROM account
     GROUP BY branch_name
   HAVING SUM (balance) !
              ( select avg (tot_balance)
              from (select branch_name, sum (balance)
              from account
              group by branch_name) as branch_total (branch_name,
                tot_balance)
```

Q.4. Consider once again the Employee database of Q1 and write an SQL schema definition. Choose appropriate domain for each attribute and an appropriate primary key for each relation schema.

Ans. **create domain** *company_names* **char**(20)

```
create domain       city_names char(30)
create domain       person_names char(20)
create table        employee
(employee_name      person_names,
street              char (30),
city                city_names,
primary key         (employee_name))

create table        works
(employee_name      person_names,
company_name        company_names,
salary              numeric (8,2),
primary key         (employee_name))

create table        company
(ecompany_name      company_names,
city                city_names,
primary key         (company_name))
create table        manages
(employee_name      person_names,
manager_name        person_names,
primary key         (employee_name))
```

Q.5. Referential-integrity constraints as defined in this chapter involve exactly two relations. Consider a database that includes the following relations:

***salaried-worker* (*name, office, phone, salary*)**
***hourly-worker* (*name, hourly-wage*)**
***address* (*name, street, city*)**

Suppose that we wish to require that every name that appears in address appear in either salaried-worker or hourly-worker, but not necessarily in both.

(*a*) Propose a syntax for expressing such constraints.

(*b*) Discuss the actions that the system must take to enforce a constraint of this form.

Ans. (*a*) For simplicity, we present a variant of the SQL syntax. As part of the **create table** expression for *address* we include

foreign key (*name*) **references** *salaried-worker* or *hourly-worker*

(*b*) To enforce this constraint, whenever a tuple is inserted into the *address* relation, a lookup on the *name* value must be made on the *salaried-worker* relation and (if that lookup failed) on the *hourly-worker* relation (or vice-versa).

Q.6. Consider an employee database with two relations

***employee* (<u>*employee-name*</u>, *street, city*)**
***works* (<u>*employee-name*</u>, *company-name, salary*)**

where the primary keys are underlined. Write a query to find companies whose employees earn a higher salary, on average, than the average salary at First Bank Corporation.

(*a*) Using SQL functions as appropriate.

(*b*) Without using SQL functions.

Ans. (*a*)

```
Create function avg-salary (cname varchar(15))
    returns integer
    declare result integer;
        select avg (salary) into result
        from works
        where works. company-name= cname
    return result;
end
select company-name
from works
where avg-salary (company-name) > avg-salary ("First Bank Corporation")
```

(*b*)

```
Select company-name
from works
group by company-name
having avg (salary) > (select avg (salary)
    from works
    where company-name = "First Bank Corporation")
```

Q.7. Compare the use embedded SQL with the use in SQL of functions defined in a general-purpose programming language. Under what circumstances would you use each of these features ?

Ans. SQL functions are primarily a mechanism for extending the power of SQL to handle attributes of complex data types (like images), or to perform complex and non-standard operations. Embedded SQL is useful when imperative actions like displaying results and interacting with the user are needed.

These cannot be done conveniently in an SQL only environment. Embedded SQL can be used instead of SQL functions by retrieving data and then performing the function's operations on the SQL result. However a drawback is that a lot of query-evaluation functionality may end up getting repeated in the host language code.

Q.8 What are pseudo-columns?

Ans. A pseudo column behaves like a table column but is not actually stored in the table. We can SELECT from pseudo columns but we cannot INSERT, UPDATE or DELETE their values. We have the following pseudo-columns –

(*a*) CURRVAL
(*b*) NEXTVAL
(*c*) LEVEL
(*d*) ROWID
(*e*) ROWNUM

For example, the ROWNUM pseudo-column can be used in queries to retrieve rows like,

```
SELECT * FROM CUSTOMER
WHERE ROWNUM < 5 ;
```

This query will retrieve the first four rows from the table.

Q.9. Explain the usage of the sign ( ) of oracle?

Ans. We have a sign function, whose **syntax** is –

SIGN (<n>)

Where '*n*' is a number. This function returns –1 if *n* is negative, 1 if *n* is positive and 0 if n is 0.

For example,

```
SQL > SELECT SIGN (-3.1) SIGN (0), SIGN (5)
  FROM dual;
```

Output is :

SIGN(−3.1)	SIGN(0)	SIGN(5)
−1	0	1

Q.10. What is Join?

Ans. Joins allows us to join two or more related tables to retrieve information from tables based on a relationship between certain columns in these tables.

Q.11. What is Inner Join ?

An inner join requires each record in the two joined tables to have a matching record. An inner join essentially combines the records from two tables (A and B) based on a given join-predicate. The result of the join can be defined as the outcome of first taking the Cartesian product (or cross-join) of all records in the tables (combining every record in table A with every record in table B) - then return all records which satisfy the join predicate.

Q.12. What is Natural Join ?

Ans. Natural join between two relations is written as ($R \bowtie S$). The result of the natural join is the set of all combinations of tuples in R and S that are equal on their common attribute names. For an example consider the tables *Employee* and *Department* and their natural join:

Department

DeptId	DeptName
d-01	Finance
d-02	Sales
d-03	Marketing

Employee

Name	EmpId	DeptId
Khanak	e-01	d-01
Kavita	e-02	d-02
Alpesh	e-03	d-01
Aruna	e-04	d-02

∴ *Employee* $\bowtie$ *Department is –*

Name	EmpId	DeptId	DeptName
Khanak	e-01	d-01	Finance
Kavita	e-02	d-02	Sales
Alpesh	e-03	d-01	Finance
Aruna	e-04	d-02	Sales

Q.13. What is Outer Join ?

Ans. An outer join operation returns all the rows returned by an inner join plus all the rows from one table that do not match any row from the other table. An outer join can be left, right, or full, depending on whether rows from the left, right, or both tables are retained.

Q.14. What is Left Outer Join ? **[GGSIPU, B.Tech. (CSE/IT); 5th Sem., 2012]**

Ans. The left outer join for relation *R* and *S* is the set of all combinations of tuples in R and S that are equal on their common attribute names, in addition (loosely speaking) to tuples in *R* that have no matching tuples in *S*.

For an example consider the tables *Employee* and *Department* and their left outer join :

Employee

Name	EmpId	DeptId
Khanak	e-01	d-01
Kavita	e-02	d-02
Alpesh	e-03	d-01
Aruna	e-04	d-02
Anand	e-05	d-04

Department

DeptId	DeptName
d-01	Finance
d-02	Sales
d-03	Marketing

Employee LEFT OUTER Department

Name	EmpId	DeptId	DeptName
Khanak	e-01	d-01	Finance
Kavita	e-02	d-02	Sales
Alpesh	e-03	d-01	Finance
Aruna	e-04	d-02	Sales
Anand	e-05	d-04	Null

Q.15. What is Right Outer Join ?

Ans. The right outer join behaves almost identically to the left outer join, but the roles of the tables are switched.

The right outer join for relation *R* and *S* is the set of all combinations of tuples in *R* and *S* that are equal on their common attribute names, in addition to tuples in S that have no matchig tuples in *R*.

For example consider the tables *Employee* and *Department* and their right outer join:

Employee

Name	EmpId	DeptId
Khank	e-01	d-01
Kavita	e-02	d-02
Alpesh	e-03	d-01
Aruna	e-04	d-02

Department

DeptId	DeptName
d-01	Finance
d-02	Sales
d-03	Marketing

∴ *Employee* RIGHT OUTER *Department is –*

Name	EmpId	DeptId	Manager
Khanak	e-01	d-01	Finance
Kavita	e-02	d-02	Sales
Alpesh	e-03	d-01	Finance
Aruna	e-04	d-02	Sales
NULL	Null	d-03	Marketing

Q.16. What is Full Outer Join ?

Ans. The **outer join** or **full outer join** in effect combines the results of the left and right outer joins. The full outer join for relation *R* and *S* is the set of all combinations of tuples in *R* and *S* that are equal on their common attribute names, in addition to tuples in *S* that have no matching tuples in *R* and tuples in *R* that have no matching tuples in *S* in their common attribute names.

For an example consider the tables *Employee* and *Department* and their full outer join:

Employee

Name	EmpId	DeptId
Khanak	e-01	d-01
Kavita	e-02	d-02
Alpesh	e-03	d-01
Aruna	e-04	d-02
Anand	e-05	d-04

Department

DeptId	DeptName
d-01	Finance
d-02	Sales
d-03	Marketing

∴ *Employee* ⋈ *Department is –*

Name	EmpId	DeptId	DeptName
Khanak	e-01	d-01	Finance
Kavita	e-02	d-02	Sales
Alpesh	e-03	d-01	Finance
Aruna	e-04	d-02	Sales
Anand	e-05	d-04	Null
NULL	Null	d-03	Marketing

Q.17. What is a self-join? What is its syntax? Give an example to explain self-joins?

Ans. Self-joining is the process of joining a table to itself *i.e.,* each row of the table is combined with itself and with every other row of the table. Please note that the self-join can be viewed as a join of two copies of the same table. Also note that the table is not actually copied but SQL performs the command as though it were.

Syntax : For self-joining of a table to itself, we use the same syntax as that for joining of two different tables. As both the tables have the same name, so aliases for the actual table name are used in order to distinguish the column names from one another. These table name aliases are defined in the FORM clause of the query.

For example, Consider an employee table-empl with this schema—

EMP NO	ENAME	MGR
39	AMIT	40
40	AJAY	39
41	MAYUR	88
43	SAHIB	82

empl. dbf

In this table, empno is the primary key. Details of each employee's manager is the 3rd column of the empl-table whose id is stored in MGR column of some other row. So, every employee except manager has a Manager. Thus, MGR is a foreign key that references empno. **Please note that in order to display the names of the manager with the employee record, we need to join EMPL to itself.**

How to self-join the EMPL-table?

```
SQL > SELECT WORKER. Ename "Ename",
    MANAGER. Ename "Manager"
FROM emp WORKER, emp MANAGER
WHERE WORKER. mgr = MANAGER, empno;
```

Here, WORKER and MANAGER are two aliases for the EMPL table. So, these tables act as **virtual tables.**

For example,

WORKER

EMPNO	ENAME	MGR
39	AMIT	40
40	AJAY	39

MANAGER

EMPNO	ENAME	MGR
39	ATUL	19
40	RAJIV	20

∴ The output of the above query is—

Ename	Manager
Amit	Rajiv
Ajay	Atul

2 rows selected

Q.18. What is chaining? Why are chains so popular?

Ans. Chaining is accomplished by using pointers along with the data to indicate where to go next. Practically, chaining is used broadly. Nearly all DBMS employ chains in one way or another. **For example,** IMS, system R, system 2000 etc all use pointers to create chains.

The chains are so popular as we know that records can only be stored physically in a sequential manner with respect to only one field. Chaining is a mechanism that makes possible another sequence of search with respect to another field. **For example**, a specific application of chains occurs in DBTG systems where rings or networks are created.

Q.19. Compare various Access methods on the basis of their selection criteria.

Ans. **Binary search** is the least useful method for secondary storage but is useful for in-core search. However, binary tree method has found applications in storage devices, particularly for index file organization. Though **sequential search** is inflexible, yet it is used very frequently. This is because of three reasons.

1. Inspite of the advances in storage device, tape is still used widely.
2. Many applications are naturally oriented to sequential processing like customer billing processing in a utility company falls under this category.
3. If one is required to process more than 10 of the records in a file, sequential access will be faster than random or indexed accessing.

Many DBMS like IMS, system 2000 etc tend to use a combination of different access methods to their advantage. Like, IMS uses a combination of indexed and sequential search techniques.

A database system must store information to indicate where a user file is stored. To do this, an **index file/directory** is created. **If the directory is small**, a sequential organization may be best. **If the directory is large**, then an indexed structure on a binary tree can be used to advantage. This data access structure is widely referred to as the B-tree. This technique has been used by system-R to manage its directories and indexes.

Q.20. What is the 'Create sequence' command in Oracle? Give its syntax and an example to explain.

Ans. In Oracle, a sequence of unique numbers can be generated for primary key fields by create sequence command.

Syntax : CREATE SEQUENCE ID START WITH 100 INCREMENT BY 1;

Here, ID is a sequence that is stored in the database. The sequence is made use of in the insert statement to generate the actual data.

The numbers will be generated during an insert/update operation, using this **syntax** :

```
INSERT INTO < table_name >
    VALUES (ID.NEXTVAL, .....);
```

For example,

```
INSERT INTO EMP VALUES
    (ID.NEXTVAL, 'TITANIC' '06-MAY-74', 3500, 'MGR');
```

Here, a new row will be added to the EMP table and EMP_NO will be 100 as this is the starting number of the sequence named, ID. 'NEXTVAL' above will generate the next number in sequence.

If the data has to be entered into subsidiary tables the same number which has already been generated then we use ID. CURRVAL.

Actually, a sequence is a database object from which multiple users may generate unique integers. We can use sequences to automatically generate primary key values.

Q.21. The Oracle server performs certain steps when we use the HAVING clause. What are those steps?

Ans. The steps are as follows :

(*a*) Rows are grouped.

(*b*) The GROUP function is applied to the group.

(*c*) The GROUPS that match the criteria in the HAVING clause are displayed.

The HAVING clause can precede the GROUP BY clause but it is recommended that you place the GROUP BY clause first because it is more logical. **Please note that groups are formed and group functions are calculated before the HAVING clause is applied to the groups in the SELECT list.**

Q.22. How can you lock your tables?

Ans. We can lock tables in one of the following modes :

(*a*) ROW SHARE (*b*) ROW EXCLUSIVE

(*c*) SHARE UPDATE (*d*) SHARE

(*e*) SHARE ROW (*f*) EXCLUSIVE.

A table can have multiple SHARE locks but only one EXCLUSIVE lock. Lock determines how different users can commit or rollback

Syntax :

LOCK TABLE [user.] tablename [[user.] tablename....]
IN lock mode MODE [NOWAIT]

where,**Lockmode,** can be one of the modes listed above

Nowait—If table is already locked, the call returns instead of quering for the table to be unlocked.

Share—It allows concurrent queries but disallows updates to tables.

Exclusive—It allows queries only on the locked tables.

Row share—It prevents locking the entire table for exclusive access, thereby allowing concurrent access.

For example,

LOCK TABLE cust IN EXCLUSIVE MODE

This will make oracle wait, if for some reason the table is not available for locking. The table may be locked by another user.

Example. LOCK TABLE CUST
IN EXCLUSIVE MODE NOWAIT

This statement will immediately return to the application if the table lock cannot be executed.

Q.23. Explain various data types that are available in oracle?

Ans. Oracle recognizes the following data types –

S. No.	Data Type	Meaning
1.	NUMBER	Allows 40 digits, decimal point, sign.
2.	NUMBER (W)	Number column of specified size.
3.	NUMBER (W, D)	Number column of specified width out of which 2 is reserved for decimals.
4.	Char (w)	Fixed length character date. Maximum size 255. Default is 1.
5.	DATE	Date
6.	VARCHAR 2(w)	Variable length character string of width w. Maximum width is 2000 bytes.

7.	LONG	Any printable character. The length can vary from 0 to 2GB. Only one LONG column may be defined per table. It cannot be used in functions, expressions or in WHERE clause.
8.	RAW (W)	Binary data in whatever form the host computer stores.
9.	LONG RAW	Raw binary data and in other ways is like LONG data.
10.	ROWID	A value that uniquely identifies a row in an oracle database. It is returned by the pseudo-column ROWID. Table columns may not be assigned this type.

Q.24. How can you generate subtotals for a particular group of data?

Ans. We use the BREAK ON statement in our PL/SQL code in order to generate subtotals for a group of data.

For example, BREAK ON DEPARTMENT SKIP 1

Here, BREAK ON DEPARTMENT will group and print the rows for a particular department, at the end of which a subtotal will be printed. The SKIP 1 option will print a blank line after a group of related rows are printed and before printing the rows for the next group.

Please note that we can also use –

(*a*) SKIP *n*—where '*n*' is the number for the number of blank lines required.

(*b*) SKIP PAGE will start printing the next group on a new page.

Q.25. What is the purpose of SPOOL statement. Write a PL/SQL code to generate a DEPARTMENTWISE salary Report using SPOOL statement.

Ans. DEPARTMENTWISE SALARY REPORT

```
SET FEEDBACK OFF
SET PAGESIZE 20
SET LINESIZE 60
COLUMN EMP_NO FORMAT 9999
COLUMN BASIC FORMAT 99999.99
COLUMN COMMISSION FORMAT 99999.99
COLUMN DEDUCTION FORMAT 99999.99
COLUMN EMP_NAME FORMAT A10 TRUNC
COLUMN EMP_NO HEADING "EMPLOYEE" ¦ NUMBER"
COLUMN EMP_NAME HEADING "EMPLOYEE ¦ NAME"
TTITLE CENTER 'SALARY REPORT–DEPAR TMENT WISE' SKIP 1 –
    RIGHT 'PAGE' FORMAT 99 SQL. PNO
    SKIP 2
BREAK ON REPORT ON DEPARTMENT SKIP 2
COMPUTE SUM OF COMMISSION ON DEPARTMENT
COMPUTE SUM OF DEDUCTION ON DEPARTMENT
COMPUTE SUM OF BASIC ON DEPARTMENT REPORT
COMPUTE SUM OF "NET SALARY" ON DEPARTMENT
SPOOL SALREP
```

```
SELECT DEPARTMENT, SALARY. EMP_NO,
    INITCAP(EMP_NAME) "EMP_NAME",
    BASIC, COMMISSION, DEDUCTION,
    BASIC + COMMISSION- DEDUCTION
    "NET SALARY"
FROM SALARY, EMP
WHERE SALARY. EMP_NO_EMP. EMP_NO
    ORDER BY DEPARTMENT;
SPOOL OFF
CLEAR COLUMN
TTITLE OFF
CLEAR BREAK
CLEAR COMPUTE
END OF PROGRAM.
```

Please note that here the SPOOL statement is used to spool the output of the SQL file, the report, to a file in the secondary storage. This file can be printed on paper.

To start spooling we have a **syntax** given below –

SPOOL < filename >

(File is given. LST extension)

To stop spooling, we write –

SPOOL OFF

Q.26. Explain the variable attributes—% TYPE AND % ROW TYPE,

Ans. (*a*) **% TYPE :** It is used in PL/SQL to declare a variable to be of the same type as a previously declared variable or to be of the same type as a column in a table

For example,

```
DECLARE
TOTBAS SALARY. BASIC % TYPE;
```

Here, TOTBAS will now be of the same type as BASIC column from the table SALARY.

(*b*) **% ROW TYPE :** It declares a variable which is actually a record (which has the same structure as a row from a table).

For example, SALREC SALARY % ROW TYPE;

Here, SALREC is a record variable equivalent to the row from the table-SALARY.

Q.27. What is query processing ? What steps do you follow for query processing?

Ans. The procedure of selecting the best plan or strategy to be used in responding to a database request and executing the plan to generate the response is known as query processing. It is a stepwise process. The SQL query is first of all scanned, parsed and validated. Let us draw a flow chart now.

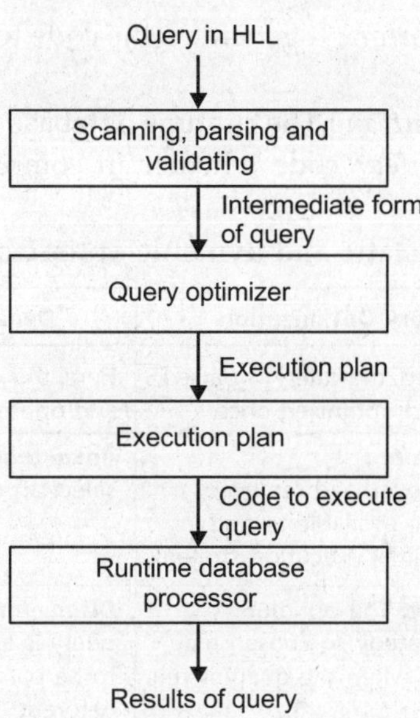

Fig. 3.5. *Flowchart for Query Processing*

The scanner identifies the language tokens such as SQL key words, attribute names and relation names in the text of query. The parser checks the query syntax to determine whether it is formulated according to the syntax rules of the query language. The query must also be validated by checking that all attributes and relation names are valid. An internal representation of the query is then created usually as a tree data structure called as a **query_tree. Please note that it is also possible to represent the query using a graph data structure called as a query graph**. A query graph has many possible execution strategies and **the process of choosing a suitable one for processing a query is known as query optimization.**

Q.28. Query processing involves 4 main phases. What are these phases and their purpose?

Ans. Four main phases of query processing are as follows :

Phase I : ***Query Decomposition.*** In this phase, **a high-level query is transformed into a relational algebra query to check whether that query is syntactically and semantically correct**. It involves—**Analysis, Normalization, semantic analysis, simplification and Query Restructuring**. **Analysis** means to lexically and syntactically analyze the query using parser. **Normalization** means converting a query into a normalized form, for easy manipulation. Semantic analysis means incorrectly formulated queries or contradictory queries are rejected. **Simplification** means to find out redundant information and to transform the query to semantically equivalent but more easily and efficiently computed form. Query Restructuring is the final stage of decomposition. Herein, the query is restructured to provide a more efficient implementation rules to convert one relational algebra expression into an equivalent form that is more efficient.

Phase II : ***Query Optimization.*** **In general, we try to reduce the total execution time of the query. The total execution time of a query is the sum of the execution times of all individual operations of that query**. Query optimization' is the activity of choosing an efficient execution strategy for processing a query.

Phase III : ***Code Generator :*** It generates the code to execute the plan created by query optimizer.

Phase IV : ***Query Execution :*** The runtime database processor has to perform the task of running the query code whether in compiled or interpreted mode to produce query result.

Q.29. Distinguish between static and dynamic optimization?

Ans.

S. No.	Static Query Optimization	Dynamic Query Optimization
1.	In this method, the query is parsed, validated and optimized once.	Here, the query is dynamically decomposed and optimized every time the query is run.
2.	***Advantages are :*** (*a*) Runtime overhead removed. (*b*) More time available to find most optimal execution strategy.	***Advantage*** is—All information required to select an optimum strategy is up-to-date.
3.	***Disadvantage:*** The optimum execution strategy so chosen may no longer be when the query is run.	***Disadvantage :*** The performance of the query is affected because the query has to be parsed, validated and optimized before it can be executed .

Q.30. What are temporal databases? Give some examples.

Ans. Temporal databases are those that store information about states of the real world across time. So, they are those databases that provide specific support for operation involving time. **Please note that a time temporal database is the one that has specific, in-built support for temporal processing.**

Examples of temporal databases.

1. **Scientific databases :** Where data collected from experiments includes the time when each data is measured.
2. **University database :** Where time is already included in the semester and year of each section of a course.
3. **Patient database** where patient histories are to be maintained.
4. **Project scheduling :** Where timing diagrams are drawn.
5. **Reservation systems** (Railway, hotel, airline etc.) Where information on dates and time is definitely required.

Please note that all these applications involve the management of temporal data.

Q.31. Depending upon the temporal aspects of tables, tables are put under four categories. Name them and define them.

Ans. Temporal aspects tables can be put under four categories.

(*a*) **Snapshot table : It is defined as a non-temporal relation showing only the current snapshot or current state of the database.**

(*b*) **Valid-time table :** It keeps track of the history of changes and thus support queries about past, present and future.

(*c*) **Transaction-time table :** In these tables, we store the information of the time when the change is applied to the database.

(*d*) **Bitemporal table : It is defined as a table which includes both valid time and transaction time.**

Q.32. Give some features of embedded SQL.

Ans. Some features of embedded SQL are as follows :

1. Embedded SQL is prefixed by EXEC SQL to distinguish it from host language.
2. Delimiter terminates every embedded SQL.
3. If embedded SQL statements extend over multiple lines then same strategy is used for continuation as used by the host language
4. Embedded SQL code is submitted to SQL precompiler.
5. Variables of host language can be referenced in embedded SQL statements to allow the values calculated by the program to be used.

Q.33. Write down the differences between SQL and PL/SQL in a tabular form ?

Ans. We tabulate the differences between SQL and PL/SQL now.

S. No.	SQL	PL/SQL
1.	SQL does not have any procedural capabilities.	Oracle provides all procedural capabilities in PL/SQL to allow for data filtration.
2.	SQL statements are passed to oracle engine (server) one at a time.	A group of SQL statements is sent to the Oracle server (called as BLOCK).
3.	Slower execution of SQL statements.	Faster execution of SQL statements.
4.	Exception handling is not feature of SQL.	PL/SQL allows us to write procedures/ functions to handle exceptions too.
5.	SQL does not support PL/SQL statements.	PL/SQL is a superset of SQL statements.
6.	We cannot store the intermediate results of a query in variables.	It allows us to store intermediate results of query for later use.

Q.34. Distinguish between Implicit cursor and Explicit cursor?

Ans. Implicit cursor : Implicit cursors are declared by PL/SQL implicitly *i.e.,* they are opened and managed by oracle engine internally and auto matically.

Explicit cursor : They are user-defined cursors for processing of multiple records returned by a query. They are declared explicitly, along with other identifiers to be used in a block. These are user-defined cursors. They are declared in the DECLARE section of the PL/SQL block. These cursors needs to be opened, before reading rows, after which the cursor is closed.

Q.35. What is the difference between a trigger and a procedure?

Ans. We tabulate some differences between triggers and procedures.

S. No.	Triggers	Procedures
1.	They donot accept parameters.	They can accept parameters.
2.	A trigger is automatically executed.	A stored procedure needs to be explicitly invoked.

Q.36. Consider the following relational database schema for a LIBRARY data base –

BOOK (BookId, Title, Publisher Name)
BOOK_AUTHORS (BookId, Author Name)
PUBLISHER (Name, Address, Phone)
BOOK_COPIES (BookId, BranchId, No_of_copies)
BOOK_LOANS (BookId, BranchId, CardNo, DateOut, Duedate)
LIBRARY_BRANCH (BranchId, BranchName, Address)
BORROWER (CardNo, Name, Address, Phone)
Now, write SQL queries for the following :

(a) How many copies of the book titled 'The Lost Tribe' are owned by the library branch whose name is "sharpstown" ?

(b) How many copies of book titted 'The Lost Tribe' are owned by each library branch?

(c) Retrieve the names of all borrowers who do not have any books checked out.

(d) For each book that is loaned out from the "Sharpstown" branch and whose Duedate is today, retrieve the book tittle, the borrower's name and the borrower's address.

(e) For each library branch, retrieve the branch name and the total number of books loaned out from that branch.

(f) Retrieve the names, addresses and number of books checked out for all borrowers who have more than five books checked out.

(g) For each book authored (or coauthored) by "Stephen king", retrieve the title and the number of copies owned by the library branch whose name is "Central".

Ans. The SQL queries are as follows :

(a)
```
SELECT NO_OF_COPIES
FROM ((BOOK ⋈ BOOK_COPIES)⋈
    LIBRARY_BRANCH)
WHERE title = 'The Lost Tribe' AND
    Branch_Name = 'Sharpstown':
```

(b)
```
SELECT BranchName, No_Of_copies
FROM ((BOOK ⋈ BOOK_COPIES) ⋈ LIBRARY_BRANCH)
WHERE Title = 'The Lost Tribe';
```

(c)
```
SELECT NAME
FROM BORROWER B
WHERE NOT EXIST (SELECT * FROM BOOK_LOANS
L WHERE B. Card No = L. CardNo;
```

(d)
```
SELECT B. Title, R.Name, R.Address
FROM Book B, BORROWER R, BOOK_LOANS BL,
LIBRARY_BRANCH LB
WHERE LB. BranchName = 'Sharpstown' AND
LB. BranchID = BL. Branch ID AND BL. Duedate = 'today' AND
BL. CardNo = R.CardNO AND BL. BOOKID = B. BOOKID;
```

(e)
```
SELECT L. BranchName, COUNT (*)
FROM BOOK_COPIES B, LIBRARY_BRANCH L
WHERE B. BranchId = L.Branch Id
GROUP BY L. Branch Name;
```

(f)
```
SELECT B. CardNo, B. Name, B.Address, COUNT (*)
FROM BORROWER B, BOOK_LOANS L
WHERE B.Card No = L.Card No
GROUP BY B.CardNo
HAVING COUNT (*) > 5;
```

(g) SELECT Title, No_Of_copies
FROM (((BOOK_AUTHORS ⋈ BOOK) ⋈
BOOK_COPIES) ⋈
LIBRARY_BRANCH) ⋈
WHERE Author_Name = 'Stephen king' and
BrandName = 'Central';

Q.37. How can the key and foreign key constraints be enforced by the DBMS? Is the enforcement technique you suggest difficult to implement? Can the constraint checks be executed in an efficient manner when updates are applied to the database?

Ans. One possible technique that is often used to check efficiently for the key constraint is to create an index on the combination of attributes that form each key (primary or secondary). Before inserting a new record (tuple), each index is searched to check that no value currently exists in the index that matches the key value in the new record. If this is the case, the record is inserted successfully.

For checking the foreign key constraint, an index on the primary key of each referenced relation will make this check relatively efficient. Whenever a new record is inserted in a referencing relation, its foreign key value is used to search the index for the primary key of the referenced relation, and if the referenced record exists, then the new record can be successfully inserted in the referencing relation.

For deletion of a referenced record, it is useful to have an index on the foreign key of each. Referencing relation so as to be able to determine efficiently whether any records reference the record being deleted.

If the indexes described above do not exist, and no alternative access structure (for example, hashing) is used in their place, then it is necessary to do linear searches to check for any of the above constraints, making the checks quite inefficient

Q.38. Consider the following COMPANY relational schema and answer the queries that follow

EMPLOYEE (FNAME, MINIT, LNAME, <u>SSN</u>, BDATE, ADDRESS, SEX, SALARY, SUPERSSN, DNO)
DEPARTMENT (DNAME, <u>DNUMBER</u>, MGRSSN, MGRSTARTDATE)
DEPT_LOCATIONS (<u>DNUMBER</u>, <u>DLOCATION</u>)
PROJECT (PNAME, <u>PNUMBER</u>, PLOCATION, DNUM)
WORKS_ON (<u>ESSN</u>, <u>PNO</u>, HOURS)
DEPENDENT (<u>ESSN</u>, <u>DEPARTMENT_NAME</u>, SEX, BDATE, RELATIONSHIP)

(a) **Retrieve the names of employees in department 5 who work more than 10 hours/week on the 'Product X' project.**
(b) **List the names of employees who have dependent with the same first name as themselves.**
(c) **Find the names of employees that are directly supervised by 'Franklin Wong'.**
(d) **For each project, list the project name and the total hours per week (by all employees) spent on that project.**
(e) **Retrieve the names of employees who work on every project.**
(f) **Retrieve the names of employees who do not work on any project.**

(g) For each department, retrieve department name and the average salary of employees working in that department.

(h) Retrieve the average salary of all female employees.

(i) Find the names and addresses of employees who work on atleast one project located in Houston but whose department has no location in Houston.

(j) List the last names of department managers who have no dependents.

Ans. (a) Retrieve the names of employees in department 5 who work more than 10 hours per week on the 'Product X' project.

SELECT LNAME, FNAME
FROM EMPLOYEE, WORKS_ON, PROJECT
WHERE DNO = 5 AND SSN=ESSN AND PNO=PNUMBER AND PNAME= 'ProductX' AND HOURS > 10;

Another possible SQL query uses nesting as follows:

SELECT LNAME, FNAME
WHERE DNO = 5 AND SSN IN (SELECT ESSN
FROM WORKS_ON
WHERE HOURS >10 AND PNO IN (SELECT PNUMBER
FROM PROJECT
WHERE PNAME = 'ProductX'));

(b) List the names of employees who have a dependent with the same first name as themselves.

SELECT LNAME, FNAME
FROM EMPLOYEE, DEPENDENT
WHERE SSN = ESSN and
FNAME = DEPENDENT_NAME

Another possible SQL query uses nesting as follows:

SELECT LNAME, FNAME
FROM EMPLOYEE
WHERE EXISTS (SELECT*
FROM DEPENDENT
WHERE FNAME = DEPENDENT-NAME AND SSN = ESSN);

(c) Find the names of employees that are directly supervised by 'Franklin Wong'.

SELECT E.LNAME, E.FNAME
FROM EMPLOYEE E,EMPLOYEE S
WHERE S.FNAME='Franklin' AND S.LNAME= 'Wong' AND E.SUPERSSN= S.SSN

Another possible SQL query uses nesting as follows:

SELECT LNAME, FNAME
FROM EMPLOYEE
WHERE SUPERSSN IN (SELECT SSN
FROM EMPLOYEE
WHERE FNAME='Franklin' AND LNAME= 'Wong');

(d) For each project, list the project name and the total hours per week (by all employees) spent on that project.

```
SELECT PNAME, SUM (HOURS)
FROM PROJECT, WORKS_ON
WHERE PNUMBER = PNO
GROUP BY PNAME;
```

(*e*) Retrieve the names of employees who work on every project.

```
SELECT LNAME, FNAME
WHERE NOT EXISTS (SELECT PNUMBER
FROM PROJECT
WHERE NOT EXISTS (SELECT*
FROM WORKS_ON
WHERE PNUMBER=PNO AND ESSN=SSN));
```

(*f*) Retrieve the names of employees who do not work on any project.

```
SELECT LNAME, FNAME
FROM EMPLOYEE
WHERE NOT EXISTS (SELECT*
FROM WORKS_ON
WHERE ESSN=SSN);
```

(*g*) For each department, retrieve the department name, and the average salary of employees working in that department.

```
SELECT DNAME, AVG (SALARY)
FROM DEPARTMENT, EMPLOYEE
WHERE DNUMBER = DNO
GROUP BY DNAME;
```

(*h*) Retrieve the average salary of all female employees.

```
SELECT AVG (SALARY)
FROM EMPLOYEE
WHERE SEX = 'F';
```

(*i*) Find the names and addresses of employees who work on at least one project located in Houston but whose department has no location in Houston.

```
SELECT LNAME, FNAME ADDRESS
FROM EMPLOYEE
WHERE EXISTS (SELECT*
FROM WORKS_ON, PROJECT
WHERE SSN = ESSN AND PNO =PNUMBER AND PLOCATION ='Houston')
AND
NOT EXISTS (SELECT*
FROM DEPT_LOCATIONS
WHERE DNO=DNUMBER AND DLOCATION = 'Houston');
```

(*j*) List the last names of department managers who have no dependents.

```
SELECT LNAME, FNAME
FROM EMPLOYEE
WHERE EXISTS (SELECT*
FROM DEPARTMENT
```

```
WHERE SSN = MGRSSN)
AND
NOT EXISTS (SELECT*
FROM DEPENDENT
WHERE SSN = ESSN);
```

Q.39. Consider the same database as above in Example 31. Write SQL queries to do the following :

(*a*) For each department whose average employee salary is more than $30,000, retrieve the department name and the number of employees working for that department.

(*b*) Suppose we want the number of male employees in each department rather than all employees (as in previous example). Can we specify this query in SQL ? Why or why not ?

Ans. (*a*)
```
SELECT DNAME, COUNT (*)
FROM DEPARTMENT, EMPLOYEE
WHERE DNUMBER=DNO
GROUP BY DNAME
HAVING AVG (SALARY) > 30000;
```

(*b*)
```
SELECT DNAME, COUNT (*)
FROM DEPARTMENT, EMPLOYEE
WHERE DNUMBER=DNO AND SEX='M' AND DNO IN (SELECT DNO
FROM EMPLOYEE
HAVING AVG (SALARY) > 30000)
GROUP BY DNAME;
```

Q.40. Consider the following database schema –

STUDENT (Name, StudentNumber, Class, Major)

COURSE (Course Name, CourseNumber, CreditHours, Department)

SECTION (SectionIdentifier, CourseNumber, Semester, Year, Instructor)

GRADE_REPORT (StudentNumber, SectionIdentifier, Grade)

PREREQUISITE (CourseNumber, PrerequisiteNumber)

Now, answer these queries :

(*a*) Retrieve the names of all senior students majoring in 'COSC' (computer science).

(*b*) Retrieve the names of all courses taught by professor King in 85 and 86.

(*c*) For each section taught by professor King, retrieve the course number, semester, year, and number of students who took the section.

(*d*) Retrieve the name and transcript of each senior student (Class = 5) majoring in COSC. Transcript includes course name, course number, credit hours, semester, year, and grade for each course completed by the student.

(*e*) Retrieve the names and major departments of all straight A students (students who have a grade of A in all their courses).

(*f*) Retrieve the names and major departments of all students who do not have any grade of A in any of their courses.

[GGSIPU, B.Tech. (CS)—5th Sem., Dec. 2007]

Ans. (*a*)
```
SELECT Name
FROM STUDENT
WHERE Major = 'COSC';
```
(*b*)
```
SELECT CourseName
FROM COURSE, SECTION
WHERE COURSE. Course Number = SECTION. Course Number AND
Instructor='King'
AND (Year='85' OR Year='86');
```
Another possible SQL query uses nesting as follows:
```
SELECT CourseName
FROM COURSE
WHERE CourseNumber IN (SELECT CourseNumber
FROM SECTION
WHERE Instructor = 'King' AND (Year='85' OR Year='86'));
```
(*c*)
```
SELECT CourseNumber, Semester, Year, COUNT (*)
FROM SECTION, GRADE_REPORT
WHERE Instructor= 'King' AND SECTION. SectionIdentifier=
GRADE_REPORT. SectionIdentifier GROUP BY CourseNumber, Semester,
Year;
```
(*d*)
```
SELECT Name, CourseName, C.Course Number, CreditHours, Year, Grade
FROM STUDENT ST, COURSE C, SECTION S,GRADE_REPORT G
WHERE Class= 5 AND Major = 'COSC' AND ST. StudentNumber =
G. Student Number AND G.SectionIdentifier = S.SectionIdentifier AND
S.Course Number = C.Course Number;
```
(*e*)
```
SELECT Name, Major
FROM STUDENT
WHERE NOT EXISTS (SELECT*
FROM GRADE_REPORT
WHERE StudentNumber= STUDENT. StudentNumber AND NOT
(Grade='A'));
```
(*f*)
```
SELECT Name, Major
FROM STUDENT
WHERE NOT EXISTS (SELECT*
FROM GRADE_REPORT
WHERE StudentNumber=STUDENT. StudentNumber AND Grade= 'A');
```

Q.41. For the above schema, write SQL update statements for the following :

(*a*) Insert a new student <'Johnson' 25,1, MATH'> in the database.

(*b*) Change the class of student 'Smith' to 2.

(*c*) Insert a new course <"Knowledge Engineering', COSC4390', 3, 'COSC'>.

(*d*) Delete the record for the student whose name is 'Smith' and sudent number is 17.

Ans. (*a*)
```
INSERT INTO STUDENT
VALUES ('Johnson', 25, 1, 'MATH');
```
(*b*)
```
UPDATE STUDENT
```

SET CLASS =2
WHERE Name = 'Smith';

(*c*) INSERT INTO COURSE
VALUES ('Knowledge Engineering', 'COSC4390', 3, 'COSC');

(*d*) DELETE FROM STUDENT
WHERE Name = 'Smith' AND StudentNumber = 17;

Q.42. Consider the following Insurance database

person (<u>driver_id</u>, name, address)

car (<u>license</u>, model, year)

accident (<u>report_number</u>, date, location)

owns (<u>driver_id, license</u>)

participated (<u>driver_id</u>, <u>car</u>, <u>report_number</u>, damage_amount)

Here, the PKs are underlined. Construct the following SQL queries for this relational database –

(*a*) Find the number of accidents in which the cars belonging to "John Smith" were involved.

(*b*) Update the damage amount for the car with license number "AABB2000" in the accident with report number "AR2197"to $3000.

[GGSIPU, B.Tech. (CS); 2nd Term Exam., Nov. 2005]

Ans. NOTE : The **participated** relation relates drivers cars, and accidents.

(*a*) SQL query :

```
select   count (distinct*)
from     accident
where    exists
         (select*
         from participated, person
         where participated. driver_id= person.driver_id
             and person. name= 'John Smith'
             and accident.report_number=participated. report_number);
```

(*b*) SQL query :

```
         update participated
         set damage_amount = 3000
         where report_number = "AR2197" and driver_id in
             (select driver_id
             from owns
             where license = "AABB200");
```

Q.43. Consider the following employee database, PKs are underlined. Write SQLs for the queries given below.

employee (<u>employee_name</u>, street, city)

works (<u>employee_name</u>, company_name, salary)

company (<u>company_name</u>, city)

manages (<u>employee_name</u>, manager_name)

(*a*) Find the names of all employee who work for First Bank Corporation.

(b) Find all employees in the database who live in the same cities as the companies for which they work.

(c) Find all employees in the database who live in the same cities and on the same streets as do their managers.

(d) Find all employees who earn more than the average salary of all employees of their company.

(e) Find the company that has the smallest payroll.

[GGSIPU, B.Tech (CS)—5th Sem., Sept. 2007]

Ans. (a) Find the names of all employees who work for First Bank Corporation.

```
SELECT employee_name
  FROM works
 WHERE company_name = 'First Bank Corporation';
```

(b) Find all employees in the database who live in the same cities as the companies for which they work.

```
SELECT e.employee_name
  FROM employee e, works w, company c
 WHERE e.employee_name = w.employee_name and e.city = c.city and
       w.company_name = c.company_name;
```

(c) Find all employees in the database who live in the same cities and on the same streets as do their managers.

```
SELECT P.employee_name
  FROM employee P,employee R, manages M
 WHERE P.employee_name = R.employee_name and
       M.manager_name = R.employee_name and
       P.street= R.street and P.city = R.city;
```

(d) Find all employees who earn more than the average salary of all employees of their company.

The following solution assumes that all people work for at most one company.

```
SELECT employee_name
  FROM works T
 WHERE salary> (SELECT AVG (salary)
                  FROM works S
                 WHERE T.company_name = S.company_name);
```

(e) Find the company that has the smallest payroll.

```
      SELECT company_name
        FROM works
    GROUP BY company_name
  HAVING SUM (salary) <= ALL (SELECT SUM (salary)
                                FROM works
                               GROUP BY company_name);
```

Q.44. Consider the above employee database and answer the queries given below–

(a) Give all employees of First Bank Corporation a 10 percent raise.

(b) Give all managers of First Bank Corporation a 10 percent raise.

(c) Delete all tuples in the works relation for employees of Small Bank Corporation.

Ans. (*a*) Give all employees of First Bank Corporation a 10-percent raise. (the solution assumes that each person works for at most company.)

```
UPDATE works
    SET salary = salary *1.1
WHERE company_name = 'First Bank Corporation';
```

(*b*) Give all managers of First Bank Corporation a 10-percent raise.

```
UPDATE works
    SET salary = salary *1.1
WHERE employee_name IN (SELECT manager_name
                        FROM manages)
      and company_name = 'First Bank Corporation';
```

(*c*) Delete all tuples in the works relation for employees of Small Bank Corporation.

```
DELETE works
WHERE company_name = 'Small Bank Corporation';
```

Q.45. Let the following relation schemas be given:

R = (A, B, C)

S = (D, E, F)

Let relations *r*(R) and *s*(S) be given. Give an expression in SQL that is equivalent to each of the following queries.

(*a*) $\Pi_A(r)$

(*b*) $\sigma_{B=17}(r)$

(*c*) $r \times s$

(*d*) $\Pi_{A,F}(\sigma_{C=D}(r \times s))$

Ans. (*a*) $\Pi_A(r)$

```
select distinct A
from r
```

(*b*) $\sigma_{B=17}(r)$

```
select*
from r
where B = 17
```

(*c*)

```
select distinct*
from r, s
```

(*d*) $\Pi_{A,F}(\sigma_{C=D}(r \times s))$

```
select distinct A, F
from r, s
where C = D
```

Q.46. Let R = (A, B, C), and let r_1 and r_2 both be relation on schema R.Give an expression in SQL that is equivalent to each of the following queries.

(*a*) $r_1 \cup r_2$

(*b*) $r_1 \cap r_2$

(*c*) $r_1 - r_2$

(*d*) $\Pi_{AB}(r_1) \bowtie \Pi_{BC}(r_2)$

Ans. (*a*) $r_1 \cup r_2$

```
(select*
from r1)
union
(select*
from r2);
```

(*b*) $r_1 \cap r_2$

We can write this using the **intersect** operation, which is the preferred approach, but for variety we present an solution using a nested subquery.

```
select*
from r1
where (A, B, C) in (select * from r2);
```

(*c*) $r_1 - r_2$

```
select *
from r1
where (A, B, C) not in (select * from r2);
```

This can also be solved using the **except** clause.

(*d*) $\Pi_{AB}(r_1) \bowtie \Pi_{BC}(r_2)$

```
select r1.A, r2.B, r3.C
from r1, r2
where r1.B = r2.B;
```

Q.47. Consider the relational database of above example. Using SQL, define a view consisting of *manager_name* and the average salary of all employees who work for that manager. Explain why the database system should not allow updates to be expressed in terms of this view.

Ans.

```
create view salinfo as
select manager_name, avg (salary)
from manages m, works w
where m.employee_name = w.employee_name
group by manager_name
```

Updates should not be allowed in this view because there is no way to determine how to change the underlying data. **For example**, suppose the request is "change the average salary of employees working for Smith to $200". Should everybody who works for Smith have their salary changed to $200? Or should the first (or more, if necessary) employee found who works for Smith have their salary adjusted so that the average is $200? Neither approach really makes sense.

EXERCISE QUESTIONS

Q.1. State true or false

(*i*) ORDER BY clause cannot be used in subquery.

(*ii*) In all group functions NULLs are ignored.

(*iii*) One block can have only one exception handler.

(*iv*) Explicit cursor attributes are defined with SQL%.

(*v*) The parameter passed in an INOUT mode cannot be referenced inside a procedure.

(*vi*) A sequence cannot be altered.

(*vii*) NVL function can be used for counting total number of null values in the table.

[GGSIPU, B.Tech. (CS)—5th Sem., Dec. 2006]

Q.2. (*a*) Write the syntax and use of DECODE function.

(*b*) What is OUTER JOIN operation.

(*c*) Explain the concept of a cursor.

(*d*) What is Trigger in database. **[GGSIPU, B.Tech. (CS)—5th Sem., Dec. 2006]**

Q.3. (*a*) What is the difference between truncate table and delete table in SQL?

(*b*) What is the disadvantage of indexes in SQL?

[GGSIPU, B.Tech. (CS/IT/ECE)—2nd term Exam, Sept. 2007]

Q.4. (*a*) Define and discuss :

(*i*) B* trees

(*ii*) What is NULL value? What type of value is it? Is a NULL value of one column similar to that of the other column?

[GGSIPU, B.Tech. (CS)—5th Sem., Dec. 2007]

Q.5. Explain the concept of method and trigger in Oracle with the help of suitable example.

[GGSIPU, B.Tech. (CS)—5th Sem., Dec. 2007]

Q.6. Consider the following two tables from a DBMS :

A	B	C
10	a	5
15	b	8
25	a	6

A	D	E
10	b	6
25	c	3
10	b	5
	a	7

(*a*) Give the result of join of these two tables.

(*b*) Write your query in SQL to produce the same output as in part (*a*).

(*c*) Is there any way to determine the primary key of the above two tables.

(*d*) Write an SQL query to produce the following output—

A	B	C
10	a	5
15	b	8
25	a	6
10	b	6
25	c	3
10	b	5
	a	7

[GGSIPU, B.Tech. (CS/IT/ECE); 5th Sem., Dec. 2008]

Q.7. Create the following tables and answer the queries : (Take appropriate data types to define the columns and then insert relevant data).

(*a*) SUPPLIER (<u>SNO</u>, SNAME, STATUS, CITY)

(*b*) PARTS (<u>PNO</u>, PNAME, COLOR, WEIGHT, CITY)

(*c*) PROJECT (<u>JNO</u>, JNAME, CITY)

(*d*) SPJ (<u>SNO, PNO, JNO</u>, QTY)

SQL Queries :

(*i*) Get sno values for suppliers who supply project *j*1.
(*ii*) Get sno values for suppliers who supply project *j*1 with part *p*1.
(*iii*) Get jname values for projects supplied by supplier *s*1.
(*iv*) Get color values for parts supplied by supplier *s*1.
(*v*) Get pno values for parts supplied to any project in London.
(*vi*) Get sno values for suppliers who supply project *j*1 with a red part.
(*vii*) Get sno values for suppliers who supply a London or Paris project with a red part.
(*viii*) Get pno values for parts supplied to any project by a supplier in the same city.
(*ix*) Get pno values for parts supplied to any project in London by a supplier in London.
(*x*) Get jno values for projects supplied by at least one supplier not in the same city.
(*xi*) Get all pairs of city values such that a supplier in the first city supplies a project in the second city.
(*xii*) Get sno values for suppliers who supply the same part to all projects.
(*xiii*) Get pno values for parts supplied to all projects in London.
(*xiv*) Get sname values for suppliers who supplies at least one red part to any project.
(*xv*) Get total quantity of part *p*1 supplied by supplier *s*1.
(*xvi*) Get the total number of projects supplied by supplier *s*3.
(*xvii*) Change color of all red parts to orange.
(*xviii*) Get sname values for suppliers who supply to both projects *j*1 and *j*2.
(*xix*) Get all city, pno, city triples such that a supplier in the first city supplies the specified part to a project in the second city.
(*xx*) Get jnames for those project which are supplied by supplier XYZ.

[GGSIPU, B.Tech. (CS) and M.Tech (IT); 5th Sem., Dec. 2008]

[UPTU, MBA; 4th Sem., 2006–2007 and GGSIPU, MCA; 2nd Sem., May 2003]

Q.8. What is a view? What are its advantages? Explain the syntax for creating views.

[GGSIPU, B.Tech. (CS); 5th Sem., Dec. 2008]

Q.9. (*a*) SQL is a very powerful DML and DDL. If so, what is the need of host languages in DBMS? Your explanation should include an example. Also describe the static embedding of SQL with the help of an example.

(*b*) What are four restrictions that update a database through a view? Describe them with the help of an example. Do the database forms represent the same concept as that of views? Give two reasons in support of your answer.

(*c*) Define with one example of each—

(*i*) Access plan in Query Evaluation.
(*ii*) B-tree index. **[IGNOU,MCA, 3rd Year, June 2004]**

Q.10. Consider the following database :

EMPLOYEE (emp_code, emp_name, desig, head, DOJ, basic, dept_code)
DEPARTMENT (dept_code, dept_name, floor)

Write SQL queries for the following :

(*i*) List the different positions available in the EMPLOYEE table.
(*ii*) List all department names, their locations from the DEPARTMENT TABLE.
(*iii*) List the names and designation of those employees who work on FLOOR 2 of the building. **[Delhi University, B.Sc., (MS); 3rd Year, 2008]**

Q.11. Given the relational schema :

ENROLL (S#, C#, Section)
TEACH (Prof, C#, Section)
ADVISE (Prof, S#)
PRE-REQ (C#, pre-C#)

GRADE (S#, C#, grade, year)
STUDENT (S#, sname)
Give queries expressed in SQL—
(*i*) List of students taking courses with Smith or Jones.
(*ii*) List all students taking atleast one course that their advisor teaches.
(*iii*) List those professors who teach more than one section of the same course.
(*iv*) List all students number and course number.
(*v*) List the student number and course number who got grade A.

[UPTU, B.Tech. (CS); 4th Sem., 2006–2007]

Q.12. (*a*) What are the various characteristics of SQL? Discuss five aggregate functions with a suitable example.
(*b*) Discuss the selection, projection and join operator with suitable example.
(*c*) What do you mean by Query and Sub-query? Discuss cursors in SQL also.

[UPTU, B.Tech. (CS); 4th Sem., 2006–2007]

Q.13. Let the following relational schema be given—
Employee (SSN, name, age, dno)
Salary (SSN, Salary)
Work_on (Project#, SSN)
Project (Project#, project_name, location)
Write SQL queries to—
(*a*) Display the names of projects at "Delhi".
(*b*) Find the project_name of employee whose salary is greater than 10,000.
(*c*) Retrieve the name and SSN of employees working on Project#A100.

[UPTU, MBA; 4th Sem., 2006–2007]

Q.14. Consider the following tables—

A	B	C
3	7	9
8	6	5

A	B	C
5	8	1
8	2	6

Show the semantics and the output of the following query—

```
SELECT *
FROM S, R
WHERE S.A = R.A AND S.B = R.B;
```

[BPUT, Orissa, B.Tech. (CS); 4th Sem., 2008]

Q.15. (*a*) Explain the following DML commands using appropriate examples : INSERT INTO, DELETE FROM, SELECT FROM.
(*b*) Explain the join and selection operations in an RDBMS. How can join operation be used to stimulate a selection?
(*c*) Explain the SQL construction for selections, projections and joins.
(*d*) What do you understand by query optimization? How is it achieved?

[BPUT, Orissa, B.Tech. (CSE); 4th Sem., April 2005]

Q.16. Explain with example the following SQL commands—
(*i*) CREATE—both view and table
(*ii*) ALTER—both add and modify
(*iii*) SELECT—group by, having apart from FROM and WHERE.

[BPUT, Orissa, B.Tech. & MCA; 2nd Year, June 2005]

Q.17. (*a*) What is the purpose of GROUP BY, ORDER BY and HAVING clause in the SELECT statement?
(*b*) Illustrate the use of SUM ( ) and AVG ( ) and COUNT ( ).
(*c*) What are unions? When two tables are said to be union compatible. How are the results ordered in a union compatible.

[GGSIPU, BCA/BIS(H); 3rd Sem., Dec. 2002]

Q.18. (*a*) What are DDL and DML commands? Explain with examples.
(*b*) Illustrate the use of SUM ( ), AVG ( ), COUNT ( ), MIN ( ), MAX ( ).
(*c*) Explain the query processing process with the help of a diagram.
[GGSIPU, BCA/BIS (H); 3rd Sem., Dec. 2002 and 2003]

Q.19. "NULL value concept is useful one but a large use of NULL VALUE in implemented database is not desirable." Comment. **[GGSIPU, MCA; 2nd Sem., May 2004]**

Q.20. Consider the following schema—
Faculty (Fno, Name, Date-of-Birth, DNO)
Deptt (DNO, Name,c Bldg)
Course (CNO, Name)
Teaches (FNO, CNO)
Write SQL statements to do the following :
(*a*) Find the names of the faculty members who work in the same building as faculty member with no. '104' works.
(*b*) Find the names of faculty members who are teaching atleast one course which the faculty member no. '101' is not teaching. **[GGSIPU, MCA; 2nd Sem., May 2004]**

Q.21. Consider the following relations—
Employee (emp_name, street, city)
Works (emp_name, company_name, salary)
Company (company_name, city)
Manages (emp_name, manager_name)
Write SQL queries for the following :
(*a*) Find the names of all employee who live in the same city as the company for which they work for.
(*b*) Find the names of all employees who live in same city as do their managers.
(*c*) Find the names and cities of residence for all employee who work for company "XYZ".
(*d*) Find the name of city where employee "X" works.
[GGSIPU, M.Tech. (IT); 3rd Sem., Dec. 2004]

Q.22. (*a*) What are the restrictions that are put on update operations using a view?
(*b*) List the reasons as why the null values might be introduced into the database.
[GGSIPU, M.Tech. (IT); 3rd Sem., Dec. 2005]

Q.23. Explain what is meant by repetition of information and inability to represent information? Also, explain why each of these properties may indicate a bad relational database design?
[GGSIPU, B.Tech. (CSE); 5th Sem., Dec. 2008]

Q.24. (*a*) What is a view? What are its advantages? Explain the syntax for creating views.
(*b*) Write a short note on query optimization.
[GGSIPU, B.Tech. (CSE); 5th Sem., Dec. 2008]

Q.25. (*a*) List the operations of relational algebra. Explain in detail function of each with suitable examples.
(*b*) Explain the role of SQL. What are the various components of SQL ? Explain in detail.
[GGSIPU, MCA-3rd Sem., Dec. 2010]

Q.26. Given the following schema :-
SUPPLER(SNO, SNAME, CITY)
PART CPNO, PANO, QTY)
Formulate SQL statements for the following :-
(*a*) Get supplier names for the suppliers who supply part no. 3.
(*b*) Get supplier names for the suppliers who do not supply part no. 3.
(*c*) For each part supplied, get the part number and the total supplied quantity.
(*d*) Get all pairs of supplier numbers such that the two suppliers are located in the same city.
(*e*) Get the maximum and minimum supplied quantity for part no. 3.
[GGSIPU, M.Tech. sem., Jan. 2011]

UNIT-III

Normalization

4.0 INTRODUCTION

Normalization is a design technique that is widely used as a guide in designing relational databases. To design a relational model system, we have to design a logical structure of the database. Normalization is a two step process. **In first step**, data is put in a tabular form by removing repeating groups. **In second step**, the duplicated data is removed from the relational tables. Our Normalization theory is based on the concepts of Normal forms. So, **Normalization is defined as the process of decomposing the redundant relation schemas by breaking up their attributes into smaller relation schemas that posses desirable properties**. This method of splitting is known as **projection**. **Please note that the goal is to have only primary keys on the left-hand side of a functional dependency**. Actually, this decomposition (splitting) has to be lossless. **This means that the new tables can be recombined back again by a natural join to recreate, the original table without creating any spurious or redundant data**. We will be discussing about functional dependencies a bit later. Let us first of all see the objectives of Normalization.

Objectives of Normalization Process : Normalization process has certain objectives which are discussed below :

1. To create a **formal framework** for analyzing relation schemas based on their keys.
2. To obtain **powerful relational retrieval algorithms** based on a collection of primitive relational operators.
3. To **free relations** from undesirable insertion, update and delete anomalies.
4. To reduce the **need for restructuring** the relations as new data types are introduced.
5. To carry out a **series of tests** on individual relation schema so that the relational database can be normalized to some degree. When a test fails, then the relation violating that test must be decomposed into relations that individually meet the normalization tests.

Please note the the entire process of normalization is based on the analysis of relations, their schemas, their primary keys and their functional dependencies (to be discussed). This process of Normalization was proposed by Dr. E.F. Codd. It is a bottom-up design technique for the relational database.

Basic Comcepts Associated with Normal Forms : A relation is said to be in a particular normal form if it satisfies a certain specified set of constraints. Please understand that each normal form has a set of constraints and if our data follows these constraints then our database is in that particular normal form. There are some characteristics expected by these decomposed relations :

1. They should have a **minimal number of attributes** necessary to support the data requirements of the enterprise.
2. The attributes with a close logical relationship are found in the same relation.
3. It has a **minimal redundancy**, which requires that the value of no attribute of a database instance is replicated except where tuples are linked by foreign keys.

Initially, Dr. E.F. Codd proposed three Normal forms—1st, 2nd and 3rd normal forms. The **basic idea** behind these forms is to make 2NF better than 1NF and 3NF better than 2NF. 3NF has two versions, both given by R.Boyce and Dr. E.F. Codd. Actually, the new version of 3NF is stronger than old form and named as BCNF to distinguish it from the old 3NF.

4.1 TERMINOLOGIES RELATED TO NORMALIZATION

There are some basic terms associated with normalization. They are discussed below :

1. **Functional Dependancy (FD) : A functional dependency is an association between two attributes of the same table (relation).** One of the attributes is called as the **determinant** and the other attribute is called as the **determined. Please note here that for each value of the determinant there is associated one and only one value of the determined.**

Notation used : If A is the determinant and B is the determined then we say that '**A functionally determines B**' and is graphically represented as :

$$A \to B$$

We can also say, **that B is functionally determined by A.**

For example, Consider the table below :

A	B
10	60
11	70
12	80
13	90
14	100

Here, A → B, because **for each value of A there is an associated one and only one value of B.**

Now, consider another table,

	A	B
	10	60
→	11	70
	12	80
	13	90
→	11	100

Here, A does not functionally determines B. This is because, for A = 11 there is associated more than one value of B *i.e.,* 70 as well as 100.

So, FD is defined as follows—"**An attribute in a relational model is said to be functionally dependent on another attribute in the table if it can take only one value for a given value of the attribute upon which it is functionally dependent**".

Consider the following database now.

SUPPLIER table (SP)

Sno	Sname	Status	City
S1	Ajay	11	Delhi
S2	Mayur	12	Gurgaon
S3	Rahul	13	Delhi

Here, **Sname is FD on Sno.** why ?

This is because Sname can take only one value for the given value of Sno (eg, S2 for Mayur). We can also say that there must be one Sname for supplier number, S2.

∴ This FD is represented as :

Sno → Sname

Here, FD is shown by an arrow (→) which shows that Sname is functionally dependent on Sno.

Similarly, city and status are also FD on Sno, because for each value of Sno, there will be only one city and status. These FDs are represented as follows :

Sno → City
Sno → Status

We can combine these FDs also and write them as follows :

SP. Sno → SP (Sname, City, Status)

Now, consider another table (SH) below.

SHIPMENT table (SH)

Sno	Pno	Qty
S1	P1	150
S1	P2	200
S1	P3	300
S2	P1	350
S2	P2	400
S3	P2	450

Here, Qty is FD on combination of (Sno, Pno) because **each combination of** *(Sno, Pno)* **results** only for one quantity. So, we write.

(Sno, Pno) → Qty

We can also represent all these FDs in form of a diagram called as a **Dependency diagram**. It consists of the attributes (fields) and all FDs in a given table.

For example, in our first table–SUPPLIER (SP) we have the following FDs existing

Sno → Sname
Sname → Sno

$$Sno \rightarrow City$$
$$Sno \rightarrow Status$$
$$Sname \rightarrow City$$
$$Sname \rightarrow Status$$
$$City \rightarrow Status$$

Now, we can draw its Dependency Diagram (DD) also. It is shown in Fig. 4.1.

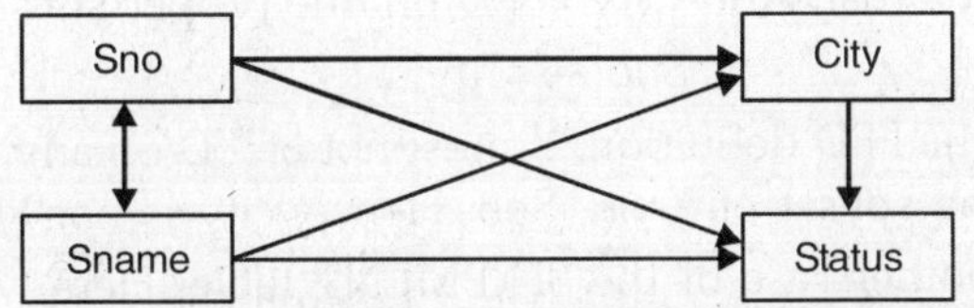

Fig. 4.1. *Dependency diagram for the SUPPLIER table*

On the other hand, the DD for the second table *i.e.*, SHIPMENT table (SH) will be as shown in Fig. 4.2.

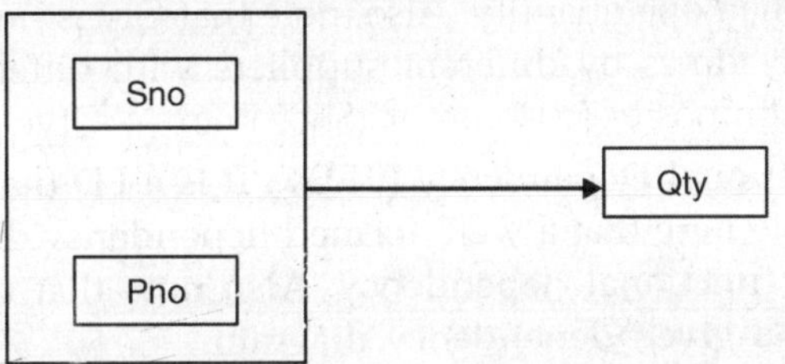

Fig. 4.2. *DD for the SHIPMENT table*

Now, consider another relation–PARTS (PT) :

Pno	Pname	Color	Weight	City
P1	Nut	Black	10	Delhi
P2	Bolt	Red	12	Gurgaon
P3	Screw	Blue	15	Delhi

Here,
$$Pno \rightarrow Pname$$
$$Pno \rightarrow Color$$
$$Pno \rightarrow Weight$$

∴ It's DD or FD diagram is as follows :

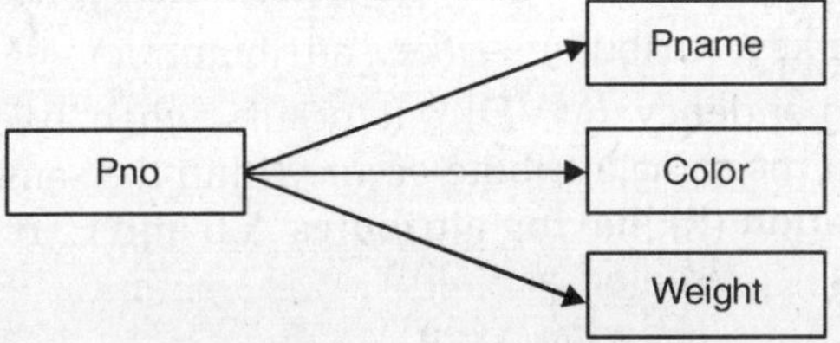

Fig. 4.3. *DD for the PARTS table*

2. Fully Functionally Dependent (FFD) : We define FFD as follows— **"An attribute, 'Y', is FFD on attribute 'X', if it is FD on X and not FD on any proper subset of X."**

For example, As already discussed, in the SHIPMENT table,

$$(Sno, Status) \rightarrow City$$

It means that city is FD on composite attribute (Sno, Status) but city is not FFD no this composite attribute. Why ?

This is explained as follows :

$$\underbrace{(\text{Sno, Status})}_{X} \rightarrow \underbrace{\text{City}}_{Y}$$

Let these be represented by X and Y. Now, Y is FD on X. But X has two proper subsets (*i.e.*, Sno and Status). And City is FD on one proper subset of X *i.e.*, Sno, that is,

$$\text{Sno} \rightarrow \text{City}$$

But according to the FFD definition, Y must not be FD on any proper subset of X but, here, city is FD on one subset of X *i.e.*, Sno. Hence, city is not FFD in (Sno, Status).

Now, consider another case of the SHIPMENT table. Here, we found an FD that

$$\underbrace{(\text{Sno, Pno})}_{X} \rightarrow \underbrace{\text{Qty}}_{Y}$$

Here, also X has two proper subsets Sno and Pno. Qty is **not FD** on Sno because one Sno can supply more than one quantity. Also, note that Qty is **not FD** on Pno as one Pno may be supplied many times by different suppliers with different or same quantities. Here, Qty is FFD on composite attribute of (Sno, Pno) → Qty.

3. Candidate Functional Dependency (CFD) : It is a FD that includes all attributes of the table. Please note here that a well–formed dependency diagram (DD) must have atleast one candidate functional dependency. Also note that there can be more than one candidate FD for a given dependency diagram.

4. Primary Functional Dependency (PFD) : It is a candidate FD that is selected to determine the primary key. The determinant of the PFD is the primary key of the table. Each dependency diagram must have one and only one primary FD. If a table has only one CFD then it automatically becomes the PFD. Once the primary key has been determined, there will be three possible types of FDs :

(*a*) PFD is a FD where **determinant** consists of key attributes but not the entire primary key and the **determined** consists of non-key attributes *i.e.*,

(Key-attributes) → (Non-key attributes)

(*b*) **Transitive Functional Dependency** is a FD where the **determinant** consists of non-key attributes and the **determined** also consists of non-key attributes *i.e.*,

(Non-key attribute) → (Non-key attribute)

(*c*) **Boyce-Codd functional dependency** (BCFD) is a FD where the **determinant** consists of non-key attributes and the **determined** consists of key-attributes *i.e.*,

(Non-key attribute) → (key attribute)

5. Multivalued Dependency (MVD) : It occurs when two or more independent multi-valued facts about the same attribute occur within the same table. **Please note that it means that if in a relation (R), having attributes A,B and C, B and C are multi-valued facts about A**, which is represented as

$$A \twoheadrightarrow B$$

and

$$A \twoheadrightarrow C$$

then MVD exists only if B and C are independent of each other.

6. Join Dependency (JD) : A JD exists if a relation (R) is equal to the join of the projections X, Y, ... Z where X, Y, ... Z are projections of R.

We are in a position to solve some questions now.

Example 1. For the given relation R, which of the following FDs are satisfied by the instances—

Relation, R

X	Y	Z
1	4	2
1	5	3
1	6	3
3	2	2

(*a*) XY → Z and Z → Y

(*b*) YZ → X and Y → Z

(*c*) YZ → X and X → Z

(*d*) XZ → Y and Y → X

Solution. Z → Y, X → Z are incorrect because attributes Z and X do not contain unique values, Similarly, XZ → Y is incorrect because the pair {X, Z} has the same values {1, 3} at multiple records (tuples).

Thus, the only set of FDs that are satisfied by R is (c).

Example 2. Write short notes on Trivial and non-trivial dependencies.

Solution. In general, **dependencies that are satisfied by all relations are called as trivial dependencies.**

For eg., The dependency X → X is satisfied by any relation having attribute, X. Again, XY → X is satisfied by any relation having attribute X.

> **NOTE :** In general, a dependency X → Y is trivial it Y ⊆ X. Trivial dependencies are not concerned with database consistency. Hence, they do not have much significance.

However, not-trivial dependencies are very significant as they correspond to essential integrity constraints of the database.

4.2 FIRST NORMAL FORM (1NF)

"A relation is said to be in INF if and only if every entry of the relation has at most a single (or atomic or indivisible) value only".

Please understand that the objective of normalizing a table is to remove its repeating groups and ensure that all entries of the resulting table have at most a single value. Also note that by simply removing the repeating groups of the unnormalized tables, they do not become relations automatically. Some further manipulations of the resulting tables may be necessary to ensure that they are indeed relations. Many a times, it is desired during database designing that we need to make our database atomic.

Table entries that have more than one value are called as **multivalue** entries. **Such tables with multivalue entries are known as un-normalized tables.**

Let us consider an example of an **un-normalized table**-STUDENT.

Course Code	Course_name	Tname	RNo	SName	System	Rate	Total_Hrs
A1	DBMS	Ajay	1	Rahul	P-II	10	2
			2	Rajiv	P-iv	12	1
			3	Raman	AMD	15	2
			4	Rohit	Celeron	20	1
B2	OS	Rajiv	2	Rajiv	P-IV	5	3
			5	Mayur	AMD	40	7
			6	Nimit	P-I	10	1
			3	Raman	AMD	40	2

We can see so many repeating groups here. **This tupe of table cannot be considered as a relation because there are entries with more than one value.** So, we need to normalize this table, firstly, to its 1NF. There are basically two approaches for the same –

First Method : Flattening of the table

In this method, **we remove repeating groups by filling in the missing entries of each incomplete row of the table with the copies of their corresponding non-repeating attributes.** So, the normalized representation of the above STUDENT table is as follows:

Course Code	Course_name	Tname	RNo	SName	System	Rate	Total_Hrs
A1	DBMS	Ajay	1	Rahul	P-II	10	2
A1	DBMS	Ajay	2	Rajiv	P-IV	12	1
A1	DBMS	Ajay	3	Raman	AMD	15	2
A1	DBMS	Ajay	4	Rohit	Celeron	20	1
B2	OS	Rajiv	2	Rajiv	P-IV	5	3
B2	OS	Rajiv	5	Mayur	AMD	40	7
B2	OS	Rajiv	6	Nimit	P-I	10	1
B2	OS	Rajiv	3	Raman	AMD	40	2

Please note that this normalized table is not a relation because it does not have primary key. The attribute (field): Course_code now no longer identifies any row uniquely. **To transform this table into a relation, a primay key (PK) needs to be defined. And a suitable PK of this table is the composite key:** (Course_code, RNo).

Second Method : Decompose the table

In this approach of normalization of a table, **we decompose the table into two new tables that will replace the original table.** Decomposition of a table involves separating the attributes of the relation to create two or more new relations. Naturally, this requires a careful selection of the attributes from the original table to form the attributes of new tables.

In this approach, we follow certain **rules of decomposition** –

Rule 1. One of the two tables contains the tables-identifier (PK) of the original table + all the non-repeating attributes.

Rule 2. The other table contains a copy of the table identifier (PK) + all repeating attributes.

Please understand that in order to transform these tables into relations, it may be necessary to identify a PK for each table. **Also note that the tuples of the new relations are the projections of the original relation into their respective schemes.** So, using this scheme, if we try to normalize our STUDENT table then we need to replace it by two tables. That is—

1st table, named as COURSE with the fields as a table-identifier (or PK) and the non-repeating groups *i.e.,*

COURSE (Course-code, Course_Name, Tname)
↑
This field is a table identifier/PK
for COURSE relation.

2nd table, named as, say, COURSE_STUDENT with the fields as a table_identifier (or PK) and all the repeating groups *i.e.,*

COURSE_STUDENT (Course_code, RNo, SName, System, Rate, Total_Hrs)

NOTE : you can add records from the original STUDENT table on your own.

However, to transform this 2nd table into a relation, it is necessary to assign a primary key (PK) to it. Please note that for the 2nd table COURSE_STUDENT, the most appropriate primary key is (Course_code, RNo).

Which out of these two schemes is better and why?

Both the approaches are correct as they transform an un-normalized table into 1NF relation. **But the second approach is more efficient because the relations produced are less redundant**.

However, the table in 1NF do suffer from insert, delete, update anomalies and thus we go in for the Second Normal Form (2NF). **We are in a position to solve some examples now.**

Example 1. Consider the following relation – LIVED_IN. Is it a normalized relation? If not normalize it.

PERSON	CITY	DATE_MOVED
Abhishek	Calcutta	14-3-2008
	Mumbai	14-4-2008
	Delhi	06-5-2009
Thomas	Singapore	5-5-2006
	Chennai	9-4-2007
	Bangalore	9-9-2008

Solution. We need to flatten the tables to convert it to 1NF (*i.e.,* method -I). So, we have

PERSON	CITY	DATE_MOVED
Abhishek	Calcutta	14-3-2008
Abhishek	Mumbai	14-4-2008
Abhishek	Delhi	06-5-2009
Thomas	Singapore	5-5-2006
Thomas	Chennai	9-4-2007
Thomas	Bangalore	9-9-2008

Example 2. In the employee table given below, identify the primary key (PK), all repeating and non-repeating attributes. Flatten the table and state if the resulting table is a relation. If not, how can you make it a relation

EID	Name	Department	Dependents_Name	Dependent_ID
A1	Mayur	Sales	Nishita	D10
			Nishant	D11
A2	Rahul	MIS	John	D12
			Mary	D13

Solution. It is clear from the table that if we use method -1 of flattening of our table, then the **suitable primary key (PK) is EID**. The **non-repeating attributes are**–EID, Name and Department. The **repeating attributes** are–Dependent_Name and Dependent_ID.

To flatten this tables, we fill the missing entries –

EID	Name	Department	Dependents_Name	Dependent_ID
A1	Mayur	Sales	Nishita	D10
A1	Mayur	Sales	Nishant	D11
A2	Rahul	MIS	John	D12
A2	Rahul	MIS	Mary	D13

Now, EID is no longer a PK. To transform this table into a relation, we need to identify a suitable PK. We observe that the composite key (EID, Dependent_ID) seems to be a suitable choice of the PK

Example 3. Consider the same table as in Example -2 above. Normalize it using decomposition technique now.

Solution. The given relation EMPLOYEE is EMPLOYEE (EID, Name, Department, Dependents_Name, Dependent_ID).

Now, to normalize this, we need to create two new relations using our 2 rules of decomposition. So, we get –

1st table = PK + all non-repeating attributes.

2nd table = PK + all repeating attributes.

That is, EMPLOYEE (EID, Name, Department)

and DEPENDENT (EDID, Dependent_Name, Dependent_ID)

Please note here that EID of 1st table has been renamed as EDID. This EDID along with Dependent_ID will form a composite PK for the 2nd relation.

4.3 SECOND NORMAL FORM (2NF)

Definition : "A relation R is in second Normal form (2NF),if and only if it is in 1NF and every non-key attribute is fully dependent on the primary key".

Rule used to convert a relation from 1NF to 2NF is as follows :

If A, B, C and D are four fields or attributes and if A and B are PKs. 'Now, A and B attributes determine all other attributes. C and D are non-key (or non-prime) attributes. Attribute C is **fully dependent** on the key. Attribute D is **partially dependent** on the key, because we only need attribute A to functionally determine it. Here, the rule is

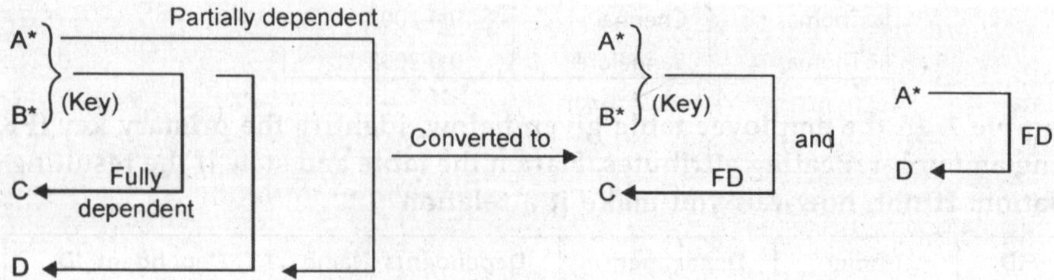

Fig. 4.4

These resultant 2-relations are both fully dependent on the PK now. So,

$$(A^*, B^*) \rightarrow C$$

$$A^* \rightarrow D$$

Here, '*' denotes that it is a PK. So, we observe that the **first-new relation** has 3 attributes: A*, B* and C where (A*, B*) is the PK of this relation (same as that of original relation) And the **second relation** has A* and D as its 2 attributes. So, A* is the PK of second relation and D is now fully dependent on the key.

This process can be extended to any number of attributes.

We are in a position to solve problems now.

Example 1. Trans_form the STUDENT table with fields as – (Course_code Course_Name, Tname, RNO, System, Rate, Total_Hrs) into a 2NF.

Solution. We consider the same relation that we had in 1NF and use the above rule to convert it to 2NF. We need to decompose it into three tables :

1. **HOURS_ASSIGNED (Course_code, RNo, Total-Hrs) :** This is so because the primary key of STUDENT (Course_code, RNo) and the remaining attributes of this relation that fully depends on this composite key is Total_Hrs. Hence, the above relation.
2. **STUDENT_SYSTEM_CHARGE (RNo, NAME, System, Rate) :** Here, RNo is it's PK because RNo fully determines the Name, System and the Rate.
3. **The third relation could be—COURSE (Course_code, Course_Name, Tname) :** It contains Course_code as its PK, because Course_code fully determines the Course_Name, Tname.

Example 2. Consider the relation scheme and FD given below. What is the highest normal form of this relation ? Transform this relation to its next higher form. Can the information of the given relation be recovered ? What operation is necessary to recover it?

Programmer_Task (PID, PackID, PackName, Tot_Hrs_Worked)

and Pack ID → PackName

Solution. The highest form of this relation is 1NF because there are partial dependencies on the composite key, as shown in the given FD. The next highest form of this relation is 2NF. To transform this relation, we use rule of decomposition, as stated earlier. This is shown below :

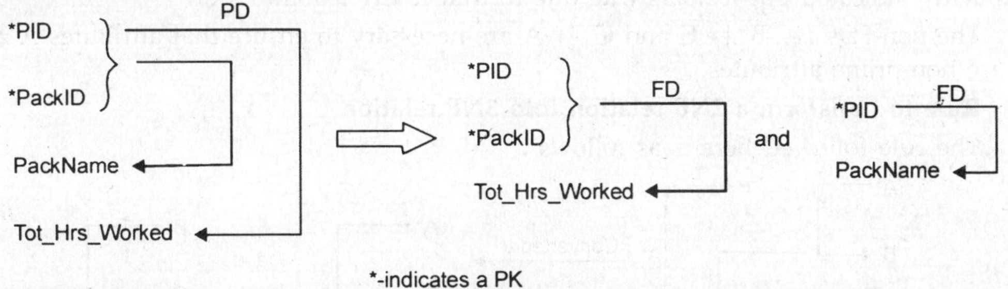

Fig. 4.5

Note that these two sub-relations are in 2NF now because as per our definition of 2NF, every non_key attribute is fully dependent on PK. Here, now the attribute Tot_Hrs_Worked is FD on (*PID,*PackID) primary key. Similarly, in 2nd relation, PackName is FD on *PID. So, we can say that we have removed all partial dependencies that were these in the orginal table.

Also note that the information of the original relation can be recovered by means of a join operation on the common attribute *i.e.,* *PackID.

4.4 THIRD NORMAL FORM (3NF) AND BCNF

Definition : "A relation R is said to be in 3NF if and only if the following conditions are simultaneously satisfied :

1. **R is already in 2NF.**
2. **No non-prime attribute (*i.e.,* non-key attribute) is transitively dependent on the key or we can say that no non-prime attribute functionally determines any other non-prime attribute."**

So, we observe that the **objective** of transforming relations into 3NF is to **remove transitive dependencies.**

Before we discuss further, let us describe what is transitive dependency (TD)?

Consider a relation (R) that has a set of three attributes –A, B and C. Also, assume that the following FDs for this R, exists –

$$A \to B,\ B \to C \text{ and thus } A \to C$$

Please note here that C → B is neither required nor prohibited. And if all these conditions are true, we say that the attribute C is TD on attribute A. **Also note that these FDs determine the conditions for having a TD of attribute – C on A.** This is shown in Fig. 4.6.

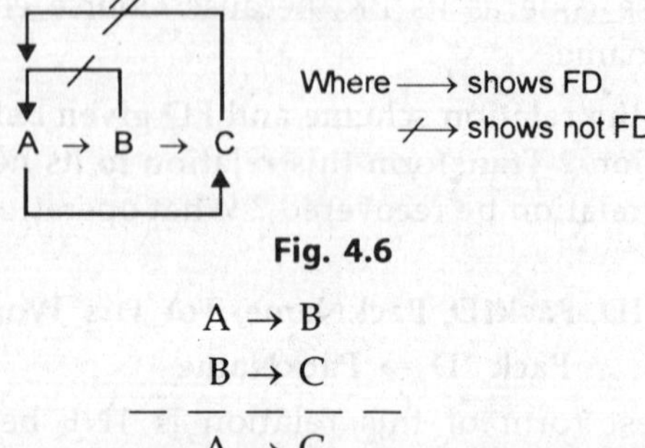

Fig. 4.6

i.e.,

$$A \to B$$
$$B \to C$$
$$\overline{A \to C}$$

∴ TD exists but $B \not\to A$, $C \not\to A$ means B will not functionally determine A and similarly, C will not functionally depend on A. Also note that the FD, $A \to C$ may not be explicitly indicated but it holds true due to transitivity axiom.

The non-FDs *i.e.,* $B \not\to C$ and $C \not\to A$ are necessary to ensure that attributes A and B are non-prime attributes.

Rule to transform a 2NF relation into 3NF relation

The **rule** followed here is as follows :

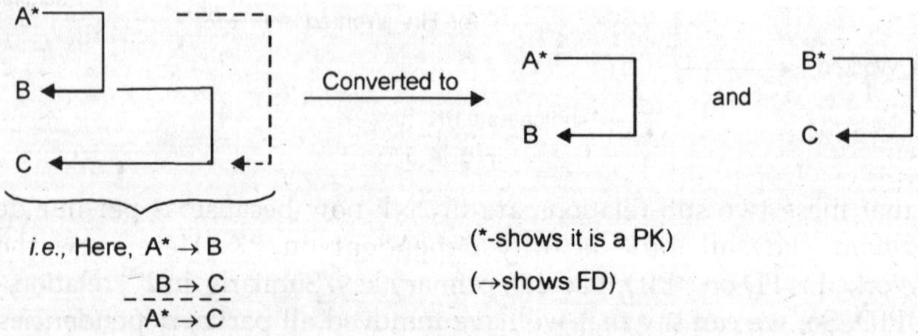

Fig. 4.7

⇒ Transitive dependency (TD) exists.

We assume here that any FD not implicitly indicated does not hold. The **dashed line** shows an FD, A → C which may not be explicitly given but it is always present because we can derive it using the inference axioms.

Finally, we get 2 new tables and in the 2nd table, B is made the PK of this table. **We are in a position to solve some problems now.**

Example 1. Consider the Manufacturer relation-MANU. Each manufacturer has a unique ID and name. Manufacturers produce items. They may produce more than one item and different manufacturers may produce the same items. The relation schema is:

MANU (<u>MID</u>, MNAME, <u>ITEM_NO</u>, QTY).

Solution. This MANU relation has two candidate keys: (MID, ITEM_NO) and (MNAME, ITEM_NO) that overlap on the attribute ITEM_NO. This relation is in 3NF because there is only one non-prime attribute and therefore it is impossible that this attribute can determine another non-prime attribute.

Example 2. Consider the following relation R(Rno, Name, System, Rate) again and convert it to 3NF if it is not in 3NF.

Solution. The given relation, R, is not in 3NF because there is a TD of a non-prime attribute on the PK of the relation. Here, Rate attribute (non-prime or non-key) is TD on primary-key, RNo, through the FD, System → Rate. **Please note that all other conditions required by the definition are met by this set of FDs**. So, we have RNo → System and System → Rate. How to transform this relation into 3NF now?

To do so, we need to remove any transitive dependency (TD) of a non_prime attribute on the key. So, following our rule, we get two new relations –

1. R_1(<u>RNo</u>, Name, System)
2. R_2 (<u>System</u>, Rate).

Please note that in the second relation, R_2, the System attribute has been made the PK of this relation (as per our rule). Also note that we have another reason to say that R was not in 3NF. As is clear, in System → Rate FD, both the attributes are non-prime (non_key) in R. So, we get the above two relations—R_1 and R_2. 3NF also suffers from some anamolies and thus we need to carry out the normalization process to the next higher step called as **Boyce-Codd Normal Form**.

Boyce Codd Normal Form (BCNF) : Actually, BCNF is a stronger form of 3NF as it eliminates all anomalies associated with 3NF.

Definition : "A relation R is said to be in BCNF if and only if every determinant is a candidate key". Here, determinant is a simple attribute or composite attribute on which some other attribute is fully functionally dependent.

For example, in FD, (Sno, Pno) → Qty (Sno, Pno) is a **composite determinant** whereas in FD, Sno → Sname , Sno is **simple determinant**.

Let us consider two cases now.

Case I. Similarities between 3NF and BCNF.

Case II. Dissimilarities between 3NF and BCNF.

Case I. Similarities between 3NF and BCNF.

Any relation which is in 3NF is always in BCNF.

For example, consider a relation, STUD as follows :

STUD (<u>RNO</u>, Name, System, Rate)

Here, RNo → Name ¦ System ¦ Rate

and System → Rate

Now, System attribute is also a determinant but it is not unique (or candidate key). So, this relation STUD is not in BCNF.

Please understand that the relation STUD is not in 3NF and hence are not in BCNF also. Now, consider another example, where we formed 2 relations–R_1 and R_2 from the above STUD relation and both were in 3NF *i.e.,*

R_1(<u>RNo</u>, Name, System)
and R_2 (<u>System</u>, Rate) } are in 3NF (done earlier)

Now, these relations are in BCNF also because

RNo → Name | System
and System → Rate.

Here, each determinant is unique in its relation, R_1 and R_2.

Thus, we conclude that in these relations which have only single candidate key, can be normalized both with 3NF and BCNF without any problem.

Case II. Dissimilarities between 3NF and BCNF.

The difference between 3NF and BCNF is that for a FD, A → B, 3NF allows this dependency in a relation if B is a PK and A is not a candidate key. Whereas BCNF insists that for this dependency to remain in a relation, A must be a candidate key. Therefore, BCNF is stronger form of 3NF, such that every relation in BCNF is also in 3NF.

To understand this further, we must understand the concept of overlapping of candidate keys first.

Overlapping of candidate keys : "Two candidate keys overlap if they involve two or more attributes each and have an attribute in common."

For example, consider the MANU relation again with this schema.

MANU (<u>MID</u>, MNAME, <u>ITEM_NO</u>, QTY)

Now, for this relation, FDs are –

(MID, ITEM_NO) → QTY
(MNAME, ITEM_NO) → QTY
ITEM_NO → MNAME
MNAME → ITEM_NO

This relation has two overlapping candidate keys because there are two composite candidate keys – (MID, ITEM_NO) and (MNAME, ITEM_NO) out of which ITEM_NO is a common attribute in both the candidate keys. So, this is a due case of overlapping of candidate keys. We can now draw it's FD diagram as shown in Fig. 4.8.

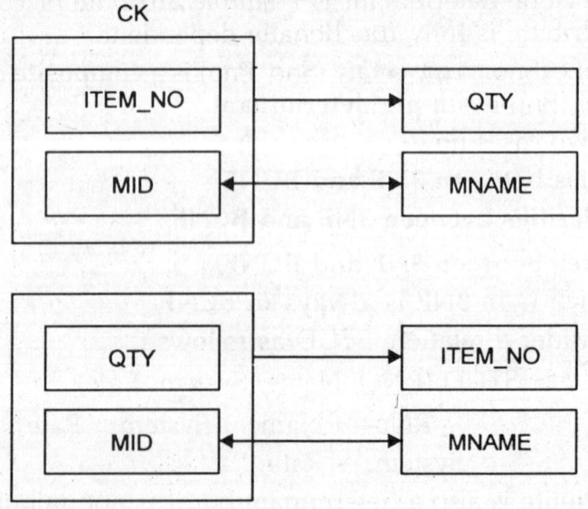

Fig. 4.8. *FD diagram*

Please note here that both the relations are in 3NF because every non-key attribute is non-transitively fully functional dependent on the primary key. Also note that in the above relation, there is only one non-key attribute *i.e.,* QTY and it is FFD and non-transitively dependent on the PK. Also, MNAME and ITEM_NO are not **non-key attributes** because they can participate into the primary key (shown in Fig). But the **MANU relation is not in BCNF** because this relation has four determinants *i.e.,*

(*a*) (MID, ITEM_NO)
(*b*) (MNAME, ITEM_NO)
(*c*) ITEM_NO
(*d*) MNAME
(See FD's)

Now, out of these four determinants, two determinants :

(*a*) (MID, ITEM_NO) and
(*b*) (MNAME, ITEM_NO)

are unique but ITEM_NO and MNAME (determinants) are not the candidate keys. So, MID is made the candidate key.

Now, in order to convert this MANU relation into BCNF, we have to non-loss decompose this relation into two projections –

(*a*) MIN (MID, MNAME)
(*b*) QID (MID, ITEM_NO, QTY).

∴ MIN relation has two determinants (MID, MNAME) and both are unique. Also, QID has one determinant (MID, ITEM_NO) and is also, unique.

So, now these two relations are in BCNF, will remove all anomalies of MANU relation.

Algorithm for BCNF decomposition :

If relation scheme R is not in BCNF, we can decompose R into a collection of BCNF schema R_1, R_2, ...R_n. Using the algorithm given below :

result : ={R}
done:=false;
Compute F^+;
while (not done) do
if (there is a schema R_i in result that is not in BCNF) then begin
    let $\alpha \rightarrow \beta$ be a non_trival functional dependency that holds on R_i such that
    $\alpha \rightarrow R_1$ is not in F+, and $\alpha \cap \beta = \phi$;
    result:=(result-R_1) $\cup$ (R_1–β) $\cup$ (α ,β);
end
else
    done:=true

BCNF decomposition algorithm.

This algorithm generates BCNF decomposition which is also loss-less-join decomposition.

We are in a position to solve some problems now.

Example 1. Consider the following relation–USE :

PROJECT	PROJ_MANAGER	MACHINE	QTY_USED
P1	Rajiv	Drill	3
P2	Mayur	Weld	5
P3	Deepak	Drill	3
P1	Rajiv	Drill	10

Is this relation in 2NF or in 3NF or both ? Is it in BCNF? How can you do the required transformations?

Solution. This relation-USE has two primary keys :

(*a*) (PROJECT, MACHINE)

(*b*) (PROJ_MANAGER, MACHINE)

Here, the keys **overlap** because the attribute MACHINE appears in both keys whereas PROJECT and PROJ_MANAGER, each appear in one primary key only.

Please note that the relation, USE, has only one non-prime (non-key) attribute, QTY_USED, which is fully functionally dependent on each of the relations. So, this relation (USE) is in 2NF.

Also note that there is only one non-prime attribute, QTY_USED, **so there can be non dependencies between non-prime attributes.**

Thus, the relation USE is **also in 3NF.**

However, this relation is not in BCNF as it contains the following two FDs :

PROJ_MANAGER → PROJECT

PROJECT → PROJ_MANAGER

But neither PROJ_MANAGER or PROJECT is a super key. So, to get it into BCNF, we decompose these relations as follows –

R_1 (PROJECT, MACHINE, QTY_USED)

R_2 (PROJECT, PROJ_MANAGER)

Here, the only FD between the R_1 attributes is –

(PROJECT, MACHINE) → QTY_USED

and (PROJECT, MACHINE) is a super key. So, both of the above relations are in BCNF. The two FDs between the PROJECTS attributes are :

PROJECT → PROJ_MANAGER

PROJ_MANAGER → PROJECT

Both PROJECT and PROJ_MANAGER are super keys of the relation R_1 and R_1 is in BCNF.

Example 2. Consider a relation given below SP(Sno, Sname, Pno, Qty)

Here, Sname is considered unique for each Sno. So, FD of above relation is –

(Sno, Pno) → Qty

(Sname, Pno) → Qty

Sno → Sname

Sname → Sno

Is this relation in 3NF ? Check for it to be in BCNF ? How can you solve this problem?

Solution. Given : FDs of SP relation –

(Sno, Pno) → Qty
(Sname, Pno) → Qty
Sno → Sname
Sname → Sno

This relation has two overlapping candidate keys because there are two composite candidate keys (Sno, Pno) and (Sname, Pno) out of which Pno is common attribute in both the candidate keys. So, this is a due case of overlapping of candidate keys. Now, we can draw, its FD diagram also.

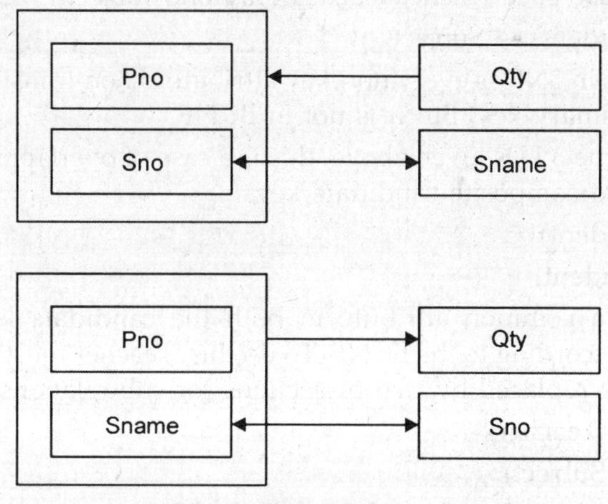

Fig. 4.9

Please note here that both the relations are in 3NF because every non-key attribute is non-transitively fully functional dependent on the primary key. In the above relation, there is only one non-key attribute *i.e.*, Qty and it is FFD and non-transitively dependent on the primary key. Sname and Sno are not non-key attribute they can participate into the primary key (shown in FD diagram).

But, **please note that this relation, SP is not in BCNF because it has four determinants –**

(*a*) (Sno, Pno)

(*b*) (Sname, Pno)

(*c*) (Sno)

(*d*) (Sname)

Out of these four determinants, two determinants (Sno, Pno) and (Sname, Pno) are unique but Sno and Sname determinants are not candidate keys.

Now, to make this relation in BCNF, we have to non-loss decompose this relation into two projections :

(*a*) SN (Sno, Sname)

(*b*) SPP (Sno, Pno, Qty)

∴ SN relation has two determinants and that both are unique.

SP has one determinant (Sno, Pno) and is also unique.

Thus, all anomalies are removed.

Example 3. Consider a relation, SST with attributes (Student, Subject, Teacher). For each subject, each student of that subject is taught by only one teacher. Each teacher teaches only one subject. Each subject is taught by several teachers. It's schema is—

SST (Student, Subject, Teacher). Find all FD's. Is this relation in BCNF or not ? How can you transform it to BCNF?

Solution. From the given rules, we find the following FDs :

1. (Subject, Student) → Teacher.

   This is because it is given that (Subject, Student) combination gives only one teacher.

2. Teacher → Subject

   This is because each teacher teaches only one subject.

3. (Teacher, Student) → Subject

So, this relation is in 3NF as every non-key attribute is non-transitively fully functional dependent on the primary key. But it is not in BCNF.

Now, observing the 3 FDs given above, this is a case of overlapping of candidate keys because there are two composite candidate keys :

(*a*) (Subject, Student)

(*b*) (Teacher, Student)

And Student is a common attribute in both the candidate keys. So, we need to normalize this table according to the BCNF. To do this, Teacher must be the candidate key, so original relation is replaced by two projections (or sub-relations) :

(*a*) ST (Student, Teacher)

(*b*) TJ (Teacher, Subject)

This removes all anomalies from the original table.

Example 4. Let, **R = (A, B, C, D) and**

F = {AB → C,

C → A}

Find BCNF decomposition of R using the algorithm.

Solution.

Consider, AB→ C

R_1 = (A, B, C.)

F_1 = {AB → C, C → A}

R_2 = (A, B, D)

F_2 = { }

R_2, can be again decomposed using.

C → A

R_{11} = (A, C)

F_{11} = {C → A }

R_{12} = {B, C}

F_{12} = { }

Example 5.Find BCNF decomposition of the relation schema shipping with the following set of functional dependencies.

Shipping_schema = (ship, capacity, Data, Cargo, Value)

Ship	→	Capacity
Ship Date	→	Cargo
Cargo capacity	→	Value
Consider cargo capacity	→	Value FD.

Solution:

It gives

R_1 = (Cargo, Capacity, Value)

R_{11} = (Cargo, Capacity, Ship, Date)

Now using ship → capacity FD,

R_{11} can be decomposed as :

R_2 = (Ship, Capacity)

R_3 = (Ship, date, cargo)

Hence, the shipping is decomposed as follows:

R_1 (Cargo, Capacity, Value) with F.D.

Cargo capacity → value

R_2 (Ship, Capacity) with the FD

Ship → Capacity

R_3 (Ship, Date, Cargo) with FD

Ship Date → Cargo

This decomposition is loss-less-join decomposition and also dependency preserving.

Not every decomposition is dependency preserving :

Consider the Banker_schema and set of functional dependencies.

Banker_schema = (branch_name, customer_name, banker_name)

Banker_name → branch_name

branch_name customer_name → banker_name

The above given Banker_schema is not in BCNF since, banker_name is not a super key.

Using BCNF decomposition algorithm and banker name → branch_name dependency, it can be decomposed into:

Banker_branch_schema = (banker_name, branch_name)

With FD F_1 = banker_name → branch_name

Customer_banker_schema = (customer_name, banker_name)

and FD F_2 = { }.

$F' = F_1 \cup F_2$ = {banker_name → branch_name}

The decomposed schema preserve only,

banker_name → branch_name

F'^{+} does not contain,

Customer_name branch_name banker_name.

$F'^{+} \neq F^{+}$

Hence, it is not a dependency preserving decomposition.

This example demonstrates that not every BCNF decomposition is dependency preserving.

We cannot always satisfy all three design goals:

1. BCNF
2. Loss-less Join
3. Dependency Preservation

This algorithm generates decomposition into 3NF of a given relation schema. The decomposition is dependency preserving and loss-less join decomposition.

Example 6. Find 3NF decomposition of given relation schema and FDs.

Banker_info_schema = (branch_name, customer_name, banker_name, office_no.)

Functional dependencies are :

banker_name → branch_name, office_no.

customer_name, branch_name, banker_name

Solution:

Using the algorithm and FD

Result of for loop:

- banker_name → branch_name office_no.

  α = banker-name, β = branch_name office_no.

  R_1 = (banker_name, branch_name, office_no)
- Customer_name, branch_name → banker_name

  R_2 = (customer_name, branch, name, banker_name
- Second if condition is not satisfied since, candidate key for R is {customer name, branch_name} which is present in R_2.

R_1 and R_2 given 3NF decomposition of schema which is loss-less and dependency preserving.

Example 7. Find 3NF decomposition of given relation schema.

Shipping (ship, capacity, Date, Cargo, Value)

Functional dependencies:

Ship → Capacity

Ship date → Cargo

Cargo capacity → Value.

Solution. Using the algorithm and functional dependencies.

- ship → capacity

  R_1 = (ship, capacity)
- ship date → Cargo

  R_2 = (ship, Date, Cargo)
- Cargo capacity → value

  R_3 = (Cargo, Capacity, value)

R_1, R_2 and R_3 give 3NF decomposition which is loss-less and dependency preserving.

Comparison of BCNF and 3NF

1. Decomposition Properties

3NF design is always dependency preserving and loss-less.

But, it is difficult to achieve all three design goals: BCNF, loss-less-join and dependency preservation.

2. Transitive Dependencies :

BCNF schema cannot have transitive dependencies.

But, if we do not eliminate transitive dependencies in 3NF, we may have to use null values to represent some of the possible meaningful relationships among data items and there is a problem of repetition of information.

It is generally preferable to output for 3NF with dependency preservation. If we cannot test for dependency preservation efficiently, we either pay high penalty in system performance or risk the integrity of the data in our database.

A relation schema is in BCNF, then it is also in 3NF:

From the definitions of BCNF and 3NF, it is clear that a relation schema which is in BCNF can satisfy at least one of the first two conditions of 3NF definition. Hence, it is also in 3NF.

If a relation schema is in BCNF then all functional dependencies are of the form **"super key determines a set of attributes"** or the dependency is trival. Thus, a BCNF schema cannot have any transitive dependencies. As a result, every BCNF schema is also in 3NF.

4.5 FOURTH NORMAL FORM (4NF) AND MVDS

Definition : "A relation R is in Fourth Normal Form (4NF) if and only if the following conditions are satisfied simultaneously:

1. **R is already in 3NF or BCNF.**
2. **If it contains no multi-valued dependencies.**

Now, the question is *what are* **multi-valued dependencies (MVDs)?**

MVD is the dependency where one attribute value is potentially a 'multi-valued fact' about another. It was introduced by R. Fagin. A MVD is a functional dependency where the dependency may be to a set and not just a single value. **Please note two things about MVDs :**

1. In order for a relation to contain an MVD, it must have three or more attributes.
2. It is possible to have a table containing two or more attributes which are inter – dependent multivalued facts about another attribute.

Please note that this does not make the relation an MVD. For a relation to be MVD, the attributes must be independent of each other.

For example, Consider a table cust as follows :

Cust_name	CAddr
Rajiv →	New Delhi
Rajiv →	Patiala
Shahid ←	Patiala
Amit	Calcutta

Here, we can see that CAddress (CAddr) is a multivalued fact about Cust_name and the converse is also true. Like, here CAddr can take two values 'New Delhi' and 'Patiala' for the single (same) customer, Rajiv Hence, we conclude that, **"MVDs occur when two or more independent multivalued facts about the same attribute occur within the same table.**

This means that if in a relation, R, having A, B and C as attributes, B and C are the multivalued facts about A, which is represented as $A \to \to B$ and $A \to \to C$, then the multivalue dependency exists only if B and C are independent of each other."

For example, Consider the following table :

Book table

Sname	Librarian	Text	Data_of_issue
Rajiv	Paramjit	OS	1-1-2009
AJay	Gurucharan	ACA	2-1-2009
Sahib	Atul	Testing	5-6-2009
Nitin	Akash	SPM	6-5-2009
Rajiv	Atul	SE	12-2-2009

Here, we know that there is an association between librarians, books issued by them and the date of issue. **These multivalued facts are not independent of each other. Hence, there are no MVDs in this table**, as per our definition above. **Also note that there is no redundancy in this table**, even though the student 'Rajiv' takes books twice, yet they are different books and their dates issue are also different.

Now consider another table–COURSE as shown below :

Course table

Course	Sname	Book
B.Tech.	Rajiv	O.S.
M.Tech	Rajiv	ACA
MCA	Ajay	S.E.
BCA	Abhay	SPM
BIS	Ajay	Testing

Here, the attributes—Sname and Book are multivalued facts about the attribute 'Course'. **Please note here that the student has no control over the books to be used for their course, these multivalued facts about courses are independent of each other.**

Thus, this table contains MVDs. These MVDs are as follows –

1. Course $\rightarrow\!\!\!\rightarrow$ Sname
2. Course $\rightarrow\!\!\!\rightarrow$ Book.

Note, here, that Sname and Book are independent of each other.

However, this form of table is full of anomalies. There is a high degree of redundancy in this database which may result in update problems. But, **this database** *is in BCNF as* all the three attributes concatanated together constitute its key. However, it has certain anomalies and hence, needs to be decomposed.

Rule to transform a relation to 4NF?

According to the *Fagin's rule*—**"A relation ,R, having attributes A, B, and C can be non-loss decomposed into projections R_1 (A, B) and R_2 (A, C) if and only, if the MVD. A → → B¦C holds in R."**

Now, consider the 2 MVDs of the COURSE table given above *i.e.,*

Course → → Sname

Course → → Book.

To transform the COURSE-table into it's 4NF, we form 2 separate tables –

(*a*) CSTUDENT (COURSE, Sname)

(*b*) C Book (Course, Book)

Now, this removes redundancy.

4NF and BCNF: 4NF is more restrictive than BCNF.

4NF differ from the definition of BCNF is only the use of mutivalued dependencies instead of functional dependencies. Every 4NF schema is in BCNF.

If schema R is not in BCNF, then it cannot be in 4NF:

If a schema R is not in BCNF, then there is a non-trival functional dependency $\alpha \rightarrow \beta$ holding on R, where α is not a super key.

$\alpha \rightarrow \beta$ implies $\alpha \rightarrow\rightarrow \beta$ by replication rule

Hence $\alpha \rightarrow\rightarrow \beta$ is a non-trival functional dependency and α is not a super key, which means that R is not in 4NF.

But there are BCNF schemas that are not in 4NF eliminates the problem encountered in BCNF.

Fourth Normal Form decomposition algorithm:

```
result :={R};
done :=false;
compute D+;
while (not done) do
if (there is a schema R1 in result that is not in 4 NF) then
begin
let α → β be a non-trival multivalued dependency that holds on R1 such that α → β
R1 is not D+ and α ∩ β = ϕ′. result := (result – Ri) ∪ (Ri – β) (α , β);
end
else
done:=true.
```

It generates loss-less join decomposition.

Example: Let R = (A, B, C, G, H, I) with

$$D = \{A \rightarrow\rightarrow B, B \rightarrow\rightarrow HI, CG \rightarrow H\}$$

R is not in 4NF. Lets apply 4NF decomposition algorithm and test resulting decomposition for dependencies preservation

$A \rightarrow\rightarrow B$ is non-trival dependency and A is not a super-key. The first iteration of while loop will replace R with two schcemas:

(A, B) and (A, , G, H, I)

(A, B) is in 4NF since all multivalued dependencies that hold on (A, B) are trival. But (A, C, G, H, I) is not in 4 NF.

Applying the multivalued dependency $G \rightarrow\rightarrow$ Hwhich follow from $CG \rightarrow H$ functional dependency, second iteration of while loop will replace the (A, C, G, H, I) schema into two schemas:

(C, G, H) and (A, C, G, I). Schema (C, G, H) is in 4NF , but schema (A, G, C, I) is not in 4NF.

Now using the productions,

$$A \rightarrow\rightarrow B$$

$$B \rightarrow\rightarrow HI$$

And transitivity rule,

A →→ HI

i.e., A →→ H and A →→ I

Using A →→ I (A, C, G, I) can be decomposed into (A, I,) (A, C, G)

Thus the algorithm terminates resulting in following relation schemas in 4NF.

(A, B) { A →→ B}

(C, G, H) (G →→ H)

(A, I) {A →→ I}

(A, C, G) { }.

This decomposition is loss-less join decomposition. But, it is not a dependency preserving decomposition, since it fails to preserve the multivalued dependency B →→ HI.

If we are given a set of multivalued and functional dependencies, it is advantageous to find database design that meets the three criteria of:

1. 4NF
2. Dependency Preservation
3. Loss-less join

But, if all dependencies are the functional dependencies, then the first criteria is just BNF. When we cannot achieve all three goals, we compromise on 4NF and accept BCNF or even 3NF with dependency preservation.

Before we go further, we shall solve some problems now.

Example 1. Consider the following table, STUD, STUD (Sname, Computer_used, Language) with the following records :

Sname	Computer_used	Language
Rajiv	P–IV Celeron	English Spanish
Sahib	P–III	English Russian

Normalize this table. Is this table in 4NF? If no, decompose it to 4NF?

Solution. Firstly, to normalize this given table we flatten it :

Sname	Computer_used	Language
Rajiv	P–IV	English
Rajiv	P–IV	Spanish
Rajiv	Celeron	English
Rajiv	Celeron	Spanish
Sahib	P–III	English
Sahib	P–III	Russian

We can observe here that 'Computer used' and 'Language' attributes are independent multi-valued facts about Sname. So, it has MVDs. So, redundancies are there.

This table is in BCNF because all three attributes concatenated together form its key but it still has anomalies and hence needs decomposition. We will use **Fagin's rule** for this. Now, this database contains 2 MVDs –

(*a*) Sname → → Computer_used

(*b*) Sname → → Language.

So, we decompose it. We form 2 tables now –

(*a*) R1 (Sname, Computer_used)

(*b*) R2 (Sname, Language)

Example 2. Consider the following employee table. Suppose that employees can be assigned to multiple projects. Also assume that employees can have multiple job skills.

Eno	Pno	Skill
A1	100 109	Coding Testing Maintenance

Try to normalize this table.

Solution. Firstly, we flatten the above table – emp, in order to normalize it.

Eno	Pno	Skill
A1	100	Coding
A1	100	Testing
A1	100	Maintenance
A1	109	Coding
A1	109	Testing
A1	109	Maintenance

This table has lot of redundancies. It contains MVDs also, we need to remove them. And this can be done by decomposing it. Now, the MVDs are :

1. Eno → → Pno
2. Eno → → Skill.

So , we decompose now.

EPROJECT (Eno, Pno)

ESKILL (Eno, Skill)

4.6 FIFTH NORMAL FORM (5NF)/PJNF

Definition : "A relation R is in 5th Normal Form (5NF) if and only if the following conditions are satisfied simultaneously –

1. **R is already in 4NF.**
2. **It cannot be further non-loss decomposed."**

Actually, 5NF is of little practical use for a database designer.

In all the normal forms, that we have studied so far, **no loss decomposition was possible by decomposing a single table into two separate tables. And this non-loss decomposition was possible because of the availability of the join operator in this relational model.** Whereas, in 5NF we try to achieve non-loss decomposition only if we decompose it into three or more separate tables. But this decomposition is not always possible.

For example, Consider the following table,

Agent table

Aname	Company	Pname
Raman	HCL	Bolt
Rajiv	IBM	Nut
Ajay	HCL	Nut
Ravi	Daksh	Bolt
Kunal	Infosys	Bolt

We see here that HCL makes Bolts as well as Nuts. Now, this table can be decomposed into 3 projections without any loss of information –

1. R1 (Aname, Company)
2. R2 (Aname, Pname)
3. R3 (Company, Pname)

Here, all redundancies get removed. Also, if we take natural join, (⋈) of R_1, R_2 & R_3 then we get :

$$R1 \bowtie R2 \bowtie R3 \xrightarrow{\text{we get}} R \text{ (back)}$$

Now, **please note that this is the correct recomposition of the original table and a no-loss decomposition into 3 projections was achieved. Also note that the order in which joins are performed will not affect the final result.**

Actually, detecting whether a table violates 5NF is very difficult, practically and it is for this reason that 5NF has very little practical application.

We call this rule as a **Join-Dependency Rule** because it holds good only if a table can be retransformed back without any loss of information from the join of certain specified projections of it. The notation used to represent a join dependency on a table, T, is –

*(X, Y, - - -Z)

Where X, Y, ... Z are the projections of T. Now, a table, T is said to satisfy the above join dependency if it is equal to the join of the projections X, Y, ... Z.

Hence, we define now : "A table (T) is in 5NF if every join dependency in T is a consequence only of the candidate keys of T."

The table-Agent, considered earlier, violated 5NF because the join dependency *(Aname, company, Pname) was not a consequence only of the primary key for the table but also a consequence of the tuple formulation rule that we studied earlier.

So, our **objective** is to find JDs in a table and if they exist then the table is not in 5NF. So, try to remove JDs. Because a table in 5NF should not be further non-loss decomposable.

But the **problem** is that detecting JDs is not practically easy. Also, many times, recomposition may not give the same table but may give some spurious rows also. This is because our decomposition of R into R_1, R_2, ... R_3 depends on us. The differences lay in some semantic properties of the information being represented.

We are in a position to solve an example now.

Example 1. Consider the following relation-PERSONS, PERSON (Pname, Skill, Job)

Pname	Skill	Job
Ajay	DBA	J-1
Amit	Tester	J-2
Aakask	Programmer	J-3
Sahib	Analyst	J-1

Is this table in 5NF?

Solution. We can decompose this further and hence it is not in 5NF. The three relations are as follows :

1. R_1 (Pname, Skill)
2. R_2 (Skill, Job)
3. R_3 (Pname, Job)

Now, by applying the definition of 5NF, the JD is as given below :

*{(Pname, Skill), (Skill, Job), (Pname, Job)}

This statement is **true** because a join relation of these three relations is equal to the original relation-PERSONS. The consequence of these JDs is that the skill, Job or Pname is not a relation key and hence the relation is not in 5NF. Now, say, Row-2 is removed from the PERSONS table then a new relation is created that no longer has any join dependencies (JDs). Thus, the new relation will be in 5NF.

4.7 CLOSURE OF A SET OF FDS AND MVDS

Let F be a set of FDs. The closure of F is the set of all FDs logically implied by F. We denote the closure of F by F^+. Given F, we can compute F^+ directly from the formal definition of FD. If F were large then this process would be lengthy and difficult.

The technique used to find F^+ is based on some axioms or rules of inference for FDs. We assume that (α, β, γ, ...) are the set of attributes for a relation, R. We use $\alpha\beta$ to denote $\alpha \cup \beta$. So, R(α, β, γ...).

Then we have these rules :

1. **Reflexivity rule :** If α is a set of attributes and $\beta \subseteq \alpha$, then $\alpha \rightarrow \beta$ holds.
2. **Augmentation rule :** If $\alpha \rightarrow \beta$ holds and γ is a set of attributes then $\gamma \alpha \rightarrow \gamma \beta$ holds.
3. **Transitivity rule :** If $\alpha \rightarrow \beta$ holds and $\beta \rightarrow \gamma$ holds, then $\alpha \rightarrow \gamma$ holds.

   These rules are collectively known as **Armstrong's axioms. These rules are sound as they do not generate any incorrect FDs**. Also these **rules are complete** because for a given set F of FDs we can find all F^+.
4. **Union rule :** If $\alpha \rightarrow \beta$ holds and $\alpha \rightarrow \gamma$ holds, then $\alpha \rightarrow \beta\gamma$ holds.
5. **Decomposition rule :** If $\alpha \rightarrow \beta\gamma$ holds, then $\alpha \rightarrow \beta$ holds, and $\alpha \rightarrow \gamma$ holds.
6. **Pseudotransitivity rule :** If $\alpha \rightarrow \beta$ holds and $\gamma\beta \rightarrow \delta$ holds, then $\alpha\gamma \rightarrow \delta$ holds.

This approach takes exponential time to find F^+. So, we deal with one attribute or a set of attributes at a time and find its closure. Please understand that the closure of a set of attributes X is all the attributes that are FD on X, given some FDs (F). Whereas the closure of F was all FDs that are implied by F. So, computing the closure of a set of attributes is a much simpler task if we are dealing with a small number of attributes.

Assume that the closure of a set of attributes, X, given F, is denoted by X^+. Then, we state an algorithm to find the closure –

Step 1. Let $\hat{X}c \leftarrow X$

Step 2. Let the next dependency by $A \rightarrow B$. If A is in $\hat{X}c$ and B is not,

$$\hat{X}c \leftarrow \hat{X}c + B.$$

Step 3. Continue step -2 until no new attributes can be added to $\hat{X}c$.

Output : The result of this algorithm is $\hat{X}c$ that is equal to X^+.

This algorithm may be used to remove redundant dependencies also.

For example, to check if X → A is redundant, we find closure of X without using X → A. If A is in X^c, we can eliminate X → A as redundant.

We are in a position to solve some examples now

Example 1. Let R be a relation with attributes as shown – R = (A, B, C, G, H, I) and you are given a set of FDs –

$$A \rightarrow B \qquad CG \rightarrow I$$
$$A \rightarrow C \qquad B \rightarrow H.$$
$$CG \rightarrow H \qquad \text{Find } F^+?$$

Solution. ∵ A → B
B → H
∴ A → H (transitivity rule)

Also, CG → H
CG → I
∴ CG → HI (Union rule)

And A → C
CG → I
∴ AG → I (Pseudo transitivity)

Example 2. Consider the following relation – Stud (Sno, Sname, Cno, Cname). Find closure of (Sno, Cno). Given FDs are :

(a) **Sno → Sname**

(b) **Cno → Cname?**

Solution. We apply the algorithm discussed above. We use X^*c* as the placeholder for all the attributes that have been found to be dependent on X so far.

Step 1. X^*c* ← X,

i.e., X^*c* ← (Sno, Cno)

Step 2. Consider FD, Sno → Sname.

Since, Sno is in X^*c* and Sname is not, we have X^*c* ← (Sno, Cno) + Sname.

Step 3. Consider 2nd FD, Cno → Cname. Since, Cno is in X^*c* and Cname is not, we have X^*c* ← (Sno, Cno, Sname) + Cname.

Step 4. Again consider FD, Sno → Sname but this does not change X^*c*.

Step 5. Again consider FD, Cno → Cname but this does not change X^*c*.

∴ X^+ = X^*c* = (Sno, Cno, Sname, Cname)

This example shows that the attributes in the relation - Student (Sno, Cno, Sname, Cname) are dependent on (Sno, Cno) and therefore, (Sno, Cno) is a candidate key of the present relation. Here, it is only the candidate key.

> **NOTE :** We may find closure of (Sname, Cname) also by using this algorithm. We find that the closure of (Sname, Cname) is (Sname, Cname) only. So, these attributes together cannot form the key of the above relation.

To get a **complete and minimum set of FDs,** we need to do the following:

(*a*) To derive the complete set of FDs (result is a closure of FDs).

(*b*) To minimize the complete set of FDs result is a canonical set of FDs).

The **complete set of FDs** can be obtained from closure of FDs. We can define the closure of some set of FDs. F, as the set of FDs that are implied by F including F itself.

Please understand that to compute the closure of a set of FDS. Computation of closure of attributes of each FDS is very important. Also understand that the closure of an attribute can be similarly defined as that of the closure of FDS , **closure of an attribute is the set of all attribute that can be derived from the concerned attribute.**

> NOTE : By computing all possible FDS, followed by rejection of redundant ones, we can compute a minimal or canonical set of FDS.

We are in a position to solve some problems now.

Example 1. Let R be a relation: R = (A, B, C, D, E, F,) having the functional dependencies:

(*a*) A → BC

(*b*) B → E

(*c*) C → EF

(*d*) E → CF

Find the closure of {A, B} over the given set of FDs.

Solution. We start with initial closure for {A, B} and then proceed as follows

$[AB]^+$ = {A, B}
= {A, B, C} (as A → Bc)
= {A, B, C, E} (as B → E)
= {A, B, C, E, F} (as C → E F)
= {A, B, C, E, F} (cas E → C F)

All FDs are considered and no more inclusion in the set $\{AB\}^+$ is possible

∴ [AB] + = {A,B,C,E,F}

Example 2. Let R be a relation:

R = (A, B, C, D, E, F,) having the FDs

(*a*) C → F

(*b*) E → A

(c) EC → E

d) A → B

Which of the following is a key for R ?

(a) CD

(*b*) EC

(*c*) AE

(*d*) AC ?

Solution. $[CD]^+$ = {C, D} = { C, D} = {C,D, F}

$[EC]^+$= [E, C] = {E, C, A, F} = {E, C, A, F, D, B}

$[AE]^+$ = {A, E} = {A, E, B}

$[AC]^+$ = {A, C} = {A, C, F, B}

ie, only combination EC determines all other attributes of R.

∴ {E, C} is the PK for relation, R

Example 3. Let R be a relation: R = (A, B, C, D, E, F, G,) having the FDs—

(*a*) A → B

(*b*) BC → D

(*c*) BC → E

(*d*) AEF → G

(*e*) B → G

Find out candition keys of R.

Solution. Here,

$$[A]^+ = \{A, B, G\}$$
$$[B]^+ = \{B, G\}$$
$$[BC]^+ = \{B, C, D, E, G\}$$
$$[AEF]^+ = \{A, B, C, E, F, G\}$$
$$\therefore \quad [ACEF]^+ = \{A, B, C, E, F, G\}$$
$$= \{A, B, C, D, E, F, G\}$$

Because A → B and BC → E

∴ AC → E

∴ we can write $[ACF]^+ = \{A, B, C, D, E, F, G\}$

Therefore, {A, C, F} is a candidate key.

Example 4. Given a relation R= {A, B, C, D, E} and the corresponding set of FDS: F = {A → BC, CD → E, B → D, E → A}.

Find out candidate keys of relation, R.

Solution. Here,

$$[A]^+ = \{A\} = \{A, B, C\} = \{A, B, C, D, E\}$$
$$[B]^+ = [B] = \{B, D\}$$
$$[C]^+ = \{C\}$$
$$[D]^+ = \{D\}$$
$$[CD]^+ = \{C, D\} = \{C, D, E\} = \{C, D, E, A\}$$
$$= \{A, B, C, D, E\}$$
$$[E]^+ = \{E\} = \{E, A\} = \{A, B, C, D, E\}$$

∴ A, E and CD are candidate Key of relation R

Example 5. When are the FDS said to be equivalent? Consider two sets of FDs:

$$\mathbf{F_1 = \{A \to C, AC \to D, E \to AD, E \to H\}}$$

&

$$\mathbf{F_2 = \{A \to CD, E \to AH\}}$$

Check whether F_1 and F_2 are equivalent.

Solution. From F_1:

$$A \to C \text{ (given)}$$
$$AC \to D$$
$$\therefore \quad A \to CD$$

Also, E → AD, E → H implies E → AH.

∴ F_1 covers F_2

From F_2:

$$[A]^+ = \{A, C, D\} \text{ and } [AC]^+ = \{A, C, D\}$$
$$[E]^+ = \{A, E, H\} = \{A, C, D, E, H\}$$
$$\therefore \quad [F_1]^+ = [F_2]^+$$

Closure of MVDs : We follow a same approach as we followed for FDs. Let D denote a set of functional and MVDs. Then, the closure, D^+ of D is the set of all FDs and MVDs logically implied by D. Our objective is to find D^+. we follow certain rules here :

1. **Reflexivity rule :** If α is a set of attributes and $\beta \subseteq \alpha$ then $\alpha \to \beta$ holds.
2. **Augmentation rule :** If $\alpha \to \beta$ holds, and γ is a set of attributes, then $\gamma\alpha \to \gamma\beta$ holds.
3. **Transitivity rule :** If $\alpha \to \beta$ holds and $\beta \to \gamma$ holds then $\alpha \to \gamma$ holds.
4. **Complementation rule :** If $\alpha \to \beta$ holds, then $\alpha \to\to R-\beta-\alpha$ holds.
5. **Multivalued transitivity rule :** If $\alpha \to\to \beta$ holds and $\beta \to\to \gamma$ holds then $\alpha \to\to \gamma - \beta$ holds.
6. **Multivalued augmentation rule :** If $\alpha \twoheadrightarrow \beta$ holds and $\gamma \subseteq R$ and $\delta \subseteq \gamma$ then $\gamma\alpha \twoheadrightarrow \delta\beta$ holds.
7. **Replication rule :** If $\alpha \to \beta$ holds, then $\alpha \to\to \beta$.
8. **Coalescence rule :** If $\alpha \to\to \beta$ holds and $\gamma \subseteq \beta$ and there is a δ such that $\delta \subseteq R$ and $\delta \cap \beta = \phi$ and $\delta \to \gamma$ then $\alpha \to \gamma$ holds.
9. **Multivalued union rule :** If $\alpha \twoheadrightarrow \beta$ holds, and $\alpha \twoheadrightarrow \gamma$ holds, then $\alpha \twoheadrightarrow \beta\gamma$ holds.
10. **Intersection rule :** If $\alpha \twoheadrightarrow \beta$ holds and $\alpha \to\to \gamma$ holds then $\alpha \to\to \beta \cap \gamma$ holds.
11. **Difference rule :** If $\alpha \to\to \beta$ holds and $\alpha \to\to \gamma$ holds then $\alpha \to\to \beta-\gamma$ holds and $\alpha \to\to \gamma-\beta$ holds.

We are in a position to solve an example now.

Example 1. Given a relation, R with attributes – R(A, B, C, G, H, I) and you are given a set of FDs and MVDs as

$$A \twoheadrightarrow B$$
$$B \twoheadrightarrow HI$$
$$CG \to H$$

Find D^+?

Solution.

$\because$ $A \twoheadrightarrow B$ (given)

$\therefore$ $A \twoheadrightarrow R\text{-}B\text{-}A$ [from complementation rule 4]

But $R\text{-}B\text{-}A = CGHI$

$\therefore$ $A \twoheadrightarrow CGHI.$

Also, as given, $A \twoheadrightarrow B$

$A \twoheadrightarrow HI$

$A \twoheadrightarrow HI - B$ [from multivalued transitivity rule]

But $HI - B = HI$

$\therefore$ $A \twoheadrightarrow HI.$

Now, $B \twoheadrightarrow HI$

$CG \to H$

$B \to H$ (from coalescence rule)

Also, $A \twoheadrightarrow CGHI$

And $A \twoheadrightarrow HI$

$A \twoheadrightarrow CGHI - HI$ (by difference rule).

But $CGHI - HI = CG$

$\therefore$ $A \twoheadrightarrow CG$ holds.

4.8 MINIMAL OR CANONICAL COVER OF FDs

A data base designer needs to consider only the minimal set of FDs. **Please understand** that when a database relation is updated, **we must be careful so that none of the existing FDS are violated** ***ie*****, all FDs must be preserved** and to check for this, we must have a minimal equivalent set of FDs, **Also understand that this minimal set can be obtained by elimination of extraneous FDs or extraneous attributes from given FDs.** But these extraneous attributes many appear either on the LHS or RHS of a FDs.

How to Identify extraneous FDs or attributes?

Assume that X and Y represent group of attributes and A and B represent individual attributes only. Then,

Rule 1: Extraneous FD

If {F – {X → A }} is equivalent to F then FD, X → A is extraneous.

Rule 2: Extraneous Right Attribute

If {(F – (X → Y)} U {X → (Y – A)}} is equivalent to F then attribute A is extraneous in FD X → Y.

Rule 3: Extraneous Left Attribute

If {{F – {X → A}} U {(X – B) → A}}

is equivalent to F then attribute B is extraneous in FD, X → A.

Please note that now if we reduce all the given FDs into a form like X → A, then there will be no extraneous attributes on RHS. This will further simply the procedure

Algorithm: To find complete, minimal set of FDs

Inputs: F_1: Initial (arbitrary) set of FDs

user supplied or designer specified at intial stages

Outputs: (1) It eliminates redundancy present in any determinant.

(2) Eliminate any extreneous FD.

Algorithm: Minimal cove of FDs

```
begin
    Set F2: = F1;
    replace an FD X → {A1, A2, ... An} in F2 by following smaller FDs X → A1,
    X → A2, ...., X → An;
    for each FD X → A in F2 do
    begin
        for each attribute B that is an element of X do
        begin
            if {{F2 – {X → A}} ∪ {(X – B) → A}} is equivalent to F2
            then replace X → A with (X → B) in F2;
        end
    end
    for each remaining FD X → A in F2 do
        begin
            if { F2 – {X → A} ∪ {(X – B) → A}} is equivalent to F2
            then replace X → A with (X – A) in F2,
        end
    end
 For each remaining FD X → A in F2 Do begin
    If {F2 – {X → A } is equivalent to F2 then remove FD X → A from F2;
    end
    end
```

We are in a position to so we some problems now.

Example 1. Given a relation, R = {A, B, C, D, E, F, G, H, I,} and the corresponding set of FDs:

{ABCD → E, AB → G, B → F, C → J, CJ → I, G → H}.

Minimize the set of FDs. Determine the PK for R and then find out a minimal cover for given FDs.

Solution. Given FD: CJ → I

The **determinant** CJ has redundancy because C → J it already available

∴ CJ → I should be replaced by J → I.

There is no other FD or deteminant having similar characteristic.

∴ Minimal cover is:

{ABCD → E, AB → G, B → F, C → J, J → I, G → H}

It is found that: $[A\ B\ C\ D]^+ = [A, B, C, D, E, F, G, H, I, J\}$.

∴ {A, B, C, D} is the PK.

To find minimal cover, the following steps are followed:

Step 1: Old FD Set was:

ABCD → E
AB → G
B → F
C → J
CJ → I
G → H

New FD set is:

ABCD → E
AB → G
B → F
C → J
J → I
G → H

Reasons: {F – {CJ → I}} ∪ {J → I}is equivalent to F.

Step 2: Old FD set was:

ABCD → E
AB → G
B → F
C → J
J → I
G → H

New FD set is:

ABCD → E
AB → G
B → F
C → J
J → I
G → H

Reasons: No other reduction is possible. So, step-2 is not needed.

∴ The minimal cover is:

{ABCD → E, AB → G, B → F, C → J, J → I, G → H].

Example 2. Given a relation R = {A, B, C, D}

The corresponding set of FDs:

{A → BC, AC → D, D → B, AB → D}. Find out A^+ B^+, C^+, D^+ and hence determine PK for R.

Minimize the set of FDs.

Solution.

$A^+ = \{A\} = \{A, B, C\} = \{A, B, C, D\}$
$B^+ = \{B\}$
$C^+ = \{C\}$

$D^+ = \{D\} = \{D, B\}$

∴ {A} is the P.K

Given set of FDs is

{A → BC, AC → D, D → B, AB → D}

or {A → B, A → C, AC → D, D → B, AB → D}

In FD, AC → D, the determinant AC is found to have a redundancy because A → C is already available. Henre, AC → D should be replaced by C → B. Similarly, AB → D should be replaced by B → D.

∴ Equivalent set of FDs =

{A → B, A → C, C → D, D → B, B → D}

∴ Minimal cover is:

{A → B, A → C, C → D, D → B, B → D}

To find find minimal cover, the following steps are thus followed:

Step 1: Old FD set was:

A → BC
AC → D
D → B
AB → D

New FD set is:

A → B
A → C
AC → D
D → B
AB → D

Reason (s): A → BC → A → B (Decomposition)
A → C

Step-2: Old FD set was:

A → B
A → C
AC → D
D → B
AB → D

New FD set is:

A → B
A → C
A → D
D → B
AB → D

Reasons: {F – {AC – D}} ∪ {A → D} is equivalent to F.

Step-3: Old FD set was:

A → B
A → C
A → D
D → B
AB → D

New FD set is:

A → B

$$A \rightarrow C$$
$$A \rightarrow D$$
$$D \rightarrow B$$
$$B \rightarrow D$$

Reasons (S): {F – {AB → D}} ∪ {B → D} is equivalent to F.

∴ Minimal cover is

{A → B, A → C, A → D, D → B, B → D}

NOTE : Two different solutions are possible for the given minimization problem.

Example 3. Given a relation R = {A, B, C, D} and the corresponding set of FDs: F = {A → BC, B → C, A → B, AB → C}. Minimize the set of FDs.

Solution. Step-1: Old FD set was:

$$A \rightarrow BC$$
$$B \rightarrow C$$
$$A \rightarrow B$$
$$AB \rightarrow B$$

New FD set is:

$$A \rightarrow B$$
$$A \rightarrow C$$
$$B \rightarrow C$$
$$A \rightarrow B$$
$$AB \rightarrow C$$

Reasons: A → BC → A → B (Decomposition)

A → C

Step-2: Old FD set was:

$$A \rightarrow B$$
$$A \rightarrow C$$
$$B \rightarrow C$$
$$A \rightarrow B$$
$$AB \rightarrow C$$

New FD set is

$$A \rightarrow B$$
$$A \rightarrow C$$
$$B \rightarrow C$$
$$AB \rightarrow C$$

Reason(s): A → B was present in duplicate.

Step-3: Old FD set was:

$$A \rightarrow B$$
$$A \rightarrow C$$
$$B \rightarrow C$$
$$AB \rightarrow C$$

New FD set is:

$$A \rightarrow B$$
$$A \rightarrow C$$
$$B \rightarrow C$$
$$A \rightarrow C$$

Reasons: {F – {AB → C}} ∪ {A → C} is equivalent to F.

Step-4: Old FD set was:

A → B
A → C
B → C
A → C

New FD set is:

A → B
A → C
B → C

Reasons: A → C was present in duplicate.

Step-5: Old FD set was:

A → B
A → C
B → C

New FD set is:

A → B
B → C

Reasons: **A → B**
B → C → A → C

∴ **Minimal set of FDs is:** {A → B, B → C}

Example 4. Given a relation, R = {A, B, C, D}. The corresponding set of FDs:

F = {A → BC, B → AC, C → AB}.

Minimize the set of FDs.

Solution. Step-1: Old FD set was:

A → BC
B → AC
C → AB

New FD set is:

A → B
A → C
B → A
B → C
C → A
C → B

Reasons (s): A → BC → A → B, A → C
B → AC → B → A, B → C
C → AB → C → A, C → B (Decompsition)

Step-2: Old FD set is:

A → B
A → C
B → A
B → C
C → A
C → B

New FD set is

A → B

B → A
B → C
C → A
C → B

Reason (s): A → B, B → C → A → C.

Step-3: Old FD set is:

A → B
B → A
B → C
C → A
C → B

New FD set is

A → B
B → C
C → A
C → B

Reasons: B → C
C → A → B → A

∴ Minimal set of given FDs is:
{A → B, B → C, C → A, C → B}.

Exapmle 5. Given a relation, R = {A, B, C, D, E}.The corresponding set of FDs:
F = {A → BC, CD → E, B → D E → A}.

Minimize the set of FDs.

Solution. Step1: Old FD set was:

A → BC
CD → E
B → D
E → A

New FD set is:

A → B
A → C
CD → E
B → D
E → A

Reason: A → BC → A → B (decomposition).
A → C

Step-2: Old FDs set was:

A → B
A → C
CD → E
B → D
E → A

New FD set is

A → B
A → C

$$A \to E$$
$$B \to D$$
$$E \to A$$

Reasons:

$$E \to A$$
$$A \to B, B \to D \to A \to D$$
$$A \to C, A \to D \to A \to CD$$

∴ Replace $CD \to E$ with $A \to E$.

∴ Minimal set of given FDs is:

$\{A \to B, A \to C, A \to E, B \to D, E \to A\}$

4.9 LOSS LESS JOIN

A relational table is decomposed or factored into two or more smaller tables in such a manner that it is possible to get back the original table by joining these decomposed tables. This is called as **loss less join or non-additive join decomposition**. In general, the decomposition of R(A, B, C) into R_1 (A, B) and R_2 (A, C) is lossless if for attributes A (common to R_1 and R_2) either $X \to Y$ or $Y \to Z$. **Please note here that all decompositions must be lossless, that is, there should not be any loss of information. Also note that the lossless join decomposition is a property of decomposition which ensures that no spurious tuples are generated when a natural join operation is applied to the relations in the decomposition.** So, we can say, if R is decomposed into R_1 and R_2 *i.e.,*

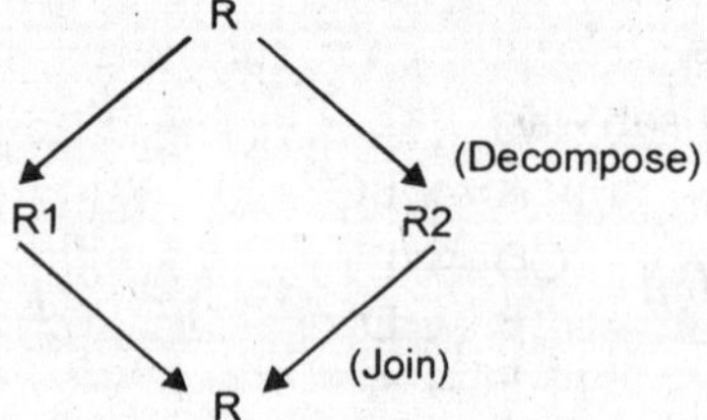

4.10 DEPENDENCY PRESERVING DECOMPOSITION

The dependency preservation decomposition is another property of decomposed relational database schema, D in which each FD, $X \to Y$, specified in F either appeared directly in one of the relation schemas R_i in the decomposed, D or could be inferred from the dependencies that appear in some R_i.

The Decomposition, $D = \{R_1, R_2, R_3 \ldots R_m\}$ of R is said to be dependency preserving with respect to F if the union of the projections of F on each R_i in D is equivalent to F. That is,

$$R \subset \text{join of } R_1, R_1 \text{ over } X$$

The dependencies are preserved because each dependency in F represents a constraint on the database. If decomposition is not dependency preserving, some dependency is lost in the decomposition.

4.11 OVERALL FLOWCHART OF NORMALIZATION

Let us summarize this process of Normalization with a flowchart now :

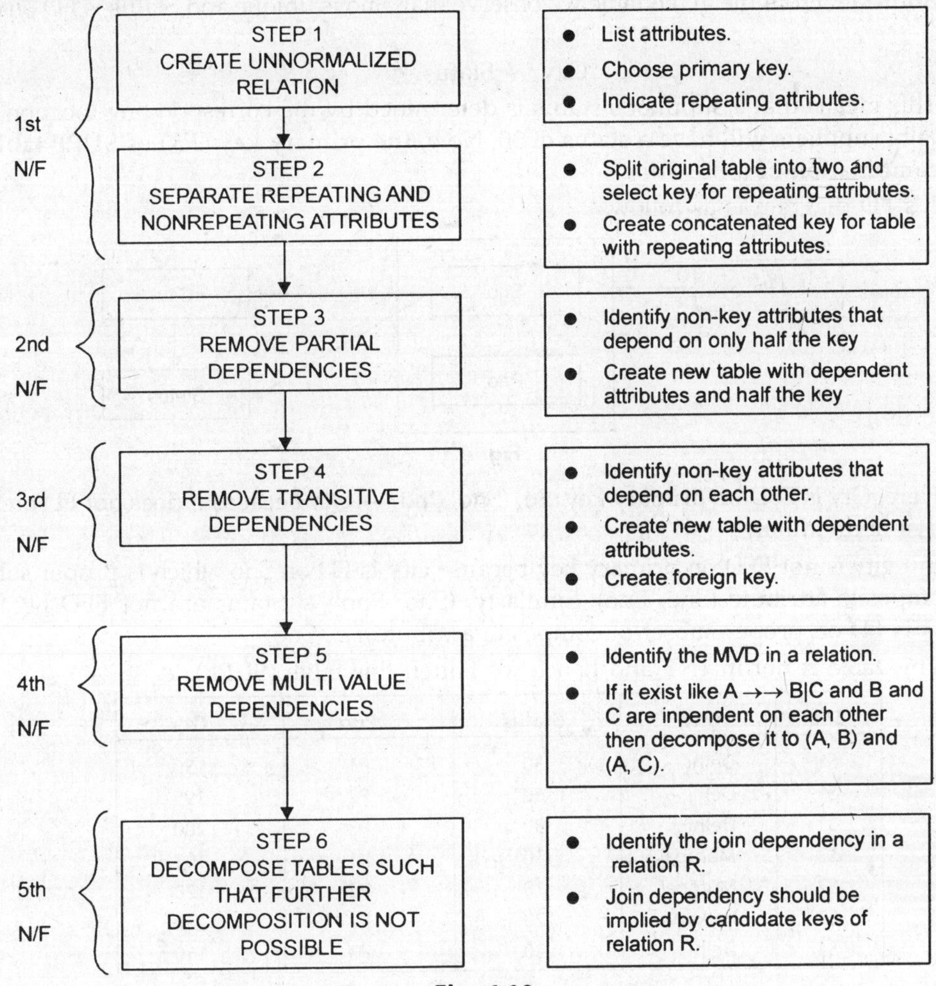

Fig. 4.10

The students are advised to learn this flowchart.

4.11 EXAMPLES ON NORMALIZATION BASED ON FDS AND MVDS

Example 1. Consider the following SUPP table

SUPP (Sno, City, Status, Pno, Qty)

The records in this table are –

Sno	City	Status	Pno	Qty
S1	Delhi	30	P1	150
			P2	195
			P3	200
S2	Mumbai	10	P1	101
			P2	120
S3	Kolkatta	20	P2	250
S4	Delhi	30	P3	150

Is this table in 1NF ? If not, transform it to 1NF. Is it in 2NF, 3NF. If not then transform it ? Draw functional dependency diagrams also.

Solution. From the given table we observe that, Sno is unique and Status is FD on city. So,

$$City \rightarrow Status$$

This means that a supplier's status is determined by the corresponding location like all Delhi suppliers will have a status of 30. Now, **the primary key (*PK*) of SUPP table is the combination of (*Sno, Pno*).**

It's FD diagram is as follows :

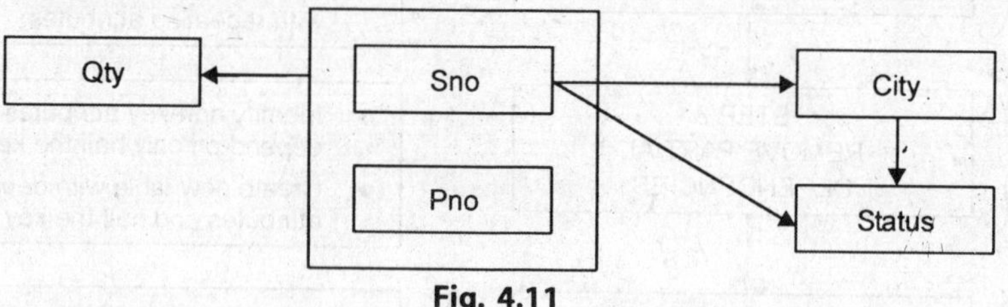

Fig. 4.11

Here, Qty is FFD on primary key. So, (Sno, Pno) → Qty because it does not FD on Sno and Pno individually.

But city is not FFD on primary key because city is FD on Sno which is proper subset of composite attribute (Sno, Pno). Similarly, (Sno, Pno) → Status are not FFD because status is FD on proper subset of composite attribute *i.e.*, Sno.

This table is not in 1NF and hence we flatten this table (SUPP).

Sno	City	Status	Pno	Qty
S1	Delhi	30	P1	150
S1	Delhi	30	P2	195
S1	Delhi	30	P3	200
S2	Mumbai	10	P1	101
S2	Mumbai	10	P2	120
S3	Kolkatta	20	P2	250
S4	Delhi	30	P3	150

This table is in 1NF but it suffers from insertion, deletion and updation anomalies. To remove these anomalies, we should convert this table into 2NF. To convert this SUPP table into 2NF, we move the columns - (Sno, Status, City) to a new table (say, S_Second) and the second table (SP) will be (Sno, Pno, Qty). Now, attribute Sno becomes the primary key of this new table, S_Second. SUPP table is in 2NF now, because in both these sub-relations, all the non-key attributes like (Status, City) in 1st table and Qty (in 2nd table) are fully functionally dependent on the primary key. The PK of 2nd table is (Sno, Pno).

In general, a relation that is in 1NF and not in 2nd NF can always be reduced to an equivalent collection of 2NF relations. Please note that a 1NF relation that is not also 2NF must have a composite primary key. The process of reduction consists of replacing the relations by suitable projections. The collection of these projections is equivalent to the original relation. Thus, this process is reversible *i.e.*,

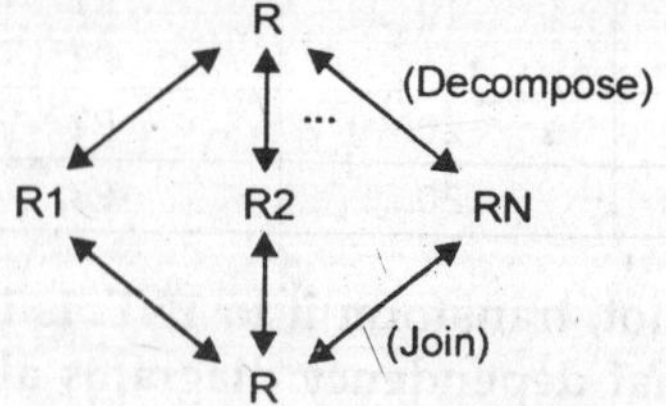

Now, how many subrelations ($R_1, R_2, ..., R_N$) will be there, depends on the fact that it should be possible for us to **rejoin** these projections (Sub-relations) back to get the original relation, R.

$\therefore$ $$\text{SUPP} \Longleftrightarrow \text{S\_second} \bowtie \text{SP}$$

From the second relation (SP) it is clear that it is not only in 2NF but also in 3NF, as there are no transitive dependencies here. So, we leave this table as it is.

But the first table, S_Second is not in 3NF as it has transitive dependencies as follows–

$$\text{Sno} \rightarrow \text{Status}$$
$$\text{Sno} \rightarrow \text{City}$$
$\therefore$ $$\text{City} \rightarrow \text{Status}$$

That is, non-key attribute, status, is FD on primary key (Sno) directly and also on city. This is actually transitive dependency. To convert this table (S-Second) into 3NF we non-loss decompose it into two relations as follows :

S_second

SC (Sno, City) CS (City, Status)

$$\text{S\_Second} \Longleftrightarrow \text{SC} \bowtie \text{CS}$$

Now, SC and CS are in 3NF as no TD exists. **Please note again that the relation that is in 2NF and not in 3NF can always be reduced to an equivalent collection of 3NF relations. Also note that process is reversible and non-lossy meaning that no information is lost during reduction (or decomposition or Normalization).**

The overall flowchart is shown next.

Given :

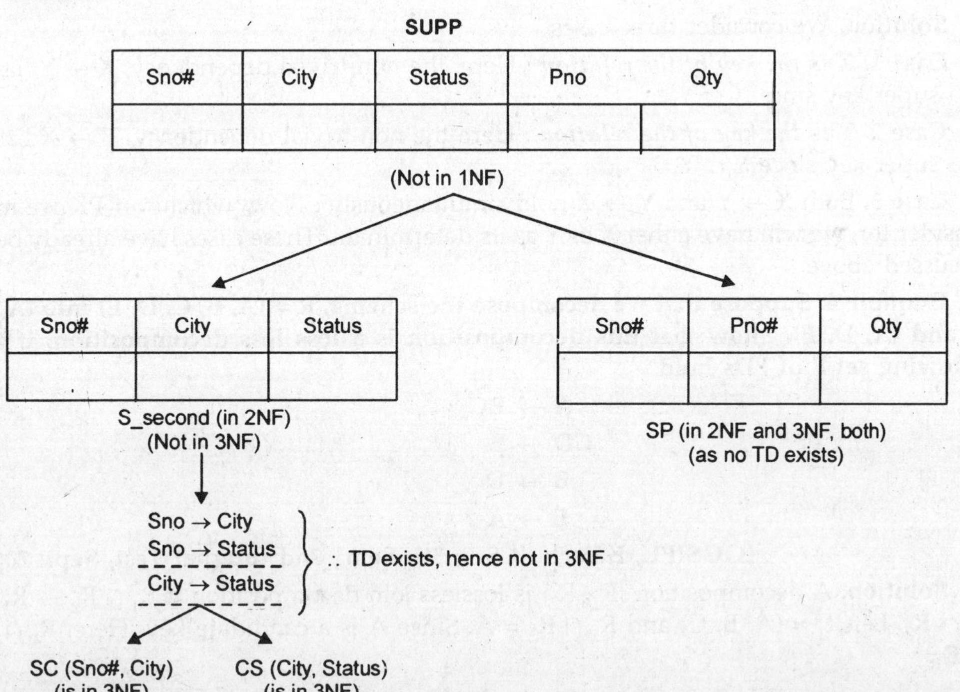

Example 2. Normalize the following table of employees to 3NF. Primary keys are marked by*.

EMP (*Emp_code, Dept_code, Mgr_code, Course_code, Course_title).

Solution. The first_step of normalization is to remove all repeating groups. So, we decompose.

Employee (*Emp_code, Dept_code, Mgr_code)

Training (*Emp_code, *Course_code, Course_title)

But they are not in 2NF. So, we need to remove partial key dependencies. In our example, Course_title relates only to Course_code, so it is moved to another table–

Course (*Course_code, Course_title)

It is in 2NF now with 3 relations but is not in 3NF, as Dept_code and Mgr_code are mutually dependent because the manager is same. So, we create another new table, Dept with Dept_code as its PK, *i.e.,*

DEPT (*Dept_code, Mgr_code)

So, overall chart is

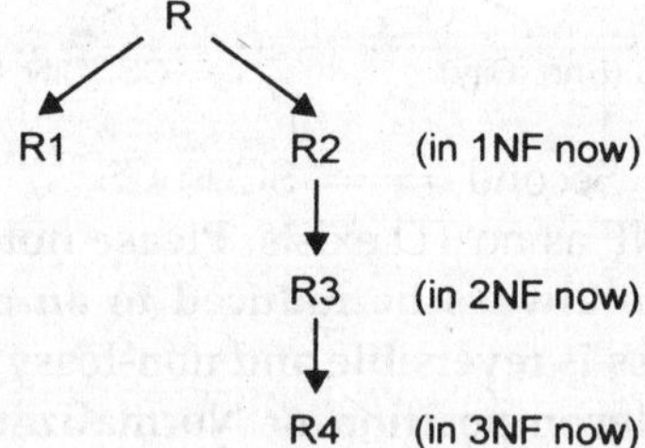

Example 3. Show that every two attribute relation is in BCNF. That is, if r(x, y) then r(x,y) is in BCNF.

Solution. We consider three cases

Case 1. ***X is the key of the relation :*** Here, the non-trivial dependency, $X \rightarrow Y$ has X as a super key since $X \subset Y$.

Case 2. ***Y is the key of the relation :*** Here the non-trivial dependency, $Y \rightarrow X$ has Y as a super key since $Y \subset Y$.

Case 3. Both $X \rightarrow Y$ and $Y \rightarrow X$ hold simultaneously : Now, whichever PK we may consider for, we will have either X or Y as its determinant. These cases have already been discussed above.

Example 4. Suppose that we decompose the schema, R = (A, B, C, D, E) into (A, B, C) and (A, D, E). Show that this decomposition is a loss less decomposition, if the following set F of FDs hold –

$$A \rightarrow BC$$
$$CD \rightarrow E$$
$$B \rightarrow D$$
$$E \rightarrow A \text{ ?}$$

[GGSIPU, B.Tech. (CSE); 5th Sem., 2nd Internal Test, Sept. 2007]

Solution. A decomposition $\{R_1, R_2\}$ is lossless join decomposition if $R_1 \cap R_2 \rightarrow R_1$ or $R_1 \cap R_2$. Let R_1 = (A, B, C) and $R_1 \cap R_2$ = A. Since A is a candidate key. Here, $R_1 \cap R_2 \rightarrow R_1$.

Example 5. Prove the soundness of :

(a) Union Rule.

(b) Pseudotransitivity Rule.

Use Armstrong's axioms to prove.

Solution. (a) *Soundness of Union Rule*

To prove. if $\alpha \to \beta$ and $\alpha \to \gamma$ then $\alpha \to \beta\gamma$

Proof. $\alpha \to \beta$ (given)

$\therefore$ $\alpha\,\alpha \to \alpha\beta$ (augmentation rule)

$\alpha \to \alpha\beta$ (union rule)

$\alpha \to \gamma$ (given)

$\therefore$ $\alpha\beta \to \gamma\beta$ (augmentation rule)

$\alpha \to \beta\gamma$ (transitivity rule)

(b) *Soundness of pseudotransitivity Rule*

To prove. If $\alpha \to \beta$ and $\gamma\beta \to \delta$ then $\alpha\gamma \to \delta$.

Proof. $\alpha \to \beta$ (given)

$\therefore$ $\alpha\gamma \to \beta\gamma$ (augmentation rule)

Also, $\gamma\beta \to \delta$ (given)

$\therefore$ $\alpha\gamma \to \delta$ (tansitivity of above two FDs).

Example 6. Consider the following relation – SUPP (Sno, Pno, Sname, SControl, Price). Also assume that the following FDs hold –

Sno → Sname

Sno → SControl.

What normal form is this table in? Transform it to 3NF if it is not in 3NF?

Solution. To transform this table into 3NF we non-loss decompose it :

(a) R_1 (Sno, Sname, SControl)

(b) R_2 (Pno, Sno, Price)

This removes transitive dependencies also and hence, R_1 and R_2 are in 3NF.

Example 7. Consider a relation, R, as follows : R(title, Performer, style, price, label, producer).

The FDs are :

title → label, style

style → price

Performer → producer.

What is the highest normal form of R?

Solution. The PK of given R is a composite attribute (title, Performer). R is in 1NF because there is atleast one partial dependency on the key like Performer → producer. So, we non - loss decompose, R, as follows –

1. R_1 (title, Performer).
2. R_2 (title, Label, style).
3. R_3 (Performer, Producer_Name).
4. R_4 (Style, Price).

Example 8. Consider the relational schema, R = {A, B, C, D, E}. The FDs defined over R are given by set F:

$$\{A \rightarrow CD, B \rightarrow D, CD \rightarrow E, E \rightarrow A\}$$

Determine whether the following decomposition of R is losseless or not. Decomposed relations are: R_1 = {A, B, C} and R_2 = {A, D, E}.

Is dependency preserved in this case?

Solution. Here, $R_1 \cap R_2 = \{A\}$.

From the FD set F, we see that

$[A]^+ = \{A, C, D, E\}$.

∴ A is super key of R_2 and the decomposition is lossless. But after decomposition, the FD, $B \rightarrow D$ is no longer implied. Hence, the decomposition is not dependency preserving.

Example 9. Consider the relational schema, R = {A, B, C, D}. The FDs defined over R are given by the set F : {A → B, C → D}. Determine whether the following decomposition of R is lossless or not.

Decomposed relations are: R_1 = {A, B} and
R_2 = {C, D}.

Solution. Here, $R_1 \cap R_2 = \phi$.

∴ Decomposition is NOT lossless.

From the FD set F, we find that the dependencies $A \rightarrow B$, $C \rightarrow D$ hold even after decomposition. Therefore, the decompostion is dependency preserving.

Example 10. Consider the relation schema , R = {U, V, X, Y,Z}. The FDs defined over R are given by the set F:

{Z → U, V → Y, XY → Z , U → VX}. Determine whether the following decomposition of R is lossless or not. Decomposed relations are:

R_1 = {U, V, X} and
R_2 = {U, Y, Z}.

Solution. Here, $R_1 \cap R_2 = \{U\}$. The closure of U is:
$[U]^+ = \{U\} = \{U, V, X\}$ since $U \rightarrow VX$.

Hance, we can write, $R_1 \cap R_2 \rightarrow R_1$.

∴ Decomposition is lossless.

From the FD set F, we see that the dependencies $V \rightarrow Y$, $XY \rightarrow Z$ does not hold after decomposition. Thus, the decomposition is not dependency preserving.

4.13 DOMAIN KEY NORMAL FORM (DKNF)

Definition : "A relation is in DKNF, if every general constraint can be inferred from the knowledge of the attributes involved in the scheme, their underlying domains and the sets of attributes that form the keys." Please note that DKNF is considered to be the highest form of normalization, since all insertion and deletion anomalies are eliminated and all general constraints can be verified by using only the domain constraints and the key constraints.

The **central requirements** in DKNF are not FDs or MVDs or JDs but a concept of domains, keys and general constraints. We define a **domain constraint** as a statement that the values of a certain attribute lie within some prescribed set of values. Also, a **key constraint** is a statement that a certain attribute or its combination is a candidate key. However, a **general constraint** is expressed as a simple statement or predicate and specifies some special requirement. **Please note that each tuple of a relation must specify this predicate** *i.e.,* general constraint for it to be a valid tuple.

Anomalies in DKNF :

1. **Insertion anomaly :** It occurs when a tuple is inserted in a relation and the resulting relation violates one or more general constraints.
2. **Deletion anomaly :** It occurs when a tuple from a relation is deleted and the remaining relation violates one or more general constraints.

We are in position to solve an example now.

Example 1. Consider the relation TRANS (Sno, Course, Grade). Suppose that the attributes Sno and Course are numeric and Grade attribute is a letter which could be A, B, C, D, E or F. The general constraint is that for course 000 to 900, grades can only be A, B, C, D, E or F. The domain constraint is Sno has to be 8 digits long,

Course is 3-digit long,

Grade is from the set {A, B, C, D, E, F}.

The key constraint is that no two tuples can exist with the same values for the key attributes which are Sno and Course. So, (Sno, Course) → Grade

Now, what will happen if a tuple like (12345678, 200, B) is inserted in the relation, R ? How to normalize it ?

Solution. The tuple (12345678, 200, B) satisfies the domain and key constraints, given to us. But, this tuple does not satisfy the general constraint. So, Trans becomes illegal after its insertion–Not in DCNF.

Now, we need to decompose TRANS relation into two relations given below –

1. **R_1 (Sno, Course, Grade) :** Here, the domain constraint is Sno being 8-digit, course being 3-digit in the range 000 to 900 and Grade in the set = {A, B, C. D, F}. The PK is (Sno, Course).
2. **R_2 (Sno, Course, Grade) :** Here the domain constraint is all satisfied but the Grade is in set = {E, F}. The PK is (Sno, Course) only.

SUMMARY

One of the main challenges during database design is to design a non-redundant and in-consistent database. With minimum redundancy, our query becomes efficient. In this chapter, emphasis has been made on the normalization of databases. We have discussed about 1NF, 2NF, 3NF, 4NF, 5NF and finally, DKNF.

MULTIPLE CHOICE QUESTIONS [MCQs]

1. The process of decomposition of a table is known as

   (*a*) Specialization (*b*) Generalization

   (*c*) Normalization (*d*) None of the above.

2. The process of Normalization was proposed by
   (*a*) Dr. E.F. Codd (*b*) Dr. Berry Boehm
   (*c*) Jacobson (*d*) None of the above.
3. An association between two attributes of the same table is known as
   (*a*) FD (*b*) MVD
   (*c*) JD (*d*) None of these.
4. A table which is in 2NF, must be in
   (*a*) 1NF (*b*) 2NF
   (*c*) 3NF (*d*) 4NF.
5. After normalization, the original table can be obtained by –
   (*a*) Delete operation (*b*) Cascade operation
   (*c*) Join operation (*d*) None of the above
6. A table in 3NF must not have
   (*a*) FDs (*b*) MVDs
   (*c*) TDs (*d*) JDs
7. BCNF stands for
   (*a*) Babbage-codd Normal Form (*b*) Boyce-codd Normal Form
   (*c*) Bakus-codd Normal Form (*d*) None of the above.
8. MVD stands for
   (*a*) Multi-Valued Dependency (*b*) Many-Value Dependency.
   (*c*) Many-Volume Dependent (*d*) None of the above.
9. A rule to transform a relation into 4NF was given by
   (*a*) Fagin (*b*) E.F Codd
   (*c*) Jacobson (*d*) None of these
10. 5NF is also known as
    (*a*) PJNF (*b*) DKNF
    (*c*) BCNF (*d*) None of the above
11. The process of Normalization is
    (*a*) Reversible (*b*) Non-reversible
    (*c*) Iterative (*d*) Recursive.
12. Every BCNF is in
    (*a*) 1NF (*b*) 2NF
    (*c*) 3NF (*d*) None of the above.
13. Which normal form is most desirable
    (*a*) DKNF (*b*) 3NF
    (*c*) BCNF (*d*) 4NF.
14. Let F_1 and F_2 be two sets of FDs. Then F_1 and F_2 are equivalent if
    (*a*) $F_1 + F_2 = F_1$ (*b*) $F + 1 = F + 2$
    (*c*) $F_1 - F_2 = F_1$ (*d*) $F_1 = F_2$
15. If a relation has 7 attributes then there will be how many subsets of these attributes
    (*a*) 2^7 (= 128) (*b*) 2^4 (= 16)
    (*c*) 2^2 (= 4) (*d*) None of these.

ANSWERS

1. (*c*) **2.** (*a*) **3.** (*a*) **4.** (*a*) **5.** (*c*) **6.** (*c*) **7.** *b*) **8.** (*a*)
9. (*a*) **10.** (*a*) **11.** (*a*) **12.** (*c*) **13.** (*a*) **14.** (*b*) **15.** (*a*)

CONCEPTUAL SHORT QUESTIONS WITH ANSWERS

Q.1. What are the characteristics of FDs?

Ans. FDs used during normalization have some attributes which are listed below :

(*i*) There is a *one-to-one relationship* between the attributes on LHS, *i.e.,* **determinant** and those on RHS of a FD. Whereas a relationship from right to left (opposite direction) may be one-to-one or one-to-many type.

(*ii*) They hold for all **time**.

(*iii*) The determinant (LHS) has the **minimal number of** attributes that are necessary to maintain the dependency with the attributes on RHS.

Q.2. What are the problems with BCNF?

Ans. Some problems with BCNF are :

(*i*) Some undesirable internal dependencies exist between elements of compound keys (composed of 3 or more attributes).

(*ii*) Violation of BCNF may occur in a relation, R, that contains two or more composite candidate keys, or if the candidate keys overlap *i.e.,* have atleast one attribute in common.

Q.3. What do you mean by a non-trivial and a trivial FD?

[GGSIPU, B.Tech. (CSE) 5th Sem., Dec. 2008]

Ans. A relation, R is said to be BCNF, if for every non-trivial FD: $X \rightarrow Y$ between attributes X and Y holds in R. This means that :

(*a*) X is a super key of R,

(*b*) $X \rightarrow Y$ is a trivial FD, that is $Y \subset X$.

Q.4. What are trivial MVDs?

Ans. An MVD, $X \rightarrow\rightarrow Y$ in relation, R, is called as a trivial MVD if

(*a*) Y is a subset of X, or

(*b*) $X \cup Y = R$.

It is called as **trivial** because it does not specify any significant or meaningful constraint on R. An MVD that satisfies neither (*a*) nor (*b*) is called **non-trivial** *MVD.*

Q.5. Consider a relation; R (A, B, C, D, E, F) with FDs and MVDs, $A \rightarrow \rightarrow B$ and $CD \rightarrow \rightarrow EF$. Is R in BCNF or 4NF?

Ans. We decompose the relation, R as follows:

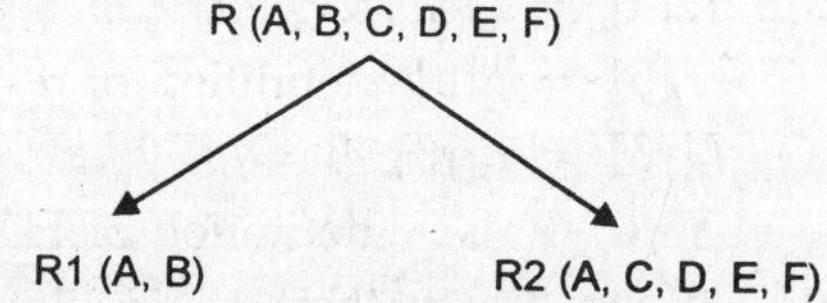

Now, R_1 is in 4NF as $A \rightarrow \rightarrow B$ is trivial and is the only MVD in the relation. However, R_2 is still in BCNF because of the non-trivial MVD: $CD \rightarrow \rightarrow EF$ (given). So, we decompose R_2 into R_{21} and R_{22} as follows :

(*a*) R_{21} (C, D, E, F)

(*b*) R_{22} (C, D, A)

i.e., by applying MVD : $CD \rightarrow \rightarrow EF$ and its compliment $CD \rightarrow \rightarrow A$. Both R_{21} and R_{22} are in 4NF now.

Q.6. Explain what is meant by *repetition of information* and *inability to represent information*. Explain why each of these properties may indicate a bad relational-database design.

Ans.
- Repetition of information is a condition in a relational database where the values of one attribute are determined by the values of another attribute in the same relation, and both values are repeated throughout the relation. This is a bad relational database design because it increases the storage required for the relation and it makes updating the relation more difficult.
- Inability to represent information is a condition where a relationship exists among only a proper subset of the attributes in a relation. This is bad relational database design because all the unrelated attributes must be filled with null values otherwise a tuple without the unrelated information can't be inserted into the relation.
- Loss of information is a condition of a relational database which results from the decomposition of one relation into two relations and which cannot be combined to recreate the original relation. It is a bad relational database design because certain queries cannot be answered using the reconstructed relation could have been answered using the original relation.

Q.7. Why are certain functional dependencies called *trivial* functional dependencies?
[BPUT, Orissa, B.Tech (CSE) and Nagpur Univ., B.Tech (CS) 2007]

Ans. Certain functional dependencies are called trivial functional dependencies because they are satisfied by all relations.

Q.8. Use the definition of functional dependency to argue that each of Armstrong's axioms (reflexivity, augmentation, and transitivity) is sound.

Ans. The definition of functional dependency is: $\alpha \rightarrow \beta$ holds on R if in any legal relation r(R), for all pairs of tuples t_1 and t_2 in r such that $t_1[\alpha] = t_1[\alpha]$, it is also the case that $t_1[\beta] = t_2[\beta]$.

Reflexivity rule : if α is a set of attributes and $\beta \subseteq \alpha$, then $\alpha \rightarrow \beta$. Assume $\exists\ t_1$ such that $t_1[\alpha] = t_2[\alpha]$

$$t_1[\beta] = t_2[\beta] \quad \text{since } \beta \subseteq \alpha$$
$$\alpha \rightarrow \beta \quad \text{definition of FD}$$

Augmentation rule : if $\alpha \rightarrow \beta$, *and* γ *is a set of attributes, then* $\gamma\alpha \rightarrow \gamma\beta$. *Assume* $\exists\ t_1, t_2$ such that $t_1[\gamma\alpha] = t_2[\gamma\alpha]$

$$t_1[\gamma] = t_2[\gamma] \quad \gamma \subseteq \gamma a$$
$$t_1[\alpha] = t_2[\alpha] \quad \alpha \subseteq \gamma\alpha$$
$$t_1[\beta] = t_2[\beta] \quad \text{definition of } \alpha \rightarrow \beta$$
$$t_1[\gamma\beta] = t_2[\gamma\beta] \quad \gamma\beta = \gamma \cap \beta$$
$$\gamma\alpha \rightarrow \gamma\beta \quad \text{definition of FD}$$

Transitivity rule: If $\alpha \rightarrow \beta$ and $\beta \rightarrow \gamma$, then $\alpha \rightarrow \gamma$.
Assume $\exists\ t_1, t_2$ such that $t_1[\alpha] = t_2[\alpha]$

$$t_1[\beta] = t_2[\beta] \quad \text{definition of } \alpha \rightarrow \beta$$
$$t_1[\gamma] = t_2[\gamma] \quad \text{definition of } \beta \rightarrow \gamma$$
$$\alpha \rightarrow \gamma \quad \text{definition of FD}$$

Q.9. Consider the following proposed rule functional dependencies : if $\alpha \rightarrow \beta$ and $\gamma \rightarrow \beta$, then $\alpha \rightarrow \gamma$. Prove that this rule is *not sound* by showing a relation r that satisfies $\alpha \rightarrow \beta$ and $\gamma \rightarrow \beta$, but does not satisfy $\alpha \rightarrow \gamma$.

Ans. Consider the following rule: If A → B and C → B, then A → C. That is, α = A, β = B, γ = C. The following relation *r* is a counterexample to the rule.

r :

A	B	C
a_1	b_1	c_1
a_1	b_1	c_2

NOTE : A → B and C → B, (since no 2 tuples have the same C value, C → B is true trivially). However, it is not the case that A → C since the same A value is in two tuples, but the C value in those tuples disagree.

Q.10. Use Armstrong's axioms to prove the soundness of the decomposition rule.

Ans. The decomposition rule, and its derivation from Armstrong's axioms are given below:

if $\alpha \to \beta\gamma$, then $\alpha \to \beta$ and $\alpha \to \gamma$.

$\alpha \to \beta\gamma$ given
$\beta\gamma \to \beta$ reflexivity rule
$\alpha \to \beta$ transitivity rule
$\beta\gamma \to \gamma$ reflexive rule
$\alpha \to \gamma$ transitive rule

Q.11. Given FDs as :

A → BC
CD → E
B → D
B → A Compute B^+?

Ans. Computing B^+ we start with result = {B}. Considering FDs of the form $\beta \to \gamma$ in F, we find that the only dependencies satisfying $\beta \subseteq$ result are B → B and B → D. Therefore result = {B, D}. No more dependencies in F apply now. Therefore B^+ = {B, D}.

Q.12. Say, R = (A, B, C, D, E) is decomposed into (A, B, C) and (C, D, E). Show that this decomposition is not a lossless join decomposition.

[Hint. Give an example of a relation *r* on schema R such that = $\Pi_{A,B,C}$ (*r*) ⋈ $\Pi_{C,D,E}$ (*r*) ≠ *r*]

Ans. Following the hint, use the following example of *r* :

A	B	C	D	E
a_1	b_1	c_1	d_1	e_1
a_2	b_2	c_1	d_2	e_2

With R_1 = (A, B, C), R_2 = (C, D, E):

(*a*) Π_{R1} (*r*) would be:

A	B	C
a_1	b_1	c_1
a_2	b_2	c_1

(*b*) $\Pi_{R2}(r)$ would be:

C	D	E
c_1	d_1	e_1
c_1	d_2	e_2

(*c*) $\Pi_{R1}(r) \bowtie \Pi_{R2}(r)$ would be:

A	B	C	D	E
a_1	b_1	c_1	d_1	e_1
a_1	b_1	c_1	d_2	e_2
a_2	b_2	c_1	d_1	e_1
a_2	b_2	c_1	d_2	e_2

Clearly, $\Pi_{R1}(r) \bowtie \Pi_{R2}(r) \neq r$. Therefore, this is a lossy join.

Q.13. List the three design goals for relational databases, and explain why each is desirable.

Ans. The three design goals are lossless-join decompositions, dependency preserving decompositions, and minimization of repetition of information.They are desirable so we can maintain an accurate database, check correctness of updates quickly, and use the smallest amount of space possible.

Q.14. Given R = (A, B, C, D, E). Give its loss-less join decomposition into BCNF.

Ans. We know that $B \rightarrow D$ is nontrivial and the left hand side is not a superkey. By the algorithm we derive the relations {(A, B, C, E) (B, D)}. This is in BCNF.

Q.15. In designing a relational database, why might we choose a non-BCNF design?

Ans. BCNF is not always dependency preserving. Therefore, we may want to choose another normal form (specifically, 3NF) in order to make checking dependencies easier during updates. This would avoid joins to check dependencies and increase system performance.

Q.16. Give a lossless -join, dependency preserving decomposition into 3NF of schema, R of above example 12.

Ans. Firstly, we see that the dependencies given in *e.g.,* 12, form a canonical cover. Generating the schema, we get

$$R' = \{(A, B, C), (C, D, E), (B, D), (E, A)\}.$$

Schema (A, B, C) contains a candidate key. Therefore R′ is a third normal form dependency-preserving lossless-join decomposition.

Note that the original schema R = (A, B, C, D, E) is already in 3NF. Thus, it was not necessary to apply the algorithm as we have done above. The single original schema is trivially a lossless join, dependency-preserving decomposition.

Q.17. Given the three goals of relational-database design, is there any reason to design a database schema that is in 2NF, but is in no higher-order normal form?

Ans. The three design goals of relational databases are to avoid

- Repetition of information
- Inability to represent information
- Loss of information.

2NF does not prohibit as much repetition of information since the schema (A, B, C) with dependencies A → B and B → C is allowed under 2NF, although the same (B, C) pair could be associated with many A values, needlessly duplicating C values. To avoid this we must go to 3NF. Repetition of information is allowed in 3NF in some but not all of the cases where it is allowed in 2NF. Thus, in general, 3NF reduces repetition of information. Since we can always achieve a lossless join 3NF decomposition, there is no loss of information needed in going from 2NF to 3NF.

Note that the decomposition{(A, B), (B, C)} is a dependency-preserving and lossless-join 3NF decomposition of the schema (A, B, C). However, in case we choose this decomposition, retrieving information about the relationship between A, B and C requires a join of two relations, which is avoided in the corresponding 2NF decomposition.

Thus, the decision of which normal form to choose depends upon how the cost of dependency checking compares with the cost of the joins. Usually, the 3NF would be preferred. Dependency checks need to be made with *every* insert or update to the instances of a 2NF schema, whereas, only some queries will require the join of instances of a 3NF schema.

Q.18. Explain why 4NF is a normal form more desirable than BCNF.

Ans. 4NF is more desirable than BCNF because it reduces the repetition of information. If we consider a BCNF schema not in 4NF, we observe that decomposition into 4NF does not lose information provided that a lossless join decomposition is used, yet redundancy is reduced.

Q.19. Compute the closure of the following set F of FDs for the relation schema, R = (A, B, C, D, E), A → BC, CD → E, B → D, E → A. List the candidate keys for R ? [GGSIPU, B.Tech. (CSE)-5th sem, 2nd internal Test, Sept. 2007].

Ans. *Given :* A → BC, So, A → B and A → C.

Since A → B and B → D, So A → D (transitivity rule)

Now, A → CD and CD → E, A → E

(union, decomposition, transitivity rule)

Since A → A, we have (reflexive property)

A → ABCDE (union rule)

Since, E → A, E → ABCDE (transitivity rule)

Since CD → E, So, CD → ABCDE (transitivity rule)

Since, B → D and BC → CD

So, BC → ABCDE

(augmentation rule & transitivity rule)

Also, C→ C, D → D → D, BD → D and so on.

Therefore, we find that any FD with A, E, BC or CD on the LHS of arrow is in F^+, no matter which other attributes appear in the FD. Say, * represents any set of attributes in R, then F^+ is

BD → B

BD → D

C → C

D → D

BD → BD

$$B \rightarrow D$$
$$B \rightarrow B$$
$$B \rightarrow BD$$

and all FDs of the form

$$A^* \rightarrow \alpha$$
$$BC^{**} \rightarrow \alpha$$
$$CD^* \rightarrow \alpha$$
$$E^* \rightarrow \alpha$$

Where α is any subset of {A, B, C, D, E}. The candidate keys are A, BC, CD and E.

Q.20. Using the FDs of above example 19, find the canonical cover, F_C?

Ans. Given : Set of FDs, F is

$$A \rightarrow BC$$
$$CD \rightarrow E$$
$$B \rightarrow D$$
$$E \rightarrow A$$

Here, LHS (determinant) of all FDs is unique. Also, none of the attributes in the left or right side of any FDs is extraneous. Therefore, the canonical cover F_C is equal to F.

Q.21. Give an example of a relation schema R′ and F′ of FDs such that there are atleast three distinct lossless decompositions of R′ into BCNF?

Ans. Given : Relation, R′ = (A, B, C, D), the set of FDs (F′) as

$$A \rightarrow B,\ C \rightarrow D,\ B \rightarrow C.$$

It allows 3 distinct BCNF decompositions

$$R_1 = \{(A, B), (C, D), (B, C)\}$$
$$R_2 = \{(A, B), (C, D), (A, C)\}$$
$$R_3 = \{(B, C), (A, D), (A, B)\}$$

Q.22. Give an example of a relation schema, R and a set of dependencies such that R is in BCNF but is not in 4NF?

Ans. The relation schema, R = (A, B, C, D, E) and the set of dependencies –

$$A \rightarrow\rightarrow BC$$
$$B \rightarrow\rightarrow CD$$
$$E \rightarrow\rightarrow AD$$

Constitute a BCNF decomposition as all FDs are trivial. But, it is not in 4NF.

Q.23. Given the database schema, R **(*a, b, c*) and a relation *r* on the screen R, write an SQL query to test whether the FD, *b* → C holds on relation *r*. Also write an SQL assertion that enforces the FD. Assume that no null values are present?**

Ans. (*a*) The Query given below gives a non-empty result if and only if *b* → *c* does not hold on *r*.

```
SELECT b
FROM r
GROUP BY b
HAVING COUNT (DISTINCT c) > 1;
```

(*b*) CREATE ASSERION *b*-to-*c* check

```
(not exist
    (Select b
    from r
    group by b
    having count (distinct c) > 1
    )
);
```

Q.24. Let R_1, R_2 ..., R_n be a decomposition of schema, U. Let μ(U) be a relation and let $r_i = \Pi\ R_1\ (\mu)$. Show that

$$\mu \subseteq r_i \bowtie r_2 \bowtie ..... \bowtie r_n.$$

Ans. Consider some tuple, *t*, in *u*.

Note that $r_i = \Pi_{Ri}$ (u) implies that $t[R_i] \in r_i$ $(1 \leq i \leq n)$. Thus,

$$t[R_1] \bowtie t[R_2] \bowtie .... \bowtie t[R_n] \in r_i \bowtie r_2 \bowtie .... \bowtie r_n$$

by the definition of natural join,

$$t[R_1] \bowtie t[R_2] \bowtie ... \bowtie t[R_n] = \Pi_\alpha\ (\sigma_\beta\ (t[R_2] \times t[R_2] \times ... \times t[R_n]))$$

Where the condition, β, is satisfied if values of attributes with the same name in a tuple are equal and where α = U. The cartesian product of single tuples generates on tuple. The selection process is satisfied because all attributes with the same name must have the same value since they are the projections from the same tuple. Finally, the projection clause removes duplicate attribute names.

As per the definition of decomposition, $U = R_1 \cup R_2 \cup .... \cup R_n$.

It means that all attributes of t are in $t[R_1] \bowtie t[R_2] \bowtie ... \bowtie t[R_n]$. That is,

t = Result of this join. Since *t* is any arbitrary tuple in *u*, so

$$u \subseteq r_1 \bowtie r_2 \bowtie ... \bowtie r_n.$$

Q.25. Show that the decomposition of R = (A, B, C, D, E) into (A, B, C) and (A, D, E) is not a dependency preserving decomposition.

[KUD, B.E(CSE); 6th Sem., 1996]

Ans. The dependency B → D is not preserved.

(*a*) F_1, the restriction of F to (A, B, C) is –

A → ABC	AB → ABC
A → AB	AB → BC
A → AC	AB → AB
A → BC	AB → A
A → B	AB → B
A → C	AB → C
A → A	AC (same as AB)
B → B	BC (same as AB)
C → C	ABC (same as AB)
AB → AC	

(*b*) F_2, the restriction of F to (C, D, E) is –

A → ADE	A → A
A → AD	A → D

$A \rightarrow AE$	$A \rightarrow E$
$A \rightarrow DE$	$D \rightarrow D$
E (same as A)	AD, AE, DE, ADE (same as A)

Now, $(F_1 U F_2)^+$ is easily seen not to contain $B \rightarrow D$ since the only FD in F_1 U F_2 with B as the left side, is $B \rightarrow B$, a trivial FD. We say that $B \rightarrow D$ is indeed in F^+. Thus, $B \rightarrow D$ is not preserved. Please note that $CD \rightarrow ABCDE$ is also not preserved.

Arguments : F_1 contains no dependencies with D on the RHS of the arrow. F_2 contains no dependencies with B on the LHS of the arrow. So, for $B \rightarrow D$ to be preserved there must be an FD, $B \rightarrow \alpha$ in F^1_+ and $\alpha \rightarrow D$ in F^2_+. So, $B \rightarrow D$ would follow by transitivity. Since the intersection of the two schemes is A, $\alpha = A$. Note that $B \rightarrow A$ is not F^1_+ since $B^+ = BD$.

Q.26. Show that it is possible to ensure that a dependency preserving decomposition into 3NF is a lossless decomposition by guaranteeing that atleast one schema contains a candidate key for the schema being decomposed ?

[IGNOU, MCA; 3rd year, June, 2004]

Ans. Let F be a set of FDs that hold no schema, R. Let $S = \{R_1, R_2, ... R_n\}$ be a dependency–preserving 3NF decomposition of R. Let X be a candidate key for R. Consider a legal instance r of R. Let

$$j = \pi_x(r) \bowtie \pi_{R1}(r) \bowtie \pi_{R2}(r) .... \bowtie \pi_{Rn}(r).$$

We want to prove that $r = j$.

We claim that if t_1 and t_2 are two tuples in j such that $t_1[X] = t_2[X]$, then $t_1 = t_2$. To prove this, we use the following inductive argument.

Let
$$F' = F_1 \cup F_2 \cup ... \cup F_n$$

where each F_i is the restriction of F to the schema R_i in σ. Considering the algorithm to find F′ (*i.e.*, closure of X), and using induction on the number of times that the for-loop in this algorithm is executed.

Step 1. Basis : In the 1st step of the algorithm, result is assigned to X and hence given that

$$t_1[X] = t_2[X], \text{ we know that}$$
$$t_1[\text{result}] = t_2[\text{result}] \text{ is true}$$

Step 2. Induction : Let t_1 [result] = t_2 [result] be true at the end of the kth execution of the For-loop.

Suppose that the FD considered in the (K + 1)th execution of the For -loop is $\beta \rightarrow \gamma$ and that $\beta \subseteq$ result. $\beta \subseteq$ result implies that $t_1[\beta] = t_2[\beta]$ is true. The facts that $\beta \rightarrow \gamma$ holds for some attribute set R_i in σ and that $t_1[R_i]$ and $t_2[R_i]$ are in $\Pi_{Ri}(r)$ imply that $t_1[\gamma] = t_2[\gamma]$ is also true. Since γ is now added to result by the algorithm, we know that t_1 [result] = t_2 [result] is true at the end of (k + 1)th execution of the For-loop.

Since σ is dependency preserving and X is a key for R , all attributes in R are in result, when the algorithm terminates. Thus, $t_1[R] = t_2[R]$ is true, *i.e.*, $t_1 = t_2$ (as claimed earlier.

Our claim implies that the size of $\Pi_x(j)$ is equal to the size of j. Note also that $\Pi_x(j) = P_x(r) = r$ (as X is a key for R). Thus, we have proved that the size of j equals that of r. Using the result, we know that $r \subseteq j$. Hence, we conclude that $r = j$. Please note that since X is trivially in 3NF, σ U{X} is a dependency-preserving lossless-join decomposition into 3NF.

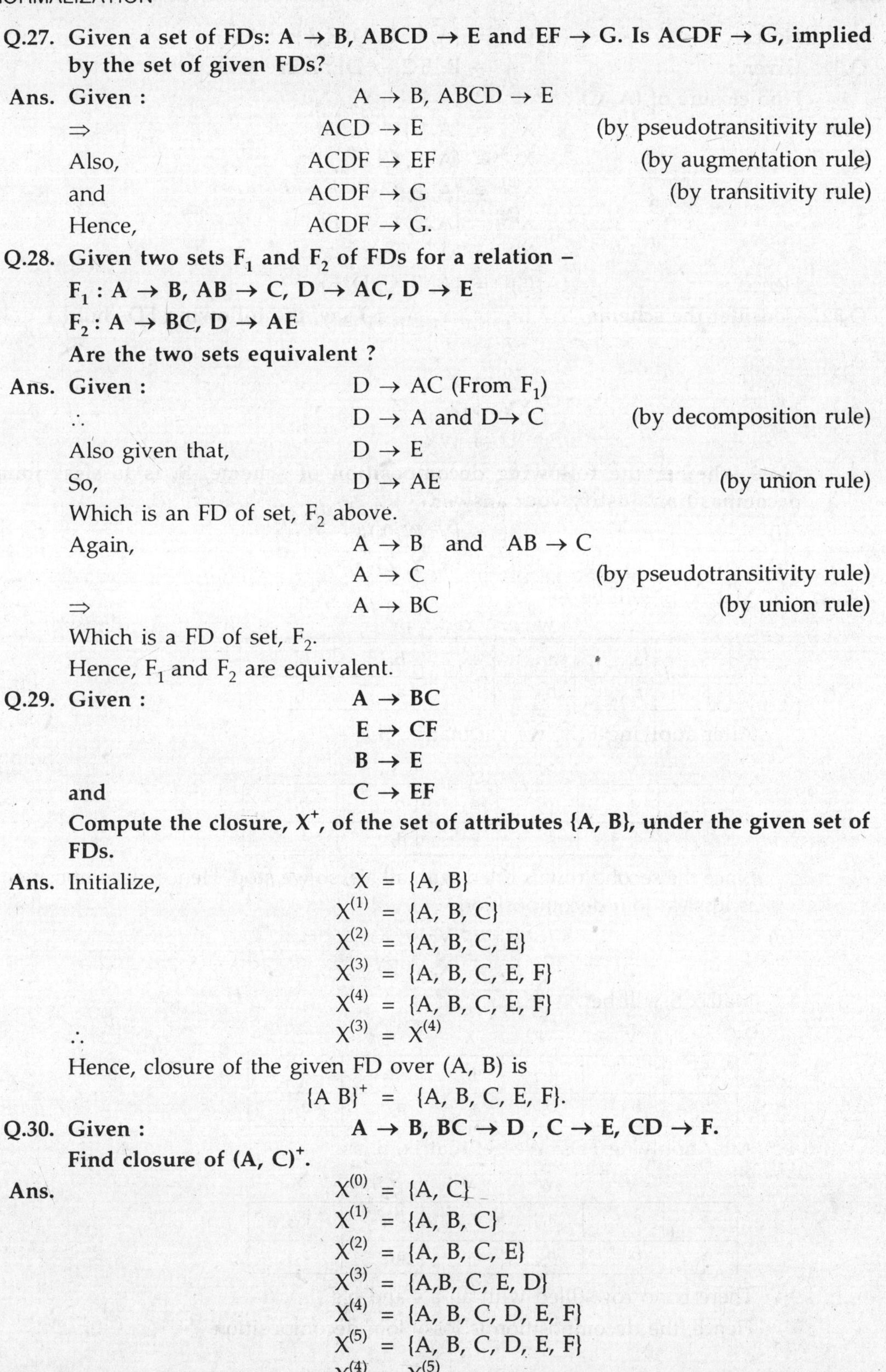

Q.27. Given a set of FDs: $A \rightarrow B$, $ABCD \rightarrow E$ and $EF \rightarrow G$. Is $ACDF \rightarrow G$, implied by the set of given FDs?

Ans. Given : $A \rightarrow B$, $ABCD \rightarrow E$

$\Rightarrow$ $ACD \rightarrow E$ (by pseudotransitivity rule)

Also, $ACDF \rightarrow EF$ (by augmentation rule)

and $ACDF \rightarrow G$ (by transitivity rule)

Hence, $ACDF \rightarrow G$.

Q.28. Given two sets F_1 and F_2 of FDs for a relation –

$F_1 : A \rightarrow B$, $AB \rightarrow C$, $D \rightarrow AC$, $D \rightarrow E$

$F_2 : A \rightarrow BC$, $D \rightarrow AE$

Are the two sets equivalent ?

Ans. Given : $D \rightarrow AC$ (From F_1)

$\therefore$ $D \rightarrow A$ and $D \rightarrow C$ (by decomposition rule)

Also given that, $D \rightarrow E$

So, $D \rightarrow AE$ (by union rule)

Which is an FD of set, F_2 above.

Again, $A \rightarrow B$ and $AB \rightarrow C$

$A \rightarrow C$ (by pseudotransitivity rule)

$\Rightarrow$ $A \rightarrow BC$ (by union rule)

Which is a FD of set, F_2.

Hence, F_1 and F_2 are equivalent.

Q.29. Given : $A \rightarrow BC$

$E \rightarrow CF$

$B \rightarrow E$

and $C \rightarrow EF$

Compute the closure, X^+, of the set of attributes {A, B}, under the given set of FDs.

Ans. Initialize, $X = \{A, B\}$

$X^{(1)} = \{A, B, C\}$

$X^{(2)} = \{A, B, C, E\}$

$X^{(3)} = \{A, B, C, E, F\}$

$X^{(4)} = \{A, B, C, E, F\}$

$\therefore$ $X^{(3)} = X^{(4)}$

Hence, closure of the given FD over (A, B) is

$$\{A\ B\}^+ = \{A, B, C, E, F\}.$$

Q.30. Given : $A \rightarrow B$, $BC \rightarrow D$, $C \rightarrow E$, $CD \rightarrow F$.

Find closure of $(A, C)^+$.

Ans. $X^{(0)} = \{A, C\}$

$X^{(1)} = \{A, B, C\}$

$X^{(2)} = \{A, B, C, E\}$

$X^{(3)} = \{A, B, C, E, D\}$

$X^{(4)} = \{A, B, C, D, E, F\}$

$X^{(5)} = \{A, B, C, D, E, F\}$

$\therefore$ $X^{(4)} = X^{(5)}$

Hence, $(A, C)^+ = \{A, B, C, D, E, F\}$.

Q.31. Given : $A \rightarrow B, BC \rightarrow DE, AEF \rightarrow G$.

Find closure of (A, C) ?

Ans.

$$X^{(0)} = \{A, C\}$$
$$X^{(1)} = \{A, B, C\}$$
$$X^{(2)} = \{A, B, C, E\}$$
$$X^{(3)} = \{A, B, C, D, E\}$$
$$\therefore \quad X^{(2)} = X^{(3)}$$

Hence, $(A, C)^+ = \{A, B, C, D, E\}$.

Q.32. Consider the scheme, S = $(v_1, w_1, x_1, y_1, z_1)$ say, the following FDs hold

$$Z \rightarrow V$$
$$W \rightarrow Y$$
$$XY \rightarrow Z$$
$$U \rightarrow WX$$

State whether the following decomposition of scheme, S, is lossless join decomposition. Justify your answer.

(*i*) $S_1 = (V, W, X)$

(*ii*) $S_2 = (V, Y, Z)$

Ans. (*i*) Matrix, S, will be –

	V	W	X	Y	Z
S_1	a_{11}	a_{12}	a_{13}	b_{14}	b_{15}
S_2	a_{21}	b_{22}	b_{23}	a_{24}	a_{25}

After applying FDs, we get matrix, S as –

	V	W	X	Y	Z
S_1	a_1	a_2	a_3	b_{14}	b_{15}
S_2	a_{21}	a_{22}	a_{23}	a_{24}	a_{25}

Since the second row is filled with all a's, so we stop. Hence, decomposition is lossless join decomposition.

(*ii*)

$$S_1 = (V, W, X)$$
$$S_2 = (X, Y, Z)$$

Matrix S will be :

	V	W	X	Y	Z
S_1	a_{11}	a_{12}	a_{13}	b_{14}	b_{15}
S_2	b_{21}	b_{22}	a_{23}	a_{24}	a_{25}

After applying FDs, We get matrix, S, as :

	V	W	X	Y	Z
S_1	a_{11}	a_{12}	a_{13}	b_{14}	a_{15}
S_2	b_{21}	b_{22}	a_{23}	a_{24}	a_{25}

There is no row filled with all a's and b's.

Hence, the decomposition is lossy join decomposition.

Q.33. Prove or disprove the following inference rules for functional dependencies. A proof can be made either by a proof argument or by using inference rules IR1 through IR3. A disproof should be done by demonstrating a relation instance that satisfies the conditions and functional dependencies in the left hand side of the inference rule but do not satisfy the conditions or dependencies in the right hand side.

(a) {W -> Y, X -> Z}| = {WX -> Y}

(b) {X -> Y} and Z subset-of Y| = {X -> Z}

(c) {X -> Y, X -> W, WY -> Z} | = {X -> Z}

(d) {XY -> Z, Y -> W} | = {XW -> Z}

(e) {X -> Z, Y -> Z} | = {X, Y}

(g) {X -> Y, XY -> Z} | = {X -> Z}

[GGSIPU, B.Tech (CSE); 5th Sem., 2nd Internal Test, Nov. 2007]

Ans. (*a*) **Proof :**

(*i*) W -> Y (given)

(*ii*) X -> Z (given)

(*iii*) WX -> YX (using IR2 (augmentation) to augment (1) with X)

(*iv*) YX -> Y (using IR1 (reflexivity), knowing that Y subset-of YX)

(*v*) WX -> Y (using IR3 (transitivity) on (3) and (4))

(*b*) **Proof :**

(*i*) X -> Y (given)

(*ii*) Y -> Z (using IR1 (reflexivity), given that Z subset-of Y)

(*iii*) X -> Z (using IR3 (transitivity) on (1) and (2))

(*c*) **Proof :**

(*i*) X -> Y (given)

(*ii*) X -> W (given)

(*iii*) WY -> Z (given)

(*iv*) X -> XY (using IR2 (augmentation) to augment (1) with X)

(*v*) XY -> WY (using IR2 (augmentation) to augment (2) with Y)

(*vi*) X -> WY (using IR3 (transitivity) on (4) and (5))

(*vii*) X -> Z (using IR3 (transitivity) on (6) and (3))

(*d*) **Disproof :** XYZW

$$t1 = x1\ y1\ z1\ w1$$
$$t2 = x1\ y2\ z2\ w1$$

The above two tuples satisfy XY -> Z and Y -> W but do not satisfy XW -> Z.

(*e*) **Disproof :** XYZ

$$t1 = x1\ y1\ z1$$
$$t2 = x1\ y2\ z1$$

The above two tuples satisfy X -> Z and Y -> Z but do not satisfy X -> Y.

(*f*) **Proof :**

(*i*) X -> Y (given)

(*ii*) XY -> Z (given)

(*iii*) X -> XY (using IR2 (augmentiation) to augment (1) with X

(*iv*) X -> Z (using IR3 (transitivity) on (3) and (2).

Q.34. Consider the following two sets of functional dependencies F = {A -> C, AC -> D, E -> AD, E -> H} and G = {A -> CD, E -> AH}. Check whether or not they are equivalent.

Ans. To show equivalence, we prove that G is covered by F and F is covered by G.

Proof that G is covered by F :

{A} + = {A, C, D} (with respect to F), which covers A -> CD in G

{E} + = {E, A, D, H, C} (with respect to F), which covers E -> AH in G

Proof that F is covered by G :

{A} + = {A, C, D} (with respect to G), which covers A -> C in F

{A, C} + = {A, C, D} (with respect to G), which covers AC -> D in F

{F} + = {E,A, H, C, D} (with respect to G), which covers E -> AD and E -> H in F.

Q.35. Prove that any relation schema with two attributes is in BCNF.

[GGSIPU, B.Tech (CSE)-5th sem, Dec 2007]

Ans. Consider a relation schema R = {A, B} with two attributes. The only possible (non-trivial) FDs are {A} -> {B} and {B} -> {A}. There are four possible cases:

(*i*) No FD holds in R. In this case, the key is {A, B} and the relation satisfies BCNF.

(*ii*) Only {A} -> {B} holds. In this case, the key is {A} and relation satisfies BCNF.

(*iii*) Only {B} -> {A} holds. In this case, the key is {B} and relation satisfies BCNF.

(*iv*) Both {A} -> {B} and {B} -> {A} hold. In this case, there are two keys {A} and {B} and the relation satisfies BCNF.

Hence, any relation with attributes is in BCNF.

Q.36. Consider the universal relation R = {A, B, C, D, E, F, G, H, I} and the set of functional dependencies F = {{A, B} -> {C}, {A} -> {D, E}, {B} -> {F} {F} -> {G, H}, {D} -> {I, J}}. What is the key for R? Decompose R into 2NF, then 3NF relations.

[GGSIPU, B.Tech. (CSE) -5th sem., Dec. 2007] & [Delhi University (DU), B.Sc., 3rd year, 2005]

Ans. A minimal set of attributes whose closure includes all the attributes in R is a key. Since the closure of {A, B}, {A, B}+ = R, one key of R is {A, B} (in this case, it is the only key).

To normalize R intuitively into 2NF then 3NF, we take the following steps.

First, identify partial dependencies that violate 2NF. These are attributes that are functionally dependent on either parts of the key, {A} or {B}, alone. We can calculate the closures {A}+ and {B}+ to determine partially dependent attributes:

{A}+ = {A, D, E, I, J}. Hence {A} -> {D, E, I, J} ({A} -> {A} is a trivial dependency)

{B}+ = {B, F, G, H}, hence {A} -> {F, G, H} ({B} -> {B} is a trivial dependency)

To normalize into 2NF, we remove the attributes that are functionally dependent on part of the key (A or B) from R and place them in separate relations R1 and R2, along with the part of the key they depend on (A or B), which are copied into each of these relations but also remains in the original relation, which we call R3 below :

R1 = {A, D, E, I, J}, R2 = {B, F, G, H}, R3 = {A, B, C}

The new keys for R1, R2, R3 are underlined. Next, we look for transitive dependencies in R1, R2, R3. The relation R1 has the transitive dependency {A} -> {D} -> {I, J}, so we remove the transitively dependent attributes {I, J} from

R1 into a relation R11 and copy the attribute D they are dependent on R11. The remaining attributes are kept in a relation R12. Hence, R1 is decomposed into R11 and R12 as follows:

R11 = {D, I, J}, R12 = {A, D, E}

The relation R2 is similarly decomposed into R21 and R22 based on the transitive dependency {B} -> {F} -> {G, H}:

R2 = {F, G, H}, R2 = {B, F}

The final set of relations in 3NF are {R11, R12, R21, R22, R3}

Q.37. Repeat exercise 36 for the following different set of functional dependencies G = {{A, B} -> {C}, {B, D} -> {E, F}, {A, D} -> {G, H}, {A} -> {I}, {H} -> {J}}.

Ans. To help in solving this problem systematically, we can first find the closures of all single attributes to see if any is a key on its own as follows :

{A} + -> {A, I}, {B} + -> {B}, {C} + -> {C}, {D} + -> {D}, {E} + -> {E}, {F} + ->{F}, {G} + -> {G}, {H} + -> {H, J},{I} + ->{I}, {J} + -> {J}

Since none of the single attributes is a key, we next calculate the closures of pairs of attributes that are possible keys:

{A, B} + -> {A, B, C, I}, {B, D}+ -> {B, D, E, F}, {A, D}+ -> {A, D, G, H, I, J}

None of these pairs are keys either since none of the closures includes all attributes. But the union of the three closures includes all the attributes:

{A, B, D} + -> {A, B, C, D, E, F, G, H, I}

Hence, {A, B, D,} is a key.

Based on the above analysis, we decompose as follows, in a similar manner, starting with the following relation R:

R = {A, B, D, C, E, F, G, H, I}

The first-level partial dependencies on the key (which violate 2NF) are:

{A, B} -> {C, I}, {B, D} -> {E, F}, {A, D} + -> {G, H, I, J}

Hence, R is decomposed into R1, R2, R3, R4 (key are underlined):

R1 = {A, B, C, I}, R2 = {B, D, E, F}, R3 = {A, D, G, H, I, J} R4 = {<u>A</u>, <u>B</u>, <u>D</u>}

Additional partial dependencies exist in R1 and R3 because{A} ->{I}. Hence, we remove {I} into R5, so the following relations are the result of 2NF decomposition:

R1 = {A, B, C}, R2 = {B, D, E, F}, R3 = {A, D, G, H, J}, R4 = {A, B, D}, R5 = {A, I}

Next, we check for transitive dependencies in each of the relations (which violate 3NF). Only R3 has a transitive dependency {A, D} -> {H} -> {J}, so it is decomposed into R31 and R32 as follows:

R31 = {H, J}, R32 = {A, D, G, H}

The final set of 3NF relations is {R1, R2, R3, R4, R5}

Q.38. Given relation R(A, B, C, D, E) with dependencies

AB → C

CD → E

DE → B

Is AB a candidate key?

Is ABD a candidate key? [Delhi University (DU); B.Sc., 3rd year, 2005]

Ans. No, AB + = {A, B, C}, a proper subset of {A, B, C, D, E}

Yes, ABD + = {A, B, C, D, E}

Q.39. Consider the relation R, which has attributes that hold schedules of courses and sections at a university; R {CourseNo, SecNo, Offering Dept, CreditHours, CourseLevel, InstructorSSN, Semester, Year, Days_hours, RoomNo, NoOfStudents}. Suppose that the following functional dependencies hold on R:

{CourseNo} -> {Offering Dept, CreditHours, CourseLevel} {CourseNO, SecNo, Semester, year } -> {Days_Hours, RoomNO, NoOfStudents, InstructorSSN}, {RoomNo, Days_Hours, Semester, Year} -> {InstructorSSN, CourseNo, SecNo}. Try to determine which sets of attributes form keys of R. How would you normalize this relation?

Ans. Let us use the following shorthand notation :

C = CourseNo, SN = SecNo, OD = Offering Dept, CH = CreditHours, CL = CourseLevel, I = InstructorSSN, S = Semester, Y = Year, D = Days_Hours, RM = RoomNo, NS = NoOfStudents

Hence, R = {C, SN, OD, CH, CL, I, S, Y, D, RM, NS}, and the following functional dependencies hold:

{C} -> {OD, CH, CL}

{C, SN, S, Y} -> {D, RM, NS, I}

{RM, D, S, Y} -> {I, C, SN}

First, we can calculate the closures for each left hand side of a functional dependency, since these sets of attributes are the candidates to be keys:

(1) {C} + = {C, OD, CH, CL}

(2) Since {C, SN, S, Y} -> {D, RM, NS, I}, and {C} + = {C, OD, CH, CL}, we get: {C, SN, S, Y} + = {C, SN, S, Y, D, RM, NS, I, OD, CH, CL} = R

(3) Since {RM, D, S, Y} -> {I, C, SN}, we know that {RM, D, S, Y} + contains {RM, D, S, Y, I, C, SN}. But {C} + contains {OD, CH, CL} so these are also contained in {RM, D, S, Y} + since C is already there. Finally, since {C, SN, S, Y} are now all in {RM, D, S, Y} + and {C, SN, S, Y} + contains {NS} (from (2) above), we get: {RM, D, S, Y} + = {RM, D, S, Y, I, C, SN, OD, CH, CL, NS} = R

Hence, both K1 = {C, SN, S, Y} and K2 = {RM, D, S, Y} are (candidate) keys of R. By applying the general definition of 2NF, we find that the functional dependency {C} -> {OD, CH, CL} is a partial dependency for K1 (since C is included in K1). Hence, R is normalized into R1 and R2 as follows:

R1 = {C, OD, CH, CL}

R2 = {RM, D, S, Y, I, C, SN, NS} with candidate keys K1 and K2

Since neither R1 nor R2 have transitive dependencies on either of the candidate keys, R1 and R2 are in 3NF also. They also both satisfy the definition of BCNF.

Q.40. Consider the following relations for an order-processing application database at ABC, Inc.

ORDER (<u>O#</u>, Odate, Cust#, Total_amount)

ORDER-ITEM (<u>O#</u>, <u>I#</u>, Qty_ordered, Total_price, Discount%)

Assume that each item has a different discount. The Total_price refers to one item, Odate is the date on which the order was placed, and Total_amount is the amount of the order. If we apply a natural join on the relations Order-Item and Order in this database, what does the resulting relation schema look like? What will be its key? Show the FDs in this resulting relation. Is it in 2NF? Is it in 3NF? Why or why not ? (State any assumptions you make).

Ans. Given relations

Order (O#, Odate, Cust#, Total_amt)

Order_Item (O#, I#, Qty_ordered, Total_price, Discount%), the schema of Order* Order_Item looks like T_1 (O#, I#, Odate, Cust#, Total_amount, Qty_ordered, Total_price, Discount%) and its key is O#, I#. It has functional dependencies O#I#. Qty_ordered,

O#I#. Total_price,

O#I#. Discount%,

O#. Odate,

O#. Cust#,

O#. Total_amount.

It is not in 2NF, as attributes Odate, Cut#, and Total_amount are only partially dependent on the primary key, O#I#

Nor is it in 3NF, as a 2NF is a requirement for 3NF.

Q.41. Consider the following relation:

CAR_SALE (Car#, Date_sold, Salesman#, Commision%, Discount_amt)

Assume that a car may be sold by multiple salesmen and hence {CAR#, SALESMAN#} is the primary key. Additional dependencies are:

Date_sold -> Discount_amt

and

Salesman# -> Commission %

Based on the given primary key, is this relation in 1NF, 2NF, or 3NF? Why or why not? How would you successively normalize it completely?

Ans. Given the relation schema Car_Sale (Car#, Salesman#, Date_sold, Commission%, Discount_amt) with the functional dependencies

Date_sold → Discount_amt, Salesman# → Commision %, Car# → Date_sold

This relation satisfies 1NF but not 2NF (Car# → Date_sold and Car# →. Discount_amt) so these two attributes are not FFD on the primary key and not in 3NF.

To normalize,

2NF:

Car_Sale 1 (Car#, Date_Sold, Discount_amt)

Car_Sale 2 (Car#, Salesman#)

Car_Sale 3 (Salesman#, Commission%)

3NF:

Car_Sale 1-1 (Car#, Date_sold)

Car_Sale 1-2 (Date_sold, Discount_amt)

Car_Sale 2 (Car#, Salesman#)

Car_Sale 3(Salesman#, Commission%)

Q.42. Consider the following relation for published books:

BOOK (Book_title, Authorname, Book_type, Listprice, Author_affil, Publisher)

Author_affil referes to the affiliation of the author. Suppose the following dependencies exist.

Book_title -> Publisher, Book_type

Book -> type -> Listprice

Author_name -> Author-affil

(*a*) **What normal form is the relation in? Explain your answer:**

(*b*) **Apply normalization until you cannot decompose the relations further. State the reasons behind each decomposition.**

[GGSIPU, B.Tech (CSE)-5th sem., 2nd Internal Test, Nov. 2005], [Delhi University, (DU)-B.Sc., 3rd year, 2006], [UPTU, MBA-4th sem., 2006 & 07].

Ans. Given the relation

Book (Book_title, Authorname, Book_type, Listprice, Author_affil, Publisher) and the FDs

Book_title → Publisher, Book_type

Book_type → Listprice,

Authorname → Author_affil

(*a*) The key for this relation is Book_title, Authorname. This relation is in 1NF and not in 2NF as no attributes are FFD on the key. It is also not in 3NF.

(*b*) 2NF decomposition:

Book0 (Book_title, Authorname)

Book 1 (Book_title, Publisher, Book_type, Listprice)

Book 2 (Authorname, Author_affil)

This decomposition eliminates the **partial dependencies.**

3NF decomposition:

Book0 (Book_title, Authorname)

Book 1-1 (Book_title, Publisher, Book_type)

Book 1-2 (Book_type, Listprice)

Book 2 (Authorname, Auther_affil)

This decomposition eliminates the **transitive dependency** of Listprice

Q.43. Specify a template dependency for join dependencies.

Ans. The following template specifies a join dependency JD (X, Y, Z).

R = (A, B, C)

	$a \; b \; c_1$	X = (A, B)
hypothesis	$a \; b_1 \; c$	Y = (B, C)
	$a_1 \; b \; c$	Z = (A, C)
conclusion	$a \; b \; c$	

Q.44. Prove that a functional dependency is also a multivalued dependency.

[GGSIPU, B.Tech. (CSE); 5th Sem., 2nd Internal Test. Sept. 2007]

Ans. Suppose that a functional dependency X -> Y exists in a relation R = {X, Y, Z}, and suppose there are two tuples with the same value of X. Because of the functional dependency, they must also have the same value of Y. Suppose the tuples are t1 = < *x*, *y*, *z* 1> and *t*2 = < *x*, *y*, *z*2 >. Then, according to the definition of multivalued dependency, we must have two tuples *t*3 and *t*4 (not necessarily distinct from *t*1 and *t*2) satisfying: *t*3 [X] = *t*4 [X] = *t*1 [X] = *t*2[X], *t*3[Y] = *t*2[Y], *t*4[Y] = *t*1[Y], *t*3 [Z] = *t*1[Z], and *t*4[Z] = *t*2[Z]. Two tuples satisfying this are *t*2 (satisfies conditions for *t*4) and *t*1 (satisfies conditions for *t*3). Hence, whenever the condition for functional dependency holds, so does the condition for multivalued dependency.

Q.45. Consider the relation REFRIG(MODEL#, YEAR, PRICE, MANUF_PLANT, COLOR), which is abbreviated as REFRIG(M, Y, P, MP, C), and the following set of F of functional dependencies: F = {M -> MP, {M, Y} -> P, MP -> C}

(*a*) Evaluate each of the following as a candidate key for REFRIG, giving reasons why it can or cannot be a key: {M}, {M, Y}, {M, C}

(*b*) Based on the above key determination, state whether the relation REFRIG is in 3NF and in BCNF, giving proper reasons.

(*c*) Consider the decomposition of REFRIG into D = {R1 (M, Y, P), R2(M, MP, C)}. Is this decomposition lossless? Show why.

Ans. (*a*) {M} IS NOT a candidate key since it does not functionally determine attributes Y or P.

{M, Y} is a candidate key since it functionally determines the remaining attributes P, MP, and C.

i.e.,

{M, Y}, But M MP

By augmentation {M, Y} MP

Since MP C, by transitivity M $\rightarrow$ MP, MP $\rightarrow$ C, gives MC

By augmentation {M, Y} $\rightarrow$ C

Thus {M, Y} P, MP, C and {M, Y} can be a candidate key

{M, C} IS NOT a candidate key since it does not functionally determine attributes Y or P.

(*b*) REFRIG is not in 2NF, due to the partial dependency {M, Y} $\rightarrow$ MP {since {M} MP holds}. Therefore REFRIG is neither in 3NF nor in BCNF.

Alternatively: BCNF can be directly tested by using all of the given dependencies and finding out if the left hand side of each is a superkey (or if the right hand side is a prime attribute). In the two fields in REFRIG: M $\rightarrow$ MP and MP $\rightarrow$ C. Since neither M nor MP is a superkey, we can conclude that REFRIG is in neither in 3NF nor in BCNF.

(*c*)

R = {M, Y, P, MP, C}

R1 = {M, Y, P}

R2 = {M, MP, C}

F = {M MP, {M, Y} P, MP C}

F^+ = { $\{M\}^+$ {M, MP, C},

$\{M, Y\}^+$ {M, Y, P, MP, C}

$\{MP\}^+$ {MP, C} }

R1 $\cap$ R2 = M

R2 – R1 = {MP, C}

D{R1, R2} has the lossless join property since

Property : LJ1: FD ((R1 $\cap$ R2) (R2 – R1)) is in F^+ is satisfied (due to M {MP, C}).

Q.46. What do you mean by a canonical cover?

[GGSIPU, B.Tech. (CSE); 5th Sem., 2nd Internal Test, Sept. 2007]

Ans. Consider the following set, F, of FDs on schema, R (A, B, C):

A $\rightarrow$ BC, B $\rightarrow$ C, A $\rightarrow$ B, AB $\rightarrow$ C

Now, let us compute the canonical cover for F.

Now, there are two F.D.s with the same set of attributes on the left side of the arrow:

$$A \rightarrow BC, A \rightarrow B$$

We combine these FDs into $A \rightarrow BC$.

Now, A is extraneous in $AB \rightarrow C$ because F logically implies –

$$(F - \{AB \rightarrow C\} \cup \{B \rightarrow C\}$$

This assertion is true because $B \rightarrow C$ is already in our set of FD.

Also, C is extraneous in $A \rightarrow BC$, as $A \rightarrow BC$ is logically implied by $A \rightarrow B$ and $B \rightarrow C$. Thus, our canonical cover is –

$$A \rightarrow B \text{ and } B \rightarrow C$$

NOTE : An attribute of a FD is said to be extraneous if we can remove it without changing the closure of the set of FDs.

Q.47. Show that a canonical cover might not be unique.

Ans. Consider the set of FDs, F as

$$A \rightarrow BC$$
$$B \rightarrow AC$$
$$C \rightarrow AB.$$

If we apply the extraneity test to $A \rightarrow BC$, we find that both B and C are extraneous under F. But it is incorrect to delete both. The algorithm should pick one of the two and delete it. Consider 2 cases now –

Case 1. C is deleted : Here, we get the set, F′ as $\{A \rightarrow B, B \rightarrow AC, C \rightarrow AB\}$. Now, B is not extraneous in the RHS of $A \rightarrow B$ under F′. But A and B are extraneous in the RHS of $C \rightarrow AB$, leading to two canonical covers –

$$F_C = \{A \rightarrow B, B \rightarrow C, C \rightarrow A\} \text{ and}$$
$$F_C = \{A \rightarrow B, B \rightarrow AC, A \rightarrow B\}$$

Case 2. B is deleted : Here, we get the set $\{A \rightarrow C, B \rightarrow AC, C \rightarrow AB\}$ as F′. This case 2 is same as case 1, leading to the canonical covers :

$$F_C = \{A \rightarrow C, C \rightarrow B, B \rightarrow A\}$$
$$F_C = \{A \rightarrow C, B \rightarrow C , C \rightarrow AB\}$$

Q.48. Write a BCNF decomposition algorithm.

Ans. If R is not in BCNF, we can decompose R into a collection of BCNF schemas R_1, R_2....., R_n by the algorithm.

```
result := {R};
done := false;
compute F⁺;
While (not done) do
   if (there is a schema Rᵢ in result that is not in BCNF)
      then begin
         let α → β be a non-trivial FD that holds on Rᵢ such that
               α → Rᵢ is not in F⁺ and α ∩ β = ϕ;
      result:= (result – Rᵢ) ∪ (Rᵢ – β) ∪ (α, β);
   end
else done : = true;
```

Q.49. Write an algorithm for finding a dependency-preserving, lossless decomposition into 3NF. **[KUD, B.E(CSE)-6th sem., 1996]**

Ans. Let F_C be a canonical cover for F ;

i : = 0;

for each FD, $\alpha \rightarrow \beta$ in F_C do

if none of the schemas R_j, j = 1, 2, --i contains $\alpha\beta$

then begin

i : = i + 1;

R_i := $\alpha\beta$;

end

(if none of the schemas R_j , j = 1, 2, .. i contains a candidate key for R)

then begin

i : = i + 1;

R_i : = any candidate key for R;

end

return (R_1, R_2, ... , R_i)

Q.50. Discuss atleast three relational design criteria ?

Ans. In 1978, Beeri and his co-workers suggested some design criteria for a relational model. They are as follows :

1. **Representation :** The final structure must correctly represent the original specifications.
2. **Separation :** The original specifications are separated into relations that satisfy certain conditions.
3. **Redundancy :** The final structure must not contain any redundant information.

EXERCISE QUESTIONS

Q.1. (*a*) Define the following terms :

(*i*) Normalization (*ii*) FFD

(*iii*) Trivial join dependency (*iv*) BCNF

(*b*) What is a lossless decomposition?

[GGSIPU, B.Tech. (CSE); 5th Sem. 2nd Internal Test. Nov. 2005]

Q.2. Find the minimal set of FDs from the following given set :

PQ → R

PS → Q

QS → P

PR → Q

S → R

[GGSIPU, B.Tech (CSE); 5th Sem., 2nd Internal Test, Nov. 2005]

Q.3. Discuss Normalization process briefly and consider the following relation :

R (A, B, C, D, E, F, G, H) and a set of FDs:

F (AB → CEFGH, A → D, F → G, FB → H,

HBC → ADEFG, FBC → ADE).

Normalize this relation upto BCNF. **[GGSIPU, B.Tech. (CSE); 5th Sem., Dec. 2006]**

Q.4. (*a*) Define :

(*i*) FFD (*ii*) Determinant

(*iii*) MVD (*iv*) JD

(*b*) What is the need of normalization? If normalization is not done, what type to problems may arise. **[GGSIPU, B.Tech. (CSE); 5th Sem., Dec. 2006]**

Q.5. (*a*) Define and discuss—FD.

(*b*) A relation schema with only two attributes is bound to be in BCNF. Justify. **[GGSIPU, B.Tech. (CSE); 5th Sem., Dec. 2007]**

Q.6. (*a*) Is BCNF stronger than 3NF? Justify your answer.

(*b*) Define closure and minimal cover giving example. **[GGSIPU, B.Tech. (CSE); 5th Sem., Dec. 2007]**

Q.7. Create a relational schema R(A, B, C, D) with primary key AB such that R is in 2NF but not in 3NF. Show explicitly why it is in 2NF but not in 3NF. **[GGSIPU, B.Tech. (CSE); 5th Sem., 2nd Internal Test, Nov. 2007]**

Q.8. (*a*) What is functional dependency? Write down the rules for finding the FDs from a set of given FD's.

(*b*) Explain the normal forms due to FD?**[GGSIPU, B.Tech. (CS); 5th Sem., Dec. 2008]**

Q.9. What are the rules for decomposing a relation ? Explain. **[GGSIPU, B.Tech. (CS); 5th Sem., Dec. 2008]**

Q.10. A relation R (A, B, C, D, E) has the following set of FDs –

$A \rightarrow BC$ $\quad B \rightarrow E$

$C \rightarrow D$ $\quad A \rightarrow E$

$D \rightarrow B$

Is the decomposition of this relation to R_1 (A, B, C), R_2 (C, D), R_3 (B, D, E) lossless and or dependency preserving ? Justify your answer. **[IGNOU, MCA; 3rd year, June 2004]**

Q.11. What is FD? How is it different from MVD and JDs? Give an example of each of MVD and JD. **[IGNOU, MCA; 3rd year, June 2004]**

Q.12. (*a*) Given these FDs:

$F = \{A \rightarrow BC, CD \rightarrow E, E \rightarrow C, D \rightarrow AEH, ABH \rightarrow BD, DH \rightarrow BC\}$

for relational schema, R (A, B, C, D, E, F, G, H). Find minimal cover?

(*b*) Given these FDs, find primary key

$A \rightarrow B, C, D$

$A, E \rightarrow F$

$E \rightarrow G$

$D \rightarrow H$

$F, E \rightarrow I$?

(*c*) What is normalization? Why is it needed. **[Delhi University (DU); B.Sc., 3rd Year, 2006]**

Q.13. For a given relation, R = {A, B, C, D, E, F, G, H} with the following, FDs,

$F = \{A \rightarrow BCD, AE \rightarrow F, E \rightarrow G, D \rightarrow H\}$

(*i*) Find the key.

(*ii*) In which Normal form, Relation, R, is ?

(*iii*) Apply normalization on R until it cannot be decomposed further. Also give reasons for decomposition. **[Delhi University (DU); B.Sc., 3rd Year, 2006]**

Q.14. (*a*) Define the term FD. Enumerate the inference rules for FDs.

(*b*) What is the purpose of normalising data in a database application? Differentiate between 3NF and BCNF. **[Delhi University (DU); B.Sc., 3rd Year, 2007]**

Q.15. (*a*) For a relation, R(A, B, C, D, E, F) the set of FDs, F is given as follows :

F = {AB → C, C → A, BC → D, ACD → B, BE → C, CE → FA, CF → BD, D → E]

Find a Non-redundant cover for F. Is this the only Non-redundant cover? Also find its canonical cover.

(*b*) Find a BCNF decomposition of the relation schema :

SHIPPING (Ship, Capacity, DateCargo, Value)

With the following set of FDs :

Ship → Capacity

ShipDate → Cargo

Cargo, Capacity → Value

Specify the key of the relation. Also mention whether the decomposition is lossless and dependency preserving or not. **[Delhi University (DU); B.Sc., 3rd year, 2007]**

Q.16. (*a*) What do you mean by Normalization? Explain BCNF and 3NF with a suitable. Example.

(*b*) Describe the term MVD in the context of RDBMS by giving an example. Discuss 4NF and 5NF also.

(*c*) What do you mean by decomposition of a relation? Consider the relational schema, R(A, B, C, D, E, F) and FDs

A → BC, C → A, D → E, F → A, E → D.

Is the decomposition of R into R_1(A, C, D), R_2(B, C, D) and R_3(E, F, D) lossless? Explain the requirements for lossless decomposition and dependency preserving.

[UPTU, B.Tech. (CS); 4th Sem., 2006–07]

Q.17. (*a*) Let R = (A, B, C, D) and FDs be

A → C and AB → D. What is the closure of {A, B}?

(*b*) What is normalization of relation? What is the key attribute in a relation? What is the difference between 1NF, 2NF and 3NF?

[BPUT, Orissa—B.Tech (CSE); 4th Sem., 2008]

Q.18. Suppose a relation, R(A, B, C, D, E) has FDs

AB → C CD → E

D → A BE → D

AE → B

Find all the candidate keys of R? **[BPUT, Orissa; B.Tech. (CSE); 4th Sem., 2008]**

Q.19. What is normalization? Explain the first and second normal forms using appropriate examples. **[BPUT, Orissa; B.Tech. (CSE); 4th Sem., April 2005]**

Q.20. What do you mean by lossless join. **[BPUT, Orissa; MCA 2nd Year, June 2005]**

Q.21. Consider the universal relation, R = {A, B, C, D, E, F, G, H, I, J} and set of FDs

F = {{A, B} → {C}, {A} → {D, E}, {B} → {F},

{F} → {G, H}, {D} → {I, J}}

What is the key for R? Decompose R into 2NF relations.

[BPUT, Orissa, B.Tech. (CSE); 4th Sem., 2006]

Q.22. Define and explain in brief the following :

(*i*) Normalization (*ii*) 1 NF

(*iii*) 2NF (*iv*) 3NF

(*v*) BCNF (*vi*) 4NF

(*vii*) DKNF

[Nagpur University, B.E. (CSE); 7th Sem., Dec. 2008]

Q.23. (*a*) Define 1NF, 2NF, 3NF with suitable example.
(*b*) Why certain FD are called as trival FDs?
(*c*) Explain the concept of canonical cover with proper example.
[Nagpur University, B.E. (CSE); 7th Sem., Dec. 2008]

Q.24. (*a*) Explain 3NF and BCNF with appropriate examples. Prove BCNF is stronger than 3NF.
(*b*) Consider any unnormalized relation and convert it to 1NF, 2NF and 3NF.
[Nagpur University, MCA 2nd Sem., Dec. 2006]

Q.25. What is MVD? Explain 4NF. **[Nagpur University, MCA 2nd Sem., Dec. 2007]**

Q.26. (*a*) Explain 2NF with suitable example.
(*b*) Explain the following : (*i*) FD, (*ii*) MVD.
[Nagpur University, MCA 2nd Sem., Dec. 2006]

Q.27. (*a*) What is normalization? Explain in brief.
(*b*) Explain 1NF and 2NF with an example.
[Nagpur University, B.Com (Part-II)—Computer Application, June-July 2008]

Q.28. What do you mean by the term normalization? Explain.
[Nagpur University, B.Com (Part-II)—Computer Application, Dec. 2007]

Q.29. Explain FD. Why are certain FDs called as trivial FDs?
[Nagpur University, B.E. (CSE); 7th Sem., June-July 2007]

Q.30. (*a*) What do you mean by normalization? Discuss in brief, the objectives of normalization.
(*b*) Explain with suitable example, DKNF.
[Nagpur University, B.E. (CSE); 7th Sem., June-July, 2007]

Q.31. Discuss 1NF, 2NF, 3NF. Consider any unnormalized relation and bring it into 1NF, 2NF and 3NF step by step. **[Nagpur University, MCA 2nd Sem., June-July 2008]**

Q.32. (*a*) Normalize the following relation through various normal forms : (1NF, 2N, 3NF and BCNF).

Roll No	Stud_Name	Stud-Addr	Branch	Year	Subject No	Subject Name	Grade
444	Sachin	5, 4NN	CT	II	E1 E2	DBMS VC	A B
786	Nikita	26, BKKN	IT	I	E1 C5	DBMS JAVA	B A

(*b*) What constitutes a bad database design?
[Nagpur University, B.E. (CSE); 7th Sem., June-July 2007]

Q.33. (*a*) What is Normalization? Give types of normalizations.
(*b*) What are the advantages of normalized relations over the un-normalized relations?
[JNTU, B.Tech (CSE/IT; 2nd Sem., April/May, 2007]

Q.34. Give an algorithm to test for a lossless join and show that it correctly determines if a decomposition has a lossless join. **[KUD, B.E. (CSE); 6th Sem., 1996]**

Q.35. What do you mean by normalization? Define FD and MVD.
[GGSIPU, BCA; 3rd Sem., Dec. 2003]

Q.36. What is the FD? Explain with the help of an example, how a relation which exists in BCNF also exists in 2NF and 3NF? **[GGSIPU, MCA; 2nd Sem., May 2003]**

Q.37. What do you understand by the logical implication of a function dependency by a set of FDS? Suggest some algorithm that checks whether FD, $X \rightarrow Y$ is logically implied by a set of FDs, F. **[GGSIPU, MCA; 2nd Sem., May 2004]**

Q.38. With an example differentiate between 3NF and BCNF?
[GGSIPU, M.Tech. (IT); 3rd Sem., Nov. 2005]

Q.39. (*a*) What is the importance of FDs in database design?
(*b*) Write short notes on the following : (*i*) MVD, (*ii*) BCNF?
[GGSIPU, M.Tech. (IT); 3rd Sem., Dec. 2004]

Q.40. (*a*) What do you mean by decomposition? Explain the desirable properties of decomposition.

(*b*) Let R = (A, B, C, D, E) and F be the set of FDs
A → BC, B → CD, E → A, C → ED
Find closure of F (*i.e.*, F^+)? **[GGSIPU, M.Tech. (IT); 3rd Sem., Dec. 2004]**

Q.41. (*a*) What are the pitfalls of database design? Explain.
(*b*) Explain with example why PJNF is a normal form more desirable than is 4NF.
[GGSIPU, M.Tech. (IT); 3rd Sem., Dec. 2004]

Q.42. (*a*) Why are certain FDs called trivial dependencies?
(*b*) Compute the closure of the following set F of FDs for relations scheme—
R = (A, B, C, D, E)
A → BC, CD → E, B → D, E → A
What are the candidate keys for R?
(*c*) List the design goals for relational database and explain why each are desirable.
[GGSIPU, M.Tech (IT); 3rd Sem., Dec. 2005]

Q.43. Explain the concept of normalization. Why do we need normalization ? Define 1NF, 2NF, 3NF, 4NF and BCNF with the help of suitable examples.
[GGSIPU, MCA 3rd Sem., 2010]

Q.44. (*a*) Relation R(A, B, C, D, E, F) satisfies the following FDs :
AB → C BC → D BE → C CF → BD
C → A ACD → B CE → FA D → EF
Find out the closure of FDS.
(*b*) Discuss the normal forms due to FDs.
[GGSIPU, B. Tech. (CSE/IT) – 5th Sem., Dec. 2011]

Q.45. Consider the following FDs over the attribute set ABCDEFGH
A → E BE → D
AS → BE BDH → E
AC → E F → A
E → B D → H
BG → F CD → A
Find a minimal cover, then decompose into lossless 3NF.
[GGSIPU, M.Tech. (CSE/IT) — Ist Sem., Dec. 2011]

Q.46. (*i*) What are the rules of decomposition of a relation ? Suppose we decompose the schema R = (A, B, C, D, E)
R1(A, B, C)
R2(A, D, E)
Show that this decomposition is a lossless decomposition if the following FDs holds
A → BC, CD → E, B → D, E → A.
(*ii*) Why are certain FDs called as trivial FDs ?
(*iii*) In designing a relational database, why might we choose a non-BCNF design.
[GGSIPU, B. Tech. (CSE/IT) — 5th Sem., Dec. 2009]

Q.47. (*i*) Show that if a relation is in BCNF then it is also in 3NF.
(*ii*) Consider the following two sets of FDs —
F = {A → C, AC → D, E → AD, E → H} and
G = {A → DC, E → A}
Check whether they are equivalent or not. Explain with reasons.
(*iii*) Explain rules for decomposing a relation.
[GGSIPU, B. Tech. (CSE/IT) – 5th Sem., Dec. 2010]

Q.48. (*a*) What are the rules for decomposing a relation ?
(*b*) Discuss join dependency. **[Dec. 2011]**
[GGSIPU, B. Tech. (CSE/IT) — 5th Sem., Dec. 2011]

Q.49. (*a*) Explain BCNF with a suitable example.
(*b*) State Armstrong's Axions. What are their usages.
[GGSIPU, M. Tech. (CSE/IT) — Ist Sem., Dec. 2011]

Q.50. What is the best normal form of each of the following relations ? Justify —
(*i*) R1 (A, B, C) with A → B, AC → B and C → B
(*ii*) R2(A, B, C, D) with A → BC, CD → B
[GGSIPU, M.Tech. (CSE/IT) — Ist Sem., Jan. 2011]

CHAPTER

5 Oracle 8 Architecture

5.0 INTRODUCTION

Oracle is a relational database management system product of Oracle Corporation (1977). Oracle 2.0 (first version of oracle) was written in assembly language for PDP-11 machine. Oracle 3.0 database was written in C. It ran on Digital VAX/VMS systems, UNIX and other platforms. Oracle 8 was released in 1997. Oracle 8*i* (I stands for Internet) and then Oracle 9*i* was released. It had many other features of self-tuning, management and data warehousing.

5.1 ORACLE SOFTWARE STRUCTURE

When Oracle uses the names like Oracle 8 server, Oracle 8*i* server or Oracle 9*i* server to a specific database offering, it refers to what was formerly known as **work group server**. An Oracle server consists of an (*i*) **Oracle database** *i.e.,* the collection of stored data including log and control files. (*ii*) **Oracle instance** *i.e.,* the processes, including Oracle-system processes and user processes taken together, created for a specific instance of the database operation.

Oracle server supports SQL as well as PL/SQL. Oracle can also be accessed through general purpose programming languages such as C or JAVA.

Actually, the Oracle database has two primary structures :

1. **A physical structure :** It refers to the actual stored data.
2. **A logical structure :** It refers to an abstract representation of the stored data (*i.e.,* conceptual schema).

The database contains the following types of files :

(*a*) **Data files :** They have the **actual data**.

(*b*) **Redo log files :** They are 2 or more log files that are **used to record all changes made to the data**. They are used in the **process of recovering**, if certain changes do not get written to the permanent storage.

(*c*) **Control files :** These files contain control information such as database name, filenames and locations. This file like log file, is also needed for **recovery purposes**.

(*d*) **Trace files and alert log :** The background processes have a **trace file** associated with them and an **alert log** to maintain the major database events.

Please note that both, the log file and the control files may be multiplexed. It means that multiple copies may be written to multiple devices.

When we say the structure of an Oracle database then we mean what will be the definition of the database in terms of **schema objects** and **tablespaces**.

What are schema objects and tablespaces?

The **schema objects** contain definition of tables, views, sequences, stored procedures, indexes, clusters and database links.

Tablespaces are used to describe the physical storage structures of the database.

Please understand that the set of processes that constitute an instance of the server's operation is called as an Oracle Instance. It consists of

I. System Global Area (SGA)

II. Set of Background processes.

Let us now see what are these?

I. System Global Area (SGA) : Oracle uses an area of memory to store database information which is shareable and it assigns it when an instance starts. This area of memory is called as SGA. Please note that for optimal performance, the SGA is generally made as large as possible, while still fitting in the real memory. SGA has various memory structures like—

(*a*) ***Database buffer cache :*** It is a cache memory that is used to store the most frequently accessed data blocks from the database. So, now the I/O activity can be significantly reduced.

(*b*) ***Redo log buffer :*** A buffer for the redo log file. It is used for recovery purposes.

(*c*) ***Shared pool :*** It contains shared memory constructs like shared SQL areas. These areas contain the parse trees of SQL queries as well as their execution plans.

II. Set of Background Processes

(*a*) ***User processes :*** Each user process corresponds to the execution of some applications or some tool.

(*b*) ***Program Global Area (PGA) :*** It is a memory buffer that contains data and control information for a server process. It is created by Oracle when a server process is started.

(*c*) ***Oracle processes :*** A process/job/task is a thread of control or a mechanism in OS to execute a series of steps. **Please note that a process has its own private memory area where it runs**. They are divided into three types : (*i*) Server process, (*ii*) User processes, (*iii*) Background processes.

Server processes communicate with user processes and performs tasks on behalf of the users—like executing SQL statements and returning data to user processes.

User processes run on a separate machine called the **client** and the server process runs on the **server**. **Also note that every client (or user) has a corresponding or dedicated server process running on its behalf. Please note that the client and the server can be the same machine also**. If they are on separate machines then they communicate via SQL*Net.

A user process is created whenever an application or Oracle tools connect to the database.

Background processes perform the tasks related to the database, in general. There are four important background processes :

1. **Database Writer (DBWR) :** It is responsible for writing the data in the database buffers to the secondary storage. Database buffers are storage locations in the SGA.

2. **Log Writer (LGWR) :** The Log Writer writes data in the Redo buffers (storage locations in SGA) to the Redo log files in the disk. The Redo log files are used to recover the database in case of database crash.
3. **Process Monitor (PMON) :** It is responsible for managing the user processes connected to the database.
4. **System Monitor (SMON) :** It is responsible for managing the various processes associated with the database.

When Oracle is loaded from a Oracle Server, certain background processes and memory area required for Oracle to run is allocated. The memory area is allocated in the main memory or virtual memory and is called as **System Global Area (SGA). Please understand that**

SGA + Background processes = Oracle Database Instance

When the database is running, SGA is the centre of Oracle activity. It provides communication between the users and the background processes. SGA has three caches (*i.e.,* storage area) as shown below in Fig. 5.1.

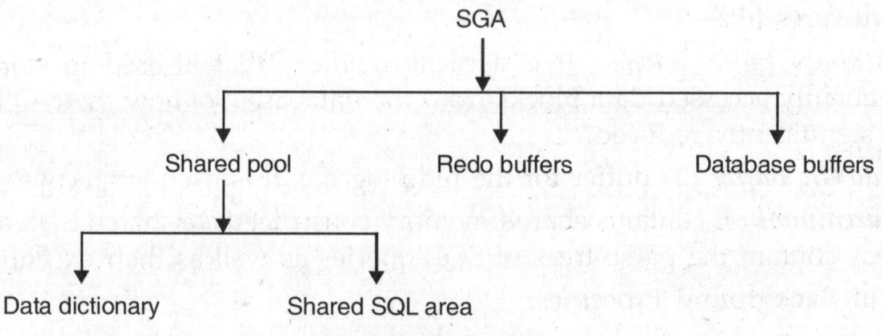

Fig. 5.1. *SGA caches*

An Oracle database is not available to users until the Oracle server has been started up and the database has been opened. Oracle database starting involves 3-steps, as follows :

Step 1. Starting an instance of the database.

In this step, SGA is allocated and background processes are created. A **parameter file** is set up to govern the initialization of the instance. This file controls the SGA size, the name of the database to which an instance can connect etc.

Step 2. Mounting a database.

Now, the Oracle instance is associated with a database. **Please note that the multiple instances of Oracle may mount the same database concurrently**. It is our DBA who chooses whether to run the database in **exclusive or parallel mode**. **When an Oracle instance mounts a database in an exclusive mode**, only that instance can access the database. On the other hand, **if the instance is started in parallel or shared mode** then other instances that are started in parallel mode can also mount the database.

Step 3. Opening a database.

This is a database administration activity. It means to open a mounted database to permit all normal database operations.

Please note that the reverse process (*i.e.,* step-3 to step-1) will be followed when you shut down an oracle instance. That is,

1. Close the database.
2. Dismount the database.
3. Shut down the Oracle instance.

5.2 DATABASE STORAGE

Oracle has 2 file representations.

1. Logical structure.
2. Physical structure.

1. Logical Structure : It is the user's view of data. A database is divided into logical storage units called as **tablespaces**. User sees data in form of 2D tables or groups of tables. The tables are created in tablespaces. These tablespaces have the following characteristics :

(*i*) Each database is divided into one or more tablespaces.

(*ii*) There is a system tablespace and users tablespace.

(*iii*) One tablespace can contain many data files. When requested data is not available in the memory cache for the database, it is read from the appropriate data file.

(*iv*) Whenever a database is created, the system tablespace is created. It contains the Oracle Data Dictionary and System Rollback segments.

(*v*) The combined storage capacity of a database's tablespace is the total storage capacity of the database.

NOTE : Oracle has CREATE TABLESPACE command to create a new tablespace.

Every Oracle database contains a tablespace called as *SYSTEM* which is used to hold the data dictionary's objects and is created automatically when the database is created.

2. Physical Structure : It is organized in terms of

(*a*) Data blocks

(*b*) Extents

(*c*) Segments.

Please note that a data block or logical block or page or Oracle block is a fixed number of bytes and is the finest level of granularity of storage.

An extent is a specific number of contiguous data blocks. And, **a segment is a set of extents allocated to a specific data structure.**

5.3 SHARED DATABASE ACCESS MECHANISM

To develop applications, Oracle offers the following tools and features.

(*a*) SQL*Plus (*b*) SQL*Forms

(*c*) SQL*Report write (*d*) Export/Import utility.

SQL*Plus : It is Oracle's implementation of SQL. It is an interactive, low-level user interface to the Oracle DBMS. It is an extension to the standard SQL. It comprises of PL/SQL which is procedural. It comprises of—SQL, SQL*PLUS and PL/SQL. It has an in built command line editor and an online command interpreter. SQL*PLUS is used by

(*a*) ***Application developers***—to create, modify database and to generate reports

(*b*) ***End-users***—to query and retrieve data from the database.

(*c*) ***DBA***—to create users, to specify rights and privileges to users and to monitor the database.

How to load SQL?

Step 1. Select SQL*PLUS from Oracle document window.

Step 2. Supply username and password (usually, SCOTT and TIGER respectively).

If both are correct, the SQL prompt appears as follows :

SQL >

This is called as the **command line**. To exit from SQL, just type

SQL > exit

SQL * Forms : It is a tool for creating forms based applications. It has provision to create default data entry forms too. SQL *Forms can be used to query a database, update or delete or add to a database.

SQL * Report Writer : It is a menu-driven formatting tool to create simple to more sophisticated reports.

Export/Import Utility : Files may be imported into a database or exported using this utility.

5.4 DATABASE PROTECTION

To prevent, loss of mission—critical data is very important for our organization. And improper backup can make recovery difficult. Oracle 8 provides various means of storing back up data. Some of them are as follows :

1. **Recovery Manager (RMAN) :** Typically, backups includes
   - Complete database backups (common).
   - Tablespace backups
   - Data file backups
   - Control file backups
   - Achieve log backups.

   Oracle 8 introduced the Recovery Manager (RMAN) for the server-managed backup and recovery of the database.
2. **Partitioning :** In this approach, we make individual partitions offline for maintenance while other partitions remain available for user access. Oracle 8*i* uses **hash partitioning** wherein data partitions are divided up based on the hashing function. Oracle 9*i* uses *list partitioning* which allows partitioning of data based on discrete values (like geography).
3. **Incremental Backup and Recovery :** RMAN can perform incremental backups of databases. Here, only the modified blocks are stored as they are smaller and faster than complete backups.
4. **Data Guard Feature :** A **stand by database** which is a copy of the production database is created. It is used if primary database is lost due to site failure or during maintenance. Oracle 9*i* Data Guard fully automates this process.
5. **Failover Features :** When the first system fails then another system or node provides access to data residing on a shared disk.

SUMMARY

Oracle is the top selling multi-user RDBMS. Oracle applications cover e-commerce, business intelligence, financial, mobiles, sales, Internet procurement, manufacturing etc. There are four main products of Oracle 8*i*.

- **Oracle 8*i* Oracle Server**—used for small number of users and small database size.
- **Oracle 8*i* Enterprise Edition**—is used when number of users are large or database size is large.

- **Oracle 8*i* Personal Edition**—is single user version of Oracle.
- **Oracle 8*i* Lite**— is a light weight database engine for mobile computing on notebooks.

MULTIPLE CHOICE QUESTIONS [MCQs]

1. Oracle is a
(*a*) RDBMS (*b*) HDBMS
(*c*) NDBMS (*d*) None of the above.

2. Oracle 2.0 was written in assembly language for
(*a*) 8086 machine (*b*) PDP-11
(*c*) IBM-370 (*d*) None of the above.

3. Oracle 3.0 database was written in
(*a*) C (*b*) JAVA 2
(*c*) C++ (*d*) None of the above.

4. Oracle server consists of
(*a*) Oracle database + DBMS (*b*) Oracle instances only
(*c*) Oracle database + Oracle instance (*d*) None of the above.

5. When multiple copies may be written to multiple devices, we say files are
(*a*) Multiplexed (*b*) Partitioned
(*c*) Protected (*d*) None of the above.

6. SGA stands for
(*a*) System Go Ahead (*b*) Software Global Area
(*c*) System Global Area (*d*) None of the above.

7. PGA stands for
(*a*) Program Global Area (*b*) Process Global Area
(*c*) Parallel Global Area (*d*) None of the above.

8. SGA has
(*a*) 2 caches (*b*) 3 caches
(*c*) 4 caches (*d*) 5 caches.

9. A file used to govern the initialization of the instance is known as
(*a*) Shared file (*b*) Parameter file
(*c*) Read-only file (*d*) None of the above.

10. A database is divided into logical storage units called as
(*a*) Tables (*b*) Records
(*c*) Tablespaces (*d*) None of the above.

ANSWERS

1. (*a*) **2.** (*b*) **3.** (*a*) **4.** (*c*) **5.** (*a*) **6.** (*c*) **7.** (*b*) **8.** (*b*)
9. (*b*) **10.** (*c*)

CONCEPTUAL SHORT QUESTIONS WITH ANSWERS

Q.1. What is row chaining in Oracle?

Ans. When we use Oracle data types like LONG or LONG RAW, a row may not fit in a datablock. In such a case, Oracle stores the data for the row in a chain of datablocks reserved for that segment. This is called as **row chaining**.

Q.2. What is migration?

Ans. If a row originally fits in one block but is updated so that it does not fit any longer, Oracle uses a technique called as **migration**. **It is the process of moving an entire row to a new data block and trying to fit it there**.

Q.3. Write short notes on Oracle Wireless Edition.

Ans. Formerly, it was known as **Oracle Portal-to-Go**. It includes the following :

(*a*) **Content adapters** for transforming content to XML.

(*b*) **Device transformers** for transforming XML to device-specific markup languages.

(*c*) **Personalisation portals** for service personalisation of alerts, alert addresses, location marks and profiles. The wireless personalisation portal is also used for the creation, servicing, testing and publishing of URL service.

Q.4. Write short notes on Oracle's data dictionary.

Ans. An Oracle's data dictionary contains all information about the structures and objects of the database such as tables, columns, users, data etc. The data stored in the data dictionary is called as **metadata**. It is a valuable source of information for end-users and developers. The data dictionary consists of two levels :

(*a*) **Internal level :** It has all base tables that are used by DBMS and not by users.

(*b*) **External level :** It provides many views on these base tables to access information. It provides users a front-end to access information relevant to the users.

Q.5. Draw the Oracle system architecture. [GGSIPU, B.Tech. (CS); 5th Sem.]

Ans.

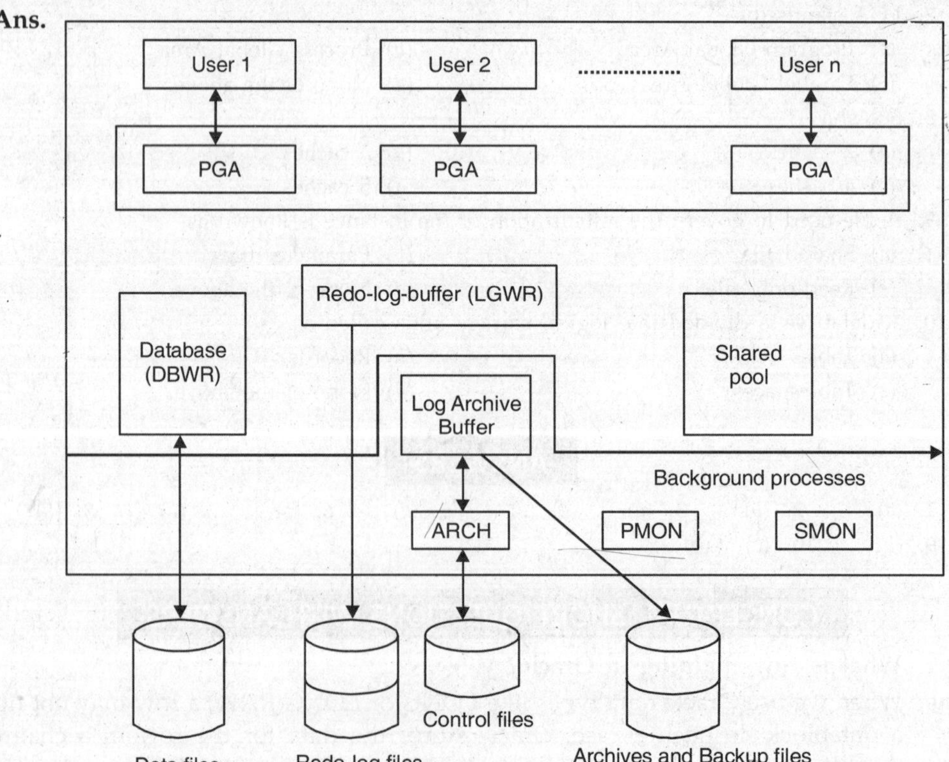

EXERCISE QUESTIONS

Q.1. Explain in brief about database system structure with the help of a diagram.
[GGSIPU, B.Tech. (CSE); 5th Sem., Sept. 2007]

Q.2. What mechanisms are used for
(*a*) database protection
(*b*) accessing shared databases. **[GGSIPU, B.Tech. (CSE); 5th Sem., Dec. 2007]**

Q.3. Explain the architecture of RDBMS Oracle in brief.
[GGSIPU, B.Tech. (CSE); 5th Sem., IInd Terminal Test, Nov. 2008]

Q.4. With a neat diagram explain the internal architecture of Oracle 8 DBMS.
[GGSIPU, B.Tech. (CSE); 5th Sem., Dec. 2008]

Q.5. Explain the Oracle 8 architecture with the help of a block diagram.
[GGSIPU, B.Tech. (CSE/IT) — 5th Sem., Dec. 2009]

Q.6. Explain the Oracle internal process architecture for a specific database instance
[GGSIPU, B.Tech. (CSE/IT) —5th Sem., 2011]

UNIT-IV

CHAPTER 6

Transaction Management

6.0 INTRODUCTION

A transaction is a set of changes that must all be made together. It is a program unit whose execution may or may not change the contents of a database. **A transaction is executed as a single unit. Please understand that if the database was in a consistent state before a transaction, then after the execution of the transaction also, the database must be in a consistent state. Also note that a transaction that changes the contents of the database must alter the database from one consistent database state to another**. So, we can say that

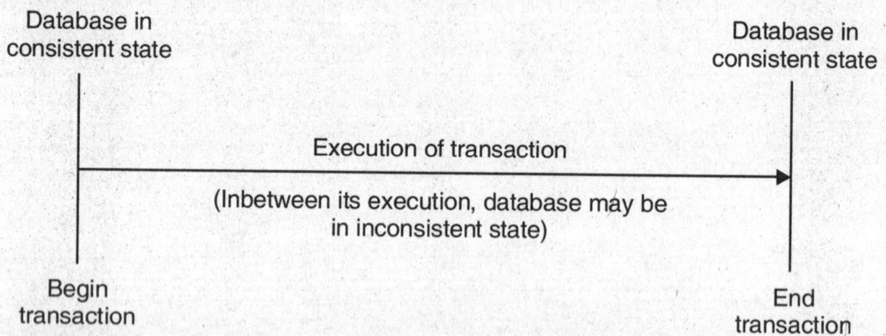

Why must a transaction be executed together (atomically)?

Say, a customer goes to an ATM and wants to transfer $100 from his saving-account to balance-account. Now, our SQL code would be—to use an UPDATE command to subtract $100 from his savings account and to add it to his balance account. This again can be done using UPDATE command.

But what will happen, if ATM crashes between these two operations. The amount of $100 that has been subtracted from his account will not be added to his balance-account. It is, therefore, lost. Now, what is the solution?

The solution is that both the changes must be made successfully. Thus, a transaction is a set of changes that must be made together.

6.1 TRANSACTION CONCEPT AND PROPERTIES

A transaction accesses data with a series of Read and Write operations.

Read Operation : Reading of a database object means that it is, firstly, brought into main memory from the disk and then its value is copied into a program variable *i.e.,*

$$\text{Disk} \xrightarrow{\text{to}} \text{Main memory} \xrightarrow{\text{to}} \text{Program variable}$$

Similarly, during write operation, the copy of the object is first modified and then written to disk.

$$\text{Program variable} \xrightarrow{\text{to}} \text{Main memory} \xrightarrow{\text{to}} \text{Disk}$$

Properties of transaction : There are four important properties of a transaction :

1. **Atomicity : A transaction is said to be atomic if a transaction always executes all of its actions in one step or not execute any actions at all.** It implies that either all or none of the transaction's operations are performed.
2. **Consistency :** A transaction must preserve the **consistency of a database** after its execution. It means that the execution of a transaction must leave a database in either its **prior stable state** or a **new stable state.** If a transaction fails then the database must be returned to it's previous state. If it is successful then the database must reflect new changes. **Please note that all resources are in a consistent state always.** Ensuring this property is the job of the user.
3. **Isolation :** It means that the data used during the execution of a transaction cannot be used by a second transaction until the first one is completed. The transactions do not interfere with each other. They must behave as if they are executed in isolation. **Please note that it means that if several transactions are executed concurrently then the results must be same as if they were executed serially in some order.** This isolation property of a transaction is used in **multi-user database environments.**
4. **Durability :** The effect of a completed or committed transaction should persist even after a system's failure (crash). **Please note that it means that once a transaction commits, the system must guarantee that result of its operations will never be lost.** It is the responsibility of the recovery subsystem of DBMS.

So, we can say that :

S. No.	Property	Meaning
1.	Atomicity	All or nothing
2.	Consistency	No violation of integrity constraints.
3.	Isolation	Concurrent changes invisible
4.	Durability	Committed update persist.

We use the acronym—**ACID** also to refer to the above four properties of transaction. **Before we go further, let us solve an example.**

Example 1. Consider a transaction, T_i, that transfers Rs 500/- from account–A to account B as defined below :

Read (A, a);

a = a – 500;

Write (A, a);

Read (B, b);

b = b + 500;

Write (B, b);

Assume that prior to the execution of transaction (T_i), the amount in account–A is Rs 2000/- and in B is Rs 3000/-. Furthermore, assume that a power failure accurs. What will happen? Will our database be in a consistent state? Apply ACID test to check whether the four properties hold or not?

Solution. Consider again the given transaction, T_i :

1. Read (A, *a*);
2. $a = a - 500$;
3. Write (A, *a*); ⟵ a power failure occurs
4. Read (B, *b*);
5. $b = b + 500$;
6. Write (B, *b*);

Say, T_i, fails after the execution of 3rd instruction. This means that changes in variable a are done but not in B. So, values of account – A and account –B are 2000 – 500 = 1500 and 3000 respectively. So, account–B is unchanged and we have lost Rs 500/- in this transaction. So, our database is in inconsistent state. To solve this problem, we use the concept of atomicity. **Please note that in order to maintain the consistency of database, either all or none of the transaction's operations are performed. Also note that in order to maintain the atomicity of transaction, the database system keeps track of the old values of any write if the transaction does not complete its execution, the old values are restored to make it appear as the transaction never executed.**

Next, property is ***consistency***.

The requirement of consistency here is that the sum of A and B must be unchanged when T_i executes. Without this, money could be lost. You can verify that if the database is consistent before an execution of the transaction, the database remains consistent after its execution also. Let us see the **isolation** of this T_i.

Now, if several transactions are executed parallely or concurrently, then each transaction must behave as if it were executed in isolation. So, it should not result in a inconsistent state.

Say, T_1 and T_2 are performed concurrently (parallel) and their schedule is :

T_1	T_2
Read (A, *a*); $a = a - 500$; Write (A, *a*);	
	Read (A, *a*); Read (B, *b*); Print $(a + b)$;
Read (B, *b*); $b = b + 500$; Write (B, *b*);	

This schedule results in inconsistency of the database. This is because it shows Rs. 4500/-. This **anomaly** occurs as the 2nd transaction (T_2), reads A and B at intermediate point and computes its sum, which is a inconsistent value. **Please recall that the data used during the execution of a transaction cannot be used by the second transaction until the first transaction is completed.** The solution to this problem is to execute T_i, serially (*i.e.*, one-after-another). We will see later how it can be done?

Another test is it's **durability. This property ensures that once transaction completes successfully, all updates that were done on the database, persist even if a system failure occurs after T_i completes its execution.**

So, after transfer of Rs 500/- from account–A to account–B, there shouldn't be any loss of data, even if system failure occurs.

6.2 STATES OF A TRANSACTION

A transaction can be in various states as shown below in Fig. 6.1.

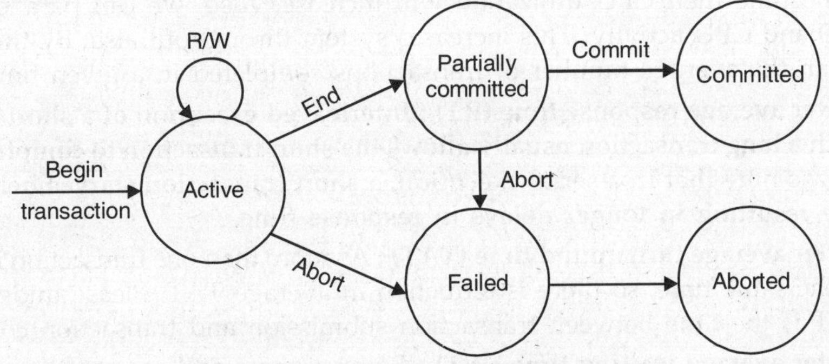

Fig. 6.1. *Transaction state diagram.*

Active state : It is the initial state. The transaction stays in this state while it is executing .

Partially committed : When the final statement has been executed, we say, transaction is in a partially committed state.

Failed : When the normal execution can no longer proceed, we say that the transaction is in a failed state.

Aborted : A transaction is aborted if the transaction has been rolled back and the database has been restored to its state prior to the start of the transaction.

Committed : When a transaction has successfully been completed.

Explanation : A transaction starts in the **active state**. When it finishes its last statement, it enters the **partially committed state**. At this time, the transaction has completed its execution but it is still possible that it may have to be aborted as the actual output may still be temporarily residing in the main memory. DBMS then writes information to disk that even if the system failure occurs, the updates performed by T_i can be recreated when the final or last of this information is written out, the transaction enters the **committed state**.

6.3 CONCURRENT EXECUTIONS

Concurrent execution of transaction means executing more than one transaction at the same time. we use the technique of interleaving execution of two transactions. **For example**, interleaving is shown below in Fig. 6.2.

T_1	T_2
Read (A); Write (A);	
	Read (B); Write (B);
Read (C); Write (C);	

Fig. 6.2. *Interleaving*

Thus, firstly, T_1 executes, then T_2 and then T_1 again. This is **interleaving**. This way multiple transactions are allowed to run concurrently in the system.

***Advantages of Concurrent Execution of Transactions* :** Naturally, concurrent execution of our transaction can result in many benefits. Some of them are listed below :

1. **Increased CPU utilization :** If a CPU executes more than one transaction at the same time then CPU utilization will increase. Also, we can parallely do both I/O and CPU activity. This increases system throughput also. By **throughput**, I mean the average number of transactions completed in a given time.
2. **Better average response time (RT) : Interleaved execution of a short transaction with a long transaction usually allows the short transaction to complete quickly. Please note that in a serial execution, a short transaction starves behind a long one resulting in longer delays in response time.**
3. **Better average turnaround time (TAT) :** As more than one transaction is executing at the same time, so there is reduction in average TAT. Please understand that TAT is the time between transaction submission and transaction completion.
4. **Better average waiting time (WT) :** Because more and more of transactions are completed in lesser time, so, WT (on average) becomes better, *i.e.*, gets reduced. By WT, I mean the time required by a transaction to wait to get executed.
5. **Better disk utilization :** The overlapping of I/O activities of CPU reduces the amount of time for which the disks are idle.

6.4 SCHEDULING OF TRANSACTIONS

A schedule is a list of actions from a set of transactions which must consist of all the instructions of those transactions. We must preserve the order in which the instructions appear in each individual transaction. When we say a series or list of actions, it means actions like reading, writing, aborting or committing. Actually, a transaction is seen by the DBMS as a series (or list) of actions. So, a transaction is also defined as a set of actions that are partially ordered *i.e.*, the relative order of some of the actions may not be important.

For example, if in a transaction (T_i), the instruction, write (A) appears before read (A), then in any **valid schedule, this sequence must also be preserved**, *i.e.*,

T_i	T_j
Read (A);	Write (A);
Write (A);	Read (A);

Then, both these sequences must be preserved. **Please note that a schedule represents an actual execution sequence. We move forward in time as we go down from one row to the next. Also note that a schedule describes the actions of transactions as seen by the DBMS. A schedule is also called as a history.**

Types of schedules

There are five types of schedules, namely :

1. Complete schedule.
2. Serial schedule.
3. Non-Serial schedule.
4. Equivalent schedule.
5. Serializiable schedule.

Let us understand these schedules one by one.

1. **Complete schedule : A schedule that contains either an abort or a commit for each transaction whose actions are listed in it is called as a complete schedule.** A complete schedule must contain all the actions of every transaction that appears in it.
2. **Serial schedule :** Each serial schedule consists of a sequence of instructions from various transactions, where the instructions belonging to one single transaction appear together in that schedule. **Please note that if the actions of different transactions are not interleaved (*i.e.,* transaction are executed from start to finish) then the schedule is called as a serial schedule.**

   For example, in the following schedule, T_1 is followed by T_2 and hence, is a serial schedule.

   Schedule-1

T_1	T_2
A = A * 10; B = B – 10;	
	A = A/100; B = B * 4.06;

   Note that this schedule is serial in which T_1 is followed by T_2.

   Can we execute T_2 first and then T_1?

   Schedule-2

T_1	T_2
	A = A/100; B = B * 4.06;
A = A * 10; B = B – 10;	

   Here, T_2 is followed by T_1 and hence, is a **serial schedule.**
3. **Non-serial schedule : A schedule in which the operations from a set of concurrent transactions are interleaved is called as a non-serial schedule.** A non-serial schedule is serializable if it is equivalent to a serial schedule of commited transaction. As we know that a schedule converts an initial state to the final state. A non-serial schedule is acceptable if the final state produced by a non-serial schedule is equivalent to some state produced by a serial schedule. **For example,**

   Schedule-3

T_1	T_2
A = A * 10;	
	A = A/100;
B = B – 10;	
	B = B * 4.06;

   This schedule is equivalent to the previous schedule and is concurrent.
4. **Equivalent schedule : Two schedules are said to be equivalent schedules if they produce the same result on any database state.** It means that for any database state, the effect on the set of objects in the database, of executing the

first-schedule is identical to the effect of executing the second schedule. **Please note that equivalent schedules always produce identical results.**

For example, the schedule-3 (given above) is an equivalent schedule to schedule-1 and schedule-2.

5. **Serializable schedule :** We define it as follows—**"A non-serial schedule that is equivalent to some serial execution of transactions is known as a serializable schedule".**

   For example, schedule-3 (given above) is a serializable schedule which is equivalent to schedule-1 and schedule-2.

Please understand that here the objective of serializability is to find non-serial schedules that allow the transactions to execute concurrently without interfering with one another and thereby producing a database state that could be produced by a serial execution. Please note that it is important to guarantee serializability of concurrent transactions in order to prevent inconsistency from transactions interfering with one another. Also note that in serializability, the ordering of read and write operations are important. Also, it is said that if each transaction preserves consistency then every serializable schedule also preserves consistency.

If a schedule is serializable, it does not mean that the schedule is a serial schedule. Being serializable implies that the schedule is a correct schedule meaning that it will have our database in a consistent state, interleaving is appropriate and the efficiency due to concurrent execution.

6.5 OPERATIONS CONFLICTS

In a given schedule, the order of read/write operations can be changed but not always. **Such read/write operations whose order cannot be changed without affecting the consistency of data are called as conflict operations.**

Rules to define conflict operations

There are some rules followed to define these conflict operations and are given below:

Rule 1. If two transactions just read a data object then they do not conflict and the order is not important.

Rule 2. If two transactions either read or write completely separate data objects then they do not conflict and the order is not important.

Rule 3. If one transaction writes a data object and another either reads or writes the same data object then the order of execution is important.

Rule 4. Two actions on the same data object conflict if atleast one of them is a write.

From these rules, we find that if I_i and I_j are two consecutive instructions of transactions, T_i and T_j respectively and that $i \neq j$. Furthermore, if I_i and I_j are read instructions then their relative order of execution does not matter. **Please note that the transactions T_i and T_j conflict, if there are presence of operations by different transactions on the same data item and atleast one of these operations is a write operation**. That is,

$I_i\downarrow$ \ $I_j \rightarrow$	**Read (*t*)**	**Write (*t*)**
Read (*t*)	No	Yes
Write (*t*)	Yes	No

i.e., Read and Read gives no conflicts but Read and Write instructions do conflict.

We are in a position to solve and example now.

Example 1. *Consider the following schedule :*

T_1	T_2
Read (A) Write A	
	Read A
Read B	
	Write (A)
Write (B)	
	Read (B) Write (B)

Are there any conflicting operations in T_1 or T_2? Find out a serial schedule for it? Make it conflict serializable?

Solution. The schedule given to us is :

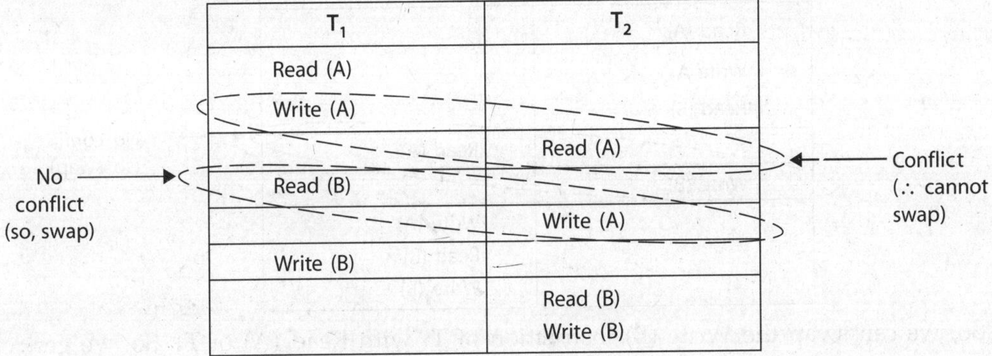

T_1	T_2
Read (A)	
Write (A)	
	Read (A)
Read (B)	
	Write (A)
Write (B)	
	Read (B) Write (B)

Here, the write (A) instruction of T_1, conflicts with the Read (A) instruction of T_2 **because both of these instructions involves Write and Read operation on the same data-item (A)**. But, Write (A) instruction of T_2 does not confict with Read (B) instruction of T_1 **because these two instructions access different data items**. Now, we find that the Write (A) instruction of T_2 *does not conflict* with Read (B) instruction of T_1. **So, we can swap these instructions to generate an equivalent schedule**. Now, consider again the schedule given to us :

T_1	T_2
Read (A) Write (A)	
	Read (A)
Read (B)	
	Write (A)
Write (B)	
	Read (B) Write (B)

No conflict (so, swap)

We can swap the Read (B) instruction of T_1 Read (A) of T_2. So, we get :

T_1	T_2
Read (A) Write (A)	
Read (B)	
	Read (A)
	Write (A)
Write (B)	
	Read (B) Write (B)

← No conflict (so, swap)

We can now swap the Write (B) instruction of T_1 with the Write (A) instruction of T_2. So, we get :

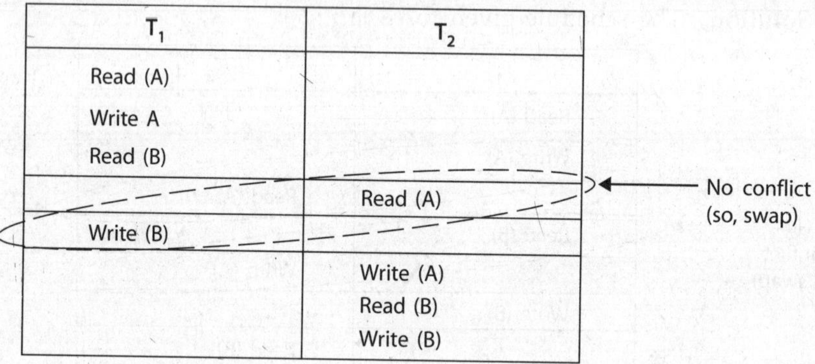

T_1	T_2
Read (A) Write A Read (B)	
	Read (A)
Write (B)	
	Write (A) Read (B) Write (B)

So, we can swap the Write (B) instruction of T_1 with Read (A) of T_2. So, we get :

T_1	T_2
Read (A) Write (A) Read (B) Write (B)	
	Read (A) Write (A) Read (B) Write (B)

This final schedule after swaps is a **serial schedule**. Thus, this schedule is equivalent to a serial schedule. We find that regardless of the initial system state, these different schedules and hence, the final schedule produces the same final system state.

Please note that if a schedule, S, can be transformed into a schedule, S′, by a series of swaps of non-conflicting instructions, we say that S and S′ are conflict equivalent. For *e.g.*,

T_1	T_2
Read (A) Write (A)	
	Read (B) Write (B)

S

⟺

T_1	T_2
	Read (B) Write (B)
Read (A) Write (A)	

S′

Here, schedule, S and S′ are **conflict** equivalent as Read and Write of T_1 can be swapped with Read and Write of T_2.

This leads us to a concept of **conflict serializability also. We say that a schedule, S, is conflict serializable if it is conflict equivalent to a serial schedule.** Like,

T_1	T_2
X = X + 5;	
	X = X * 1;
Y = Y – 100;	
	Y = Y * 20;

S

T_1	T_2
X = X + 5; Y = Y – 100;	
	X = X * 1; Y = Y * 20;

S′

Here, Schedule, S, is conflict serializable as it is conflict equivalent to S′, serial schedule.

6.6 TESTING FOR SERIALIZABILITY

It is mandatory to show that the schedules generated by the scheme are serializable. This is must to do concurrency control. So, we must firstly know the **test for conflict serializability. The test is as follows :**

Let us assume that there is a schedule, S. What we do is, we construct it's **directed graph** or **precedence graph**. This graph, G, is a pair G = (V, E) where 'V' is a set of vertices and 'E' is a set of edges.

Notations :

(*a*) **Set of vertices** consists of all the transactions participating in the schedule.

(*b*) **Set of edges** consists of all edges $T_i \rightarrow T_j$, for which one of the following **three conditions hold :**

(*i*) T_i executes Write (A) before T_j executes Read (A).

(*ii*) T_i executes Read (A) before T_j executes write (A).

(*iii*) T_i executes Write (A) before T_j executes write (A).

We also say that, if an edge, $T_i \rightarrow T_j$ exists in the precedence graph then in any serial schedule, S′, equivalent to S, T_i must appear before T_j.

For e.g., say, schedule, S, is

T_1	T_2
A = A + 100; Write (A);	
	Read (A); A = A – 100;

It's precedence graph is

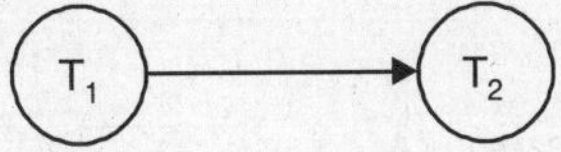

There is one edge and two vertices, T_1 and T_2 . Arrow indicates that all instructions of T_1 are executed before the execution of first instruction of T_2.

But if the schedule is

T_1	T_2
A = A + 100;	
	B = B * 10;
A = A/10;	
	B = B – 10;

Then, its precedence graph is

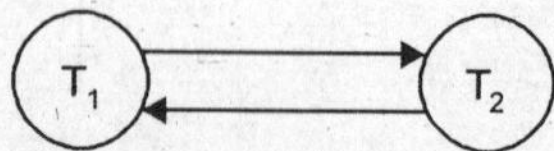

This is because, firstly T_1 is executed then T_2, then again T_1 and then T_2. Here, the graph contains a cycle. **Please note that if the precedence graph for S has a cycle, then the schedule, S, is not conflict serializable. But, if the graph contains no cycles, then the schedule, S, is confict serializable**. So, the above schedule, S, has a cycle and thus is not conflict serializable. Many cycle detection algorithms exists which take $O(n^2)$ time, where n is the number of vertices in the graph. **We are in a position to solve some problems now.**

Example :

1. Given schedule is :

	Table 1	
T_{11}	T_{12}	T_{13}
Read (A)		
	Read (B)	
A: = f_1 (A)		
		Read (C)
	B: = f_2 (B) write (B)	
		C:f_2(C) Write (C)
Write (A)		
	Read (A) A: = f_4 (A)	
Read (C)		
	Write (A)	
C:= f_5 (C) Write (A)		
		B:=f_6 (B)

Draw its precedence graph. Is the schedule conflict serializable ?

write (B)

Solution :

Precedence graph for the schedule is :

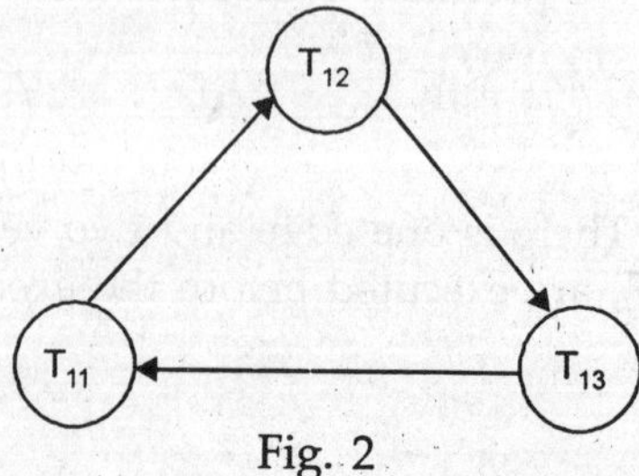

Fig. 2

This graph contains a cycle. Hence, the schedule is not conflict serializable.

Example :

2. The given schedule is :

Table 2

T_{14}	T_{15}	T_{16}
Read (A)		
A: = f_1 (A)		
Read (C)		
Write (A)		
A: = f_2 (C)		
	Read (B)	
Write (C)	Read (A)	
		Read (C)
	B: = f_3 (B)	
	write (B)	
		C: = f_4 (C)
		Read (B)
		Write (C)
	A: = f_5 (A)	
	write (A)	
		B: f_6 (B)
		Write (B)

Solution :

The precedence graph for the given schedule is :

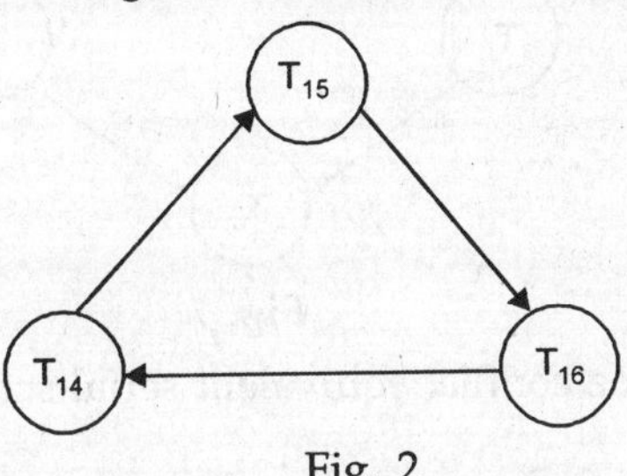

Fig. 2

The graph is acyclic. The conflict equivalent serial schedule for given schedule can be obtained using step 2 of algorithm.

T_{14} is the transaction with no arcs entering in T_{14}. Hence T_{14} is the first transaction in serial schedule. Remove T_{14} and all edges emitting from T_{14}.

T_{15} is the next schedule, since it has no incoming edges. Remove T_{15} and edges emitting from T_{15}.

T_{16} is the last schedule. Hence the serial schedule which is conflict equivalent to given schedule is :

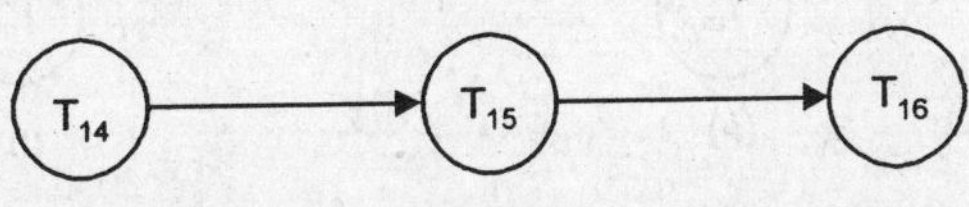

Fig. 3

Hence, the schedule is conflict serializable.

Example :

3. Consider schedule 3, the precedence graph for it is given as :

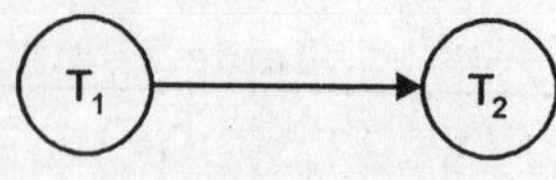

Fig. 6

Since, T_1 executes write (A) and write (B) before T_2 executes read (A) and read (B).

This graph is acyclic and the conflict equivalent serial schedule is $T_1 \rightarrow T_2$. Hence, schedule 3 is conflict serializable.

Example :

4. Consider schedule 4, the precedence graph for it is :

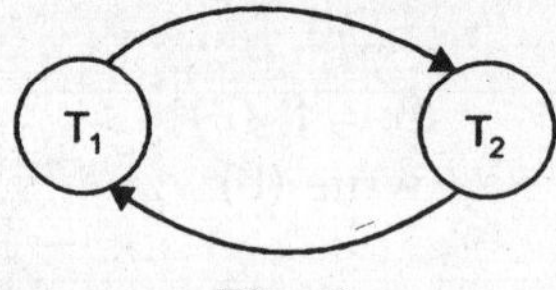

Fig. 6

which is a cyclic graph and hence it is not conflict serializable.

Example :

5. Consider the precedence graph given in Fig. 7

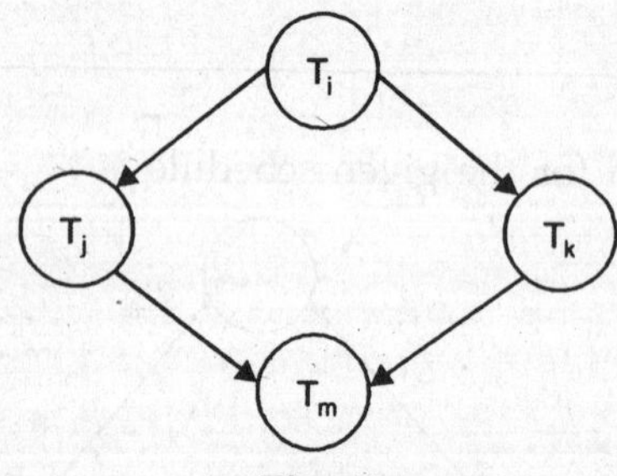

Fig. 7

The graph is acyclic. The conflict equivalent serial schedules equivalent to this are:

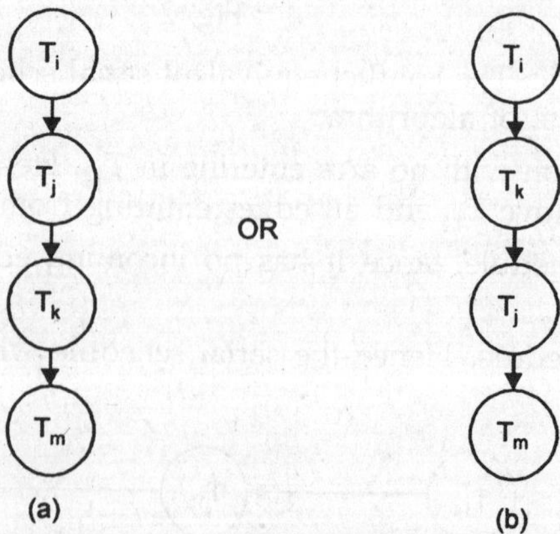

Fig. 8

Henc the schedule corresponding to precedence graph in Fig. 8 is conflict serializable

Example :

6. Consider the precedence graph in Fig. 9.

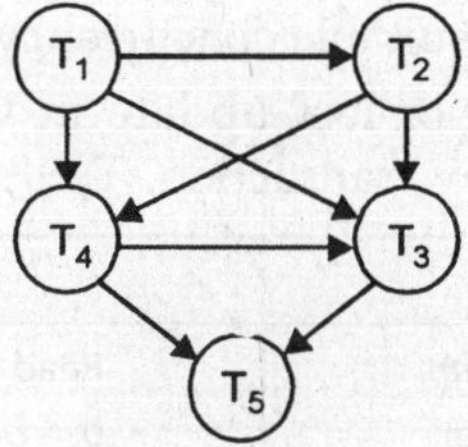

Fig. 7

The graph is acyclic. The serial schedules that are conflict equivalent to given schedule are:

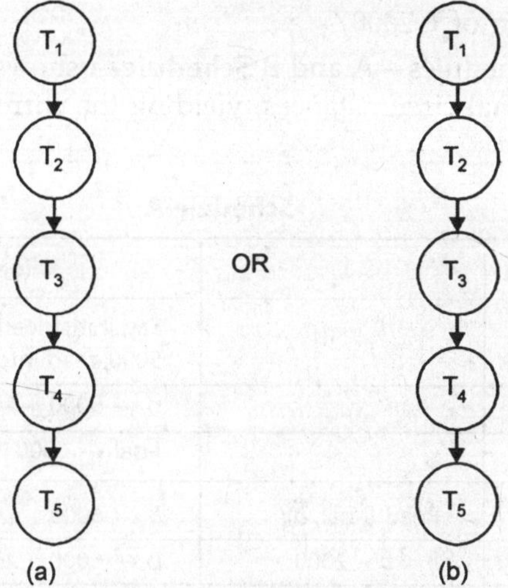

Fig. 10

Hence the schedule corresponding to given precedence graph is conflict serializable.

6.7 THREE PROBLEMS OF CONCURRENCY CONTROL–CASE STUDIES

When concurrent transactions (*i.e.*, accessing same data at same time) are executed in an uncontrolled manner then several problems can occur. The concurrency control has 3-main problems and are discussed one by one –

(*a*) Lost update problem.

(*b*) Dirty read (or uncommitted data) problem.

(*c*) Unrepeatable read (or inconsistent retrievals) problem.

Case Study 1 : Lost update problem

"A lost update problem occurs when two transactions that access the same database items have their operations in a way that makes the value of some database item incorrect. In other words, if the transactions, T_1 and T_2 both read a record and then update it, the effects of the first update will be overwritten by the second update".

Consider an example to understand this problem say, two accountants in a xyz company are updating the salary record of it's employee – 'Rajiv'. The **first accountant** is supposed to give Rajiv an annual salary adjustment. The **second accountant** is supposed to give Rajiv, conveyance charges, if any. In such a scenario, the effect of the first update will be overwritten by the second one, if there is no suitable concurrency control mechanism.

Now, consider an example of lost update in which the update performed by the transaction, T_2, is overwritten by transaction, T_1.

T_1	T_2
Read (A, *a*); Read (B, *b*); *b* = *a* + b; Write (B, *b*);	Read (B, *b*); *b* = *b* + 2; Write (B, *b*);

Now, consider two more transactions, T_4 and T_5 as shown below –

T_4 : Take additional loan of 1000/-

T_5 : Repay loan of ₹ 2000/-

Now, there are 2 schedules – A and B **Schedule-A** shows the serial execution of these transactions under normal circumstances, yielding the correct result. **Schedule-B** shows the lost-update problem.

Schedule-A

T_4	T_5	Values of variables
Read (*l*-bal, *b*);		Say, initial loan balance is 5000, read into local variable, *b*.
b = *b* + 1000;		b ← 5000 + 1000 ← 6000;
Write (b, l-bal);		*l*-bal ← 6000
	Read (l-bal, *b*);	*b* ← 6000
	b = *b* – 2000;	b ← 6000 – 2000 = 4000;
	Write (*b*, *l*-bal)	*l*-bal ← 4000

So, the result of exployee's balance of ₹ 4000/- is correct.

Schedule-B : Now, say that a transaction is able to read exployee's loan value from the table before a previous transaction for employee loan balance has been committed.

T_4	T_5	Values
Read (*l*-bal, *b*)		Say, *l*-bal is 5000 So, *b* ← 5000
	Read (l-bal, c)	*c* ← 5000
b = *b* + 2000		*b* ← 7000
	c = *c* /+ 3000	*c* ← 2000
Write (b, l-bal)		*l*-bal ← 7000
	Write (*b*, *l*-bal)	*l*-bal ← 2000

This schedule-B, actually shows the lost update problem. We observe that the first transaction, T_4, has not yet been committed and the second transaction; T_5, is executed. So, T_5 still operates on the value 7000 and its subtraction yields 2000/- in memory. In the meantime, T_4 writes the value of 7000/- to disk which is immediately overwritten by transaction, T_5. Thus, the addition of ₹ 2000/- is lost during the process. This is the reason as why it is known as a lost update problem.

Case Study 2: Dirty Read (or Uncommitted Data) Problem

"A dirty read problem occurs when one transaction updates a database item and then the transaction fails for some reason. The updated database item is accessed by another transaction before it is changed back to the original value. In other words, a transaction T_1 updates a record, which is read by the transaction T_2. Then T_1 aborts and T_2 now has values which were never formed part of the stable database.

Consider a schedule, S, in which transaction, T_5 **roll backs** after the Read (A, a) operation of transaction, T_7. Now, T_6 and T_7 have read the values of A which never committed. So, they perform the **dirty read operation**. This is so because transacations, T_6 and T_7 read the value of A modified by transaction, T_5. Since the transaction, T_5, fails and roll back, it means that T_5 obtain the original value of A and cancels the modified value of A. But other transactions, T_6 and T_7 process the modified value of A and result into incosistent state of the database. The schedule, S, is as follows :

T_5	T_6	T_7
Lock – X (A); Read (A, *a*); Lock – S(B); Read (B, *b*); Write (A, *a*); Unlock (A);		
	Lock – X (A); Read (A, *a*); Write (A, *a*); Unlock (A);	
		Lock – S(A) Read (A, *a*);
Roll back		

Please note that in a dirty read, data are not committed when two transactions, T_1 and T_2 are executed concurrently and the first transaction, T_1, is rolled back after the second transaction T_2 has already accessed the uncommitted data. Thus, it violates the isolation property of transactions.

Consider the **same example of lost-update** transaction with a difference that this time the transaction, T_4, is rolled back to eliminate the addition of ₹ 2000/-. Because transaction, T_5, subtracts ₹ 3000/- from the original, ₹ 5000, the correct answer should be ₹ 2000/-. The transactions are as follows–

T_4 : *l*-bal = *l*-bal + 2000 (Roll back)

T_5 : *l*-bal = *l*-bal – 3000.

Consider a schedule now that shows the serial execution of these transactions under normal circumstances, yielding the **correct result** of employee laon balance to ₹ 3000.

T_4	T_5	Values
Read (*l*-bal, *b*);		Say, *l*-bal = 5000
b = *b* + 1000;		*l*-bal = 6000;
Write (*b*, *l*-bal);		*l*-bal = 6000
Roll back (T_4);		*l*-bal = 5000 (restore it back)
	Read (*l*-bal, *b*);	*b* ← 5000
	b = *b* – 2000;	*b* ← 5000 – 2000 ← 3000
	Write (*b*, *l*-bal);	*l*-bal ← 3000

However, the schedule below shows the sequence of execution resulting in a dirty read (or uncommitted data) **problem** when the **Rollback** completed after T_5 has begun its execution-

T_4	T_5	Values
Read (*l*-bal, *b*);		*l*-bal = 5000 (Say)
b = *b* + 1000;		*b* = 6000;
Write (*b*, *l*-bal);		*l*-bal = 6000
	Read (*l*-bal, *b*);	*b* ← 6000
	b = *b* – 2000;	*b* ← 6000 – 2000 ← 4000
Roll back (T_4);		*l*-bal ← 5000 (Restore back)
	Write (*b* *l*-bal)	*l*-bal ← 4000

Case Study 3 : Unrepeatable read (or inconsistent retrievals)

"This problem occurs when a transaction reads several values from a database while a second transaction updates some of them. Actually, this problem occurs when a transaction calculates some aggregate function over a set of data while other transactions are updating the data. In an unrepeatable read, the transactions, T_1 reads a record and then does some other processing during which the transaction T_2 updates the record. Now, if T_1 rereads the record, the new value will be inconsistent with the previous value."

Consider an example of unrepeatable read in which of T_1 were to read the value of X after T_2 had updated X, the result of T_1 would be different. That is,

T_1	T_2
	Read X → A_2
Read Y → A_2	A_2 + 1 → A_2
	Write A_2 → X
Read X → A_1	
A_2 + A_1 → A_2	
	Roll back
Write A_2 → X	

This inconsistency occurs because T_1 reads several values from a database while a second transaction, T_2, updates some of them.

SUMMARY

We have studied in this chapter about what a transaction is? Committing means that a user has explicitly or implicity requested that the changes in the transaction be made permanent. Rollback means undoing any changes to data that have been performed by SQL within an uncommitted transaction. We have also studied when is a schedule conflict serializable.

MULTIPLE CHOICE QUESTIONS [MCQs]

1. A set of changes that must be all made together is called as a
   (a) Atom (b) Transaction
   (c) Concurrency (d) None of the above.
2. A transaction must be
   (a) Atomic (b) Small
   (c) Large (d) None of the above.
3. ACID stands for
   (a) Again, Common, Internal, Data (b) Atomic, Common, Inernal, Data
   (c) Atomic, Consistent, Isolation, Durability (d) None of the above.
4. The initial state of a transaction is known as
   (a) Active state (b) Partially committed state
   (c) Failed state (d) Aborted state.
5. A list of actions from a set of transactions is known as
   (a) Statement (b) Schedule
   (c) Transaction Set (d) None of the above.
6. A schedule in which the operations from a set of concurrent transactions are interleaved is called as a
   (a) Non-serial schedule (b) Serial schedule
   (c) Complete schedule (d) None of the above.
7. A schedule that will always produce identical results
   (a) Equivalent schedule (b) Complete schedule
   (c) Serial schedule (d) Non-serial schedule.
8. Two actions on the same data object conflict if atleast one of them is a
   (a) Write (b) Read
   (c) Read/Write (d) None of the above.
9. A schedule (S) can be transformed to a schedule (S′), by a series of swaps of non-conflicting instructions, then we say that S and S′ are
   (a) Equivalent (b) Serial
   (c) Conflict equivalent. (d) None of the above
10. If the precedence graph has no cycles, then the schedule, S, is
   (a) Conflict Serializable (b) Conflict Equivalent.
   (c) Serial (d) None of the above.

ANSWERS

1. (b) 2. (a) 3. (c) 4. (a) 5. (b) 6. (a) 7. (a) 8. (a)
9. (c) 10. (a)

CONCEPTUAL SHORT QUESTIONS WITH ANSWERS

Q.1. There are three conflict operations. What are they ?

Ans. The three conflict operations are :

(a) Reading Uncommitted Data (WR conflicts).

(b) Unrepeatable Reads (RW conflicts)

(c) Overwriting Uncommitted Data (WW conflicts).

WR conflicts: A transaction (say, T′) could read a database object – A that has been modified by another transaction (say, T), which has not yet committed. Such a read is called a **dirty read.**

RW conflicts : A transaction (say, T′) could change the value of an object – A that has been read by transaction (T) while T is still in progress.

WW conflicts : A transaction (T′) could overwrite the value of an object – A, which has already been modified by a transaction T, while T is still in progress. Even if T^1 does not read the value of A written by T, a potential problem exists.

Q.2. Gray (1976) has defined four levels of transaction consistency. What are they?

[JNTU, Hyderabad, B.Tech (CSE/IT); 2nd Sem., Apr./May 2007]

Ans. Jim Gray defines four levels of consistency

(*a*) **Level-0 consistency :** A transaction does not overwrite data updated by another user or process (dirty data) of other transactions.

(*b*) **Level-1 consistency :** Degree 0 plus a transaction does not commit any writes until it completes all its writes until the end of transaction.

(*c*) **Level-2 consistency :** Degree 1 plus a transaction does not read dirty data from other transactions.

(*d*) **Level -2 consistency :** Degree 2 plus other transactions do not read dirty data before the transaction commits.

Please note, however, that most of the conventional database applications require level-3 consistency and it is provided by all major commerical DBMSs.

Q.3. List the ACID properties. Explain usefulness of each.

Ans. The ACID properties, and the need for each of them are:

- **Consistency :** Execution of a transaction in isolation (that is, with no other transaction executing concurrently) preserves the consistency of the database. This is typically the responsility of the application programmer who codes the transactions.
- **Atomicity :** Either all operations of the transaction are reflected properly in the database, or none. Clearly lack of atomicity will lead to inconsistency in the database.
- **Isolation :** When multiple transactions execute concurrently, it should be the case that, for every pair of transactions T_i and T_j, it appears to T_i that either T_j finished execution before T_i started, or T_i started execution after T_i finished. Thus, each transaction is unaware of other transactions executing concurrently with it. The user view of a transaction system requires the isolation property, and the property that concurrent schedules takes the system from one consistent state to another. These requirements are satisfied by ensuring that only serializable schedules of individually consistency preserving transactions are allowed.
- **Durability :** After a transaction completes successfully, the changes it has made to the database persist, even if there are system failures.

Q.4. During its execution, a transaction passes through several states, until it finally commits or aborts. List all possible sequences of states through which a transactions may pass. Explain why each state transition may occur.

Ans. The possible sequences of states are :

(*a*) *active → partially committed → committed.* This is the normal sequence a successful transaction will follow. After executing all its statements it enters the **partially committed** state. After enough recovery information has been written to disk, the transaction finally enters the *committed* state.

(*b*) *active → partially committed → aborted.* After executing the last statement of the transaction, it enters the **partially committed** state. But before enough recovery information is written to disk, a hardware failure may occur destroying the memory contents. In this case the changes which it made to the database are undone, and the transaction enters the **aborted** state.

(*c*) *active → failed → aborted.* After the transaction starts, if it is discovered at some point that normal execution cannot continue (either due to internal program errors or external errors), it enters the failed state. It is then rolled back, after which it enters the **aborted** state.

Q.5. Explain the distinction between the terms *serial schedule* and *serializable schedule.*

Ans. A schedule in which all the instructions belonging to one single transaction appear together is called a **serial schedule.** A **serializable schedule** has a weaker restriction that it should be **equivalent** to some serial schedule. There are two definitions of schedule equivalence–conflict equivalence and view equivalence. Both of these are described in the chapter.

Q.6. Consider the following two transactions :

T_1 : read (A);
read (B);
if A = 0 then B := B + 1,
write (B);

T_2 : read (B);
read (A);
if B = 0 then A := A + 1;
write (A);

Let the consistency requirement be $A = 0 \vee B = 0$, with $A = B = 0$ the initial values.

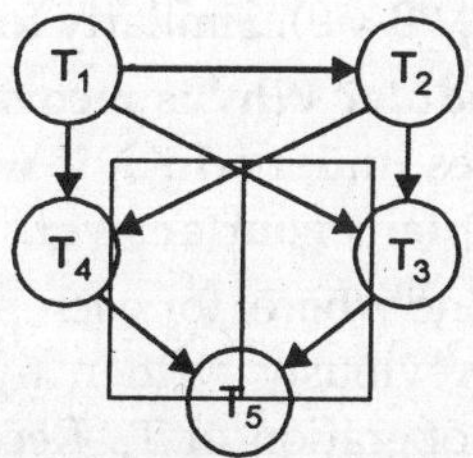

(*a*) Show that every serial execution involving these two transaction preserves the consistency of the database.

(*b*) Show a concurrent execution of T_1 and T_2 that produces a nonserializable schedule?

(*c*) Is there a concurrent execution of T_1 and T_2 that produces a serializable schedule?

[Delhi University (DU) - DCE, ME (CS) 2005 and BPUT Orissa, B.Tech (CSE); 2nd year, June 2005]

Ans. (*a*) There are two possible executions : $T_1 T_2$ and $T_2 T_1$.

Case 1.

	A	B
initially	0	0
after T_1	0	1
after T_2	0	1

Consistency met: $A = 0 \vee B = 0 \equiv T \vee F = T$

Case 2.

	A	B
initially	0	0
after T_2	1	0
after T_1	1	0

Consistency met : $A = 0 \vee B = 0 \equiv F \vee T = T$

(*b*) Any interleaving of T_1 and T_2 results in a non-serializable schedule.

T_1	T_2
read (A)	
	read (B) read (A)
read (B) if A = 0 then B = B + 1	
	if B = 0 then A = A + 1 write (A)
write (B)	

(*c*) There is parallel execution resulting in a serializable schedule. From part a we know that a serializable schedule results in $A = 0 \vee B = 0$. Suppose we start with T_1 read (A). Then when the schedule ends, no matter when we run the steps of T_2, B = 1. Now suppose we start executing T_2 prior to completion of T_1. Then T_2 read (B) will give B a value of 0. So when T_2 completes, A = 1. Thus $B = 1 \wedge A = 1 \rightarrow \neg (A = 0 \vee B = 0)$. Similarly for starting with T_2 read (B).

Q.7. What is a recoverable schedule? Why is recoverability of schedules desirable? Are there any circumstances under which it would be desirable to allow non-recoverable schedules? Explain your answer.

Ans. A recoverable schedule is one where, for each pair of transactions T_i and T_j such that T_j reads data items previously written by T_i, the commit operation of T_i appears before of commit operation of T_j. Recoverable schedules are desirable because failure of a transaction might otherwise bring the system into an irreversibly inconsistent state. Nonrecoverable schedules may sometimes be needed when updates must be made visible early due to time constraints, even if they have not yet been committed, which may be required for very long duration transactions.

Q.8. Why is an explicit transaction end statement needed in SQL but not an explicit begin statement?

Ans. A transaction is an atomic operation. It has only one way to begin, that is with "Begin Transaction" command but it could end up in two ways: Successfully installs its updates to the database (*i.e.*, commit) or Removes its partial updates (which may be incorrect) from the database (abort). Thus, it is important for the database system to identify the right way of ending a transaction. It is for this reason a "End" command is needed in SQL2 query.

Q.9. Describe situations where each of the different isolation levels would be useful for transaction processing.

Ans. Transaction isolation levels provide a measure of the influence of other concurrent transactions on a given transaction. This affects the level of concurrency, that is, the level of concurrency is the highest in Read Uncommitted and the lowest in Serializable.

Isolation level Serializable : This isolation level preserves consistency in all situations, thus it is the safest execution mode. It is recommended for execution environment where every update is crucial for a correct result. **For example,** airline reservation, debit credit, salary increase, and so on.

Isolation level Repeatable Read : This isolation level is similar to Serializable except Phantom problem may occur here. Thus, in record locking (finer granularity), this isolation level must be avoided. It can be used in all types of environments, except in the environment where accurate summary information (*e.g.*, computing total sum of a all different types of account of a bank customer) is desired.

Isolation level Read Committed : In this isolation level a transaction may see two different values of the same data items during its executing life. A transaction in this level applies write lock and keeps it until it commits. It also applies a read (shared) lock but the lock is released as soon as the data item is read by the transaction. This isolation level may be used for making balance, weather, departure or arrival times, and so on.

Isolation level Read Uncommitted : In this isolation level a transaction does not either apply a shared lock or a write lock. The transaction is not alllowed to write any data item, thus it may give rise to dirty read, unrepeatable read, and phantom. It may be used in the environment where statistical average of a large number of data is required.

Q.10. Which of the following schedules is (conflict) serializable? For each serializble schedule, determine the equivalent serial schedules.

(*a*) r1(X); r3(X); w1(X); r2(X); w3(X)

(*a*) r1(X); r3(X); w3(X); w1(X); r2(X)

(*a*) r3(X); r2(X); w3(X); r1(X); w1(X)

(*a*) r3(X); r2(X); r1(X); w3(X); w1(X)

Ans. Let there be three transactions T1, T2, and T3. They are executed concurrently and produce a schedule S. S is serializaable if it can be reproduced as at least one serial schedule (T1˜ T2˜ T3 or T1˜ T3˜ T2 or T2˜ T1˜ T3 or T2˜ T3˜ T1 or T3˜ T1˜ T2 or T3˜ T2˜ T1). (~ means →)

(*a*) This schedule is not serializable because T1 reads X (r1(X)) before T3 but T3 reads X (r3(X)) before T1 writes X (w1(X)), where X is a common data item. The operation r2(X) of T2 does not affect the schedule at all so its position in the schedule is irrelevant. In a serial schedule T1, T2, and T3, the operation w1(X) comes after r3(X), which does not happen in the question.

(*b*) The schedule is not serializable because T1 reads X (r1(X)) before T3 but T3 writes X (w3(X)) before T1 writes X (w1(X)). The operation r2(X) of T2 does not affect the schedule at all so its position in the schedule is irrelevant. In a serial schedule T1, T3, and T2, r3(X) and w3(X) must come after w1(X), which does not happen in the question.

(*c*) This schedule is *serializable* because all conflicting operations of T3 happens before all conflicting operation of T1, T2 has only one operation, which is a read on X (r2(X)), which does not conflict with any other operation. Thus this serializable schedule is equivalent to r2(X); r3(X); w3(X); r1(X); w1(X) (*e.g.*, T2 → T3 → T1) serial schedule.

(*d*) This is not a serializable schedule because T3 reads X(r3(X)) before T1 reads X (r1(X)) but r1(X) happens before T3 writes X (w3(X)). In a serial schedule T3, T2, and T1, r1(X) will happen after w3(X), which does not happen in the question.

Q.11. Consider the three transactions T1, T2 and T3, and the schedule S1 and S2 below. Draw the serializability (precedence) graphs for S1 and S2 and state whether each schedule is serializable or not. If a schedule is serializable, write down the equivalent serial schedule(s).

T1 : r1(x); r1(z); w1(x)

T2 : r2(z); r2(y); w2(z); w2(y)

T3 : r3(x); r3(y); w3(y)

S1 : r1(x); r2(z); r1(x); r3(x); r3(y); w1(x); w3(y); r2(y); w2(z); w2(y)

S2 : r1(x); r2(z); r3(x); r1(z); r2(y); r3(y); w1(x); w2(z); w3(y); w2(y)

Ans. S1: it is a serializable schedule because

- T1 only reads X (r1(X)), which is not modified either by T2 or T3,
- T3 reads X (r3(X)) before T1 modifies it (w1(X)),
- T2 reads Y (r2(Y)) and writes it (w2(Y)) only after T3 has written to it (w3(Y))
- Thus, the serializability graph is

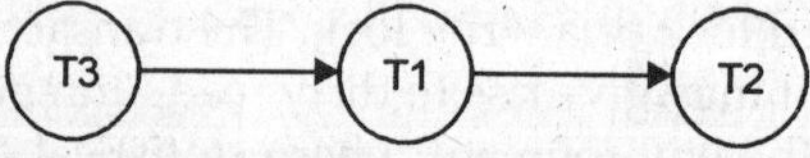

Schedule is not a serializable schedule because

- T2 reads Y (r2(Y)), which is then read and modified by T3 (w3(Y))
- T3 reads Y (r3(Y)), which then modified before T2 modifies Y (w2(Y))

In the above order T3 interferes in the execution of T2, which makes the schedule nonserializable.

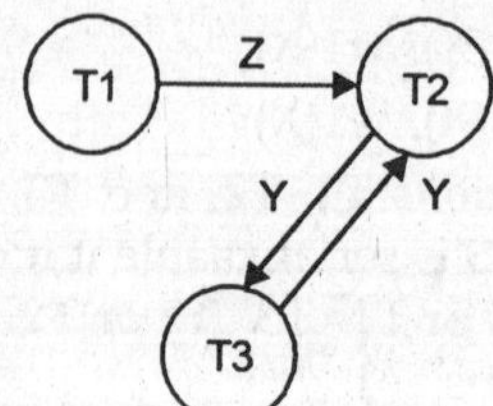

Q.12. Consider schedules S3, S4, and S5 below. Determine whether each schedule is strict, cascadeless, recoverable, or nonrecoverable. (Determine the strictest recoverability condition that each schedule satisfies).

S3 : r1(x); r2(z); r1(z); r3(x); r3(y); w1(x); c1; w3(y); c3; r2(y); w2(z); w2(y); c2

S4 : r1(x); r2(z); r1(z); r3(x); r3(y); w1(x); w3(y); r2(y); w2(z); w2(y); c1; c2; c3;

S5 : r1(x); r2(z); r3(x); r1(z); r2(y); r3(y); w1(x); w1(x); w2(y); w2(y); c3; c2;

Ans. Strict schedule : A schedule is strict if it satisfies the following conditions :

1. Tj reads a data item X **after** Ti has written to X and Ti is terminated (aborted or committed)
2. Tj writes a data item X **after** Ti has written to X and Ti is terminated (aborted or committed)

Schedule S3 is not strict because T3 reads X (r3(X)) **before** T1 has written to X (w1(X)) but T3 commits after T1. In a strict schedule T3 must read X **after** C1.

Schedule S4 is not strict because T3 reads X (r3(X)) **before** T1 has written to X (w1(X)) but T3 commits **after** T1. In a strict schedule T3 must read X **after** C1.

Schedule S5 is not strict because T3 reads X (r3(X)) **before** T1 has written to X (w1(X)) but T3 commits **after** T1. In a strict schedule T3 must read X **after** C1.

Cascadeless schedule : A schedule is cascadeless if the following condition is satisfied:

Tj reads X only ***after*** Ti has written to X and terminated (aborted or committed).

Schedule S3 in ***not cascadeless*** because T3 reads X (r3(X)) before T1 commits.

Schedule S4 in ***not cascadeless*** because T3 reads X (r3(X)) before T1 commits.

Schedule S5 in ***not cascadeless*** because T3 reads X (r3(X)) ***before*** T1 commits or T2 reads.

Y (r2(Y)) ***before*** T3 commits.

> **NOTE :** According to the definition of cascadeless schedules S3, S4, and S4 are not cascadeless. However, T3 is not affected if T1 is rolled back in any of the schedules, that is, T3 does not have to roll back if T1 is rolled back. The problem occurs because these schedules are not serializable.

Recoverable schedule: A schedule is recoverable if the following condition is satisfied:

Tj commits after T_i if Tj has read any item written by T_i.

> **NOTE:** C_i > Cj means C_i happens ***before*** Cj. Ai denotes abort T_i. To test if a schedule is recoverable one has to include abort operations. Thus in testing the recoverability abort operations will have to used in place of commit one at a time. Also the strictest condition is where a transaction neither nor writes to a data item, which was written to by a transaction that has not committed yet.

If A1>C3>C2, then S3 is ***recoverable*** because rolling back of T1 does affect T2 and T3. If C1>A3>C2, S3 is ***not recoverable*** because T2 read the vaiue of Y (r2(Y)) ***after*** T3 wrote X (w3(Y)) and T2 committed but T3 rolled back. Thus, T2 used non-existed value of Y. If C1>C3>A3, then S3 is ***recoverable*** because roll back of T2 does not affect T1 and T3. Strictest condition of S3 is C3>C2.

If A1>C2>C3, then S4 is ***recoverable*** because roll back of T1 does not affect T2 and T3. If C1>A2>C3, then S4, is ***recoverable*** because the roll back of T2 will restore the value of Y that was read and written to by T3 (w3(Y)). It will not affect T1. If C1>C2>A3, then S4 is ***not recoverable*** because T3 will restore the value of Y which was not read by T2. Strictest condition of S4 is C3>C2, but it is not satisfied by S4.

If A1>C3>C2, then S5 is ***recoverable*** because neither T2 nor T3 writes to X, which is written by T1. If C1>A3>C2, then S5 is ***not recoverable*** because T3 will restore the value of Y, which was read by T2. Thus, T2 committed with a non-existent value of Y. If C1>C3>A2, then S5 is ***recoverable*** because it will restore the value of Y to the value, which was read by T3. Thus, T3 committed with the right value of Y. Strictest conditions of S3 is C3>C2, but it is not satisfied by S5.

Q.13. Change the transaction, T2, given below :

```
Read-item(X);
X := X + M;
Write_item (X);
```

to read:

```
read _item (X);
X := X + M;
if X > 90 then exit;
else write_item (X);
```

Discuss the final result of the different schedules given below :

T_1	T_2
read_item (X); X := X – N;	
	read_item (X); X := X + M;
write_item (X); read_item (Y);	
	write_item (X);
Y := Y + N; write_item (Y);	

Where M = 2 and, N= 2, with respect to the following questions. Does adding the above condition change the final outcome? Does the outcome obey the implied consistency rule (that the capacity of X is 90)?

Ans. The above condition does not change the final outcome unless the initial value of X > 88. The outcome, however, does obey the implied consistency rule that X < 90, since the value of X is not updated if it becomes greater than 90.

Q.14. Repeat Exercise 13, adding a check in T1 so that Y does not exceed 90.

Ans. T1 T2

read_item(X);

X := X – N;

read_item (X);

X := X + M;

Write_item (X);

read_item (Y);
if X > 90 then exit
else write item (X);
Y := Y + N;
if Y > 90 then
exit
else write_item(Y);

The above condition does not change the final outcome unless the initial value of X > 88 or Y > 88. The outcome obeys the implied consistency rule that X < 90 and Y < 90.

Q.15. Add the operation commit at the end of each of the transactions, T_1 and T_2 given below and then list all possible schedules for the modified transactions. Determine which of the schedules are recoverable, which are cascadeless and which are strict. T1 and T2 are as follows :

T_1	T_2
read-item (X); X := X – N; write_item (X); read_item (Y); Y := Y + N; write_item (Y);	read_item (X); X := X + M; write_item (X);

Ans. T1 T2
read_item (X); read_item(X);
X := X – N X := X + M;
write_item (X); write_item(X):
read_item (Y); commit T2
Y := Y + N;
write_item (Y);
commit T1

The transactions can be written as follows using the shorthand notation:
T1 : r1 (X); w1 (X); r1(Y); w1 (Y); C1;
T2 : r2 (X); W2 (X); C2;

In general, given m transactions with number of operations n1, n2 , ... , nm, the number of possible schedules is: (n1 + n2 + ... + nm)! / (n1!* n2!* ... * nm!), where ! is the factorial function. In our case, m = 2 and n1 = 5 and n2 = 3, so the number of possible schedules is:

(5 + 3)!/ (5!* 3!) = 8*7*6*5*4*3*2*1/*5*4*3*2*1*3*2*1 = 56.

Below are the 56 possible schedules, and the type of each schedule:

S 1: r 1 (X); w 1 (X); r 1 (Y); w 1 (Y); C 1; r 2 (X); w 2 (X); C 2; strict (and hence cascadeless)

S 2: r 1 (X); w 1 (X); r 1 (Y); w 1 (Y); r 2 (X); C 1; w 2 (X); C 2; recoverable

S 3: r 1 (X); w 1 (X); r 1 (Y); w 1 (Y); r 2 (X); w 2 (X); C 1; C 2; recoverable

S 4: r 1 (X); w 1 (X); r 1 (Y); w 1 (Y); r 2 (X); w 2 (X); C 2; C 1; non-recoverable

S 5: r 1 (X); w 1 (X); r 1 (Y); r 2 (X); w 1 (Y); C 1; w 2 (X); C 2; recoverable
S 6: r 1 (X); w 1 (X); r 1 (Y); r 2 (X); w 1 (Y); w 2 (X); C 1; C 2; recoverable
S 7: r 1 (X); w 1 (X); r 1 (Y); r 2 (X); w 1 (Y); w 2 (X); C 2; C 1; non-recoverable
S 8: r 1 (X); w 1 (X); r 1 (Y); r 2 (X); w 2 (X); w 1 (Y); C 1; C 2; recoverable
S 9: r 1 (X); w 1 (X); r 1 (Y); r 2 (X); w 2 (X); w 1 (Y); C 2; C 1; non-recoverable
S 10: r 1 (X); w 1 (X); r 1 (Y); r 2 (X); w 2 (X); C 2; w 1 (Y); C 1; non-recoverable
S 11: r 1 (X); w 1 (X); r 2 (X); r 1 (Y); w 1 (Y); C 1; w 2 (X); C 2; recoverable
S 12: r 1 (X); w 1 (X); r 2 (X); r 1 (Y); w 1 (Y); w 2 (X); C 1; C 2; recoverable
S 13: r 1 (X); w 1 (X); r 2 (X); r 1 (Y); w 1 (Y); w 2 (X); C 2; C 1; non-recoverable
S 14: r 1 (X); w 1 (X); r 2 (X); r 1 (Y); w 2 (X); w 1 (Y); C 1; C 2; recoverable
S 15: r 1 (X); w 1 (X); r 2 (X); r 1 (Y); w 2 (X); w 1 (Y); C 2; C 1; non-recoverable
S 16: r 1 (X); w 1 (X); r 2 (X); r 1 (Y); w 2 (X); C 1; w 1 (Y); C 2; non-recoverable
S 17: r 1 (X); w 1 (X); r 2 (X); w 2 (X); r 1 (Y); w 1 (Y); C 1; C 2; recoverable
S 18: r 1 (X); w 1 (X); r 2 (X); w 2 (X); r 1 (Y); w 1 (Y); C 2; C 1; non-recoverable
S 19: r 1 (X); w 1 (X); r 2 (X); w 2 (X); r 1 (Y); C 2; w 1 (Y); C 1; non-recoverable
S 20: r 1 (X); w 1 (X); r 2 (X); w 2 (X); C 2; r 1 (Y); w 1 (Y); C 1; non-recoverable
S 21: r 1 (X); r 2 (X); w 1 (X); r 1 (Y); w 1 (Y); C 1; w 2 (X); C 2; strict (and hence cascadeless).
S 22: r 1 (X); r 2 (X); w 1 (X); r 1 (Y); w 1 (Y); w 2 (X); C 1; C 2; cascadeless
S 23: r 1 (X); r 2 (X); w 1 (X); r 1 (Y); w 1 (Y); w 2 (X); C 2; C 1; cascadeless
S 24: r 1 (X); r 2 (X); w 1 (X); r 1 (Y); w 2 (X); w 1 (Y); C 1: C 2; cascadeless
S 25: r 1 (X); r 2 (X); w 1 (X); r 1 (Y); w 2 (X); w 1 (Y); C 2; C 1; cascadeless
S 26: r 1 (X); r 2 (X); w 1 (X); r 1 (Y); w 2 (X); C 2; w 1 (Y); C 1; cascadeless
S 27: r 1 (X); r 2 (X); w 1 (X); w 2 (X); r 1 (Y); w 1 (Y); C 1; C 2; cascadeless
S 28: r 1 (X); r 2 (X); w 1 (X); w 2 (X); r 1 (Y); w 1 (Y); C 2; C 1; cascadeless
S 29: r 1 (X); r 2 (X); w 1 (X); w 2 (X); r 1 (Y); C 2; w 1 (Y); C 1; cascadeless
S 30: r 1 (X); r 2 (X); w 1 (X); w 2 (X); C 2; r 1 (Y); w 1 (Y); C 1; cascadeless
S 31: r 1 (X); r 2 (X); w 2 (X); w 1 (X); r 1 (Y); w 1 (Y); C 1; C 2; cascadeless
S 32: r 1 (X); r 2 (X); w 2 (X); w 1 (X); r 1 (Y); w 1 (Y); C 2; C 1; cascadeless
S 33: r 1 (X); r 2 (X); w 2 (X); w 1 (X); r 1 (Y); C 2; w 1 (Y); C 1; cascadeless
S 34: r 1 (X); r 2 (X); w 2 (X); w 1 (X); C 2; r 1 (Y); w 1 (Y); C 1; cascadeless
S 35: r 1 (X); r 2 (X); w 2 (X); C 2; w 1 (X); r 1 (Y); w 1 (Y); C 1; strict (and hence cascadeless).
S 36: r 2 (X); r 1 (X); w 1 (X); r 1 (Y); w 1 (Y); C 1; w 2 (X); C 2; strict (and hance cascadeless)
S 37: r 2 (X); r 1 (X); w 1 (X); r 1 (Y); w 1 (Y); w 2 (X); C 1; C 2; cascadeless
S 38: r 2 (X); r 1 (X); w 1 (X); r 1 (Y); w 1 (Y); w 2 (X); C 2; C 1; cascadeless
S 39: r 2 (X); r 1 (X); w 1 (X); r 1 (Y); w 2 (X); w 1 (Y); C 1; C 2; cascadeless
S 40: r 2 (X); r 1 (X); w 1 (X); r 1 (Y); w 2 (X); w 1 (Y); C 2; C 1; cascadeless
S 41: r 2 (X); r 1 (X); w 1 (X); r 1 (Y); w 2 (X); C 2; w 1 (Y); C 1; cascadeless
S 42: r 2 (X); r 1 (X); w 1 (X); w 2 (X); r 1 (Y); w 1 (Y); C 1; C 2; cascadeless
S 43: r 2 (X); r 1 (X); w 1 (X); w 2 (X); r 1 (Y); w 1 (Y); C 2; C 1; cascadeless

S 44: r 2 (X); r 1 (X); w 1 (X); w 2 (X); r 1 (Y); C 2; w 1 (Y); C 1; cascadeless

S 45: r 2 (X); r 1 (X); w 1 (X); w 2 (X); C 2 ; r 1 (Y); w 1 (Y); C 1; cascadeless

S 46: r 2 (X); r 1 (X); w 2 (X); w 1 (X); r 1 (Y); w 1 (Y); C 1; C 2; cascadeless

S 47: r 2 (X); r 1 (X); w 2 (X); w 1 (X); r 1 (Y); w 1 (Y); C 2l C 1; cascadeless

S 48: r 2 (X); r 1 (X); w 2 (X); w 1 (X); r 1 (Y); C 2; w 1 (Y); C 1 ; cascadeless

S 49: r 2 (X); r 1 (X); w 2 (X); w 1 (X); C 2 ; r 1 (Y); w 1 (Y); C 1; cascadeless

S 50: r 2 (X); r 1 (X); w 2 (X); C 2 ; w 2 (X); r 1 (Y); w 1 (Y); C 1; cascadeless

S 51: r 2 (X); w 2 (X); r 2 (X); w 1 (X); r 1 (Y); w 1 (Y); C 1; C 2; non-recoverable

S 52: r 2 (X); w 2 (X); r 1 (X); w 1 (X); r 1 (Y); w 1 (Y); C2 ; C 1; recoverable

S 53: r 2 (X); w 2 (X); r 1 (X); w 1 (X); r 1 (Y); C 2; w 1 (Y); C 1; recoverable

S 54: r 2 (X); w 2 (X); r 1 (X); w 1 (X); C 2; r 1 (Y); w 1 (Y); C 1; recoverable

S 55: r 2 (X); w 2 (X); r 1 (X); C 2; w 1 (X); r 1 (Y); w 1 (Y); C 1; recoverable

S 56: r 2 (X); w 2 (X); C 2; r 1 (X); w 1 (X); r 1 (Y); w 1 (Y); C 1; strich (and hence cascadeless)

Q.16. List all possible schedules for transactions T1 and T2 from example above, and determine which are conflict serializable (correct) and which are not.

Ans. T 1 T 2

read_item (X); read_item (X);

X := X - N X := X + M;

write_item(X); write_item (X);

read_item (Y);

Y := Y + N;

write_item(Y);

The transactions can be written as follows using shorthand notation:

T 1: r 1 (X); w 1 (X); r 1 (Y); w 1 (Y);

T 2: r 2 (X); w 2 (X);

In this case, m = 2 and n1 = 4 and n2 = 2, so the number of possible schedule is (4 + 2)! / (4!* 2!) = 6*5*4*3*2*1 / 4*3*2*1*2*1 = 15.

Below are the 15 possible schedules, and the type of each schedule:

S 1: r 1 (X); w 1 (X); r 1 (Y); w 1 (Y); r 2 (X); w 2 (X): serial (and hence also serializable)

S 2: r 1 (X); w 1 (X); r 1 (Y); r 2 (X); w 1 (Y); w 2 (X): (conflict) serializable

S 3: r 1 (X); w 1 (X); r 1 (Y); r 2 (Y); w 2 (X); w 1 (Y); (conflict) serializable

S 4: r 1 (X); w 1 (X); r 2 (X); r 1 (Y); w 1 (Y); w 2 (X); (conflict) serializable

S 5: r 1 (X); w 1 (X); r 2 (X); r 1 (Y); w 2 (X); w 1 (Y); (conflict) serializable

S 6: r 1 (X); w 1 (X); r 2 (X); w 2 (X); r 1 (Y); w 2 (Y); (conflict) serializable

S 7: r 1 (X); r 2 (X); w 1 (X); r 1 (Y); w 1 (Y); w 2 (X); not (conflict) serializable

S 8: r 1 (X); r 2 (X); w 1 (X); r 1 (Y); w 2 (X); w 1 (Y); not (conflict) serializable

S 9: r 1 (X); r 2 (X); w 1 (X); w 2 (X): r 1 (Y); w 1 (Y); not (conflict) serializable

S 10: r 1 (X); r 2 (X); w 2 (X); w 1 (X); r 1 (Y); w 1 (Y); not (conflict) serializable

S 11: r 2 (X); r 1 (X); w 1 (X); r 1 (Y); w 1 (Y); w 2 (X); not (conflict) serializable

S 12: r 2 (X); r 1 (X); w 1 (X); r 1 (Y); w 2 (X); w 1 (Y); not (conflict) serializable

S 13: r 2 (X); r 1 (X); w 1 (X); w 2 (X); r 1 (Y); w 1 (Y); not (conflict) serializable
S 14: r 2 (X); r 1 (X); w 2 (X); w 1 (X); r 1 (Y); w 1 (Y); not (conflict) serializable
S 15: r 2 (X); w 2 (X); r 1 (X); w 1 (X); r 1 (Y); w 1 (Y); serial (and hence also serializable)

Q.17. How many serial schedules exist for the three transactions in Figure below? What are they? What is the total number of possible schedules?

Ans. T1 T2 T3 T3 T2 T1
T2 T3 T1 T2 T1 T3
T3 T1 T2 T1 T3 T2

Total number of serial schedules for the three transactions = 6

In general, the number of serial schedules for n transactions is *n*! (*i.e.*, factorial (*n*))

T_1	T_2	T_3

read_item(X);
write_item(X);
read_item(Y);
write_item(Y);
	read_item(Z);
	read_item(Y);
	write_item(Y);
	read_item(X);
	write_item(X);
		read_item(Y);
		read_item(Z);
		write_item(Y);
		write_item(Z);

Q.18. Discuss tree protocol.

Ans. Let D = {d_1, d_2, ..., d_n} is the set of all data items. If $d_1 \rightarrow d_j$, then any transaction accessing both d_i and d_j must access d_i before accessing d_j. This partial ordering may be a result of either the logical or physical organization of data or it may be imposed solely for the purpose of concurrency control.

The partial ordering implies that the set D may be viewed as a directed acyclic graph, called database graph. For simplicity we shall consider only those graphs which are rooted trees. A simple protocol called **tree-protocol**, which is restricted to exclusive locks is stated here. Each transaction T_i can lock (lock-X (Q)) a data item at most once and observe the following rules.

1. The first lock by T_i may be on any data item.
2. Subsequently, a data item Q can be locked by T_i only if the parent of Q is currently locked by T_i.
3. Data item may be unlocked at any time.
4. A data item that has been locked and unlocked by T_i cannot subsequently be locked by T_i.

All schedules that are legal under the tree protocol are conflict serializable.

Example :

Consider the database graph in Fig. below (next page). The following four transactions follow the tree protocol on this graph.

T_{10} lock-X (B)
lock-X (E);
lock-X (D);
unlock (B);
unlock (E);
lock-X (G);

unlock (D);
unlock (G);

T_{11} lock-X (D);
lock-X (H);
unlock (D);
unlock (H);

T_{12}: lock-X (B);
lock-X (E);
unlock (E);
unlock (B);

T_{13}: lock-X (D);
lock-X (H);
unlock (D);
unlock (H).

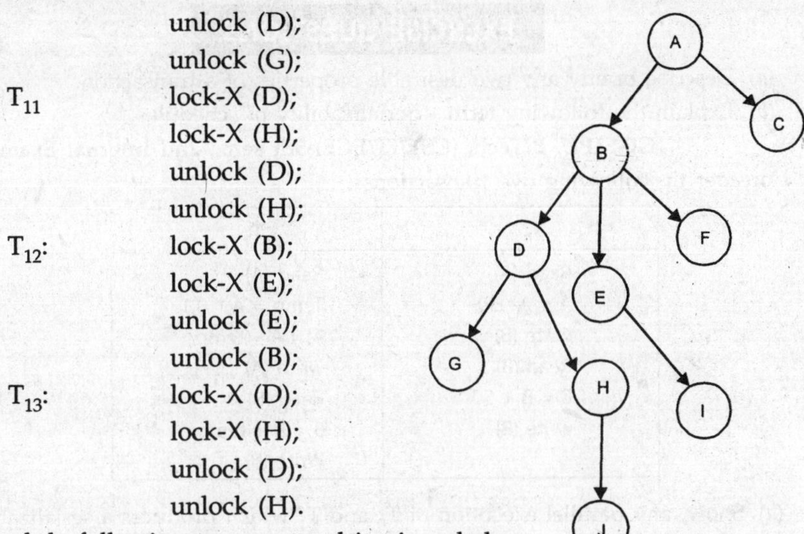

Fig. Database Graph

The schedule following tree protocol is given below :

Table 6.00

T_{10}	T_{11}	T_{12}	T_{13}
lock-X (B)			
	lock-X (D)		
	lock-X (H)		
	unlock (D)		
lock-X (E)			
lock-X (D)			
unlock (B)			
unlock (E)			
		lock-X (B)	
		lock-X (E)	
	unlock (H)		
lock-X (G)			
unlock (D)			
			lock-X (D)
			lock-X (H)
			unlock (D)
			unlock (H)
		unlock (E)	
		unlock (B)	
unlock (G)			

This schedule is conflict serializable. Tree protocol ensures conflict serializability and it is free from deadlocks.

Advantages :

Tree locking protocol has an advantage over two phase locking protocol :

1. Unlocking may occur earlier, Earlier unlocking may lead to shorter waiting times and to an increase in concurrency.
2. It is deadlock free and hence no rollbacks are required.

EXERCISE QUESTIONS

Q.1. (*a*) Describe briefly any two desirable properties of a transaction.

(*b*) Explain the following term – Serializability of schedules.

[GGSIPU, B.Tech. (CSE/IT/ECE)-5th sem., 2nd Internal Exam., Nov., 2005]

Q.2. Consider the following two transactions :

T_0	T_1
Read (A) A = A– 50 write (B) Read (B) B = B + 50 write (B)	Read (A) Temp = A * 0.1 A = A – temp write (A) Read (B) B = B + temp Write (B)

(*a*) Show, any parallel execution of T_0 and T_1 which produces a serializable schedule.

(*b*) Show any parallel execution of T_0 and T_1 which produces a non-serializable schedule.

(*c*) For concurrency control in the above case, which lock can be used and how will that lock solve the problem.

[GGSIPU, B.Tech. (CSE/IT/ECE)-5th sem., Dec., 2006]

Q.3. Since every conflict-serializable schedule is view serializable why do you emphasize conflict serializability rather than view serializability?

[GGSIPU, B.Tech. (CSE)-5th sem., Sept., 2007]

Q.4. Differentiate between a serial schedule and serializable schedule.

[GGSIPU, B.Tech. (CSE)-5th sem., Dec., 2008]

Q.5. What is a serializable schedule? Give two example, each having two transactions that access and modify the same data value, yet execute in a serializable way.

[IGNOU, MCA-3rd year, June 2004]

Q.6. (*a*) What is a serializablie schedule?

(*b*) What is a transaction? Explain ACID properties with an example.

(*c*) In the following precedence graph, is the corresponding schedule conflict serializable? Explain your answer.

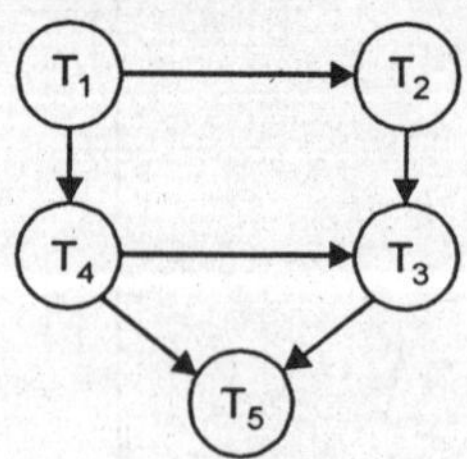

[Delhi University (DU) - DCE, M.E. (CS) - 2004]

Q.7. (*a*) Define the following terms –

(*i*) Atomicity (*ii*) Consistency. (*iii*) Isolation

(*iv*) Durability. (*v*) Schedule (*vi*) Blind write.

(*vii*) Dirty read. (*viii*) Unrepeatable reads (*ix*) Serializable schedule.

(*x*) Recoverable schedule.

(*b*) Consider the precedence graph below. Is the corresponding schedule conflict serializable? Explain your answer.

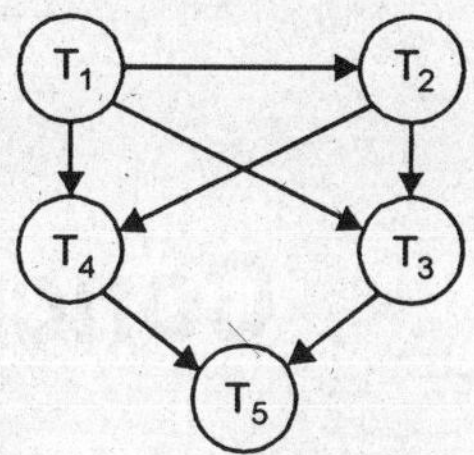

[Delhi University (DU) - DCE, M.E. (CS) - 2005]

Q.8. What do you mean by schedule in the context of concurrent execution of transactions in RDBMS? What is seriablizable schedule? Discuss the various types of serializability with a suitable example? **[UPTU, B.Tech (CSE) - 4th sem., 2006–07]**

Q.9. Define serializablility. Differentiate conflict and view serializability.

[UPTU, MBA-4th sem., 2006–07]

Q.10. (*a*) Define the term Dirty Reads.

(*b*) Explain transaction states and its property.

(c) Write short note on-conflict serializability.

[Nagpur University, B.E. (CSE)-7th sem., Dec. 2008]

Q.11. Write in detail about serializability.

[Nagpur University, B.E. (CSE)-7th sem., June-July 2007]

Q.12. Write short notes on –

(*a*) Serializability

(*b*) ACID. **[Nagpur University, B.E. (CSE)-7th sem., June–July 2007]**

Q.13. Explain the transaction management in a database.

[JNTU, Hyderabad, B.Tech. (CSE/IT)-2nd sem., Apr/May 2007]

Q.14. What is a transaction ? What are its ACID properties?

[GGSIPU, BCA-3rd sem., Dec. 2003]

Q.15. What is a transaction in database context? When a schedule is said to be view equivalent to another schedule?

[GGSIPU, MCA -2nd sem., May 2004]

Q.16. How schedules can be tested for serializability? Explain with example. What are the different techniques used for testing serializability?

[GGSIPU, M.Tech. (IT)-3rd sem., Dec. 2004]

Q.17. (i) List ACID properties. Explain the usefulness of each.

(ii) What are the different states of a transaction ? Explain concurrent executions with the help of an example.

[GGSIPU, B.Tech. (CSE/IT)—5th Sem., Dec. 2009]

Q.18. Discuss atomicity and concurrency in databases.

[GGSIPU, B. Tech. (CSE/IT) — 5th Sem., Dec. 2010]

Q.19. Discuss ACID properties of a transaction.

[GGSIPU, B. Tech. (CSE/IT)— 5th Sem., Dec. 2011]

[GGSIPU, M.Tech. (CSE/IT)— Ist Sem., Dec. 2011]

Q.20. Draw a state diagram and discuss the typical states that a transaction goes through during execution. **[GGSIPU, M. Tech. (CSE/IT) Ist Sem., Jan. 2011]**

CHAPTER 7

Concurrency Control Techniques

7.0 INTRODUCTION

Concurrency control is the process of managing simultaneous execution of transactions (like queries, updates, inserts, deletes etc.) in a multiprocessing database system without having them interfere with one another. **This property of DBMS allows many transactions to access the same database at the same time without interfering with each other**. So, the primary goal is to ensure atomicity or serializability of execution of transactions in a multi-user database environment. **Please note that the objective is to interleave executions to yield the same results as that of a serial schedule execution. Also note that this interleaving creates the impression that the transactions are executing concurrently**. Interleaving is a mechanism to achieve concurrency. Concurrency control is important because simultaneous execution of transactions over shared database can create several data integrity and consistency problems.

7.1 LOCK-BASED PROTOCOLS

Let us first of all discuss, **what is a lock?**

A lock is defined as a variable associated with a data item that describes the status of the item with respect to the possible operations that can be applied to it. Please note that generally, there is one lock for each data item in the database. Also, we say that locks are used as a means of synchronizing the access by concurrent transactions to the database items.

Locks are put under two categories :

1. Binary locks.
2. Share/Exclusive (for R/W) locks.

Let us discuss them briefly now.

1. Binary Locks : A binary lock has two states—locked or unlocked. So, if 'A' is a data-item, we refer to the current value of the lock associated with item A as lock (A).

If Lock (A) = 1 then item-A cannot be accessed.

Else if Lock (A) = 0 then item-A can be accessed.

There are 2 operations with this binary locking. A transaction (say, T) requests an access to an item-A by firstly issuing a lock-item (A) operation. If Lock (A) = 1, the transaction is forced to wait. If lock (A) = 0, then transaction is allowed to access item-A. When T's accessing is over, it issues an unlock-item (A) operation which sets Lock (A) to 0, so that the item-A may be accessed by other transactions.

Rules followed during Binary locking : Every transaction (say, T) must follow the following **rules** in general :

Rule 1. A transaction (say, T) must issue the operation, lock_item (A) before any read_item (A) or write_item (A) operations are performed in T.

Rule 2. T must issue the operation, unlock_item (A) after all read_item (A) and write_item (A) operations are completed in T.

Rule 3. T will not issue a lock_item (A) operation if it already holds the lock on item-A.

Rule 4. T will not issue an unlock_item (A) operation unless it already holds the lock on item-A.

Rule 5. At the most, only one transaction can hold the lock on a particular item. No two transactions can access the same item concurrently.

> **NOTE :** The lock manager module of DBMS can enforce these rules.

Advantages and Disadvantages of Binary Locks : Binary locking is easy to implement but it is restrictive to yield optimal concurrency conditions. DBMS will not allow two transactions to read the same database object even if neither of the transaction updates the database. In nutshell, at most one transaction can hold a lock on a given item. So, this scheme is not used for practical purposes.

2. Share/Exclusive (for R/W) Locks : When several transactions try to access the same data_item (say, A) for reading purpose only, then we should allow the access. But, if a transaction is to write an item-A, it must have exclusive access to A. For this purpose, a different type of lock called as a **multiple-mode lock** is used.

Here, there are three locking operations.

(*a*) Lock-S(A)
(*b*) Lock-X(A)
(*c*) Unlock (A)

} 'S' ≡ Shared lock
'X' ≡ Exclusive lock

Thus, a lock associated with an item-A, Lock (A), now has 3 possible states :

(*i*) read-locked,
(*ii*) write-locked, or
(*iii*) unlocked.

Please note that here a read-locked item is also called as a share-locked item because other transactions are allowed to read the item. Also note that a write-locked item is called as exclusive-locked, because a single transaction exclusively hold the lock on the item.

The exclusive lock must be used when there is a chance of conflict. **It is used when a transaction wants to write (update) a data-item and no locks are currently held on that data item by any other transaction.** It is granted if and only if no other locks are held on the data item.

A shared lock is used when a transaction wants to read data from the database and no exclusive lock is held on that data item. **It allows several read transactions to concurrently read the same data item.**

Can this lead to starvation?

Consider the following case :

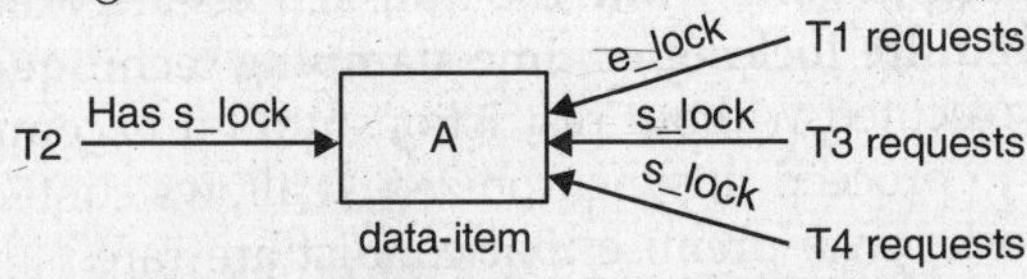

Fig. 7.1. *Starvation of T1 transaction*

Say, that a transaction, T2, has a shared lock on data-item-A. Now T1 transaction requests for exclusive lock. Now, T1 has to wait till T2 releases the lock. In the mean time, say T3 requests for shared lock (s_lock in Fig. 7.1). Now, since T2 and T3 are request compatible, so T3 is granted the shared-lock. Here, T2 may release the lock but still T1 has to wait for T3 to finish. Again, say, T4 requests for s_lock and it is granted the lock before T3 releases it. This may continue but T1 just starves (waits infinitely).

What is the solution?

Locks can be used to avoid the problem of starvation. This is done as follows :

1. **If a shared lock is requested**, the queue of requests is empty and the object is not currently locked in exclusive mode, the lock manager grants the lock and updates the lock table entry for the object.
2. **If an exclusive lock is requested**, and no transaction currently holds a lock on the object *i.e.*, the queue of requests is empty, the lock manager grants the lock and updates the lock table entry.
3. Otherwise, the requested lock cannot be immediately granted and the lock request is added to the queue of lock requests for this object. The transaction requesting the lock is suspended.

Please note that if the transaction, T1, has a shared lock on data_item-A and T2 requests an exclusive lock then its requests enters a queue. Now, if T3 requests a **shared lock**, its requests enters the queue behind that of T2, even though the requested lock is compatible with the lock held by T1. Also note that this rule ensures that T2 does not starve, while a stream of other transactions acquire shared locks and thereby prevent T2 from getting the exclusive lock that it is waiting for.

Actually, when we write concurrency control algorithms, there are 2 approaches

(*a*) Pessimistic Approach.

(*b*) Optimistic Approach.

Let us now see what these approaches are and what are their merits?

I. Pessimistic Approach : An approach in which the transaction are delayed if they conflict with each other at some point of time in future is called as a pessimistic approach.

During **pessimistic execution**, the **validate operation** is performed first. If there is a validation according to compatibility of lock then only read, compute and write operations are performed *i.e.*,

Validate → Read → Compute → Write.

Based on pessimistic (not sure) approach, there are two commonly used locking protocols, namely :

1. Two-phase locking protocol.
2. Time stamp ordering protocol.

We shall be studying these a bit later.

II. Optimistic Approach/Validation/Certification Approach : It is based on the assumption that conflicts of operations (R/W) on database are rare. It is better to run the transactions to completion and to check for conflicts only before they commit. **Please note that here no checking is done while the transactions are executing. Also note that this method does not require locking or time-stamping technique as discussed above.** Here, a transactions is executed without restrictions until it is committed. This approach allows the transactions to proceed unsynchronized. It allows conflict checking at the end only. This approach works on a premise that conflict are rare.

During **optimistic execution**, we perform read and compute operation without validation and validation just before the write operation, *i.e.*,

Read → Compute → Validate → Write.

Advantages of Optimistic Approach : The optimistic concurrency control has certain advantages and are listed below :

1. When conflicts are rare, then the transaction rollback becomes very easy.
2. There will not be any cascading rollbacks as the rollback involves only the local copy of data and not the database.

Disadvantages of Optimistic Methods : The optimistic concurrency control has certain disadvantages also and are listed below :

1. Dealing with conflicts is expensive as a conflicting transaction needs to be rolled back.
2. Whenever there is a conflict between longer and shorter transactions, longer transactions are rolled back repeatedly as they are more likely to have conflicts.

Applications of Optimistic Methods : This method is suitable for those environments where conflicts are lesser and transactions are small. Moreover, it is an acceptable method for those DBMS which require very fewer update transactions.

Let us now discuss another locking protocol *i.e.*, a two-phase locking (2PL) protocol.

III. Two Phase Locking (2PL) Protocol : If all locking operations precede the first unlock operation in the transaction then a transaction follows the two phase locking protocol. 2PL has two phases in a given schedule.

Phase-I : Growing Phase. A phase during which all locks are requested.

Phase-II : Shrinking Phase. A phase during which all locks are released.

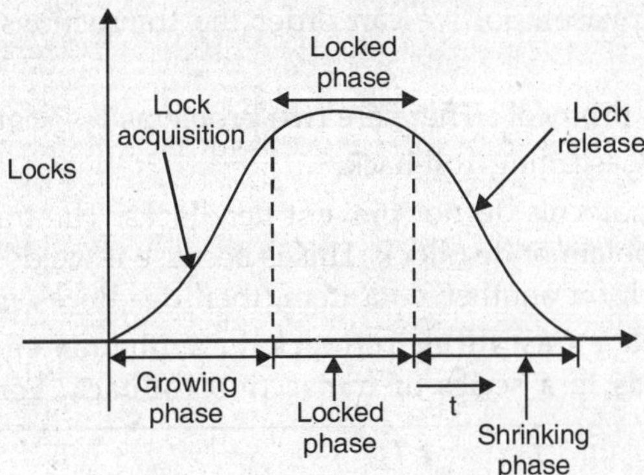

Fig. 7.2. *2PL scheme*

As shown in Fig. 7.2, initially a transaction is in the growing phase. The transactions acquire locks as needed. Once the transaction releases a lock it enters the shrinking phase and it can issue no more lock requests.

Rules for 2PL :

1. Two transactions cannot have conflicting locks.
2. No unlock operation can precede a lock operation in the same transaction.
3. No data are affected until all locks are obtained.

Please note that as per 2PL protocol, the transaction cannot acquire a new lock after it has unlocked any of its existing locked items.

For example, consider two transactions, T_1 and T_2 as shown below :

T_1	T_2

lock-X(B);
read (B, *b*);
b = *b* + 10;
write (B, *b*);
lock-X(A);
read (A, *a*);
a = *a* – 20;
write (A, *a*);
unlock (B);
unlock (A);
	lock-S(A);
	read (A, *a*)
	unlock (A);
	lock-S(B);
	read (B, b);
	unlock (B);
	display (*a* + *b*);

In T_1, we put an exclusive-lock on B (data-item), so we can read or write B. Then, we put an exclusive-lock on A and thus we can read or write to A. Finally, we unlock both B and A in that order. **So, T_1 is in two-phase**. On the other hand, T_2 is not in two-phase. This is because T_2 puts a shared-lock on data-item (A), so read operation can be performed. Then, it unlocks A. Then it locks B in shared mode and reads it. Then, it unlocks B. Finally, T_2 tries to display the result. This schedule of T_2 is not a 2-phase as it releases lock on A and locks B, immediately. And a 2PL protocol means it should acquire all locks first and then release them. So, it is not in 2-phase.

Please note that it is not necessary that unlock operations should appear at the end of transaction only. Like in T_1 above, we can move unlock (B) instruction to just after lock-X(A) instruction and still retain the two phase locking property. **Such a point is called as a lock-point of T *i.e.,* a point in the schedule where T has obtained its final lock** (end of growing phase). So, we can order the transactions now as per their lock points.

Limitations of 2PL protocol : There are two problems associated with 2PL protocols :
1. Deadlocks, 2. Cascading roll-back.

Deadlocks : 2PL protocols do not prevent deadlocks. The transaction, T_1, is in two-phase but still has a problem of deadlock. This is because if we do not unlock a data item, before requesting a lock on another data item, then deadlocks may occur.

Cascading rollback : Cascading rollback is a phenomenon in which a single transaction failure leads to a series of transaction rollback. For example,

T_1	T_2	T_3
Read (X); Read (Y) Z = X + Y; Write (Z);		
	Read (Z); Write (Z);	
		Read (Z);

Here, the transaction, T_1, writes a value of Z that is read by transaction, T_2, T_2 then writes a value of Z which is read by T_3. Suppose now that at this point, T_1 fails. So, T_1 must be rolled back. Since T_2 depends on T_1, So, T_2 must be rolled back. Since T_3 is dependent on T_2, so T_3 also must be rolled back. This is known as **cascading rollback effect**.

How to solve cascading rollback problem?

There are two solutions to this problem :

(*a*) Strict two phase locking protocol.

(*b*) Rigorous two phase locking protocol.

Let us discuss these two protocols first.

Strict two-phase locking protocol?

This protocol requires that in addition to locking being two-phase, all exclusive-mode locks taken by a transaction must be held until that transaction commits. This requirement ensures that any data written by an uncommitted transaction are locked in exclusive mode until the transaction commits, preventing any other transaction from reading the data.

Rigorous two-phase locking protocol: This protocol requires that all locks are to be held until the transaction commits. **Please note that it can be easily verified that with this protocol, transactions can be serialized in the order in which they commit**.

Most of our DBMS implement either strict or rigorous two-phase locking.

Lock Conversions : Consider two transactions, T_1 and T_2 as follows :

T_1	T_2
Read (A1, *d*1); Read (A2, *d*2); : Read (A_n, d_n); : Write (A1, *d*1);	Read (A1, *d*1); Read (A2, *d*2); print (*d*1 + *d*2);

Now, if I follow, 2PL protocol then the transaction, T_1, must lock item A1 in **exclusive mode** because it has to perform the write-operation on item A1. The other transaction, T_2, which has to read the value of A1 is unable to get shared lock on item A1 until T_1 performs write operation on A1. Since, T_1 needs an exclusive lock on A1 only at the end of its execution where it performs write operation on A1, **it is better if T_1 could initially lock A1 in shared mode and then could later change lock to exclusive mode when it has to perform write operation** and then we can get more of concurrency. This is so because then T_1 and T_2 could access the data items A1 and A2 simultaneously. So, we must refine our 2PL protocol, in which **lock conversion** are allowed. **Thus objective is to have a mechanism for upgrading a shared lock to an exclusive lock and downgrading an exclusive lock to a shared lock**. We denote the conversion from shared to exclusive modes by **upgrade** and from exclusive to shared mode by **downgrade**. **Please note that lock conversion cannot be allowed to occur arbitrarity. Also note that upgrading can take place in only the growing phase whereas downgrading can take place in only the shrinking phase**. Considering the same transactions, T_1 and T_2, we can run them concurrently using our refined two-phase locking protocol.

T_1	T_2
lock-S(A1);	
	lock-S(A1);
lock-S(A2);	
	lock-S(A2);

lock-S(A3); lock-S(A4);	
	unlock(A1);
	unlock(A2);
lock-S(An); upgrade(A1);	

Please note that a transaction trying to upgrade a lock on an item (I) may be forced to wait. This enforced wait occurs if the required data item is currently locked by another transaction in shared mode. **Algorithm for automatic generation of an appropriate lock and unlock for a transaction.**

We must have a scheme for the automatic generation of locks and unlocks for any transaction. This algorithm is as follows :

Step 1. When a transaction, T_i ($i \leftarrow 1$ to n) issues a read (I) operation, it issues a lock-S (I) instruction followed by read (I) instruction.

Step 2. When a transaction, T_i ($i \leftarrow 1$ to n) issues a write (I) operation, the system checks to see whether T_i already holds a shared lock on the data-item, I. If it does then the system can upgrade (I) instruction followed by write (I) instruction.

Step 3. Otherwise the system issues a lock-X(I) instruction followed by write (I) instruction.

Step 4. All locks obtained by the transaction are unlocked after the transaction commits or abort.

Next we shall discuss those protocols that are not based on 2PL protocol *i.e.*, non-two phase locking protocols.

Non two-phase locking protocols : We now need some additional information on how each transaction will access the database. They are of two types :

(*a*) Graph-based protocol.

(*b*) Time stamp-based protocol.

Let us discuss them one by one now.

I. Graph-based or Tree Protocol

In this protocol, we must have prior knowledge about the order in which the database items will be accessed. Here, the data-items are arranged in a tree form.

Notations used : The nodes of the tree represent data items to be accessed. If (A, B) is an arc of the tree, then A is called as the parent of B. If there is a directed path from A to B, then A is called as an **ancestor** of B. **Please note that in this protocol transactions access sub-trees. Also note that an entity can be accessed after all its ancestors in the sub-tree have been accessed**.

Rules of Graph/Tree protocol : Tree protocol follows certain rules and these are as follows :

Rule 1. No data item can be accessed unless the transaction locks it.

Rule 2. A data-item, X, can be locked by a transaction, T, only if T currently holds the lock on the parent of X, unless X is the root of sub-tree accessed by T.

Rule 3. A transaction, T, after unlocking a data item cannot subsequently relock it.

Rule 4. Transaction can unlock data items any time.

For example,

Fig. 7.3. *Tree protocol*

Where $d_0 - d_{10}$ is data.

Say, now 3-transactions follow a tree protocol on this graph –

T_1 needs exclusive lock on d_0, d_1, d_4, d_9

T2 needs exclusive lock on d_1, d_4

T3 needs exclusive lock on d_3, d_7, d_8

A schedule of transactions obeying the above locks and using tree protocol are as follows :

T_1	T_2	T_3
Lock (d_0) Lock (d_1) Lock (d_4)		Lock (d_3)
Unlock (d_1)		Lock (d_7)
Lock (d_9)	Lock (d_1)	Lock (d_8)
Unlock (d_4)		Unlock (d_3)
	Lock (d_4)	

Please understand that these transactions are not in two phase. This is because the transaction, T_1 , could release a lock on the data item, d_1, after its processing with it is over, thereby allowing T_2 to proceed concurrently. But it does not. But if we use a tree protocol then lock is released by T_1 and T_2 can proceed concurrently as shown above. So, we have a better concurrency now. Please note that the above schedule is equivalent to a serial schedule as follows :

$$T_1 \rightarrow T_3 \rightarrow T_2.$$

If we draw its precedence graph then we find that it does not have a cycle. Hence, the tree/graph protocol ensures serializability.

Advantages of tree/graph protocol : This protocol has many advantages. Some of them are given below :

1. Unlocking may occur earlier in this protocol, so there is shorter waiting time of transactions and hence increased concurrency.
2. This protocol is free from deadlocks and thus, no rollbacks are required.

Disadvantages of Tree-based protocols : This protocol has some disadvantages also and they are given below :

1. Sometimes a transaction may have to lock those data items which it does not need. This additional locking results in an increased locking overhead, additional waiting time and decreased concurrency.

2. If there is no prior knowledge of what data items will need to be locked, then in such a case, the transaction will have to lock the root of the tree. This also can reduce concurrency.

II. Timestamp-based Protocols

This protocol works on a principle that—**"we must have a prior knowledge about the order in which the transactions will be accessed"**. In graph based protocol, we require the knowledge of ordering of data items in the transactions.

How to do it?

To order the transactions, we associate a unique fixed timestamp, denoted by $TS(T_i)$ for each transaction, T_i. This time stamp is an integer (unique) value. It is assigned by DBMS before the transaction, T_i , starts execution.

Timestamps have 2 properties :

1. **Uniqueness :** This property assures that no equal timestamp values can exist.
2. **Monotonicity :** It means that timestamp values always increase.

Please note that the READ and WRITE operations of database within the same transaction must have the same timestamp. DBMS executes conflicting operations in the timestamp order, thereby ensusring serializability of the transactions. If two transactions conflict, one often is stopped, rescheduled and assigned a new timestamp value. **Please note that the fundamental goal of this protocol is to order transactions globally in such a way that older transactions get priority in the event of a conflict**. This method needs no locks and hence, results in no deadlocks.

If a transaction (T_i) has been assigned timestamp, $TS(T_i)$, and a new transaction, T_j, enters the system, then

$$TS\ (T_i) < TS\ (T_j)$$

Scheme Implementation Methods : There are two common methods for its implementation :

1. Using the **value of the system clock as the timestamp**. That is,

   Transaction's timestamp value = Value of the system clock.

   When the transaction enters the system.
2. Using a **logical counter** that is incremented after a new timestamp has been assigned. That is,

   Transaction's timestamp value = Value of the counter

   when the transaction enters the system.

These timestamps of the transactions determine the serializability order. So, if $TS\ (T_i) < TS\ (T_j)$ then the system must ensure that the produced schedule is equivalent to a serial schedule in which T_i appears before T_j.

Problems with Timestamps :

1. Each value stored in the database requires two additional timestamp fields, one for the last time the field was read and one for the last update.
2. It increases the memory requirements and the processing overhead of the database.

Implementation : To implement this scheme, we associate with each data item Q two timestamp values :

- **W-timestamp (Q)** denotes the largest timestamp of any transaction that executed write (Q) successfully.
- **R-timestamp (Q)** denotes the largest timestamp of any transaction that executed read (Q) successfully.

These timestamps are updated whenever a new read (Q) or write (Q) instruction is executed.

The Timestamp-Ordering Protocol : The timestamp-ordering protocol ensures that any conflicting read and write operations are executed in timestamp order. **This protocol operates as follows :**

1. ***Suppose that transaction T_i issues read (Q) :***

   (*a*) If TS(T_i)<W-timestamp (Q), then T_i needs to read a value of Q that was already overwritten. Hence the read operation is rejected, and T_i is rolled back.

   For example, suppose that T_i has a TS of 12.00 PM and W-timestamp (Q) is 12.02 AM. It means that if a transaction whose TS is 12 PM and wants to read the data item which is already written by transaction of TS, 12.02 PM. Thus, the read request of 12 PM transaction is **rejected** and TS(T_i) is rolled back.

   (*b*) If TS(T_i)> = W-timestamp (Q), then the read operation is executed, and R-timestamp (Q) is set to the maximum of R-timestamp(Q) *i.e.,* TS(T_i).

   For example, if a transaction of a timestamp, 12.5 PM issue instruction to read a data-item which is written by a transaction of timestamp 12.02 PM, then the read operation is allowed and R-timestamp for Q data-item set equal to 12.05 PM because transaction of timestamp, 12.05 PM performes the read operation successfully.

2. ***Suppose that transaction T_i issues write (Q) :***

   (*a*) If TS(T_i)< R-timestamp (Q), then the value of Q that T_i is producing was needed previously, and the system assumed that value would never be produced. Hence, the write operation is rejected, and T_i is rolled back.

   For example, if a transaction whose TS is 11.58 AM issues an instruction to write a data-item whose R-timestamp is 12 PM, then it means that transaction, TS(T_i) wants to write a data-item which is successfully read by a transaction of higher TS, then the write operation is rejected and T_i is rolled back.

   (*b*) If TS(T_i) < W-timestamp (Q), then T_i is attempting to write an obsolete value of Q. Hence this write operation is rejected and T_i is rolled back.

   For example, if TS(T_i) issues an instruction to write a data-item with TS of 11.58 PM which is successfully written by a transaction whose TS is 12 PM, then it means that data-item is already written by higher timestamp transaction. So, the write operation of transaction having 11.58 PM TS is rejected and TS(T_i) is rolled back.

   (*c*) Otherwise, the write operation is executed and W-timestamp (Q) is set to TS (T_i).

   For example, if TS (T_i), TS is greater than 12 PM and R-timestamp and W-timestamp is less than TS (T_i) then the transaction can perform the write operation without any problem.

Please note that a transaction, T_i, that is rolled back by the concurrency control scheme, as result of either a read or write operation being issued, is assigned a new TS and is restarted.

We are in a position to solve some examples now.

Example 1. *Consider that there are 2 transactions, T_1 and T_2, defined as follows :*

T_1	T_2
Read (B, *b*); Read (A, *a*); print (*a* + *b*);	Read (B, *b*); *b* = *b* – 10; write (B, *b*); Read (A, *a*); *a* = *a* + 20; write (A, *a*); print (*a* + *b*);

Say, now that T_1 starts at 10 AM and T_2 starts at 10.05 AM, that is,

$$TS(T_1) < TS(T_2).$$

The schedule is as under :

T_1	T_2	Comments
Read (B, *b*);		R-timestamp (B) = TS (T_1) *i.e.,* 10 AM
	Read (B, *b*);	TS (T_2) > R-timestamp (B) so read operation is performed and R-timestamp (B) = TS (T_2) *i.e.,* 10.05 AM
	b = *b* – 20;	
	write (B, *b*);	W-timespamp (B) = TS (T_2) *i.e,* 10.05 AM
Read (A, *a*);		R-timespamp (A) = TS (T_1)
	Read (A, *a*);	TS (T_2) > R-timespamp (A) so, read operation is performed and R-timespamp (A) = TS (T_2)
print (*a* + *b*);		
	a = *a* + 30;	
	write (A, *a*);	TS (T_2) = R-timestamp (A) so write operation is granted
	print (*a* + *b*);	

Please note that from this schedule we find that both the transactions perform concurrently under the timestamp schedule without giving in-consistent results. Also note that this protocol ensures freedom from deadlock, since no transaction ever waits.

Example 2. *If the order of the transactions, T_1 and T_2 given in the above example change i.e,*

T_1	T_2
Read (B, *b*);	
	Read (B, *b*); *b* = *b* – 20; Write (B, *b*); Read (A, *a*); *a* = *a* + 30; write (A, *a*); print (*a* + *b*);
Read (A, *a*); print (*a* + *b*);	

Is this schedule consistent ? Why or why not?

Solution. This schedule will result in an inconsistent state of the database because Read (A, a); operation requested by T_1 is not to be granted because TS (T_1)< W-timestamp (A) which is equal to TS (T_2). So, according to timestamp protocol, T_1 read operation is rejected and T_1 is rolled back. Then T_1 has to restart after sometime and a new timestamp is assigned to T_1.

Example 3. *Say, TS (T_1) > TS (T_2) in above example. Then what will be the schedule? Will it be consistent ?*

Solution. Now, it is given that TS (T_1) > TS (T_2). So, the schedule is :

T_1 will read the A and B modified values because R-timestamp (A), W-timestamp (A), and R-timestamp (B) and W-timestamp (B), all are equal to TS (T_2). Then, T_1 will read the value of A and B only if TS (T_1) > W-timestamp of A and B which becomes possible when it restarts. So, the consistency of the data is automatically maintained. It means that if T_1 is rolled back, it starts again after some time with a new timestamp and produces consistent results.

7.2 DEADLOCK HANDLING

Actually, the solution to inconsistency can lead to deadlocks. If we do not use locking or unlocking of data-items as soon as possible after reading or writing them, we may get inconsistent states. Also note that, if we do not unlock a data item before requesting a lock on another data item, deadlocks may occur. **Please note that deadlocks are preferable to there inconsistent states because they can be handled by rolling back of transactions. The inconsistent states may lead to real world problems that cannot be handled by DBMS.**

The rule is—**"When a transaction requests a lock on a data item in a particular mode and no other transaction has a lock on the same data item in a conflicting mode, then the lock can be granted"**.

In order to understand deadlocks, consider an example given below.

T_1	T_2	Lock granted or not granted
lock-X(A);		Lock granted as there is no other lock on data-item, A.
	lock- X(B);	Lock granted as there is no other lock on data-item-B.
lock-X(B);		Cannot grant lock as T_1 will have to wait for T_2 to unlock (release) lock on data-item, B. So, request is queued up.
	lock-X(A);	Cannot grant lock as T_2 has to wait for T_1 to release the lock on data-item, A.

Please understand that we have used the rule given above to grant/ungrant the lock. In the schedule above, T_1 waits for T_2 to release it's lock on data-item, B and T_2 waits for T_1 to release its lock. **Such a cycle of transactions waiting for locks to be released is called as a Deadlock.**

So, T_1 and T_2 will make no further progress. We now define a deadlock in a more formal way—**"A system is in a deadlock state if there exists a set of transactions such that every transaction in the set is waiting for another transaction in the set"**.

Methods of dealing with deadlock problem : There are two basic methods for dealing with the deadlock problem.

1. Deadlock prevention, 2. Deadlock detection.

Let us discuss each of these methocls now.

1. Deadlock Prevention : We can prevent deadlocks by giving each transaction a priority and ensuring that the lower priority transactions are not allowed to wait for higher priority transactions or vice versa. One way of assigning priorities is to give each transaction a timestamp when it starts. **Please note here that the lower is the timestamp, the higher is the transaction's priority**. This means that the oldest transaction has the highest prority.

Techniques used : If a transaction, T_i, requests a lock and the transaction, T_j, holds a conflicting lock, the lock manager can use one of the following techniques–

(*a*) Wait-die.

(*b*) Wound-wait.

In **wait-die method**, if T_i has a higher prority, it is allowed to wait else it is aborted. This means that when T_i requests for a data-item that is currently being held by T_j, then T_i is allowed to wait only if it has a timestamp smaller than that of T_j *i.e.*, T_i is older than T_j. Otherwise, T_i is rolled back (dies).

For example, say, T_1 requests for a data-item held by T_2 and T_3 also requests for data-item held by T_2 *i.e.*,

$$T_1 \text{ requests} \longrightarrow \boxed{T_2} \longleftarrow T_3 \text{ requests}$$

Then T_1 is made to **wait** while T_3 is **rolled back** provided that TS (T_1) = 3, TS (T_2) = 6 and TS (T_3) = 9. This scheme is non-preemptive as only a transaction requesting a lock can be aborted. As a transaction's priority increases (grows older), it tends to wait for more and more younger transactions.

In **wound-wait method**, if T_i transaction has a higher priority then we abort T_j else T_i waits. It means that when T_i requests a data-item currently held by T_j, then T_i is allowed to **wait** only if it has a TS > TS (T_j). Else T_j is rolled back. For *e.g.*, if T_1 requests a data_item held by T_2 then the data -item will be preempted from T_2 and T_2 will be rolled back *i.e.*,

$$T_1 \longrightarrow T_2 \text{ (Rollbacks)}$$

Now, if T_3 requests a data-item held by T_2, then T_3 waits *i.e.*,

$$T_2 \longleftarrow T_3 \text{ (waits)}$$

This method is preemptive one.

Please understand that in wait-die scheme, lower priority transactions can never wait for higher transactions whereas in wound-wait scheme, the higher priority transactions never wait for lower priority transactions. Also note that in either case given above, no deadlock cycle can exist.

We have to be a bit careful when a transaction is aborted or restarted. Here, a transaction should be given the same timestamp that it had originally. If we reissue timestamps (TS) like this then we ensure that each transaction will eventually become the oldest transaction and so the one with the highest priority will get the required locks. Also, whenever a transaction is rolled back, it is important to ensure that there is **no starvation** *i.e.*, no transaction gets rolled back repeatedly.

2. Deadlock Detection : It is defined as a periodic check mechanism by DBMS to determine whether a deadlock has occurred or not. Actually, the frequency of deadlocks depends upon the query load and the physical orgarization of a database. In 1981, Gray proposed that the deadlock frequency (deadlock per second) is :

(*a*) **Square** of the degree of multi-programming (DOM).

(*b*) **Fourth power** of the transaction size For this a system must maintain information about the current allocation of data items to transactions, provide an appropriate algorithm to find if the system has entered a deadlock state and to recover from deadlock if it exists.

Wait-for graph for deadlock detection : A very simple way to detect a state of deadlock is to draw **wait-for graph**. This graph is constructed and maintained by the system.

Notations used :

1. **One node is created in the wait-for graph for each transaction that is currently executing.**
2. **Whenever a transaction, T_i, is waiting to lock an item–A that is currently locked by a transaction, T_j, a directed edge ($T_i \rightarrow T_j$) is created in the wait-for graph**. when T_j releases the lock on the items that T_i is waiting for, the directed edge is **dropped** from the wait-for graph. **If the graph has cycles, deadlock is detected**. So, we need an algorithm that searches for a cycle in this wait-for graph. The invoking of this deadlock detection algorithm depends on two factors :
   (*a*) How often does a deadlock occur?
   (*b*) How many transactions will be affected by the deadlock?

If deadlocks occur frequently, then invoke this algorithm more frequently. In the worst-case scenario, we can invoke this algorithm whenever a request for allocation could not be granted immediately.

7.3 RECOVERY SYSTEM

Whenever our detection algorithm finds that the deadlock exists then we must recover from it. **The common solution to this is to roll-back one or more transactions to break the deadlock. This proceses of choosing which transactions to abort is known as victim selection. Please understand that we should rollback those transactions only that involve minimum cost**. For this, the criteria used is as follows :

1. Abort the transaction that has fewest locks.
2. Abort the transaction that has done the least work.
3. Abort the transaction that is farthest from completion.

Once we have decided that a particular transaction must be rolled back, we must find out that how far it should be rolled back. The simplest solution is a total rollback—Abort the transaction and then restart it. **Please note that it will be more effective if you rollback the transaction to the extent that it breaks the deadlock**.

So, we have to pick the transaction which is our victim. It may also happen that the same transaction is always picked as victim. So, this transaction never completes its designated task. This leads to **starvation**. Hence, we need to ensure that transaction can be picked as a victim only a small and finite number of times. To do this we try to include the number of rollbacks in the cost factor.

7.4 FAILURE CLASSIFICATION

Many types of failures have been identified related to databases Some of them are–

1. **Hardware failures :** It includes memory errors, disk crashes, had disk sectors etc. It may be due to design errors, poor quality control and wear-out of hardware parts.

2. **Software failures :** It may include OS related failures, DBMS software related failures etc.
3. **Network failures :** When multiple database servers are connected by a common network, errors will come.
4. **Natural disasters :** These are the failures caused by floods, earthquakes, fires or power failures.
5. **Sabotage :** It includes failures due to intentional corruption or destruction of data, hardware or software facilities.

Please note that in the event of failure, there are 2 things that are affected :

1. Loss of **main memory**.
2. Loss of the **disk copy** of the database. Recovery of lost data is possible only if we have a backup of data.

7.5 STORAGE STRUCTURE

Data in a database may be stored and accessed in a number of ways. There are 3 main storage types :

(*a*) Volatile storage.

(*b*) Non-volatile storage.

(*c*) Stable storage

Let us discuss these storages one by one.

Volatile storage : By volatile, we mean those storages that are lost due to system crashes.

For example, main memory and cache memory storages. Here, accessing is very fast as speed or memory is faster and access is direct.

Non-volatile storage : By non-volatile, we mean that those storages whose contents are not lost due to system crashes. **For exampie**, disk and magnetic tape storage. These storages are slower than volatile storages because tapes and disks are electromechanical devices. These storages are normally used for backup data storages only. Non-volatile memory like flash storage has insufficient capacity for most database systems.

Stable storages : The information stored in a stable storage is never lost. Theoretically, it is impossible to obtain stable storages.

The block transfers between memory and disk storage can result in either successful completion or partial failure or a total failure. Our **objective** is that if data-transfer failure occurs, the system detects it and invokes a recovery procedure to restore the block to a consistent state. To do so, the system must maintain two physical blocks for each logical database block. In the case of **mirrored disks**, both the blocks are at the same location. In case of **remote backup** one of the blocks is local, whereas the other is at a remote site. In both the methods the output operation is executed as follows :

S1 : Write the information onto the first physical block.

S2 : When the first write completes successfully write the same information onto the second physical block.

S3 : The output is completed only after the second write completes successfully,.

During recovery, the system examines each pair of physical blocks. 2 cases arise here.

Case 1. Both blocks are same, no detectable error exists then no further actions are necessary.

Case 2. If the system detects an error in one block then it replaces its content with the content of the other block.

This procedure ensures that a write to stable storage either succeeds completely or results in no change.

Please note that the database system resides permanently on non-volatile storage like disks and is partitioned into fixed-length storage units called as blocks. Also note that blocks are the units of data transfer to and from disk and may contain several data items.

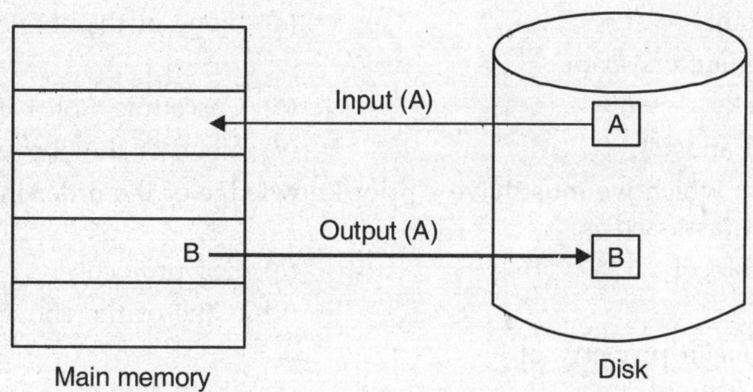

Fig. 7.4. *Block storage operations*

Transactions input information from the disk to the main memory and then output the information back onto the disk. The I/O operations are done in block units. **The blocks residing on the disk are called as physical blocks. The blocks residing temporarily in the main memory are called as buffer blocks. The area of memory where blocks reside temporarily is called as the disk buffer**. Each transaction (T) has a **private work area** in which copies of all data-items accessed and updated by T are kept. The system creates this **work area** when T is initiated and remove it when T either commits or aborts. Each data-item is kept in this work area of T. Now, T interacts with database system by transferring data to and from its work area to the system buffer.

We shall be discussing other techniques in the next chapter.

SUMMARY

Concurrency control and database recovery are intertwined as both are a part of the transaction management. The basic idea of concurrency is to control concurrent data access so that database consistency is always preserved. This chapter highlights all such features.

MULTIPLE CHOICE QUESTIONS [MCQs]

1. To synchronize the concurrent accessing of database items, we use

(*a*) Transactions (*b*) States

(*c*) Locks (*d*) None of the above.

2. When a transaction never progresses then we say that it is

(*a*) Aborted (*b*) Starved

(*c*) Shared (*d*) Locked.

3. During pessimistic approach, the order of operation execution is

(*a*) Read, Validate, Compute, Write (*b*) Validate, Read, Compute, Write

(*c*) Validate, Compute, Read, Write (*d*) None of the above

4. A phase during which all locks are requested is known as a
(*a*) Growing phase (*b*) Shrinking phase
(*c*) Aborted phase (*d*) None of the above.

5. No more lock requests can be asked for in
(*a*) Growing phase (*b*) Shrinking phase
(*c*) Aborted phase (*d*) None of the above.

6. The point in the schedule where the transaction has obtained its final lock is known as
(*a*) Deadlock (*b*) Commit point
(*c*) Lock point (*d*) None of the above.

2PL protocol suffers from :
(*a*) Deadlock (*b*) Cascading Roll back
(*c*) Both (*a*) and (*b*) (*d*) None of the above.

8. A protocol in which we must have a prior knowledge of the order in which the database items will be assessed is
(*a*) Tree protocol (*b*) OSI protocol
(*c*) TCP/IP (*d*) None of the above.

9. Timestamp has a property of
(*a*) Monotonicity (*b*) Irreducibility
(*c*) Atomicity (*d*) None of the above.

10. Timestamps can be implemented by using a
(*a*) System clock. (*b*) Logical counter
(*c*) Both '*a*' and '*b*' (*d*) None of the above.

11. Deadlock frequency is given by
(*a*) Square-root of degree of multiprogramming
(*b*) Fourth power of transaction size
(*c*) Fifth power of transaction size
(*d*) None of the above.

12. By granularity, we mean
(*a*) Size of data item being locked
(*b*) Size of locks
(*c*) Size of a transaction
(*d*) None of the above.

13. The major factor for concurrency control is
(*a*) Granularity (*b*) Locking
(*c*) Time stamping (*d*) None of the above.

14. The assumption that hardware errors and bugs in the software bring the system to halt but do not corrupt the non-volatile storage contents is known as
(*a*) Lock point (*b*) Fail-stop assumption
(*c*) Single fault assumption (*d*) None of the above.

15. Disks and tapes are the examples of
(*a*) Volatile storage (*b*) Non-volatile storage.
(*c*) Stable storage (*d*) None of the above.

ANSWERS

1. (*c*) **2.** (*b*) **3.** (*b*) **4.** (*a*) **5.** (*b*) **6.** (*c*) **7.** (*c*) **8.** (*a*)
9. (*a*) **10.** (*c*) **11.** (*b*) **12.** (*a*) **13.** (*a*) **14.** (*b*) **15.** (*b*)

CONCEPTUAL SHORT QUESTIONS WITH ANSWERS

Q.1. What are the various levels of locking?

Ans. Locking can be done at :

(*a*) Database levels. (*b*) Table levels.

(*c*) Page levels. (*d*) Row (or tuple) levels.

(*e*) Attributes (or fields) levels.

Database levels : At this level of locking, the entire database is locked. So, if T_1 uses tables then T_2 cannot use it.

Applications : This locking is very slow and is thus suitable for batch processes.

Table levels : Here, the entire table is locked. So, T_1 uses a table then at the same time T_2 cannot use it. But, two transactions can access the same database if they are accessing different tables.

Applications : Table-level locks are not suitable for multi-user DBMS.

Page levels : Here, the entire disk-page or disk-block is locked. A page has a fixed size (always power of 2 *i.e.*, 2^i type). A table can span several pages and a page can contain several tuples of one or more tables.

Applications : This type of locking is most suitable for multi-user DBMS.

Row-level : Here, at this level, a particular row is locked. A lock exists for each row in each table. DBMS allows concurrent transaction to access different rows of the same table even if the rows are located on the same page.

Application : It is a costlier method and is much restrictive.

Attribute-level : Here, a particular attribute or field is locked. It allows concurrent transactions to access the same row as long as they require the use of different attributes within the row.

Application : It provides the most flexible multi-user data access. But a high level of computation overhead is also involved.

Q.2. What is a cohort?

Ans. A cohort is a process. It may be one of a number of states like processor wait, execution wait, I/O wait, session wait, a cohort waits for data from one or more other cohorts. A **distributed deadlock** has a number of cohorts, each operating on a separate node of the system.

Q.3. Show that 2PL protocol ensures conflict seializability and that transactions can be serialized according to their lock points?

Ans. Suppose that 2PL does not ensure serializability. Then, there exists a set of transactions $T_0, T_1, \ldots T_{n-1}$ which obey 2PL and which produce an non-serializable schedule. A non-serializable schedule implies cycle in a precedence graph and we shall show that 2PL cannot produce such cycles. Without loss of generality, assume the following cycle exists in the precedence graph :

$$T_0 \rightarrow T_1 \rightarrow T_2 \rightarrow \ldots \rightarrow T_{n-1} \rightarrow T_0.$$

Let α_i be the time at which T_i obtains its last lock *i.e.*, T_i's lock point. Then for all transactions such that $T_i \rightarrow T_j$, ($\alpha_i < \alpha_j$). Then for the cycle we have

$$\alpha_0 < \alpha_1 < \alpha_2 < \ldots < \alpha_{n-1} < \alpha_0$$

Since $\alpha_0 < \alpha_0$ is a contradiction, no such cycle can thus exist. Hence, 2PL cannot produce non-serializale schedules. Because of the property, that for all transactions such that $T_i \rightarrow T_j$, $\alpha_i < \alpha_j$, the lock-point ordering of the transactions is also a topological sort ordering of the precedence graph. Thus, transactions can be serialized according to their lock points.

Q.4. Consider the following two transactions :

T_{31} : read (A);
read (B);
if A = 0 then B : = B + 1;
write (B);
T_{32} : read (B);
read (A);
if B = 0 then A : = A + 1;
write (A);

Add lock and unlock instructions to these transactions, T_{31} and T_{32}, so that they observe the 2PL protocol. Can the execution of these transactions result in a deadlock? [GGSIPU, B.Tech., (CS); 5th Sem., Dec. 2007]

Ans. (*a*) Adding Lock and Unlock instructions

T_{31} : lock-S(A);
read (A);
lock-X(B);
read (B);
if A = 0
then B : = B + 1;
write (B);
Unlock (A);
Unlock (B);

T_{32} : lock-S (B);
read (B);
lock-X(A);
read (A);
if B = 0
then A: = A + 1;
write (A);
Unlock (B);
Unlock (A);

(*b*) **Execution of these transactions can result in a deadlock. For example,** consider the following partial schedule :

T_{31}	T_{32}
lock-S(A);	
	lock-S(B); read (B);
read (A); lock-X(B);	
	lock-X (A);

These transactions, T_{31} and T_{32}, are now dead locked.

Q.5. What benefit does rigorous-2PL provide? How does it compare with other forms of 2PL?

[GGSIPU, B.Tech (CSE/IT); 5th Sem., 2nd Term Exam., Sept. 2007]

Ans. Rigorous 2PL has the advantages of strict 2PL. In addition, it has the property that for two conflicting transactions, their commit order is their serializability order. In some systems, users might expect this behaviour.

Q.6. Show by example that there are schedules possible under the tree protocol that are not possible under the 2PL protocol and vice-versa?

Ans. Consider the tree-structured database graph given below :

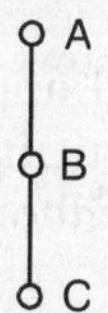

Case 1. Schedule possible under tree protocol but not under 2PL is –

T_1	T_2
lock (A); lock (B); unlock (A);	
	lock (A);
lock (c); unlock (B);	
	lock (B); unlock (A); unlock (B);
unlock (C);	

Case 2. Schedule possible under 2PL but not under tree protocol is –

T_1	T_2
lock (A);	
	lock (B);
lock (C);	
	unlock (B);
unlock (A); unlock (C);	

Q.7. For each of the following protocols, describe aspects of practical applications that would lead you to suggest using the protocol and aspects that would suggest not using the protocol:

(*a*) Two-phase locking (2PL).

(*b*) 2PL with multiple granularity locking.

(*c*) Tree protocol.

(*d*) TSO

(*e*) Validation.

(*f*) Multiversion TSO.

(*g*) Multiversion 2PL.

Ans. (*a*) **2PL :** Use it for simple applications where a single granularity is acceptable. If there are large number of read-only transactions, then multiversion protocols would do better. Also, if deadlocks must be avoided at all costs, the tree protocol would be preferable.

(*b*) **Two-phase locking with multiple granularity locking :** Use for an application mix where some applications access individual records and others access whole relations or substantial parts thereof. The drawbacks of 2PL mentioned above also apply to this one.

(*c*) **The tree protocol :** Use if all applications tend to access data items in an order consistent with, a particular partial order. This protocol is free of deadlocks, but transactions will often have to lock unwanted nodes in order to access the desired nodes.

(*d*) **Timestamp ordering :** Use if the application demands a concurrent execution that is equivalent to a particular serial ordering (say, the order of arrival), rather than any serial ordering. But conflicts are handled by roll-back of transactions rather than waiting, and schedules are not recoverable. To make them recoverable, additional overheads and increased response time have to be tolerated. Not suitable if there are long read-only transactions, since they will starve. Deadlocks are absent.

(*e*) **Validation :** If the probability that two concurrently executing transactions conflict is low, this protocol can be used advantageously to get better concurrency and good response times with low overheads. Not suitable under high contention, when a lot of wasted work will be done. Multi version timestamp ordering: Use if timestamp ordering is appropriate but it is desirable for read requests to never wait. Shares the other disadvantages of the timestamp ordering protocol.

(*f*) **Multi version two-phase locking :** This protocol allows read-only transactions to always commit without ever waiting. Update transactions follow 2PL, thus allowing recoverable schedules with conflicts solved by waiting rather than roll-back. But the problem of deadlocks comes back, though read-only transactions cannot get involved in them, keeping multiple version.

Q.8. The problem of inconsistency, as described in this text, can be solved with the help of locks. How can this be done? Will it lead to deadlock? Is it an acceptable solution?

Ans. Initial values : A = $400, B = $500, and C = $300

Begin (T1)
Lock (T1, A, S) // Granted
Read (T1, A, a) // a = 400
Lock (T1, B, S) // Granted
Read (T1, B, b) // b = 500
begin (T2)
Lock (T2, C, X) // Granted
Read (T2, C, c) // c = 300
Write (T2, C, c-100) // c = 200
Lock (T2, A, X) // Delayed

// Read (T2, A, a)
// Write (T2, A, a+100)
Lock (T1, C, S) // Delayed
// Deadlock !!!! Suppose T2 is aborted! Unlock (T2, A)!
Read (T1, C, c) // c = 300
Return a+b+c // Result = 1200
Commit (T1)

Note that the above example leads to a deadlock. Still, it is an acceptable solution because the ACID properties are preserved.

Q.9. What is Thomas write rule?

Ans. Thomas proposed a new rule named as Thomas write rule which states that "in order to increase the concurrency and to reduce the rollback of timestamp-based protocols, obsolete write operations can be ignored under certain circumstances."

So, the protocol rules for read operations remain unchanged whereas for the write operations, they are slightly different from our timestamp ordering protocol.

To understand the concept of Thomas write rule let us consider the following schedule :

T_1	T_2
read (A, *a*)	
	write (A, *a*)
write (A, *a*)	

Apply the timestamp ordering protocol on above schedule, since T1 starts before T2, so TS (T1)<TS(T2). The read (A, a) operation of T1 succceeds, as does the write (A, a) operation of T2. When T1 attempts its write (A, a) operations, we find that TS(T1)<W-timestamp (A), since W-timestamp (A) = TS(T2). Thus write (A, a) by T1 is rejected and transaction T1 must be rolled back.

Although the rollback of T1 is required by the timestamp-ordering protocol it is unnecessary. Since T2 has already written A, the value of T1 is attempting to write is one that will never need to be read. Any transcation T_i with $TS(T_i)$<TS(T1) that attempts a read (A) will be rolled back, since $TS(T_i)$<W-timestamp (A) and any transaction Tj with TS(Tj)>TS(T2) must read value of A written by T2, rather than the value written by T1.

Modified Write Rule : Suppose that transaction T_i issues write (Q)

1. If TS (T_i)<R-timestamp (Q) then the value of Q that T_i is producing was previously needed and it was assumed that the value would never be produced. Hence, the write operation is rejected, and T_i is rolled back. (Same as timestamp based protocol)
2. If $TS(T_i)$<W-timestamp (Q) then T_i attempting to write an obsolete value of Q. Hence this write operation can be ignored. (Note the difference).
3. Otherwise, the write operation is executed and W-timestamp (Q) is set $TS(T_i)$. (Same as timestamp based protocol)

The difference between the preceding rules and those of time-stamp based protocol lies in the second rule. The timestamp-ordering protocol requires that T_i be rolled back if T_i issues write (Q) and $TS(T_i)$<Timestamp (Q). However here, in this case

where TS(T_i)<W-timestamp (Q) we ignore the obsolete write. This modification to the timestamp odering protocol is called Thomas write rule.

Q.10. Timestamp ordering protocol has three basic variants. Name them and define them.

Ans. The three basic variants of TSO protocol are as follows –

(*a*) Total timestamp ordering.

(*b*) Partial timestamp ordering.

(*c*) Multiversion timestamp ordering.

Total timestamp ordering : This algorithm depends maintaining access to granules in timestamp order by aborting one of the transactions involved in any conflicting access.

Partial timestamp ordering : In this ordering, only non-permutable actions are ordered to improve upon the total timestamp ordering. This algorithm allows the granule to be read by any transaction younger than the last transaction that updated the granule.

Multiversion timestamp ordering : This algorithm stores several versions of an updated granule, allowing transactions to see a consistent set versions for all granules it accesses. A transaction that requires read access to granule sees the youngest version that is older than the transaction *i.e.,* the version having a timestamp equal to or immediately below the transaction's timestamp.

NOTE : Granule timestamp is a record of the timestamp of the last transaction to access it.

Q.11. Differetiate between wait-die and wound-wait schemes?

Ans.

S. No.	Wait-die Scheme	Wound-wait Scheme
1.	In this scheme, lower priority transaction can never wait for higher priority transactions.	In this scheme, higher priority transactions never wait for lower priority transactions.
2.	It is a non-preemptive scheme as only a transaction requesting a lock can be aborted.	It is a preemptive technique and is a counterpart to the wait-die scheme.
3.	Here, an older transaction must wait for a younger one to release its data-item.	Here, an older transaction never waits for a younger transaction.
4.	A transaction may die several times.	Few rollbacks occur here.

Q.12. What is timeout-based scheme? What are its advantages and limitations?

Ans. A simple approach for deadlock handling is based on **lock timeouts**.

Approach used : A transaction that has requested a lock waits for at most a specified amount of time. If the lock has not been granted within that time, the transaction is said to **time out**, it rolls itself back and restarts. If this was in fact a deadlock, one or more transactions involved in the deadlock will time out and rollback, allowing the others to proceed.

Advantages of timeout based scheme :

1. It is quite easy to implement.
2. It works well if transactions are short.
3. It works well if long waits are likely to be due to deadlocks.

Disadvantages of timeout-based scheme :

1. It is quite difficult to decide, how long a transaction must wait before timing out. **Please note that if the wait is longer, then it results in unnecessary delays once a deadlock has occurred. Also note that too short a wait, results in transaction rollback even when there is no deadlock.** This may lead to wasted resources also.
2. **Starvation** may also accur. Hence, these schemes have limited practical applicability.

Q.13. What is multiple granularity? Explain with an example?

Ans. Granularity means the size of the data-item being locked. **If the granularity of a data-item is very large then overhead to locking is very low.**

Two cases arise : 1. Granularity is large, 2. Granularity is small.

Case 1. ***Granularity is large :*** If we select the data-item as whole database, then a transaction, T, when accessing even a small portion of the database, will lock the entire database. So, other transactions would not be able to do concurrent accesses.

Case 2. ***Granularity is small :*** If the granularity is very small, say a field of a record, then the number of locks to be maintained would increase causing higher overhead.

For example, consider a tree having four levels of nodes *i.e.,*

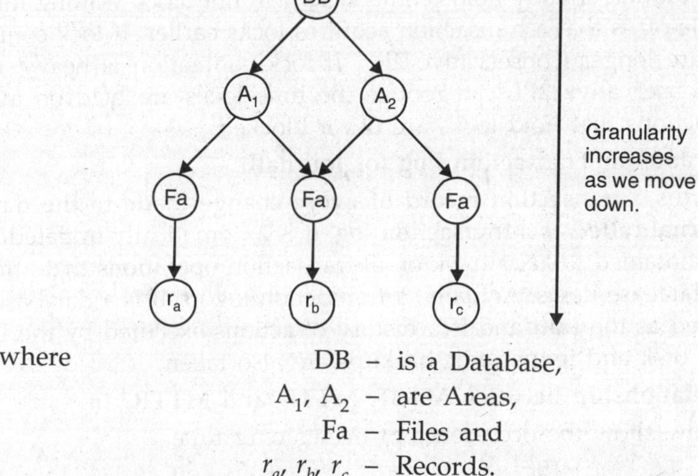

where DB – is a Database,
A_1, A_2 – are Areas,
Fa – Files and
r_a, r_b, r_c – Records.

Here, the highest level represents the entire database. Below it are the nodes of type area. **Please note that a database consists of exactly these areas**. Each area in turn has nodes of type file as its children. Each area contains exactly those files that are its child nodes. **No file is in more than one area**. Finally, each file has nodes of type record. As before, the file consists of exactly those records that are its child nodes and no record can be present in more than one file. **Also note that each node in the tree can be locked individually**.

In multiple granularity locking, each transaction may use a most appropriate granularity for its mode of operations. So, we may consider a database as the hierarchy of various modes. **Please understand that if a** node is locked in an intension mode, explicit locking is being done at the lower level of the tree *i.e.,* at a finer granularity. Intension locks are put on all the ancestors of a node before that node is locked explicitly. Thus, a transaction does not need to search the entire tree to determine whether it can lock a node successfully. In general, a transaction rolling to lock a node (say, X), must traverse a path in the tree from the root to X. While doing the traversal, the transaction, T, locks the various nodes in an intension mode.

Q.14. How is detection different from prevention?

Ans. **In prevention-based schemes**, the abort mechanism is used preemptively in order to avoid deadlocks. On the other hand, **in detection-based schemes**, the transactions in a deadlock cycle hold locks that prevent other transactions from progress. System throughput is reduced because many transactions may be blocked, waiting to obtain locks currently held by deadlocked transactions.

There is the fundamental trade-of between these prevention and detection approaches to deadlocks : loss of work due to preemptive aborts versus loss of work due to blocked transactions in a deadlock cycle. We can increase the frequency with which we check for deadlock cycles, and thereby reduce the amount of work lost due to blocked transaction, but this entails a corresponding increase in the cost of the deadlock detection mechanism.

A variant of 2PL called **Conservative 2PL** can also prevent deadlocks. Under Conservative 2PL, a transaction obtains all the locks that it will ever need when it begins, or blocks waiting for these locks to become available. This scheme ensures that there will not be any deadlocks, and, perhaps more importantly, that a transaction that already holds some locks will not block waiting for other locks. The trade-off is that a transaction acquires locks earlier. If lock contention is low, locks are longer Conservative 2PL. If lock contention is heavy, on the other hand, Conservative 2PL can reduce the time locks are held on average, because transactions that hold locks are never blocked.

Q.15. Write a short note on Transaction Log (or Journal).

Ans. **DBMS maintains a transaction record of every change made to the database into a log /journal called as a transaction log**. It is automatically updated by the DBMS. It is maintained to keep track of all transaction operations that affect the values of the database items. Actually, a transaction log itself is a database. This log is also called as the **trail** and is a history of actions executed by the DBMS. It is kept on a disk and its periodic backups are also taken.

Q.16. What is the relationship between MTBF, MTTD and MTTR?

Ans. The figure below show the occurrence of events over time.

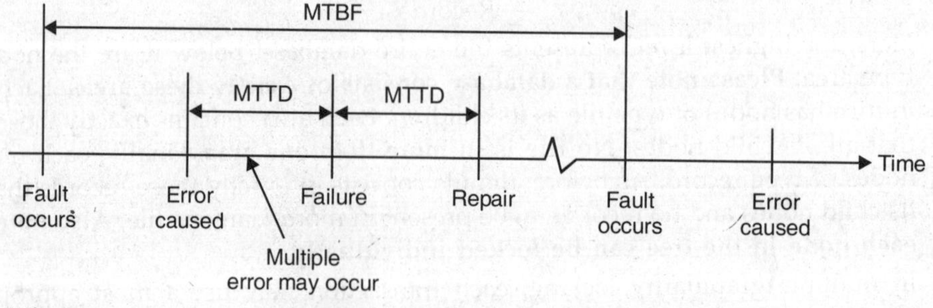

Where MTTF : Mean Time Between Failure.

MTTR : Mean Time to Repair

MTTD : Mean Time to Detect.

Q.17. What is the fail-stop assumption?

Ans. The assumption that hardware errors and bugs in the software bring the system to halt, but do not corrupt the nonvolatile storage contents, is known as the fail-stop assumption.

Q.18. What benefit does strict two-phase locking provide? What disadvantages result?

Ans. Because it produces only cascadeless schedules, recovery is very easy. But the set of schedules obtainable is a subset of those obtainable from plain two phase locking, thus concurrency is reduced.

Q.19. Most implementation of database systems are strict two-phase locking. Suggest three reasons for the popularity of this protocol.

Ans. It is relatively simple to implement, impose low rollback overhead because of cascadeless schedules, and usually allows an acceptable level of concurrency.

Q.20. Consider a variant of the tree protocol called the *forest* protocol. The database is organized as a forest of rooted trees. Each transaction T_i must follow the following rules :

- The first lock in each tree may be on any data item.
- The second, and all subsequent, locks in a tree may be requested only if the parent of the requested node is currently locked.
- Data items may be unlocked at any time.
- A data item may not be relocked by T_i after it been unlocked by T_i.

Show that the forest protocol does not ensure serializability.

Ans. Take a system with 2 trees :

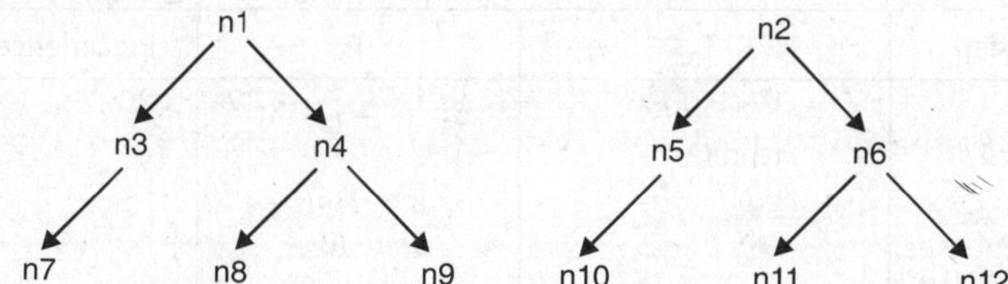

We have 2 transactions, T_1 and T_2. Consider the following legal schedule :

T_1	T_2
lock (n1) lock (n3) write (n3) unlock (n3)	
	lock (n2) lock (n5) write (n5) unlock (n5)
lock (n5) read (n5) unlock (n5) unlock (n5)	
	lock (n3) read (n3) unlock (n3) unlock (n2)

This schedule is not serializable.

Q.21. When a transaction is rolled back under timestamp ordering, it is assigned a new timestamp. Why can it not simply keep its old timestamp?

Ans. A transaction is rolled back because a newer transactions has read or written the data which it was supposed to write. If the rolled back transaction is re-introduced with the same timestamp, the same reason for rollback is still valid, and the transaction will have to be rolled back again. This will continue indefinitely.

Q.22. In multiple-granularity locking, what is the difference between implicit and explicit locking?

Ans. When a transaction *explicitly* locks a node in shared or exclusive mode, it *implicitly* locks all the descendents of that node in the same mode. The transaction need not explicitly lock the descedent nodes. There is no difference in the functionalities of these locks, the only difference is in the way they are acquired, and their presence tested.

Q.23. Although SIX mode is useful in multiple-granularity locking, an exclusive and intend-shared (XIS) mode is of no use. Why is it useless?

Ans. An exclusive lock is incompatible with any other lock kind. Once a node is locked in exclusive mode, none of the descendents can be simultaneously accessed by any other transaction in any mode. Therefore an exclusive and intend-shared declaration has no meaning.

Q.24. Show that there are schedules that are possible under the two-phase locking protocol, but are not possible under the timestamp protocol, and vice versa.

Ans. A schedules which is allowed in the two-phase locking protocol but not in the timestamp protocol is :

Step	T_0	T_1	Precedence Marks
1	lock-S(A)		
2	read (A)		
3		lock-X(B)	
4		write (B)	
5		unlock (B)	
6	lock-S(B)		$T_1 \rightarrow T_0$
7	read (B)		
8	unlock (B)		
9	unlock (B)		

This schedule is not allowed in the timestamp protocol because at step 7, the W-timestamp of *B* is 1.

A schedules which is allowed in the timestamp protocol but not in the two-phase locking protocol is:

Step	T_0	T_1	T_2
1	write (A)		
2		write (A)	
3			write (A)
4	write (B)		
5		write (B)	

This schedule cannot have instructions added to make it legal under two-phase locking protocol because T_1 must unlock (A) between steps 2 and 3 and must lock (B) between steps 4 and 5.

Q.25. Under a modified version of the timestamp protocol, we require that a commit bit be tested to see whether a read request must wait. Explain how the commit bit can prevent cascading abort. Why is this test not necessary for write requests?

Ans. Using the commit bit, a read request is made to wait if the transaction which wrote the data item has not yet committed. Therefore, if the writting transaction fails before commit, we can abort that transaction alone. The waiting read will then access the earlier version in case of a multiversion system, or the restored value of the data item after abort in case of a single-version system. For writes, this commit bit checking is unnecessary. That is because either the write is a "blind" write and thus independent of the old value of the data item or there was a prior read, in which case the test was already applied.

Q.26. Under what conditions is it less expensive to avoid deadlock than to allow deadlocks to occur and then to detect them?

Ans. Deadlock avoidance is preferable if the consequences of abort are serious (as in interactive transactions), and if there is high contention and a resulting high probability of deadlock.

Q.27. If deadlock is avoided by deadlock avoidance schema, is starvation still possible? Explain your answer.

Ans. A transaction may become the victim of deadlock-prevention rollback arbitrarily many times, thus creating a potential starvation situation.

Q.28. Explain the phantom phenomenon. Why may phenomenon lead to an incorrect concurrent execution despite the use of the two-phase locking protocol?

Ans. The phantom phenomenon arises when, due to an insertion or deletion, two transactions logically conflict despite not locking any data items in common. The insertion case is described in the book. Deletion can also lead to this phenomenon. Suppose T_i deletes a tuple from a relation while T_j scans the relation. If T_i deletes the tuple and then T_j reads the relation, T_i should be serialized before T_j. Yet there is no tuple that both T_i and T_j conflict on.

An interpretation of 2PL as just locking the accessed tuples in a relation is incorrect. There is also an index or a relation data that has information about the tuples in the relation. This information is read by any transaction that scans the relation, and modified by transactions that update, or insert into, or delete from the relation. Hence locking must also be performed on the index or relation data, this will avoid the phantom phenomenon.

Q.29. Explain the reason for the use of degree-two consistency. What disadvantages does this approach have?

Ans. The degree-two consistency avoids cascading aborts and offers increased concurrency but the disadvantage is that it does not guarantee serializability and the programmer needs to ensure it.

Q.30. Prove that the basic two-phase locking protocol guarantees conflict serializability of schedules. (Hint. Show that, if a serializability graph for a schedule has a cycle, then at least one of the transactions participating in the schedule does not obey the two-phase locking protocol).

Ans. (This proof is by contradiction, and assumes binary locks for simplicity. A similar proof can be made for shared/exclusive locks.)

Suppose we have *n* transactions T1, T2, ... , Tn such that they all obey the basic two-phase locking rule (*i.e.*, no transaction has an unlock operation followed by a lock operation). Suppose that a non-(conflict)-serializable schedule S for T1, T2, ... Tn does occur; then, the precedence (serialization) graph for S must have a cycle. Hence, there must be some sequence within the schedule of the form:

S: ... ; [o1(X);l ..; o2(X);]...; [o2(Y);] ... ; ... ; o3(Y);] [on(Z); ... ; o1(Z);]...

where each pair of operations between square brackets [o, o] are conflicting (either[w, w], or [w, r], or [r, w]) in order to create an arc in the serialization graph. This implies that in transaction T1, sequence of the following form occurs:

T1: ... ; o1(X) ; ... ; o1(Z); ....

Furthermore, T1 has to unlock item X (so T2 can lock it before applying o2(X) to follow the rules of locking) and has to lock item Z (before applying o1 (Z), but this must occur after Tn has unlocked it). Hence, a sequence in T1 of the following form occurs:

T1: ...; o1(X); ... ; unlock (X); ... ; o1 (Z); ...

This implies that T1 does not obey the two-phase locking protocol (since lock(Z) follows unlock (X)) contradicting our assumption that all transactions in S follow the two-phase locking protocol.

Q.31. Modify the data structures for multiple-mode locks and the algorithms for read_lock(X), write_lock(X), and unlock(X) so that the upgrading and downgrading of locks are possible. (Hint. the lock needs to keep track of the transaction id (s) that hold the lock, if any.)

Ans. We assume that a list of tranasaction ids that have read_locked an item is maintained, as well as the (single) transaction id that has write_locking on item. Only read_lock and write_lock are shown below.

```
read_lock (X, Tn):
B: If lock (X) = 'unlocked"
then begin lock (X) <- "read_locked, List (Tn)",
no_of _reads (X) <- 1
end
else if lock (X) = "read_locked, List"
then begin
(* add Tn to the list of transactions that have read_lock on X *)
lock (X) <- "read_locked, Append(List, Tn)";
no_of_reads(X) <- no_of _reads (X) + 1
end
else if lock(X) = "write locked, Tn"
(* downgrade the lock if write_lock on X is held by Tn itself*)
then begin lock (X) <- " read_locked, List(Tn)";
no_of_read(X) <-1
end
else begin
wait (until lock(X) = "unlocked" and
the lock manager wakes up the transaction);
goto B;
end
```

```
write_lock (X, Tn);
B : if lock (X) = "unlocked"
then lock (X) <- "write_locked, Tn"
else
if (lock(X) "read_locked, List") and (no_of_reads (X) =1)
and (transaction in List = Tn)
(* upgrade the lock it read_lock on X is held only by Tn itself*)
then lock (X) = "write_locked, Tn"
else begin
wait (until ([lock (X) = "unlocked"] or
[(lock(X) = "read_locked, List") and (no_of_reads (X) = 1)
and (transaction in List = Tn)]) and
the lock manager wakes up the transaction);
goto B;
end;
```

Q.32. Prove that strict two-phase locking guarantees strict schedules.

Ans. Since no other transaction can read or write an item written by a transaction T until T has committed, the condition for a strict schedule is satisfied.

Q.33. Prove that cautious waiting avoids deadlock.

Ans. In cautious waiting, transaction T_i can wait on a transaction Tj (and hence T_i becomes blocked) only if Tj is not blocked at the time, say time b(Ti), when T_i waits. Later, at some time $b(Tj) > b(Ti)$, Tj can be blocked and wait on another transaction T_k only if Tk is not blocked at that time. However, Tj cannot be blocked by waiting on an already blocked transaction since this is not allowed by the protocol. Hence, the wait-for graph among the blocked transactions in this system will follow the blocking times and will never have a cycle, and no deadlock cannot occur.

Q.34. Apply the TSO algorithm to the following schedules and determine whether the algorithm will allow the execution of the schedules?

[GGSIPU, B.Tech (CS); 5th Sem., Dec. 2006]

Schedule-1

T_1	T_2	T_3

	read_item(Z);
	read_item(Y);
	write_item(Y);	

		read_item(Y); read_item(Z);
read_item(X); write_item(X);		
		write_item(Y); write_item(Z);
	read_item(X);	
read_item(Y); write_item(Y);		
	write_item(X);	

Schedule 2

T_1	T_2	T_3
		read_item(Y); read_item(Z);
read_item(X); write_item(X);		
		write_item (Y); write_item (Z);
	read_item(Z);	
read_item(Y); write_item(Y);		

	read_item (Y);
	write_item(Y);
	read_item(X);
	write_item(X);	

Ans. Let us assume a clock with linear time points 0,1,2,3, ... and that the original read and write timestamps of all items are 0, without the loss of generality.

read_TS(X) = read_TS(Y) = read_TS(Z) = 0

write_TS(X) = write_TS(Y) = write_TS(Z) = 0

Let us call the schedules in Figure, Schedule 1 or S1 and that Schedule 2 or S2. The two schedules can be written as follows in shorthand notation:

S1: r2(Z); r2(Y); w2(Y); r3(Y); r3(Z); r1(X); w1(X); w3(Y); w3(Z); r2(X); r1(Y); w1(Y); w2(X);

1 2 3 4 5 6 7 8 9 10 11 12 13

S2: r3(Y); r3(Z); r1(X); w1(X); w3(Y); w3(Z); r2(Z); r1(Y); w1(Y); r2(Y); w2(Y); r2(X); w2(X);

1 2 3 4 5 6 7 8 9 10 11 12 13

Assume that each operation takes one time unit, so that the number under the operations indicate the time when each operations occurred. Also assume that each transaction timestamp corresponds to the first of its operations in each schedule, so the transaction timestamps are as follows

> **NOTE:** These values do not change during the schedule, since they are assigned as unique identifiers to the transactions):

TS (T1) = 6 TS(T1) = 3

TS(T2) = 1 TS (T2) = 7

TS(T3) = 4 TS (T3) = 1

(*a*) Applying timestamp ordering to schedule 1: Initial values (new values are shown after each operation):

read_TS(X)=0,read_TS(Y)=0,read_TS(Z)=0,write_TS(X)=0,write_TS(Y)=0, write_TS(Z)=0

TS(T1)=6, TS(T2)=1, TS(T3)=4 (These do not change)

T2: read_item(Z)

TS(T2) > write_TS(Z)

Execute read_item(Z)

Set read_TS(Z) <- max(read_TS(Z), TS(T2)) = 1

read_TS(X)=0,read_TS(Y)=0,read_TS(Z)=1,write_TS(X)=0, write_TS (Y)=0,write_TS(Z)=0

T2: read_item(Y)

TS(T2) > write_TS(Y)

Execute read_item(Y)

Set read_TS(Y) <- max(read_TS(Y), TS(T2)) = 1

read_TS(X)=0,read_TS(Y)=0,read_TS(Z)=1,write_TS(X)=0, write_TS (Y)=0,write_TS(Z)=0

T2: read_item(Y)

TS(T2) = read_TS(Y) and TS(T2) > write_TS(Y)

Execute write_item(Y)

write_TS(Y) <- max(read_TS(Y), TS(T2)) = 1

read_TS(X)=0,read_TS(Y)=1,read_TS(Z)=1,write_TS(X)=0, write_TS (Y)=0,write_TS(Z)=0

T3: read_item(Y)

TS(T3) > write_TS(Y)

Execute read_item(Y)

read_TS(Y) <- max(read_TS(Y), TS(T3)) = 4

read_TS(X)=0,read_TS(Y)=4,read_TS(Z)=1,write_TS(X)=0, write_TS (Y)=1,write_TS(Z)=0

T3: read_item(Y)

TS(T3)>write_TS(Y)

Execute read_item(Y)

read_TS(Y) <- max (read_TS(Z), TS(T3)) = 4

read_TS(X)=0,read_TS(Y)=4,read_TS(Z)=1,write_TS(X)=0, write_TS (Y)=1,write_TS(Z)=0

T1: read_item (Z)

TS(T1) > write_TS(X)

Execute read_item (X)

read_TS(X) <- max (read_TS(X), TS (T1)) = 6

read_TS(X)=6,read_TS(Y)=4,read_TS(Z)=1,write_TS(X)=0, write_TS (Y)=1,write_TS(Z)=0

T1 : write_item(X)

TS(T1) > read_TS(X) and TS(T1) > write_TS(X)

Execute write_item(X)

write_TS(X) <- max (write_TS(X), TS(T1))= 6

read_TS(X)=6,read_TS(Y)=4,read_TS(Z)=1,write_TS(X)=0, write_TS (Y)=1,write_TS(Z)=0

T3 : write_item(X)

TS(T3) = read_TS(X) and TS(T3) > write_TS(X)

Execute write_item(Y)

write_TS(Y) <- max (write_TS(Y), TS(T3)) = 4

read_TS(X)=6,read_TS(Y)=4,read_TS(Z)=1,write_TS(X)=6, write_TS (Y)=4,write_TS(Z)=0

T3 : write_item(Y)

TS(T3) = read_TS(Z) and TS(T3) > write_TS(Z)

Execute write_item(Z)

write_TS(Z) <- max (write_TS(Z), TS(T3))= 4

read_TS(X)=6,read_TS(Y)=4,read_TS(Z)=1,write_TS(X)=6, write_TS (Y)=4,write_TS(Z)=4

T2 : read_item(X)

TS(T2) < write_TS(X)

Abort and Rollback Y2, Reject Read_item(X)

Result: Since T3 had read the value of Y that was written by T2, T3 should also be aborted and rolled by the recovery technique (because of cascading rollback); hence, all effects of T2 and T3 would also be erased and only T1 would finish execution.

(*b*) Aplying timestamp ordering to schedule 2:

Initial values (new values are shown after each operation):

read_TS(X)=0,read_TS(Y)=0,read_TS(Z)=0,write_TS(X)=0, write_TS (Y)=0,write_TS(Z)=0

TS(T1) = 3, TS(T2) =7, TS(T3) = 1 (These do not change)

T3 : read_item(Y)

TS(T3) > write_TS(Y)

Execute read_item(Y)

Set read_TS(Y) <- max(read_TS(Y), TS(T3)) = 1

read_TS(X)=0,read_TS(Y)=1,read_TS(Z)=0,write_TS(X)=0, write_TS (Y)=0,write_TS(Z)=0

T3 : read_item(Z)

TS(T3) > write TS(Z)

Execute read_item(Z)

Set read_TS(Z) <- max(read_TS(Z), TS(T3)) = 1

read_TS(X)=0,read_TS(Y)=1,read_TS(Z)=1,write_TS(X)=0, write_TS (Y)=0,write_TS(Z)=0

T1 : read_item(X)

TS(T1) > write TS(X)

Execute read item (X)

read_TS(X) <- max(read_TS(X), TS(T1)) = 3

read_TS(X)=3,read_TS(Y)=1,read_TS(Z)=1,write_TS(X)=0, write_TS (Y)=0,write_TS(Z)=0

T1 : write_item (X)

TS(T1) = read_TS(X) ans TS(T1) > write_TS(X)

Execute write_item (X)

write_TS(X) <- max (write_TS(X), TS(T1)) = 3

read_TS(X)=3,read_TS(Y)=1,read_TS(Z)=1,write_TS(X)=3, write_TS (Y)=0,write_TS(Z)=0

T3: Write_item(Y)

TS(T3) = read_TS(Y) and TS(T3) > write_TS(Y)

Execute write_item(Y)

write_TS(Y) <- max(write_TS(Y), TS(T3)) = 1

read_TS(X)=3,read_TS(Y)=1,read_TS(Z)=1,write_TS(X)=3, write_TS (Y)=1,write_TS(Z)=0

T3 : write_item(Z)

TS(T3) = read_TS(Z) and TS(T3) > write_TS(Z)

Execute write_item(Z)

write_TS(Z) <- max(write_TS(Z), TS(T3)) = 1

read_TS(X)=3,read_TS(Y)=1,read_TS(Z)=1,write_TS(X)=3, write_TS (Y)=1,write_TS(Z)=1

T2 : read_item(Z)

TS(T2) > write_TS(Z)

Execute read_item(Z)

Set read_TS(Z) < - max (read_TS(Z), TS(T2)) = 7

read_TS(X)=3 read_TS(Y)=1,read_TS(Z)=7,write_TS(X)=3, write_TS (Y)=1,write_TS(Z)=1

T1 : read_item(Y)

TS(T1) > write_TS(Y)

Execute read_item(Y)

Set read_TS(Y) <- max(read_TS(Y), TS(T1)) = 3

read_TS(X)=3,read_TS(Y)=3,read_TS(Z)=7,write_TS(X)=3, write_TS (Y)=1,write_TS(Z)=1

T1 : write_item (Y)

TS(T1) = read_TS(Y) and TS(T1) > write_TS(Y)

Execute write_item(Y)

write_TS(Y) <- max(read_TS(Y), TS(T1)) = 3

read_TS(X)=3,read_TS(Y)=3,read_TS(Z)=7,write_TS(X)=3, write_TS (Y)=3,write_TS(Z)=1

T2 : read_item(Y)

TS(T2) > write_TS(Y)

Execute read_item(Y)

Set read_TS (Y) <- max(read_TS(Y), (T2)) = 7

read_TS(X)=3,read_TS(Y)=7,read_TS(Z)=7,write_TS(X)=3, write_TS (Y)=3,write_TS(Z)=1

T2 : write_item (Y)

TS(T2) = read_TS(Y) and TS (T2) > write_TS(Y)

Execute write_item(Y)

write_TS(Y) <- max(write_TS(Y), TS(T2)) = 7

read_TS(X)=3,read_TS(Y)=7,read_TS(Z)=7,write_TS(X)=3, write_TS (Y)=7,write_TS(Z)=1

T2 : read_item(X)

TS(T2) > write_TS(X)

Execute read_item (X)

Set read_TS(X) <- max(read_TS(X), TS(T2)) = 7

read_TS(X)=7,read_TS(Y)=7,read_TS(Z)=7,write_TS(X)=3, write_TS (Y)=3,write_TS(Z)=1

T2 : write_item(X)

TS(T2) = read_TS(X) and TS(T2) > write_TS(X)

Execute write_item(X)

write_TS(X) <- max(write_TS(X), TS(T2)) = 7

read_TS(X)=7,read_TS(Y)=7,read_TS(Z)=7,write_TS(X)=7, write_TS (Y)=7,write_TS(Z)=1

Result: Schedule 2 executes successfully.

Q.35. Repeat Exercise 34 above, but use the multiversion timestamp ordering method.

Ans. Let us assume the same timestamp values as in the solution for Exercise 34 above. To refer to versions, we use X, Y, Z to reference the original version (value) of each item, and then use indexes (1, 2, ...) to refer to newly written version (for example, X1 , X2, ..).

(*a*) Applying multiversion timestamp ordering to Schedule 1:

Initial values (new values are shown after each operation):

read_TS(X)=0,read_TS(Y)=0,read_TS(Z)=0,write_TS(X)=0, write_TS (Y)=0,write_TS(Z)=0

TS(T1) = 6, TS (T2) = 1 (T3)=4 (These do not change)

T2: read_item (Z)

Execute read_item(Z)

Set read_TS(Z) <- max(read_TS(Z), TS(T2)) = 1

read_TS(X)=0,read_TS(Y)=0,read_TS(Z)=1,write_TS(X)=0, write_TS (Y)=0,write_TS(Z)=0

T2 : read_item(Y)

Execute read_item (Y)

Set read_TS(Y) <- max(read_TS(Y), TS(T2)) = 1

read_TS(X)=0,read_TS(Y)=1,read_TS(Z)=1,write_TS(X)=0, write_TS (Y)=0,write_TS(Z)=0

T2 : write_item (Y)

TS(T2) = read_TS(Y)

Execute write_item(Y) (by creting a new varsion Y1 of Y)

write_TS(Y1) <- TS(T2) = 1,

read_TS(Y1) <- TS(T2) = 1

read_TS(X) = 0, read_TS(Y) = 1, read_TS(Y1) = 1, read_TS(Z)=1, write_TS(X) = 0, write_TS(Y) = 0, write_TS(Y1) = 1, write_TS(Z)=0,

T3: read_item(Y)

Execute read_item(Y) by reading the value of version Y1

read_TS(Y1) <- max(read_TS(Y1), TS(T3)) = 4

read_TS(X)=0, read_TS(Y) = 1, read_TS(Y1) = 4, read_TS(Z) = 1,

write_TS(X)=0, write_TS(Y) = 0, write_TS(Y1) = 1, write_TS(Z) = 0
T3 : read_item (Z)
Execute read_item(Z)
read_TS(Z) <- max(read_TS(Z), TS(T3))=4
read_TS(X)=0, read_TS(Y) = 1, read_TS(Y1) = 4, read_TS(Z) = 4,
write_TS(X)=0, write_TS(Y) = 0, write_TS(Y1) = 1, write_TS(Z) = 0
T1: read_item(X)
Execute read_item(X)
read_TS(X) <- max(read_TS(X), TS(T1)) = 6
read_TS(X)=6, read_TS(Y) = 1, read_TS(Y1) = 4, read_TS(Z) = 4,
write_TS(X)=0, write_TS(Y) = 0, write_TS(Y1) = 1, write_TS(Z) = 0
T1: write_item(X)
Execute write_item(X) (by creating a new version X1 of X)
write_TS(X) <- TS(T1) = 6
read_TS(X) <- TS(T1) = 6
read_TS(X)=6,read_TS(X1)=6, read_TS(Y) = 1, read_TS(Y1)=4, read_TS(Z) =4,
write_TS(X)=0,write_TS(X1)=6,write_TS(Y)=0,write_TS(Y1)=1,
write_TS(Z) =0
T3: write_item (Y)
Execute write_item(Y) creating a new version Y2 of Y)
write_TS(Y2) <- TS(T3) = 4
read_TS(Y2) <- TS(T3) = 4
read_TS(X)=6,read_Ts(X1)=6,read_TS(Y)=1,read_TS(Y1)=4,read_TS(Y2)=4,
read_TS(Z)=4,
read_TS(X)=0,write_Ts(X1)=6,write_TS(Y)=0,write_TS(Y1)=1,write_TS(Y2)=4,
write_TS(Z)=0
Execute write_item(Z) (by creating a new version Z1 of Z)
write_TS(Z1) <- TS(T3) = 4,
read_TS(Z1) <- TS(T3) = 4
read_TS(X)=6,read_TS(X1)=6,read_TS(Y)=1,read_TS(Y1)=4,
read_TS(Y2)=4, read-TS(Z)=4,read_TS(Z1)=4,
write_TS(X)=0,write_TS(X1)=6,write_TS(Y)=0,write_TS(Y1)=1,
write_TS(Y2)=4, write-TS(Z)=0,write_TS(Z1)=4
T2: read_item(X)
Execute read_item(X) by reading the value of the initial version X
read_TS(X) <- max(read_TS(X), TS(T3)) = 6
read_TS(X)=6,read_TS(X1)=6,read_TS(Y)=1,read_TS(Y1)=4,
read_TS(Y2)=4, read-TS(Z)=4,read_TS(Z1)=4,
write_TS(X)=0,write_TS(X1)=6,write_TS(Y)=0,write_TS(Y1)=1,
write_TS(Y2)=4, write-TS(Z)=0,write_TS(Z1)=4
T1: read_item(Y)
Execute read_item(Y) by reading the value of version Y2

read_TS(Y2) <- max(read_TS(Y2), TS(T3)) =6

read_TS(X)=6,read_TS(X1)=6,read_TS(Y)=1,read_TS(Y1)=4, read_TS(Y2)=6, read-TS(Z)=4,read_TS(Z1)=4,

write_TS(X)=0,write_TS(X1)=6,write_TS(Y)=0,write_TS(Y1)=1, write_TS(Y2)=4, write-TS(Z)=0,write_TS(Z1)=4

T1: write_item(Y)

Execute write_item(Y) by creating a new version Y3 of Y)

write_TS(Y3) <- TS(T3) = 4,

read_TS(Y3) <- TS(T3) = 4

read_TS(X)=6,read_TS(X1)=6,read_TS(Y)=1,read_TS(Y1)=4, read_TS(Y2)=6, read-TS(Y3)=6,read-TS(Z)=4,read_TS(Z1)=4,

write_TS(X)=0,write_TS(X1)=6,write_TS(Y)=0,write_TS(Y1)=1, write_TS(Y2)=4, write_TS(Y2)=6,write-TS(Z)=0,write_TS(Z1)=4

T2:write_item(X)

Abort and Rollback T2 read_TS(X) > TS(T2)

Result: Since T3 had read the value of Y that was written by T2, T3 should also be aborted and rolled by the recovery technique (because of cascaing rollback); hence, all effects of T2 and T3 would also be erased and only T1 would finish execution.

(*b*) Applying timestamp ordering to Schedule 2:

read_TS(X)=0, read_TS(Y)=0, read_TS(Z)=0, write_TS(X)=0, write_TS(Y)=0, write_TS(Z)=0

TS(T1)=3, TS(T2)=7,TS(T3)=1 (These do not change)

T3: read_item(Y)

Execute read_item(Y)

Set read_TS(Y) <- max(read_TS(Y), TS(T3))=1

read_TS(X)=0, read_TS(Y)=0, read_TS(Z)=0, write_TS(X)=0, write_TS(Y)=0, write_TS(Z)=0

T3: read_item(Z)

Execute read_item(Z)

Set read_TS(Z) <- max(read_TS(Z), TS(T3))=1

read_TS(X)=0, read_TS(Y)=1, read_TS(Z)=1, write_TS(X)=0, write_TS(Y)=0, write_TS(Z)=0

T1: read_item (X)

Execute read_item(X)

read_TS((X) <- max(read_TS(X), TS(T1))=3

read_TS(X)=3, read_TS(Y)=1, read_TS(Z)=1, write_TS(X)=0, write_TS(Y)=0, write_TS(Z)=0

T1: write_item(X)

Execute write_item(X) by creating a new version X1 of X

write_TS(X1) <- TS(T1) = 3, read_TS(X1) <- TS(T1) = 3

read_TS(X)=3, read_TS(X1)=3, read_TS(Y)=1, read_TS(Z)=1,

write_TS(X) =0, write_TS(X1)=3, write_TS(Y)=0, write_TS(Z) = 0
T3: write_item(Y)
Execute write_item(Y) by by creating a new version Y1 of Y
write_TS(Y1) <- TS(T3) = 1, read_TS(Y1) <- TS(T3) = 1
read_TS(X) = 3, read_TS(X1)=3, read_TS(Y)=1, read_TS(Y1)=1,read_TS(Z)=1,
write_TS(X) = 3, write TS(X1)=3, write_TS(Y)=0, write_TS(Y1)=1,
write_TS(Z)=0
T3: write_item(Z)
Execute write_item(Z) by creating a new version Z2 of Z
write_TS(Z1) <- TS(T3) = 1, read_TS(Z1) <- TS(T3) = 1
(Y1) read_TS(X)=3,read_TS(X1)=3,read_Ts(Y)=1,read_TS=1,read_TS(Z)=1,
read_TS(Z1)= 1,
write_TS(X)=0,write_TS(X1)=3,write_Ts(Y)=0,write_TS(Y1)=0,write_TS(Z)=0,
write_TS(Z1)= 1
T2 : read_item(Z)
Execute read_item(Z) by reading the value of version Z1
Set read_TS(Z1) <- max(read_TS(Z1),TS(T2))=7
read_TS(X)=3,read_TS(X1)=3,read_TS(Y)=1,read_TS(Y1)=1,read_TS(Z)=1,
read_TS(Z1)= 7,
write_TS(X)=0,write_TS(X1)=3,write_TS(Y)=0,write_TS(Y1)=1,write_TS(Z)=0,
write_TS(Z1)= 1
T1: read_item(Y)
Execute read_item(Y) by reading the value of version Y1
Set read_TS(Y1) <- max(read_TS(Y1), TS(T1)) = 3
read_TS(X)=3,read_TS(X1)=3,read_TS(Y)=3,read_TS(Y1)=1,read_TS(Z)=1,
read_TS(Z1)=7,
write_TS(X)=0,write_TS(X1)=3,write_TS(Y)=0,write_TS(Y1)=1,write_TS(Z)=0,
write_TS(Z1)=1
T1: write_item(Y)
Execute write_item(Y) by creating a new version Y2 of Y
write_TS(Y2) <- TS(T1)=3, read_TS(Y2) <- TS(T1) = 3
read_TS(X)=3,read_TS(X1)=3,read_TS(Y)=3,read_TS(Y1)=1, read_TS(Y2)=3,
read_TS(Z)=1, read_TS(Z1)=7,
write_TS(X)=0,write_TS(X1)=3,write_TS(Y)=0,write_TS(Y1)=1,
write_TS(Y2)=3, write_TS(Z)=0, write_TS(Z1)=1
T2: read_item(Y)
Execute read_item(Y) by reading the value of version Y2
Set read_TS(Y2) <- max(read_TS(Y2),(T2)) = 7
read_TS(X)=3,read_TS(X1)=3,read_TS(Y)=3,read_TS(Y1)=1, read_TS(Y2)=7,
read_TS(Z)=1, read_TS(Z1)=7,
write_TS(X)=0,write_TS(X1)=3,write_TS(Y)=0,write_TS(Y1)=1,
write_TS(Y2)=3, write_TS(Z)=0, write_TS(Z1)=1
T2: write_item(Y)

Execute write_item(Y) by creating a new version Y3 of Y
write_TS(Y3) <- TS(T2) = 7, read_TS(Y3) <- TS(T2) = 7
read_TS(X)=3,read_TS(X1)=3,read_TS(Y)=3,read_TS(Y1)=1, read_TS(Y2)=7, read_TS(Y3)=7, read_TS(Z)=1, read_TS(Z1)=7,
write_TS(X)=0,write_TS(X1)=3,write_TS(Y)=0,write_TS(Y1)=1, write_TS(Y2)=3, write_TS(Y3)=7, write_TS(Z)=0, write_TS(Z1)=1

T2: read_item(X)

Execute read_item(X) by reading the value of version X1
Set read_TS(X1) <- max(read_TS(X1), TS(T2))=7
read_TS(X)=3,read_TS(X1)=7,read_TS(Y)=3,read_TS(Y1)=1, read_TS(Y2)=7, read_TS(Y3)=7, read_TS(Z)=1, read_TS(Z1)=7,
write_TS(X)=0,write_TS(X1)=3,write_TS(Y)=0,write_TS(Y1)=1, write_TS(Y2)=3, write_TS(Y3)=7, write_TS(Z)=0, write_TS(Z1)=1

T2: write_item(X)

Execute write_item(X) by creating a new version X2 of X
write_TS(X2) <- TS(T2) = 7, read_TS(X2) <- TS(T2) = 7
read_TS(X)=3, read_TS(X1)=7, read_TS(X2)=7, read_TS(Y)=3,read_TS(Y1)=1, read_TS(Y2)=7, read_TS(Y3)=7, read_TS(Z)=1, read_TS(Z1)=7,
write_TS(X)=0, write_TS(X1)=3, write_TS(X2)=7, write_TS(Y)=0, write_TS(Y1)=1, write_TS(Y2)=3, write_TS(Y3)=7, write_TS(Z)=0, write_TS(Z1)=1

Result : Schedule 2 executes successfully.

Q.36. Explain the difference between the three storage types—volatile, nonvolatile, and stable—in terms of I/O cost.

Ans. Volatile storage is storage which fails when there is a power failure. Cache, main memory, and registers are examples of volatile storage. Non-volatile storage is storage which retains its content despite power failues. An example is magnetic disk. Stable storage is storage which theoretically survives any kind of failure (short of a complete disaster!). This type of storage can only be approximated by replicating data.

In terms of I/O cost, volatile memory is the fastest and non-volatile storage is typically several times slower. Stable storage is slower than non-volatile storage because of the cost of data replication.

Q.37. Stable storage cannot be implemented.

(*a*) **Explain why it cannot be.**

(*c*) **Explain how database systems deal with this problem.**

Ans. (*a*) Stable storage cannot really be implemented because all storage devices are made of hardware, and all hardware is vulnerable to mechanical or electronic device failures.

(*b*) Database systems approximate stable storage by writting data to multiple storage devices simultaneously. Even if one of the devices crashes, the data will still be available on a different device. Thus data becomes extremely unlikely.

EXERCISE QUESTIONS

Q.1 Differentiate between the working of time stamping techniques and locking techniques of concurrency control. **[GGSIPU, B.Tech., (CSE); 5th Sem., Nov. 2005]**

Q.2. What is wait die scheme ? **[GGSIPU, B.Tech., (CSE); 5th Sem., Nov. 2006]**

Q.3. Produce a wait-for graph for the following transaction scenario and determine whether deadlock exists :

Transaction	Data Item Locked by Transaction	Data Item Transaction is Waiting for
T1	X2	X1, X3
T2	X3, X10	X7, X8
T3	X8	X4, X5
T4	X7	X1
T5	X1, X5	X3
T6	X4, X9	X6
T7	X6	X5

Discuss two general techniques for handling deadlock (1) time out (2) deadlock detection and recovery. **[GGSIPU, B.Tech., (CSE); 5th Sem., Dec. 2006]**

Q.4. (*a*) Discuss TSO technique for concurrency control.

(*b*) How does optimistic concurrency control method differ from other concurrency control methods? Why are they also called as validation of certification methods

[GGSIPU, B.Tech., (CSE); 5th Sem., Dec. 2007]

Q.5. (*a*) What do you understand by concurrency control. Discuss two phase locking protocol. How does it guarantee serialization?

(*b*) What is a time stamp? Discuss the working of wait and die and wound-wait trasactions.

[GGSIPU, B.Tech., (CSE); 5th Sem., Dec. 2007]

Q.6. (*a*) Explain the concept of recovery in database. What is the difference between stable storage and disk.

(*b*) Compare lock-downgrades with lock-upgrades in concurrency control. Explain why lock-downgrades violate the '2PL' but are nonetheless acceptable.

[GGSIPU, B.Tech., (CSE); 5th Sem., 2nd Term Exam, Nov. 2008]

Q.7. Formulate a concurrency control protocol based on Read and Write locks.

[GGSIPU, B.Tech. (CSE); 5th Sem., Dec. 2008]

Q.8. What is timestamping? How can it be used for concurrency control? Describe this with the help of an example. **[IGNOU, MCA; 3rd Year, June 2004]**

Q.9. What is two-phase comment protocol of transactions? **[DU, B.Sc. (MS); 3rd year, 2005]**

Q.10. Describe strict 2PL ? What benefit does strict 2PL provide? What are its disadvantages?

[DU, DCE; M.E. (CS); 2nd Year, 2003]

Q.11. Explain the Plantom phenomenon. Can it occur in a database where the set of database objects is fixed and only the value of objects can be changed?

[DU, DCE, ME(CS); 2nd year, 2003]

[**Hint.** Consider a transaction, T_1, that executes the following SQL query on the bank database:

```
SELECT sum (balance)
FROM account
WHERE branch_name = 'PNB';
```

T_1 requires access to all tuples of the account relation pertaining to the PNB branch. Let T_2 be a transaction that the following SQL insertion:

INSERT INTO account
VALUES (101, 'PNB', 500);

Now, say S is a schedule involving T_1 and T_2. We expect there to be potential for a conflict for the following reasons:

Case A. If T_1 uses the tuple newly inserted by T_2 in computing sum (balance), then T_1 reads a value written by T_2. Thus, in a serial schedule equivalent to S, T_2 must come before T_1.

Case B. If T_1 does not use the tuple newly inserted by T_2 in computing sum (balance), then in a serial schedule equivalent to S, T_1 must come before T_2.

Out of these two cases, case-B is more curious. T_1 and T_2 do not access any tuple in common, yet they conflict with each other. **Please note that T_1 and T_2 conflict on a phantom tuple.** If concurrency control is performed at the tuple granularity, this conflict would go undetected. As a result, the system could fail to prevent a nonserializable schedule. **This problem is called as a phantom phenomenon.**

Q.12. (*a*) What do you mean by a deadlock? What are the various conditions under which a deadlock occurs? Discuss the wait-die and wound-wait in detail.

(*b*) What do you mean by time stamping protocols for concurrency control? Discuss multi-version scheme of concurrency control.

[UPTU, B.Tech (CS); 4th Sem., 2006–07]

Q.13. Write short notes on any two parts of the following :

(*a*) 2PL

(*b*) Need for concurrency control.

(*c*) Multiversion techniques. **[UPTU, MBA, 4th Sem., 2006–07]**

Q.14. Show an example of deadlock with 2PL. Give two techniques to prevent deadlock?

[BPUT, Orissa, B.Tech (CS); 2nd year, June 2005]

Q.15. Write a short notes on :

(*a*) Conflict serializability

(*b*) Timestamp based protocols. **[Nagpur University, B.E (CSE); 7th Sem., Dec. 2008]**

Q.16. Explain how can one resolve the deadlock?

[Nagpur University, MCA; 2nd Sem., Dec. 2006]

Q.17. (*a*) Explain lock based protocols.

(*b*) What is a deadlock? How deadlock detection and prevention is achieved in DBMS?

[Nagpur University, B.C. (CSE); 7th Sem., June 2007]

Q.18. What are the types of locks? Explain them in brief.

[Nagpur University, MCA; 2nd Sem., June 2008]

Q.19. Write short notes on:

(*a*) Deadlock handling

(*b*) Timestamp based protocols. **[Nagpur University, B.E (CSE); 7th Sem, June 2007]**

Q.20. (*a*) Explain how does granularity of locking affect performance of concurrency control algorithm.

(*b*) What is a lock ? Explain shared and exclusive locks with a suitable example.

[JUTU, Hyderabad, B.Tech (CS/IT); 2nd sem., Apr/May 2007]

Q.21. (*a*) What is a deadlock? How are deadlocks prevented?

(*b*) How does timestamp ordering protocol work? Explain with example.

[GGSIPU, BCA/BIS(H); 3rd Sem., Dec. 2002]

Q.22. Write short notes on :

(*a*) Rollback.

(*b*) Livelocks and deadlocks. **[GGSIPU, MCA; 2nd Sem., May 2003]**

Q.23. Write short notes on :

(*a*) 2PL protocol

(*b*) Reachability Mechanism of persisting objects.

[GGSIPU, MCA; 2nd Sem., May 2004]

Q.24. (*a*) Show that 2PL protocol ensures conflict serializability with the help of an example schedule.

(*b*) Explain timestamp based and validation based protocols.

[GGSIPU, M.Tech. (IT); 3rd Sem., Dec. 2005]

Q.25. What is 2PL protocol ? **[GGSIPU, MCA-3rd Sem., Dec. 2010]**

CHAPTER 8

Recovery and Atomicity

8.0 INTRODUCTION

The process of restoring the database to a correct state in the event of a failure is known as database recovery. It is a service to be provided by DBMS to ensure the database ***reliability***. Reliability here means both; the resilience of DBMS to various types of failure and its capability to recover from them. In the previous chapter, we have already studied the reasons for failure. Let us now see how to recover from it. **But please remember that the database has to be restored back to consistent state from its inconsistent state that has been caused due to failure.**

8.1 CATEGORIZATION OF RECOVERY ALGORITHMS

Conceptually, there are two main techniques for recovery from non-catastrophic transaction failures:

1. Deferred update (or NO UNDO/REDO) algorithm.
2. Immediate update (or UNDO/REDO) algorithm.

Deferred update : These techniques do not physically update the database on disk until after a transaction reaches its commit point. Then the updates are recorded in the database. Before reaching commit, all transaction updates are recorded in the local transaction work space or buffers. During commit, the updates are first recorded persistently in the *log* and then written to the database.

If a transaction fails before reaching its commit point, it will not have changed the database in any way, so UNDO is not needed. It may be necessary to REDO the effect of the operations of a committed transaction from the log, because their effect may not yet have been recorded in the database. ***Hence, deferred update is also known as the NO-UNDO/REDO algorithm.***

Immediate update : The database may be updated by some operations of a transaction before the transaction reaches its commit point. However, these operations are typically recorded in the log on disk by force writing before they are applied to the database, making recovery still possible. ***If a transaction fails after recording some changes in the database but before reaching its commit point, the effect of its operations on the database must be undone*** *i.e.,* the transaction must be rolled back. ***Please note that here both undo and redo may be required during recovery.*** This technique is known as **UNDO/REDO algorithm**.

3.2 TERMINOLOGIES USED

The recovery processes are very much similar to our O.S. functions like that of buffering and caching of disk pages in main memory. In general, it is convenient to consider recovery in terms of the database disk pages (or blocks). Disk is partitioned into fixed length storage units called as **blocks**. ***Please note that blocks are the units of data transfer to and from disk and may contain several data.*** When a transaction starts, the data required for the transaction is transferred from the disk to the main memory in blocks. When all operations are performed on the block present in the main memory, then that block is transferred from main memory to disk for final storage of results. ***The blocks residing on the disk are called as physical blocks. The block residing temporarily on main memory are called as Buffer blocks. Also note that the area of memory where block resides temporarily is called as disk buffer.***

Associated with each buffer in the cache is a **dirty bit**. A **directory** for the cache is used to keep track of which database items are in the buffers. This **dirty bit** can be included in the directory to show whether or not the buffer has been modified. Another bit called as **pin-unpin** bit is also needed. A page in a cache is pinned (*i.e.*, bit-value = 1)if it cannot be written back to disk as yet.

There are 2 methods to flush a modified buffer back to disk. They are as follows :

1. In-place updating
2. Shadowing

1. **In-place updating** will write the buffer back to the same original disk location. So, it over-writes the old value of any changed items on disk. Hence, a single copy of each database disk block is maintained.
2. **Shadowing** : It writes an updated buffer at a different disk location, so multiple versions of data items can be maintained. ***In general, the old value of the data item before updating is called as the before-image (BFIM) and the new value after updating is called as the after-image (AFIM). Please note that in this method, both AFIM and BFIM can be kept on disk.*** So, it is not necessary to maintain a log for recovering.

The following terminology is used in database recovery when pages are written back to disk :

(*a*) **Steal policy** : It allows the buffer manager to write a buffer to disk before a transaction commits. That is, the buffer is **unpinned** (page can be written back to disk). In other words, the buffer manager "**steals**" a page from the transaction. The alternative policy is **no-steal**.

(*b*) **Force policy** : It ensures that all pages updated by a transaction are immediately written to disk when the transaction commits. The alternative policy is **no force**.

Which approach to use?

We use a ***no-steal, force policy.*** With **no-steal**, we *do not* have to **undo changes** of an aborted transaction because the changes will not have been written to disk and with *force*. We ***do not*** have to ***redo the changes*** of a committed transaction if there is a subsequent crash because all the changes will have been written to disk at commit.

For example, the deferred update recovery protocol uses no-steal policy.

On the other hand, the ***steal policy*** avoids the need for a very large buffer space to store all updated pages by a set of concurrent transactions which in practice may be unrealistic. Also, the **no-force** policy has the distinct advantage of not having to rewrite a page to disk for a later transaction that has been updated by an earlier committed transaction and may stili be in a database buffer. ***This is the reason as the why most of the DBMSs employ a steal, no-force policy.***

To achieve our goal of atomicity, we firstly need to output the information regarding modifications to a stable storage without modifying the database. There are 2 ways to perform such outputs :

(*a*) Log-based recovery.

(*b*) Shadow paging.

These are discussed next.

8.3 LOG-BASED RECOVERY

It is the most common structure used for recording any modifications made to the database. In this recovery procedure, a **log-file** is maintained. A log file is a sequence of log records. A log record maintains a record of all operations of the databse. There are four types of log record, namely

(*i*) <Start> Log Record

(*ii*) <Update> Log Record

(*iii*) <Commit> Log Record

(*iv*) <Abort> Log Record.

(*i*) **<Start> Log Record** : It contains information about the start of each transaction. It has a transaction identifier, which is always unique. It's **syntax** is

$$<T_i, Start>$$

(*ii*) **<Update> Log Record** : It describes a single database write. It's **syntax** is

$$<T_i, X_j, V1, V2>$$

where T_i – transaction identifier

X_j – data item

V1 – old data-item value

V2 – New or modified value of the data item.

(*iii*) **<Commit> Log Record** : When a transaction, T_i, is successfully committed or completed, a <T_i, commit> log record is stored in the log file.

(*iv*) **<Abort> Log Record** : When a transaction, T_i, is aborted due to any reason, a <T_i, abort> log record is stored in the log file.

Please note that whenever a transaction performs a write operation, it is necessary that the log record for that write be created before the database is modified. Also understand that once a log record exists, we have the ability to undo a transaction. So, a log record plays a vital role during recovery process of the database. Hence, it must reside in stable storage. As soon as a log record is created, it must be written to stable storage. There are two technique for log-based recovery as follows :

1. **Deferred Database Modification**
2. **Immediate Database Modification.**

Let us discuss these approaches one by one

1. Deferred Database Modification: ***It ensures transaction atomicity by recording all database modification in the log, by deferring the execution of all write operations of a transaction until the transaction partially commits.***

A transaction is said to be **partially committed** once the final action of the transaction has been executed. When a transaction has performed all the actions, then the information in the log associated with the transaction is used in executing the deferred writes. In other words, at partial commits time logged updates are **"replayed"** into database item.

It means that in this case during write operation the modified values of local variable are not copied into database items, but the corresponding new and old values are stored in the log record. But when the transaction successfully performed all the operations, then the information stored at log record is used to set the value of data items, but if the transaction fail to complete, then the value of data item retain their old values and hence in that case information on the log record is simply ignored.

The execution of transaction T_i proceeds as follows :

<T_i, Start> Before T_i starts its execution, a log record is written to the log file.

<T_i, A, V2> The write operation by T_i results in the writing of new records to the log. This record indicates the new value of A *i.e.,* V2 after the write operation performed by T_i.

<T_i, Commit> **When T_i partially commits this record is written to the log.**

It is important to note that only the new value of the data item is required by the deferred modification technique because if the transaction fails before the commit then log record is simply ignored because data item already contain old value due to deferred write operation. **But if the transaction commit, the new value present in the log record are copied to the data base item.** ***Thus log record contain only the new values of data item, not the old values of data item. This approach save the stable storage space and reduce the complexity of log record.***

We are in a position to solve an example now.

Example 1. Consider two transactions, T_1 and T_2 as follows :

T_1	T_2
Read (A, *a*); *a* = *a* – 100; Write (A, *a*); Read (B, *b*); *b* = *b* + 100; Write (B, *b*);	Read (C, *c*); *c* = *c* – 200; Write (C, *c*);

Say, now that T_1 and T_2 are executed serially i.e., $T_1 \rightarrow T_2$. Assume the values of A, B and C before the execution as 1000, 2000 and 3000 respectively. What will be the state of Log Record and Database? What happens if a crash occurs :

(a) just after write (B, b)

(b) just after write (C, c)

(c) just after <T2, Commit>.

(d) During recovery action. **[DU, B. Sc. (MS), 3rd year, 1999]**

Solution. The result of the execution of T_1 and T_2 is as follows :

Log	Database	Sequence of Time
<T_1, Start> (T_1, A, 900> (T_1, B, 2100> (T_1, Commit> <T_2, Start> <T_2, C, 2800> <T_2, Commit>	(Buffer) A = 900 B = 2100 } We do not know whether A and B are there on disk or not because the system decides output operation.	↓

Please note that the value of A is changed in the database only after the record <T_1, A, 900> has been placed in the log. By using the log, the system can handle any failure that results in the loss of information on volatile storage.

The **recovery procedure** of deferred database modification is based on the **Redo operation**, Redo (T_i). It sets the value of all data items updated by T_i to the new values from the log of records. After a failure has occurred the recovery subsystem consults the log to determine which transaction need to be redone. ***Please note that a transaction, T_i, needs to be redone if and only if the log contains both the record <T_i, Start> and the record <T_i, Commit>. Also note that if the system crashes after the transaction completes its execution, then the information in the log is used in restoring the system to a previous consistent state.*** So, use redo operation to get the modified values from the log record. Otherwise, ignore the log record and re-execute the transaction.

Now, say, system crashes before the completion of the transaction :

(*a*) ***After write (B, b) :*** If this is the case, then the log record is as follows :

<T_1, Start>
<T_1, A, 900>
<T_1, B, 2100>.

Since no commit record appears in the log, it means that no write operation is performed on the database item. So, database items just retain their old values. So, A and B are 1000 and 2000 respectively. Thus, when the system comes back, no redo actions need to be taken. The log records of the incomplete transaction, T_1, can be deleted from the log.

(*b*) ***After write (C, c) :*** If this is the case, then the log record state is as follows :

<T_1, Start>
<T_1, A, 900>
<T_1, B, 2100>
<T_1, Commit>
<T_2, Start>
<T_2, C, 2800>

Since T_1 is completed successfully before the crash, when the system comes back then the new value of items must be copied from the log record to the data items. It means that redo (T_1) must be performed to recover the system after crash. The T_2 transaction is not committed, so there is no need of redo (T_2) operation. T_2 is re-executed. Again, the log record of the incomplete transaction, T_2, can be deleted for the log.

So, redo (T_1) is done as the record <T_1, Commit> appears in the log *i.e.*, A = 900 and B = 2100. T_2 must be re-executed and C = 3000.

(*c*) ***Just after <T_2, Commit>*** : In this case, the state of the log record is as follows :

<T_1, Start>
<T_1, A, 900>
<T_1, B, 2100>
<T_1, Commit>
<T_2, Start>
<T_2, C, 2800>
<T_2, Commit>

Here, when the system comes back, there are 2 commit records in the log—one from T_1 and another from T_2. So, the operation redo (T_1) and redo (T_2) must be performed. So, now values of A, B and C are 900, 2100 and 2800 respectively.

(*d*) ***During recovery action*** : In this case, some transactions recover and some may not. To remove such problems, recovery actions are restarted from the beginning.

2. Immediate Database Modification : The immediate database modification technique allows database modification to be output to the database while the transaction is still in the active state. The data modification written by active transactions are called "uncommitted modification".

If the system crash or transaction aborts, then the old value field of the log records is used to restore the modified data item to the value they had prior to the start of the transaction. This restoration is accomplished through the **undo operation**. In order to understand undo operation, let us consider the format of log record.

$$<T_i, Xj, V_{old}, V_{new}>$$

Here, T_i is transaction identifier, Xj is the data item, V_{old} is the old value of data item and V_{new} is the modified or new value of the data item Xj.

Undo (T_i) : It restores the value of all data items updated by transaction T1 to the old values. Before a transaction T1 starts its execution the record <T1, start> is written to the log. During its execution, any write (*x*) operation by T1 is performed by writing of the appropriate new update recoed to the log. When T1 partially commits the record <Ti, commit> is written to the log.

We are in a position to solve an example now.

Example 1. Consider the two transactions, T_1 and T_2 as shown below :

T_1	T_2
Read (A, *a*);	**Read (C, *c*)**
***a* = *a* – 100;**	***c* = *c* – 200;**
Write (A, *a*);	**Write (C, *c*);**
Read (B, *b*);	
***b* = *b* + 100;**	
Write (B, b);	

If we use immediate database modification technique then what will be the contents of log and Database?

What happens if crash occurs :

(a) just after write (B, b)

(b) just after write (C, c)

(c) *just after <T2, commit>?[GUSIPU, MCA-5th Sem., See 2002]*

Solution. The contents of Log and Database are as follows :

Log	Database	Sequence of Time
<T_1, Start>	(Buffer)	↓
(T_1, A, 1000, 900>		
	A = 900 } Uncommited update. If T is aborted, new values must be replaced by old values.	
(T_1, B, 2000, 2100>		
	B = 2100	
(T_1, Commit>		
<T_2, Start>		
<T_2, C, 3000, 2800>		
	C = 2800	
<T_2, Commit>		

Using the log the system can handle any failure that result in the loss of information of volatile storage. The *recovery scheme uses two-recovery procedures :*

Undo (T_i) : Restores the value of all data items updated by transaction T_i to the old values. The set of data items updated by T_i and their respective old values can be found in the log.

After a failure has occurred, the recovery scheme consults the log record to determine which transaction needs to be undone. Transaction Ti needs to be undone if the log contains the record <T_i, start> but does not contain the record <T_i, commit>. This transaction is crashed during execution. Thus, transaction T_i needs to be undone.

Redo (T_i) : Sets the values of all data items updated by transaction T_i to the new values. These new values can be found in log record. After a failure has occurred log record is consulted to determine which transaction need to be redone.

Transaction T_i needs to be redone if the log contain both the record <T_i, start> and the record <T_i, commit>. This transaction is crahsed just after partially committed. Thus transaction Ti needs to be redone.

Now, let us see what happens when a **system crashes** before the completion of transaction :

(a) ***Just after write (B, b) :*** When the system comes back, it finds the record <T_1, start> in the log, but no corresponding <T_1, commit> record. Thus, T_1 must be undone. It means that the old values are copied from the log record to database items. So, T_1 is undone. The old values of A and B are taken from the log record T_1 and T_2 must be re-executed.

(b) ***Just after write (C, c) :*** Here, when the system comes back, two recovery actions need to be taken :

(i) Undo (T_2) must be done since the record <T_2, start> appears in the log but there is no record <T_2, commit>.

(ii) Redo (T_1) must be done as the log contains both the records <T_1, start> and record <T_1, commit>.

So, now A = 900, B = 2100 and C = 3000. T_2 must be re-executed.

(*c*) ***After <T_2, commit>*** : When the system comes back, both transactions, T_1 and T_2 need to be redone because the records <T_1, start> and <T_1, commit> appears in the log as do the records <T_2, start> and <T_2, commit>. So, A = 900, B = 2100 and C = 2800.

8.4 SHADOW PAGING

Lorie in 1977 introduced this technique of shadow paging as an alternative to log-based recovery schemes. ***The database is partitioned into some number of fixed-length blocks called as pages or disk blocks.*** The pages are mapped into physical blocks of storage by means of a *page table*, with one entry for each logical page of the database. Say, there are *n* pages. There must be a way to find the ith page of the database for any given *i.* We use a page table for this purpose. The page-table has *n* entries one for each database page. *Please note that each entry has a pointer to a page on the disk, as shown* in Fig. 8.1 below.

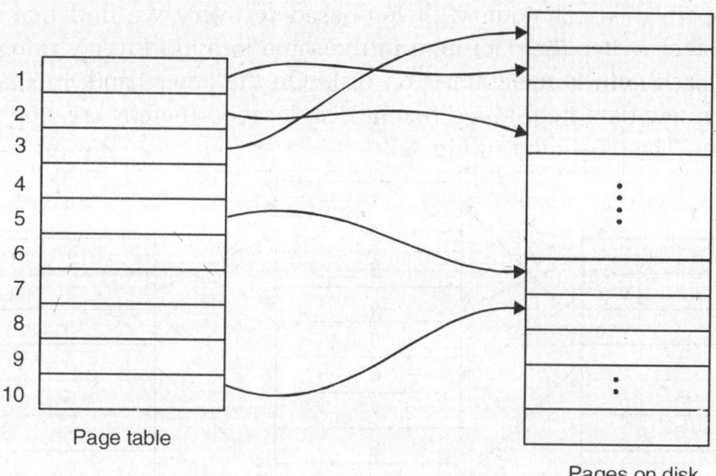

Fig. 8.1. *Page table and disk pages*

So, the first entry contains a pointer to the first page of the database, the second entry to the second page and so on.

Please note that the Fig. 8.1 above shows that the logical order of database pages does not need to correspond to the physical order in which the pages are placed on disk.

Working : The key idea here is to maintain two pages tables during the life of a transaction :

(*a*) Current page table.

(*b*) Shadow page table.

Now, when the transaction starts, both page tables are identical. The shadow page table is never changed over the duration of the transaction. The current page table may be changed when a transaction performs a write operation. All input and output operations use the current page table to locate database pages on disk.

So, we must ***remember that*** out of these two tables—***shadow table/directory is saved to the disk and the current table/directory is used by the transaction, T. Please understand that the shadow directory is never changed and is basically used to restore the database in case of a failure.*** Shadow paging is a technique for providing atomicity and durability in database systems. The page size is of the order 2^{10} to 2^{15} bytes. When a transaction completes, the current page table becomes the shadow page table.

How the write operation is performed?

Say, a transaction, T, performs a write (X) operation and that X resides on the ith page. The write operation is executed as follows :

Step 1. If the ith page (*i.e.*, page where X resides) is not already in main memory, then issue input (I).

Step 2. If first write is being done on the ith page by transaction, T, then modify the current page table as follows :

(*a*) Find an unused page on disk. DBMS has access to a list of unused (free) pages.

(*b*) Delete the page found in step 2(*a*) above from the list of free page frames.

(*c*) Modify the current page table such that the ith entry points to the page found in step 2(*a*) above.

Step 3. Assign the value of X_j to X in the buffer page.

If we compare this technique with **log-based recovery** we find that in log-based method the system writes the data item in the same location (over writing). So, only a single copy of each item is maintained on disk. On the other hand, in **shadowing**, the system writes a new data item at a different disk location thereby creating many copies of the data item. This is shown in Fig. 8.2.

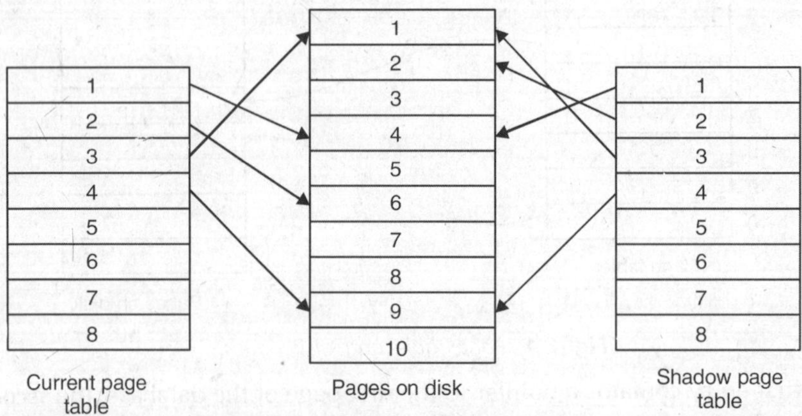

Fig. 8.2. *Write operation on page-2*

We store the shadow page table on a non-volatile storage so that the state of the database prior to the execution of the transaction can be recovered in the event of a crash or transaction abort. When a transaction commits, the current page table is written to a non-volatile storage, as it provides the only means of locating database pages. ***The current page table may be kept in the main memory i.e., volatile storage***. So, even if the current page table is lost during crash, the system recovers using shadow page table.

Use of shadow table when system crashes : One simple method is to choose one fixed location in stable storage that contains the disk address of the shadow page table. After a crash, we copy the shadow page table into the main memory and then use it for subsequent transaction processing. ***Please note that the shadow page table will point to be database pages corresponding to the state of the database prior to any transaction that was active at the time of the crash. This is the reason as to why aborts are automatic.***There is no need of invoking undo operations as required in log-based technique.

How commit operation is pereformed?

1. Flush all modified pages in main memory to disk.

2. Output current page table to disk.
3. Make the current page the new shadow page table.

Keep a pointer to the shadow page table at a fixed (known) location on disk. To make the current page table the new shadow page table, simply update the pointer to point to current page table on disk. Once pointer to shadow page table has been written, transaction is committed. No recovery is needed after a crash *i.e.,* new transactions can start right away, using the shadow page table. Pages not pointed to from current/shadow page table should be freed (garbage collected).

Advantages of Shadow Paging Technique : Shadowing has some advantages and are given below :

1. The overhead of maintaining the transaction log file is eliminated.
2. Since there is no need for undo or redo operations, recovery from crashes is significantly faster.
3. The recovery process is simpler.

Disadvantages of Shadow Paging : Shadowing has some disadvantages also and are discussed below :

1. ***Scattering (or Data Fragmentation) :*** In this shadowing technique, it is difficult to keep related database pages closer, together on the disk. This results in ***scattering of data.***
2. ***Garbage collection :*** Each time that a transaction commits, the database pages containing the old version of data changed by the transaction become inaccessible. Such pages are considered as **garbage** because they are not part of the free space and do not contain usable information. Garbage is also created during system crashing. So, we must periodically find all such garbage pages and odd them to the list of free pages. Doing this, naturally adds to more of overhead and complexity on the system.
3. ***Commit overhead :*** During shadowing, the commit of a single transaction involves three steps :
   (*a*) Copy the actual data block from RAM to hard disk by output operation.
   (*b*) Copy the current page table from main memory (RAM) to the disk by output operation.
   (*c*) Change the disk address of the current page table.

   On the other hand, **log-based schemes** need to output only log records which fit within one block if transactions are small.
4. ***Non-suitability for multi-user, concurrent applications :*** As we know that for the concurrent applications, multiple transactions run in parallel. So, now each transaction needs a separate shadow and current page tables. This makes the system very complex. So, shadowing is not suitable for a multi-user system.

We are in a position to solve an example now.

Example 1. Consider a transaction, T, as follows :

T_1		
Read (A, *a*);	// Say	A = 1000,
a = *a* – 50;		B = 2000,
Write (A, *a*);		C = 3000
Read (B, *b*);		
b = *b* + 50;		
Write (B, *b*);		

Explain how shadowing will be done here? What happens if the system crashes :

(a) Before commit of T.

(b) After commit of T? [GGSIPU, MCA-5th Sem., June 2001]

Solution. When the transaction, T, starts the shadow page table stored on the disk is copied to the main memory and becomes the current page table.

When T is executed, the first instruction is executed as follows :

I. Read (A, *a*) : Herein, the block containing the data item, A, is shifted from hard disk to RAM by input (X) operation and copies the value A to *a i.e.,* A = 1000, so $a \leftarrow 1000$. But now $a = a - 50$ (where *a* is a local variable). So, $a = 1000 - 50$ = **950.**

II. Write (A, *a*) : If the block containing data item, A, is not available in RAM, then input (X) operation is performed.

Find the unused space on the disk *e.g.,* 7th page, shown in Fig. 8.3. Delete this page from the list of free page frames. So, now the free page list is :

(7, 8, 10, 11 and 12)

Now, modify the current page-table so that the current page table entry for A now points to 7th page instead of page-2.

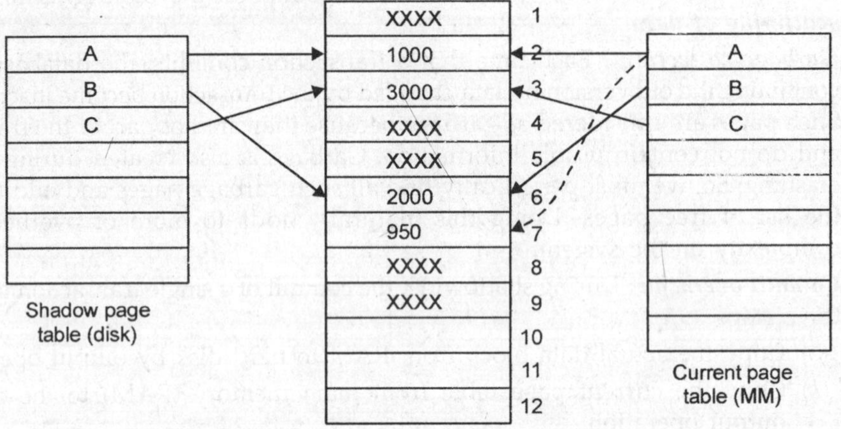

Fig. 8.3. *Unused pages on disk 7, 10, 11 and 12*

As shown in Fig. 8.3, the pointer of A block on current page table now points to 7th page on hard disk (dotted line) instead of 2nd page. So, we assign, 950 value (as $a = a - 50$); to data-item A in MM.

III. Read (B, *b*) : The block containing the data-item, A, is shifted from hard disk to RAM and the value is copied from B to *b*.

Now, $B = 2000 = b$ (say, *b* is a local variable)

$\therefore$ $b = b + 50 = 2050$

IV. Write (B, *b*) : So, now an unused page is found on the disk, as we did before. The next page free available to us is page 10. So, it is selected and the new value of B *i.e.,* 2050 is copied to page 10. This is shown in Fig. 8.4. The 10th page is thus deleted from the list of free pages and the list now becomes (10, 11, 12). So, we modify the current page table such that B now points to page-10, instead of page-6. This is shown in Fig. 8.4 below.

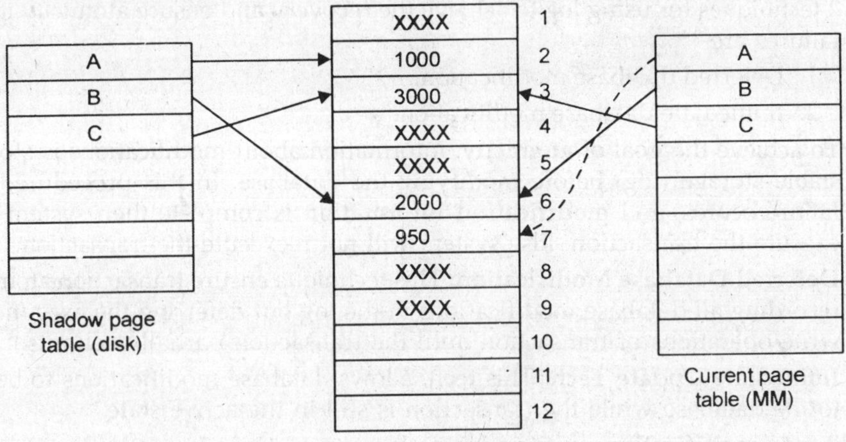

Fig. 8.4. *Value of C being written on 10th page of disk*

Please note here, how the B-pointer from the current page table is made to point to page-10, instead of page-6 where initial value of B was 2000. This process goes on.

Finally, ***commit*** is executed. This step occurring here are as follows :

1. All pages on RAM that have been changed by T are output to disk *i.e.,* A = 950 at page-7 and B = 2050 at page-10.
2. Now, output the current page table to disk without overwriting the shadow page table.
3. Also, output the disk address of the current page table to the fixed location in stable storage containing the address of shadow page table. This changes the address of old shadow page table. So, the current page table now becomes shadow page table and the transaction is completed.

Now, what happens during system crash? Two cases are given in the question.

(*a*) **Crash occurs before commit of T :** Now, the current page table stored in the main memory is crashed. When the system comes back, it gets the address of shadow page table from the fixed location on disk.
This table points to the old value of A, B and C. ***Please note that this is just equal to the undo operation of the log-based recovery technique.*** We can also say that if the system fails before the commit of transaction, T, we will get the previous state of data-item from the shadow table.

(*b*) **Crash occurs after commit of T :** Now, when the system recovers, it will get the address of shadow page table from the fixed location. This table will now point to the modified value of A and B. This is similar to the **redo operation** of log-based recovery technique. We can also say that there is no need of re-executing T and it will recover the data successfully.

2–Schemes to achieve recovery from transaction failures:

(*a*) Log based recovery
(*b*) Shadow paging.

I Log based Recovery

(*a*) It assumes that transactions are executed **serially** i e, only one T is active at a time.

(*b*) It uses a structure called **log** to store the database modifications.

(*c*) 2 techniques for using log to achieve the recovery and ensure atomicity in case of failures are–

1. Deferred database modification.
2. Immediate database modification.

(*d*) To achieve the goal of **atomicity**, information about modifications is stored to a stable storage (log) before modifying the database. In this procedure, if some failure ocures, and **modification information** is complete then system can Re-execute the transaction. Else system will not reexecute the transaction.

(*e*) **Deferred Database Modification:** This technique ensure transaction atomicity by recording all database modifications in the log but deferring the execution of all write operations of transaction until the transaction partially conmits.

(*f*) **Immediate Update Tech:** This tech. allows database modifications to be output to the database while the transaction is still in the active state.

Such data modifications writen by active transactions are called uncommitted modifications. If a failure occurs during execution, the system must use the old value field of log records.

Log is a structure used to **store** the database modifications a record of all update activities in database. Log records significant events during transaction processing and are:

1. **Start of Transaction:** Denoted as <T_i start >
2. **Update log:** It describes a single database write and is denoted as:
   <T_i, X_j, V_1, V_2>
   where $T_i \rightarrow$ Transaction identifier
   $X_j \rightarrow$ Data item identifier
   $V_1 \rightarrow$ Old value of X_j
   $V_2 \rightarrow$ New value of X_j after write operation.
3. **Transaction Commits:** Denoted as: <T_i commit>
4. **Transaction Abort:** Denoted as: < T_i abort > [log resides in stable storage]

Deferred database modification

This method stores the database modifications in the log.

Execution of write operation is done when a transaction is in partially committed state.

(As per transaction's state diagram, a transaction is in partially committed state when transaction completes executing the last instruction).

Execution of transaction, T_i, proceeds as follows

1. Before T_i starts its execution, a record <T_i start> is written to log.
2. Write (X) operation of T_i results in writing a new record <T_i, X, V_2> to the log.

NOTE : Here that it doesn't write V_1 i.e., the old value of X.

3. When T_i partially commits a record, < T_i commit> is written to log.
4. When T_i partially commits, the records associated with it in log are used in executing the deferred writes.
5. If system **crashes** before the transaction complete its execution or if the transaction **aborts**, then the information on the log is ignored.
6. If some failure occurs while updating the database using log records, the log record is written on some stable storage. Hence, T can resume its database modification.

Using log, the system can handle any failure that results in loss of information on volatile storage

The recovery scheme uses the following recovery procedure:

redo (T_i);

- This sets the value of all data items updated by T_i to the **new values**. The sets of data items & their respective new values can be found in the log.
- redo operation must be **idempotent** i.e., executing it several times must be equivalent to executing it once

A transaction can execute redo (T_i) if the log contains both the record <T_i start> and the record <T_i commit>.

Eg. Consider a transaction, T_i. It transfers ₹ 50/- from account A to account B. Original values of account A and B are ₹ 1000/- and ₹ 2000/- resp. This transaction is defined as:

T_0: read (A);
A: = A – 50;
write (A);
read (B);
B : = B + 50;
write (B).

Consider 2nd transaction (T_i) that withdraws ₹ 100/- from account – C i.e.,

T_1: read (C);
C = C – 100;
write (C).

These 2 transactions are executed serially as <T_0, T_1>

The log containing relevent information on these two transactions is given below:

<T_0 start>
<T_0, A, 950>
<T_0, B, 2050>
<T_0 commit>
<T_1 start>
<T_1, C, 600>
<T_1 commit>

It shows the log of the result from the complete execution of T_0 and T_i.

The actual output can take place in database system in various orders. One such order is given below:

log	**Database**
<T_0 start>	
<T_0, A, 950>	
<T_0, B, 2050>	
<T_0 commit>	
	A = 900
	B = 2050
<T_1 start>	
<T_1, C, 600>	
<T_1 Commit>	
	C = 600

If system crashes before the completion of transactions–

Case 1: Crash occurs just after the log record for write (B) operation.

Log contents after the crash are–

<T_0 start>
<T_0, A, 950>
<T_0, B, 2050>

<T_0 commit> is not written, hence no redo operation is possible. The values of amount remain unchanged i.e.,

amount A = ₹1000
& amount B = ₹2000

Case 2: Crash occurs just after log record for write (C) operation.

The log contents after the crash are:

<T_0 start>
<T_0, A, 950>
<T_0, B, 2050>
<T_0 Commit>
<T_1, Start>
<T_1, C, 600>

when the system comes back it finds <T_0 start> and <T_0 commit>. But there is no <T_1 Commit> for <T_0 Start>. Hence, system can execute redo (T_0) but not redo <T_1>. Hence, the value of account C remains unchanged.

Case 3: Crash occurs just after the log record <T_1 commit>.

The log contents after the crash are:

<T_0 start>
<T_0, A, 950>
<T_0, B, 2050>
<T_0, Commit>
<T_1, start>
<T_1, C, 600>
<T_1 commit>

When the system comes back it can execute both redo (T_0) and redo (T_1) operations. For each commit record, the redo (T_i) operation is performed. Redo (T_i) write the values to the values to the detabase independent of the values currently in the database. Hence the redo (T_i) is idempotent.

Eg. Consider the database graph in fig. below:

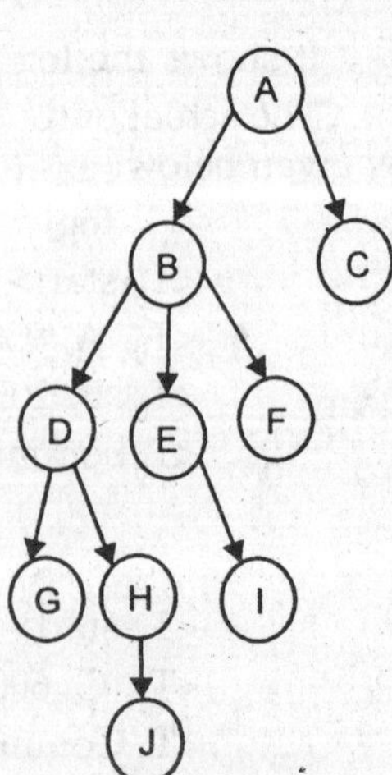

The following four transactions follow the tree protocol on this graph –

T_{10}:
lock_X(B);
lock_X(E);
lock_X(D);
Unlock (B);
Unlock (E);
lock_X(G);
Unlock (D);
Unlock (G);

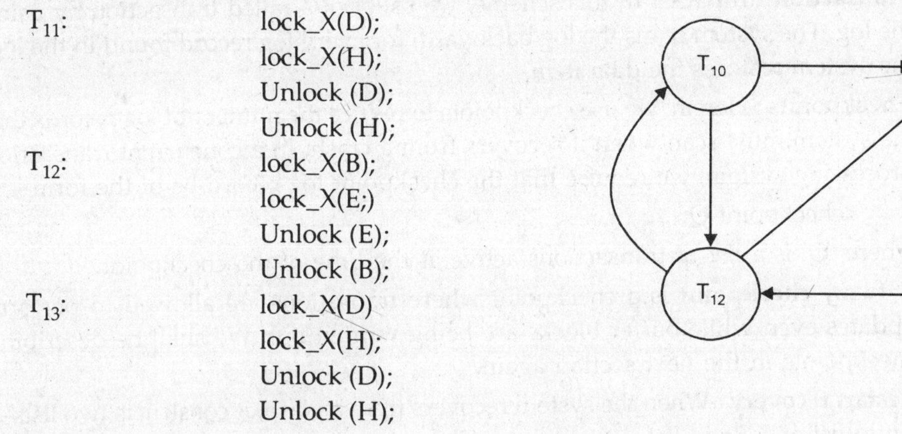

T_{11}: lock_X(D);
lock_X(H);
Unlock (D);
Unlock (H);

T_{12}: lock_X(B);
lock_X(E;)
Unlock (E);
Unlock (B);

T_{13}: lock_X(D)
lock_X(H);
Unlock (D);
Unlock (H);

The schedule following tree protocol is as follows:

T_{10}	T_{11}	T_{12}	T_{13}
lock_X(B);			
	lock_ X (D)		
	lock X (H)		
	Unlock (D)		
lock_X(E)			
lock_X(D)			
Unlock (B)			
Unlock (E)			
		lock_X(B)	
		lock_X(E)	
	Unlock (H)		
lock_X (G)			
Unlock (D)			
			lock_X (D)
			lock_X (H)
			Unlock (D)
			Unlock H
		Unlock (E)	
		Unlock (B)	
Unlock (G)			This Sch. Is conflict serialiable
			∴ Tree protocol ensures conflict serializability

A transaction needs to access data items A and J in the database graph of above eg.1, must lock which other data items ? With it affect concurrency?

Solution. Say transaction T wants to access data item A and J in graph given then it (T) must lock only A and J but also data items B, D, and H(on the path).

This addition locking results in increased locking overhead, the possibility of additional waiting time and potential decrease in concurrency

Prior knowledge of which data item is to be locked is must else T will have to lock the root of the tree itself and this can reduce concurrency greatly.

8.5 RECOVERY WITH CONCURRENT TRANSACTION

There are four ways of recovery from concurrent transactions. They are as follows :

1. **Interaction with concurrency control :** In this scheme, recovery depends upon the concurrency control scheme being used. So, to rollback a failed transaction, we must undo the updates performed by the transaction.

2. **Transaction rollback :** In this scheme, we rollback a failed transaction by using the log. The system scans the log backward, for every log record found in the log, the system restores the data item.
3. **Checkpoints :** Herein, we use checkpoints to reduce the number of log records that the system must scan when it recovers from a crash. In a concurrent transaction processing system, we require that the checkpoint log record be of the form—

   <checkpoint Q>

   where 'Q' is a list of transactions active at the time of the checkpoint.

   A **fuzzy checkpoint** is a checkpoint where transations are allowed to perform updates even while buffer blocks are being written out. We shall be describing checkpoints in the next section again.
4. **Restart recovery :** When the system recovers from a crash, it constructs two lists—Undo-list and Redo-list

   The **undo-list** consists of transactions to be undone. The **redo-list** consists of transaction to be redone. It is our system that constructs these two lists, as follows :

   (*a*) Initially, both lists are empty.

   (*b*) The system scans the log backwards, examining each record, until it finds the first <checkpoint> record.

8.6 CHECK POINTS/SYNCPOINTS/SAVE POINTS

The checkpoint (or syncpoint) is defined as the point of synchronisation between the database and the transaction log file. As we know that the general method of database recovery is using information in the transaction log. So, we need to search the entire log. This is time consuming. So, we use checkpoints. ***A checkpoint is like a snapshot of the DBMS state.*** By taking checkpoints periodically, DBMS can reduce the amount of work to be done during restart in the event of a system crash. The **approach** is to find a point that is sufficiently far back to ensure that any item written before that point has been done correctly and stored safely. This method is called as **checkpointing.** ***Please note that in checkpointing, all buffers are forced-written to the secondary storage.*** The following actions are performed when a system issues a checkpoint :

1. Output onto stable storage, all log records currently residing in main memory.
2. Output on the disk, all modified buffer blocks.
3. Output on the stable storage, a log record <checkpoint>.

Please understand that the presence of a <checkpoint> record makes the recovery process more streamlined. The checkpoint record gives a list of all the transactions that were in progress at the time the checkpoint was taken. Thus, the checkpoints help the system to provide the information at the restart time, which transaction to undo and which to redo.

For example, say, a transaction, T, commits prior to the checkpoint. It implies that <T, commit> must appear in the log before the <checkpoint> record. Any database modifications made by T must have been written to the database either prior to the checkpoint or as part of checkpoint itself. Thus, at the recovery time, there is no need to perform a redo operation on T.

Let us see as to how this information is used.

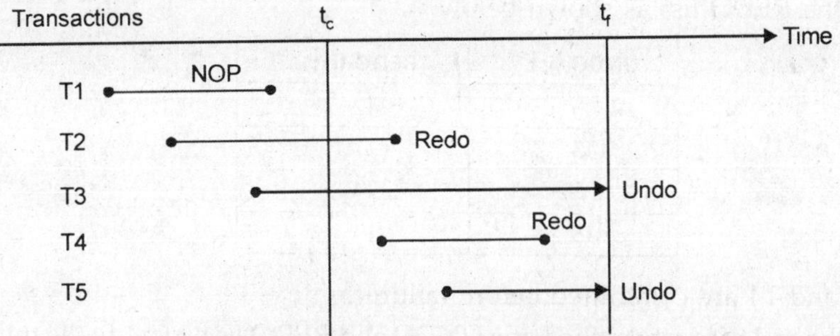

Fig. 8.5. *Checkpointing example*

Let us assume that a system failure occurs at time, t_f. And the most recent checkpoint prior to time, t_f, was taken at time, t_c.

TIP : Checkpoint can be taken at a fixed interval of time, say, every 15 mins. or 30 mins. or 1 hr and so on.

Now, referring to Fig. 8.5, we observe that T1 completed successfully prior to time, t_c. T2 started prior to t_c and completed successfully after time, t_c but before time, t_f. T3 also started prior to t_c but could not complete by time, t_f. T4 started after time, t_c, and completed successfully before time, t_f. Also, T5 transaction started after time, t_c, but did not complete by time, t_f.

Please understand that in case of immediate modification technique, those transactions that have <T, start> and <T, commit> must be **'redone'** and those transactions that have only <T, start> (and not <T, commit>) must be **'undone'**. So, when the system is restarted in case of immediate database modification, ***T3 and T5 must be undone and T2 and T4 must be redone,*** in our example. ***Please note, however, that the transactions of type T1, do not enter in the restart-process at all, because their updates were forced to the database at time t_c, as a part of the checkpoint process.***

How are UNDO and REDO lists maintained?

During **restart time**, the system firstly goes through the following procedure in order to identify all transaction of types T2 to T5 :

1. (*a*) Set UNDO list equal to the list of all transactions executing at the time of most recent checkpoint record.

   (*b*) Set the REDO list to empty as shown below :

   Undo-list :

T2	T3	

   Redo-list :

2. Search forward through the log, starting from the checkpoint record.
3. If a BEGIN TRANSACTION log entry is found for transaction, T, then add T to the UNDO-list *i.e.,*

   Undo-list :

T2	T3	T4	T5

   And Redo-list is still empty.

   Note that T4 and T5 begin its operations after checkpoint.

4. If a COMMIT log entry is found for transaction, T, then move T from the UNDO-list to the REDO-list as shown below :

UNDO list	REDO-list
	T2
T3	
	T4
T5	

So, T2 and T4 are committed before failure.

5. When the end of log is reached, the UNDO and REDO lists identify the transactions, T3 and T5 and T2 and T4 respectively.

Please note that the system works backward through the log, undoing the transactions in the UNDO and then it works forward again, redoing the transactions in the REDO list. Also note that this process of restoring the database to a consistent state by undoing work is known as backward recovery. And restoring it to a consistent state by redoing work is known as forward recovery.

It is after this that when all such recovery activity is complete, then only the system is ready to accept the new task.

SUMMARY

When a transaction starts, the data required for the transaction is transferred from the disk to the main memory (RAM) in blocks. When all the operations are performed on the blocks present in the main memory then that block is transferred from main memory to disk for the final storage of results. The blocks residing on the disk are **physical blocks** and those residing temporarily in the main memory are the **Buffer blocks.** The area where blocks reside temporarily is called as a **disk buffer**. Input operation is to transfer the physical block to the main memory. Output operation is to transfer the buffer block in main memory to the disk. These concepts have been dealt in detail in this chapter.

MULTIPLE CHOICE QUESTIONS [MCQs]

1. The process of restoring the database to a correct state in the event of a failure is known as :

(*a*) Database recovery (*b*) Database modification
(*c*) Reliability of database (*d*) None of the above.

2. The blocks residing on the disk are called as

(*a*) Physical blocks (*b*) Buffer blocks
(*c*) Disk buffer (*d*) None of the above.

3. A sequence of log record is called as a

(*a*) File (*b*) Database
(*c*) Log-file (*d*) None of the above

4. Shadow paging was introduced by

(*a*) Boehm (*b*) E.F. Codd
(*c*) Lorie (*d*) None of the above.

5. Shadowing maintains

(*a*) 2 tables (*b*) 3 tables
(*c*) 4 tables (*d*) None of the above.

6. The page size in shadowing technique is of the order
   (*a*) 2^{10} to 2^{15} bytes (*b*) 2^{11} to 2^{15} bytes
   (*c*) 2^{12} to 2^{16} bytes (*d*) 2^{13} to 2^{17} bytes
7. Shadowing may result in
   (*a*) Page loss (*b*) Data scattering
   (*c*) Page swap (*d*) None of the above
8. A checkpoint where transactions are allowed to perform updates even while buffer blocks are being written out is called as a
   (*a*) Buffer (*b*) Fuzzy checkpoint
   (*c*) Shadow paging (*d*) None of the above
9. The point of synchronisation between the database and the transaction log file is called as a
   (*a*) Checkpoint (*b*) Fuzzy checkpoint
   (*c*) UNDO and REDO (*d*) None of the above.
10. Shadow paging is used for
    (*a*) Writing same item at same location
    (*b*) Writing same item it different location
    (*c*) Creaing shadows
    (*d*) None of the above.

ANSWERS

1. (*a*) **2.** (*a*) **3.** (*c*) **4.** (*c*) **5.** (*a*) **6.** (*a*) **7.** (*b*) **8.** (*b*)
9. (*a*) **10.** (*b*)

CONCEPTUAL SHORT QUESTIONS WITH ANSWERS

Q.1. What is WAL rule?

Ans. It is a fundamental rule and is stated as follows—"***It ensures that a record of every change to the database is available while attempting to recover from a crash.***" Before a block of data in the main memory can be output to the database (in non-volatile storage), all log records pertaining to data in that block must have been output to stable storage. This is ***write-ahead logging (WAL) rule.***

So, before writing a page to disk, every update log record that describes a change to this page must be forced to stable storage. This is accomplished by forcing all by records to a stable storage before writing a page to disk.

Q.2. How do we recover when a failure results in loss of data from the non-volatile storage?

Ans. The basic technique for non-volatile storages is to dump the entire content of the database to stable storage periodically (say, once per day). ***For example,*** we may dump the database to one or more magnetic tapes. If a failure occurs that results in the loss of physical database blocks, then the most recent dump is used in restoring the database to a previous consistent state. Once this restoration is accomplished, the system uses the log to bring the database system to the most recent consistent state. To recover from the loss of non-volatile storage, we restore the database to disk using the most recent dump. Then the log is consulted and all the transactions that have committed since the most recent dump occurred are redone. ***Please note here that no UNDO operations need to be executed because dump already contains the old values of data items. Also note that a dump of the***

database contents is called as an archival dump because we can archieve the dumps and use them later to examine old states of the database. Dumps of a database and checkpointing of buffers are similar.

Q.3. Assume that immediate modification is used in a system. Show, by an example, how an inconsistent database state could result if log records for a transaction are not output to table storage prior to data updated by the transaction being written to disk.

Ans. Consider a banking scheme and a transaction which transfer $50 from account A to account B. The transaction has the following steps :

(*a*) **read** (A, a_1)

(*b*) $a_1 : a_1 - 50$

(*c*) **write** (A, a_1)

(*d*) **read** (B, b_1)

(*e*) $b_1 : b_1 + 50$

(*f*) **write** (B, b_1)

Suppose the system crashes after the transaction commits, but before its log records are flushed to stable storage. Further assume that at the time of the crash the update of A in the third step alone had actually been propagated to disk whereas the buffer page containing B was not yet written to disk. When the system comes up it is in an inconsistent state, but recovery is not possible because there are no log records corresponding to this transaction in stable storage.

Q.4. Explain the purpose of the checkpoint mechanism. How often should checkpoints be performed? How does the frequency of checkpoints affect

- **System performance when no failure occurs**
- **The time it takes to recover from a system crash**
- **The time it takes to recover from a disk crash**

Ans. Checkpointing is done with log-based recovery schemes to reduce the time required for recovery after a crash. If there is no checkpointing, then the entire log must be searched after a crash, and all transactions undone/redone from the log. If checkpointing had been performed, then most of the log-records prior to the checkpoint can be ignored at the time of recovery.

Another reason to perform checkpoints is to clear log-records from stable storage as it gets full.

Since checkpoints cause some loss in performance while they are being taken, their frequency should be reduced if fast recovery is not critical. If we need fast recovery, checkpointing, frequency should be increased. If the amount of stable storage available is less, frequent checkpointing is unavoidable. Checkpoints have no effect on recovery from a disk crash; archival dumps are the equivalent of checkpoints for recovery from disk crashes.

Q.5. Explain how the buffer manager may cause the database to become inconsistent if some log records pertaining to a block are not output to stable storage before the block is output to disk.

Ans. If a data item x is modified on disk by a transaction before the corresponding log record is written to stable storage, then the only record of the old value of x is in main memory where it would be lost in a crash. If the transaction had not yet finished at the time of the crash, an unrecoverable inconsistency will result.

Q.6. Explain the benefits of logical logging. Give examples of one situation where logical logging is preferable to physical logging and one situation where physical logging is preferable to logical logging.

Ans. Logical logging has less log space requirement, and with logical undo logging it allows early release of locks. This is desirable in situations like concurrency control for index structures, where a very high degree of concurrency is required. An advantage of employing physical redo logging is that fuzzy checkpoints are possible. Thus in a system which needs to perform frequent checkpoints, this reduces checkpointing overhead.

Q.7. Explain the difference between a "system crash" and a "disaster."

Ans. In a system crash, the CPU goes down, and disk may also crash. But stable-storage at the site is assumed to survive systm crashes. In a "disaster", *everything* at a site is destroyed. Stable storage needs to be distributed to survive disasters.

Q.8. For each of the following requirements, identify the best choice of degree of durability in a remote backup system :

(*a*) Data loss must be avoided but some loss of availability may be tolerated.

(*b*) Transaction commit must be accomplished quickly, even at the cost of loss of some commited transactions in a disaster.

(*c*) A high degree of availability and durability is required, but a longer running time for the transaction commit protocol is acceptable.

Ans. (*a*) Two very safe is suitable here because it gurantees durability of updates by committed transactions, though it can proceed only if both primary and backup sites are up. Availability is low, but it is mentioned that this is acceptable.

(*b*) One safe committing, is fast as it does not have to wait for the logs to reach the backup site. Since data loss can be tolerated, this is the best option.

(*c*) With two safe committing, the probability of data loss is quite low, and also commits can proceed as long as at least the primary site is up. Thus availability is high. Commits take more time than in the one safe protocol, but that is mentioned as acceptable.

Q.9. What implications would a no-steal/force buffer management policy have on checkpointing and recovery?

Ans. No-steal means that the cache (buffer) page updated by a transaction cannot be written to disk before the transaction commits. Force means that updated pages are written to disk when a transaction commits.

With No-steal, the checkpoint scheme that writes all modified main memory buffers to disk would not be able to write pages updated by uncommitted transactions.

With Force, once a transaction is done, its updates would be pushed to disk. If there is a failure during this, REDO is still needed, however, no UNDO is needed since uncommitted updates are never propagated to disk.

Q.10. Consider the following transaction, T with these statements

Transaction T

read (A);
write (90, B);
write (100, C);
commit

If deferred update is used, what will be values of A, B and C, before and after T is executed?

Ans. Using deferred update, the process is

Time	Action	Log
*t*1	Start	–
*t*2	read (A);	–
*t*3	write (90, B)	B = 90
*t*4	write (100, C);	C = 100
*t*5	Commit	Commit

Here, while the transaction T, runs, no changes are recorded in the database but when a commit is encountered then—

(*a*) New data is recorded in a log file and flushed to disk.

(b) The new data is then recorded in the database itself.

(c) On an abort, do nothing, so database has not been changed.

(d) On a system restart after a failure, REDO the log.

So, the contents of A, B, and C are as follows :

Disk :	Before	After
	B = 6	B = 90
	A = 5	A = 5
	C = 2	C = 100

Q.11. Let us consider a banking system with three accounts A, B and C. The initial amounts in the three accounts are `1000, `2000 and `700 respectively. Let two transactions T_1 and T_2 are executed on the banking database serially in the same order. Transaction T_1 and T_2 are specified as given in Table 1.

Table 1: Specified Transaction

Time	Transaction: T_1	Transaction : T_2
1	Read (A, *a*);	
2	$a \leftarrow a - 50$	
3	Write (A, *a*);	
4	Read (B, *b*);	
5	$b \leftarrow b + 50$;	
6	Write (B, *b*);	
7		Read (C, *c*);
8		$c \leftarrow c - 100$;
9		Write (C, *c*);

Solution:

If both the transactions are successfully completed then the log file should contain the following as given in Table 2.

Table 2: Log File

T_1	Start	–
T_1	A	950
T_1	B	2050
T_1	Commit	–
T_2	Start	–
T_2	C	600
T_2	Commit	–

Now, let us suppose that the system crashes before completion of the transactions. Depending on the time of crash, three different situations are possible.

(a) System crash before completion of the first transaction

- Let the crash occurs just after the log record for the step "write (B, *b*)" of transaction T_1 has been written to permanent storage. The log file at this time should look like as given in Table 3.

Table 3: Log File of Transaction T_1

T_1	Start	–
T_1	A	950
T_1	B	2050

- When the system comes back again, no recovery action needs to be taken since there is no commit record for transaction T_1. in the log. Values in accounts A and B will remain fixed at ₹1000 and ₹ 2000 respectively.

(b) System crash before completion of the second transaction

- Let the crash occurs just after the log records for the step "write (C, *c*)" of transaction T_1 has been written to permanent storage. The log file at this time should look like as given in Table 4.

Table 4: Log File

T_1	Start	–
T_1	A	950
T_1	B	2050
T_1	Commit	–
T_2	Start	–
T_2	C	600

- When the system comes back, transaction T_1 is redone, i.e., the recovery subsystems performs *redo* (T_1) as the record < T_1, commit > is present in the log. But no action is taken regarding transaction T_2. The values of accounts A, B and C will be ₹ 950, ₹ 2050 and ₹ 700 respectively.

(c) System crash just after writing < T_2, commit > in the log

If the crash occurs just after the log record < T_2, commit > is written to the log in stable storage, then when the system comes back, we must perform both *redo* (T_1) and *redo* (T_2) as both .< T_1, commit > and < T_2, commit > are now present in the log (Figure 1).

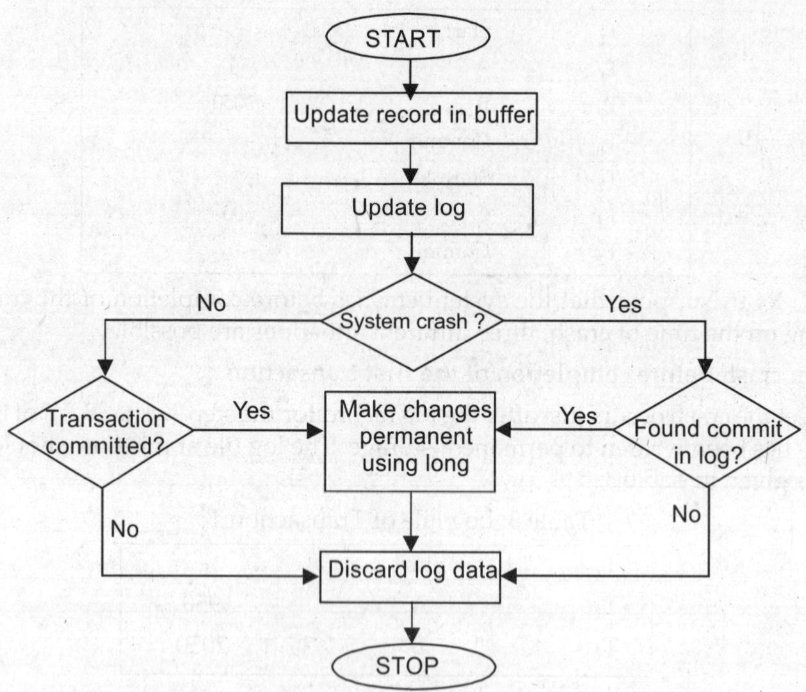

Figure 1. Incremental log with deferred updation.

(d) Incremental log with immediate updation

" Here all the updation operations are directly applied to the database immediately and the incremental log reflects the changes in the system states. If a crash occurs, the information in the log file is used in restoring the state of the system to a previous consistent state. Execution of a transaction, in this scheme, proceeds as follows.

- Before a transaction T_i starts its execution, a record < T_i, start > is written on the log file. During execution of T_i, any "write(X, x_i)" operation by T_i, is preceded by writing a new record to the log. Each such record has four fields:
  - – Transaction name (here, T_i)
  - – Data item name (here, X)
  - – Old value of the data item (here, $x_{i\text{-old}}$)
  - – New value of the data item (here, $x_{i\text{-new}}$)
- When T_i partially commits, a record < T_i, commit > is written to the log.

Using the log file the system can handle any failure causing event which does any loss of information in non-volatile storage. The recovery scheme utilizes two recovery procedures *undo* and *redo*.

- *Undo* (T_i): This restores the values of all data items updated by transaction T_i to their old values.
- *Redo* (T_i): This sets the values of all data items updated by the transaction T_i to new values using the log file.
- After a failure has occurred, the recovery subsystem consults the log to determine which of the transactions need to be redone and which to be undone.

- The transaction T_i for which both the log records < T_0, commit > and < T_1 commit > are present need to be redone and the remaining transactions to be undone.

The *undo* and *redo* operations must be idempotent in order to guarantee the correct behaviour even if a failure occurs during the recovery process itself.

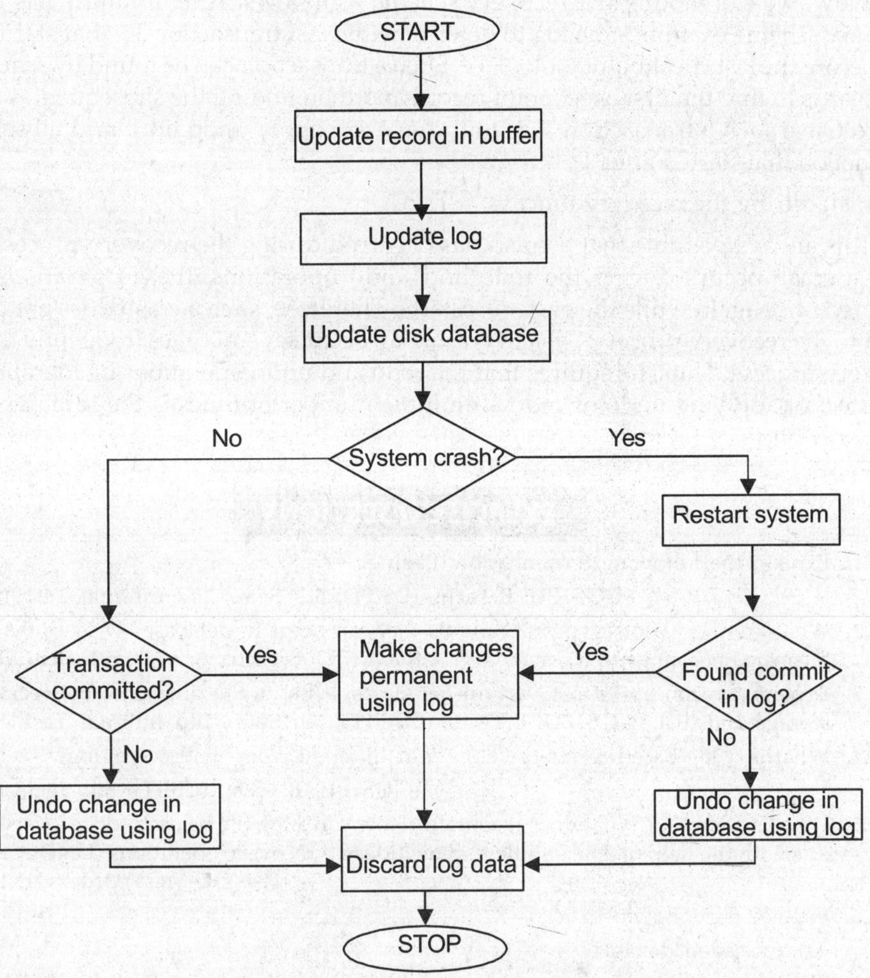

Figure 2. Incremental log with immediate updation.

(e) Incremental log with checkpoints

When a system failure occurs, it is necessary to consult the log in order to determine v of the transactions need to be redone and which to be undone. That is the entire log file i to be searched. Two major difficulties in this approach are:

- The search process is time consuming.
- Most of the transactions that need to be redone have already actually written updates in the database, and do not actually need to be redone. Redoing will cause harm, but will take longer time for recovery process to complete.

This overhead time can be reduced by the use of checkpoints. During execution, the system maintains the log, and in addition, the system periodically performs checkpointing which required the following sequence of actions to take place.

- Output all the log records currently residing in the main memory onto stable storage.
- Output all modified buffer blocks to the disk.
- Output a log record <checkpoint> onto stable storage.

Now, we can modify the recovery scheme as follows. After a failure has occurred, recovery scheme examines the log to determine the last transaction T_i, that started execution before the last checkpoint took place. Such a transaction can be found by searching the backwards to find the first checkpoint record and then finding the subsequent $< T_i$, start $>$ record Once such a transaction T_i is found, we can apply undo on T_i and all subsequent transaction that started after T_i.

(f) Crash during the recovery process

It is always possible that a crash has occurred during the recovery process itself. If such a crash occurs during the redo and undo operations, these operations may be repeated once again while the system restarts. Therefore, such a crash does not cause any harm to the recovery process. System crash may occur several times frequently during the recovery process. Thus, it requires that the redo and undo operations be idempotent, *i.e.*, the effect of applying undo or redo a multiple number of times is the same as applying them only once.

EXERCISE QUESTIONS

Q.1. Explain the following term-Shadow Paging.
[GGSIPU, B.Tech., (CS/IT); 5th Sem., 2nd Internal Test, Nov. 2005]

Q.2. What are the various types of failures that can occur in database? Discuss the log based recovery mechanism? **[GGSIPU, B.Tech., (CS/IT); 5th Sem., Dec. 2007]**

Q.3. Explain the concept of recovery in databases. What is the difference between the stable storage and disk.**[GGSIPU, B.Tech., (CSE/IT); 5th Sem., 2nd Internal Test, Nov. 2008]**

Q.4. What is a log-based recovery? How is it different from shadow-paging?
[GGSIPU, B.Tech., (CS/IT); 5th Sem., Dec. 2008]

Q.5. What is a log file? What does it contain? How can a log file be used for recovery? Describe this with the help of an example that includes all recovery operations (UNDO, REDO etc).
[IGNOU-MCA; 3rd Year, June 2004]

Q.6. Explain the following :
(*a*) Cascaded delete.
(*b*) Write-ahead by rule. **[Delhi University, B.Sc (MS); 3rd Year, 2005]**

Q.7. (*a*) What is the need for log file? When is log file used and how?
(*b*) Why should by writing be ahead of data block writing? How can this be implemented?
(*c*) Explain the purpose of checkpoint mechanism. What is done during checkpoint?
[DU, DCE—ME (CS); 3rd Sem., 2004–05]

Q.8. (*a*) When the system recovers from a crash, it constructs an undo-list and a redo-list. Explain why log records for transactions on the undo-list must be processed in reverse order while those log records for transactions on the redo-list are processed in a forward direction.
(*b*) Compare the shadow-paging recovery scheme with log-based recovery schemes in terms of implementation and overhead cost. **[DU, DCE—ME (CS); 3rd Sem., 2005]**

Q.9. Compare and contrast the features of log-based recovery mechanism versus checkpointing based recovery. Suggest applications where you will prefer log-based recovery scheme over checkpointing. Give an example of check pointing based recovery scheme. Discuss the recoverable schedule also. **[UPTU, B.Tech., (CS); 4th Sem., 2006–2007]**

Q.10. Explain the following term—Shadow Paging. **[UPTU, MBA; 4th Sem., 2006–2007]**

Q.11. Explain the database recovery technique based on deferred update?

[BPUT, Orissa, B.Tech (CSE); 4th Sem., 2006]

Q.12. (*a*) Explain log-based recovery in detail.

(*b*) Explain in brief—Checkpoints.

[Nagpur University, B.E. (CSE); 7th Sem., Dec. 2008]

Q.13. Explain Backward and Forward Recovery.

[Nagpur University, B.E. (CSE); 7th Sem., Dec. 2006]

Q.14. Explain shadow paging with an example.

[Nagpur University, B.E. (CSE); 7th Sem., June 2007]

Q.15. (*a*) Explain the following terms :

(*i*) Log-based recovery

(*ii*) Shadow paging.

(*b*) Write short notes on :

(*i*) Checkpoints

(*ii*) Recoverability. **[Nagpur University, B.E. (CSE); 7th Sem., June 2007]**

Q.16. Write short notes on :

(*i*) Write-ahead by protocol.

(*ii*) Checkpointing. **[JNTU, B.Tech (CSE); 2nd Semester, April/May 2006]**

Q.17. What is database recovery? What are the contents of a redo-type log entry?

[GGSIPU, BCA/BIS (H); 3rd Sem., Dec. 2002]

Q.18. What is database recovery? How are databases recovered from catastrophic failures?

[GGSIPU, BCA/BIS(H); 3rd Sem., Dec. 2003]

Q.19. Discuss the shadow paging scheme of database recovery?

[GGSIPU, M.Tech (IT); 3rd Sem., Dec. 2004]

Q.20. Compare the shadow paging recovery scheme with the log-based recovery scheme.

[GGSIPU, M.Tech (IT); 3rd Sem., Dec. 2005]

Q.21. Write short notes on :

(a) Concurrency control techniques (b) Recovery techniques

[GGSIPU, MCA-3rd Sem., Dec. 2010]

Q.22. (*i*) State the working of multi-version time stamp based protocol. Suggest a scheme to avoid the phantom phenomenon.

(*ii*) Discuss the procedure of deadlock detection and recovery in transactions with the help of an example.

[GGSIPU, B. Tech. (CSE/IT)— 5th Sem., Dec. 2009, 2010]

Q.23. (*a*) Explain the working of lock based protocols in shared and exclusive scenarios with examples.

(*b*) How a non-serializable schedule can be changed into a serializable schedule ?

(*c*) What is log-based recovery ? How is it different from shadow paging ?

[GGSIPU, B. Tech. (CSE/IT) — 5th Sem., Dec. 2010 & Dec. 2011]

Q24. Explain shadow paging scheme for database recovery.

[GGSIPU, M. TEch. (CCSE/IT)—Ist Sem., Dec. 2011]

Q25. Give recovery technique based on deferred update assuming concurrent execution.

[GGSIPU, M. Tech. (CSE/IT)—Ist Sem., Jan. 2011]

CHAPTER 9

Buffer Management

9.0 INTRODUCTION

Typical, I/O operations use buffers to match the CPU speed and the fast main memory. The **buffer manager** component of the OS does the assignment and management of memory blocks. It is responsible for the efficient management of the database buffers that are used to flush pages between buffer and secondary storage. The buffer management provides a temporary copy of a database page. Both the transaction log and the data pages are written to the buffer pages in virtual memory. The commit operation takes place in two phases and hence is called as a two-phase commit.

1. **1st phase of Commit :** The transaction log buffers are written out (WAL, as done earlier).
2. **2nd phase of Commit :** Here, data buffers are written out.

9.1 QUERY PROCESSING OVERVIEW

Query processing means a range of activities involved in extraction data from a database. It is a procedure of selecting the strategy to be used in responding to a database request. This component of DBMS is called as a **Query process**. It is a stepwise process. These steps are shown below in Fig. 9.1.

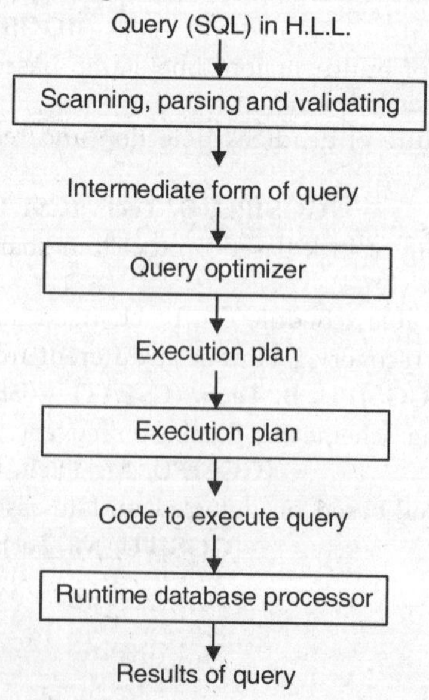

Fig. 9.1. *Query processing procedure*

Explanation : A query expressed in high level language like SQL is firstly scanned, parsed and validated. **Scanner** identifies the language tokens like SQL keywords, attributes and relation names. **Parser** checks the sytax of the query. **Validation** of the query means to check that all attributes and relation names are valid. An internal representation of this query is then created which is a tree-data structure called as a **query tree**. We can also draw a **query graph** here. A query graph has many possible execution strategies. **The process of choosing a suitable execution strategy for processing a query is known as query optimization.**

We have already discussed the phases of query processing in previous chapters also.

9.2 MEASURES OF QUERY COST

Our **objective** is to choose the most efficient way of implementing the relational algebra operations at the lowest possible cost. **This method of optimising the query by choosing a strategy that results in the minimum cost is called as cost-based query optimization.** Please note that the cost functions used in query optimizations are just the estimates !!! The cost of an algorithm depends on the cardinality of its input and also of its output because in the query tree, this forms the input to the next operation in the tree.

The cost of executing the query includes the following costs :

1. **Cost of access to secondary storage : The cost of searching for reading and writing data blocks that reside on secondary storage like disk is called as an access cost.**

   The cost of searching for tuples in a database relation depends on the type of access structures on that relation like ordering, hashing etc.
2. **Cost of storage :** It is the cost of storing any intermediate relations that are generated by the execution strategy for the query.
3. **Cost of computation :** It is the cost of performing in-memory operations on the data buffers during query execution. **For example**, searching and sorting records, merging them (for join) etc.
4. **Cost of memory usage :** It is the cost pertaining to the number of memory buffers needed during query execution.
5. **Cost of communication :** It is the cost of transferring query and its results from the database site to the site of query origination.

Please note that, out of these five cost components, the most important cost is the access cost to secondary storage. Also note that cost minimization depends on the size and the type of database applications. 3 cases arise :

Case 1. Smaller databases : Here, the emphasis is on minimising computation costs because most of the data in files, involved in query, can be completely stored in the main memory.

Case 2. Larger databases : Here, the emphasis is on minimizing the access cost to the secondary storage.

Case 3. Distributed databases : Here, the communication cost needs to be minimized because many sites are involved for data transfer.

Finally, to estimate the costs of various execution strategies, we must keep track of any information that is needed for the cost functions. **Please remember that this information may be stored in the DBMS catalog, from where it is accessed by the query optimizer.** The query optimizer needs close values of the frequently changing parameters like the number of tuples in a file, everytime a record is inserted or deleted.

9.3 EVALUATION OF EXPRESSIONS

There are two approaches used here :

(*a*) Pipelining

(*b*) Materialization.

Let us discuss these one by one.

Pipelining : As we know that a query is composed of several relational algebra operators. **The process of sending the result of one operator to another operator without creating a temporary relation to hold the intermediate results is known as pipelining or on-the-fly processing**. It improves the query performance. The results of the intermediate algebra operations are stored on secondary storage like disk, temporarily.

Materialization : If the output of an operator operation is saved in a temporary relation for processing by the next operator then we say that the tuples are materialized. **This process of temporarily writing intermediate algebra operations is called as materialization**. This process starts from the lowest level operations in the expression which are at the bottom of the query tree. **The inputs to the lowest level operations are the tables/relations in the database**. Now, the lowest level operations on the input relations are executed and stored in the temporary relations. These temporary relations are in turn used to execute the operations at the next level up in the tree. **Please note that in this process of materialization, the output of one operation is stored in a temporary relation for processing for the next operation**. The process is repeated and finally, the operation at the root of the query tree is evaluated giving the final result of the expression. **Also note that this process is called materialization because the results of each intermediate operation are created or materialized and then used for evaluation of the next-level operations.** The cost of this process of materialization includes the cost of writing the result of each operation i.e., temporary relations to the secondary storage.

Actually, the efficiency of the query evaluation can be improved by reducing the number of temporary files that are produced. Pipelining helps in this. Each pipeline takes a stream of tuples from its input and creates a stream of tuples as its output. Hence, pipelining eliminates the cost of reading and writing temporary realations.

Query Evaluation Plans : A sequence of primitive operations that can be used to evaluate a query is called as a query-execution plan or query-evaluation plan. It defines exactly what algorithm should be used for each operation and how these operations be coordinated. Let us consider an example and see how queries are evaluated –

```
SELECT bal
FROM account
WHERE bal < 3000;
```

Now, this query can be translated into either of the following relation-algebra expressions :

1. $\sigma_{bal<3000}$ (π_{bal} (account))
2. π_{bal} ($\sigma_{bal<2500}$ (account))

The *query evaluation plan* for this query is as follows –

π_{bal}

|

$\sigma_{bal<2500\text{; use index 1}}$

|

account

Herein, a particular index (as 1) is specified for the selection operation.

Please understand that the query-execution engine takes a query-evaluation plan, executes that plan and returns the answers to the query. Also note that different execution plans for a given query can have different costs. It is our systems responsibility.

9.4 TRANSFORMATION RULES

These rules are used by the query optimiser to transform one relational algebra expression into an equivalent expression that is more efficient to execute. But, one must ensure that these steps of transformation must always lead to an equivalent query tree and the desired output is achieved. A relation is considered as equivalent of another relation, if two relations have the same set of attributes in a different order but representing the same information. These rules are used to restructure the initial relational algebra query tree generated during query decomposition.

Cosider three relations —R, S and T.

R is defined over attributes, $A = \{A_1, A_2, ..., A_n\}$

S is defined over attributes, $B = \{B_1, B_2, ... B_n\}$

C denotes predicates, $C = \{C_1, C_2, ..., C_n\}$

$L, L_1, L_2, M, M_1, M_2, N$ denote a set of attributes. Then the transformation rules are as follows–

Rule 1. Cascading of selection (σ)

$$\sigma_{c_1 \wedge c_2 ... \wedge c_n} (R) \equiv \sigma_{c_1}(\sigma_{c_2}(...(\sigma_{c_n}(R))...))$$

(≡ means is equivalent to)

For example, $\sigma_{loc\ =\ 'Delhi' \wedge Sal > 28,000} (EMP) \equiv \sigma_{loc\ =\ 'Delhi'} (\sigma_{sal > 2800}(EMP))$

Rule 2. Commutativity of selection (σ)

$$\sigma_{c_1}(\sigma_{c_2}(R)) \equiv \sigma_{c_2}(\sigma_{c_1}(R))$$

For example, $\sigma_{loc\ =\ 'Delhi'} (\sigma_{sal > 28000)} (EMP))) (\sigma_{Sal > 28000} (\sigma_{loc\ =\ 'Delhi'} (EMP)))$

Rule 3. Cascading of Projection (π)

$$\pi_L\ \pi_m\ ...\ \pi_N\ (R) = \pi_L$$

For example, $\pi_{Ename}\ \pi_{loc}\ (EMP) \equiv \pi_{Ename}\ (EMP)$

Rule 4. Commutativity of Selection (σ) and projection (π)

$$\pi_{A_1, A_2 ... A_n} (\sigma_C (R)) \equiv (\sigma_c(\pi_{A_1, A_2 ... A_n(R)})$$

For example, $\pi_{Ename,\ Dob} (\sigma_{Ename\ =\ 'Rajat'} (EMP))$

$\equiv \sigma_{Ename\ ='Rajat'} (\pi_{Ename,\ Dob}(EMP))$

Rule 5. Commtativity of Join (⋈) and cartesian product (X)

$R \bowtie S \equiv S \bowtie R$

and $R \times S \equiv S \times R$

For example, $EMP \bowtie_{EMP.\ LOC=BRANCH.LOC} (BRANCH)$

$\equiv BRANCH \bowtie_{EMP.\ BRANCH\_NO\ =\ BRANCH.BRANCH\_NO} (EMP)$

Rule 6. Commutativity of selection (σ) and join (⋈) or cartesion product (X)

$\sigma_C\ R \bowtie S = (\sigma_C \bowtie S)$

and $\sigma_C\ (R \times S) \equiv (\sigma_C\ (R)) \times S$

For example, $\sigma_{position\ =\ 'Manager' \wedge city='London'} (Staff \bowtie_{staff\text{-}branch\_No\ =\ Branch\_branch\_no}$ (BRANCH)

$$= (\sigma_{position='Manger'} (staff) \bowtie_{staff.branch\_No = Branch.\ branch\_No} (\sigma_{city = 'London'} (Branch)$$

Rule 7. Commutativity of projection (π) and join (⋈) or cartesaon product (X)

$$\pi_{L_1 \cup L_2} (R \bowtie S) = \pi_{L_1} (R)) \bowtie \pi_{L_2} (s))$$

For example,

$$\pi_{position,\ city,\ branch,No} (Staff)) \bowtie_{staff.branch\ No = Branch.\ branch\ No} (Branch)$$

$$\equiv \pi_{position,\ branch} (Staff)) \bowtie_{staff.\ branch\ No = Branch.\ branch\ No} (\pi_{city,\ branch.No} (Branch))$$

Rule 8. Commutativity of Union and Intersection

$$R \cup S \equiv S \cup R$$

and

$$R \cap S \equiv S \cap R$$

Rule 9. Commutativity of selection (σ) and set of operations such as Union (∪), Intersection (∩) and set difference (–).

$$\sigma_C (R \cup S) \equiv \sigma_C(S) \cup \sigma_C (R)$$

$$\sigma_C (R \cap S) \equiv \sigma_C(S) \cap \sigma_C (R)$$

$$\sigma_C (R - S) \equiv \sigma_C(S) - \sigma_C (R)$$

In general,

$$\sigma_C(R\ \theta\ S) \equiv (\sigma_C (R))\ \theta\ (\sigma_C (S))$$

Where θ may be Union (∪), Intersection (∩) and Set difference (–) operation.

Rule 10. Commutativity of projection (π) and Union(∪)

$$\pi_L (R \cup S) \equiv (\pi_L (R)) \cup (\pi_L (S))$$

Rule 11. Associativity of join (⋈) and cartesian product (X)

$$(R \bowtie S) \bowtie T \equiv R \bowtie (S \bowtie T)$$

and $(R \times S) \times T \equiv R \times (S \times T)$

In general, $(R\ \theta\ S)\ \theta\ T \equiv R\ \theta\ (S\ \theta\ T)$

Rule 12. Associativity of Union (∪) and Intersection (∩)

$$(R \cup S) \cup T \equiv S \cup (R \cup T)$$

and $(R \cap S) \cap T \equiv S \cap (R \cap T)$

Rule 13. Converting a selection and Cartesian product (σ, X) sequence into join(⋈)

$$\sigma_C (R \times S) \equiv (R \bowtie_C S)$$

9.5 ESTIMATING CARDINALITIES

We shall now consider the cost estimates for selection, Join and projection operations, one by one.

I. Cost Function for SELECT Operation : Firstly, let us see the types of information in DBMS system catalog. For each base relation, R, we say –

(*a*) ***n* Tuples (R) :** Shows the number of tuples in R *i.e.,* its cardinality.

(*b*) ***b* Factor (R) :** Shows the blocking factor of R *i.e.,* the number of tuples of R that fit into one block.

(*c*) ***n* Blocks (R) :** Shows the number of blocks required to store R. If the tuples of R are stored physically together then –

n Blocks (R) = [*n* Tuples (R) /*b* Factor (R)] where [ ] means round this result to the smallest integer.

Also, for each attribute, A, of base relation, R, we have this statistics—

1. **n Distinct$_A$ (R)** : means the number of distinct values that appear for attribute A in relation, R.
2. **min$_A$ (R), max$_A$ (R) :** means the minimum and maximum possible values for the attribute A in relation, R.
3. **SC$_A$ (R)** : means the selection cardinality of attribute A in relation, R. It is the average number of tuples that satisfy an equality condition on attribute, A.

Now,
$$SC_A(R) = \begin{cases} 1 & \text{if A is key attribute of R} \\ n\ \text{Tuples}(R)/n\ \text{Distinct}_A(R)] & \text{otherwise.} \end{cases}$$

This is a **complete database statistics** stored in system catalog. Now, the cost of the selection operation depends on the strategy being used.

Let us summarize them in a tabular form.

Table 9.1

S. No.	Strategies	Cost
1	Linear Search	[n Blocks (R)/2], if record is found and n Block (R) otherwise
2	Binary Search	[$\log_2$ (n Block (R))], for equity condition on key as SC$_A$ (R) = 1 in this case
3	Equality on hash key (using primary index) or hash key to retrieve a single record.	1, assuming no overflow
4	Equality condition an primary key.	n Levels$_A$ (I) + 1
5	Inequality condition on primary key.	n Levels$_A$ (I) + [n Blocks (R)/2]
6	Equality condition on clustering *i.e.,* secondary index	n Levels$_A$ (I) + [SC$_A$(R)/b Factor(R)]
7	Equality condition on non-clustering index	n Levels$_A$ (I) + [SC$_A$ (R)]
8	Inequality condition on a secondary B^+ tree index	n Levels$_A$ (I) + [n/f Blocks$_A$ (I)/2 + n Tuples (R)/2]

We are in a position to solve an example now.

Example 1. *Consider an EMP relation with the following attributes—EMP (EMP_ID, DEPT_ID, POSITION, SALARY) Assume that –*

(a) There is a hash index with no overflow on the primary key attribute, EMP_ID.

(b) There is a clustering index on the foreign key attribute, DEPT_ID.

(c) There is a B^+– tree index on the salary attribute.

Also, assume that the EMP relation has the following statistics (in system catalog of DBMS) :

$$n\ Tuples\ (EMP) = 6000$$
$$b\ Factor\ (EMP) = 60$$
$$n\ Blocks\ (EMP) = \frac{n\ Tuples\ (EMP)}{b\ factor\ (EMP)} = \frac{6000}{60} = 100$$
$$n\ Distinct_{DEPT\_ID}\ (EMP) = 1000$$
$$SC_{DEPT\_ID}(EMP) = [n\ Tuples\ (EMP)/n\ Distinct_{DEPT\_ID}\ (EMP)]$$
$$= 6000/1000 = 6$$

$$n\ Dishinct_{POSITION}\ (EMP) = 20$$
$$SC_{POSITION}\ (EMP) = [n\ Tuples\ (EMP)/n\ Distinct_{POSITION}\ (EMP)]$$
$$= 6000/20 = 300$$
$$n\ Distinct_{SALARY}\ (EMP) = 1000$$
$$SC_{SALARY}\ (EMP) = [n\ Tuples\ (EMP)/n\ Distinct_{SALARY}(EMP)]$$
$$= \frac{6000}{1000} = 6$$
$$n\ Distinct_{POSITION}\ (EMP) = 20$$
$$min_{SALARY}\ (EMP) = 20{,}000$$
$$max_{SALARY}\ (EMP) = 80{,}000$$
$$n\ Levels_{DEPT\_ID}(I) = 2$$
$$n\ Levels_{SALARY}(I) = 2$$
$$nLf\ Blocks_{SALARY}(I) = 50$$

Given that the estimated cost of a linear search on the key attribute, # Emp_Id is 50 blocks. The cost of a linear search on a non-key attribute is 100 blocks. Now, consider the following SELECT operation —

$S1 : \sigma_{EMP\_IDO = '101'}\ (EMP)$

$S2 : \sigma_{POSITION\ =\ 'Analyst'}\ (EMP)$

$S3 : \sigma_{DEPT\text{-}ID\ =\ 'A\text{-}04'}\ (EMP)$

$S4 : \sigma_{SALARY\ \not> 30000}(EMP)$

$S5 : \sigma_{POSITION\ =\ 'Analyst'\ \wedge\ DEPT\_ID\ =\ 'A\text{-}04'}\ (EMP)$

What will be costs of query executions ? Use the known strategies to improve on these two costs?

Solution. Selection-1 (S1) : This selection operation has an equality condition on the primary key, EMP_ID of the table EMP. Therefore, as the attribute EMP_ID is hashed, we can use the strategy-3 defined in table, to estimate the cost as **1 block**. The estimated cardinality of the result relation is –

$$SC_{EMP\_ID}\ (EMP) = 1$$

Selection-2 (S2) : The attribute in the predicate is a non key, non-indexed attribute. Therefore, we can improve on the linear search method, giving an estimated cost of 100 blocks. The estimated cardinality of the result relation is $SC_{POSITION}$ (EMP) = 300.

Selection-3 (S3) : The attribute in the predicate is a foreign key with a clustering index. So, we can use strategy-6, to estimate the cost as (2 + [6/30]) = *3 blocks*. The estimate cardinality of the result relation is –

$$SC_{DEPT\_ID}\ (EMP) = 6$$

Selection-4 (S4) : The predicate here involves a range search on the salary field, which has a B^+ -tree index. So, we can use strategy-8 to estimate the cost as (2 + [50/2] + [6000/2]) = 3027 blocks. **Please note, however, that is significantly worse than the linear search strategy. So, a linear search strategy may be used in this case**. The estimated cardinality of the result relation is –

$$SC_{SALARY}\ (EMP) = \left[600 * \frac{(80000 - 20000 * 2)}{(80000 - 2000)}\right]$$
$$= 4000$$

Selection 5 (S5) : While retrieving each tuple using the clustering index, we can check whether it satisfies the first condition (POSITION = 'Analyst'_). We know that the estimated cardinality of the 2nd condition is :

$$SC_{DEPT\_ID}\ (EMP) = 6$$

Say, that this intermediate condition is S. Then, the number of distinct values of POSITION in S can be estimated as = [(6 + 20)/3] = 9.

Let us now apply, the 2nd condition using the clustering index on DEPT_ID (S3 above), which has an estimated cost of 3 blocks.

$$\therefore \quad \text{Estimated cardinality of the result relation} = SC_{POSITION}\ (S) = 6/9 \approx 1$$

Which would be correct if there is one analyst for each branch.

II. Cost Function for JOIN Operation : It is very difficult to estimate the cardinality of any JOIN because it depends on how the values are distributed in the joining attributes. Worst case can be that the cardinality of the join cannot be greater than the cardinality of the cartesian product *i.e.,*

$$\underbrace{n\ \text{Tuples (T)}}_{\substack{\text{Cardinality}\\ \text{of JOIN}}} \geq \underbrace{n\ \text{Tuples (R)} * n\ \text{Tuples (S)}}_{\substack{\text{Cardinality of Cartesian}\\ \text{product of R and S } i.e., (R \times S)}}$$

Some systems use this as an upper bound (but is quite pessimistic estimate !!!). If we assume a uniform distribution of values in both the relations then we can improve on this estimate for Equijoin with a predicate, R.A = S.B, as follows :

1. If A is a PK of R, then a tuple of S can only join with one tuple of R. So, the cardinality of the Equijoin cannot be greater than the cardinality of S *i.e.,*

$$\boxed{n\ \text{Tuples (T)} \leq n\ \text{Tuples (S)}.}$$

2. If B is a key of S, then

$$\boxed{n\ \text{Tuples (T)} \leq n\ \text{Tuples (R)}}$$

3. If neither A nor B are keys, then we could estimate the cardinality of the join as–

$$n\ \text{Tuples (T)} = SC_A\ (R) * n\ \text{Tuples (S)}.$$

or

$$n\ \text{Tuples (T)} = SC_B\ (R) * n\ \text{Tuples(R)}$$

Let us now see the estimated costs of strategies for JOIN operation in a tabular form :

Table 9.2

S. No.	Strategies	Cost Estimates
1	Block nested -loop join	(*a*) *n*Blocks(R) + (*n* Block(R) * *n*Blocks(S)), if the buffer has only block (*b*) *n*Blocks(R) + [*n*Blocks (S) * (*n*Buffer (R)/(*n*Buffer-2), if (nBuffQ-2)block for R (*c*) *n*Blocks (R) + *n*Blocks (S), if blocks of R can be read into databse buffer

2	Indexed nested-loop join	(*a*) nBlock(R) + nTuple(R) * (nLevels$_A$ (I) + 1), if join attribute A in S is the primary key (*b*) nBlocks(R) + nTuples(R)*(nLevels$_A$ (R)/b Factor (R)]),
3	Sort-merged join	(*a*) nBlock (R)* [log$_2$(nBlock(R) +nBlock(S)*[log$_2$(nBlocks(R)], for sorts (*b*) nBlocks(R) + nBlocks(S), for merge
4	Hash join	(*a*) 3(nBlocks(R) + nBlocks(S), for merge (*b*) 2(nBlock(R) + nBlock(S)) * [log (nBlocks(S))-1] + nBlocks (R) + nBlocks(S), otherwise

We are in a position to solve an example now.

Example 1. *Consider the following 3 relations –*

EMP (<u>Emp_id</u>, Dept_id, position, salary)

DEPT (<u>Dept_id</u>, Emp_id)

PROJ (<u>Proj_id</u>, Dept_id, Emp_id)

Assume that :

(*a*) *There are separate hash indexes with no overflow on the primary key attribute,* <u>Emp_id</u> *of relation EMP and* <u>Dept_id</u> *of relation DEPT.*

(*b*) *There are 200 database buffer blocks.*

Solution. Also assume the following database statistics –

$$n \text{ Tuples (EMP)} = 12000$$
$$b \text{ Factor (EMP)} = 120$$
$$n \text{ Blocks (EMP)} = [n \text{ Tuples (EMP)}/b \text{ Factor (EMP)}]$$
$$= 12000/120 = 200$$
$$n \text{ Tuples (DEPT)} = 600$$
$$b \text{ Factor (DEPT)} = 60$$
$$n\text{Block (DEPT)} = [n\text{Tuples (DEPT)}/b\text{Factor (DEPT)}]$$
$$= \frac{600}{60} = 10$$
$$n\text{Tuples (PROJ)} = 80000$$
$$b\text{Factor (PROJ)} = 40$$
$$n \text{ Block (DEPT)} = [n \text{ Tuples (PROJ)}/b\text{Factor (PROJ)}]$$
$$= 80000/40 = 2000$$

Now, Consider the following two joins :

$$\text{J1 : EMP} \bowtie_{\text{Emp\_id}} \text{PROJ}$$
$$\text{J2 : DEPT} \bowtie_{\text{Dept\_id}} \text{PROJ}$$

What is the estimated I/O cost of join operations given above?

Let us tabulate our results :

Strategies	Join 1	Join 2	Comments
Block nested-loop join	(*a*) 400200 (*b*) 4282 (*c*) N/A	(*a*) 20010 (*b*) N/A (*c*) 2010	(*a*) buffer has only one block (*b*) (nBuffer -2) blocks for R (*c*) all blocks of R can be read into database buffer

Indexed nested-loop join	12200	610	Key hashed
Sort-merged join	(*a*) 25800 (*b*) 2200	(*a*) 24240 (*b*) 2010	(*a*) Unsorted (*b*) Sorted
Hash join	6600	6030	Hash table fits in memeory

Please note that in both the joins J1 and J2, the cardinality of the resultant relation can be no larger than the cardinality of the first relation because we are joining over the key of the first relation. Also note that no one strategy is best for both of the join operations. The sort-merge join is the best for the join 1 provided both relations are already sorted. The indexed nested -loop join is the best for the Join-2 (J2).

III. Cost Function for PROJECT Operation : Project operation is a wary operation. It defines a relation, S, containing a vertical subset of a relation, R, extracting the values of specified attributes. It eliminates duplicates. To implement projection, the following steps are followed –

S1 : Remove the attributes that are not required.

S2 : Eliminate any duplicate tuples that are produced from the previous step – using either hashing or sorting.

When the projection contains a PK attribute, then since no elimination of duplicates is required, the cardinality of the projection is –

$$n \text{ Tuples (S)} = n \text{ Tuples (R)}$$

If the projection consists of a single non-key attribute, $S = \pi_A (R)$, we can estimate the cardinality of the projection as follows :

$$n \text{ Tuples (S)} = SC_A \text{ (R)}$$

(*a*) The total cost of duplicate elimination using sorting is – nBlokcs(R) + nBlocks(R) * [$\log_2$ (nBlock (R)]

(*b*) The total cost of duplicate elimination using hashing is

$$n\text{Blocks (R)} + nb$$

SUMMARY

We have studied in this chapter, how a user query (SQL) is processed. We have seen how this query is transformed into a query-tree or query-graph using some rules of transformation. Also, we discussed about the cost-based approach to query optimization.

MULTIPLE CHOICE QUESTIOS [MCQs]

1. The assignment and management of memory blocks is done by

(*a*) Buffer (*b*) Buffer manager

(*c*) DBMS (*d*) None of the above.

2. The process of choosing a suitable execution strategy for processing a query is known as

(*a*) Query optimization (*b*) Query evaluation

(*c*) Query execution plan (*d*) None of the above.

3. The process of sending the result of one operator to another operator without creating a temporary relation to hold the intermediate results is known as

(*a*) Query (*b*) Relation

(*c*) Pipelining (*d*) None of the above.

4. The process of temporarily writing the intermediate algebra operations is called as
   (a) Pipelining (b) Query execution plan
   (c) Materialization (d) None of the above.
5. The syntax of the query is checked by
   (a) Parser (b) Compilar
   (c) Assembler (d) None of the above.
6. The first phase of query processing is
   (a) Decomposition (b) Restructuring
   (c) Analysis (d) None of the above.
7. The result of a query, in a query tree is represented by
   (a) Root node (b) Leaf node
   (c) Intermediary node (d) None of the above.
8. Which is false rule from the following :
   (a) $R \cup S \equiv S \cup R$ (b) $R \cap S \equiv S \cap R$
   (c) $R - S \equiv S - R$ (d) None of the above.
9. A query execution strategy is evaluated by
   (a) Execution plan (b) Query tree
   (c) Database catalog (d) None of the above.
10. Which of the following query processing method is more efficient :
   (a) Pipelining (b) Materialization
   (c) Tunnelling (d) None of the above.

ANSWERS

1. (b) 2. (a) 3. (c) 4. (c) 5. (a) 6. (a) 7. (a) 8. (c)
9. (a) 10. (a)

CONCEPTUAL SHORT QUESTIONS WITH ANSWERS

Q.1. Distinguish between the demand-driven and producer-driven pipeline executions.

Ans. Let us tabulate the differences between the two.

S. No.	Demand-driven Pipeline	Producer-driven Pipeline
1.	In this method, the system makes repeated requests for tuples from the operation at the top of the pipeline.	In this m,ethod, the operations do not wait for requests to produce tuples, but instead generate tuples **eagerly**.
2.	It can be thought of as **pulling data up** an operation tree from the top.	It can be thought of as **pushing data up** an operation tree from the below.
3.	Tuples are generated **lazily** on demand.	Tuples are generated **eagerly**.
4.	It is easier to implement.	It is difficult to implement.

Q.2. Write an algorithm for projection using sorting.

Ans. //Algorithm for projection using sorting

// Say, R is project over attributes $a_1 \ldots a_m$

// Firstly, remove unwanted attributes

// Return resultant relation, *s*

for *i* block = 1 to *n* Block (R){

block = read-block (R, iblock);

```
        for (i = 1 to n Tuples (block)}
              copy block.tuple [i]. a1,
                    block.tuple [i]. a2, .....
                    blcok. tuple [i]. am to output T.
              }
        }
   // Now sort T, if necessary
      if {a1, a2, .... ,am} contains a key then
          S = T;
      else {
          Sort (T);
   // Finally, remove duplicates
          i = 1 ; j = 2;
          while (i < = n Tuples (T))}
                output T[i] to S;
   // Skip over duplicates for this tuple, if any
      while  (T [i] = T[j])
      {
          j = j + 1;
      }
          i = j;
          j = i + 1;
      }
   }
```

Q.3. Why is it not desirable to force users to make an explicit choice of a query-processing stratetgy? Are there cases in which it is desirable for users to be aware of the costs of competing query-processing strategies? Explain your answer.

Ans. In general it is not desirable to force users to choose a query processing strategy because native users might select an inefficient strategy. The reason users would make poor choices about processing queries is that they would not know how a relation is stored, nor about its indices. It is unreasonable to force users to be aware of these details since ease of use is a major object of database query languages. If users are aware of the costs of differents strategies they could write queries efficiently, thus helping performance. This could happen if experts were using the system.

Q.4. Design a variant of the hybrid merge-join algorithm for the case where both relations are not physically sorted, but both have a sorted secondary index on the join attributes.

Ans. We merge the leaf entries of the first sorted secondary index with the leaf entries of the second sorted secondary index. The result file contains pairs of addresses, the first address in each pair pointing to a tuple in the first relation, and the second address pointing to a tuple in the second relation.

The result file is first sorted on the first relation's addresses. The relation is then scanned in physical storage order, and addresses in the result file are replaced by the actual tuple values. Then the result file is sorted on the second relation's addresses, allowing a scan of the second relation in physical storage order to complete the join.

Q.5. Estimate the number of block accesses required by your solution to question –4 above for $r_1 \bowtie r_2$ where r_1 and r_2 are defined as follows –

(*a*) r_1 (A,B,C) has 20,000 tuples, 25 tuples of r_1 fit on one block.

(*b*) r_2 (C,D,E) has 45,000 tuples, 30 tuples of r_2 fit on one block.

Ans. r_1 occupies 800 blocks, and r_2 occupies 1500 blocks. Let there be n pointers per index leaf block (we assume that both the indices have leaf blocks and pointers of equal sizes. Let us assume M pages of memory, $M < 800$. r_1's index will need $B_1 = \left\lceil \frac{20000}{n} \right\rceil$ leaf blocks, and r_2's index will need $B_2 = \left\lceil \frac{45000}{n} \right\rceil$ leaf blocks. Therefore the merge join will need $B_3 = B_1 + B_2$ accesses, without output. The number of output tuples is estimated as $n_0 = \left\lceil \frac{20000 * 45000}{\max(V(C, r_1), V(C, r_2))} \right\rceil$. Each output tuples will need two pointers, so the number of blocks of join output will be $B_{01} = \left\lceil \frac{n_0}{n/2} \right\rceil$. Hence the join needs $B_j = B_3 + B_{01}$ disk block accesses.

Now we have to replace the pointers by actual tuples. For the first sorting, $B_{s1} = B_{01}(2\{\log_{M-1} (B_{01}/M)] + 2)$ disk accesses needed, including the writing of output to disk. The number of blocks of r_1 which have to be accessed in order to replace the pointers with tuple values is **min**$(800, n_0)$. Let n_1 pairs of the form **(r_1 tuple, pointer to r_2)** fit inone disk block. Therefore the intermediate result after replacing the r_1 pointers will occupy $\mathbf{B_{02} = [(n_0/n_1)]}$ blocks. Hence the first pass of replacing the r_1-pointers will cost $B_f = B_{s1} + B_{01} + \min(800, n_0) + B_{02}$ disk accesses.

The second pass for replacing the r_2-pointers has a similar analysis. Let n_2 tuples of the final join fit in one block. Then the second pass of replacing the r_2-pointers will cost $B_s = B_{s2} + B_{02} + \min(1500, n_0)$ disk accesses, where $B_{s2} = B_{02} [\log_{M-1} (B_{02}/M)] + 2$.

Hence the total number of disk accesses for the join is $B_j + B_f + B_s$, and the number of pages of output is $[n_0/n_2]$.

Q.6. Write pseudocode for an iterator that implements indexed nested-loop join, where the other relation is pipelined. Use the standard iterator functions in your pseudocode. Show what state information the iterator must mainain between calls.

Ans. Let **outer** be the iterator which returns successive tuples from the pipelined outer relation. Let **inner** be the iterator which returns successive tuples of the inner relation having a given value of the join attributes. The **inner** iterator returns these tuples by performing an index lookup. The functions **Indexed NLJoin::open, IndexedNLJoin:: close** and **IndexedNLJoin:: next** to implement the indexed nested-loop join iterator are given below. The two iterators **outer** and **inner**, the value of the last read outer relation tuple t_r and a flag **done**$_r$ indicating whether the end of the outer relation scan has been reached are the state information which need to be remembered by **IndexedNLJoin** between calls.

```
IndexedNLJoin::open()
being
        outer. open();
        innter. open();
        if (outer.next() ≠ false)
                move tuples from outers output buffer to t_r;
        else
                done_r: = true;
end
boolean IndexedNLJoin::next()
begin
        while (¬done_r)
        begin
                if (inner. next (t_r [Join Attrs]) ≠ false)
                begin
                        move tuple from inner's output buffer to t_s;
                        compute t_r ⋈ t_s and place it in output buffer:
                        return true;
                end
                else
                        if (outer. next () ≠ false)
                        begin
                                move tuple from outer' output buffer to t_r;
                                rewind inner to first tuples of s;
                end
                else
                        done_r : = true;
        end
        return false;
end
```

Q.7. Suppose that a B⁺ -tree index on (*branch-name, branch-city*) is available on relation *branch*. What would be the best way to handle of the following selection?

$\sigma_{(\text{branch-city}<\text{"Brooklyn"}) \wedge (\text{assets}<5000) \wedge (\text{branch-name} = \text{"Downtown"})}$ **(branch)**

Ans. Using the index, we locate the first tuple having **branch-name** "Downtown". We then follow the pointers retrieving successive tuples as long as **branch-city** is less then "Brooklyn". From the tuples retrieved, the ones not satisfying the condition (assets < 5000) are rejected.

Q.8. Show how to derive the following equivalences by a sequence of transformations using the equivalence rules.'

(*a*) $\sigma_{\theta_1 \wedge \theta_2 \wedge \theta_3} (E) = \sigma_{\theta_1} (\sigma_{\theta_2} (\sigma_{\theta_3} (E)))$

(*b*) $\sigma_{\theta_1 \wedge \theta_2} (E_1 \bowtie_{\theta_3} E_2) = \sigma_{\theta_1} (E_1 \bowtie_{\theta_3} (\sigma_{\theta_2} (E)))$, **when θ_2 involves only attributes from E_2**

Ans. (*a*) Using rule 1, $\sigma_{\theta_1 \wedge \theta_2 \wedge \theta_3}$ (E) become $\sigma_{\theta_1} (\sigma_{\theta_2 \wedge \theta_3} (E))$. On applying rule 1 again, we get $\sigma_{\theta_1} (\sigma_{\theta_2} (\sigma_{\theta_3} (E)))$.

(*b*) $\sigma_{\theta_1 \wedge \theta_2}(E_1 \bowtie_{\theta_3} E_2)$ on applying rule 1 becomes $\sigma_{\theta_1}(\sigma_{\theta_2}(E_1 \bowtie_{\theta_3} E_2))$. This on applying rule 7.*a* becomes $\sigma_{\theta_1}(E_1 \bowtie_{\theta_2}(\sigma_{\theta_2}(E2)))$.

Q.9. A set of equivalence rules is said to be *complete if*, whenever two expressions are equivalent, one can be derived from the other by a sequence of uses of the equivalence rules. Is the set of equivalence rules that we considered complete, [Hint. Consider the equivalence $\sigma_{3=5}$ (*r*) = {}]

Ans. Two relational expressions are defined to be **equivalent** when on all input relations, they give the same output. The set of equivalence rules so considered is not complete. The expressions $\sigma_{3=5}(r)$ and { } are equivalent, but this cannot be shown by using just these rules.

Q.10. Describe how to incrementally maintain the results of the following operations, on both insertions and deletions.

(*a*) Union and set difference

(*b*) Left outer join

Ans. (*a*) Given materialized view $v = r \cup s$, when a tuples is inserted in r, we check if it is present in v, and if not we add it to v. When a tuple is deleted from r, we check if it is there in s, and if not, we delete it from v. Inserts and deletes in s are handled in symmetric fashion.

For set difference, given view $v = r - s$, when a tuple is inserted in r, we check if it is present in s, and if not we add it to v. When a tuple is deleted from r, we delete it from v if present. When a tuples is inserted in s, we delete it from v if present. When a tuple is deleted from s, we check if it is present in r, and if so we add it to v.

(*b*) Given materialized view $v = r ⟕ s$, when a set of tuples i_r is iserted in r, we add the tuples $i_r ⟕ s$ to the view. When i_r is deleted from r, we delete $i_r \bowtie s$ from the view. When a set of tuples i_s is inserted in s, we compute $r \bowtie i_s$. We find all the tuples of r which previously did match any tuples from s (*i.e.*, those padded with **null** in $r ⟕ s$) but which match i_s. We remove all those **null** padded entries from the view and add the tuples $r \bowtie s$ to the view. When i_s is deleted from s, we delete from s, we delete the tuples $r \bowtie i_s$ from the view. Also we find all the tuples in r which match i_s but which do not match any other tuples in s. We add all those to the view, after padding them with **null** values .

Q.11. Give an example of an expression defining a materialized view and two situations (sets of statistics for the input relations and the differentials) such that incremental view maintenance is better than recomputation in one situation, and recomputation is better in the other situation.

Ans. Let r and s be two relations. Consider a materialized view on these defined by $(r \bowtie s)$. Suppose 70% of the tuples in r are deleted. Then recomputation is better than incremental view maintenance. This is because in incremental view maintenance, the 70% of the deleted tuples to be joined with s while is recompution, just remaining 30% of the tuples in r have to be joined with s.

However, if the number of tuples in r is increased by a small percentage, for example 2% then incremental view maintenance is likely to be better than recomputation.

Q.12. A file of 4096 blocks is to be sorted with an available buffer space of 64 blocks. How many passes will be needed in the merge phase of the external sort-merge algorithm?

Ans. We first need to compute the number of runs, *n*, in the merge phase, R, by a formula given belows :

$$n_R = \left\lceil \frac{b}{n_B} \right\rceil$$

Where b = 4096 (blocks in file)

and n_B = 64 (buffer blocks)

∴ n_R = 64 (number of sorted runs on disk)

In the merge phase, the number of passes is dependent on the degree of merging, M_d

where $M_d = \text{MIN}(n-1, n) = (63, 64) = 63$

∴ Number of passes $= [\log_{Md} n]$

$= [\log_{63} 64]$

$= 2.$

Q.13. Can a non dense (sparse) index be used in the implementation of an aggregate operator? why or why not?

Ans. A nondense (sparse) index contains entries for only some of the search values. A primary index is an example of a nondense index which includes an entry for each disk block of the data file rather than for every record.

If the keys in the index correspond to the smallest key value in the data block then the sparse index could be used to compute the MIN function. However, the MAX function could not be determined from the index. In addition, since all values do not appear in the index, AVG, SUM and COUNT could not be determined from just the index.

Q.14. Extend the sort-merge join algorithm to implement the left outer join.

Ans. The left outer join of R and S would produce the rows from R and S that join as well as the rows from R that do not join any row from S. The sort-merge join algorithm would only need minor modifications during the merge phase. During the first step, relation R would be sorted on the join column(s).

During the second step, relation S would be sorted on the join column(s).

During the third step, the sorted R relation and S relation would be merged. That rows would be combined if the R row and S row have the same value for the join column(s). In addition, if no matching S row as found for an R row, then that R row would also be placed in the left outer join result, except that the corresponding attributes from the S relation would be set to NULL values. (How a null value is to be represented is a matter of choice out of the options provided in a DBMS.)

Q.15. Compare the cost of two different query plans for the following query:

$\sigma_{SALARY > 400}$ **(EMPLOYEE** $\bowtie_{DNO = DNUMBER}$ **DEPARTMENT)**

The database statistics is :

Table A

Table_name	Col_name	Num_distinct	Low	High
PROJECT	Ploc	200	1	200
	Pnumber	2000	1	200
	Dnum	50	1	50
DEPARTMENT	Dnumber	50	1	50
	MGRSSN	50	1	50
EMPLOYEE	SSN	10000	1	10000
	DNO	50	1	50
	SALARY	500	1	500

Table B

Table_name	Num_Rows	BLocks
PROJECT	2000	100
DEPARTMENT	50	5
EMPLOYEE	1000	2000

Table C

Index_name	Uniqueness	Blevel	Leaf Blocks	Distinct Keys
Proj_ploc	non-unique	1	4	200
Emp_SSN	Unique	1	50	10000
Emp_Sal	non_unique	1	50	500

Ans. One plan might be for the following query tree :

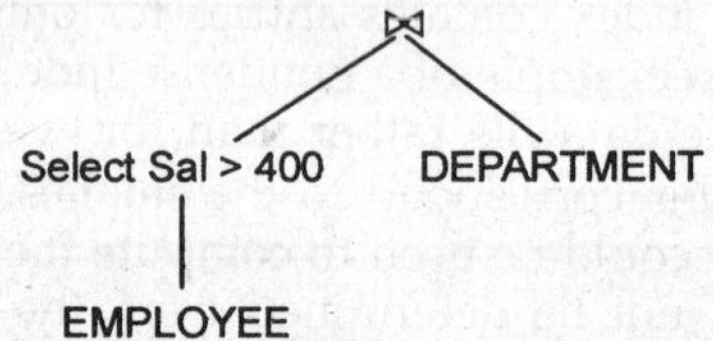

We can use the salary index on EMPLOYEE for the *select operation*:
The table (*a*) in Figure indicates that there are 500 unique salary values, with a low value of 1 and a high value of 500. (It might be in reality that salary is in units of 1000 dollars, so 1 represents $1000 and 500 represents $500,000.)
The selectivity for (Salary > 400) can be estimated as

$$(500 - 400)/500 = 1/5$$

This assumes that salaries are spread evenly across employees. So the cost (in block accesses) of accessing the index would be Blevel + (1/5) * (LEAF BLOCKS = 1 + (1/5) * 50 = 11
Since the index is nonunique, the employees can be stored an any of the data blocks. So that the number of data blocks to be accessed would be (1/5) * (NUM_ROWS) = (1/5) * 10,000 = 2000
Since 10,000 rows are stored in 2000 blocks, we have that 2000 rows can be stored in 400 blocks. So the TEMPORARY table (i.e., the result of the selection operator) would contain 400 blocks.
The cost of writing the TEMPORARY table to disk would be 400 blocks.
Now, we can do a nested loop join of the temporary table and the DEPARTMENT table, The cost of this would be

$$b + (b * b)$$

DEPARTMENT DEPARTMENT TEMPORARY
We can ignore the cost of writing the result for this comparision, since the cost would be the same for both plans, we will consider.
We have 5 + (5 * 400) = 2005 block accesses

1822 (continued)

Therefore, the total cost woul be 11 + 2000 + 400 + 2005 = 4416 block accesses
NOTE: If we have 5 main memory buffer pages available during the join, then we could store all 6 blocks of the DEPARTMENT table there. This would reduce the cost of the join to 5 + 400 * 405 and the total cost would be reduced to 11 + 2000 + 400 + 405 = 2816. A second plan might be for the following query tree.

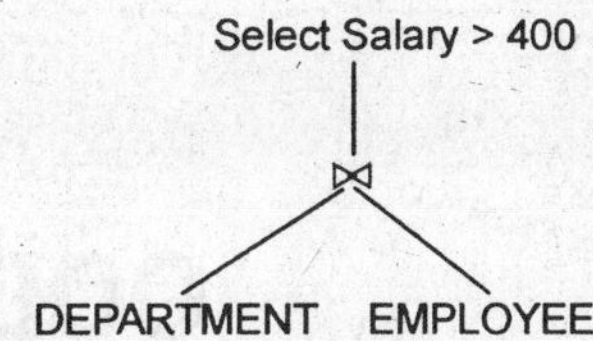

Again, we could use a nested loop for the join but instead of creating a temporary table for the result we can use a pipelining approach and pass the joining rows to the select operator as they are computed. Using a nested loop join algorithm would yield the following 50 + (50 * 2000) = 100,050 blocks We would pipeline the result to the selection operator and it would choose only those rows whose salary value was greater than 400.

NOTE : If we have 50 main memory buffer pages available during the join, then we could store the entire DEPARTMENT table there. This would reduce the cost of the join and the pipelined seleect to 50 + 2000 = 2050.

EXERCISE QUESTIONS

Q.1. Write a short note on any query optimization.
[GGSIPU, B.Tech., (CSE); 5th Sem., Dec. 2008]

Q.2. Define the following term— Access plan in query evaluation
[IGNOU, MCA; 3rd Year, June 2004]

Q.3. What are different algorithms to perform join operation? What is the cost of join operation in each of them? **[Delhi University; DCE, ME (CSE); 2005]**

Q.4. What is the role of size estimation and equivalence rules in query optimization ?
[Delhi University; DCE, ME (CSE); 2005]

Q.5. (*a*) What is the goal of query optimization ? Why is optimization important?
(*b*) What is the cost parameter for query optimization?
(*c*) What is query execution plan?
(*d*) What information is stored in the system catalogs?
[Delhi University, DCE, ME (CSE); 2006]

Q.6. What is the role of following in query optimization?
(*a*) Size estimation (*b*) Equivalence rules.
(*c*) Materialized views
(*d*) Heuristics. **[Delhi University, DCE, ME (CSE); 2006]**

Q.7. For the query expression over the given relation, draw the initial tree and write the transformed expression and corresponding tree after possible optimization. Justify the proposed plan.
Branch (branch_name, branch_city, assets)
Account (account_number, branch_name, balance)
Depositor (custome_name, account_number)
$\pi_{customer\_name}(\sigma_{branch\_city= \text{"Brooklyn"} \wedge balance > 1000}$ (branch ⋈ (account ⋈ depositor)))\
[Delhi University, DCE, ME (CSE), 2006]

Q.8. What do you understand by query optimization? How is it achieved?
[BPUT, Orissa; B.Tech. (CSE); 4th Sem., April 2005]

Q.9. (*a*) Explain equivalence rules in detail.
(*b*) Write short notes on – 'Cost based optimization.'
[Nagpur University, B.E. (CSE); 7th Sem., Dec. 2008]

Q.10. (*a*) Expain typical steps of query processing with proper diagram.
(*b*) Define the term Query optimization.
[Nagpur University, B.E (CSE); 7th Sem., Dec. 2008]

Q.11. (*a*) Explain equivalence of expression.
(*b*) State equivalance rules. **[Nagpur University, B.E (CSE); 7th Sem., Dec. 2007]**

Q.12. Discuss the Query Processor of Database system structure.
[JNTU, B.Tech., (CSE/IT); 2nd Sem. April/May 2007]

Q.13. Write short note on query processing. **[GGSIPU, BCA; 3rd Sem., Dec. 2002]**

Q.14. Define hashing – How is it used in query processing ? Explain with the help of an example.
[GGSIPU, B.Tech. (CSE/IT) – 5th Sem., Dec. 2009]

Q.15. What are the various techniques for query processing and optimization ?
[GGSIPU, B. Tech. (CSE/IT)– 5th Sem., Dec. 2011]

OODBMS—Object Oriented DBMS

10.0 INTRODUCTION

Software Engineering models the dynamic aspects of software whereas the database technology models the static aspects of information storage. The third generation of DBMS includes – Object-Oriented DBMS and Object-Relational DBMS that are used today.

10.1 CONCEPTS OF OODBMS

The evolution of OODBMS and ORDBMS is shown in Fig. 10.1.

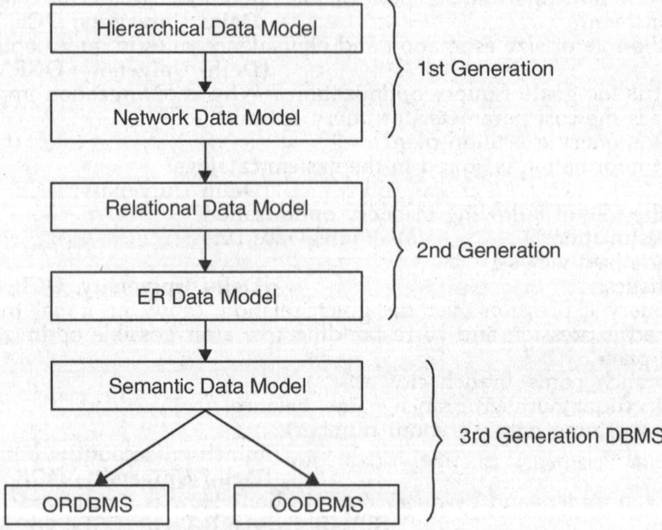

Fig. 10.1. *Evolution of data models*

Let us now discuss the characteristics of **OODBMS**. They are as follows :

1. To maintain a direct correspondence between real world and database objects so that objects do not loose integrity and identity.
2. They provide a unique system generated object identifier (OID) for each object. This simplifies object identification.
3. They are extensible meaning that they are capable of defining new data types as well as operations on them.
4. They support encapsulation *i.e.,* wrapping up of data and functions together into a single unit.

5. They exhibit inheritance also. It means that an object inherits the properties of other objects.

Oracle 8*i* is a data base, that is referred to as an ORDBMS—an object relational DBMS. The traditional Oracle is extended to include objects-oriented concepts and structures like abstract data types, nested tables, varying arrays, object views and References.

Advantages and Disadvantages of OODBMS : Let us tabulate the advantages and the disadvantages of OODBMS now.

S.No.	Advantages	Disadvantages
1.	Enriched modeling capabilities	Lack of universal data model
2.	Extensibility	Lack of experience
3.	Removal of impedance mismatch	Lack of standards
4.	More expressive query language	Competition
5.	Support for schema evolution	Query optimization compromises encapsulation
6.	Support for long-duration transaction	Locking at object level may impact performance
7.	Applicability to advanced database applications	Complexity
8.	Improved performance	Lack of support for views
9.	Improved Security	Lack of support for security

Let as discuss ORDBMS now.

Relational	The traditional ORACLE relational database (RDBMS).
Object-relational	The traditional ORACLE relational database, extended to include object-oriented concepts and structures such as abstract datatypes, nested tables, and varying arrays.
Object-oriented	An object-oriented database whose design is based solely on object-oriented analysis and design.

The combination of data and methods makes up an object. The methods of the object are used to interact with the data of the object. An object has a name, a standard representation, and a standard collection of operations that affect it The operations that effect the object are called methods.

Oracle supports many different types of objects.

Abstract Datatypes : Abstract datatypes are datatypes that consists of one or more subtypes. Rather than being constrained to the standard oracle datatypes of NUMBER, DATE, and VARCHAR2, the abstract datatypes can be used to describe the data accurately. Abstract datatypes can be nested and can contain references to other abstract datatypes.

Abstract dataypes offers both the benefits for Objects—reuse and standards adherence. When an abstract data type is created, a standard for the representation data elements is created. If you use the same abstract datatypes in multiple places, then you can be sure that the same logical data is represented in the same manner in those places. The reuse of the abstract datatype leads to the enforcement of standard representation for the data.

Nested Table : A nested table is a table within a table. A nested table is a collection of rows, represented as a column within the main table. For each record within the main table, the nested table may contain multiple rows. In one sense, it is a way of storing a one-to-many relationship within one table. Consider a table that contains information about Students. Each Student may attend different courses and answer exams for the different courses. In a strictly relational model, you would create two separate table – COURSE and MARKS.

A nested table allows us to store the information about marks of different courses within the COURSE table. The marks record of the different courses can be accessed directly via the COURSE table, without the need to perform a join. The ability to select the data without traversing joins may make the data easier to access for users. In a strictly relational model, the association between the tables would be accomplished via foreign key relationships.

Varying Arrying : A varying array is, like a nested table, a collection. A varing array is a set of objects, each with the same datatype. The size of the array is limited when it is created. When you create a varying array in a table, the array is treated as a column in the main table. Conceptually, a varying array is a nested table with a limited set of rows.

Varying arrays, also known as VARRAYS, allows us to store repeating attributes in tables. For example, you want to store the information of the different Courses undergone by each student. You can use varying arrays to store the different Courses names udergone by the student in the STUDENT COURSE table.

Large Objects : A large object (LOB) is capable of storing large volumes of data. The LOB **datatypes available are BLOB, CLOB, NCLOB, and BFILB**. The BLOB datatype is used for binary data, and can **extend to 4GB in length**. The CLOB datatype stores character data and can store data up to 4GB in length. The NCLOB datatype is used to store CLOB data for multibyte character sets. The data for BLOB, CLOB, and NCLOB datatypes is stored inside the database. Thus, you could have a single row in the databases that is 4GB in length.

The fourth LOB datatype, BFILE, **is a pointer to an external file**. The files referenced BFILEs exist in the file system; the database only maintains a pointer to the file. The size of the external file is limited only by the operating system. Since the data is stored outside the database, ORACLE does not maintain the concurrency or integrity of the data.

You can use multiple LOBs per table. **For example**, you can have a table with a CLOB column and two BLOB columns. This is an improvement over the LONG datatype, since you can only have one LONG per table. ORACLE provides a number of functions and procedures you can use to manipulate and select LOB data.

References : Nested tables and varying arrays are embedded objects - they are physically embedded within another object. Another type of objects called referenced objects are physically separate from the objects that refer to them. References also known as REFs, are essentially pointers to row objects. A "row object" is different than a "column object".

An example of a "column object" would be a varying array - it is an object that is treated as a column in a table. A "row object", on the other hand, always represents a row. References are typically among the last OO features implemented when migrating a relational application to an object-relational or OO approach.

Object Views : Object views are to add OO concepts on top of the existing relational tables. For example, you can create on abstract datatype based on an existing table's definition. Thus, object views give us the benefits of relational table storage and OO structures. Object views allow us to begin to develop OO features within relational database—a bridge between relational and OO worlds.

ABSTRACT DATATYPE - EXAMPLE

The **Create Type** command is used to create an abstract datatype.

```
CREATE TYPE STUDENT_NAME_TY AS OBJECT
(FIRST_NAME VARCHAR2 (15), LAST_NAME VARCHAR2 (15));
```

Within the **Create Type** command, the **as object** clause explicity identifies STUDENT_NAME_TY as an OO implementation.

Now the table can be created using the abstract datatype as one of the columns.

```
CREATE TABLE STUDENT (
STUDENT_ID  NUMBER (4) PRIMARY KEY,
NAME        STUDENT_NAME_TY)
```

The student table is created. The structure of the table can be listed with the DESC command.

```
DESC STUDENT
NAME            Null? Type
-------------------------------------------------
STUDENT_ID      NOT NULL NUMBER (4)
NAME            STUDENT_NAME_TY
```

To list the datailed information about the columns within the tables and views owned by us, the USER_TAB COLUMNS is used.

```
SELECT COLUMN_NAME, DATA_TYPE FROM USER_TAB_COLUMNS
WHERE TABLE_NAME = 'STUDENT'
COLUMN_NAME       DATA_TYPE
-- - - - - - - - - - - - - - - - - - - - - - - - - -
STUDENT_ID        NUMBER
NAME              STUDENT_NAME_TY
```

To see the construction of abstract datatype, the USER_TYPE_ATTRS is used. The columns of an abstract datatype are referred to as its **attributes**. The USER_TYPE_ATTRS displays information about the attributes of a user's abstract datatype.

```
SELECT ATTR_NAME, LENGTH, ATTR_TYPE_NAME
FROM USER_TYPE_ATTRS
WHERE TYPE_NAME = 'STUDENT_NAME_TY;
ATTR_NAME         LENGTH  ATTR_TYPE_NAME
- - - - - - - - - - - - - - - - - - - - - - - - -
FIRST_NAME          15    VARCHAR2
LAST_NAME           15    VARCHAR2
```

Inserting Records : ORACLE creates methods, called **constructor methods**, for data management when you create an abstract datatype. A constructor method is a program that is named after the datatype; its parameters are the names of the attributes defined for the datatype. When you need to insert record into a table based on abstract datatypes, you can use the constructor methods.

In order to insert a record into the STUDENT table, you will have to insert a record using the STUDENT_NAME_TY datatype. To insert records using this datatype, you will need to use the constructor methods for the datatype.

In the following example a record is inserted into STUDENT using the constructor method for the STUDENT_NAME_TY datatype. The constructor method for datatype, has the same name as the datatype.

```
INSERT INTO STUDENT VALUES
(1, STUDENT_NAME_TY ('SHANKAR','NARAYANA'));
```

You can insert records into the tabe, interactively using the following command.

```
INSERT INTO STUDENT VALUES
(& STUDENT_ID, STUDENT_NAME_TY (&FIRST_NAME',' &LAST_NAME'))
```

Selecting from Abstract datatypes : When the column in a table, is a normal datatype, you can use the simple query to view the datails from the table. But when the column uses an abstract datatype, you cannot query it directly.

Suppose you want to view only the FIRST_NAME from the STUDENT table. ORACLE treats FIRST_NAME as an attribute within the STUDENT_NAME_TY abstract datatype. You need to query the FIRST_NAME attribute within the NAME column as ORACLE does not treat FIRST_NAME as a column from STUDNET table. The query will be as follows:

```
SELECT STUDENT_ID, NAME.FIRST_NAME FROM STUDENT;
```

The dot(.) Operator is used to indicate that FIRST_NAME is part of Name.

OBJECT VIEWS : ORACLE provides Object Views as a means for defining objects used by existing relational relational tables. **For example**, there is a previously created relational database application and you want to implement object-relational concepts into your application without rebuilding and recreating the entire application. You need to overlay object-oriented (OO) structures such as abstract datatypes on existing relational tables. Object views allow us to create abstract datatypes within tables that already exist.

If the STUDENT table is already created as a relational table, you could create the STUDENT_NAME_TY dataype, and use Object Views to relate them to STUDENT table.

In the following example, let us assume that the STUDENT table has been created as a relational table with the following commands.

```
CREATE TABLE STUDENT
(STUDENT_ID NUMBER (4) PRIMARY KEY,
FIRST_NAME VARCHAR2 (15),
LAST_NAME VARCHAR2(15));
```

Although the STUDENT table is already created, you can create the abstract datatype, STUDENT_NAME_TY for FIRST_NAME and LAST_NAME as given :

```
CREATE OR REPLACE TYPE STUDENT_NAME_TY AS OBJECT
(FIRST_NAME VARCHAR2(15),
LAST_NAME VARCHAR2 (15);
```

Lastly, you can optionally create an object that is based on all of the columns of the STUDENT table. This object will be named as STUDENT_TY:

```
CREATE OR REPLACE TYPE STUDENT_TY AS OBJECT
(STUDENT_ID NUMBER(4),
NAME_STUDENT_NAME_TY);
```

Now the object view can be created, based on the STUDENT table using the datatypes you have defined. An object view starts with the CREATE VIEW command. The following is the command to create STUDENT_OV object view:

```
CREATE VIEW STUDENT_OV (STUDENT_ID, NAME)
AS SELECT
STUDENT_ID, STUDENT_NAME_TY (FIRST_NAME, LAST_NAME)
FROM STUDENT;
```

For creating object views based on existing relational tables, the order of operations is :

1. Create the STUDENT table.
2. Create the STUDENT_NAME_TY datatype.
3. Create the STUDENT_TY using the STUDENT_NAME_TY datatype.
4. Create the STUDENT_OV object view, using the defined datatypes.

The two main benefits to using object views are :

1. They allow us to create abstract datatypes within tables that already exist.Since you can use the same abstract datatype in multiple tables within your application, you can improve your application's adherence to standard representation of data and ability to reuse existing objects.
2. Object views allow two different ways to enter data into the base table. You can enter data into STUDENT table via the STUDENT_OV object view, or you can enter data into the STUDENT table directly. The flexibility of data manipulation for object views – being able to treat the base table as either a relational table or an object table – is a significant benefit for application developers.

METHODS : A method is a block of PL/SQL code used to encapsulate the data access method for an object. Within ORACLE, methods are specified as part of the abstract datatype specification and their body is specified as part of the CREATE TYPE BODY command. Users can execute methods on the datatypes for which the methods are defined.

In the case of object views, when you define methods that apply to abstract datatype, by applying those datatypes to existing tables, you can apply those methods to the data in those tables.

When you create an abstract datatype, you use the **Create Type** command. When you create a method, you use the **Create Type Body** command.

Before creating the body for a method, you must name the method within the type declaration. **For example**, a new datatype MARKS_TY is created in the following listing:

```
    CREATE OR REPLACE TYPE MARKS_TY AS OBJECT
    (M1     NUMBER(3),
    M2      NUMBER(3),
    M3      NUMBER(3),
MEMBER FUNCTION TOTMARKS (M1 IN NUMBER, M2 IN NUMBER,
    M3 IN NUMBER)
RETURN NUMBER);
```

TOTMARKS is function since it returns a value. It is a member of the MARKS_TY datatype. To define the TOTMARKS function, the **CREATE TYPE BODY** command is used. Now, to create TOTMARKS function as a member function within the MARKS_TY datatype.

```
CREATE OR REPLACE TYPE BODY MARKS_TY AS
MEMBER FUNCTION TOTMARKS (M1 NUMBER, M2 NUMBER,
    M3 NUMBER)
RETURN NUMBER IS
BEGIN
RETURN (M1 + M2 + M3);
END;
END;
/
```

After the TOTMARKS function is created, it is associated with the MARKS_TY datatype. If a table uses this datatype, then it can use the TOTMARKS function.

If MARKS_TY is used as a datatype for a column named MARKS in the STDMARKS, then the table structure will be:

```
CREATE TABLE STDMARKS
(STUDENT_ID NUMBER(4),
MARKS MARKS_TY);
```

Now to invoke the TOTMARKS function, which is part of the MARKS_TY datatype,

```
SELECT MARKS. TOTMARKS(MARKS.M1.MARKS.M2,MARKS.M3)
FROM STDMARKS;
```

Like the attributes of an abstract datatype, the member methods are referenced via the column names that use the datatypes.

> **NOTE** : *When you create an Object View on a existing table, you defined abstract datatypes that the table used. Those datatypes help to standardize the representation of data, but they serve another purpose as well. You can define methods that apply to datatypes, and by applying those datatypes to existing tables, you can apply those methods to the data in those tables.*

COLLECTORS (NESTED TABLES AND VARYING ARRAYS : Collectors are sets of elements that are treated as part of a single row. The two types of collectors available are called **Nested tables** and **Varying arrays**.

Varying Arrays : A varying array allows us to store repeating attributes of a record in a single row. Varying arrays allow repeating only those column values that change, potentially saving storage space. You can create a varying array based on either an abstract datatype or one of ORACLE's standard datatypes (such as NUMBER).

For example, you want to create a varying array for COURSENAME which stores the different courses undergone by a student in STDCOURSE table. Before creating an varying array in the STDCOURSE table, you need to decide the maximum number of courses taken up by a student.

To create the varying array, the as varray () clause of the create type command is used.

```
CREATE OR REPLACE TYPE COURSE_VA AS VARRAY(5) OF
VARCHAR2 (20);
```

When this **create type** command is executed, a type named COURSE_VA is created. The **as varray(5)** clause tells ORACLE that a varying array is being created, and it will hold a maximum of five entries per record.

Now that you have created the varying array COURSE_VA, you can specify that as part of the creation of either a table or an abstract datatype. In the following example, the STDCOURSE table is created using the COURSE_VA, the varying array as a datatype for its COURSENAME column:

```
CREATE TABLE STDCOURSE
(ST_ID          NAMBER(4),
COURSENAME      COURSE_VA);
```

Describing the Varying Array : The STDCOURSE table will contain one record for each student, even if that student undergoes different courses. The different courses will be stored in the COURSENAME column, using COURSE_VA varying array.

```
DESC STDCOURSE
Name            Null? Type
- - - - - - - - - - - - - - - - - - - - - - - - -
ST_ID           NUMBER(4)
COURSENAME      COURSE_VA
```

You can use the USER_TAB_COLUMNS data dictionary also to view the structure.

```
SELECT COLUMN_NAME, DATA_TYPE FROM USER_TAB_COLUMNS
WHERE TABLE_NAME='STDCOURSE';
COLUMN_NAME             DATA_TYPE
- - - - - - - - - - - - - - - - - - - - - - - - - - - - - -
ST_ID                   NUMBER
COURSENAME              COURSE_VA
```

USER_TYPES data dictionary view is used to see the datatype of COURSE_VA, which is given below;

```
SELECT TYPECODE, ATTRIBUTES FROM USER_TYPES
WHERE TYPE_NAME = 'COURSE_VA';
TYPECODE            ATTRIBUTES
- - - - - - - -     - - - - - - - - -
COLLECTION               0
```

The USER_TYPES output shows that COURSE_VA is a collector, with no attributes.

Since COURSE_VA is a collector, there may be an upper limit to the number of entries it can contain per record. You can query the USER_COLL_TYPES data dictionary view to see the characteristics of the varying array, including the abstract datatype on which it is based:

```
SELECT COLL_TYPE, ELEM_TYPE_OWNER,
ELEM_TYPE_NAME, UPPER_BOUND,
LENGTH FROM USER_COLL_TYPES
WHERE TYPE_NAME = 'COURSE_VA';
COLL_TYPE               ELEM_TYPE_OWNER
-- - - - - - - - - - -  - - - - - - -  - - - - -
ELEM_TYPE_NAME          UPPER_BOUND         LENGTH
-- - - - - - - - - - -  - - - - - - - - - - -   - - - - - -
VARYING ARRAY
VARCHAR2                     5                  20
```

From the queries of data dictionary, you can see that COURSENAME column uses the COURSE_VA varying array, and that array contains a maximum of five values whose structure is defined as VARCHAR2(20). You need to know this information in order to insert records into the STDCOURSE table.

Inserting Records into the Varying Array : When a datatype is created, the database automatically creates a method called a constructor method for the datatype. You need to use the constructor method when inserting records into columns that uses abstract datatype. Since a varying array is an abstract datatype, you need to use constructor method in order to insert records into tables that use varying arrays.

The following command will insert a single record into the STDCOURSE table. In this example, the record will have a single Student id column and three Course names.

```
INSERT INTO STDCOURSE VALUES
(1, COURSE_VA ('EXCEL', 'WORD',' WINDOWS'));
```

In the insert command, since the COURSENAME column uses the COURSE_VA varying array, you can pass multiple values to the COURSE_VA constructor method.

Selecting Data from Varying Arrays : When you insert records into a varying array, you need to make sure that the number of entries you insert into the varying array does not exceed its maximum. The maximum number of entries in the varying array is specified when the varying array is created and can be queried from USER_COLL_TYPES as discussed earlier. You can also query the varying array directly to determine its maximum number of entries per row, called its LIMIT, and the current number of entries per row, called its COUNT.

You cannot, however, query the varying array directly via a select command. In order to retrieve the COUNT, LIMIT, and data from a varying array, you need to use PL/SQL. To query the data from a varying array, you can use a set of nested Cursor FOR loops, as given below :

```
EDIT COURSE.SQL (will display an editor for typing the PL/SQL code):
SET SERVEROUTPUT ON
DECLARE
CURSOR COURSE_CURSOR IS SELECT * FROM STDCOURSE;
BEGIN
    FOR COURSE_REC IN COURSE || CURSOR
    LOOP
        DBMS_OUTPUT. PUT_LINE ('STUDENT ID : U COURSE_REC.ST_ID);
        FOR I IN 1 .. COURSE_REC.COURSENAME.COUNT
        LOOP
        DBMS_OUTPUT.PUT_LINE ('SUBJECT:' || COURSE_REC.
            COURSENAME(I));
        END LOOP;
        DBMS_OUTPUT.PUT_LINE (' .- - - - - - - - - - ');
    END LOOP;
END;
/
```

The output of this PL/SQL script is :

```
STUDENT ID :1
SUBJECT :EXCEL
```

```
SUBJECT: WORD
SUBJECT :WINDOWS
- - - - - - - - - - - --
STUDENT ID :2
SUBJECT :ORACLE
SUBJECT :VISUAL BASIC
SUBJECT :JAVA
SUBJECT :C
- - - - - - - - - - - - -
STUDENT ID :3
SUBJECT :WINDOWS
SUBJECT :FOXPRO
SUBJECT :TALLY
SUBJECT :DOS
SUBJECT :EXCEL
-------------------------
```

Nested Tables : You can use varying arrays to create collectors within the tables and datatypes. While varying arrays have a limited number of entries, a second collector, **nested tables**, has no limit on the number of entries per row. A **nested table** is, as its name implies, a table within a table. In this case, it is a table that is represented as a column within another table. You can have multiple rows in the nested table for each row in the main table.

For example, if you want to store the COURSENAME and MARKS of each course for each student along with the Student id, you could use a nested table. Using a nested table you could store the information of all students and their entire course marks details within the same table.

```
CREATE OR REPLACE TYPE COURSE_TY AS OBJECT
(COURSENAME VARCHAR2(20),
    MARKS NUMBER(3));
/
```

The COURSE_TY datatype contains a record for each course - Course name and Course marks. To use this datatype as the basis for a nested table, you need to create a new abstract datatype:

```
CREATE TYPE COURSE_NT AS TABLE OF COURSE_TY;
/
```

The **as table** of clause of this **create type** command tells ORACLE that you will be using this type as the basis for a nested table.

You can now create COURSEMARKS table using the COURSE_NTdatatype:

```
CREATE TABLE COURSEMARKS
(ST_ID NUMBER(4), COURSE_MARKS COURSE_NT)
NESTED TABLE COURSE_MARKS STORE AS COURSE_NT_TAB;
```

In this **create table** command, the COURSEMARKS table is created. The first column of the COURSEMARKS table is Student Id column. The second column is a column named COURSE_MARKS, whose definition is the nested table COURSE_NT.

When creating a table that includes a nested table, you must specify the name of the table that will be used to store the nested table's data. That is, the data for the nested table is not stored "in-line" with the rest of the tables's data. Instead, it is stored apart from the main table. Thus, the data in the Course marks column will be stored in one table, and the data in the Student id column will be stored in a separate table. ORACLE maintain pointers between the tables. In this example, the "out-of-line" data for the nested table is stored in a table named COURSE_NT_TAB.

Inserting Records into a Nested Table: You can insert records into a nested table by using the constructor methods for its datatype. For the Course marks column, the datatype is COURSE_NT; thus, you will use the COURSE_NT constructor method. The COURSE_NT type, in turn, uses the COURSE_TY datatype. In the following example, inserting a record into the COURSEMARKS table requires the use both COURSE_NT and COURSE_TY constructor methods.

```
INSERT INTO COURSEMARKS VALUES
( 1, COURSE_NT(
COURSE_TY ('EXCEL',50), COURSE_TY ('WORD',60),
COURSE_TY ('CONCEPTS',70))
);
```

In the above example, three course marks details are stored for Student id, 1. Since the course marks column uses the COURSE_NT nested table, the COURSE_NT constructor method is invoked. The COURSE_NT nested table uses the COURSE_TY constructor method is invoked for each record inserted. To query the definitions of the columns, the USER_TAB_COLUMNS is used.

SELECT COLUMN_NAME, DATA_TYPE FROM USER_TAB_COLUMNS is used.

```
WHERE TABLES_NAME = 'COURSEMARKS';
COLUMN_NAME          DATA_TYPE
- - - - - - - - - - - - - - - - - - - - - - - - - - -
ST_ID                NUMBER
COURSE_MARKS         COURSE_ NT
```

The USER_TAB_COLUMNS output shows that the course marks column uses the COURSE_NT datatype. To verify that the COURSE_NT datatype is a collector, you have to check USER_TYPES:

```
SELECT TYPECODE, ATTRIBUTES FROM USER_TYPES
WHERE TYPE_NAME= 'COURSE_NT';
TYPECODE            ATTRIBUTES
- - - - - - - - - - - - - - -   - - - - - - -
COLLECTION                 0
```

To see the datatype used as the basis for the nested table, query USER_COLL_TYPES:

```
SELECT COLL_TYPE, ELEM_TYPE_OWNER, ELEM_TYPE_NAME,
UPPER_BOUND, LENGTH FROM USER_COLL_TYPES
WHERE TYPE_NAME = 'COURSE_NT';
COLL_TYPE            ELEM_ TYPE_OWNER
- - - - - - - - - - - - - - - - - - - - - - - - - - - -
ELEM_TYPE_NAME       UPPER_BOUND        LENGTH
------------------   ----------------   -----------
TABLE                PRACTICE
```

COURSE_TY

The output from USER_COLL_TYPES shows that the COURSE_NT nested table is based on the COURSE_TY abstract datatype. You can query USER_TYPE_ATTRS to see the attributes of COURSE_TY :

```
SELECT ATTR_NAME, LENGTH, ATTR_TYPE_NAME
FROM USER_TYPE_ATTRS
WHERE TYPE_NAME ='COURSE_TY';
ATTR_NAME            LENGTH ATTR_TYPE_NAME
-------------------  ---------------------------------------
COURSENAME           20 VARCHAR2
MARKS                NUMBER
```

Thus, you can use the data dictionary views to determine the datatype structure of nested tables. You will need to know the datatype structures and the nested table structures and the nested table structures in order to effectively use the COURSEMARKS table.

Querying Nested Table : Unlike varying arrays, queries for nested tables are not limited to PL/SQL; however, in order to query nested tables you will need to be familiar with several new extensions to SQL. Nested tables support a great variety of queries. A nested table is a column within a table. To support queries of the columns and rows of a nested table, ORACLE provides a new keyworkd, **THE**. In order to select columns (such as MARKS)from the nested table, you first have to **"flatten"** the table so it can be queried. That is where **THE** function is used.

```
SELECT NT.MARKS FROM
THE (SELECT COURSE_MARKS FROM COURSEMARKS
WHERE ST_ID = 1) NT
WHERE NT. COURSENAME='EXCEL';
MARKS
- - - - - -
   50
```

In the above example, the **THE** function "flattens" the query of the nested table and allows us to query the entire COURSEMARKS table. The **FROM** (outer query) clause contains the query of nested table column, and the resulting "table" is given the alias "NT". The **where** (outer query) clause of the query specifies limiting conditions for the query. SELECT NT.MARKS, column list in the query specifies the nested table column to display.

THE Function With INSERT Command : You can use the THE function whenever you need to perform **inserts** or **updates** directly against the nested table. For example, when the marks for the other courses for the existing students will have to be recorded, you need to insert new records to the COURSE_NT nested table within the COURSEMARKS table. You will have to **insert** records into the nested table without adding new records into the COURSEMARKS table, and you will need to relate the new course marks records to students who are already in COURSEMARKS table.

```
INSERT INTO
THE (SELECT COURSE_MARKS FROM COURSEMARKS
WHERE ST_ID=1)
VALUES(
COURSE_TY('TALLY', 95));
```

In the above example, the **THE** function is used in place of the table name. The **Select** command selects the nested from within the main COURSEMARKS table for the row in which the Student id column has the value 1. You can insert into the nested table using the constructor method for the nested table's datatype (COURSE_TY).

You can use the same method for performing **updates**; you have to use the **THE** function in place of the table name and you will be able to work with the data within the nested table.

LARGE OBJECTS : The long data type can be used to store character data up to 2 GB in length per row. The Long Row datatype provides storage for long binary data.

Available Datatypes : There are 4 types of large objects (LOB's) available.

LOB Datatype	Description
BLOB	Binary LOB, Binary data, up to 4 GB in length, stored in the database.
CLOB	Character LOB character data up to 4GB in length, stored in the database.
BFILE	Binary file; read only binary data stored outside the database, length is limited by the operating system.
NCLOB	A CLOB column that supports a multibyte character set..

Multiple LOBs can be created on a table. For example, you will create a proposal table to store the data of proposals that you submit.

```
CREATE TABLE PROPOSAL
(PROPOSAL_ID          NUMBER(10) PRIMARY KEY,
PROPOSAL_TAXT CLOB,
BUDGET                BLOB,
COVER_LETTER          BFILE);
```

A Proposal_Id assigned because multiple proposals are sent to the same recipient.

Proposal_text	A CLOB containing the text of the proposal
Budget	A BLOB containing a spreadsheet showing calculations of the cost and profit for the proposed work.
Cover_letter	A Binary file stored outside the database that contains cover letter that accompanied the proposal.

For each row in the proposal table, there will be up to 3 LOB values stored. Oracle will use the normal database capabilities to support data integrity and concurrency for the proposal and budget entries but not for the Cover_letter values. Since the Cover_letter column uses BFILE datatype, data is stored outside the database. Internally, the database stores only a locator value that allows it to find external file. Oracle does not guarantee the data integrity of BFILE files stored outside the database. Oracle does not even validate that the file exists when you insert a record using a BFILE datatype. Data concurrency and integrity is only maintained for internally stored LOBs. The data for LOB columns whether stored inside or outside the database, is not physically stored within the proposal table. Within the proposal table, ORACLE stores locator values that point to data locations. For BFILE datatype, the locator points to an external file and for BLOB and CLOB datatypes the locator points to a separate data location that the database creates to hold the LOB data. Thus, the LOB data is not necessarily stored directly with the rest of the data in the proposal table.

Storing the data out-of-line like this allows the database to avoid having to scan LOB data each time it reads multiple rows from the database. The LOB data is read only when required. Otherwise the locator values will be read.

Manipulating and Selecting LOB values : LOB data can be selected and manipulated via the DBMS_LOB package. Other methods for manipulating LOB data include using API (Application Programming Interfaces) and OCI (ORACLE Call Interface) programs. LOB are much more flexible, than long datatypes in terms of data manipulation possibilities.

Intitializing Values : The PROPOSAL_ID column is the primary key column for the proposal table. There are three LOB columns identified in the proposal table, one BLOB column, one CLOB and one BFILE. For each of the LOB column, ORACLE will store a locator value that tells it where to find any out of line data stored for the record.

When inserting a record into a table that contains LOBs, use DBMS_LOB package to tell ORACLE to create an empty locator value for internally stored LOB columns. An empty locator value is different from a NULL value. If an internally stored LOB column's value is NULL, then set it to an empty locator value before updating it to a non_NULL value.

```
INSERT INTO PROPOSAL
VALUES (2,'THIS IS THE NEW PROPOSAL TEXT', EMPTY_BLOB()
BFILENAME ('C:/RAJ',' DOC'));
```

The inserted record has a Proposal_ID of 2. The Proposal_text column is set equal to a short character string for now. In order to set the budget column to an empty locator value, the EMPTY_BLOB function is used. To set a CLOB datatype column to an empty locator value, the EMPTY_CLOB function is used. The BFILE_NAME() tells ORACLE exactly where to find the Cover_letter - *i.e.,* in the 'C:/RAJ ' directory and its name is RAJ.DOC. Within the BFILENAME function, the first parameter is always the directory name and the second parameter is the name of the file within that directory.

When you select the value from a LOB column, ORACLE will use the locator value to find the data that is associated with the LOB data. The user does not know or specify the locator values.

Updating LOB Values : Before modifying an LOB value, the row must be located. Normally row locking occurs in the background when an **update** command is executed, ORACLE dynamically locks the row, performs the transaction and then unlocks the row. If you are updating a row that contains a LOB value, then you need to explicitly lock the row before you execute the **update** command or the command will fail.To lock the record, the record is selected using the for UPDATE clause.

```
SELECT PROPOSAL_TEXT FROM PROPOSAL
    WHERE PROPOSAL_ID = 2 FOR UPDATE;
```

Now the record with Proposal_ID 2 has been selected for update and has an exclusive lock on the row.

```
UPDATE PROPOSAL SET PROPOSAL ='This column is updated today'
WHERE PROPOSAL_ID = 2;
```

To release the lock, **commit** the change:

```
COMMIT;
```

The Cover_letter column can also be updated. You can use the BFILENAME function to change the filename.

```
UPDATE PROPOSAL SET COVER_LETTER=
BFILENAME(('C:\ORACLE',' ABC. DOC'));
WHERE PROPOSAL_ID =2;
```

Since the Cover_letter column uses BFILE datatype, the row need not be locked before performing update. Exclusive lock is only needed for update of internally stored LOBs. The BFILE columns can be updated with NULL value without first setting them to empty locator values. If you had inserted a record with a NULL value for Budget (a BLOB column), you cannot update the Budget column's value unless it is set to a value of EMPTY_BLOB() via an **update** command. After setting the value of EMPTY_BLOB() and establishing an empty locator value, you can update the Budget column value.

Using DBMS_LOB to Manipulate LOB Values : The DBMS_LOB package can be used to change or select LOB values. SQL function SUBSTR and INSTR can be performed on LOB values, and for appending to LOB values, comparing LOB values and reading them. The string comparison and manipulation procedures and functions are available within DBMS_LOB package.

Function	Description
SUBSTR	Function used to perform the SQL SUBSTR function on a LOB value.
INSTR	Function used to perform the SQL INSTR on a LOB value.'
GETLENGTH	Function used to perform the SQL LENGTH function on a LOB value.
COMPARE	Function used to compare two LOB values.
READ	Procedure used to read a piece of a LOB value.
WRITE	Procedure used to write data into the LOB value at a specified point within the LOB value.

Procedure	Description
APPEND	Procedure used to append the contents of one LOB value to another LOB value.
ERASE	Procedure used to erase all or part of a LOB value.
TRIM	Procedure used to perform the SQL RTRIM function on a LOB value.
COPY	Procedure used to copy all or part of a LOB value from one LOB column to another.

When using BFILEs, the maximum number of files that can be opened is limited by the setting of the SESSION_MAX_OPEN_FILES parameter in the database's Init. Ora, file. The default maximum number of concurrently open BFILE files is 10.

BFILE - specific Procedures and Functions within the DBMS_LOB package.

Procedure	Description
FILEOPEN	Procedure used to open files for reading.
FILECLOSE	Procedure used to close specific files. For every FIEOPEN call, there must be a matching FILECLOSE call.
FILECLOSEALL	Procedure used to close all open files.
FILEGETNAME	Procedure used to get the name of the external file referenced by a BFILE locator value.
FILEEXISTS	Function used to determine if the external file referenced by a BFILE locator value exists.
FILESOPEN	Function used to determine if the external file is open.

READ : The READ procedure reads a piece of a LOB value. In the proposal table, example, the PROPOSAL_TEXT which is a CLOB column can be retrieved using the SELECT statement.

```
SELECT PROPOSAL_TEXT
FROM PROPOSAL
WHERE PROPOSAL_ID=2;
```

However, since a CLOB column can contain a large amount of data (4GB), the SELECT statement is not normally used. Instead the READ procedure is used to read any portion of the column.

The same functions and operations can be used against longer CLOB strings. The read procedure has 4 parameters, which must be specified in this order.

1. The LOB locator.
2. The number of bytes or characters to be read.
3. The offset (starting point of the read) from the beginning of the LOB value.
4. The output data from the READ procedure.

If the end of the LOB value is reached before the specified number of bytes is read, the READ procedure will return an error. As the READ procedure requires to LOB locator as input, the READ procedure is executed within PL/SQL blocks. You will need to select the LOB locator value, provide that as input to the READ procedure, and then display the text read via DBMS_OUTPUT package.

A READ Example : To use the READ procedure, you need to know the locator value of the LOB you want to read. The locator value must be selected from the table that contains the LOB. Since the locator value must be supplied as input to the READ procedure, you should use PL/SQL variables to hold the locator value. The READ procedure, in turn, will place its output in a PL/SQL variable. You can use the DBMS_OUTPUT package to display the output value

From the PROPOSAL table, to select first 50 characters from PROPOSAL_TEXT column.

```
--READING INFORMATION FROM CLOB DATA TYPE.
SET SERVEROUTPUT ON
DECLARE
LOCATOR_VAR CLOB;
AMOUNT_VAR INTEGER;
OFFSET_VAR INTEGER;
OUTPUT_VAR VARCHAR2(50);
BEGIN
AMOUNT_VAR:=50;
OFFSET_VAR:=1;
SELECT PROPOSAL_TEXT INTO LOCATOR_VAR
FROM PROPOSAL WHERE PROPOSAL_ID=2;
DBMS_LOB. READ(LOCATIOR_VAR,AMOUNT_VAR, OFFSET_VAR.
    OUTPUT_VAR);
DBMS_OUTPUT.PUT_LINE('START OF PROPOSAL TEXT:
    || OUTPUT_VAR);
```

```
END;

SET SERVEROUTPUT OFF
```

The locator value was selected from the Proposal table and stored in a variable named **locator_var**. Then the READ procedure was called, using the values that has been assigned. As a result of the execution of the READ procedure, the **output_var** variable will be populated with the data that was read.

To select a different portion of the Proposal_Text CLOB, you have to just change the amount and offset variable. If you want to change the number of characters read, you will need to change the size of the output variable, too. If 20 characters are to be read from the Proposal_Text, starting from the 10th character onwards, then the amount_var : = 20 and offset : = 10 in the PL/SQL block.

If the proposal_text is created as VARCHAR2 column, then SUBSTR function is used. However, for a VARCHAR2 column, the maximum length is limited to 4000 characters. LOB columns can contain Binary data (BLOB datatypes). The READ procedure can be used to select data BLOBS the same way as selecting CLOBs. For BLOBs, the output buffer is declared to use RAW datatype. In PL/SQL raw and VARCHAR2 datatype (used for output variable for CLOB and BLOB reads) have a maximum length of 32,767.

TABLESPACE: A tablespace is an area of disk consisting of one or more disk files. A tablespace can contain many tables, indexes, or clusters. Because a tablespace has a fixed size, it can get full as rows are added to its tables. When this happens, the tablespace can be expanded by someone who has DBA authority. The expansion is accomplished by creating a new disk file and adding it to the tablespace or by extending the existing datafiles. New rows can then be added to existing tables, and those tables will therefore have rows in both files. One or more tablespaces, together, make up a database.

Each table has a single area of disk space called a **segment** set aside for it in the tablespace. Each segment, in turn, has an initial area of disk space set aside for it in the tablespace called the initial extent. Once it has used up this space, the next extent, another single area of disk space, is set aside for it. When it has used up as well, yet another next extent is set aside. This process continues with every table until the whole tablespace is full. At that point, someone has to add a new file to the tablespace to extend the tablespace's files before any more growth in the tables can take place.

Every database also contains a system tablespace, where the ownership records and addresses are kept. It contains the dictionary, and the names and locations of the tablespaces, tables, indexes, and clusters for this database.

The database is created and named by the system database administrator, who usually also sets up tablespaces and grants use of them to individual users.

Create Tablespace : The create tablespace command allows one or more files to be assigned immediately to the tablespace. It also specifies a default space for any tables created without an explicit storage clause mentioned in the create table statement.

```
CREATE TABLESPACE MYSPACE DATAFILE'HOME.ONE'SIZE 1000 K
DEFAULT STORAGE (INITIAL 25K NEXT 10K
MINEXTENTS 1 MAXETENTS 100
PCTINCREASE 0)
PERMANENT;
```

The initial file assigned to this tablespace is included in the command, as well as its size in **bytes**. The number of bytes is an integer and can be followed by a k (to multiply by 1024 — about a thousand) or an M (to be multiplied by 1048576 – about a million). Default storage sets up the storage a table will get if storage is not specified in the **create table** statement. Here the initial default extent is 25k bytes and the next (incremental) extent is 10K bytes.

Minextents allows us to set aside additional extents beyond the first at the time a table is created. These will not necessarily be contiguous (physically adjacent) with the initial extent, or with each other, but the space will at least be reserved.

Maxextents is the limit of additional extents allowed.

Pctincrease is a growth factor for extents. When set to a non-zero value, each incremental extent will be the specified percentage larger than the one before it. This has the affect of reducing the number of extents, and noncontiguous space, used by a table that grows at a constant rate, you should set **pctincrease** to 0.

```
CREATE TABLESPACE MYSPACE1 DATAFILE 'HOME.TWO' SIZE 1000K
DEFAULT STORAGE (INTIAL 25 NEXT 10K
MINEXTENTS 1 MAXEXTENTS 100
PCTINCREASE 0)
PERMANENT;
```

> **NOTE :** The permanent keyword in the create tablespace command tells ORACLE that you will be storing permanent objects (such as tables) in the tablespace. If the tablespace is only used for temporary segments, then you can specify the temporary keyword instead. The default value is permanent.

The create table command for the STUDENT table using the tablespace is as follows:

```
CREATE TABLE STUDENT
(
STUDNET_ID          NUMBER (4) PRIMARY KEY,
STUDENT_NAME        VARCHAR2 (20)
)
TABLESPACE MYPACE
;
```

Let us now compare RDBMS, ORDBMS and ODBMS in a tabular form.

A Comparison of Database Management Systems

Criteria	RDBMS	ORDBMS	ODBMS
Defining standard	SQL2 (ANSI X3H2)	SQL3/4 (in process)	ODMG_V2.0
Support for object-oriented programming	Poor; programmers spend 25% of coding time mapping the program object to the database	Limited mostly to new data types	Direct and extensive
Simplicity of use	Table structures easy to understand; many end-user tools available	Same as RDBMS, with some confusing extensions	OK for programmer; some SQL access for end users

Simplicity of development	Provides independence of data from application, good for simple relationship	Provides independence of data from application, good for simple relationships	Objects are a natural way to model; can accommodate a wide variety of types and relationships
Extensibility and content	None	Limited mostly to new data types	Can handle arbitrary complexity; users can write methods and on any structure
Complex data relationships	Difficult to model	Difficult to model	Can handle arbitrary complexity; users can write methods on any structure
Performance versus interoperability	Level of safety varies with vendor, must be traded off; achieving both requires extensive testing	Level of safety varies with vendor, must be traded off; achieving both requires extensive testing	Level of safety varies with vendor; most ODBMSs allow progr-mmers to extend DBMS functionality by defining new classes
Distribution, replication, and federated databases	Extensive	Extensive	Varies with vendor; a few provide extensive support
Product maturity	Very mature	Immature; extensions are new, are still being defined, and are relatively unproven	Relatively mature
Legacy people and the universality of SQL	Extensive supply of tools and trained developers	Can take advantages of RDBMS tools and developers	SQL accommodated, but intended for object-oriented programmers.
Software ecosystems	Provided by major RDBMS companies	Provided by major RDBMS companies	ODBMS vendors beginning to emulate RDBMS vendors, but none offers large markets to other ISVs
Vendor viability	Expected for the major established RDBMS vendors	Expected for the major RDBMS vendors: UniSQL is struggling	Less of an issue than it was; some shakeout still expected

10.2 DISTRIBUTED DBMS

A logically interrelated collection of shared data physically distributed over a computer network is called as a distributed database. And the software system that permits the management of the distributed database and makes it transparent to the users is called as a ***distributed DBMS.***

Characteristics of DDBMS : DDBMS has the following characteristics :-

1. It is a collection of logically related shared data.
2. The data is split into a number of fragments.
3. Fragments may be replicated.
4. Fragments-replicas are allocated to sites.

5. The sites are linked by a communication network.
6. The data at each site is under the control of a DBMS.
7. At each site, the DBMS can handle local applications, autonomously.
8. Each DBMS participates in at least one global application.

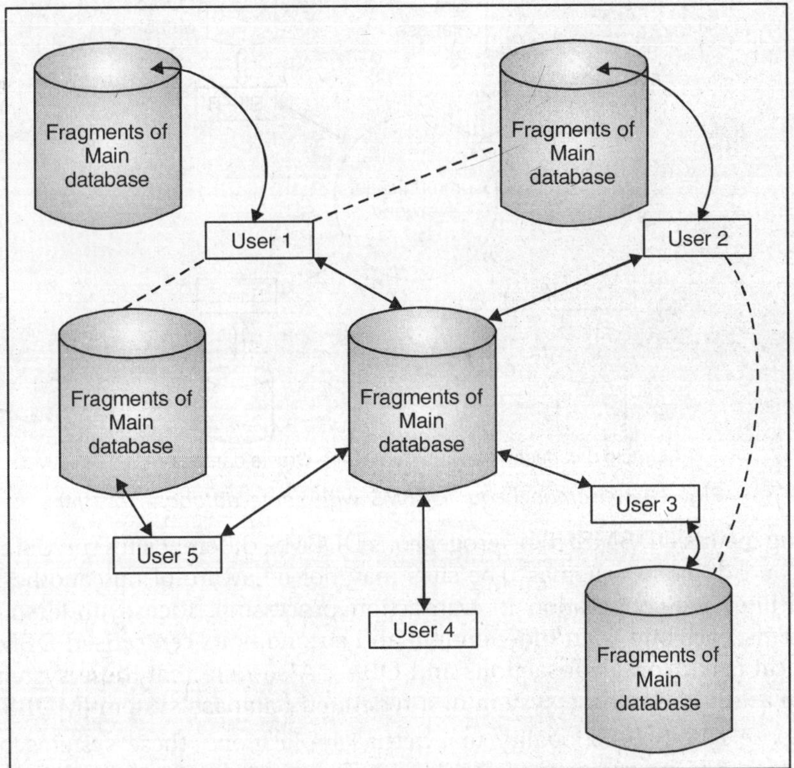

Fig. 10.2. *DDBMS topology*

Let us see the advantages and the disadvantages of DDBMS in a tabular form now.

S.No.	Advantages	Disadvantages
1	Reflects organizational structure	Complexity
2	Improved share ability and local autonomy	Cost
3	Improved availability	Security
4	Improved reliability	Integrity control more difficult
5	Improved performance	Lack of standards
6	Economics	Lack of experience
7	Modular growth	Database design more complex

DDBMS are of two types, namely :

(*a*) Homogeneous DDBMS

(*b*) Heterogeneous DDBMS.

Homogeneous DDBMS : In a homogeneous DDBMS, all sites have **identical DBMS software**. They are **aware of one another** and agree to cooperate in processing user's request. In these systems, the local sites surrender a portion of their autonomy in terms of their rights to change schemas or DBMS. **Please note that there is location transparency in these systems**. This is shown in Fig. 10.3 below.

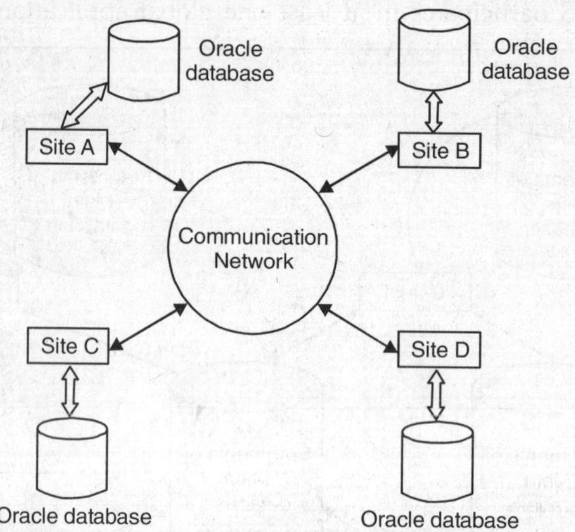

Fig. 10.3. *Homogeneous DDBMS with same database (oracle)*

Heterogeneous DDBMS: In heterogeneous DDBMS, different sites run different DBMS softwares and different schemas. The sites may not be aware of one another. There are limited facilites for cooperation in transaction processing. **Please understand that in these systems, each site is an independent and autonomous centralised DBMS that has its own local users, local transactions and DBAs. Also note that these systems are also referred to as multi-database system or a federated database system (MDBS or FDBS)**.

To expose DBMS functionality to external applications, these systems have well - accepted standards for **gateway protocols** also. These gateways will fill the gaps between different servers in a distributed system. This is shown in Fig. 10.4 below.

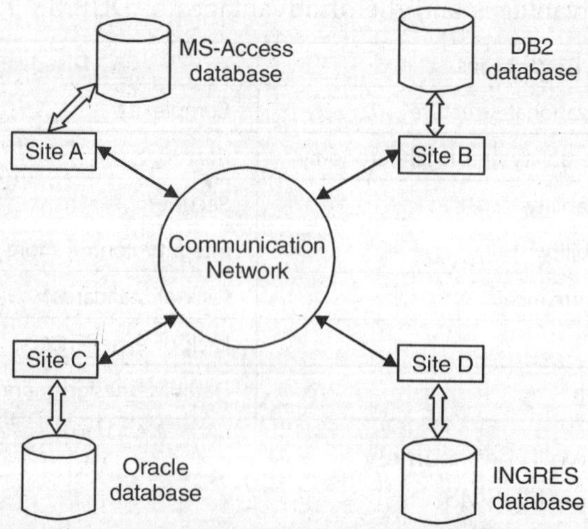

Fig. 10.4. *Heterogeneous DDBMS with different DBMS*

C.J. Date gave 12 rules for any system to claim for being a DDBMS. The basic assumption here is that even a DDBMS must make a user feel like a non-DDBMS only. So, we list Date's 12 rules now.

Rule 1. Local autonomy : The sites in a DDBMS should be autonomous. By autonomous, we mean three things here.

(*a*) Local data is locally owned and managed.

(*b*) Local operations remain purely local.

(*c*) All operations at a given site are controlled by that site.

Rule 2. No reliance on a central site : There should be no one, central site without which the systems cannot operate.

Rule 3. Continuous operation : Ideally, there should never be a need for a planned system shutdown, for operations such as :

- Adding or removing a site from the system;
- The dynamic creation and detection of fragment at one more sites.

Rule 4. Location independence : Location independence is equivalent to location transparency. The user should be able to access the database from the site. Furthermore, the user should be able to access all data as if it were stored at the user's site, no matter where it is physically stored.

Rule 5. Fragmentation independence : The user should be able to access the data, now matter how it is fragmented.

Rule 6. Replication independence : The user should be unaware that has been replicated. Thus, the user should not be able to access a particular copy of a data item directly, nor should the user have to specifically update all copies of a data item.

Rule 7. Distributed query processing : The system should be capable of processing queries that reference data at more than one site.

Rule 8. Distributed transaction processing : The system should support the transaction as the unit of recovery. The system should ensure that both global and local transactions conform to the ACID rules for transactions, namely: atomicity, consistency, isolation and durability.

Rule 9 : Hardware independence : It shoud be possible to run the DDBMS on a variety of hardware platforms.

Rule 10. Operating system independence : As a corollary to the previous rule, it should be possible to run the DDBMS on a variety of operating system.

Rule 11. Network independence : Again, it should be possible to run the DDBMS on a variety of disparate communication networks.

Rule 12. Database independence : It should be possible to have a DDBMS made up of different local DBMSs, perhaps supporting different underlying data models. In other words, the system should support heterogeneity.

Desired functions of a DDBMS : Some main functions of DDBMS are as follows :

1. Better communication services to provide access to remote sites and to transfer queries and data among multiple sites.
2. Better distributed system catalogue management.
3. Better distributed query processing.
4. Better security control to maintain access privileges.
5. Better distributed transaction management.
6. Better concurrency control for data consistency.

7. Better recovery services during system failures.
8. Support for gateways.
9. Support for fragmentation independence.
10. It should be hardware and OS independent.

Architecture of DDBMS : The ANSI – SPARC 3-level architecture is for a **centralized DBMS only**. We do not have any equivalent architecture for a DDBMS but we have a possible reference architecture of a DDBMS. It is shown in Fig. 10.5.

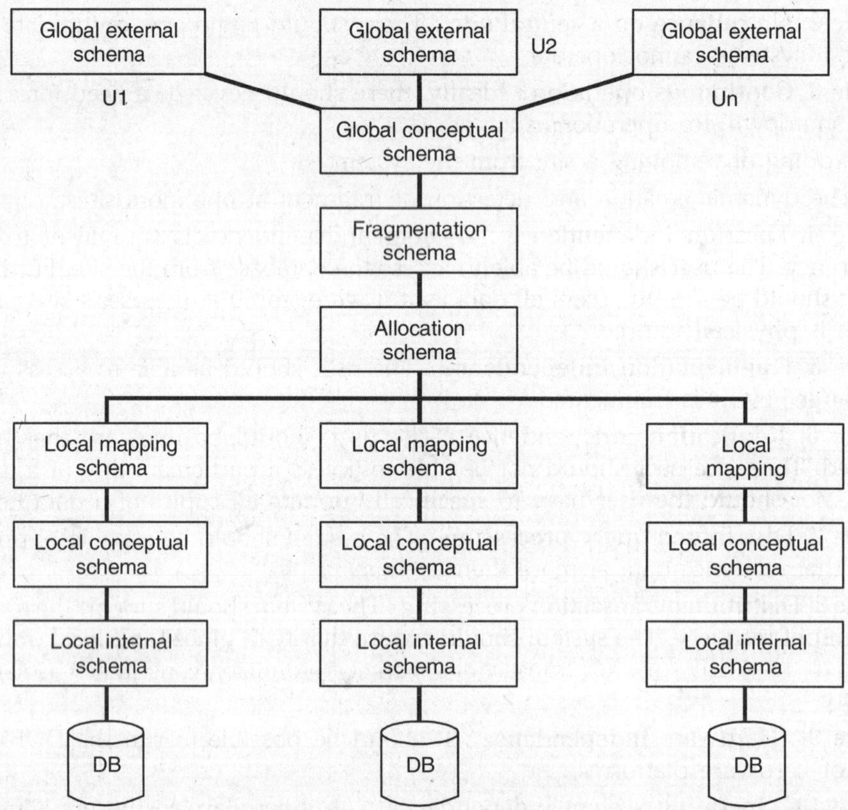

Fig. 10.5. *Architecture of a DDBMS*

Explanation : As shown in this figure, the edges represent a mapping between the different schemas. It shows various schemas, which are discribed one by one below :

I. **Global conceptual schema :** The global conceptual is a logical description of the whole database, as if it were not distributed. This level corresponds to the conceptual level of the ANSI, SPARC architecture and contains definitions of entities, relationships, constraints, security and integrity information. It provides physical data independence from the distributed environment. The global external schemas provide logical data independence.

II. **Fragmentation and allocation schemas :** The fragmentation schema is a description of how the data is to be logically partitioned. The allocation schema is a description of where data is to be located, taking account of any replication.

III. **Local schemas :** Each local DBMS has its own set of schemas. The local conceptual and local internal schemas correspond to the equivalent levels of the ANSI,

SPARC architecture. The local mapping schema maps fragments in the allocation schema into external objects in the local database. It is DBMS independent and is the basis for supporting hetergeneous DBMSs.

To design a relational-DDB, we consider 3 main strategies :

1. Fragmentation
2. Allocation
3 Replication.

During fragmentation, a relation is divided into a number of subrelations called as fragments that are distributed.

We shall be discussing about this a bit later.

During **allocation**, each fragment is stored at the site with optimal distribution.

During **replication**, DDBMS may maintain a copy of a fragment at several different sites.

Fragments are defined and allocated on the basis of how a database is used. This will involve analysis of transactions. **Please note that the design should be based on both quantitative and qualitative information which is used in allocation and fragmentation respectively. Also note that the quantitative information includes the frequency with which a transaction is run**, the site from which a transaction is run and the performance criteria of the transactions. On the other hand, qualitative information includes information like locality of reference of a transaction, acceptable performance, optimal communication costs and so on. **Please note that the retrieval costs are minimum when locality of reference is maximized**.

Allocation of data involves four strategies :

(*a*) Centralized (*b*) Fragmented
(*c*) Complete replication (*d*) Selective replication.

Let us compare these strategies in a tabular form based on five parameters, namely :

(*a*) Locality of reference (*b*) Reliability and availability
(*c*) Performance (*d*) Storage costs
(*e*) Communication costs.

	Locality of reference	**Reliability and availability**	**Performance**	**Storage costs**	**Communication costs**
Centralized	Lowest	Lowest	Unsatisfactory	Lowest	Highest
Fragmented	HIgh	Low for item; high for system	Satisfactory	Lowest	Low
Complete replication	Highest	Highest	Best for read	Highest	High for Update; low for read
Selective replication	High	Low for item; high for system	Satisfactory	Average	Low

Data Repication, however, is the process of storing data in more than one site or node. It may be of two types :

(*a*) **Partial replication** : In this scheme, some important frequently used fragments are only replicated.

(*b*) **Full replication** : In this scheme, a copy of the whole database is stored at every site.

Replication of data enhances the performance of read operations and increases the availability of data. But update transactions incur greater overhead. We can manage these replicas by choosing one of them as the primary copy of *r*. **For example**, in an airline reservation system, a flight can be associated with the site at which the flight orginates.

Let us define what is fragmentation now?

The process of dividing the whole of the database into several subrelations so that data can be stored in different computers is known as fragmentation and these pieces of subrelations are called as fragments. Each of this piece is then stored at a different site. **Please understand that these fragments** are logical data units that are stored at various sites of a distributed system.

If a relation, *r*, is fragmented, *r* is divided into a number of fragments *r*1, *r*2, r3,.... *rn*. These fragments contain sufficient information to allow the reconstruction of the original relation, *r*. This reconstruction can take place through the use of UNION or JOIN operation on various fragments. This is known as **data fragmentation**. *But please note that all of these fragments are independent i.e.*, these fragments cannot derived from the others. Users need not be logically concerned about fragmentation *i.e.*, they should not feel at all that the data is fragmented. This called as **fragmentation independence or fragmentation transparency**.

There are three methods of data fragmenting of a relation : –

(*a*) Horizontal fragmentation

(*b*) Vertical fragmentation

(*c*) Mixed fragmentation.

We shall discuss these schemes one by one now.

I. Horizontal Fragmentation : The process of splitting of a relation horizontally by assigning each tuple (or group of tuples) of a relation to one or more fragments is called as horizontal fragmentation. These fragments can then be assigned to different sites in the distributed system. So, some of the tuples of the relation are placed in one computer and the rest are placed in other computers.

Please note that the tuples that belong to horizontal fragments are specified by a condition on one or more attributes of the relation. In relational algebra, horizontal fragmentation on a relation, R, can be represented as follows :

$$\sigma_p(R)$$

where σ = relational algebra operator for selection

p = condition satisfied by a horizontal fragment.

Also note that a, UNION operation can be performed on the fragments to construct the relation, R. Such a fragment containing all the tuples of relation, R, is called as a **complete horizontal fragment.**

For example, consider an EMPLOYEE relation (*r*) as follows :

Eno	Ename	Desig	Sal	Dept_no
1001	Raman	Tester	80,000	1
1002	Rajat	SA	40,000	1
1003	Rahul	CA	20,000	2
1004	Mayur	Manager	10,000	2
1005	Ajay	CEO	15,000	2

This Employee relation can be divided into different fragments as follows –

$$\text{EMP 1} = \sigma_{\text{Dept\_no} = 1} \text{(EMPLOYEE)}$$
$$\text{EMP 2} = \sigma_{\text{Dept\_no} = 2} \text{(EMPLOYEE)}$$

These two fragments are :

r_1 fragment of Dept_no = 1

Eno	Ename	Desig	Sal	Dept_no
1001	Raman	Tester	80,000	1
1002	Rajat	SA	40,000	1

Similarly, r_2 fragment on the basis of Dept_no = 2 is :

Eno	Ename	Desig	Sal	Dept_no
1003	Rahul	CA	20,000	2
1004	Mayur	Manager	10,000	2
1005	Ajay	CED	15,000	2

Now, here it is also possible to get back r as follows :

$$r = r_1 \cup r_2 \cup \ldots \cup rn$$

II. Vertical Fragmentation : The prcess of decomposing a relation vertically by columns (attributes) is called as vertical fragmentation. In this technique, some of the columns are stored in one computer and the rest are stored in other computers. This is so because each site may not need all the attributes of a relation. The fragmentation should be in such a manner that we can reconstruct relation, r, from the fragments by taking the natural join. Because there is no common attribute between the two fragments, **so we need not get the original relation back again**. To do this, we need to include a special attribute called as **tuple-id**, to the schema R. Any superkey can be used. So, now tuples can be linked. The physical or the logical address for a tuple can be used as a tuple-id because each tuple has a unique address. Vertical fragmention corresponds to the relational algebra operation.

Projection and is defined as follows :

$$\pi_{a_1, a_2, \ldots, an} \text{(R)}$$

where π = relational algebra operator for projection

$a_1, \ldots a_n$ = attributes of R

R = *a* relation (table)

For example, for the EXPLOYEE table we have r_1 as :

Eno	Ename	Desig	Tuple_id
1001	Raman	Tester	1
1002	Rajat	SA	2
1003	Rahul	CA	3
1004	Mayur	Manager	4
1005	Ajay	CEO	5

And the second subrelation after vertical fragmentation is as follows :

Sal	Dept_no	tuple-id
80000	1	1
40000	1	2
20000	2	3
10000	2	4
15000	2	5

This is r_2. To get back the original R, we join these two fragments r_1 and r_2 as follows :

$$\pi_{EMPLOYEE} (r_1 \bowtie r_2)$$

III. Mixed (or Hybrid) Fragmentation : Sometimes, horizontal or vertical fragmentation is not sufficient to adequately distribute data for some applications. So, we need a mixed fragmentation. **Thus, the borizontal (or vertical) fragmentation of a relation followed by further vertical (or horizontal) fragmnetation of some of the fragments is called as mixed fragmentation.** A mixed fragmentation is defined using the SELECT and PROJECT operauons of the relational algebra. **Please note here that the orignal relation is obtained by a combination of JOIN and UNION operations.** So, it is given as –

$$\sigma_p(\pi_{a_1, a_2, \ldots an}(R))$$

or $$\pi_{a_1, a_3, \ldots an}(\sigma_p(R))$$

For example, for our EMPLOYEE relation, an example of mixed fragmentation is –

$$\pi_{Ename, Desing}(\sigma_{Eno>1002} (EMPLOYEE)$$

The result of this fragmentation is :

Ename	Desig
Rahul	CA
Mayur	Manager
Ajay	CEO

Please understand this that data replication and data fragmentation can be applied successively to the same relation, that is, a fragment can be replicated, replicas of fragments can be fragmented further and so on. We can get many fragmentations as per our requirements.

Transparencies in DDBMS : Any DDBMS must provide four types of transparencies. They are follows :

1. Distribution transparency
2. Transaction transparency
3. Performance transparency
4. DBMS transparency

Let us define these terms one by one now.

1. Distribution Transparency : It allows the user to perceive the database as a single, logical entity. **Please note that if a DDBMS exhibits distribution transparency then the user does not need to know that the data is fragmented (fragmentation transparency) or the location of data items (local transparency).** It is classified into 5 types :

(*a*) Fragmentation transparency
(*b*) Location transparency
(*c*) Replication transparency
(*d*) Local mapping transparency
(*e*) Naming transparency

(*a*) ***Fragmentation transparency :*** If a DDBMS provides this type of transparency then the user need not know that the data is fragmented. This is the reason as to why database accesses are based on the global schema. Users need not specify the fragment names or data locations. **Please understand that fragmention is the highest level of distribution transparency**.

(*b*) ***Location transparency :*** If a DDBMS provides this type of transparency then the user must know how the data has been fragmented but still does not have to know the location of the data. **Please understand that location is the middle level of distribution transparency**.

(*c*) ***Replication transparency :*** In this type of transparency, the user is unaware of the replication of fragments. **Please note that the replication transparency is implied by the location transparency only**.

(*d*) ***Local mapping transparency :*** In this type of transparency, the user needs to specify both the fragment names and the location of data items, taking into account any replications that may exists. **Please note that it is the lowest level of distribution transparency. Also note that this is a more complex and time-consuming query for the user to enter than the first two transparencies.**

(*e*) ***Naming transparency :*** As we know that our DBMS is a contralized database system. And so should be our DDBMS also. It means that each item in a distributed database must have a unique name. **Please note that this means that DDBMS must ensure that no two sites create a database object with the same name**. To achieve this goal, either we can create a central name server which ensures unique names of objects in the system or another way is to prefix an object with the identifier of the site that created it. **But both these methods have problems** like performance problem which occur if the central site fails. So, the solution is to use aliases (or similar names) for each database object. **Also note that it is the responsibility of our DDBMS to map the alias name to its corresponding database object**.

II. Transaction Transparency : It ensures that all distributed transactions maintain the distributed database integrity and consistency. **Please understand that a distribution transaction accesses the data stored at more than one location**. Each transaction is divided into a number of **Subtransactions** (one of each site) and a **subtransaction** is represented by an agent. **Also note that our DDBMS must ensure the atomicity of each subtransaction**.

III. Performance Transparency : It requires that a DDBMS should perform as if it were a centralized DBMS. Also, the system should not suffer from any performance degradation due to the distributed architecture. As we know that in our DBMS, a query processor evaluates every query. Similarly a DDBMS must have distributed query processor that maps a data request into an ordered sequence of operations on the local database. It has an added complexity of taking into account the fragmentation, replication and allocation schemas. In this system also, we have various associated costs like I/O costs, CPU time costs and communication costs.

IV. DBMS Transparency : It hides the fact that the local DBMSs may be different. So, it is only applicable to heterogeneous DDBMS.

10.3 Comparison of DBMS and DDBMS

DBMS	DDBMS
1. A DBMS is a generalized software for managing and manipulating the databases.	1. DDBMS is a software that manages a distributed database and make distribution transparent to the user.
2. DBMS have the capability to process the query at a single site.	2. DDBMS have the capability to handle remote sites and transmit query and data among various sites.
3. Data replication is minimum.	3. Data replication is necessary to improve availability, reliability and performance.
4. DBMS may be categorized into DDBMS and parallel DBMS according to location of storage and it may be categorized into RDBMS, Hierarchial DBMS and Network DBMS according to its structure.	4. DDBMS may be catagorized into homogeneous and heterogeneous data bases according to the type of DBMS used at different sites.
5. There is only directory and has no concept of local and global directory.	5. DDBMS maintains two types of directories, Global for the entire DDB and local for each site.
6. Data may not be distributed in case of DBMS.	6. Data is distributed at different sites that may be geographical apart.

10.4 QUERY PROCESSING IN DISTRIBUTED DATABASES

A query in a DDBMS generally requires data from more than one site. This need of data from other sites means transmission of the data that causes communication costs. The query processing in DDBMS is different from query processing in centralized DBMS due to this communication cost of data transfer over the network. The transmission cast is low when site are connected through high speed network and is quite significant in other networks.

I. Costs (Transfer of data) of Distributed Query Processing

The data transfer costs of distributed query processing involves cost of transferring intermediate files to other sites for processing and the cost of transferring the final result files to the site where that result is required.

Let us assume, that a user gives a query at site S_1, that requires data from its own as well as another site S_2, There are three strategies to process this query as given below.

1. Transfering data from S_2 to S_1 and process for query there.
2. Transfering data from S_1 to S_2 and process the query there.
3. Transfering data from S_1 and S_2 to S_3 and process the query there.

The choice depends on many factors such as :

– The size of relations and the results.

– The communication costs between different sites *i.e.*, between S_1 and S_2, S_1 and S_3, S_2 and S_3 etc.

– At which site the result will be utilized.

Generally, the data transfer cost is calculated in terms of the size of messages. The data transfer cost can be calculated using the formula.

$$\text{Data Transfer Cost} = C * \text{Size}.$$

where C is the cost per byte of transferring data and Size is the number of bytes transmitted.

Example : Consider the following relations EMPLOYEE And DEPARTMENT.

Site 1 :

EMPLOYEE

EID	NAME	SALARY	DID

EID-5 bytes SALARY-10 bytes

Name-20 bytes DID-5 bytes

Total records - 1000

Record size-40 bytes

Site 2:

DEPARTMENT

D-ID	DNAME

SITE 2: D-ID-5 bytes

D Name 20 bytes

Total records-50

Record size-25 bytes

Query : Find the name of employees and their department name.

Determine the amount of data transfered to execute this query when the query is submitted at Site 3.

Solution. Since the query is submitted at SITE 3 and neither of the two relations *i.e,.* EMPLOYEE and DEPARTMENT reside at site 3. We have three strategies to execute this query.

1. Transfer both the relations *i.e.,* EMPLOYEE and DEPARTMENT at site 3 and then join the relations there. The total cost in this case in 1000* 40 + 50 * 25 = 40,000 + 1250 = 41,250 bytes.

2. Transfer the relation EMPLOYEE to Site 2, join the relation at Site 2 and then transfer the result at Site 3. The total cost is $40 \times 1000 + 40 \times 4000 = 80{,}000$ bytes, since we have to transfer 1000 tuples having NAME and DNAME from site 1 to site 3 that are of 40 bytes each.

3. Transfer the relation DEPARTMENT to site 1, join the relation at site 1 and then transfer the result at site 3. The total cost is $25 \times 50 + 40 \times 1000 = 41{,}250$ bytes, since we have to transfer 1000 tuples having NAME and DNAME from site 1 to site 3 that are of 40 bytes each.

We can choose startegy 1 or 3, if optimization criteria is to minimize the amount of data transfer.

II. Using Semijoin in Distributed Query Processing

The Semijoin operation is used in distributed query processing to reduce the number of tuples in a relation before transmitting it to another site. This reduction in the number of tuples, reduces the number and total size of the transmission that ultimately reduces the total cost of data transfer.

Let us assume, that we have two relations R_1 and R_2 on site S_1 and S_2. We will send the joining column of one relation (say R_1) to the site where the other relation (say R_2) is located. This column is joined with R_2 at that site. The decission as to whether to reduce R_1 or R_2 can only be made after comparing the advantages of reducing R_1 with that of reducing R_2. Thus semijoin is an efficient solution to minimize the data transfer in distributed query processing.

Note *The semijoin operation is not commutative i.e.,* $R_1 \bowtie R_2 \neq R_2 \bowtie R_1$.

Example. Determine the amount of data transferred to execute the query given in the previous example using semijoin. Assume that the query is submitted at site 3.

Solution. The following startegy can be used to execute the query.

1. Project the attributes of EMPLOYEE at site 1 and transfer them to site 3. We transfer NAME, DID (EMPLOYEE) and the size is $25 \times 1000 = 25{,}000$ bytes.

2. Transfer the relation DEPARTMENT to site 3 and join the projected attributes of EMPLOYEE with this relation. The size of DEPARTMENT relation is $25 \times 50 = 1250$.

Using the above strategy, the amount of data transferred to execute the query is 25000 + 1250 = 26250

10.5 COMPARISION OF PARALLEL AND DISTRIBUTED DATABASES (DDB'S)

Sr. No.	Parallel Databases	Distributed Databases
1.	Processors are tightly coupled and constitute a single database system *i.e.*, parallel databases are centralized databases and data reside in single location.	Sites are loosely coupled and share no physical components i.e., distributed databases are geographically separted and data are distributed at several locations.
2.	Query processing and transaction processing is complicated in parallel database systems.	Query processing and transaction is more complicated in distributed database systems.
3.	This is not applicable here	Local and global transaction can be differentiated in distributed database systems.
4.	Data are partitioned among different disks so that it can be retrieved faster.	Each site maintains a local database system for faster processing because of slower interconnection between sites.
5.	Parallel databases have three types of architectures; shared memory, shared disk and shared nothing.	DDB's are generally a kind of shared nothing architecture.
6.	Query optimization is more complex in parallel databases.	Query optimization techniques may be different at different sites and are easy to maintain.
7.	Data is generally not replicated.	Data is replicated at any number of sites to improve the performance of the systems and availability of data.
8.	Parallel databases are generally homogeneous in nature.	Distributed databases may be homogeneous or hetrogeneous..
9.	Skew is the major issue with increasing degree of parallelism.	Blocking due to site failure and transparency are the major issues.

10.6 CASE STUDY ON–DB2

DB2–UDB is a universal database. It has various Editions like :

- DB2 Everyplace Edition.
- DB2 Satellite Edition.
- DB2 Personal Edition.
- DB2 Workgroup Edition.
- DB2 Enterprise Edition.
- DB2 Enterprise Extended Edition.

DB2 Everyplace : Is a tiny "fingerprint" database of about 100k. It is designed for low-cost, low power, small form-factor devices like personal digital assistants (PDAs), handheld Personal computers. It allows mobile workers to access DB2 data sources through handheld devices. Relational data can be synchronized to the handheld device from other DB2 data sources.

DB2 Satellite Edition : Is a fully functional database for PCs on windows OS. It supports systems that operate disconnected from the corporate system for most of the time and connects occassionally to the corporations central database for data exchange **Please**

note that it is a fully functional database working on window OS. It provides mobility for your applications.

DB2 Personal Edition : Is a fully functional database for systems in OS/2, windows and Linux OS. It allows local users to create database on the workstation where the product is installed. No connection request is accepted by remote users. It can be used as a remote client to a DB2 server also because it also contains the DB2 client components.

DB2 Workgroup Edition : It provides full DB2 database server capacity for departmental LANS runing OS/2, WIN-NT/2000, UNIX, LINUX, AIX and solaris. It is designed for use in a LAN environment. It provides support to both remote and local clients.

DB2 Enterprise Edition : It is a fully Web-enabled, scalable from single processors to symmetric multiprocessors to massively parallel clusters. It also supports unstructured data like image, audio, video, text, XML etc. It provides full user access to the enterprise data on OS/2, WIN-NT/2000 and UNIX OS.

DB2 Enterprise Extended Edition : It is more scalable that enables DB2 to partition data across clusters or massively parallel computers. All SQL statements are processed in parallel. This increases the execution speed of any given query.

DB2 Product Components :

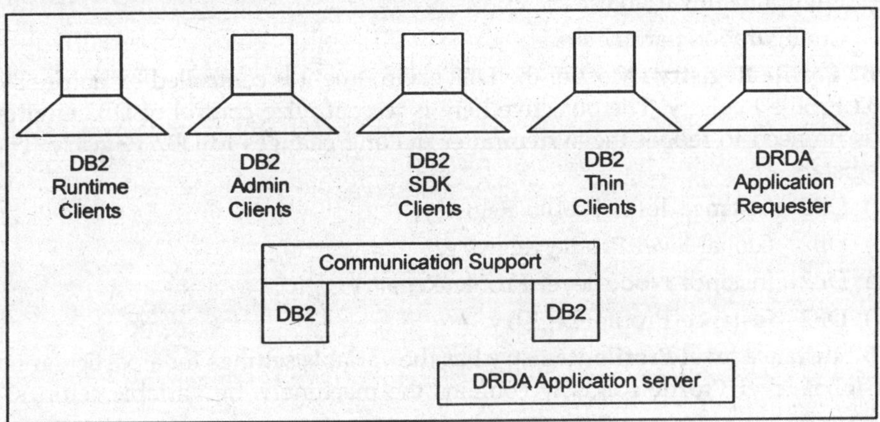

Fig. 10.6

DB2 provides a full-function, robust, relational database management system (RDBMS), along with a set of relations for universal database platforms . DB2 brings to these platforms the support of the IBM SQL technology that is available on all members of the DB2 family.

In the diagram, DB2 identifies as the database engine. The database engine is responsible for managing and controlling all data access, generating packages (stored access paths to the data), providing transaction management, ensuring data integrity and data protection, providing concurrency control.

All remote database client connectivity is through the DB2 Communication Support via protocols such as TCP/IP, SNA, or IPX/SPX. This then allows access from remote clients running the Administration Client, Run-Time Client, Thin Client SDK or Client.

DB2 Connect provides Distributed Relational, Database Architecture (DRDA) Application Requester (AR) function. With Communications Support, DB2 Connect enables applications running on DB2 UDB for UNIX, OS/2, and Windows client platforms to access and update data DB2 on MVS, OS/390, VM and VSE, OS/400.

DB2 Instances : *A* **DB2 instance is defined as a logical database server environment**. DB2 databases are created within DB2 instances on the database server. **Please understand that the creation of multiple instances on the same physical server provides a unique database server enivronment for each instance. For example**, you can maintain a **test environment** and a **production environment** on the same machine.

DB2 Admin Server (DAS) :

1. It is a special DB2 instance to manage local and remote DB2 servers.
2. It is used by the DB2 administration tools including the control center, Client Configuration Assistant etc.
3. It provides a scheduler to execute jobs locally or remotely.
4. Collect information results from DB2 discovery.
5. No database can be created within a DAS instance
6. Only one DAS instance can be created in each machine.

DB2 environment : DB2 environment controls many database related factors by several different mechanisms :

— DB2 profile registry.

— Environment variables.

— Configuration parameters.

DB2 Profile Registry : Most of the DB2 ervironment is controlled by entries stored in the DB2 Profile Registry. The objective here is to centralize control of DB2 environment. There is no need to reboot the system after making changes to DB2 Registry. There are four registers –

(*a*) DB2 Instance–level Profile Registry.

(*b*) DB2 Global-level Profile Registry.

(*c*) DB2 Instance Node–level Profile Registry.

(*d*) DB2 Instance Profile Registry.

DB2 Instance level Profile Registry has the variable settings for a particular instance, **DB2 Global-level Profile Registry** contains the machine wide variable settings.

DB2 Instance Node_level Profile Registry : It resides on every node if the database is divided into database partitions.

DB2 Instance Profile Registry : It contains the list of instance names recognized by this system.

Environment Variables : DB2 Profile Registry Controls most of the environment varibles. Those variables that are not stored in the DB2 Profile Registry can be called as ***system environment variables***. They are set in a location where the platform stores its system variables.

DB2 Configuration Parameters : Database Manager Configuration (DBMCFS) parametess affect resources and performances at an instance level.

DB2's Command Center : The command center is a graphical interface for SQL commands. You can access the other DB2 tools through the toolbar across the top of the command center. You can enter the SQL statements either interactively or by writing a script and scheduling that script for a later time. Any DB2 messages appear in the bottom window while query results, if any, appear on the Query results tab. For a single statement on either the Interactive or script tabs you can create an access plan which will give you an "explain" of the steps the engine will perform to access your data. This plan will appear on the Access plan table and is shown on the next page :

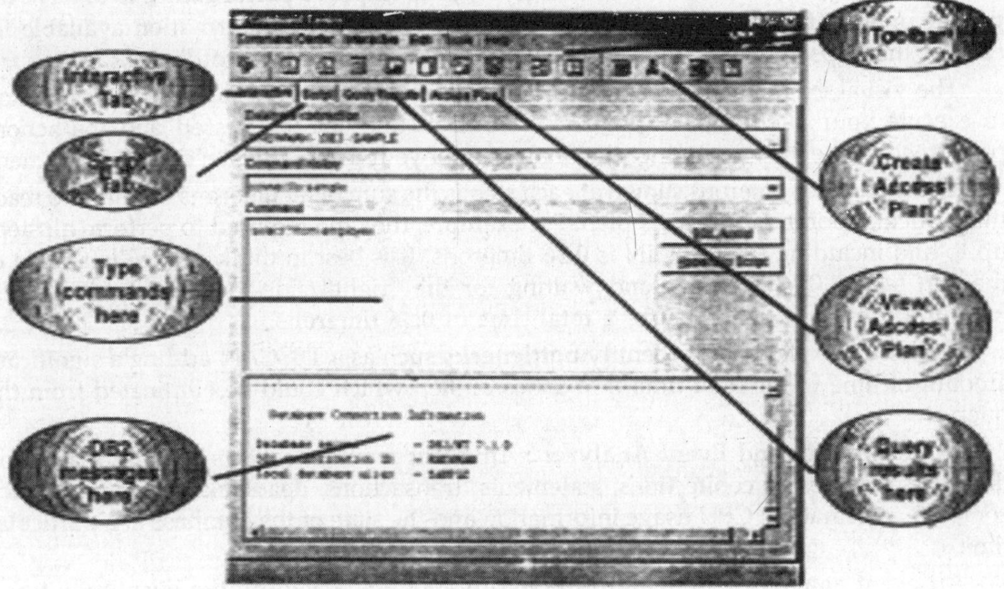

Fig. 10.7. *The DB2 command center*

Query Result Processing : It is also possible to work with data directly from a command center Resultset. You can add or remove rows from the resultset. You can also alter any data within the current resultset. It is possible to either commit or rollback a set of changes. Auto-commit is always an option. You can export the data in the resultset as either text, HTML or a comma delimited file.

What DB2 explains? It explains :

1. A description of the steps that the engine will perform to process a query.
2. The execution of the "explain" is measured in **timerons. A timeron gives a relative estimate of the resources (cost) required by the database manager to execute.**But it doesnot include the time required for the statement compilation steps like query rewrite.

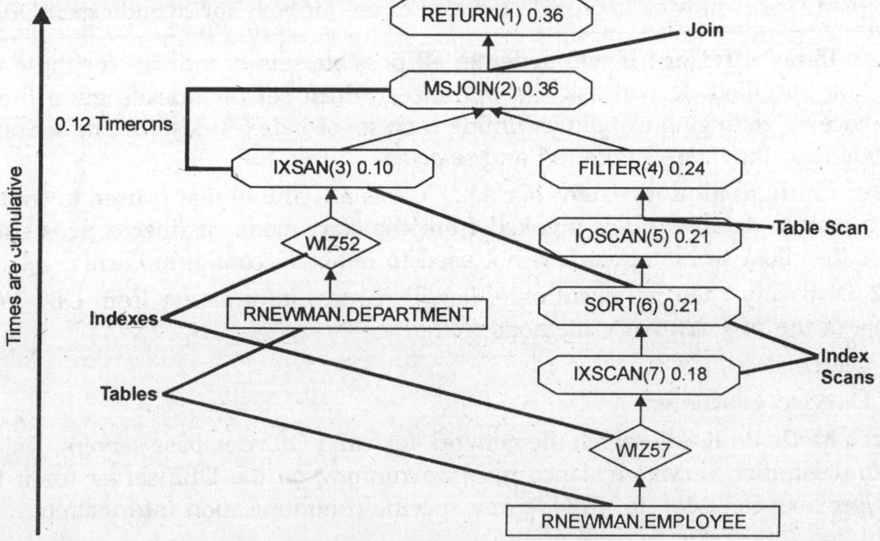

Fig. 10.8. *DB2 visual explain*

Please understand that one of the best ways to improve performance is to have the proper indexes for the queries being executed. The detailed information available for each of the steps shown in Fig. 10.8 below, allows us to analyze bottlenecks.

The visual explain provides a **graphical representation** of the access plan necessary to execute your query. An explain describes both the object accessed and the actions performed on the data to produce the final result of your insert, update, or select statement.

The number of timerons shown at each step is the sum of all timerons required to reach the particular point in the access plan. **For example**, the time required to perform all steps up to and including the MSJOIN is 0.36 timerons. It is best to think of the "left" side of the join taking 0.10 timerons and waiting for the "right" side to catch up. **Then the MSJOIN takes 0.12 timerons for a total time of 0.36 timerons.**

The visual explain helps identify **bottlenecks** such as a TBSCAN adding a significant amount of time to the total time or a series of step which could be eliminated from the query.

Event Monitor and Event Analyzer : An **event monitor** collects the information on database activities eg connections, statements, transactions, deadlocks etc. It provides a complete information, CPU usage information and the state of the database at a particular time.

An **event analyzer** will analyze the information generated by the event monitor.

Stored Procedure Builder [SPB] : It is a graphical application that suports the rapid development of DB2 stored procedures. We use SPB to :

(*a*) Create new stored procedures.

(*b*) Build stored procedures on local and remote DB2 servers.

(*c*) Modify and rebuild existing stored procedures.

(*d*) Test and bebug the execution of installed stored procedures.

It is available on sun solaris, windows 32bit OS. The languages supported are **JAVA** (on OS/2, HP-UX, Linus, Solaris and WIN 32-bit OS) and **SQL** on these (same) environments.

Smart Guides : It guides you step-by-step through common DBA tasks. It uses expert system to make recommendations or changes to our database.

TIP : Smart Guides provide unprecedented ease of use for both novice and expert DBAs.

DB2's Index Advisor : It will generate all possible sets of indexes for these set of queries you specified. It will ask the optimizer which set of indexes gives the best performance by getting an explain assuming each set of indexes existed. The scripts will be provided for the index suggested and selected.

Client Configuration Assistant (CCA) : CCA is a GUI tool that is used to configure access to remote database. It is invoked from the start menu or dbzcca. It is used to configure the client workstation. It is not used to remotely configure clients.

DB2 Discovery : On the client side, it will request information from DB2 servers using one of the two discovery methods :

(*a*) Search.

(*b*) Directed or Known.

Search Method : It will search the network for valid DB2 database servers. The DAS (DB2 Administration server) instance must be running on the DB2 server for it to be found. User does not have to provide any specific communication information.

Directed or Known Method : It needs to provide communication information such as the protocol that is running on the admin server and protocol's configuration information.

Comparisons : Search may appear to be a simpler discovery method. However, in large networks, routers and bridges can filter the messages. So, you may get an incomplete list. With directed method, the messages are not filtered.

DB2 Process Model : db2 on UNIX platform employs a dedicated **Process-based architecture**. The database engine is comprised of a list of processes. These processes are dispatchable units. For each active connection, there is a dedicated server process serving that connection. Each b2 agent works on behalf of the database application and handles all SQL requests. **Please understand that the application and database agents communicate using Inter Process communication**. (IPC) **techniques** like message queries, shared memory and semaphores. Each db2 server has a suite of **background processes** each of which has a dedicated purpose like logging or writing to the database files. Also note that oracle implements a similar architecture called as the **dedicated server architecture.** The applications run in the application process. Like DB2, Oracle has a dedicated server process for each active connection to the db as well as a number of background server processes performing specific tasks such as logging or writing to db files. Oracle also supports the multithreaded server architecture which implements a pooled-agents architecture with a number of server processes serving the applications.

DB2 Memory Model : DB2 and Oracle have direct mappings between each other. It is shown in Fig. 10.9 below.

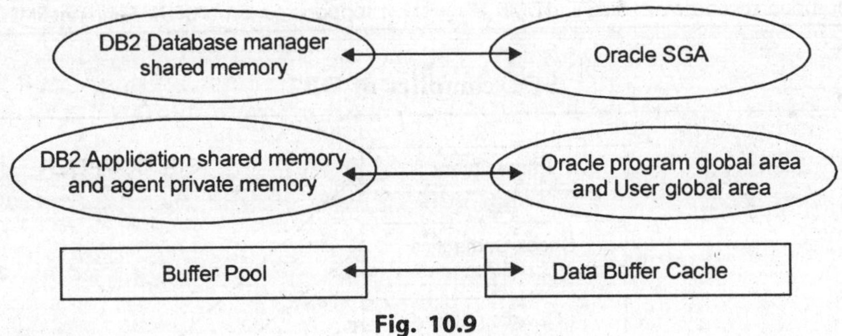

Fig. 10.9

DB2 Storage Model

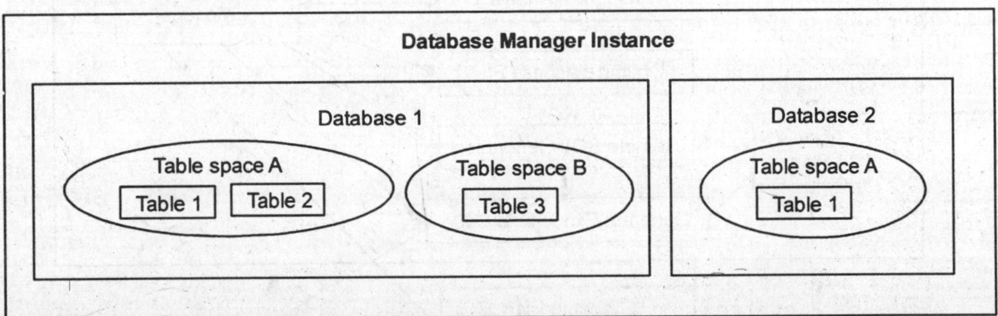

Here, tablespace are a logical layer created within a database. Tables are created within table spaces. We define these terms now :

1. **DB2 instance :** It is a logical database server environment. There can be multiple DB2 instances on a server. And databases are created within a DB2 instance on the database server.

2. **Database :** It is created within an instance. Please note that there may be multiple database managed by a DB2 instance.
3. **Tablespace :** It is a logical layer between data and storage devices. Tables reside in tablespaces. It has one or more containers. 2 types of storages are done –
   (*a*) System Managed Storage (SMS)
   (*b*) Database Managed Storage (DMS).
4. **Table :** It consists of regular data, indexes and long data.
5. **Container :** It is file or raw device name. It can be a directory or any other device also.

Let us now compare the storage models of DB2 and Oracle in a tabular form.

S.No.	DB2	Oracle
1.	Here, data is stored in **pages**.	Data is stored in **data blocks**.
2.	A **tablespace** is defined to have a single page size (4k, 8k, 16k, 32k).	Data block size is defined when a database is created. All **tablespaces** will have the **same block size**, from 2k to 4k
3.	An *extent* is a number of **contiguous pages**.	An *extent* is a number of **contiguous data blocks**.
4.	Objects like tables, indexes are made up of pages.	Segments like data, index, rollback segments are made up of data blocks.
5.	It supports concepts of SMS and DMS.	It supports concepts of DMS and not SMS.

SQL compiler of DB2

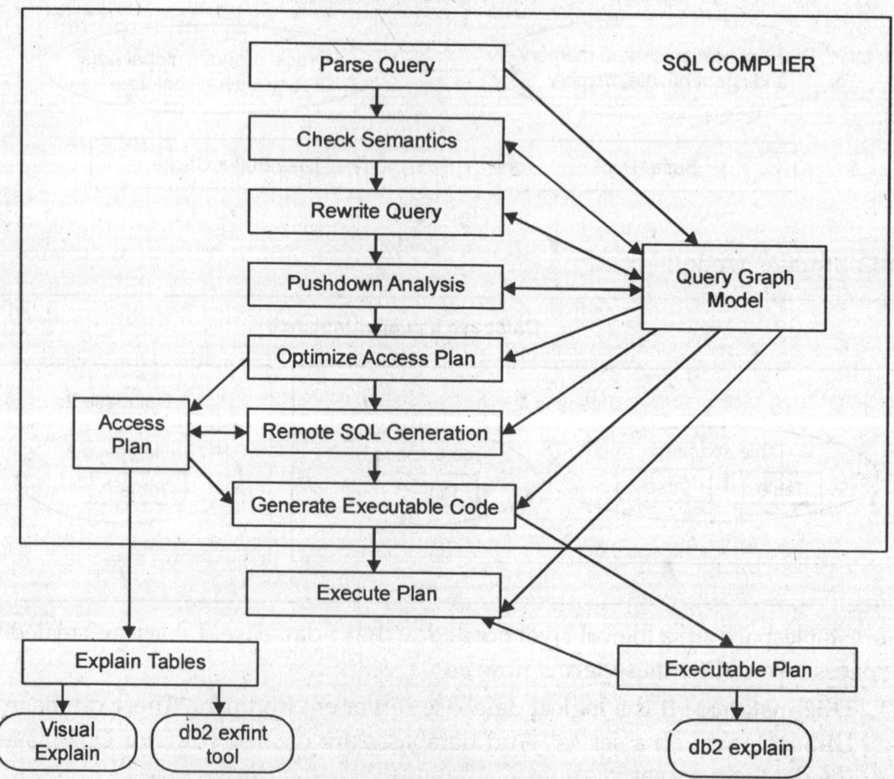

Fig. 10.10

Summary of DB2 Database Layout : DB2 containers can be defined as SMS or DMS. By default, when a db is created, SMS is assumed for all containers. Oracle does not have the concept of SMS. **Please note that the data files in oracle resemble DB2 DMS containers**. Oracle's data is stored in ***data blocks and pages*** in DB2. An **extent** is the specific number of contiguous datablocks obtained in a single allocation. **Also note that, segments are made up of extents to store a particular type of information**. A segment grows one extent at a time.

The SQL Compiler performs a number of tasks during the creation of the compiled form of the SQL statements. The representation of the query is stored in an internal in-memory structure known as the Query Graph Model.

Various tasks of the SQL compiler are :

1. **Task-1:** To analyze the SQL query to validate the syntax. If any syntax errors are detected, the SQL compiler stops processing and the appropriate SQL error is returned to the application attempting or compile the SQL statement. When parsing is complete, an internal representation of the query is created.
2. **Task-2:** To further validate the SQL statement by checking to ensure that parts of the statement make sense given the other parts. **For example**, ensuring that the data-types of the columns input into scalar functions are correct for those functions.

The SQL compiler uses global semantics provided in the query graph model to transform the query into a form that can be optimized more easily.

For example, the compiler might move a predicate, altering the level at which it is applied, in an attempt to improve query performance.

The **SQL optimizer** part of the SQL compiler uses the query graph model as input and generates many alternative execution plans for satisfying the user's request. It estimates the execute cost of each alternative plan using the statistics for tables, indexes, columns and functions. And it chooses the plan with the smallest estimated execution cost.

The *final step* uses the access plan and the query graph model to create an executable access plan for the query. **Please note that the information about the access plans for static SQL is stored in the system catalog tables.**

Let us summarize this now.

SQL Compiler-Tasks

- **Parse Query**
  - ❖ SQL compiler analyzes the SQL query to validate the syntax
- **Check Semantics**
  - ❖ Make sure database objects referenced in the statement are correct (*e.g.*, data types of the columns match the actual table definition)
  - ❖ Add behavioural semantics (*e.g.*, RI, constraints, triggers, and etc)
- **Rewrite Query**
  - ❖ Transform the query so that is can be optimized more easily
- **Optimize Access Plan**
  - ❖ The SQL optimizer (portion of SQL compiler) generates many alternative execution plans and chooses the plan with the least estimated execution cost
  - ❖ Based on current statistics of the tables, indexes, columns, etc.
- **Generate Executable Code**
  - ❖ Create executable access plan for the query
  - ❖ Access plans are stored in the system catalog

DB2 Security Issues

- Three levels of security that control access to a DB2 system
  - ❖ Instance Level
  - ❖ Database level
  - ❖ Database Object Level
- All acccess to the instance is managed by a security facility external to DB2
- The security facility can be part of the operating system or a separate product
- Database manager security parameters, administrative autorities and user privileges are used to control access of database and data objects

When working with a RDBMS, access to it needs to be controlled. You need to consider, who will access it, what will be accessed and what type of access is allowed?

Let us compare the security issues of DB2 and Oracle –

S. No.	DB2	Oracle
1.	User authenication is validated externally by OS/external facility.	User authentication validated by OS or database.
2.	OS defined username with appropriate access right is used to execute DB2 programs and connect to databases for data manipulations.	OS defined username with appropriate access right is used to execute oracle binaries like imp, exp etc.
3.	Database role is not supported, privileges are to be granted to users or groups separately.	Data role is supported to group multiple database privileges.

Actually, a privilege is the right to create or access a database object. It is of three types in DB2.

(*a*) Ownership privilege (*b*) Individual privilege

(*c*) Implicit privilege

Ownership privilege has full access to the object

Individual privilege allows user to perform specific function on a database object eg SELECT, DELETE, INSERT and UPDATE.

Implicit privilege is automatically granted when that user is explicitly granted certain higher level privileges.

DB2 Programming Methods : It includes

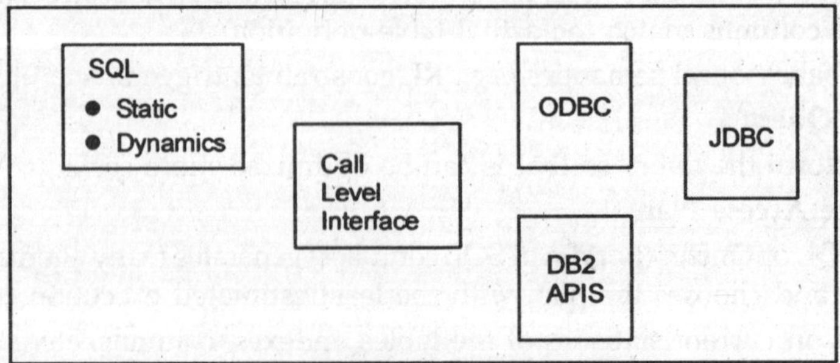

Fig. 10.11

Let us see these various programming methods of DB2:

Static Embedded SQL

- Application development involves combination of SQL with 3GL programming language
- When executed in a program, pre-defined SQL statements bound to a database as application packages.

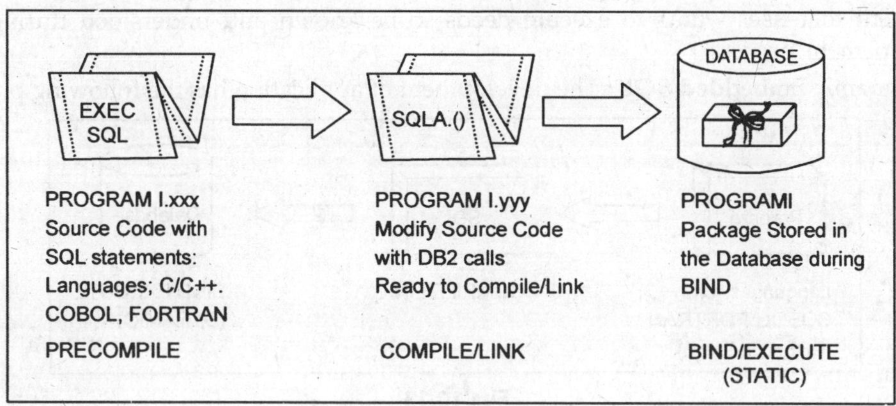

Fig. 10.12

Static SQL statements are ones where the SQL statement type and the database objects accessed by the statement, such as column names, are known prior to running the application. The only unknown are the data values the statement is searching for or modifying.

The db objects being accessed must exist when a static embedded application module is bound to the db.

When the embedded SQL program is executed, it uses pre-defined SQL statements that have been bound to the db as application packages. Thus, the access plan to data is retained in the db, is a ready-to-execute package.

The txns are grouped into packages and stored in the db. The SQL statement are embedded within programming modules. The programming modules must be precompiled. The modified programming modules, created by the precompiler, are then compiled and linked to create the application. During the precompile phase, the SQL statements are analyzed and packages are created.

The Embedded SQL steps involves the following tasks.

Task	Statement
Connect to DB	db2 connect to eddb
Prepare Source code	db2 prep myapp. Sqc bind-file
Compile and link	icc myapp. cdb2 api.lib
Bind to DB	db2 bind myapp.bnd blocking all
Execute object code	myapp>mayapp.out

Static Embedded SQL (SES) : It is supported by C/C++, JAVA, COBOL, and FORTRAN.

Advantages of SES : SES has the following advantages.

1. Optimized packages available at run-time.
2. They are persistent.

Disadvantages of SES :

1. You must know what SQL is needed.
2. It requires precompilation.

Static embedded SQL programs have the least run-time overhead and execute faster. But this method of developing applications is not most flexible because every SQL statement that user wants to execute needs to be known and understood during the developement process.

Dynamic Embedded SQL : The development of application has the following phases.

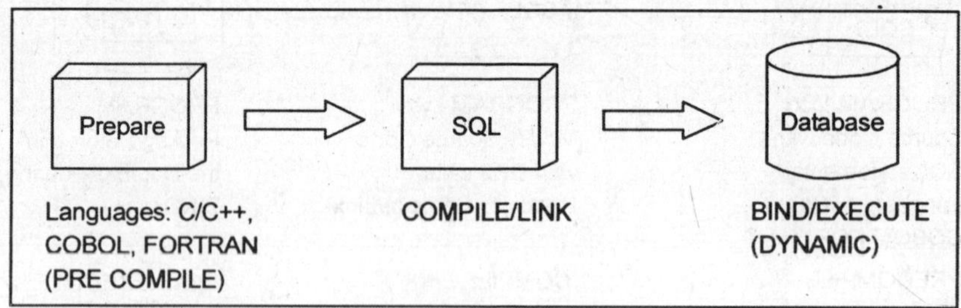

Fig. 10.13

Dynamic SQL statements are defined as those statements that your application builds and executes at runtime. It has various phases as shown above. SQL statements are dynamically prepared. **Please note that an embedded static SQL Programming module will have its data access method determined during the static binding phase and will use the database statistics available at the bind time. On the other, hand, note that an embedded dynamic SQL programming module will have its data access method determined during the statement preparation and will utilize the database statistics available at query execution time.**

Dynamic Embedded SQL supports various languages like C/C++, JAVA, COBOL, FORTRAN, REXX, etc.

Advantages of Dynamic Embedded SQL :

1. It provides execution of dynamic SQL statements.
2. Database objects do not have to exist before runtime.
3. It is more flexible than static SQL statements.

Distvantages of Dynamic Embedded SQL : It takes more time to execute.

DB2 Call Level Interface (CLI) : It is defined as a programming interface that your C/,C++ application can use to access DB2. It is based on MS-ODBC, X/open and ISO call Level Interface standards. It is dynamic SQL application development environment. **Please note that now instead of embedding SQL statements, your application passes dynamic SQL statements as function arguments to the db using C/C++ API provided with DB2 UDB.** So, CLI programs are not precompiled CLI applications use common access packages provided with DB2 UDB. So, there is no need to bind the program modules separately. **Also note that you can only bind CLI packages once to each db, you want to access using any CLI or ODBC application on a client.**

Advantage of CLI :

1. Precompile or Binding is not required.
2. Current statistics are used.
3. Can store and retrieve sets of data.

4. Application can be multi-threaded.
5. Easy application porting.

Disadvantages of CLI :

1. It is confined to C/C++.
2. Dynamic bindings are slower.

DB2 API : It is used to directly manipulate DB2 instance and database.

(*a*) Backup/recovery.
(*b*) Database monitoring
(*c*) Database configuration.
(*d*) Table space management.

Advantages of DB2 APIs :

1. It can be used to do tablespace administration
2. No precompilation or binding is required.

Disadvantages of DB2 APIs :

1. It requires host language compiler.
2. It can be more difficult to use.
3. It cannot issue SQL statements.
4. It cannot be easily ported to other database servers.

Declared Temporary Tables : Tables that are created and used by on application and dropped automatically when the application terminates are known as Declared Temporary Tables. It's features are as follows :

1. They can only be accessed by the application that created the table
2. No entry of this table will exist in any catalog table.
3. If different applications all create a table with the same name then each application has a unique instance of that declared temporary table.
4. No table locking or row locking is allowed.
5. Changes are not logged

Need of Declared Temporary Tables :

1. They are required to hold intermediate results during complex processing.
2. Better performance as it –
   (*a*) Avoids catalog contention.
   (*b*) Requires no locking of rows.
   (*c*) Requires no logging.
   (*d*) Requires no authority checking.
3. There are no namespase collisions between instances of application.
4. They provide automatic cleanup.

Where they reside ? How are they created?

Declared temporary tables reside in a user temporary tablespace. They are created using CREATE TABLESPACE statement as follows :

```
CREATE USER TEMPORARY TABLESPACE apptemps
MANAGED BY SYSTEM USING ('apptemps');
```

DECLARED GLOBAL TEMPORARY TABLE : It is a statement that defines a temporary table for the current session. No authority is required to issue this statement, when issuing DML against the table.

TRIGGERS in DB2 : A trigger defines a set of actions that are activated or triggered by an update operation on a specified base table. The actions may cause other changes to the database or raise an exception. They are used to

(*a*) Define busines rules.

(*b*) Automatically update summary data.

(*c*) Validate input data.

(*d*) Generate values for inserted rows.

(*e*) Read from other tables.

(*f*) Write to other tables for audit-trail purposes.

(*g*) Alerts.

For example,

```
CREATE TRIGGER NEW_HIRE
    AFTER INSERT ON EMP
    FOR EACH   ROW   MODE   DB2 SQL
    UPDATE COMPANY_STATS
    SET NBEMP = NBEMP + 1;
```

This is an example of a simple trigger named NEW_HIRE. **It is activated after the insert operation. This is called as the trigger activation time**. You can specify BEFORE or AFTER.

A trigger is associated with a table called the subject table. The subject table of this trigger is EMP.

Now, this trigger is activated when an insert operation is performed on the EMP table. **Please note that every trigger is associated with an event like insert, update or delete operation. Also note that a trigger associated with an update operation can be associated with specific columns of the subject table.**

FOR EACH ROW clause shows that this trigger runs for each row in the set of affected rows. We can also use FOR EACH STATEMENT which means it runs once for the entire trigger statement. The **trigger** action is performed when the trigger event occurs.

Transition Variables : They are defined as those variables that are used to refer to the value of the set of affected rows for the currently executing trigger. They are of two types.

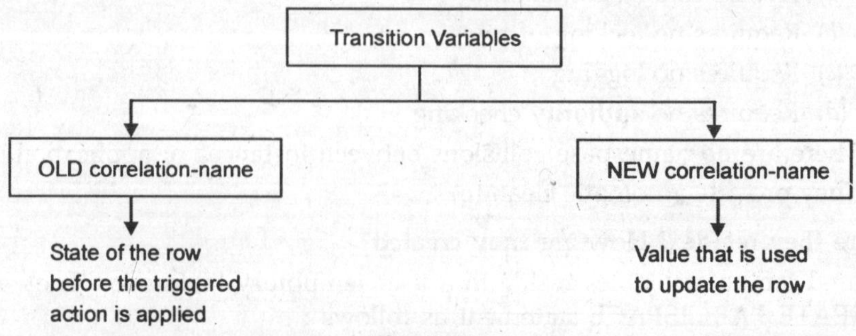

Fig. 10.14

But for every trigger, every transition variable cannot be defined. This is shown below.

Trigger \ Transition Variables	OLD	NEW	Meaning
UPDATE	✓	✓	Both OLD and NEW transaction variables can be defined.
INSERT		✓	Can define NEW transaction variable only.
DELETE	✓		Can define OLD transaction variable only.

Accordingly, the transition tables are of two types :

(*a*) OLD_TABLE

(*b*) NEW_TABLE

Transition tables are read only

DB2 provides 16-levels of cascading. If level 17 is activated then SQLCODE-724 will be returned. Trigger can be activated as a result of referential constraint enforcement. If multiple triggers are defined for a table then both before-triggers and after-triggers are activated in the order that they were created.

User Defined Functions (UDFs) : UDF is a mechanim for creating extensions to SQL. They build customized functions for specific application. They are usable by all authorized users. They are accessed through DML only and are executed on the server only. This is shown below.

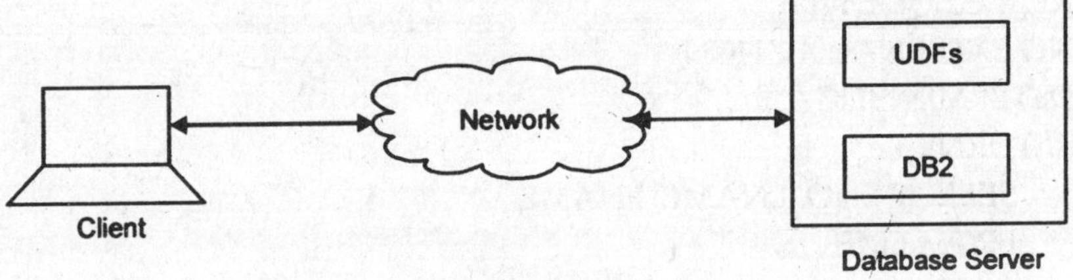

Fig. 10.15

So, UDFs must be built and installed in each database. They have to be installed in every database that will be using them.

Steps to implement an external UDF are :

Writing the UDF
↓
Compiling the UDF
↓
Linking the UDF
↓
Debugging the UDF
↓
Registering UDF with DB2

What is an SQL_UDF?

It is a function body written in SQL. It is defined together with the registration of the database. It returns a scalar value, a table or a single row.

Example 1.

```
CREATE FUNCTION TAN (X DOUBLE)
RETURNS DOUBLE
```

```
LANGUAGE SQL
CONTAINS SQL
NO EXTERNAL ACTION
DETERMINISTIC
RETURN SIN(X)/cos (X)
```

Example 2.

```
CREATE FUNCTION PERSON (P PERSON)
RETURNS ROW (NAME    VARCHAR, (10), FNAME VARCHAR(10))
LANGUAGE SQL
CONTAINS SQL
NO EXTERNAL ACTION
DETERMINISTIC
RETURN VALUES (P... NAME, P.. FNAME)
```

Example 3.

```
CREATE FUNCTION DEPEMP (DEPNO CHAR (3))
RETURNS TABLE (ENO CHAR (6),
    LNAME VARCHAR (15)
    FNAME VARCHAR (10))
LANGUAGE SQL
READS SQL DATA
NO EXTERNAL ACTION
DETERMINISTIC
RETURN
    SELECT ENO, LNAME, FNAME
    FROM EMP
    WHERE EMP. WORKDEPT = DEPEMP. DEPNO
```

So, RETURN clause may return an expression, NULL, full select etc.

STORED PROCEDURES : They execute on the database server. They perform intermediate processing. So, there is no need to transmit data across the network. An application consists of

(*a*) Stored procedure on database server

(*b*) Client application that involves the stored procedure.

This is shown below.

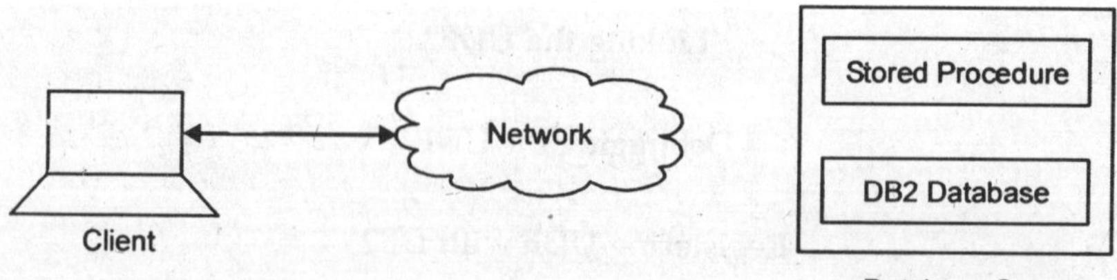

Fig. 10.16

Advantages of Stored Procedures :

1. They **reduce network traffic** as they perform intermediate processing on the server and transmit only those records that are required by the client side.

2. They impove performance
3. The access to features is only available on the database server like memory and disk space, software etc.
4. Better improved security.
5. Reuse of common routines.
6. Centralized administration and maintenance

How to implement stored procedures ?

Before you can use SPs, you have to build them and install them in the database. They have to be installed in every database that will be using them.

Steps to implement an external SP are :

Writing the SP
↓
Compiling the SP
↓
Linking the SP
↓
Registering SP with DB2

SQL Procedures : They are created with a CREATE PROCEDURE statement. Every SQL procedure has :

(*a*) Procedure name
(*b*) Parameters
(*c*) SQL
(*d*) Procedure Body

For example,

```
CREATE PROCEDURE update_sal
    (IN     eno     CHAR (5),
    IN      rate    INTEGER)
    LANGUAGE SQL
    BEGIN
        UPDATE EMP
        SET SAL = SAL* (1.0 + RATE/100.0)
        WHERE ENO1 = eno;
    END
```

The **name** of SP is update_sal. There are 2 **input parameters** to types CHAR and INT.

LANGUAGE SQL indicates that this is an SQL procedure. So, a procedure body follows other parameters.

BEGIN ... END has the procedure body. Here, we have a single SQL UPDATE statement in its body. An SQL procedure statement can be an SQL control statement or SQL statement.

SQL control statements like assignment, CASE, compound, FOR, GOTO, IF, ITERATE, LEAVE, LOOP, REPEAT, RESIGNAL, RETURN, SIGNAL statements, can be used.

All SQL statements except, CONNE CT, CREATE, DESCRIBE, DISCONNECT, DROP, REFRESH, RENAME, RELEASE, REVOKE, SET CONTECTION, SET INTEGRITY, cannot be used.

NOTE : SQL procedures can call only stored procedures written in SQL or C. 16 Levels of nesting are allowed. It can even call itself recursively (upto 16 levels).

Resultsets can be returned to the client or caller. To do so, we use –

WITH RETURN TO CLIENT in the DECLARE CURSOR statement.

And to return Resultsets to the caller, we use –

WITH RETURN TO CALLER in the DECLARE CURSOR statement.

Stored Procedure Builder : It is a new GUI tool for rapid development of DB2 Java and SQL stored procedures. It supports static (SQLJ) and dynamic (JDBC) SQL. Currently, only JAVA language is supported. It supports all DB2 UDB server platforms. This simplifies our development of stored procedures and increases portability across DB2 family. It's other uses are :

(*a*) SPs can be built for local or for remote systems.

(*b*) You can modify and rebuild existing stored procedures.

(*c*) You can test and debug stored procedures.

DB2 Protection : DB2 provides different levels of protection to isolate data. Cursor stability is the default isolation level. Isolation level can be specified for a session, a client connection or an application before a database connection. **Please note that for enbedded SQL, the level is set at bind-time whereas for dynamic SQL, the level is set at run-time.**

Isolation Levels–DB2 v/s Oracle

S. No.	DB2 UDB	Oracle
1.	Repeatable Read.	Transaction-level read consistency.
2.	Read Stability	Not applicable
3.	Cursor stability (default)	Statement-level read consistency.
4.	Uncommitted Read.	Not Applicable.

DB2 Locking : By default, DB2 uses row-level locking. Database, tablespaces and tables can be implicitly as well as explicitly locked.

SQL server has page-level locking. DB2 and Oracle have row-level locking. But there are some differences also. Let us tabulate them.

S. No.	DB2	Oracle
1.	A reader will never get a 'before image'.	A reader gets a 'before image' by default, through the use of rollback segments.
2.	It has deadlock detector that periodically checks for deadlock.	It does not have a deadlock detector
3.	We use db2 lock timeout database parameter to avoid exclusive lock wait.	We specify NOWAIT in the cursor declaration.

Recovery in DB2 : There are three ways of recovery. They are as follows :

I. **Crash/Restart Recovery**

- Uses the RESTART DATABASE command or the automatic restart enable configuration parameter (autorestart) to protect a database from being left in a inconsistent, or unusable, state.

II. **Version/Image Recovery**

- Uses the BACKUP command in conjunction with the RESTORE command to put the database in a state that was previously saved.
- Used for non-recoverable database or databases for which there are no archived logs.

III. **Rollforward Recovery**

- Uses the BACKUP command in conjunction with the RESTORE and ROLLFORWARD command to recover a database or table space to a specified point in time.

SUMMARY

An ORDBMS is a relational DBMS that allows developers to integrate the database with their own custom data types and methods. In this chapter we have discussed about OODBMS as well as Distributed DBMS. Also, a case-study on IBM's DB2 has been dealt in detail.

MULTIPLE CHOICE QUESTIONS [MCQs]

1. The third generation DBMS includes
   (*a*) Relational Data Model (*b*) ER Data Model
   (*c*) ORDBMS and OODBMS (*d*) None of the above.

2. LOB stands for
   (*a*) Large object Base (*b*) Large Object
   (*c*) List Object (*d*) None of the above.

3. A pointer to an external file is
   (*a*) BLOB (*b*) CLOB
   (*c*) BFILE (*d*) None of the above.

4. Fragmentation is used in
   (*a*) ORDBMS (*b*) DDBMS
   (*c*) ODBMS (*d*) RDBMS.

5. Indentical DBMS software is found in
   (*a*) Homegeneous DDBMS. (*b*) Heterogeneous DDBMS
   (*c*) Both '*a*' and '*b*' (*d*) None of the above.

6. FDBS stands for
   (*a*) Future Database System (*b*) Federated Database System
   (*c*) Final Database System (*d*) None of the above.

7. C.J Date gave
   (*a*) 10-rules. (*b*) 11 – rules.
   (*c*) 12-rules. (*d*) 13 – rules.

8. ANSI—SPARC architecture is for
   (*a*) Centralized DBMS (*b*) Distributed DBMS
   (*c*) Decentralized DBMS (*d*) None of the above.

9. Data allocation involves which of these strategies
   (*a*) Replication (*b*) Duplication
   (*c*) Selection (*d*) None of these

10. Size of DB2 is
   (*a*) 10 k (*b*) 100 k
   (*c*) 1000 k (*d*) 10,000 k

ANSWERS

1. (*b*) 2. (*b*) 3. (*c*) 4. (*b*) 5. (*a*) 6. (*b*) 7. (*c*) 8. (*a*)
9. (*a*) 10. (*b*)

CONCEPTUAL SHORT QUESTIONS WITH ANSWERS

Q.1. Compare different DBMS Models in a tabular form?

Ans.

S. No.	Database Model	Organisation	Relationship Organization	Identity	Access Language
1.	Hierarchical	Files, Records	Linear tree	Record-based	Procedural
2.	Network	Files, Records	Networks	Record-based	Procedural
3.	Relational	Tables	PK of one table embedded as attributes in another table	Value-based	Non-procedural
4.	Object-Oriented	objects	Recursive examination of attributes of an project	Record-based	Procedurals
5.	Object-Relational	Object, Functions & Rules	Supports image retrievals advanced text searching.	Value-based	Non-Procedural
6.	Deductive	Facts, Rules	Inference rules	Value-based	Now-Procedural

Q.2. Compare OO data model and ER data model?

Ans. Let us tabulate the differences between the two.

S. No.	OO Data Model	ER Data Model
1.	We talk of type.	We talk of entity definition.
2.	We use the term object here.	We use the term Entity here.
3.	Classes are defined.	Entity sets are defined.
4.	If supports inheritance, encapsulation and associations.	It supports entity and relationships only.
5.	We draw class diagrams here.	We draw ER diagrams here.

Q.3. Name some OODBMS and their vendors.

Ans.

OODBMS	Vendor
Gemstone	Gemstone system Inc
Poet	Poet software corporation
Jasmine	Computer Associates
IRIS	HP
Orion	MCC
O2	Leeluse

Q.4. What is ODL?

Ans. Object definition language (ODL) is used to support the semantic constructs of the ODMG object model. It is similar to DDL of traditional RDBMS. ODL is programming language independent. It is used to facilitate probability of schemas between complaint systems.

Q.5. What is OQL?

Ans. **Object query language** (OQL) is the query language proposed for ODMG object model. An OQL query is embedded into these programming languages. The OQL syntax is similar to the syntax of our standard SQL.

Q.6. Compare KBMS and DBMS in a tabular form.

Ans.

S. No.	KBMS	DBMS
1.	It is a system that handles **small amount** of knowledge.	It is a system that handles **large amount** of shared data.
2.	The starting point, here is a **knowledge representation** schema.	The starting point is a **data model** used to represent data and interrelationships between them.
3.	We stress more on **robust knowledge** representation schema. By 'robust', we mean a schema rich in expressive power and efficient.	We stress more on **efficient access** *and* **management** of data that model a portion of real world.
4.	It is concerned with the **meaning** of information.	It is concerned with the **information** contained in data.
5.	It uses the concept of **knowledge independence**. It means that the knowledge stored in the system must be independent from physical or logical structure.	It uses the concept of **data independence**.

Q.7. Discuss the relative advantages of centralized and distributed databases.

Ans.
- A distributed database allows a user convenient and transparent access to data which is not stored at the site, while allowing each site control over its own local data. A distributed database can be made reliable than a centralized system because if one site fails, the database can continue functioning, but if the centralized system fails, the database can no longer continue with its normal operation. Also, a distributed database allows parallel execution of queries and possibly splitting one query into many parts to increase throughput.
- A centralized system is easier to design and implement. A centralized system is cheaper to operate because messages do not have to be sent.

Q.8. Explain how the following differ : fragmentation transparency, replication transparency, and location transparency.

Ans. (*a*) With fragmentation transparency, the user of the system is unaware of any fragmentation the system has implemented. A user may formulate queries against global relations and the system will perform the necessary transformation to generate correct output.

(*b*) With replication transparency, the user is unaware of any replicated data. The system must prevent inconsistent operations on the data. This requires more complex concurrency control algorithms.

(*c*) Location transparency means the user is unaware of where data are stored. The system must route data requests to the appropriate sites.

Q.9. When is it useful to have replication or fragmentation of data? Explain your answer.

Ans. Replication is useful when there are many read-only transactions at different sites wanting access to the same data. They can all execute quickly in parallel, accessing local data. But updates become difficult with replication. Fragmentation is useful if transactions on different sites tend to access different parts of the database.

Q.10. Explain the notions of transparency and autonomy. Why are these notions desirable from a human-factors standpoint?

Ans. Autonomy is the amount of control a single site has over the local database. It is important because users at that site want quick and correct access to local data items. This is especially true when one considers that local data will be most frequently accessed in a database. Transparency hides the distributed nature of the database. This is important because users should not be required to know about location, replication, fragmentation or other implementation aspects of the database.

Q.11. If we apply a distributed version of the multiple-granularity protocol of Chapter 10 to a distributed database, the site responsible for the root of the DAG may become a bottleneck. Suppose we modify that protocol as follows :

- **Only intention-mode locks are allowed on the root.**
- **All transactions are given all possible intention-mode locks on the root automatically.**

Show that these modifications alleviate this problem without allowing any nonseriablizable schedules.

Ans. Serializability is assured since we have not changed the rules for the multiple granularity protocol. Since transactions are automatically granted all intention locks on the root node, and are not given other kinds of locks on it, there is no need to send any lock requests to the root. Thus the bottleneck is relieved.

Q.12. Consider the relations –

employee (name, addrees, salary, plant_number)

machine (machine_number, type, plant_number)

Assume that the *employee* relation is fragmented horizontally by *plant_number*, and that each fragment is stored locally at its corresponding plant site. Assume that the *machine* relation is stored in its entirety at the Armonk site. Describe a good strategy for processing each of the following queries.

(*a*) Find all employees at the plant that contains machine number 1130.

(*b*) Find all employees at plants that contain machines whose type is "milling machine".

(*c*) Find all machines at the Almaden plant.

(*d*) Find employee ⋈ machine.

Ans. (*a*) (*i*) Perform $\pi_{\text{plant\_number}}$ ($\sigma_{machine\_number=1130}$)) at Armonk.

(*ii*) Send the query π_{name} (*employee*) to all site (*s*) which are in the result of the previous query.

(*iii*) Those sites compute the answers.

(*iv*) Union the answers at the destination site.

(*b*) This strategy is the same as 0.a, except the first step should be to perform π_{plant_number} ($\sigma_{type="milling\ machine"}$(*machine*)) at Armonk.

(*c*) (*i*) Perform $\pi_{\text{plant\_number}=\ x}$ (*machine*) at Armonk, where *x* is the plant_number for Almaden.

(*ii*) Send the answers to the destination site.

(*d*) Strategy 1:

(*i*) Group **machine** at Armonk by plant number.

(*ii*) Send the groups to the sites with the corresponding plant_number.

(*iii*) Perform a local join between the local data and the received data.

(*iv*) Union the results at the destination site.

Strategy 2: Send the **machine** relation at Armonk, and all the fragments of the **employee** relation to the destination site. Then perform the join at the destination site.

There is parallelism in the join computation according to the first strategy but not in the second. Nevertheless, in a WAN the amount of data to be shipped is the main cost factor. We expect that each plant will have more than one machine, hence the result of the local join at each site will be a cross-product of the employee tuples and machines at that plant. This cross-product's size is greater than the size of the *employee* fragment at that site. As a result the second strategy will result in less data shipping, and will be more efficient.

Q.13. For each of the strategies of Exercise 12, state how your choice of a strategy depends on:

(*a*) The site at which the query was entered

(*b*) The site at which the result is desired

Ans. (*a*) Assuming that the cost of shipping the query itself is minimal, the site at which the query was submitted does not affect our strategy query evaluation.

(*b*) For the first query, we find out the plant number where the machine number 1130 is present, at Armonk. Then the employee tuples at all those plants are shipped to the destination site. We can say that this strategy is more or less independent of the destination site. The same can be said of the second query. For the third query, the selection is performed at Armonk and results shipped to the destination site. This strategy is obviously independent of the destination site.

For the fourth query, we have two strategies. The first one performs local joins at all the plant sites and their results are unioned at the destination site. In the second strategy, the **machine** relation at Armonk as well as all the fragments of the **employee** relation are first shipped to the destination, where the join operation is performed. There is no obvious way to optimize these two strategies based on the destination site. In the answer to Exercise 12 we saw the reason why the second strategy is expected to result in less data shipping than the first. That reason is independent of destination site, and hence we can in general prefer strategy two to strategy one, regardless of the destination site.

Q.14. Is the expression $r_i \ltimes r_j$ necessarily equal to $r_j \ltimes r_i$? Under what conditions does $r_i \ltimes r_j = r_j \ltimes r_i$ hold?

Ans. In general, $r_i \ltimes r_j \neq r_j \ltimes r_i$. This can be easily seen that $r \ltimes s \neq s \ltimes r$. $r \ltimes s$ was given in 22.11 while

$s \ltimes r =$

C	D	E
3	4	5
3	6	8
2	3	2

By definition, $r_i \ltimes r_j = \pi_{Ri} (r_i \bowtie r_j)$ and $r_j \ltimes r_i \; \pi_{Ri} (r_i \bowtie r_j)$, where R_i and R_i are the schemas of r_i and r_j respectively. For $\pi_{Ri} (r_i \bowtie r_j)$ to be always equal to $\pi_{Rj} (r_i \bowtie r_j)$ to be always equal to $\pi_{Rj} (r_i \bowtie r_j)$, the schemas R_i and R_j must be the same.

Q.15. Describe how LDAP can be used to provide multiple hierarchical views of data, without replicating the base level data.

Ans. This can be done using referrals. For example an organization may maintain its information about deparments either by geography (*i.e.,* all departments in a site of the the organization) or by structure (*i.e.,* information about a department from all sites). These two hierarchies can be maintained by defining two different schemas with department information at a site as the base information. The entries in the two hierarchies will refer to the base information entry using referrals.

Q.16. Discuss the advantages and disadvantages of the two methods that we presented for generating globally unique timestamps.

Ans. The centralized approach has the problem of a possible bottleneck at the central site and the problem of electing a new central site if it goes down. The distributed approach has the problem that many messages must be exchanges to keep the system, fair, or one site can get ahead of all other sites and dominate the database.

Q.17. (*a*) What are the three broad levels at which a database system can be tuned to improve performance?

(*b*) Given two example of how tuning can be done, for each of the levels.

Ans. (*a*) We refer to performance tuning of a database system as the modification of some system components in order to improve transaction response times, or overall transaction throughput. Database systems can be tuned at various levels to enhance performance. viz.

(*i*) Schema and transaction design

(*ii*) Buffer manager and transaction manager

(*iii*) Access and storage structures.

Hardware-disks, CPU, busses etc.

(*b*) We describe some examples for performance tuning of some of the major components of the database system.

(*i*) Tuning the schema-

In this chapter we have seen two example to schema tuning, viz vertical partition of a relation (or conversely-join of two relations), and denormalization (or conversely-normalization). These examples reflect the general scenario, and ideas therein can be applied to tune other schemas.

(*ii*) Tuning the transactions –

One approach used to speed-up query execution is to improve the its plan. Suppose that we need the natural join of two relations-say **account** and **depositor** from our sample bank database. A **sort-merge-join** (Section 13.5.4) on the attribute **account-number** may be quicker than a simple nested-loop join on the relations.

Other ways of tuning transactions are-breaking up long update transactions and combining related sets of queries into a single query. Generic examples for these approaches are given in this chapter.

For client-server systems, wherein the query has to be transmitted from client to server, the query transmission time itself may form a large fraction of the total query cost. Using *stored* **procedures** can significantly reduce the queries response time.

(*iii*) Tuning the buffer manager –

The buffer manager can be made to increase or decrease the number of pages in the buffer according to changing page-fault rates. However it must be noted that a larger number of pages may higher costs for latch management and maintenance of other data-structures like free-lists and page map tables.

(*iv*) Tuning the transaction manager –

The transaction schedule affects system performance. A query that computes statistics for customers at each branch of the bank will need to scan the relations **account** and **depositor**. During these scans, no updates to any customer's balance will be allowed. Thus, the response time for the update transactions is high. Large queries are best executed when there are few updates, such as at night.

Checkpointing also incurs some cost. If recovery time is not critical, it is preferable to examine a long log(during recovery) rather than spend a lot of (checkpointing) time during normal operation. Hence it may be worthwhile to tune the checkpointing interval according to the expected rate crashes and the required recovery time.

(*v*) Tuning the access and storage structures –

A query's response time can be improved by creating an appropriate index on the relation. **For example**, consider a query in which a depositor enquires about her balance in a particular account. This query would result in the scan of the relation **account** if it has is no index on **account-number**. Similar indexing consideration also apply to computing joins. *i.e.*, an index on **account-number** in the **account** relation saves scanning **account** when a natural join of account is taken with *depositor*.

In contrast, performance of update transactions may suffer due to indexing. Let us assume that frequent updates to the balance are required. Also suppose that there is an index on **balance** (presumably for range queries) in **account**. Now, for each update to the value of the balance, the index too will have to be updated. In addition, concurrent updates to the index structure will require additional locking overheads. Note that the response time for each update would not be more if there were no index on balance.

The type of index chosen also affects performance. For a range query, an order preserving index (like B-treees) is better than a hashed index.

Clustering of data affects the response time for some queries. For example, assume that the tuples of the **account** relation are clustered on **branch-name**. Then the average execution time for a query that finds the total balance amount deposited at a particular branch can be improved. Even more benefit accrues from having a clustered index on **branch-name**.

If the database system has more than one disk, **declustering** of data will enable parallel access. Suppose that we have five disks and that in a hypothetical situation where each customer has five accounts and each account has a lot of historical information that needs to be accessed.

Storing one account per custromer per disk will enable parallel access to all accounts of a particular customer. Thus, the speed of a scan on depositor will increase about five-fold.

(*vi*) Tuning the hardware –

The hardware for the database system typically consists of disks, the processor, and the interconnecting architecture (buses etc). Each of these components may be a bottleneck and by increasing the number of disks or their block-sizes, or using a faster processor, or by improving the bus architecture, one may obtain an improvement in system performance.

Q.18. What is the motivation for splitting a long transaction into a series of small ones? What problems could arise as a result, and how can these problems be averted?

Ans. Long update transactions cause a lot of log information to be written, and hence extend the checkpointing interval and also the recovery time after a crash. A transaction that performs many updates may even cause the system log to overflow before the transaction commits.

To avoid these problems with a long update transaction it may be advisable to break it up into smaller transactions. This can be seen as **group transaction** being split into many small *mini-batch* transactions. The same effect is obtained by executing both the group transaction and the mini-batch transactions, which are scheduled in the order that their operations apperar in the group transaction.

However, executing the mini-batch transactions in place of the group transaction has some costs, such as extra effort when recovering from system failures. Also, even if the group transaction satisfies the **isolation** requirement, the mini-batch may not. Thus the transaction manager can release the locks held by the mini-batch only when the last transaction in the mini-batch completes execution.

Q.19. Suppose the price of memory falls by half, and the speed of disk access (number of accesses per second) doubles, while all other factors remain the same. What would be the effect of this change on the 5 minute and 1 minute rule?

Ans. There will be no effect of these changes on the 5 minute or the 1 minute rule. The value of *n, i.e.,* the frequency of page access at break-even point, is proportional to the product of memory price and speed of disk access, other factors remaining constant. So when memory price falls by half and access speed doubles, n remains the same.

Q.20. List at least 4 features of the benchmarks that help make them realistic and dependable measures.

Ans. Some features that make the TPC benchmarks realistic and dependable are –

(*a*) Ensuring full support for ACID properties of transactions,

(*b*) Calculating the throughput by observing the *end-to-end* performance,

(*c*) Making sizes of relations proportional to the expected rate of transaction arrival, and

(*d*) Measuring the dollar cost per unit of throughput.

Q.21. Why was the TPCD benchmark replaced by the TPCH and TPCR benchmarks?

Ans. Various TPCD queries can be significantly speeded up by using materialized views and other redundant information, but the overheads of using them should be properly accounted. Hence TPCR and TPCH were introduced as refinements of TPCD, both of which use same schema and workload. TPCR models periodic reporting queries, and the database running it is permited to use materialized views. TPCH, on the other hand, models and-hoc querying, and prohibits materialized views and other redundant information.

EXERCISE QUESTIONS

Q.1. Write short notes on—'Problems in distributed databases'.
[GGSIPU, B.Tech., (CSE); 5th Sem., Dec 2006]

Q.2. Wrie short notes on-'object oriented Database'.
[GGSIPU, B.Tech., (CSE); 5th Sem., Dec 2007]

Q.3. What mechanisms are used for - 'accessing shared databases:
[GGSIPU, B.Tech. (CSE); 5th Sem., Dec 2007]

Q.4. What is an object-oriented database ? What are its advantages compared to relational database? Explain some applications where an object-oriented database may be useful.
[BPUP Orissa, B.Tech., (CSE); 4th Sem., 2008]

Q.5. What is distributed DBMS? How is different from client-server DBMS?
[BPUT, Orissa, B.Tech (CSE); 4th Sem., 2008]

Q.6. What is object-oriented data model?
[BPUT, Orissa, MCA; 2nd year, June 2005]

Q.7. Explain in detail distributed database
[Nagpur University, MCA; 2nd Sem., Dec .2006]

Q.8. Write short note on DDBMS?
[Nagpur University, B.Tech., 2nd Sem., June 2008]

Q.9. Elaborate on the popularity of OODBS. State its advantages and disadvantages.
[Nagpur University, MCA; 2nd Sem., June 2008]

Q.10. Explain how node failures are handled in a distributed dbms. What activities need to be performed when a crashed node is to be restared? **[KUD, B.E (CSE); 6th Sem., 1995]**

Q.11. Explain the advantages and disadvantages of OODBS?
[GGSIPU, BCA, BIS(H); 3nd Sem., Dec. 2002]

Q.12. Write short note on OODBS. **[GGSIPU, BCA; 3nd Sem., Dec. 2003]**

Q.13. (*a*) Explain logical data structure and physical data structure with reference to DB2

(*b*) What are tiggers and how they are used in DB2.
[GGSIPU, MCA; 2nd Sem., May 2003]

Q.14. "Cursor construct in any database support language is to provide the procedural extension to a non-procedural language."Explain with example, in context of DB2 product.
[GGSIPU, MCA; 2nd Sem., May 2004]

Q.15. Explain the internal memory structure of DB2.
[GGSIPU, M.Tech (IT); 3nd Sem., Dec. 2004]

Q.16. (*a*) Explain the notions of transparency and autonomy with reference to the distributed database.

(*b*) How does the concept of an object in object-oriented model differ from the concept of an entity in ER-model.

(*c*) Explain the internal architecture of DB2 database.
[GGSIPU, M.Tech. (CSE/IT); 3nd Sem., Dec. 2004]

Q.17. Write short notes on distribution data bases.
[GGSIPU, M.Tech. (CSE/IT); 5th Sem., Dec. 2011]

Q.18. Describe objects, literals, ODL and Fragmentation in distributed databases.
[GGSIPU, M.Tech. (CSE/IT); 1st Sem., Jan. 2011]

CHAPTER 11

Parallel Databases

11.0 INTRODUCTION

Parallel database system is a DBMS running across multiple processors and disks that is designed to perform various tasks concurrently like loading data, building indexes and evaluating queries, when we have large databases and a large number of transactions have to be executed per second. It has to provide shared resource management.

To meet the changing requirements of the users, the modern database systems operate with an architecture where multiple CPU's are working in parallel on the database to provide the services. These multiple CPU's are working in parallel and are located in the same building and communicating with each other at very high speed. The databases used in such systems are called **parallel databases.** Parallel systems improve processing and I/O speeds by using multiple CPU's and disks in parallel. Parallel processing divides a large task into many smaller tasks and executes the smaller tasks concurrently on several CPU's and completes it more quickly. Parallel computers with hundreds of CPU's and disks are available commercially.

A **distributed database system** is a database that is physically stored on several computer systems across various sites connected through the network. The computer systems in a distributed system do not share main memory or disks. The computers may vary in size and function also.

The main differences between **parallel databases and distributed databases** are that the former is ***tightly coupled*** and the later is ***loosely coupled.*** This means the distributed databases are geographically separated, separately administered and have a slower interconnection. Another major difference is that, we differentiate between ***local*** and ***global*** transactions in a distributed database system.

11.1 DESIGN OF PARALLEL DATABASES

There are three main architectural designs for parallel DBMS. They are as follows :

(*a*) Shared Memory Architecture

(*b*) Shared Disk Architecture

(*c*) Shared Nothing Architecture.

Let us discuss these one by one.

I. Shared Memory Architecture : In this architecture, there are many (multiple) CPUs that are attached to an interconnection network. They can share a single or global main memory and common disk arrays (storages). **Please note that in this architecture, a single copy of a multithreaded OS and multithreaded DBMS can support these multiple**

processors (CPUs). Also note that shared memory is a tightly coupled architecture in which multiple CPUs share memory. It is shown in Fig. 11.1. It is also known as **Symmetric Multiprocessing (SMP)**. This approach has a very wide range starting from personal workstations that support a few microprocessors in parallel via RISC, to largest main frames.

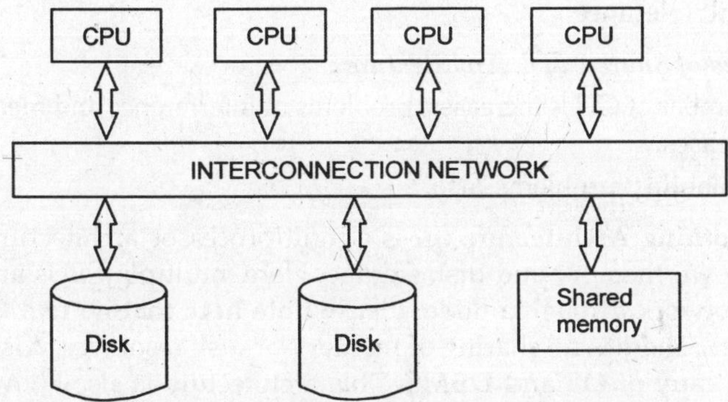

Fig. 11.1. *Shared-memory architecture*

Advantages of Shared-Memory Architecture :

1. High speed data access for a limited number of processors.
2. Communication is efficient, lesser overheads.

Disadvantages of Shared-Memory Architecture :

1. It is not scalable beyond 80 or 100 CPUs in parallel as the interconnection network is shared by all CPUs.
2. The bus or the interconnection network becomes a bottleneck as the number of CPUs increases.

II. Shared Disk Architecture : In this method, multiple CPUs are attached to an interconnection network. Each CPU has its own memory but all have access to the same disk. **Please note that here the memory is not shared among CPUs, so each node has its own copy of O.S. and DBMS. Also note that it is a loosely coupled architecture optimized for application that are inherently centralized.** Each CPU can access all disks directly but each has its own private memory. *So, shared disk systems are sometimes referred to as clusters.* This is shown in Fig. 11.2 below.

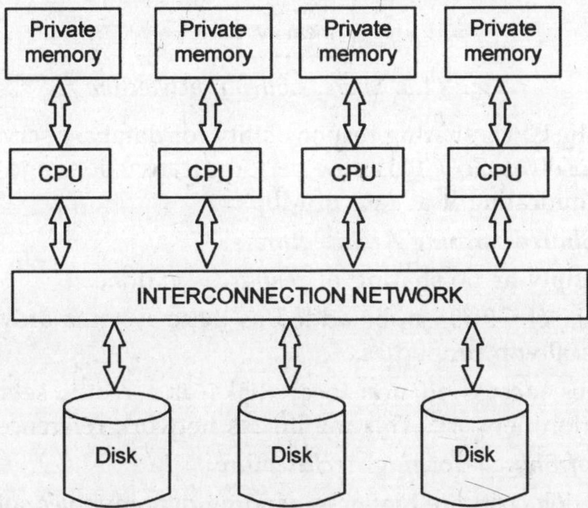

Fig. 11.2. *Shared-disk architecture*

Advantages of Shared-disk Architecture :

1. The interconnection network is no longer a bottleneck as each CPU has its own memory.
2. Load balancing is easy.
3. Better fault tolerance.

Disadvantages of Shared-disk Architecture :

1. As the number of CPUs increases, problems of interference and memory contentions also increases.
2. It has scalability problems also.

III. Shared-nothing Architecture : It is a multiprocessor architecture in which each processor has its own memory and disk storage. Here, multiple CPUs are attached to an interconnection network through a node. **Please note here that no two CPUs can access the same disk area**. There is no sharing of memory or disk resources. **Also note that each CPU has its own copy of OS and DBMS**. This architecture is also known as **Massively Parallel Processing (MPP)**. This is shown in Fig. 11.3.

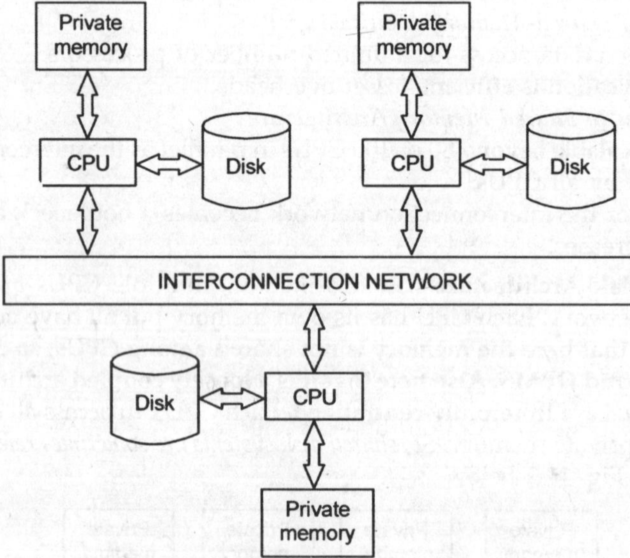

Fig. 11.3. *Shared-nothing architecture*

In this scheme, the CPUs sharing responsibility for database services usually split up the data among themselves. So, CPUs now perform transactions and queries by dividing the work and communicating it at rate of Mbps.

Advantages of Shared-nothing Architecture :

1. Better scalability as no sharing of resources is done.
2. More number of CPUs can be added as these systems provide linear speed-up and linear scale-up properties.
3. Only queries, access to non-local disks and result sets pass through the interconnection network. This minimizes network references.

Disadvantages of Shared-nothing Architecture:

1. Communication costs are higher as sending data involves software interaction at both ends.

2. Costs of non-local disk access are higher than the costs of shared-disk architectures.
3. Adding more CPUs and disks means that data may need to be redistributed and reorganized.

We *conclude* by saying that this technology is typically used for very large databases (of the size of 10^{12} bytes or terabytes) or the systems that have to process thousands of transactions per second. A parallel DBMS can use the underlying architecture to improve the performance of complex query execution using parallel scan, join and sort techniques.

11.2 PARALLEL QUERY EVALUATION

The cost of parallel evaluation of operations includes :

(*a*) **Start-up costs :** Costs for initiating the operation at multiple processors.

(*b*) **Skew** in the distribution of work among the processors. Some processors get a large number of tuples than others.

(*c*) **Contention :** Resources (like memory, disk, network etc.) results in delays.

(*d*) **Cost of assembling :** It includes the final result by transmitting partial results from each processor.

∴ Time taken by a parallel operation is given by the formula :

$$T_{part} + T_{asm} + \max(T_0, T_1, ..., T_{n-1})$$

where T_{part} – time for partitioning relation

T – time for assembling results

T_i – time taken for the operation at processor, P_i.

Now, if we assume that the tuples are distributed without any skew, the number of tuples sent to each processor can be estimated as $1/n$ of the total number of tuples.

Please note that even though breaking down of a single query into a number of parallel steps reduces the size of the average step, it is the time for processing the single slowest step that determines the time taken for processing the query as a whole.

11.3 ADVANTAGES OF PARALLEL DATABASES

There are many advantages of parallel databases. They are as follows :

1. Parallel databases have increased the throughput i.e., more number of tasks can be completed in a given time interval using parallel databases.
2. Parallel databases improve the response time i.e., the amount of time needed to complete a single task is reduced with the use of parallel databases.
3. Using several resources (CPU's and disks) in parallel can significantly improve performance.
4. *Increased availability* : If a site containing a relation goes down, the relation continues to be available if a copy is maintained at another site.
5. It is possible to serve large number of users.

11.4 DISADVANTAGES OF PARALLEL DATABASES

There are many disadvantages of parallel databases. The important one are as follows :

1. The start up costs are comparatively high.
2. *Interference problem* : Existing CPU's get slow down, as more CPU's are added, due to increased contention of memory and network bandwidth.

3. *Data skew* : Multiple disks contain partitions with widely varying number of tuples. Skew causes CPU's dealing with large partitions to become performance bottleneck.

11.5 ELEMENTS OF PARALLEL DATABASE PROCESSING

There are four key elements of any parallel database processing. They are as follows :

1. Speed-up
2. Scale-up
3. Synchronization
4. Locking

Let us define them one by one now.

1. **Speed-up (S_k) : It is a property of running a given task in less time by increasing the degree of parallelism.** Mathematically,

$$S_k = \frac{T_s}{T_p}$$

where T_s – time serial execution

T_p – time parallel execution

2. **Scale-up : It is the ability of handling larger tasks by increasing the degree of parallelism in the same time period as the original system.** Mathematically,

$$\text{Scale-up} = \frac{V_p}{V_o}$$

where V_p – parallel or large processing volume

V_o – original or small processing volume

3. **Synchronisation : It means the coordination of concurrent tasks for a successful operation of the parallel database systems.** It depends upon :

   (*a*) Amount of resources (CPUs, disks, memory, databases, etc.)

   (*b*) Number of users and tasks working on these resources.

   Please note that more are the concurrent tasks, more synchronisation is required to coordinate these larger number of parallel tasks.

4. **Locking : *It is defined as a method of synchronising current tasks.***

   A distributed lock manager (DLM) is used for external locking. DLM is a part of our O.S.

11.6 PARALLELISM IN QUERY

The real challenge today is to allow parallel execution of multiple queries by **decomposing** it into the parts that act in parallel. To some extent, this has been achieved by shared-nothing architecture.

Parallelism in Queries has been achieved by the following methods :

1. I/O parallelism
2. Intra-query parallelism
3. Inter-query parallelism
4. Intra-operation parallelism
5. Inter-operation parallelism.

Let us discuss these one by one now.

1. I/O Parallelism : A form of parallelism in which the relations are partitioned on multiple disks so as to reduce the retrieval time of relations from the disk. Herein, the input data is partitioned and then each partition is processed in parallel. These results are combined after the processing of all partitioned data. This form of processing is also known as *data-partitioning*.

It is of four types :

(*a*) Hash partitioning (*b*) Range partitioning
(*c*) Round-Robin partitioning (*d*) Schema partitioning

(*a*) ***Hash partitioning :*** As we know that a hash function is a fast, mathematical function. Each row (or tuple) of the original relation is hashed on the partitioning attributes.

For example, assume that there are *n*-disks $d_1, d_2, d_3, ..., d_n$ across which the data is to be partitioned. Now, if our hash function returns 3, then the tuple is placed on disk, d_3.

This schema has an **advantage**. It provides even distribution of data across the disk. This prevents skewing problem also. Skewing as done earlier can slow the performance caused by one or more CPUs and disks getting more work than others. Also, this technique is best suited for those point queries that are based on the partitioning attribute. **Please note that hash partitioning is useful for the sequential scans of the entire relation placed on '*n*' number of disks. Also note that the time taken to scan the relation is approximately 1/*n* of the time required to scan the relation in a single disk system.**

For example, if a relation is partitioned on the telephone-number attribute, then we can answer the query, "Find the record of employee with telephone-number = 9811276099" by applying the partitioning hash function to 9811276099 and then searching that disk.

But this scheme is not well suited for those queries that are point queries on non-partitioning attributes. It is not well suited for range queries. *For example,*

```
SELECT *
FROM EMP
WHERE EID > 100 AND EID < 1000;
```

In this case, the search would have to involve most of the disks over which the relation has been partitioned.

(*b*) ***Range partitioning :*** This technique distributes contiguous attributes-value ranges to each disk.

For example, range partitioning with three disks numbered 0, 1 and 2 may assign tuples with values less than 5 to disk-0, values between 5 and 40 to disk-1 and values greater than 40 to disk-2.

It has some advantages also. It involves placing tuples containing attribute values that fall within a certain range on disk.

For point queries, (involving exact matches), the partitioning vector is used to locate the disk where tuples reside.

For range queries, the partitioning vector is used to find the range of disks on which the tuples may reside.

But range partitioning can cause skewing also. **For example**, say there is an EMP relation that is partitioned across disk according to EID. Say, tuples containing numbers 1000 to 1500 are placed on disk-0 and tuples containing number 1501 to 2000 are placed on disk-1, then data will be **evenly distributed** *i.e.,*

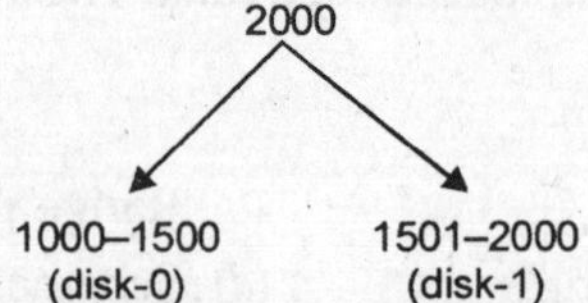

But if a company employs only 1800 employees currently and most of them are assigned EIDs from 1000–1500, then in this case most of the tuples for this relation will be skewed towards disk-0 only.

(*c*) ***Round-Robin partitioning :*** In this technique, the relations are scanned in any order. The ith tuple is send to disk number (d_i % n). So, disks take turns receiving new tuples of data. Herein, a system with *n*-disks would place tuple-A on disk-0, tuple-B on disk-1, tuple-C on disk-2 and so on. This technique ensures an even distribution of tuples across disks. This method is ideally suitable for applications that wish to read the entire relation sequentially for each query. But with this method, both point and range queries are complicated to process since each of the *n*-disks must be used for search.

(*d*) ***Schema partitioning :*** In this technique, different relations within a database are placed on different disks. That is,

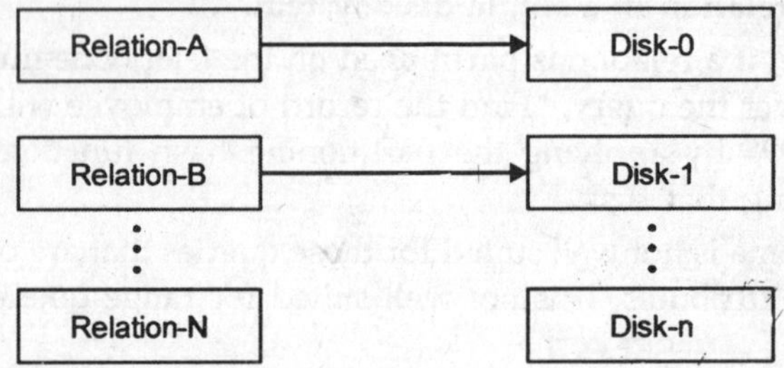

This scheme is more prone to data skewing. So, it is used in conjunction with other techniques.

2. Intra-query Parallelism : It refers to the execution of a single query in parallel on multiple CPUs using shared-nothing parallel architecture technique. It uses two approaches :

(*a*) ***First approach :*** Each CPU can execute the same task against some portion of the data.

(*b*) ***Second approach :*** The task can be divided into different subtasks with each CPU executing a different subtask.

But, in both the approaches, the data must be divided among disks in a most appropriate manner.

3. Inter-query Parallelism : In this method, multiple transactions are executed in parallel by each CPU. It is also known as **parallel transaction processing.** DBMS uses transaction dispatching to support inter-query parallelism. The incoming requests are routed to the least busy CPU. So, overall workload is kept balanced. Another method that can be used here is efficient lock management. In this technique, each query is run sequentially. This slows down the running of long queries. In such scenario, DBMS must understand the locks held by different transactions, running on different processors. Inter-query parallelism on shared-disk architecture performs best when transactions that execute in parallel do not access the same data. Oracle 8 is a shared-disk parallel DBMS that support inter-query parallelism. This is shown below.

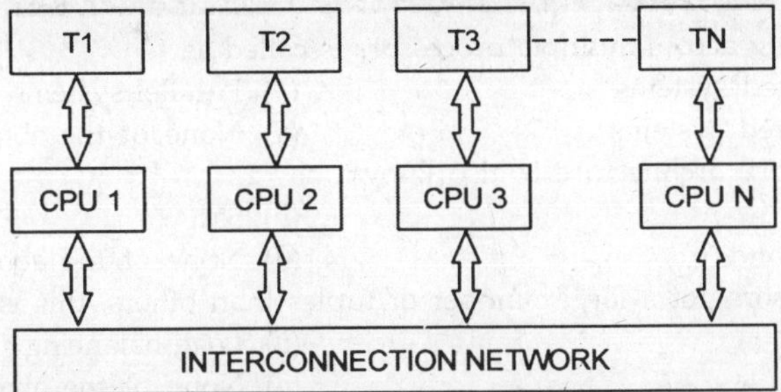

It is an easiest form of parallelism in DBMS systems. There is an increased transaction throughput. On the other hand, it has some disadvantages also. It is more complicated in a shared-disk or shared-nothing architecture. Even response times are slower.

4. Intra-operation Parallelism : A sort of parallelism in which we parallelise the execution of each individual operation of a task such as sorting, joins, projections and so on. As we know that the number of operations in a typical query is small, compared to the number of tuples processed by each operation, intra-operation parallelism scales better with increasing parallelism. This type of parallelism is natural in a database. Also, the degree of parallelism is quite high.

5. Inter-operation Parallelism : When different operations in a query expression are executed in parallel then it is known as inter-operation parallelism. It is of two types

(*a*) Pipelined parallelism

(*b*) Independent parallelism.

(*a*) ***Pipelined parallelism :*** In this parallelism, the output tuples of one operation are consumed by a second operation, even before the first operation has produced the entire set of tuples in its output. Also, it is possible to run these two operations simultaneously on different CPUs, so one operation consumes tuples in parallel with another operation producing them. It is useful with a small number of CPUs. Also, it avoids writing of intermediate results to disk. But, it does not scale up well. There are three reasons for this—

(*i*) Pipeline chains do not achieve sufficient lengths to provide a high degree of parallelism.

(*ii*) It is not possible to pipeline relational operators that do not produce output until all inputs have been accessed.

(*iii*) Only, marginal speed-up is obtained for the frequent cases in which one operator's execution cost is much higher than are those of the others.

(*b*) ***Independent parallelism :*** In this parallelism, the operations in a query expression that do not depend on one another can be executed in parallel. It is very useful with a lower degree of parallelism. It does not provide a high degree of parallelism.

SUMMARY

In this chapter, we have seen how parallel DBMS works. We can estimate the cost of parallel query evaluation. Query optimization is also more complex here than in sequential databases.

MULTIPLE CHOICE QUESTIONS [MCQs]

1. DBMS running across multiple processors is called as
   (*a*) Distributed systems (*b*) Parallel systems
   (*c*) Centralized systems (*d*) None of the above.
2. Shared-memory architecture is also known as
   (*a*) MPP (*b*) SMP
   (*c*) Both '*a*' and '*b*' (*d*) None of the above.
3. Some processors get a large number of tuples than others, this is called as a
   (*a*) Skew (*b*) Load balancing
   (*c*) Speed-up (*d*) None of the above.
4. Which of the following is a benefit of a parallel database system
   (*a*) Better performance (*b*) Better flexibility
   (*c*) Better availability (*d*) None of the above.
5. A global locking system is required in
   (*a*) Shared-disk architecture (*b*) Shared-nothing architecture
   (*c*) Shared-memory architecture (*d*) None of the above.
6. Parallelism in which the relations are partitioned on multiple disks to reduce the retrieval time of relations from disk is called as
   (*a*) I/O parallelism (*b*) Inter-operation parallelism
   (*c*) Intra-query parallelism (*d*) Inter-query parallelism.
7. Hash partitioning prevents
   (*a*) Skewing (*b*) Loss of data
   (*c*) Speed-up (*d*) None of the above.
8. Synchronisation is the coordination of
   (*a*) Concurrent tasks (*b*) Serial tasks
   (*c*) Larger tasks (*d*) None of the above.
9. The architecture that is easy to load-balance is
   (*a*) Shared-disk architecture (*b*) Shared-nothing architecture
   (*c*) Shared-memory architecture (*d*) None of the above.
10. A method of synchronising concurrent tasks is
    (*a*) Synchronisation (*b*) Locking
    (*c*) Speed-up (*d*) None of the above.

ANSWERS

1. (*b*) **2.** (*b*) **3.** (*a*) **4.** (*d*) **5.** (*a*) **6.** (*c*) **7.** (*a*) **8.** (*a*)
9. (*a*) **10.** (*b*)

CONCEPTUAL SHORT QUESTIONS WITH ANSWERS

Q.1. What is the most common form of data partitioning in a parallel database environment?

Ans. The most common form of data partitioning is **horizontal partitioning.** In this technique, the tuples of a relation are divided or declustered among many disks so that each tuple resides on one disk.

Q.2. Define the following terms :

(*a*) Attribute-value skew

(*b*) Partition skew.

Ans. (*a*) **Attribute-value skew** occurs when some values appear in the partitioning attributes of many tuples.

(b) **Partition skew** occurs when there is load imbalance in partitioning even if there is no attribute skew.

Q.3. Show that the loss of speed up takes place due to skew?

Ans. A small skew can also result in a significant decrease in performance. Skew becomes an increasing problem with a higher degree of parallelism.

For example, if a relation of 1000 tuples is divided into 10 parts and the division is skewed, then there may be some partitions of size less than 100 and some partitions of size more than 100. If, even one partition happens to be of size 200, the speed-up is only 5 instead of 10. Now, if the same relation has to be partitioned into 100 parts, a partition will have 10 tuples on average. If even one partition has 40 tuples, the speed-up is 25, rather than 100. Thus, we say that the loss of speed-up due to skew increases with parallelism.

Q.4. Write a short note on parallel Query optimization

Ans. Query optimizers for parallel query evaluation are more complicated than query optimizers for sequential query evaluation. This is so because the cost models are more complicated as we need to consider the partitioning costs and also the issues like skewing and resource contention. To evaluate an operator tree in a parallel system we need to consider :

(a) How to parallelize each operation and how many CPUs to use for it.

(b) Which all operations to execute parallely and which all sequentially?

Please understand that these decisions constitute the task of scheduling the execution tree.

The number of parallel execution plans from which to choose is much larger than the number of sequential evaluation plans. Optimization of parallel queries is much more expensive.

Q.5. Why long pipelines should be avoided?

Ans. Long pipelines do not lend themselves to good resource utilization. Unless the operations are coarse grained, the final operation of the pipeline may wait for a long time to get inputs while holding precious resources like memory.

Q.6. For each of the three partitioning techniques, namely round-robin, has partitioning, and range partitioning, give an example of a query for which that partitioning technique would provide the fastest response.

Ans. Round robin partitioning : When relations are large and queries read entire relations, round-robin gives good speed-up and fast response time.

Hash partitioning : For point queries, this gives the fastest response, as each disk can process a query simultaneously. If the hash partitioning is uniform, even entire relation scans can be performed efficiently.

Range partitioning : For range queries which access a few tuples, this gives fast response.

Q.7. What factors could result in skew when a relation is partitioned on one of its attributes by :

(a) Hash partitioning

(b) Range partitioning

In each case, what can be done to reduce the skew?

Ans. (a) **Hash partitioning** : Too many records with the same value for the hashing attribute, or a poorly chosen has function without the properties of randomness and uniformity, can result in a skewed partition. To improve the situation, we should experiment with better hashing functions for that relation.

(*b*) **Range partitioning :** Non-uniform distribution of values for the partitioning attribute (including duplicate values for the partitioning attribute) which are not taken into account by a bad partitioning vector is the main reason for skewed partitions. Sorting the relation on the partitioning attribute and then dividing it into *n* ranges with equal number of tuples per range will give a good partitioning vector with very low skew.

Q.8. Give an example of a join that is not a simple equi-join for which partitioned parallelism can be used. What attributes should be used for partitioning?

Ans. We give two examples of such joins.

(*a*) $r \bowtie_{(r.A=s.B) \wedge (r.A < s.C)} s$

Here we have extra conditions which can be checked after the join. Hence partitioned parallelism is useful.

(*b*) $r \bowtie_{(r.A \geq (\lfloor s.B/20 \rfloor) * 20) \wedge (r.A < ((\lfloor s.B/20 \rfloor) + 1) * 20)} s$

This is a query in which an *r* tuple and an *s* tuple join with each other if they fall into the same range of values. Hence partitioned parallelism applies naturally to this scenario.

For both the queries, *r* should be partitioned on attribute A and *s* on attribute B.

Q.9. Describe a good way to parallelize each of the following :

(*a*) The difference operation

(*b*) Aggregation by the count operation

(*c*) Aggregation by the count distinct operation

(*d*) Aggregation by the avg operation

(*e*) Left outer join, if the join condition involves comparisons other than equality.

(*f*) Left outer join, if the join condition involves comparisons other than equality

(*g*) Full outer join, if the join condition involves comparison other than equality.

Ans. (*a*) We can parallelize the difference operation by partitioning the relations on all the attributes, and then computing differences locally at each processor. As in aggregation, the cost of transferring tuples during partitioning can be reduced by partially computing differences at each processor, before partitioning.

(*b*) Let us refer to the group-by attribute as attribute A, and the attribute on which the aggregation function operates, as attribute B. **count** is performed just like **sum** (mentioned in the book) except that, a count of the number of values of attribute B for each value of attribute A) is transferred to the correct destination processor, instead of a sum. After partitioning, the partial counts from all the processors are added up locally at each processor to get the final result.

(*c*) For this, partial counts cannot be computed locally before partitioning. Each processor instead transfers all unique B values for each A value to the correct destination processor. After partitioning, each processor locally counts the number of unique tuples for each value of A, and then outputs the final result.

(*d*) This can again be implemented like **sum**, except that for each value of A, a **sum** of the B values as well as a **count** of the number of tuples in the group, is transferred during partitioning. Then each processor outputs its local result, by dividing the total sum by total number of tuples for each A value assigned to its partiti n.

(*e*) This can be performed just like partitioned natural join. After partitioning, each processor computes the left outer join locally using any of the strategies of Chapter 13.

(*f*) The left outer join can be computed using an extension of the Fragment-and-Repliate scheme to compute non equi-joins. Consider $r ⟕ s$. The relations are partitioned, and $r \bowtie s$ is computed at each site. We also collect tuples from r that did not match any tuples from s; call the set of these dangling tuples at site i as d_i. After the above step is done at each site, for each fragment of r, we take the intersection of the d_i's from every processor in which the fragment of r was replicated. The intersections give the real set of dangling tuples; these tuples are padded with nulls and added to the result. The intersections themselves, followed by addition of padded tuples to the result, can be done in parallel by partitioning.

(*g*) The algorithm is basically the same as above, except that when combining results, the processing of dangling tuples must done for both relations.

Q.10. Describe the benefits and drawbacks of pipelined parallelism.

Ans.
- **Benefits :** No need to write intermediate relations to disk only to read them back immediately.
- **Drawbacks :**
  (*a*) Cannot take advantage of high degrees of parallelism, as typical queries do not have large number of operations.
  (*b*) Not possible to pipeline operators which need to look at all the input before producing any output.
  (*c*) Since each operation executes on a single processor, the most expensive ones take a long time to finish. Thus speed-up will be low inspite of parallelism.

Q.11. How query parallelism is obtained ?

Ans. The major challenge in parallel databases is how to achieve query parallelism? That is, the question is how to design an architecture that allow parallel execution of multiple queries. This goal can be achieved very easily in the share-nothing parallel database architectures.

Some of the query parallelism techniques are as follow :

(*i*) I/O Parallelism
(*ii*) Inter-query Parallelism
(*iii*) Intra-query Parallelism
(*iv*) Intra-operation Parallelism
(*v*) Inter-operation Parallelism

I. I/O Parallelism

It is the simplest form of parallelism that reduces the time required to access the relations from disk by partitioning the relations on several disks. In this, the data is partitioned and stored on different disks and then each partition is processed in parallel and results are combined later on to produce the final result. There are several partitioning strategies. Some of them are as follows.

(i) Round Robin partitioning
(ii) Hash partitioning
(iii) Range partitioning

(i) **Round Robin partitioning :** In this technique, the relation is scanned in any order and the ith row of the relation is sent to the disk number D_i Mod n. This technique, partitions the relation tuples equally in all the disks *i.e.,* the tuples are distrubuted evenly among the various disks.

Advantages

1. It is well suited for the applications that read the entire relation sequentially for each query.
2. The distribution of tuples among the disks are even.

Disadvantages

Both point queries (where specified value required) and range queries (value lies within range) are very difficult to process, since all the *n* disks are required to process the query.

(ii) **Hash partitioning :** This technique selects one or more attributes from given relation's attributes and designate them as partitioning attributes. A hash function is defined whose range is {0, 1, ..., n – 1}. Now every tuple of the original relation is hashed on the designated partitioning attributes. The tuple t_k is placed on disk *Di,* if the hash function returns the value *i.*

Advantages

1. Best suited for point queries that are based on partitioning attributes.
2. It is useful for sequential scans of the entire relation.
3. If the hash function is a good randomizing function, then the tuples are evenly distributed among the multiple disks.

Disadvantages

1. It is not well suited for point queries that are not based on partitioning attributes.
2. It is also not well suited for range queries since all the disks need to be scanned to give the answer.

(iii) **Range partitioning :** This technique distributes contiguous attribute-value ranges to each disk. Thus the attribute-values within a certain ran *be* are to be placed on a certain disks. Here the tuples are sorted before distribution.

Advantages

1. Best suited for point and range queries that are based on partitioning attributes.
2. It gives higher throughput while maintaining good response time since different disks can be used to answer different queries.

Disadvantages

If there are many tuples in the queried range, many tuples have to be retrieved from small number of disks, causing I/O bottleneck at those disks. This situation is called **execution skew.**

II. Inter-query Parallelism

In inter-query parallelism, multiple queries (Transactions) execute in parallel at different CPU's. This type of parallelism increases the transaction throughput. The response time of individual transactions is almost same as if they were run in isolation. The basic reason of using the inter-query parallelism is to scale up a transaction processing system.

Advantages

1. It is the easiest form of parallelism to support in a database system, particularly in shared memory parallel system.
2. It increases the transaction throughput.

3. It scales-up a transaction processing system to support a larger number of transactions per second.

Disadvantages

1. The response time of individual transaction remains almost same as if the transactions were run in isolation.
2. It is more complicated to support in a shared disk or share nothing architecture.
3. It does not help in speeding up long running queries, since each query runs sequentially.

III. Intra-query Parallelism

In Intra-query parallelism, a single-query is executed in parallel on multiple CPU's and disks. It speeds-up the long running queries. The individual query can be parallized by parallelizing the individual operations involved in the query. There are two main ways by which a single query can be parallelized. These are **intraoperation parallelism** and **Interoperation parallelism**. Both are discussed below:

Advantages

1.It speeds up long running queries.
2.It is useful in decision support application.

Intra-operation Paralleism. In Intra-operation parallelism, the execution of each individual operation such as sort, selection, projection and join of a query is parallelized. The dugree of parallelism may be high, since the number of tuples in a relation can be large. This type of parallelism is natural in a database system.

Advantages

1. It speeds up the query processing by parallely executing the individual operations in the query.
2. It can scale better with increasing parallelism.

Disadvantages

1. The cost of parallel evaluation of operations is considerable.
2. A partitioned parallel evaluation is only as fast as slowest of the parallel executions.
3. Any skew in the distribution of work across CPU's greatly affects the performance.

V. Inter-operation Parallelism

In Inter-operation parallelism, the different operations in a query expression are executed in parallel to speed up the processing of the query. There are two types of Interoperation parallelism. These are

(i) Pipelined parallelism

(ii) Independent parallelism.

(i) **Pipelined parallelism :** In pipelined parallelism, the output tuples of one operation, A, acts as input to a second operation, B, even before the first operation has produced the entire set of tuples in its output. Thus it is possible to run operations A and B simultaneously on different CPU's, so that the tuples produced by A is taken by B as input in parallel.

Advantages

1. It is useful with a small number of CPU's.
2. Writing intermediate results to disk can be avoided.

Disadvantages

1. It does not scale-up well.
2. When the degree of prallelism is high, it is less important than partitioning.

3. Only marginal speed-up is obtain, when one operator's cost is much higher than others.

4. It is not possible to pipeline relational operators that do not produce output until all inputs have been accessed e.g., set difference operation.

(ii) **Independent parallelism** : In independent parallelism, the operations in a query expression that do not depend on one another can be executed in parallel.

Advantages

It is useful with a lower degree of parallelism.

Disadvantages

1. It does not provide a high degree of parallelism.

2. The operations in a query expression can be parallelized only if they are independent.

EXERCISE QUESTIONS

Q.1. What do you understand by the term parallel databases? Discuss some of its applications.

Q.2. Discuss the architecture of parallel databases.

Q.3. Explain the following with a neat sketch :
(*a*) Shared-memory architecture
(*b*) Shared-disk architecture
(*c*) Shared-nothing architecture.

Q.4. Define synchronization, locking and query parallelism.

Q.5. What is data partitioning? What are its different types?

Q.6. What form of parallelism is most important for each of the following tasks:
(*a*) Increasing system throughput with many small queries.
(*b*) Increasing system throughout with a few large queries.

Q.7. Discuss key elements of parallel data processing.

Q.8. What is pipelined parallelism? Give its advantages and disadvantages.

Q.9. Write short notes on :
(*a*) Hash partitioning
(*b*) RR partitioning
(*c*) Range partitioning
(*d*) Schema partitioning.

Q.10. Write short notes on :
(*a*) Intra-query parallelism
(*b*) Inter-query parallelism
(*c*) Intra-operation parallelism
(*d*) Inter-operation parallelism.

CHAPTER 12

Web Databases

12.0 INTRODUCTION

Web is used as a front-end to databases. Database information can be published on the web in two ways :

(*a*) Static web publishing, (*b*) Dynamic web publishing.

Let us define these two terms :

Static Web Publishing : It inolves creation of a list (or report) based on the information stored in a database and publishing it online. **Please note that it is a good way to publish information that does not change often and does not need to be fittered or searched.**

Dynamic Web Publishing : It involves the creation of pages "on the fly" based on information stored in the database.

There are two common tools that are used to create database —CGI and XML and will be discussed here.

12.1 ACCESSING DATABASE THROUGH THE WEB

What makes our **website dynamic** is actually the inclusion of database at our back-ends. **The web server uses a standard interface called as Common Gateway Interface (CGI) to act as middleware**. It is this layer that we say exists between user-interface front-end and the DBMS back-end. This makes access to our heterogeneous database easier. Let us see how it works. Details are shown in Fig. 12.1.

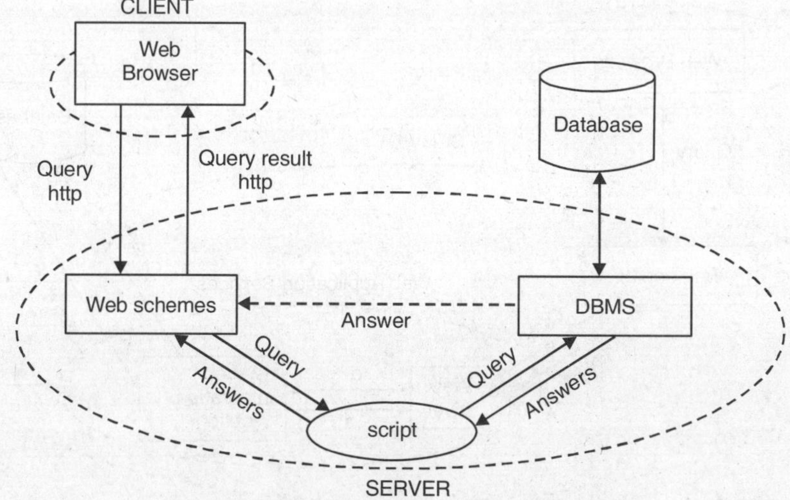

Fig. 12.1. *Web database access (using CGI)*

Here, the CGI middleware executes external programs or scripts to obtain dynamic information and it returns the information to the server in HTML, which is given back to the browser.

Working : The database server can be made to interact with the web server via CGI. (See Fig. 12.1). CGI scripts are written in PERL, or C or Tcl. The problem here is that for each user request, the web server must start a new CGI process. Each process makes a new connection with the DBMS. The Web server must wait until the results are delivered to it. By grouping multiple users request, no efficiency is achieved. Also, learning PERL or Tcl to write scripts is a drawback. What if the scripts are scattered every where? Here, also the manageability of scripts is a big problem

So, we have another method. This is known as *JDBC-ODBC* **bridge**. JDBC has capabilities to connect to the database, send SQL statements to a database and to retrieve the results of a query. **Please note that the Java code is DBMS transparent**.

This is because of two reasons :

1. **If the JDBC driver is on the server-side**, then driver specific to the DBMS will carry on the task of interaction with that DBMS.
2. **If the JDBC driver is on the client-side**, the application runs on the client and its requests are communicated to the DBMS directly by the driver.

> **NOTE :** Besides CGI, many other web server vendors are creating their own middleware products like Internet Server API (ISAPI) by Microsoft and Netscape API (NSAPI) from Netscape.

12.2 INFORMIX—WEB SERVERS

Informix has created the Integration Option (WIO) as its solution to address the limitations of CGI and the incompatibilities of CGI, NSAPI and ISAPI.

WIO eliminates the need for scripts. Developers use tools to create intelligent HTML pages called Application Pages (or App pages) directly within the database. They execute SQL statement dynamically, format the results inside HTML, and return the resulting web page to end users. The Fig. 12.2 below shows its CGI implementation.

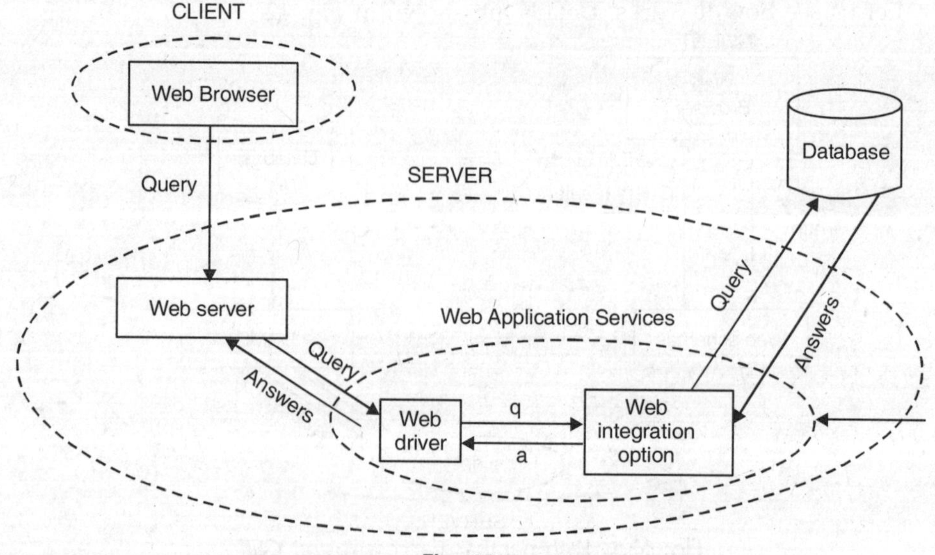

Fig. 12.2

Schematic architecture is shown in Fig. 12.2. B WIO creates a lightweigh CGI process called the Web Driver which is invoked when a URL request it received by the web server. A unique session identifier in generated for each request but the WIO applications is persistent and does **not** terminate after each request.

When the WIO application receives a request from the web driver, it connects to the database and executes a function called Web Exoplode. Web Explode executes the queries within web pages and formats results as a web page which goes back to the browser via the web driver.

Informix HTML tag extensions allow web authors to create applications that can dynamically construct web page templates from Informix Dynamic Server and present them to the end users. The WIO also lets users create their own customizable tags to perform specialized tasks. Thus, without resorting to any programming or scripts development, powerful applications can be designed. Another feature of WIO helps transaction-oriented applications. It provides an application programming interface (API) which offers a collection of basic services such as connection and session management which can be incorporated into web application.

WIO supports application developed in C, C++ and Java. This flexibility lets developers port existing applications to the web or develop new applications in these languages. The WIO is integrated with web server software and utilizes the native security mechanism of Informix Dynamic Server. The open architecture of WIO allows use of various web browsers and web servers.

12.3 XML DATABASE

As we know that some prominent applications of intranet and WWW are **databases** to support electronic storefronts, parts and product catalogs, directories, schedules, newsstands and book stores. We define **E-commerce as the process of purchasing of products and services electronically on the Internet which is supported by databases as back-end**.

Efforts are underway to address the limitations of the current data structuring technology, particularly by the World Wide Web Consortium (W3C). A Web Object Model is being designed. W3C is also proposing an Extensible Markup Language (XML) for structured document interchange on the web. XML defines a subset of SGML (the Standard Generalized Markup Language), allowing customization of markup languages with application-specific tags. XML is rapidly gaining ground due to its extensibility in defining new tag. W3C's Document Object Model (DOM) defines as object-oriented API for HTML or XML documents presented by a web client. W3C is also defining metadata modeling for describing Internet resources.

Overall, the web servers have to gain robustness as a reliable technology to handle production level database for supporting 24×7 (24 hours a day, 7 days a week) applications. The technology to model information using above standards and to find information on the web is undergoing a major evolution. Security remains a critical problem for supporting applications involving financial and medical database. Moreover, transition from existing database application environments to those on the web will need adequate support for existing users to continue their current mode of operation, and an expensive infrastructure of handling migration of data among systems without introducing inconsistencies. The traditional database functionality of querying and transaction processing must undergo appropriate modifications to support web-based applications. One such area is mobile-databases which we address in the next chapter.

12.4 CASE STUDY ON INTERNET HISTORY

With exponentially increasing number of people accessing the Internet, the day isn't far enough when the Internet would be clogged and access speeds would decrease to a fraction of the speeds todays. The Internet has grown at nearly 100 percent per year since 1988 and Internet traffic has been growing at 400 percent per year. The Internet has created jobs and whole new industries. Business and government organizations are increasingly dependent on it More than 50 million people worldwide access the Internet which has seen an almost vertical growth within the past 2 decades.

12.4.1 Introduction

In 1997 the Clienton administration flagged the Next Generation Internet (NGI) project for research and development of more stable, secure and faster networks than today's internet addressing the problems and challenges faced by today internet.

The R&D needed to address these requirements is beyond the scope of any single institution, company, or industry. The Next Generation Internet (NGI) initative with its broad agenda and abillity to involve government, research institutions, and the business sector, is a timely program that will address these challenges. The goal of the NGI initiative is to conduct R&D in advanced networking technologies, to demonstrate those technologies in testbeds that are 100 to 1,000 times faster than today's Internet, and to develop and demonstration on those testbeds revolutionary applications that meet important national needs and that cannot be achieved with today's Internet.

The NGI initiative is supported by various R&D institutions across the United States of America. These are :

- Advaned Research Projects Agency (DARPA)
- National Science Foundation (NSF), National
- Aeronautics and Space Administration (NASA)
- National Institute of Standards and Technology (NIST)
- National Library of Medicine (NLM).

Fig. 12.3

The NGI Initiative has three goals

1. To advance research, development, and experimentation in the next generation of networking technologies to add functionality and improve performance.

2. To develop a (1) Next Generation Internet testbed, emphasizing end-to-end perfomance. (2) To support networking research and demonstrate networking technologies.
3. To develop and demonstrate revolutionary applications

GOAL 1: Experimental Research For Advanced Network Techologies

Goal 1 activities focus on research, development, and testbed deployment and demonstration, of the technologies necessary to permit the effective, robust, and secure management, provisioning, and end-to-end delivery of differentiated service classes.

These activities cluster into three major tasks :

1. network growth engineering
2. end-to-end quality of serivce QoS
3. security.

These technologies along with increased bandwidth will help meet the needs for dependability, differentiation of service, security, and for the real time demands of emerging and next generation applications such as collaboration, wide area distributed computing, and teleoperation and telecontrol

Goals 1, 2, and 3 are interdependent. The challenge for Goal 1 is to develop the advanced capabilities required for the Goal 2 testbed networks and ensure the advanced capabilities of Goal 2.

GOAL 2 : NGI Testbed

The networks developed under the NGI initiative will connect at least 100 sites—universities, Federal research institutions, and other research partners at speeds 100 times faster end-io-end than those of today's Internet, and will connect on the order of 10 sites at speeds 1,000 times faster end-to end than the current Internet. This end-to-end connectivity (such as between two workstations) will be at speeds from 100+ million bits per second (Mbps) to 1+billion bits per second (Gigabits per second or Gbps). Some networks have already achieved OC-12 (Optical Carrier) speeds (622 Mbps) on their backbone links and some experimental links are running at 1+Gbps, but end to-end usable connectivity is typically limited to less than 10 Mbps because of bottlenecks or incompatibilities in switches, routers, local area networks, and workstations.

Subgoal 2.1: High Performance Connectivity. The Goal 2.1 testbed will functions as a distributed laboratory. It delivers at a minimum 100 times faster speeds than current Internet performance on an end-to-end basis to at least 100 interconnected NGI participating universities, national laboratories, and Federal research sites conducting networking and applications research that require such a testbed. This network is designed to be large enough to provide a full system, proof-of-concept testbed for hardware, software, protocols, security, and network management that will be required in the future commercial Internet. This testbed will include easily accessible sites, remote sites, and sites in EPSCoR (Experimental Program to Stimulate Competitive Research) states.

Subgoal 2.2: NGI Technologies and Ultra High Performance Connectivity. Goal 2.2 addresses the development of ultrahigh speed switching and transmission technologies and of end-to-end network connectivity at 1 + Gbps. Because of its high risk and pioneering nature, networks involved are limited initially to approximately 10 NGI sites and a limited number of applications. Attaining this goal, together with the technologies developed in Goal 1, lays the groundwork for terabit per second (trillions of bits per second,Tbps) networks operated by appropriate network management and control and guaranteeing end-to-end quality of service.

GOAL 3 : Revolutionary Applications

To achieve Goal 3, the participating agencies have established a coordinated selection process to identify appropriate applications to be developed and tested. These applications require the advanced networking capabilities of Goal 1 and 2. Agencies will be asked to adapt their applications to take advantage of these capabilities. The resulting NGI applications will integrate advanced networking and application technologies. The selection process is used to ensure that applications tested and demonstrated on the NGI network provide robust, realistic, complete tests of technologies that are extensible and adaptable to other applications. The selection of NGI applications will be an iterative process with Federal, academic, and industry participation. Applications are derived from the Federally focused applications in appropriate technology classes such as digital libraries, remote operation of medical instruments, environmental monitoring, crisis management, manufacturing, basic sciences, and Federal information services.

Resources

The skills and experience that the participating agencies bring to the initiative, provide the base upon which the NGI is built. This strong base increases the likelihood that the initiative will succeed without that base the initiative would involve much risk. Specific agency strengths include:

1. **DARPA :** Pioneer of long term networking research; developed cutting-edge network techologies; great strength in network management and services.
2. **DoE :** Long term experience in managing production and research networks; specialized in networking technology; great strength in mission-driven applications and system integration.
3. **NASA :** Experience in network management and in specialized network testbeds strength in mission driven applications involving high data rates; great strength in system engineering and integration.
4. **NSF :** Special relationships with the academic community ; experience in network research and in managing networks; great strength in scientific applications.
5. **NIST :** Long experience in standards development, networking research, metrology, computer systems security, systems integration for manufacturing applications, and in testbeds involving many industrial partners.
6. **National Library of Medicine (NLM)/National Institute of Health (NIH):** Extensive experience in medical research; great strength in health care applications.

12.4.2 Goal 1 : Experimental Research for Advanced Network Technologies

Introduction and Strategy : The Next Generation Internet (NGI) program is the pathway to terabit-per-second network speeds over wide area advanced capbility networks.

This is done by means of a partnership with industry leading to shared infrastructure that can be used profitably to support new, experimental services for high end users, as well as large numbers of typical commerical users. Although the highspeed communication capability (developed under Goal 2.2) will enable advanced applications for the Department of Defense (DoD), the National Aeronautical and Space Administration (NASA), the National Science Foundation (NSF), and other agency users, increased bandwidth alone will be insufficient to meet the dependebility, security, and real time demands of emerging next generation applications, such as collaboration, wide area distributed computing, and teleoperation and control. The challenge for Goal 1, then is to ensure that the advanced capabilities of both Goal 2.1 and Goal 2.2 networks can be made predictably and reliably accessible to broad range of users sharing a common infrastructure.

Goal 1 activities will therefore focus on multiagency coordinated research, development, deployment, and demonstration of the technologies necessary to permit the effective, robust, and secure management, provisioning, and end-to-end delivery of differentiated service classes. These activities cluster into three major tasks : network growth engineering, end-to-end quality of service (QoS), and security. The NGI strategy focuses on developing the most important and highly leveraged aspects of internetworking technology: network growth engineering, end-to-end QoS, and security.

Network Growth Engineering: The goals of this task are to

1. Create and deploy tools and algorithms for planning and operations that guarantee predicatable end-to-end performance at scales and complexities of 100 times those of the current Internet
2. Facilitate management of large scale internetworks operating at gigabit to terabit speeds supporting a range of traffic classes on a shared infrastructure.
3. Create an infrastructure partnership through which lead users (government and research) share facilities with the general public, thereby accelerating the development and penetration of novel network applications.

This task will develop and integrate technologies for

- Network planning and simulation
- Network monitoring
- Analysis and control
- Innovative data delivery
- shared infrastructure mangement for lead users. The highly automated services envisioned in this task lead to the goal of building strong securitymechanisms into the components.

Planning and Simulation : Under this subtask, a network planning description language will be developed as a community standard facilitating not only the initial planning but also maintenance of requirements throughout the network life cycle.

Metrics : Ability to plan, coordinate, and maintain 100 organizational networks.

Monitoring, Control, Analysis, and Display : Current practice uses planned analysis based on protocol headers and aggregated statistics. This subtask will take on the challenge of pressenting runtime analysis based on distributed communication patterns and very high communication speeds that would overwhelm current tools.

Metrics : Demonstrate monitoring and analysis at speeds of Optical Carrier (OC)- 48 (2.5 Gbps) and higher.

Integration : The goal of this subtask is to ensure that the network engineering tools and the high performance transmission and switching technologies work smoothly together for accomplishing end-to-end management of leading edge user requirements.

Metrics : Demonstrate 25 percent utilization improvement in Goal 2.1 network over 3 month and 100 percent utilization improvement in Goal 2.2 network

Data Delivery : The management software will work in a tightly bound interlock with new strategries for managing and controlling data delivery in networks. This subtask will develop network interior nodes that combine methods previously seen as disjoint or mutually exclusive: routing and switching, best effort and priority traffic, dynamic routing and virtual circuits, greedy admission versus guaranteed delivery, and flat-rate versus variable costing. Tools that permit network engineers to adjust the strategy trade-offs to best meet their requirements will be prototyped and tested in the high speed arena.

Metrics : Demonstrate 100 percent improvement in throughput using heterogeneous, application specific routing strategies.

Managing Lead User Infrastructure : The DoD, NASA, NSF, and other government agencies, as well as the research community at large, typically have led user requirements for telecommunication facilities that require speed and complexity that are orders of magnitude beyond those of the typical users. This task will investigate architectural concepts, management strategies, and operational arrangements that will allow lead users to concurrently share the same infrasturcture as conventional users at a variety of levels. Extension of this dual modality into the campus infrastructure for end-to-end support will also be investigated.

Metrics : Demonstrate lead user support by striping, that is, partitioning a data stream across multiple low bandwidth channels to emulate a high bandwidth channel, over 100 ordinary channels without performance loss.

End-to-End Quality of Service : The goals of this task are to facilitate the delivery of end-to-end ensured QoS to applications and to ensure that these technologies can be tailored for use by and made available to lead users who have demanding requirements. The strategy is to allow users to negotiate application specific trade-offs among such parameters as bandwith, latency, precision, and reliability in order to obtain predictable performance at a known quality level. Exploiting emerging network level mechanisms is difficut, however, as they are semantically far removed from the applications they are intended to support and are accessible only through many layers of software. End-to-end QoS assurance requires an approach that spans these layers of operating system and middleware in order to effectively deliver network level QoS guarantees. This task will develop and demonstrate a comprehensive QoS management architecture, drill down technologies to facilitate propagation of QoS constraints across software layers, and next generation network technologies to support QoS.

Baseline Quality of Serivce Architecture : The baseline QoS management architecture will provide the framework of models, languages, and protocols to permit distributed applications to specify multidimensional QoS requirements, negotiate acceptable trade-offs and confidence levels, and receive feedback on delivered QoS enablig adaptation. Application Program Interfaces (APIs) supporting the propagation of QoS constraints and feedback through software layers will be developed, as well as the requisite admission control, accounting/costing, security, and priority mechanisms both within network infrastructure and the periphery ingress/egress environments.

Metrics : Demonstrate ability to handle differentiated service classes and to reduce variance in end-to-end performance by factors of three to five for multimedia traffic.

Drill Down Technologies : Current technolgies support composition of functionality across layers but not the composition of their QoS properties. This subtask will develop technologies that can be used to drill down and expose interfaces to QoS and network management capabilities that are presently hidden within the individual layers. Emphasis will be on techniques appropriate for operating systems, communications libraries, and middleware services, including distributed objects, and providing direct access from the applications to network layer components and objects.

Metrics : Demonstrate factor of 3 of 5 reduction in communications overhead attributable to systems software.

Next Generation Network Technologies : Next generation network technologies, particularly those supporting QoS, are critical to the success of the Internet, but they lack an adequate experience base at the speeds and scale envisioned for NGI. This subtask will accelerate pilot deployment of and experimention with technologies such as class based queuing, Resource Reservation Protocol (RSVP), and Internet Protocol Version6 (IPv6), as well as research and develop new technologies for admission control, accounting/costing, scheduling, prioritization in both IP and Asynchronous Transfer Method (ATM) networks.

Security

Public Key and Key Management Infrastructure : The use of cryptographic services across the global internet requires the use of "certificates" that bind cryptographic keys and other security information to specific users or entities in the network. Comprehensive certificate management mechanisms and underlying support infrastructure are required for all of this to work.

Internet/Internetwork Security : The viability and success of the NGI will depend on the existence of new, more secure protocols. Current protocols have limited and demonstrably weak security mechanisms. New protocols being developed will include advanced methods to authenticate communications, nodes, and users, and will provide other security services such as confidentiality protection, extended audit trials, and threat monitoring.

Security Criteria, Test Methods, and Testing : Unlike other types of standards and open specifications, security standards have an implict requirement for special testing. In addition to traditional functionality and interoperability tests, security products and services need to be tested to ensure that they cannot be subverted by intentional acts or attacks and that they do not contain functionality beyond that specified (for example, "trap doors"). This subtask will continue efforts to develop a common set of security product/system evaluation and testing criteria to meet this need.

Agency Specifics

Defense Advanced Research Projects Agency

Introduction : DARPA'S goals in network research mesh well with those of the initiative in key areas. Together with the terabit-per-second (Tbps) network speeds enabled by Goal 2.2 technologies, the network management and end-to-end QoS technologies developed under Goal 1 will be the pathway to a robust, scalable, shared infrastructure supporting lead DoD users, other government agencies, and the research community, as well as large numbers of commercial users. This will be accomplished through a partnership with industry. Specifically, the DARPA NGI program goals are :

1. Develop network growth engineering and end-to-end QoS technologies and put them into the hands of the research community
2. Ensure that these technologies can be tailored for use in mission critical environments
3. Create an infrastructure partnership through which lead users (government and research) share facilities with the general public, thereby accelerating the development and penetration of novel network applications.

Network Growth Engineering : The goals of this task are to

1. Create and deploy tools and algorithms for planning and operations that guarantee predictable end-to-end performance at scales and complexities that are 100 times those of the current Internet.
2. Facilitate management of large scale internetworks operating at terabit speeds supporting a range of traffic classes on a shared infrastructure
3. Create an infrastructure partnership through which lead users share facilities with the general public to accelerate the development and penetration of novel network applications.

This task will develop and integrate technologies for network planning and simulation; network monitoring, analysis, and control; innovative data delivery; and shared infrastructure management for lead users. The highly automated services envisioned in this task lead to the goal of building strong security mechanisms into the components.

Planning and Simulation : Planning large network interconnections is at present mainly a manual process that is not tied to any runtime tools or distributed efforts. Under this subtask, a network planning description language will be developed as a community standard. The target goals to show that

1. 100 small organizational networks can be planned and coordinated into an Internet
2. The plan can be validated against the requirements
3. Requirements can be maintained during the life cycle of the resulting network

Monitoring, Control and Display : Network engineering and management requires tools for gathering and analyzing data and for issuing control commands based on the results. Current practice uses planned analysis based on protocol headers and aggregated statistics. This subtask will take on the challenge of presenting runtime analysis based on distributed communication patterns and communication speeds so high that they would over when current tools. This will be accomplished by developing the following capabilities :

1. Monitoring and analytical tools and capabilities at all protocol levels for all speeds, but especially those at OC-48 and higher
2. Distributed control of all configuration parameters at distributed management stations
3. Large screen visualization of runtime data showing deviation from planning models, efficiency of distributed computing communication, and available command options for all hardware
4. Control of wavelength division multiplexing (WDM) cross domain circuit assignments for at least two optical networks

Integration : The goal of this subtask is to ensure that the network engineering tools and the high performance transmission and switching technologies work smoothly together for accomplishing end-to-end management of leading edge user requirements. The requirements will be developed with the users, and the tools will be integrated into the NGI testbed, developing 10 distributed management stations with monitoring and command interfaces to all connected equipement; half of the management stations will be in the Goal 2.1 testbed and half will be in the Goal 2.2 testbed. The management stations will demonstrate the scalability nature of the design and its capability to adjust to varying levels of granularity of information, organizational responsibility, and active versus passive monitoring and control. Analysis and control functions will work smoothly among cooperating organizations, and the ability to implement wide area, distributed interoperation will be demonstrated as an ongoing NGI effort.

Data Delivery : The management software will work in a tightly bound interlock with new strategies for controlling data delivery in network research effort under this subtask will develop network interior nodes that combine methods previously seen as disjoint or mutually exclusive : routing and switching, best effort and priority traffic, dynamic routing and virtual circuits, greedy admission versus guaranteed delivery, and flat rate versus variable costing. In addition, schemes that use generalized or alternative addressing methods will be explored. Tools that permit network engineers to adjust the strategy tradeoffs to best meet their requirements will be prototyped tested in the high speed arena.

End-to-End Quality of Serivce : The goals of this task are to facilitate the delivery of end-to-end ensured QoS to applications and to ensure that these technologies can be tailored for use by lead users who have demanding requirements. The strategy is to allow users to negotiate application specific trade-offs among such parameters as bandwidth, latency, percision, and reliability in order to obtain predictable performance at a known quality level. Exploiting emerging network level mechanisms is difficult, however, for they are semantically far removed from the applications they are intended to support and are accessible only through layers of software. End-to-end QoS assurance requires an approach that spans these operating system and middleware layers in order to effectively deliver network level QoS guarantess. This task will develop and demonstrate a comprehensive QoS management architecture; drill down technologies to facilitate propagation of QoS constraints across software layers; and next generation network technologies to support QoS.

Baseline QoS Architecture : The baseline QoS management architecture will provide the framework of models, languages, and protocols to permit distributed applications to specify multidimensional QoS requirements, to negotiate acceptable trade-offs and confidence levels, and to receive feedback on delivered QoS enabling adaptation. Specific areas to be investigated under this subtask include:

1. Specification and translation of application specific views QoS into constraints on individual resources and propagation of those constraints through software layers to network sevices.
2. Negotiation of QoS "contracts" providing applications with quantitative confidence bounds onthe level of service to expect and explicit characterization of the trade offs involved.
3. Monitoring and feedback technology to continually measure delivered QoS and to notify applications when QoS contracts can no longer be honored.

Drill Down Technologies : Current technologies support composition of functionality across system layers, but not the composition of their QoS properties. This task will develop technologies that can be use to drill down and expose interfaces to QoS and network management capabilities that are presently hidden within the individual layers. Emphasis will be on techniques appropriate for operating systems, communications libraries, and middleware serivces, including distributed objects. Specific topics to be addressed include:

1. Adaptation mechanisms, such as specialization, "on-the-fly" code generation, and dynamic module substitution.
2. Efficient triggering and assurance mechanisms, including event and exception handling, guarded execution, monitoring .
3. Coordinated adaptation across layers and cross layer optimization

Security : The NGI security goals are to provide the basis for implementing and enforcing appropriate security policies among organizations, users, and infrastructure components under shared control. Interoperable authentication methods are a prerequisite.

12.4.3 Goal 2 : Next generation network testbed

Goal 2.1 : High performance connectivity

Introduction : NGI Goal 2.1 will perform R&D on advanced interconnection technology to develop and deploy a wide area demonstration network fabric that will support network research and advanced network capable applications as defined in NGI Goals 1 and 3. This fabric will function as a distributed laboratory delivering a minimum of 100 times the current Internet performance on an end-to-end basis (typically greater than 100+Mbps end-to-end) to at least 100 interconnected NGI universities, national laboratories, and Federal research sites that demonstrate research and applications that require such an infrastructure. This demonstration network fabric will be large enough to provide a full system, proof-of concept testbed for hardware, software, protocols, and network management that is required in the commercial NGI.

Strategy and Subgoals : To implement this goal, strategy and metrics will be defined for each of the following subgoals :

- Infrastructure
- Common bearer services
- Applications feedback
- Interconnections
- Site selection
- Network management
- Information distribution and training

Infrastructure Subgoal : The large scale development of advanced applications calls for a network that is relatively stable in order to provide a consistent environment to which developers can build, and one that is also leading edge in order to incorporate new technologies as soon as they are available.

A balance must be achieved between a stable "production"environment and one that allows for research and new technology insertion so as to enable both. For the most part this can be accomplished with existing technology. It is envisioned that : (1) a relatively stable but leading edge infrastructure will be developed that will have some downtime as new technologies are developed and introduced; (2) sites will have backup commodity serivce; (3) a sevice definition will exist between the end user and providers—this will include such items as latency, demand, and scheduled service.

The performance metrics that will be used to determine if the infrastructure subgoal has been achieved are:

1. Does the network infrastructure perform to expectations, that is, end-to-end 100x the present Internet speed?
2. Can users get the required bandwith and capabilities that they cannot get anywhere else?
3. Does the network infrastructure accommodate Goal 1 research needs?
4. Can the testbed support the development of and experimentation with advanced NGI applications?

5. Has the connectivity to site met user requirements?
6. Do the sites have access to a 100x infrastructure that support Goals 1 and 3?

Common Bearer Services Subgoal : In order to create a relatively stable infrastructure that can be quickly deployed, IPv4 with "best effort" services will be the initial and minimum common bearer service for all agency network infrastructure. IPv6 and other advanced technologies for QoS, etc., will be deployed on the networks as soon as they demonstrate a "leading edge, but stable" performance. Direct connections in ATM, IP over SONET, and other services will be introduced on the basis of feasibility,support for Goal 1 research activities, and application demand. The use of virtual backbones over the existing agency networks to perform the required R&D will assist in developing these technologies and services, provide a relatively leading edge but stable infrastructure for applications development, and assist in solving problems of interagency and intercarrier connectivity at the ATM level.

Application Feedback Subgoal : One of the basic failures of previous high end testbeds was that although the infrastructure may have been a success, the initiative did not attain its potential because there were virtually no applications that could effectively use the infrastructure . This subgoal will help to ensure that this does not occur in the NGI initiative.

The strategy that will be used to facilitate applications development and migration onto the 100x testbed is to provide feedback from application developers to network researchers, and implementors by means of regularly scheduled coordination meetings and conferences among these groups.

The metrics that will be used to determine if this subgoal has been met are:

1. Satisfaction of advanced applications requirements
2. The number of applications using advanced services.

Interconnection subgoal : In order for the NGI initiative to lay the foundation for the future Internet, it is imperative that the Federal networks provide end-to-end QoS, interconnecting with advanced services at the IP and lower layers as appropriate. It is also recognized that different levels of QoS will exist as dictated by the needs of the applications, for example, e-mail does not require the same QoS as does a real time collaborative environment used to control an experiment at a remote site. Implementation of NGI Goal 2.1 will create a nationwide seamless NGI fabric that provides appropriate levels of QoS, as well as necessary internetwork management security.

The metrics that will be used to determine success are:

1. Ability to change network and carriers while remaining transparent to applications
2. Number of applications that successfully operate among nodes supported by at least two different carriers.
3. Number of applications that successfully operate among nodes
4. A network is supported by at least two different carriers
5. Statistics and trends gathered on bandwidth and interconnects that show the migration
6. Number of users/customers who indicate they became aware of and engaged with NGI as a result of NGI information distribution or training activities

Site Selection Subgoal : Since NGI research crosses sites and agencies, a coordinated mechanism is needed to ensure that the sites have valid applications and the required infrastructure to promote the NGI Goal 2.1 success. To achieve this, each agency will identify its NGI sites and will work in a coordinated manner with the other agencies and the application group in the site selection process.

The metrics that will be used to determine success of this subgoal are :

1. Percent of the 100 sites awarded for connection.
2. End-to-end bandwidth and service level delivery at the site.

Network Management Subgoal : In order to make NGI Goal 2.1 a success, the various testbed operators must be able to ensure that the testbed is manageable and performing to the required levels. To achieve this, network management must be addressed early in the NGI initiative. It is envisioned that the agencies will have distributed, yet coordinated, network management efforts that build on existing agency efforts.

The key features of this network management effort are :

1. Distributed help desk
2. Security/authentication methods
3. A disributed GigaPOP Network operation Center (NOC)
4. Internet 2 and NGI coordination for engineering and network management
5. Capability of applications to schedule end-to-end bandwidth
6. Network monitoring and management tools consisting of existing tools, emerging tools for newservices and higher speeds, and scaling of tools to many sites and across carriers

The metrics that will be used to determine the success of this subgoal are:

1. How much control the network operator has of network
2. The effectiveness of distributed NOCs and help desks
3. Flow measurement and the ability to diagnose problems
4. Develpment of standards for completely portable performance metrics and diagnostics
5. The effectivences of the distributed help desk

Information Distribution and Training Subgoal : One of the key items necessary to ensure that an initiative succeeds is to provide a mechanism for information dissemination and training. The effort under this subgoal is to ensure that information distribution occurs on a regular basis and that mechanisms are put in place to provide the required level of training to ensure that the NGI can succeed. These efforts will consist of, but are not limited to:

1. Web information dissemination
2. Training opportunities
3. Conferences
4. Agency network/information distribution mechanisms
5. Statistics/measurement information dissemination
6. Interagency program manager meetings

The metrics that will be used to determine success of this subgoal are :

1. Number of coordinated confereces held
2. Customeer survey (appliciations and campus network operators)

3. Number of users/customers who indicate (through any of our feedback mechanisms) that they became aware of and engaged with NGI as a result of NGI
4. Information distribution or training activities
5. How many technologies from Goal 1 are implemented into Goal 2.1
6. How quickly applications from Goal 3 use Goal 2.1 networks.

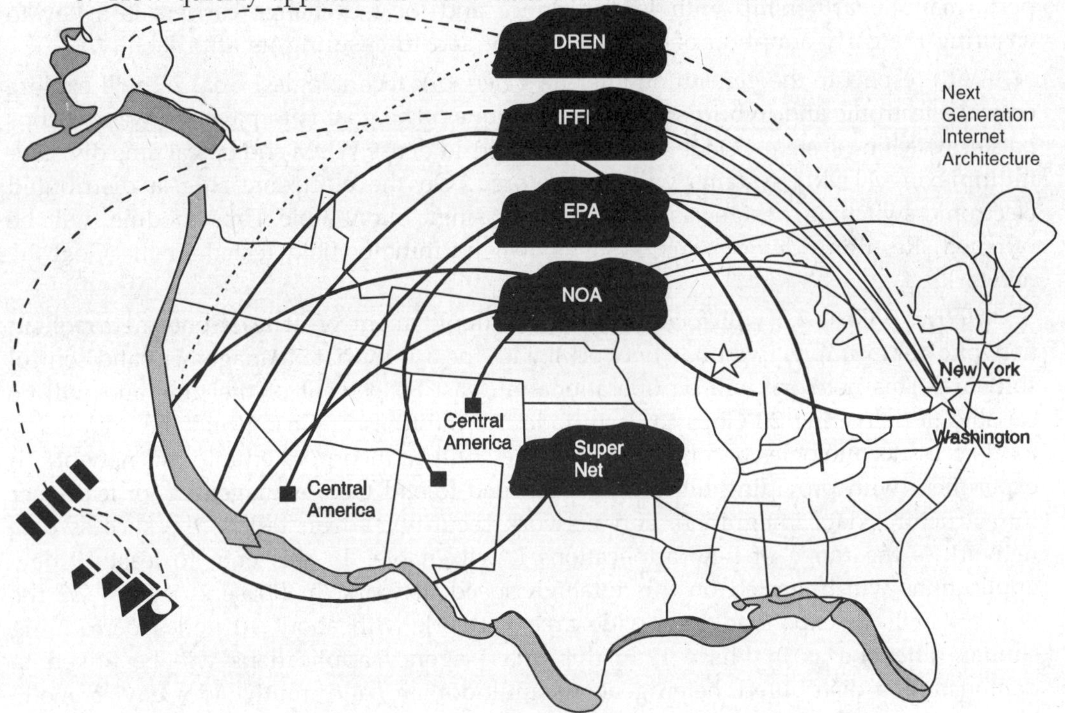

Fig. 12.4. *Proposed NGI architecture*

Goal 2.2 : Next Generation Network Technologies and Ultrahigh Performance Connectivity

Introduction : This Goal 2.2 addresses the development of ultrahigh speed switching and transmission technologies, and the demonstration of end-to-end network connectivity at 1+Gbps. Because of its high risk and pioneering nature, networks involving about 10 NGI sites and applications will be implemented. Attaining this goal, together with the technologies developed in Goal 1 will be the pathway to terabit – persecond (Tbps) networks, operated with the appropriate network management and control and guaranteed end-to-end QoS. Working in partnership with industry is the key to a shared infrastructure that can be profitably used to support high end scientific users and large numbers of commercial users.

Strategy : The technology of choice to achieve a Tbps network is wavelength division multiplexing (WDM), which is a **technique of mixing many wavelengths onto the same optical fiber.** This is equivalent to opening up the narrow communication links into multiple-lane communication highways. DARPA's Broadband Information Technology (BIT) program has pioneered much of today's WDM effort. **Whereas WDM is currently implemented at the physical layer,** the aim here is to integrate WDM and its management with the upper layers of ATM and IP. To this end, a new network architecture that specifically addresses the access loop will be designed. These technologies and architectures hold the promise of eventually satisfying the goal of an infrastructure that is shared by both high end users, typical users, and network researchers. Some of the network nodes will be chosen to coincide with some Goal 2.1 nodes. The architecture will be designed such that portions of the Goal 2.1 networks can interconnect to and gracefully evolve into Goal 2.2 network and further demonstrate the continuing evolution of network performance. Partnership with long distance and local exchange carriers is a key to ensuring the early adoption of this technology and to ensuring its affordability.

With respect to the generation-after-next network technologies, Goal 2.2 will explore optical, electronic and hybrid switching techniques. The goal is to pave the way to Tbps packet switching systems. On the optical side, hydrid dense WDM and opical time division-multiplexing (TDM) systems will be explored. On the electronic side, a distributed electronic switching design, as opposed to a single monolithic Tbps module, will be pursued, Resulting devices and systems will be initially field tested in the Goal 2.2 network.

Metrics : Goal 2.2 will focus first on the deployment of at least one metropolitan network (for example, five-node network), with the appropriate management and control software. This network will be operational at least 80 percent of the time and will be capable of delivering 20 Gbps to each node. As the tools of Goal 1 and the broadband local access technologies become available, they will be incorporated into this network to experiment with providing ultra-high speed end-to-end QoS, management of lead user infrastructure, data integration, and network security. A trun test of the success of a network is the range of new applications it wil enable. To this end, to least 10 new applications will be tested on this ultahigh speed network. In Phase 2 of Goal 2.2 the network will be expanded to a wide area network with about 10 nodes performing similar functions as in Phase 1. In this phase agency applications will be linked to demonstrate a distributed, heterogeneous, multidomain, and multivendor environment. Since the number of nodes that can be built is limited by the available resources, the scalability and network management of hundreds of ultrahigh speed nodes will be examined by simulation and modeling. The following is a description of the implementation plans and milestones by participating agencies.

Agency Specifics

Defense Advanced Research Projects Agency : **Wide Area Broadband Core :** DARPA's Broadband Information Technology (BIT) program has developed basic WDM transmission capabilities and will soon demonstrate a metropolitan network of five nodes, with link transmission capacities of 20 Gbps. DARPA will extend these technolgies and deploy them in more complex, mesh-like topologies that involve long distance links. The metropolitan testbed will be expanded into a wide area network with about 10 nodes using WDM technology. This wide area backbone will have sufficient aggregate transmission and switching resources to support hundreds of users at Gbps rates. This network will share the fiber facilities with the general public.

Tbps Multiplexing and Switching : DARPA will develop the generation-after-next multiplexing, switching, and routing technologies that will bridge the gap among packet-based Gbps tributaries and the WDM-based optical core. This task will also lay the groundwork for the direct optical support to packetbased communication. A major component of this task will be to investigate statistically sound techniques for performing "space-division"-like spreading of the resultant TDM traffic across a set of wavelengths.

A second component will be the design and demonstration of a highly parallel and distributed switching fabric.

Taken together, these efforts will enable the development of a highly distributed the approach to Tbps switching, based on a combination of optical and electronic technologies, with many-to-many multicast capability.

Broadband Local Trunking : The need to provide select sites with "orders -of-magnitude-aboveaverage" access to the network core has been a recurring source of delay in commissioning advanced research facilities. This task explore novel and cost effective approaches to delivering broadband access to select sites within a geographically restricated area. DARPA will examine the terrestrial extension of Super Net rate facilities to the building and explore the effectiveness of high capacity (>150 Mbps) radio frequency (RF)-based trunking. In addition, wireless broadband local access will be addressed as one of the DARPA tasks in Goal 2.2.

Technology Demonstration and Field Trials : Most of the technologies to be developed by the previous tasks are associated with the physical, link, and networking layers. This task will seek opportunities to demonstrate the newly developed capabilities through collaboration with some of DARPA's application oriented activities, such as the Human Computer Interaction, Information Management, and Intelligent Collaboration and Visualization programs.

12.4.4 Goal 3 : Revolutionary applications

Introduction : Applications are the ultimate success metric of this program. Faster and more advanced networks will enable a new generation of applications that include crisis response, distance education, environmental monitoring, health care, scientific research, and national security. To achieve this goal, agencies will leverage the NGI investments significantly with other major application investments. Agencies will demonstrate new applications, as well as enhance and enable current mission applications that meet important national goals and missions. Each demonstration will partner the advanced networking technologies developed in Goals 1 and 2 with modern applications technologies. Each community will bring its knowledge, skills, and methods to the partnership. The applications partner will provide the bulk of the resources and support needed to implement its applications. The partner will work within the framework of the NGI initiative to develop and demonstrate its applications over the high performance networking infrastructure by using advanced network technologies provided by other parts of the NGI. The applications demonstrations will primarily be proofof-concept demonstrations. Many of these demonstrations will suggest new ways for the application partners to meet their mission needs. The demonstrations are part of a research effort, as such they will initially be built on less-than-fully-robust technologies and be operating in less-than-bullet proof networking environments. Many agencies have critical signature applications that will benefit from advanced networking services and capabilities. Both the Federal Government's information technology services and the Federally supported R&D community have networking requirements that cannot be met with today's networking technology. Higher speed networks with more advanced services and functionality will enable a new generation of applications that support fundamental governmental interests including disaster response; distance education; environmental monitoring, prediction and warning; national security; scientific research; and health care. As the NGI initiative develops capabilities such as QoS nomadicity, and adaptive networking for the NGI, advanced demonstration applications will take advantage of these new services. It is expected that additional agencies will participate in these applications. For example, the Environmetal Protection Agency (EPA) and the National Oceanic and Atmospheric Administration (NCAA) have identified key applications requiring NGI speed and services. The education community is putting significant effort into connecting K-12 schools to the current generation Internet. Advanced education applications such as distance learning are expected to be major partners as the NGI matures. NGI applications prototypes will test these new capabilities to ensure that the protocols developed in Goals 1 and 2 are complete, robust, and useful in real applications and to provide a road map to future governmental and commerical services.

Success in reaching Goal 3 depends on success in Goals 1 and 2. Hence, Goal 3 drives the selection of the capabilities and designs for the other goals. In addition it requires integrating the new networking capabilities with the application domain. Although this program will not provide substantial direct funding for applications, it will partner with and leverage resources of the NGI community to incorporate new networking technologies and capabilities into applications to improve the R&D and service delivery to the public and private sectors. The essential and common features required by applications and demonstrated by this program will be identified and included in the feature set available via the NGI.

Applications

Health Care : Doctors at university medical centers will use large archives of radiology images to identify the patterns and features associated with a particular disease. With remote access to supercomputers, they will also be able to improve the accuracy of mammography by detecting subtle changes in three-dimesional images.

- ***Crisis Management, Crisis Response :*** Crisis managers will access wide range of information under the most difficult and unpredictable circumstances. Networks will be self-configuring to enable rapid return of services after a disaster; and information from multiple levels of government and the public sector will be immediately available. The results of remote models will be available for failure diagnosis and prediction of effects during natural or man-made disasters.
- ***Education, Distance Education :*** Universities are now experimenting with technologies such as twoway video to remote sites, VCR-like replay of past classes, modeling and simulation, collaborative environments, and on-line access to interactive, multimedia instructional software. Distance education will improve the ability of universities to serve working Americans who want new skills but who cannot attend a class at a fixed time during the week.
- ***Basic Science, Scientific Research :*** Scientists and engineers across the country will be able to work with each other and access remote scientific facilities as if they were in the same building "Collaboratories" that combine videoconferencing, shared virtual work spaces, networked scientific facilities, and database will increase the efficiency and effectivencess of our national research enterprise.
- ***Environment : Climate Research :*** Scientists, researchers, and policy makers will be able to examine the effects of proposed actions on the long term evolution of our environment. Models will become availale to and usable by all interested users.
- ***Health Care : Biomedical Research :*** Researchers will be able to solve problems in large scale DNA sequencing and gene identification that were previously impossible, opening the door to breakthroughs in curing human genetic diseases.
- ***Environment : Environmental Monitoring :*** Researchers are constructing virtual worlds to model and monitor defined ecosystems. **For example**, one project models the Chesapeake Bay ecosystem, which serves as a nursery area for many commercially important species.

- *Manufacturing :* Collaborative engineering, distributed data sharing, and teleoperation of unique manufacturing resources will dramatically reduce the time required to develop new, higher quality products in distributed enterprises and in virtual enterprises. Enhancing manufacturing applications such as design, analysis, modeling, simulation, virtual reality, equipment/process control, and monitoring with NGI-based capabilities will enable system-wide improvements for geographically distributed manufacturers, suppliers, and customers.

12.4.5 NGI Initiative Accomplishments at DARPA

So far chapter paper discussed the implementation plan of the NGI. This section evaluates and describes the accomplishments attained DARPA the team leader of the NGI project.

The three goals have been achieved although not completely and thus the NGI program is extended to the year 2002-2003 by the US government.

The implementation of the NGI plan has led to the development of SUPERNET at DARPA which is the testbed developed according to goal 2 of the NGI implementation plan.

As per section 2 of this paper DARPA implemented and suggested the following architecture for the testbeds to be created in order to accomplish goal 2.

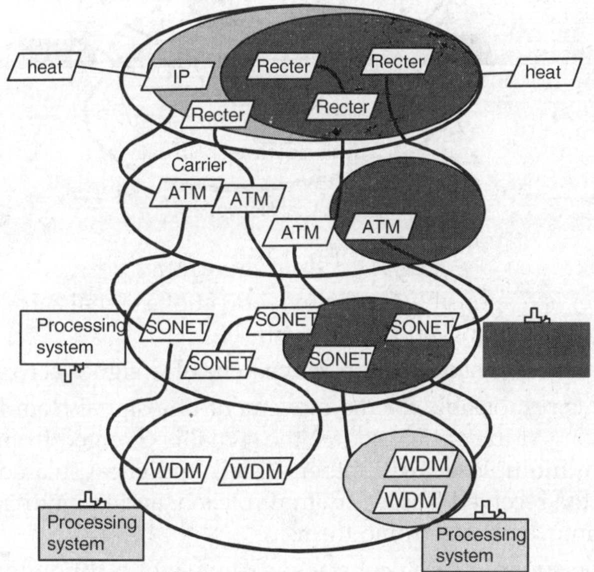

Fig. 12.5

In this architecture the each layer has a provisioning system that provides control over the a part of the layout in order to monitor the data transfer and errors is any in the link.

WDM stands for Wave division multiplexing in which light signals are multiplexed and demultiplexed through fiber optic cables. Multiple source of light are combined into one single light at the multiplexes and the reverse is done at the demultiplexer. This allows for speed upto 16,40 λ's

The layer of protocol stack over this is the SONET which again has various provisioning systems for the same reasons as for the WDM layer.

SONET stands for Synchronous Optical network

The SONET standard includes four functional layers namely the photonic layer, section layer, line layer and the path layer.

The photonic layer includes the physical specifications for the optical fiber channel, the sensitivity of the receiver, multiplexing functions and so on.

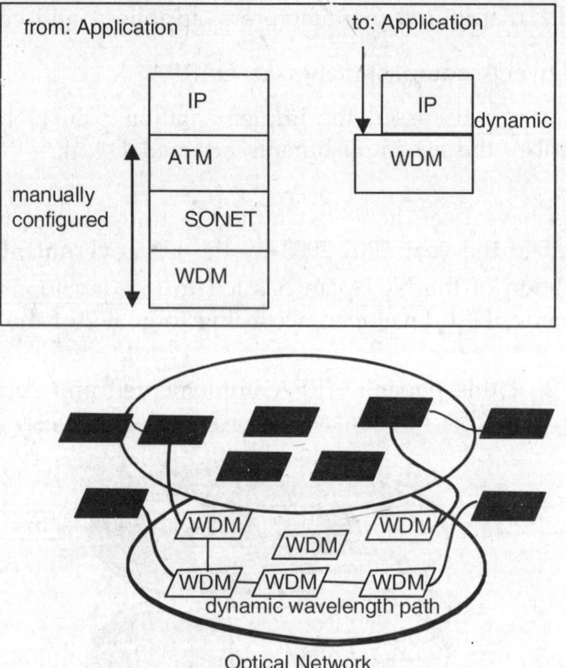

Fig. 12.6

The section layer is responsible for the movement of a signal across a physical section, it handles framing, scrambling and error control.

The line layer is responsible for the movement of a signal across a physical line.

The path layer is responsible for the movement of a signal from its optical source to its optical destination. At the optical source the signal is changed from an electronic form into an optical form multiplexed with other signals and encapsulated in a frame. At the optical destination the received frame is demultiplexed, and the individual optical signals are changed back into their electronic forms.

This layer in the supernet protocol stack is capable of a bandwidth of upto 2.5 to 10 Gbps .

The next layer in the protocol stack is the ATM (Asynchronous Transfer Mode) which is a cell relay protocol.

ATM is a cell switched network. The user access devices are connected through a user to network interface (UNI) to the switches inside the network and the switches are connected through a network to network interface.

Connection between two end points is accomplished through transmission paths (TPs), Virtual paths (VPs) and Virtual circuits (VCs).

A transmission path is the physical connection between an end point and a switch and between two switches.

A transmission path is divided into several virtual paths. A virtual path provides a connection or a set of connections between two switches

Cell networks are based on virtual circuits. All cells belonging to a single message follow the same virtual circuit and remain in their original order until they reach their destination. The basic data unit in an ATM network is called a cell which is only 53 bytes long. Each all carries in it a 5 byte header having the Virtual path and Virtual circuit identifier.

ATM uses switches to route the cell from a source end point to the destination end point. This layer of the supernet protocol stack has a capacity of 45,155 Mbps.

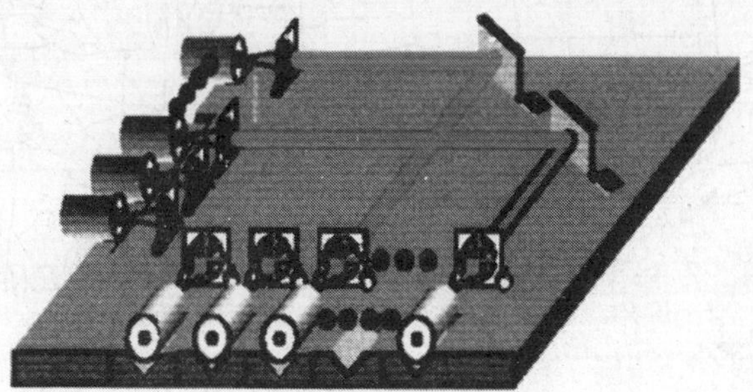

Fig. 12.7

The switching used for the Super Net is optical flow switching which has a capacity of 1-10 GBPS end to end. This has been made possible by using the MEMS (Micro-electro mechanical system) switch where large 32X32 optical Cross-connect or a crossbar switch on a single chip of silicon which is less then one inch square. This switch is independent of wave length, bit rate, protocol polarization, modulation format.

This switch is a 100 times better in speed power and size as compared to the traditional cross bar switch.

The final layer in the supernet protocol stack is the IP layer. This layer is implemented using the Ipv6 protocol so that to enable access to the current generation of systems connecting to the internet and maintaining a possible wide spread use of the Super Net.

The QoS or quality of service in as proposed in the NGI implementation plan is achieved with high level of both user oriented and network oriented QoS. One indicator of it is the cell loss ratio which is constant in the supernet testbed.

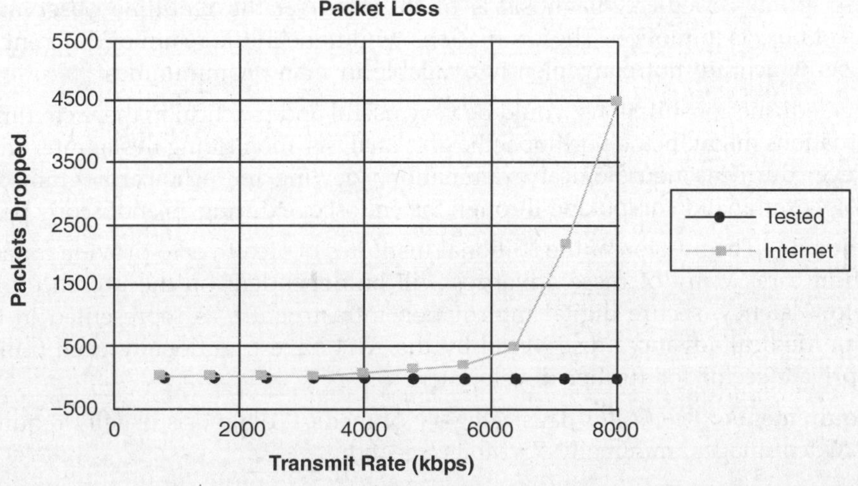

Fig. 12.8

This brings us to the current level of the testbed deployment as per Goal 2 of the NGI initiative at DARPA. The architecture of the supernet in given below along with the participating organizations and the network links between them.

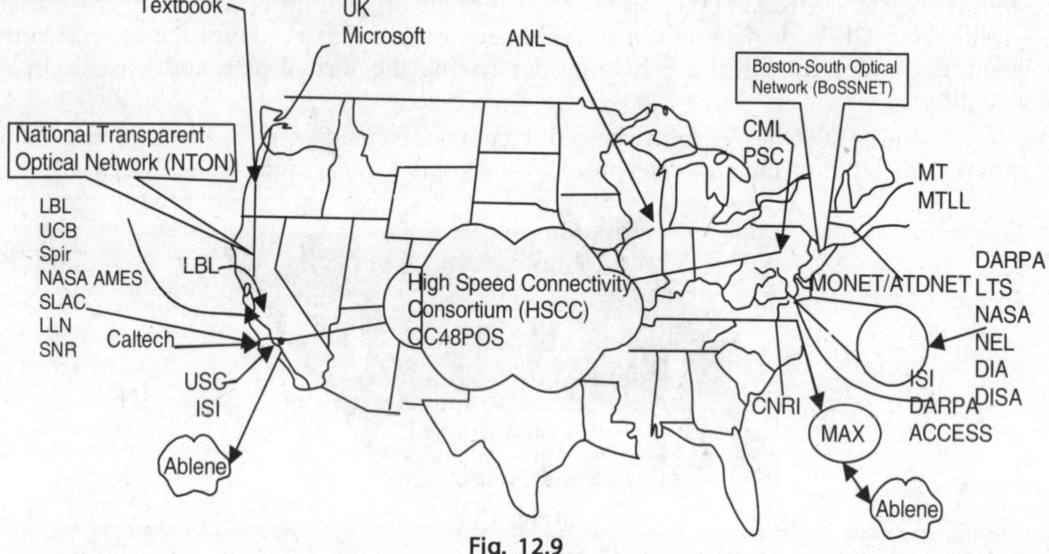

Fig. 12.9

Thus now the revolutionary applications which is the fourth and the final goal of the NGI is left to be achieved-one of the few candidate applications for the supernet is the following.

Real-time Telemedicine : Sponsored by The National Institutes of Health

Categories : Medicine, Collaboration

Vision : Provide a means of remote medical consultations through the use of real-time analysis of medical diagnostic procedures involving motion.

Why NGI ?

For accurate medical diagnosis, real-time telemedicine require 75 Mbits/sec transmission speeds for video sequences such as echo-cardiography. In addition, latency must be maintained at a constant rate to prevent errors in diagnosis.

Description : Medical diagnosis is often based on the real-time observation and analysis of objects in motion. These situations tend to be in the realm of different medical specialists which are not conveniently available in many communities.

Telemedicine consultations would be very useful and practical in these circumstances. Such situations might include orthopaedic gate analysis, monitoring nystagmus (vibrations of the eye) during a neurological examination, viewing the echo-cardiogram during a cardiology examination or looking through the endoscope during an endoscopy procedure.

Rationale : The mission of the National Institutes of Health is to provide for advances in medical care. Many of these advances will be dependent on the presence of a high speed, low latency, secure digital information infrastructure as represented in the NGI program. Medical advances discovered by the NIH have traditionally been transitioned to the private sector for further development.

Requirements : *Bandwidth*. This category of medical diagnosis usually requires VHS quality video images, minimally 75 Mbits/second.

Latency. Absolute latency is not a factor in these applications. In order to maintain a feeling of interactivity, the latency should be less then 250 msec. However, whatever the latency is, it must be kept constant through the consultation as real-time motion analysis is the goal of this telemedicine consult. Very often the motion being looked at is not very smooth and the irregularites in the motion are often a clue to the diagnosis. Introduction of a variable latency may lead to erroneous diagnosis. Fortunately most biological motions are of relatively low frequency and so a variation in latency of less than 5 msec would probably be acceptable.

Security. These applications involve the transmission of real patient data which the patient may consider sensitive. It requires a high level of transmission security to be sure that it cannot be viewed or altered during transmission.

Reliability. The network should be highly reliable but absolute reliability is not a requirement for most of these applications as lack of network reliability will not result in life threatening situations. If there is a network problem, although it is inconvenient for all concerned, the patient and care given can reschedule their appointment together. However, some real-time applications require that the data being transmitted be collected byinvasive means such as endoscopy or colonoscopy. These special applications require as close to 100% network reliability as possible.

Scalability. This group of applications tend to be point to point applications and so will initially not require scalability. However, if viewed as a successful telemedicine applications, the bandwidth available on the network should be scalable so that the capacity can be increased in the future in response to potential increases in demand. Likewise, in the future additional interactive monitoring sites may be added so that such telemedicine consultations can also serve a useful teaching function which will require a degree of network scalability.

Latest Review of the NGI : The latest report on the NGI was by the PITAC (Presidents Information Technology Advisory Committee) in December 2000 the report was as follows :

PITAC Year 2000 Report To Congress Reviewing The Next Generation Internet Program And Related Issues

(Updated December 2002)

The Next Generation Internet Research Act of 1998, requires President's Information Technology (IT) Adivsory Committee (PITAC) to review the implementation of the Next Generation Internet (NGI) initiative and report annually on:

Advanced Networking Research: Progress in NGI-funded advanced networking research, NGI Testbeds : Progress in implementing high-performance network testbeds, NGI Applications: Progress in developing high-performance network applications, Geographic Reach: Addressing geographic penalties faced by rural institutions, Minority-and- Small-College Reach : Addressing access by historically black and Hispanic-serving institutions, colleges and universities with fewer than 5,000 Technology Transfer: Flow of NGI ideas to industry, Agency Coordination: Effectiveness of coordination among the NGI agencies, and IT Leadership: The extent to which federal research support will maintain U.S IT leadership.

The Committer reviewed the NGI initiative with DARPA, DOE, NASA, NIH, NIST, and NSF.

The NGI agencies have made excellent progress over the last year. We are gratified that they have responded to advice from Congress and from the PITAC. We recommend Congress extend funding of the NGI program for two more years at the proposed level of $ 104 million. Advanced networking research: The NGI program has initiated a broad networking research plan that addresses the need for critical technology. NGI research activites, especially the DARPA and NSF programs, are producing exciting results that are likely to be cornerstones of the new communications infrastructure. For example, DARPA's Super Net program will provide guaranteed ultra high-bandwidth on demand for national, regional, metropolitan, and local networks. They are pioneering work on dynamically controlled optical networks.

NGI Testbeds : NSF and DARPA are deploying two NGI Testbeds. In FY 2000 NSF, DOE, and NASA have connected more than 150 sites to a testbed providing a 100-fold increase in network performance, and DARPA is deploying a testbed with 1000-fold increased performance at more than 15 sites to support networking research and applications development. Currently, the maximum desktop-to-desktop performance has been measured at about 900 million bits per second more than a ten-fold increase over the 80 Mbps reported to us last year. There is still much more to do, but the agencies have an excellent plan and they are executing it very well. The agencies have also cooperated in setting up the Qbone network to experiment with applications that need Quality of Service guarantees.

NGI Applications : The NGI agencies are exploring network applications that require NGI services and performance. NIH's National Library of Medicine, for example, has funded many promising application pre-proposals. Many agencies (NASA, DATPA, USGS, NOAA, NEMA, and ACE) are cooperating on the Digital Earth framework to make all US geo-referenced data available via a point-and-click user interface via a high-speed network. Today, there are few applications that will use the low latency, quality of serivce, or high bandwith that NGI will offer. Only 20 percent of NGI's FY 2000 funding is for applications, hence progress has been disappointing. We again recommend increased emphasis on and investments in new applications that use NGI-level capabilities. It is necessary to fund such applications explicitly. Congress might consider doing this as part of other agency funding bills.

Reach : The NGI initiative cannot directly address reach to rural, inner-city, minority, or small institutions. NGI is a research and development program to provide the technologies and applications required as foundations for the next generations of the Internet. It is a relatively small initiative that funds peer-reviewed research proposals. The announced NGI awards cover 177 of the nation's 2,200 four-year, college-level educational institutions. It cannot fund istitutions where research is not emphasized and where there is little experience developing advanced networking or applications. The end of this report makes a specific recommendation to address this issue.

Geographic Reach : While the NGI intiative was not planned or directed to address reach in general, access for otherwise qualified universities with fundable research proposals must not be disadvantaged merely because of their location. NSF expanded the High Performance Connentions program to cover all 50 states and has made 40 grants in 18 EPSCoR states. Eventually, NGI research on wireless, hybrid, and satellite technologies may reduce the cost and improve the services available to all users including those in geographically remote areas.

Minority-and-Small-College Reach : The NGI was not funded to address Internet access for historically black, Hispanic-serving, Native American, or small colleges and universities. Based on its standard peer review process, NSF has awarded High performance Connection grants to two historically black and five Hispanic-serving institutions. In addition,unrelated to the NGI effort, NSF has granted 6 million dollars to Educause to work with disadvantaged minority colleges to develop their IT infrastructure.

Technology Transfer: Industry, universities, and Federal agencies collaborate on NGI research, testbeds, teams, and workshops. This creates substantial technology transfer opportunities. Indeed, a quick survey found about a dozen startups capitalized at nearly $30 billion that have sprung up from the NGI program.

Agency Coordination : NGI agencies coordinate their activities through the Large Scale Networking Coordinating Group and its specialized teams that focus on the NGI goals. The agencies seem to be cooperating effectively in implementing the NGI goals.

IT Leadersphip : The Committee's Report to the President, February 1999, concluded that Federal support for research in information technology is seriously inadequate. The PITAC recommended the Federal government increase IT research funding by $1.4B per year by FY 2004. The President's FY 2000 Budget includes an Information Technology for the 21st Century (IT2) initiative that begins to address this recommendion.

Recommendations : The Committee recommends that the NGI Program be extended through FY 2002 at the proposed funding levels. Planning for follow-on activities should begin now. In particular, more applications should be funded that demonstrate utility of the NGI's gigabit badwidth to end-users, its increased security, and its expanded quality of service.

The Committee shares Congress' concern that on Federal program addresses the reach issue. We recommend Congress consider additional funding for a program where the NGI research institutions act as aggregators and mentors for nearby smaller or disadvantaged institutions. This is primarily infrastructure, not networking research and, hence, not part of the current NGI program.

Raj Reddy

Co-Chair PITAC lrving Wladawsky-

Berger

CoChair PITAC

12.4.6 Conclusion

To conclude the NGI project is the most likely direction that the internet will take in the coming years with more and more networks emulating the SuperNet.Although the R&D cost of such networks is considerably high and thus there hasn't been such a widespread deployment of such a network. Although the NGI implementation plan and the Supernet show us the right path whether we travel it or not remains to be seen in the future.

SUMMARY

Web databases are platform independent, Standard, Scalable as well as transparent. Web enables organizations to provide new and innovative services and reach new customers through globally accessible applications. On the other hand, internet is not very reliable as security is a very big concern. Also, HTML has limited functionality.

MULTIPLE CHOICE QUESTIONS [MCQs]

1. Web is used as a

(*a*) Front-end (*b*) Back-end

(*c*) Both '*a*' and '*b*' (*d*) None of the above

2. CGI stands for
   (a) Common Global Interface
   (b) Common Gateway Interoperability
   (c) Common Gateway Interface.
   (d) None of the above.
3. CGI scripts are written in
   (a) C
   (b) PERL
   (c) Both 'a' and 'b'
   (d) None of the above.
4. ODBC stands for
   (a) Open database connectivity.
   (b) Open data case
   (c) Over database case.
   (d) None of the above.
5. ISAPI is a product by
   (a) Microsoft
   (b) Netscape
   (c) IBM
   (d) HCL.

ANSWERS

1. (a) 2. (c) 3. (c) 4. (a) 5. (a)

CONCEPTUAL SHORT QUESTIONS WITH ANSWERS

Q.1. How oracle supports web access to database?

Ans. The oracle's web server components are shown in Fig. 12.10 below.

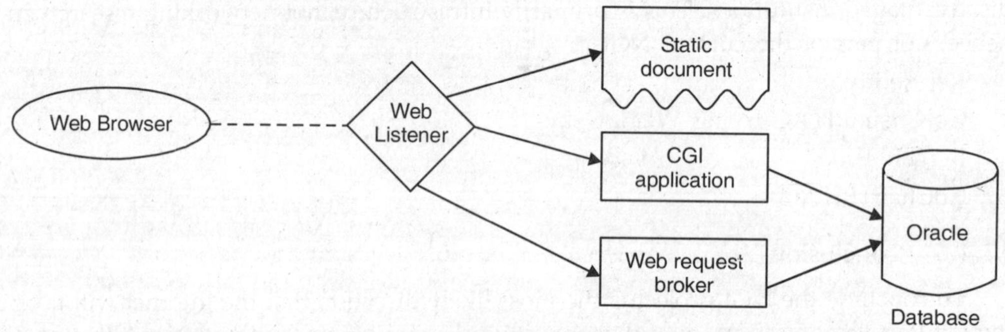

Fig. 12.10

Herein, the client requests files that are either **static** or **dynamic files** from the web server. Static files have fixed contents whereas dynamic files may have content that includes results of queries to the database. *Web Listener is an HTTP demon i.e., a process that runs continously on the server.* It listens for the requests originating in the clients. A static file is retrieved from the file system of the server and displayed on the web browser at the client. The request for a dynamic page is passed by the listener to a web request broker (WRB). WRB is a multi-threaded dispatcher that adheres to cartridges. **Cartridges are defined as those software modules that perform specific functions on specific types of data and can communicate among themselves :** *For e.g.,* We have cartridges for PL/SQL, Java2 and so on.

Our web server has been fully integrated with PL/SQL, making it efficient and scalable. Further more, cartridges adds to flexibility and interoperability. **For example**, Designer 2000 (development tool) has a web generator to port applications working on LAN to the Internet and Intranet environments.

Q.2. Give some advantages and disadvantages of Web databases.

Ans. ***Advantages of web databases*** are as follows :

1. HTML used in Web database designing is quite simple.
2. They are platform independent.
3. They provide good GUI (Graphical User Interface).
4. They provide interoperability also *i.e.,* one application can communicate with another one.
5. It is a transparent and scalable approach

Disadvantages of Web database are as follows :

1. Internet, itself, is unreliable *i.e.,* may fail anytime.
2. Communications are slow.
3. Security is an open challenge as it is easy for the hackers to hack information now.
4. HTML, itself, has a limited functionality
5. When peak loads are high, scalability becomes a problem.

Q.3. Do we need to integrate web technology with the object technology?

Ans. Yes, we need to integrate them. Presently, the *Web* can be viewed as a distributed object system and *HTML-pages* as objects identified by the URL (Uniform Resource Locators).

EXERCISE QUESTIONS

Q.1. What is meant by web-databases?

Q.2. What are web database tools? Explain.

Q.3. Discuss some advantages and disadvantages of a web database.

Q.4. What is Web publishing ? Distinguish between Static and Dynamic web publishing.

Q.5. Write short notes on :

(*a*) CGI

(*b*) XML.

Advanced Topics in DBMS

13.0 INTRODUCTION

If we can store data and text information in our databases, then why not our images, audio, video and almost the entire multimedia? Can't we make our database digital and mobile? These issues are dealt in this chapter.

13.1 DEDUCTIVE DATABASES

A deductive database system is a database system which can make deductions i.e., conclude additional facts based on rules and facts stored in the deductive database. Datalog is the language typically used here. We state an equation to understand this :

Deductive Databases = Logic Programming + Relational Databases

These database are more expressive than relational databases but less expressive than logic programming systems.

Let us tabulate the differences between deductive and logic programming.

S.No	Features	Logic Programming	Deductive Database
1.	**Order sensitivity and procedurality.**	In prolog programs, it depends on the order of rules in a program.	Here, program execution is independent of the order of rules and facts.
2.	**Special predicates**	Prolog programmers can directly influence the procedural evaluation with special predicates.	No correspondence exists in deductive databases.
3.	**Function Symbols**	Logic programming languages allow function symbols to build up complex symbols.	This is not allowed in deductive databases.
4.	**Tuple-oriented processing**	Logic programming languages concentrate on one tuple at a time.	Deductive database use set-oriented processing.

13.2 MULTIMEDIA DATABASES

Multimedia databases provide us a facility to store and query multimedia information like images, videos, audios and documents like books, journals etc.

Multimedia Database Queries : In multimedia databases, **content-based queries** are used. It is also known as a content-based retrieval because the multimedia source is being retrieved based on its containing certain objects. It's applications includes :

(*a*) Medical imaging (*b*) Art galleries
(*c*) Museums (*d*) Fashion design
(*e*) Interior design.

Another approach is to use the method of identification of multimedia sources. We may here, use either manual identification or automatic identification.

Let us now see some of the applications of multimedia databases :

1. **Repository applications** like repository of satellite images, engineering drawings, designs, space photographs and radiology scanned pictures.
2. **Presentation applications** like our audio and video applications where data is consumed as it is delivered.
3. **Collaborative works** like intelligent healthcare networks as Nell as telemedicine work together.
4. **Knowledge dissemination** for public use like books, catalogue, journals etc on NET.
5. **Real-time applications** like nuclear power plants, patients in ICU, transportation systems etc.

Examples of DBMS Supporting Multimedia : DB2, Informix, Oracle 8i, CA-JASMINE, Sybase etc.

13.3 MOBILE DATABASES

A mobile database is a portable database and is physically separate from a centralized database server. Now, the users can access remote and corporate data on their laptops, PDAs (Personal Digital Assistant) etc.

General Architecture of Mobile Databases : It is a distributed architecture where several computers or hosts are interconnected through a high-speed communication network.

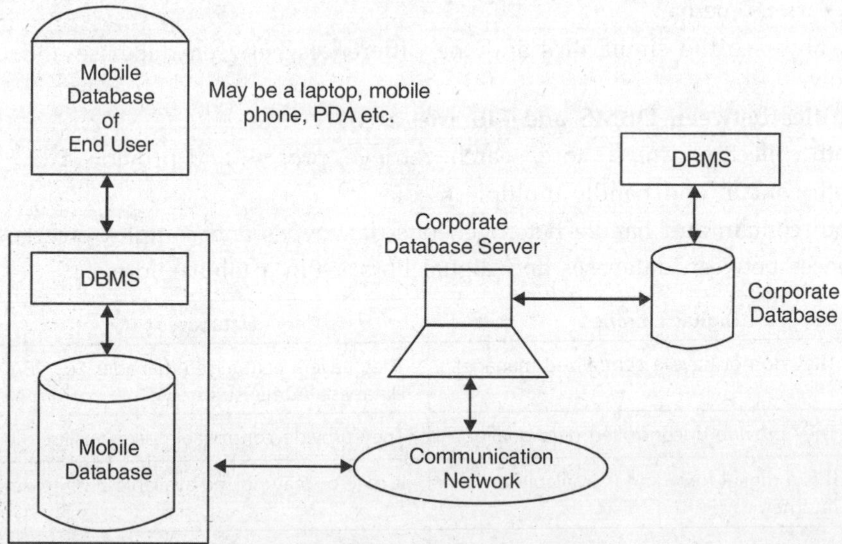

Fig. 13.1. *Mobile database system*

The mobile DBMS are capable of communicating with a range of major relational DBMS. A mobile DBMS must be able to communicate with centralized databases server through wireless access. Today, most mobile DBMS, provide Pre-Packaged SQL functions for the mobile application as well as support extensive database querying. Mobile database replicate data among themselves and with a centralized database.

Examples of Mobile Databases

- SQL Any where by sybase.
- SQL server 2000 by MS.
- DB2 Every place 7 by IBM.
- Oracle 9i lite by Oracle.

NOTE : Mobile database are smaller parts of their Server-based counter parts. Their database engines require from 125KB 1MB only.

Let us now compare mobile and distributed databases in a tabular form –

S.No	Distributed Databases	Mobile Databases
1	Data is not disconnected for long periods.	Data is unevenly distributed among the Base Stations (BS) and the mobile units. Data may be disconnected for long periods.
2.	Traditional, ACID properties apply.	Central coordination of transaction execution is lacking. New transaction properties need to be defined.
3.	No such problem as they are not mobile.	Due to mobility, the global name resolution problem for handling queries is more.
4.	Location updations are not required.	Location updations are required.
5.	Cost of query evaluation does not need special data location awareness.	Cost of query evaluation needs special data location awareness also.

13.4 DIGITAL DATABASES

A digital database or a digital library is an analog of a traditional library, coupled with the advantages of digital technologies. They are a large collection of information sources in various media.

Let us now see the similarities and the differences between database and digital libraries now.

Similarities between DBMS and Libraries :

1. Both collect, organize, store, search, retrieve, process and provide data.
2. Both contain and handle multiple media.
3. Both contain and handle heterogeneous data types and complex objects.

Differences between databases and digital libraries in a tabular form :

S.No	Digital Libraries	Databases
1.	They do not have a centralized manager.	They have a centralized manager, *i.e.,* DBA-Database Administrator.
2.	They provide uncontrolled data quality.	They provide controllable data quality.
3.	It is a digital form and is available on Internet.	It may or may not be available on Internet.
4.	Data access is faster.	Data access is slower as compared to digital libraries.
5.	Information is always available (24 × 7).	Information may not be available everywhere.

SUMMARY

In this chapter, we have studied how database are used and accessed from Internet using web technologies, use of mobile databases, multimedia databases and digital databases (libraries).

MULTIPLE CHOICE QUESTIONS [MCQs]

1. A database system that can make deductions based on facts and rules is known as

(*a*) Digital library (*b*) Multimedia database

(*c*) Deductive database (*d*) None of the above.

2. Deductive database use a language

(*a*) C (*b*) PERL

(*c*) Datalog (*d*) None of the above.

3. Which is true for deductive databases

(*a*) Deductive databases = Logic programming + Relational Databases

(*b*) Deductive databases = Logic programming – Relational Databases

(*c*) Deductive databases = Logic programming * Relational Databases

(*d*) None of the above.

4. Logic programming performs :

(*a*) Set-oriented processing (*b*) Tuple-oriented processing

(*c*) Table oriented processing. (*d*) None of the above.

5. Which of the following has a centralized manager –

(*a*) Databases (*b*) Digital libraries

(*c*) Records (*d*) None of the above.

ANSWERS

1. (*c*) **2.** (*c*) **3.** (*a*) **4.** (*b*) **5.** (*a*)

CONCEPTUAL SHORT QUESTIONS WITH ANSWERS

Q.1. What are GIS databases?

Ans. GIS systems are used to collect, model, store and analyze information describing the physical properties of the geographical world as well as to combine it with related non-spatial data.

Q.2. Discuss some GIS applications?

Ans. GIS applications are put under 3 categories –

(*a*) Cartographic applications.

(*b*) Digital terrain modeling based.

(*c*) Geographic-objects based.

This may further include various fields and is shown below.

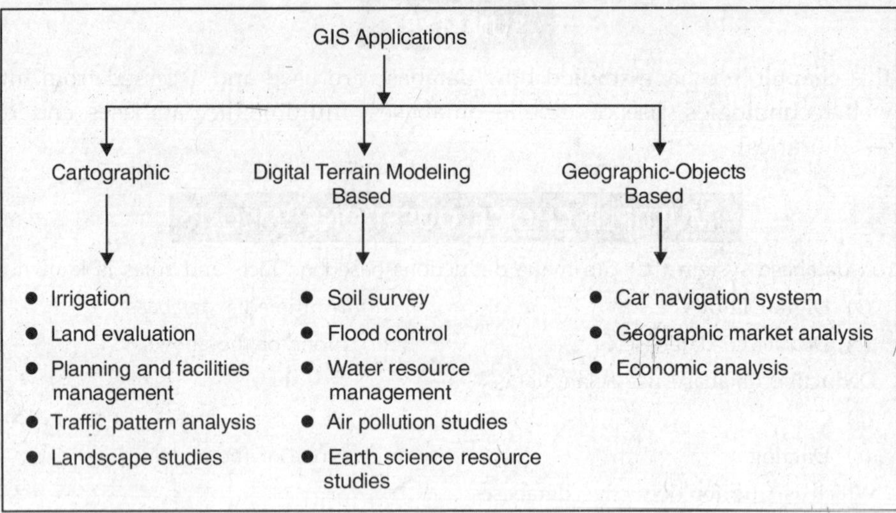

Fig. 13.2

Q.3. Will functional dependencies be preserved if a relation is converted to a temporal relation by adding a time attribute? How is the problem handled in a temporal database?

Ans. Functional dependencies may be violated when a relation is augmented to include a time attribute. **For example**, suppose we add a time attribute to the relation **account** in our sample bank database. The dependency **account-number→ balance** may be violated since a customer's balance would keep changing with time.

To remedy this problem temporal database systems have a slightly different notion of functional dependency, called **temporal functional dependency. For example**, the temporal functional dependency **account-number → balance** over **Account-schema** means that for each instance **account of Account-schema**, all snap-shots of account satisfy the functional dependency **account-number • balance**, *i.e.*, at any time instance, each account will have a unique bank balance corresponding to it.

Q.4. Consider two-dimensional vector data where the data items do not overlap. Is it possible to convert such vector data to raster data? If so, what are the drawbacks of storing raster data obtained by such conversion, instead of the original vector data?

Ans. To convert non-overlapping vector data to raster data, we set the values for exactly those pixels that lie on any one of data items (regions); the other pixels have a default value.

The disadvantages to this approach are : loss of precision in location information (since raster data loses resolution), a much higher storage requirement, and loss of abstract information (like the shape of a region).

Q.5. What problems can occur in a continuous-media system if data is delivered either too slowly or too fast?

Ans. Continuous media systems typically handle a large amount of data, which have to be delivered at a steady rate. Suppose the system provides the picture frames for a television set. The delivery rate of data from the system should be matched with the frame display rate of TV set. If the delivery rate is too low, the display would periodically freeze or blank out, since there will be no new data to be displayed for some time. On the other hand, if the delivery rate is too high, the data buffer at the destination TV set will overflow causing loss of data; the lost data will never get displayed.

Q.6. List three main features of mobile computing wireless networks that are distinct from traditional distributed systems.

Ans. Some of the main distinguishing features are as follows.

- In distributed systems, disconnection of a host from the network is considered to be a **failure**, whereas allowing such disconnection is a **feature** of mobile systems.
- Distributed systems are usually centrally administered, whereas in mobile computing, each personal computer that participates in the system is administered by the user (owner) of the machine and there is little central administration, if any.
- In conventional distributed systems, each machine has fixed location and network address (es). This is not true for mobile computers, and in fact, is antithetical to the very purpose of mobile computing.
- Queries made on a mobile computing system may involve the location and velocity of a host computer.
- Each computer in a distributed system is allowed to be arbitrarily large and may consume a lot of (almost) uninterrupted electrical power. Mobile systems typically have small computers that run on low wattage, short-lived batteries.

Q.7. List three factors that need to be considered in query optimization for mobile computing that are not considered in traditional query optimizers.

Ans. The most important factor influencing the cost of query processing in traditional database systems is that of disk I/O. However, in mobile computing, minimizing the amount of energy required to execute a query is an important task of a query optimizer. To reduce the consumption of energy (battery power), the query optimizer on a mobile computer must minimize the size and number of queries to be transmitted to remote computers as well as the time for which the disk is spinning.

In traditional database systems, the cost model typically does include connection time and the amount of data transferred. However, mobile computer users are usually charged according to these parameters. Thus, these parameters should also be minimized by a mobile computer's query optimizer.

Q.8. Give an example to show that the version-vector scheme does not ensure serializability. (Hint: Use the assumption that documents 1 and 2 are available on both mobile computers A and B, and take into account the possibility that a document may be read without being updated).

Ans. Consider the example given in the previous exercise. Suppose that both host A and host B are not connected to each other. Further, assume that identical copies of document 1 and document 2 are stored at host **A** and host **B**.

Let **{X = 5}** be the initial contents of document 1, and **{X = 10}** be the initial contents of document 2. Without loss of generality, let us assume that all version-vectors are initially zero.

Suppose host A updates the number its copy of document 1 with that in its copy of document 2. Thus, the contents of both the documents (at host A) are now **{X = 10}**. The version number $\mathbf{V_{1.A,A}}$ is incremented to 1.

While host B is disconnected from host A, it updates the number in its copy of document 2 with that in its copy document 1. Thus, the contents of both the documents (at host B) are now {X = 5}. The version number $V_{2.B,B}$ is incremented to 1.

Later, when host A and host B connect, they exchange version-vectors. The version-vector scheme updates the copy of document 1 at host B to {X = 10}, and the copy of document 2 at host A to {A = 5}. Thus, both copies of each document are identical, viz. document 1 contains {X = 10} and document 2 contains {X = 5}.

However, note that a serial schedule for the two updates (one at host A and another at host B) would result in both documents having the *same* contents. Hence this example shows that the version-vector scheme does not ensure serializability.

Q.9. Explain how a TP monitor manages memory and processor resources more effectively than a typical operating system.

Ans. In a typical OS, each client it represented by a process, which occupies a lot of memory. Also process multi-tasking over-head is high.

A TP monitor is more of a service provider, rather than an environment for executing client processes. The client processes run at their own sites, and they send requests to the TP monitor whenever they wish to avail of some service. The message is routed to the right server by the TP monitor, and the results of the service are sent back to the client.

The advantage of this scheme is that the same server process can be serving several clients simultaneously, by using multithreading. This saves memory space, and reduces CPU overheads on preserving ACID properties and on scheduling entire processes. Even without multi-threading, the TP monitor can dynamically change the number of servers running, depending on what-ever factors affect good performance. All this is not possible with a typical OS setup.

Q.10. If the entire database fits in main memory, do we still need a database system to manage the data? Explain your answer.

Ans. Even if the entire database fits in main memory, a DBMS is needed to perform tasks like concurrency control, recovery, logging etc, in order to preserve ACID properties of transactions.

Q.11. In the group-commit technique, how many transactions should be part of a group? Explain your answer.

Ans. As log-records are written to stable storage in multiples of a block, we should group transaction commits in such a way that the last block containing log-records for the current group is almost full.

Q.12. In a database system using write-ahead logging, what is the worst-case number of disk accesses required to read a data item? Explain why this presents a problem to designers of real-time database systems.

Ans. In the worst case, a read can cause a buffer page to be written to disk (preceded by the corresponding log records), followed by the reading from disk of the page containing the data to be accessed. This takes two or more disk accesses, and the time taken is several orders of magnitude more than the main-memory reference required in the best case. Hence transaction execution-time variance is very high and can be estimated only poorly. It is therefore difficult to plan schedules which need to finish within a deadline.

Q.13. What is the purpose of compensating transactions? Present two examples of their use.

Ans. A compensating transaction is used to perform a semantic undo of changes made previously by committed transactions. For example, a person might deposit a cheque in their savings account. Then the database would be updated to reflect the new balance. Since it takes a few days for the cheque to clear, it might be discovered later that the check bounced, in which case a compensating transaction would be run to subtract the amount of the bounced check from the depositor's account. Another example of when a compensating transaction would be used is in a grading program. If a student's grade on an assignment is to be changed after it is recorded, a compensating program (usually an option of the grading program itself) is run to change the grade and redo averages, etc.

Q.14. Why is it relatively easy to port a database from a single processor machine to a multiprocessor machine if individual queries not be parallelized?

Ans. Porting is relatively easy to a shared memory multiprocessor machine. Database designed for single-processor machines already provide multitasking, allowing multiple processes to run on the same processor in a time-shared manner, giving a view to the user of multiple processes running in parallel. Thus, coarse-granularity parallel machines logically appear to be identical to single-processor machines, making the porting relatively easy.

Porting a database to a shared disk or shared nothing multiprocessor architecture is a little harder.

Q.15. Transaction server architectures are popular for client-server relational databases, where transactions are short. On the other hand, data server architectures are popular for client-server object-oriented database system, where transactions are expected to be relatively long. Given two reasons why data servers may be popular for object-oriented database but not for relational database.

Ans. Data servers are good if data transfer is small with respect to computation, which is often the case in applications of OODBs such as computer aided design. In contrast, in typical relational database applications such as transaction processing, a transaction performs little computation but may touch several pages, which will result in a lot of data transfer with little benefit in a data server architecture. Another reason is that structures such as indices are heavily used in relational database, and will become spots of contention in a data server architecture, requiring frequent data transfer. There are no such points of frequent contention in typical current-day OODB applications such as computer aided design.

Q.16. What is lock de-escalation, and under what conditions is it required? Why is it not required if the unit of data shipping is an item?

Ans. In a client-server system with page shipping, when a client requests an item, the server typically grants a lock not on the requested item, but on the **page** having the item, thus implicitly granting locks on all the items in the page. The other items in the page are said to be **prefetched**. If some other client subsequently requests one of the prefetched items, the server may ask the owner of the page lock to transfer back the lock on this item. If the page lock owner doesn't need this item, it de-escalates the page lock that it holds, to item locks on all the items that it is actually accessing, and returns the locks on the unwanted items. The server can then grant the latter lock request.

If the unit of data shipping is an item, there are no coarser granularity locks; even if prefetching is used, it is typically implemented by granting individual locks on each of the prefetched items. Thus when the server asks for a return of a lock, there is no question of de-escalation, the requested lock is just returned if the client has no use for it.

Q.17. Suppose you were in charge of the database operations of a company whose main job is to process transactions. Suppose the company is growing rapidly each year, and has outgrows its current computer system. When you are choosing a new parallel computer, what measure is most relevant—speedup, batch scaleup, or transaction scaleup? Why?

Ans. With increasing scale of operations, we expect that the number of transactions submitted per unit time increases. On the other hand, we wouldn't expect most of the individual transactions to grow longer, nor would we require that a given transaction should execute more quickly now than it did before. Hence transactions scale-up is the most relevant measure in this scenario.

Q.18. What are the factors that can work against linear scaleup in a transaction processing system? Which of the factors are likely to be the most important in each of the following architectures: shared memory, shared disk, and shared nothing?

Ans. Increasing contention for shared resources prevents linear scale-up with increasing parallelism. In a shared memory system, contention for memory (which implies bus contention) will result in falling scale-up with increasing parallelism. In a shared disk system, it is contention for disk and bus access which affects scale-up. In a shared-nothing system, inter-process communication overheads will be the main impeding factor. Since there is no shared memory, acquiring locks and other activities requiring message passing between processes will take more time with increased parallelism.

Q.19. Consider a bank that has a collection of sites, each running a database system. Suppose the only way the database interact is by electronic transfer of money between one another. Would such a system qualify as a distributed database? Why ?

Ans. In a distributed system, all the sites typically run the same database management software, and they share a global schema. Each site provides an environment for execution of both global transactions initiated at remote sites and local transactions. The system described in the question does not have these properties, and hence it cannot qualify as a distributed database.

EXERCISE QUESTIONS

Q.1. Write short notes on—Multimedia databases

[GGSIPU, B.Tech., (CSE); 5th Sem., Dec. 2006]

Q.2. Write short notes on—Digital Libraries.

[GGSIPU B.Tech. (CSE); 5th Sem., Dec. 2007]

Q.3. What are the different multimedia sources?

Q.4. What is a mobile database? With the help of a neat sketch, explain its architecture.

Q.5. What are GIS applications?

CHAPTER

14

CASE STUDY—Dataware Housing and Data Mining

Definitions of Data warehouse

Data warehouse is a collection of data designed to support management decision-making.

Another definition: Data warehousing is the process, whereby, organizations extract meaning from their informational assets through the use of data warehouses. (Barguin, 1996).

Another definition: A data warehouse is a subject oriented, integrated, time variant, non-volatile collection of data used in support of management decision making processes (Inmon and Hackathorn, 1994). The meaning of the key terms in this definition is as follows:

(i) **Subject oriented:** In data warehouse, data is organized and optimized according to specific subjects or areas of interest of the organization rather than simply as computer files. Examples of major subject areas include Customers, Products, Accounts, Transactions etc. It provides capability to provide answers to various queries coming from various functional areas within an organization.

(ii) **Integrated :** Data warehouse is integrated. A single source of information for and about understanding multiple areas of interest. It provides information about a variety of subjects at one place. The input data comes from various sources in inconsistent form. Data warehouse refines the data to make it consistent and provides a unified view of overall organizational data to users. So, data warehouse is a centralized depository of data of the entire organization which helps in better understanding of organization's operations for strategic business opportunities and hence increase decision making capabilities.

(iii) **Non-volatile:** Data warehouse contains stable information that doesn't change each time an operational process is executed. The data in the data warehouse are loaded and refreshed from operational systems, but cannot be changed by end users. New data is always added as a supplement to database, rather than a replacement.

(iv) **Time-variant:** The data in data warehouse is only accurate and valid at some point in time or over some time interval. Data contains a time-dimension so that they may be used as a historical record of business' *i.e.*, sales statistics of previous week.

(v) **Accessible:** The primary purpose of a data warehouse is to provide readily accessible information to end users.

A number of separate technologies have come together to make Data warehousing possible to implement. However, it may be deployed physically, the data warehouse may be viewed as a single, consistent state of information with appropriate tools to provide valuable information about a business.

Distinctive Characteristics of Data Warehouses

The data warehouses have many characteristics that make them different from others.

It typically integrates several resources e.g., sales databases from various regions/states/years.

Acquisition of Data: All the data warehouses must have a source from where the data is acquired. Most of the data in the data warehouse is derived from the operational data of the organization. The required data is extracted, filtered, translated and integrated into the data storage environment.

Storage of Data: The large amounts of operational data that is historical in nature are defined, indexed and then partitioned to allow for economic and efficient access.

Data Access: A number of data mining applications allow many users throughout the organization to retrieve, analyze, query and generate reports. The ability to access data is fundamental to the concept of data warehouse in the organization.

Data Warehouse Components

There are mainly six components of a data warehouse. These are as follows:

(*i*) Summarized data
(*ii*) Operational data-store
(*iii*) Integration/Transformation programs
(*iv*) Detailed data
(*v*) Meta data
(*vi*) Archives

(*i*) **Summarized data:** The raw data generated by a transaction-processing system may be too large to store online. However, many queries can be answered by just maintaining the summary data obtained by aggregation on a relation, rather than maintain the entire relation. Summary data is classified into two categories-Light'y summarized and Highly summarized.

(*a*) Lightly summarized data: This represents data distilled from current detailed data. It is summarized according to some unit of time and always resides on disk.

(*b*) Highly summarized data: This represents data distilled from lightly summarized data. It is more compact and easily accessible and resides on disk.

(*ii*) **Operational data store :** Operational databases are the source data for the data warehouse. Operational data store is a repository of operational data.

(*iii*) **Integration/transformation programs:** The integration and transformation programs convert the operational data that is applications specific into enterprise data. The major functions performed by these programs are as follows:

— Reformatting, re-evaluation or changing key structures.

— Adding time elements.

— Default values identification.

— Providing logic to choose between multiple data sources.

— Summarizing, tallying and merging data from multiple sources.

These programs are modified when operational or data warehouse environments change to reflect the changes.

(*iv*) **Detailed data:** Detailed data is of two types–*Older detail data* and *current detail data*. The older detail data represent data that is not very recent, may be as old as ten years or longer. It is voluminous and most frequently stored on mass storage such as tape. It can be voluminous; it is almost always stored on disk to permit faster access.

(*v*) **Meta data:** Meta data is data about data. Meta data for data warehouse users are part of the data warehouse itself and controls access and analysis of the data warehouse contents. The meta data repository is a key data warehouse component. It contains both technical and business meta data. The technical meta data cover details about acquisition, processing, storage structure, data descriptions, warehouse operations and maintenance and access support functionality. The business meta data covers the relevant business rules and organizational details supporting the warehouse.

(*vi*) **Archives:** These contain old or historical data of significant interest and have value to the enterprise. It is generally used for forecasting and trend analysis, thus, these archives store old data and the meta data that describe the characteristics of the old data.

Advantages of Data Warehouse

The data warehouse has many advantages for an enterprise. The most important one are as follows.

1. *Effective decision making*: The major benefit of a data warehouse is its ability to analyze and execute business decisions based on data from multiple sources. By using data warehouse, one can look at past trends and may be do some predictions of what is going to happen in the future.

2. *Increases the productivity of business analysts*: The data warehouse can provide analysts with pre-calculated reports and graphs, that increase the productivity of business analysts.

3. An enterprise can maintain better customer relationships by correlating all customer data through a single data warehouse.

4. It provides supplementing disaster recovery plans with another data backup source.

5 .Business and information re-engineering: By knowing what information is important to the enterprise, that is possible by using data warehousing, the re-engineering efforts become more directional and have priorities. Also the data warehouse development is the effective first step in re-engineering the enterprise's legacy system.

Disadvantages/Limitations of Data Warehouse

The data warehouse have some limitations, these are as follows:

1. The data warehouse is very expensive solution and generally found in large firms.
2. Performance tuning is hard due to very large size of the data warehouse.
3. The cost of maintaining the data warehouse is very high.
4. Data warehouse has a high demand of various resources.
5. Scalability can be a problem with the data warehouse.
6. Complexity of integration in data warehouse.
7. Data warehouse is query intensive.

Data Analysis, Tools And Application

- Provides capabilities as mathematical and statistical function, MD modeling and forecasting.
- OLAP allows users to analyze and slice and dice data across multiple dimensions.
- OLAPs now provides the advantage of GUIS and client/server computing.
- Provides historical data also, so useful for trend analysis.
- There are 2 Multidimensional Data Analysis client tools.
- Those accessing data stored in MD Base systems. (MDBMSs).
- Those accessing data stored in relational DBMSs.
- MDBMS has both decision making and data management server capabilities.
- It is useful for only summarized data while less suited for handling large amounts of detailed data.
- While RDBMS provide data management capability, while front and client tool provides the analysis engine.
- So in RDBMS, both summarized and detailed data can be stored.
- Thus, to improve performance, vendor moving analytical processing into a separate analytical server positioned between MDA client and RDBMS server.
- Data Analysis tools work with summarized data.
- Summaries are build during analytical processing, but it is efficient to prebuild them, stored in form of data marts.

Types of End user Tools

3 main user tasks are revered here :

- Querying and reporting of Known facts.
- Analysis of known facts: Data Mining
- Discovery of unknown facts.

D.W. Applications

Application served by D.W can be placed in one of 3 main categories:

1. **Personal Productivity Application :** Spreadsheets, statistical packages and graphics tools are useful for manipulating and presenting data on individual PCs. These tools address applications requiring only small volumes of warehouse data.

2. **Data Query and Reporting Application :** Deliver warehouse wise data across, through simple, list oriented queries and generation of basic reports. This , do not fulfill the enterprise's need for in-depth analysis and planning.
3. **Planning and Analysis Application :** Address essential business requirement as budgeting, forecasting, customer profitability etc.
   OLAPs are used for this application.

Requirements for OLAP Application

- An application specific analytical model.
- Consolidation of actual, projected and derived data.
- Read and write environment to support "what-if" analysis.
- Fast Response Times.
- Ability to be deployed and adapted quickly.
- Ability to share and manage large volumes of data

Impact of D.S.S. Architecture

- Decision makers need answers to a host of questions.
- Ideal arch has a distinct purpose in delivery of data, can access normalized data marts.
- Should leverage metadata to facilitate application construction. Engine that inter prets data requests and generates SQL queries.

MDDs Performance

- Queries here cross all arrays, so they are similar in response time to full table scans in RDB.

Scalability

- MDDs can be easily scaled, by keeping underlying databases Bases intact.

OLAP Components

- Physical Data storage
- Data storage in MDD
- Relational OLAP Data storage.
- Storage Efficiency : Storage and efficiency
- Data Management : security
- MD Manipulation and Calculation.

Relational OLAP Solutions

- Generates SQL optimize for target database Base
- Provides a mechanism to describe the model through metadata.
- Has powerful SQL generator, capable of generating nested queries.
- Partition the application between clients, servers and middle tier.
- Capable of creating non-trivial ranking.

Important Relational/OLAP Characteristics:

- **Data Ware Housing :** and RD Bases are inseparable. Subsetting data ware housing into smaller pieces data marts is best suited for MDDs.
- **Rapidly changing dimensions :** On the fly dimensional view of a relational/OLAP can be changed.
- **Data rich application :** Large amounts of data and simple relationships are best covered by RD Bases
- **Development :** Is a difficult task and requires lots of learning.
- **Fat client/Thin client :** Means placing burden on the server, by keeping client thin.
- **Network Impact :** Closely related.

Relational OLAP

OLAP systems allow users to quickly manipulate operational data, and help in decision making process by performing "slice and dice" operation. To enable full-functioned business analysis, OLAP systems need to :

1. **Devise sophisticated analysis :** The key to performance of OLAP are the metrices in user-customizable format. These metrices are obtained from transactional Data Bases, precalculated or generated on demand.
2. **Scale to a large number of dimensions :** Users analyze data from a number of different perspectives or dimensions. A dimension is any element or hierar chical combination of elements that can be displayed in various forms.
3. **Support analysis against large atomic data sets :** Atomic data refers to the lowest level of data granularity required for effective decision making. OLAP systems should be such designed as they fulfill such requirement.

OLAP Concepts

Why required-as organisation, structures have became flatter and front-line managers have to make quick, intelligent decisions that significantly by impact business directions.

1. **Multidimensional View**
   - Much more relevant to decision making.
   - Decision makers at all levels can see the big picture of all applications.
   - Has information from all operational systems as well.
   - Ability to compare any part of business against any other and define new analysis.
   - As the number of analyses required are large and the time duration is short, the response times must be T, this is achieved here.
   - OLAP application requirements require more than just viewing history, but analysis are made on different levels of aggregation.
   - Decisions are made on comparisons and trends, so calculating % or ratios differences must be feasible.
   - OLAP makes D.W. Read and Access.
   - OLAP tools work with databases or D.W. to provide reliable, robust data for fast, flexible analysis of data.
   - OLAP application have query and response time characteristics.
   - OLAP provides the management, with the data, that is efficient for taking up decisions.

2. **First Generation Analysis Solutions :** These include Eis is solution and PC based drill down tools.
   - ***Eis solution*** : Executive information systems. It was designed to provide predefined analysis a very simple screen to encourage user acceptance.
   - ***PC based drill down tools*** : Here large relational data bases and conventional relational reporting and query tools are used directly.
3. **Second Generation Analysis Solution :**
   - To make OLAP successful it must be deployable throughout many layers of organization and should have the ability to scale as enterprise grows.

Third Generation

- Users need to use query tools, reporting and analysis techniques to make best use of OLAP. This gives users the autonomy and time-efficient way to perform data analysis.

MDD

- MDDs logically store the data in form of arrays.
- Unlike Relational model, MDDs, have no agreed upon MD model.
- MDDs have no standard access method (such as SQL) or APIs.

2 MD. Database Capabilities

1. **Cube :** Implies that each side is of equal length, which is rarely the case in real life.
2. **Hypercube :** This term describes a similar object of greater than 3D, with flat sides.
   - MDD. provide stunning query performance
   - Here indexes are stored and then used for getting the results.

   Disadvantage :
   - Minor changes require a complete reorganization of the data bases.
   - Difficult to understand, how to use these elements and creating a table to hold aggregates for all combinations is a difficult maintenance task.
3. When, some new information, is to be added to be fact table, building aggregates will become difficult.

The Right Aggregates

1. **Usage Patterns :** Which aggregates would most improve performance for specific queries run most often by end user.
2. **Data Density :** Where is data concentrated. If a given dimension element represents a large number, of rows, then aggregating by that dimension element improves performance.

   This analysis can turn more meaningful and complicated as dimensions combine. It is the range of data retrieved and also the density.

Simple Aggregation Sizing

Two factors are considered before aggregation operations are performed:

1. Total amount of space occupied.
2. Total number, of aggregate tables.

Data Partitioning

- Denormalization of DB design that repeatitively stores data in tables, minimizing number, of time consuming joins.
- **Summarization :** Technique for aggregating information in advance, eliminating need to do so at run time.
- **Partitioning :** The ability to divide a single large fact table into many smaller tables so as to improve response time of queries.

Aggregating the D.W.

The data in the main fact table, which is stored in most detailed form, is needed to be aggregated. Fact tables tend to be very large, resulting in serious performance challenges. Summing large data, takes lot of time. So we need to aggregate the data and store it for DSS.

Problems While Aggregating

1. Storing summary information at every possible level consumes enormous amount of disk space.
2. D.W. have thousands of Combinations of dimension overall structure and Planning process.
   - Extraction
   - Monitoring
   - Investigation : (*a*) At senior level, (*b*) At business analyst level.

Multidimensional vs. Relational Model

- Transactions view vs. Slice of Time.
- Internally vs. globally Consistent.
- Relations modeled implicity vs. explicitly

Local Consistency vs. Global Consistency

- Relational model has local consistency.
- M.D. model starts from a globally consistent view of enterprise.

Audit Trail vs. Big Picture

- Solves local problems.
- Enterprise related problems, solved here.

Explicit vs. Implied Relationships

In Relational model, relations exist implicitly, while in M.D. models relationships or implied by existence of facts.

Operational vs. Warehouse Data

Because of differences between various operational systems, the data captured must under go:

- Conditioning
- Validating mapping from source to target.

Operational	D.W.
• Current values	• Archival data,
• Application oriented	• Subject oriented
• Dynamic	• Static
• Complex	• Single
• Suitable for operational computation	• For business analysis.
• Access is high	• Low.
• Structured architecture	• unstructured.
• Response time 2–3 Sec	• Seconds to minutes.
• Plan	
• Source data	
• Scrub	

What is D.W Model ?

- This model describes the target data structures and their data relationships.
- Industry specific D.W model is derived directly form same-industry enterprise data model.
- The parent data structures are foundation for development of corresponding D.W. structure.

The D.W. Model for each industry has following characteristics

- Summarized data for decision support and analysis.
- Multiple levels of summarization.
- Integrated data from multiple sources.
- Oriented by business area, function or subject.
- Provides integrated information, across entire enterprise.
- Provides clean, reliable data to business area "data marts"

As data move from central D.W. to Local decision support systems, control of data is transferred to local administrators.

Goal of Data Model

- Convey the meaning of data.
- Relationships among data.
- Attributes of data.

The data model does not change greatly over time unless business organization changes fundamental business. The organization. within same industry tend to be very similar.

So, data models have basic stability and process models have basic stability while process models are relatively unstable.

Enterprise Data Model

EDM for each industry specific data environment represents all integrated primary data requirements of a typical organization, operating within that industry.

The subjects covered here are business subject area, business functional area and the dominent relationships between key data. This model is supported by data dictionary (metadata.)

Data Modeling

Done to manage large amounts of data.

Features:

- Modelling is not tied to any physical representation of data.
- Is not inseparable from MDD Bases.
- Does not involve squeezing information into cubes.

What is a Data Model ?

It is a graphic representation of the data within a specific area of interest. This area may be as broad as all integrated data requirements of enterprise or as focussed as a single business area.

Generally data model represents a business functional area or a business area that is to be analyzed.

Good Data Model describer :

- Entities
- Attributes
- Complete definition entities and attributes.
- Relationships among data.
- Primary, secondary or alternate keys.
- Large-format, clear graphics.

Metadata Repository

- Descriptions and structures of D Base are stored here.
- Details of all fields in D.W schemes, the field's origination; the operation data source used and what transformations the data go through are stored.

Benefits

- Provides a standard way of entering and representing metadata.
- Helps in better integration between different stages of D.W.

Tools for Designing Metadata Repository

- Intutive interface.
- Transparent access to data.
- Support for a catalog of information.
- Multiple queries and analysis methods.
- Multiple presentation styles for information.

Technology Issues

- Hardware
- DBase
- Middleware—gluts DBases together.
- End user Tools—include DSS tools, neutral net's, mining tools, warehouse management, tools-organize, reorganize data, form new views etc.
- Services—Providing the end user systems with complete results.

Decision Support Tools

- Use every conceivable type of query and investigation.
- Spreadsheets and preferred query and reporting tools should be used.

Middleware

The effective technologies should be selected to provide flexibility for strategic changes

D Base

- Relational D-Bases., MD-D Bases
- Transactional processing on established D Bases also help in rapid response time.

Parallel H/W

Modest systems with parallel processing lan activate productivity of a D.W.

- The precalculated results.
- The indening structured required to access data quickly.
- Metadata describes and manages physical data structures.

Helps in

- Mapping MD structures to relational tables.
- Determining nearest stored results, tables that are having data
- Helps in records to dimensions mapping.

Applications

- Managing data extract.
- Warehouse data discovery, by using metadata, to describe D.W structure and contents.
- Making data available to D.W based on data extract scheduling.
- Data synchronization by tracking the imported data and using rules on that data.
- Measuring and reporting on the quality of data imported into warehouse.

Metadata

- It is the information required to make scientific data useful.
- It is the term used to describe the definition of data that is stored in D.W.
- It describes the conceptual or logical data structures of all objects/entites with the database.
- Metadata is the additional data that is invoked to implement change in content.

Importance :

- Provides a catalog of data in D.W and pointers to this data.
- Data extraction/transformation history.
- Column aliases.
- D.W. table sizes.
- Data usage statistics

In a well designed architecture, metadata has :

- Dimension, attribute, metric definitions.
- Attribute hierarchies – mapping of parent/child relationships among attributes.

- Attribute to Dimension Mapping
- Metric to attribute mapping indicates which metric quality attribute.
- Performance metrices : explains rows in table and indexes existing on the table.
- Distinct elements per attribute: need of the knowledge of available elements within attribute to formulate queries is fulfilled here.

Role of Metadata

Describe different aspects of applications:

- Hierarchical relationships
- Stored formulae
- Currency conversions
- Time series information
- Item description.

Operational Environment

- Same level of importance as documentation and is optional, while in D.W. is important.
- O.S. used by computer literates, while D.W by computer illiterates.
- Transformations from operational to D.W. environments.
- Track of changing structures

External and Unstructured Data Environments

- Metadata takes entirely different dimensions in storing and managing external and unstructured data.
- Through metadata external data is registered, accessed and controlled in D.W environment.

Contents of Metadata for External Data

- Document Identification.
- Source of document.
- Description of document.
- Classification of document.
- Data of entry into warehouse.
- Document length.
- References for Location of external used/unstructured data.

Components of Metadata

Several components of stored data are :

1. **The data characteristics**
   - — Data Format
   - — When the data is acquired and Compiled.
   - — Who Compiled it
   - — Method of compilation and accuracy
   - — Interpretation of data items.
   - — Where data is available.

2. **Incremental DBase Refresh**
   — Should allow updates to any subset of D Base with out restricting access to unaffected parts.
3. **Multiple Array Support :** MD D Bases do not support the creation of multiple, related MD arrays within a single D Base structure.
4. **D Base Joins :** MD Dbases do not support the logical joining of multiple multidimensional arrays. This limits query flexibility by eliminating possibility of dynamic data access by users.
5. **Subset Selection :** Allows for subset selection, by limiting the amount of data for analysis.
6. **Local Data Support :** Should support local storage and data manipulation, enabling users to select subsets of data for local processing.
7. **SQL Interface :** Do not support SQL interfaces, have their own APIs for data access.

DSS Topologies

Requirements :

- These have moved from trapping the data and making lists to performing complex analysis.
- These help in producing competitively useful information.

One-Tier Stand Alone

- PCs or PC like devices connected to a central server, are used here for OLAP analysis.
- The client and server are on the same processor.

Two-Tier Architecture

- Involves a client and a server.
- The client interfaces with user and plays role of a requester, while server has all data and software to run queries.
- This isolates non-technical users from SQL code generation.
- The SQL code is written by developers and embedded under Give or executed as stored procedures.
- Limitation that decision makers lack the ability to use large amount of data and use it accordingly.

Three-Tier Architecture

- Addresses performance, reliability, resource management by moving complex applied, logic to a **decision support server**, independent of D-Bases and PCs.
- The server provides efficient data access, accelerated response; scheduled background processing.
- Maintenance is simplified as complex applied logic is centralized on the server.
- Here the client is dedicated to presentation logic.
- The database server is dedicated to data services and file services.
- The middle layer is application server on which business logic exists.

Considerations while Developing Three Tired Systems

- Consistency of the data should be maintained.
- Each function should define its own business rule; which is used with applied serve.
- GOI should be separate from applied Logic so, that when logic is changed, the front end remains intact.

Multidimensional D Bases

- Here data can be stored relationally and still be viewed multi dimensionally.

Challenges :

1. **Dbase Management Tools :** MD Bases need to have management. tools that have following abilities:
   — Ensure D Base integrity.
   — Provides user security at multiple levels.
   — Tune D Bases for optimum performance.
2. Support for drill down to atomic level detail
   — enables to access row-level detail and relational details for decision support systems.

D.W. Architectural Model

This model is a way of representing the overall structure of data, communication, processing and presentation that exists for end user computing within the enterprise.

Layers

- Extensible DB, Layer/Operation D.B Layer
- Information Access Layer
  1. With this layer the end user deals directly.
  2. It represents the tools that end user normally uses day to day. eg. Excel, Access, V.B.
  3. This layer includes the h/w and s/w involved in displaying and printing, reports, graph, charts for analysis and presentation.
- Data Access Layer
  1. It enables the information access layer to communicate with the operational layer.
  2. The mostly commonly used language today for this layer is SQL.
  3. For this layer there is growth of data-access filters such as EDA/SQL that enables us to access all DBMS and data file systems, relation or non relational.
  4. It also spans manufactures and network protocols.

  One of the key to D.W. strategy is to provide users with "universal data access".

Data Directory (Metadata) Layer

Here variety of metadata is available : *i.e.,* data about the end user views of data about the operational databases.

e.g., CREATE statement in SQL.

- **Process Management Layer**
  1. Helps in scheduling various tasks that are must to be accomplished to build maintain the D.W.

     e.g., updating data, adding new records.
- **Application Messaging Layer**
  1. Involved in transporting information around the enterprise compiling networking.
  2. Referred to an middle ware, but can involve more than just net working protocols.
  3. Used to deliver messages called transactions and deliver them to certain location.
- **D.W. (Physical layer)**
  1. A D.W. is where the actual data used primarily for informational user occurs.
  2. We can also think of it as a virtual or logical view.
  3. Many copies of operational and or external data are stored in form that is easy to access.
- **Data Staging Layer**
  1. It include all processes necessary to select, edit, summarize, combine and load data. Warehouse and information access data from operational and on or external D Bases.
  2. Involves complex programming. It may also include data quality analysis programs and filters that identify patterns.

Implementation Options

1. **Rechosing mainframe application :** It means taking inisting application. and moving them to microprocessor based servers. The servers may run under UNIX, Windows NT.
2. **1 tier architecture :** The D.W., DSS engine and DSS client all reside on same G/W platform
3. **2 tier architecture :** Here the SQL is hidden beneath GUI, or executed as stored procedures.
4. **3 tier architecture :** Here the D.S.S is at the server.
5. **4 tier architecture**

Justification for a D.W.

- Single repository makes sense if volumes of data is available.
- The data is to be integrated from multiple sources and single is to be used.

Factors Affecting a D.W.

1. **Business Factors :** The following business factors are considered.
   (*a*) ***Business objectives :*** Affect the location, frequency of use and maintenance of D.W.
   (*b*) ***Location of current data :*** Where is the data, what its characteristics are.
   (*c*) ***Need to move data :***
   - Quality of existing data.
   - Size of usable data.
   - Performance Impact of a direct query.

(*d*) ***Movement of data :*** Types of tools to be used, the form in which it can be stored.

(*e*) ***Location to which data is to be moved :*** In a single computer host band/ Server LAN.

(*f*) ***D.S.S. requirements***

(*g*) ***Data preparation:***

- Refresh the data.
- Encoding of data.
- Coordinate transactions and master files.

(*h*) ***Query and reporting requirements:***

- Types of query tools available and deployable.

(*i*) ***Integration of data model:*** Various models of data for use in a D.W are combined and used thereafter.

(*j*) ***Management and administration:***

- Policies to manage and maintain the D.W. are built. *e.g.*, Refreshing the current data, removing historical data.

Types of D.W.

1. **Host Based D.W.**
   - These are DWs that reside on a high volume data bases.
   - Have Complex source systems.
   - Require constant maintenance.

   To make it more efficient, we require to follow the under mentioned steps ·
   - Select and clean the operational data.
   - Translate the data to appropriate form and defining rules.
   - Moving data directly into DB2 tables by following refinement rules.

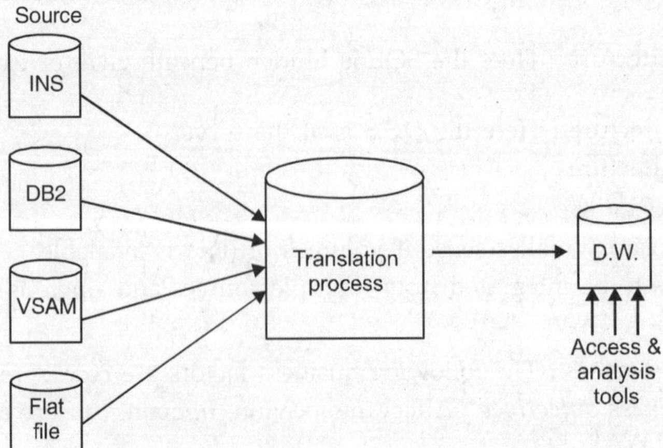

Fig. 14.1. *Host based data warehouse*

2. **LAN Based Single Stage Ware house**
   - Supports data from many sources.
   - Requires minimal initial investment.

- Minimal technical know-how.
- Supports single metadata store and
- Supports existing DSS applications.
- Provides business users with a complete data to information solution.
- Designed, using a common data repository called data mart.

Challenger

- Limited by DBMS and h/w scalability factors.
- Do not have adequate recovery management, organized maintenance and perfomance monitoring procedures.

3. **LAN Based Work Group Data Warehouses**
   - It is an integrated architecture for building and maintaining a D.W in a LAN environment.
   - Ideal for any business organization. that wishes to build a DW, often called a data mart.
   - Minimal investment, know-how.
   - Low startup cost and ease of use.
   - As needs of work group grow, this warehouse can grow or integrate with a larger, more centralized warehouse.

   Data Delivery—Transparent access to the data in the D.W. Data is transformed into meaningful terms on requirements.

   Metadata—Helps us to track where your decision-support data comes from and understand what it means at the source.

   Administrative Tool—Basically used for internal business processes, enables business users to find metadata to better understand the aggregation, sources for data in warehouse.

4. **Multistage D.W.**
   - Suits environment, where end users require access to both summarized, cumulative data for long term decisions and summarized data for up-to-minute tactical decisions.
   - Both ODS and D.W. may reside on host-based or LAN based databases.
   - Tactical decisions are based on data present and in ODS and strategic decisions on historical trends present in D.W.

   Challenges :

   - Must maintain data once loaded.
   - Require frequent updates to ODS.
   - More volumes of storage and activity.
   - More skilled personnel and technology.

5. **Stationary D.W.**
   - Here data is not moved from the sources. Instead users are given direct access to the data.

   Features

   - Require highly specialized and sophisticated "middleware".
   - Facility to display the extracted data for the user.

Challenges

- Identifying the location of data for users.
- Ability to query different DBMS as if they were all a single DBMS with a single API.
- Impacts performance, since users compete with production data stores.

6. **Distributed D.W.**
   - There are two types of D.D.W. and there are variations of their types for different organizations:
     (*a*) Local D.W. (*b*) Global D.W.
   - Sense to make DDW if there are diverse businesses under the same enterprise umbrella.

   Features :

   - Activity occurs at local level.
   - Local site is autonomous.
   - The data is unique and is of prime importance to that locality only.
   - Local sites serve different geographic regions.
   - Majority of data is local and not replicated,
   - Majority of operational processing is done at the local site.

Virtual D.W.

- Here the virtual view of databases is created, allowing the creation of a virtual warehouse.
- There is logical description of all databases and their structures and individual did not had any knowledge about them.

For this we define four kinds of information.

1. **Data Dictionary**—contain various data bases, their structures and the information present in them.
2. Description of the Relationship among the data elements.
3. Description of way user interfaces with system.
4. Business Rules and algorithms.

So here the data sources can be local or remote. The data is not moved from the sources, instead the users are given direct access to the data. This access may be through simple SQL queries, complex SQL queries. Virtual warehouse enables users to develop a virtual, enterprise-wide relational database. Middleware access s/w can provide a single database image of all the available data.

Benefits

- No replication of data in the physical DW databases.
- Drawbacks
- Queries compete with the production data transactions, so performance is degraded.
- Here no metadata, summarized data is available, so queries are replicated to the databases.
- No cleansing or refreshing process.

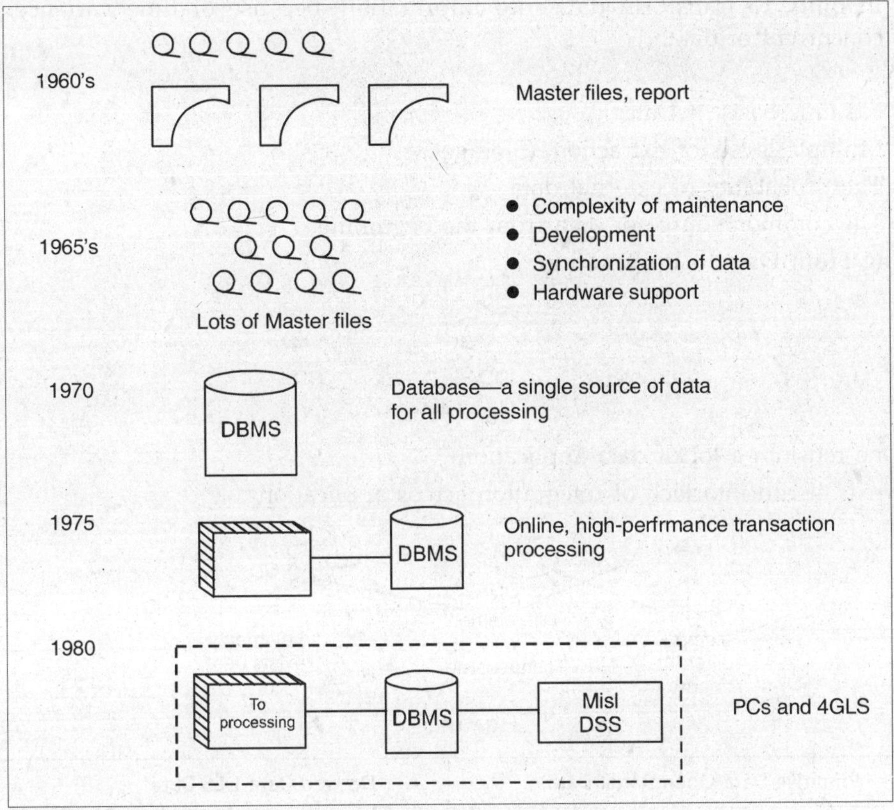

Fig. 14.2. *D.W. and D.M.*

The single database serving all purpose.

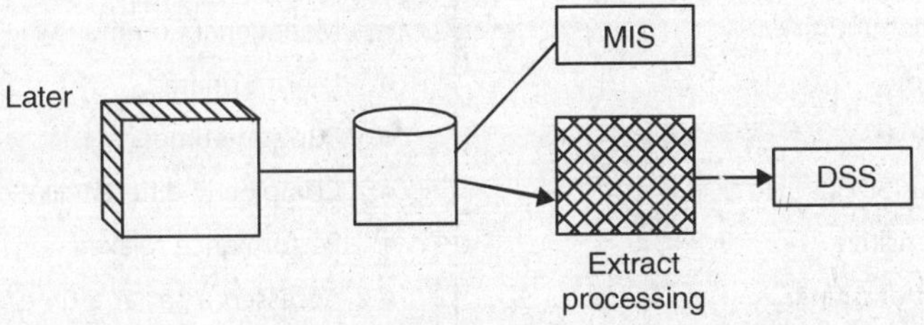

Fig. 14.3

Extract Processing

- start with some parameters, search a file based on the parameters, then pull the data else where.

Why Extract Processing

- Performance
- Control

E.P lead to SPIDER WEB of information that is a naturally evolving architecture

Challenges for SPIDER WEB

(*a*) Data creadibility

(*b*) Productivity by duplication

(*c*) Inability to transform data into information, because of time variance, less concurrent of data.

Why?

(*a*) No time basis of Data.

(*b*) Multiple levels of extraction. (Storage).

(*c*) The probability of external data.

(*d*) The common source of data from the beginning.

Going From Data to Information

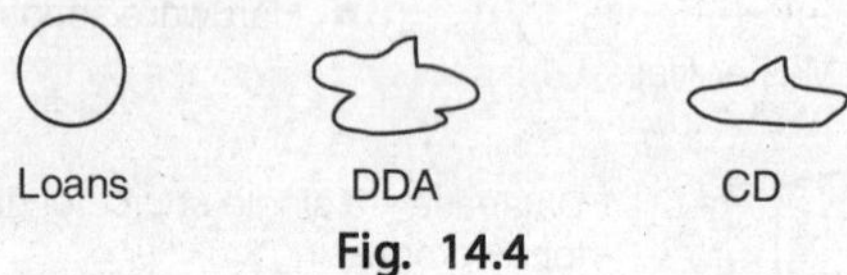

Fig. 14.4

- One rensinto a lot of data application
- Next 'u' run into lack of integration across applications.

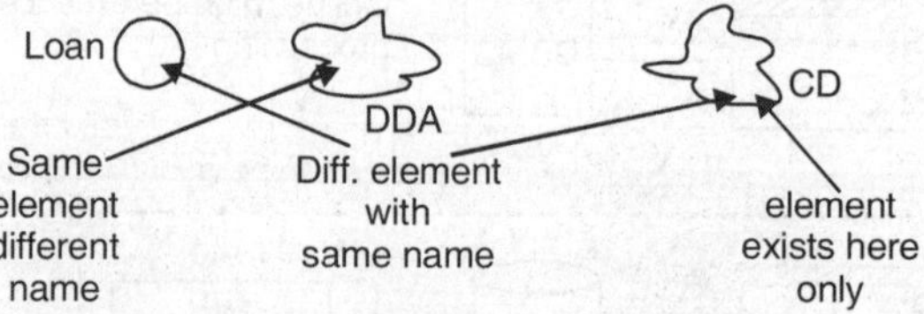

Fig. 14.5

Primitive Data/Operational Data	Derived Data/DSS Data
• Applications oriented	• Subject oriented
• Detailed	• Summarized
• Accurate, at moment of access	• Represents values over time.
• Server clerical community	• Managerial Community
• Can be updated	• Is not updated.
• Run repetitively	• Run sometimes.
• Compatible with SDLC.	• Completely different like cycle
• Performance sensitive	• Performance relaxed.
• Accessed a unit at a time.	• Accessed a set at a time.
• Transaction driven	• Analysis driven.
• High availability	• Relaxed availability.
• Managed in its entirety	• Managed by subsets.
• Non redundant.	• Redundancy is a fact.
• Static structure-variable content	• Flexible structure
• Small amount of data used in a process	• Large amount of data used in a process.
• Supports day -to-day operations.	• Support managerial needs.
• High probability of access.	• Low probability of access.

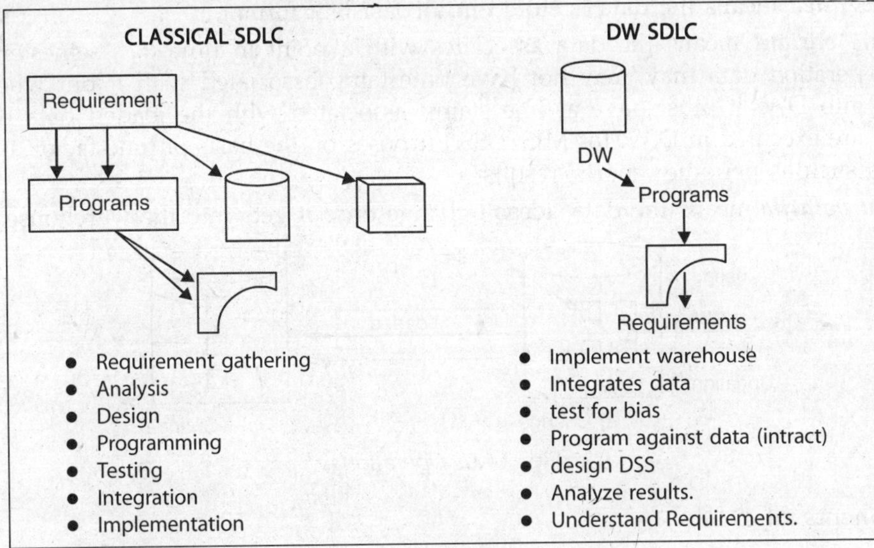

Fig. 14.6

The Data Warehousing Environment

"A data warehouse is a subject oriented integrated, time variant and non volatile collection of data in support of managements decision making process.

The D.W. contains granular corporate data.

Subject Oriented : Means the DW focusses on the high level entities of the business.

SUBJECT ORIENTATION OF DATA : Subject oriented means D.W. focusses on the high level entities of the business. This is in contrast to operational systems, which deal with processes low level entities.

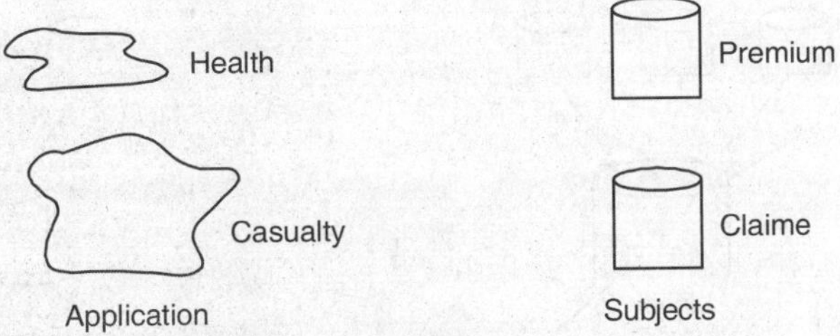

Fig. 14.7

INTEGRATION : Here data is read from multiple disparate sources into D.W. As data is fed, it is converted reformatted, resequenced, summarized and so forth.

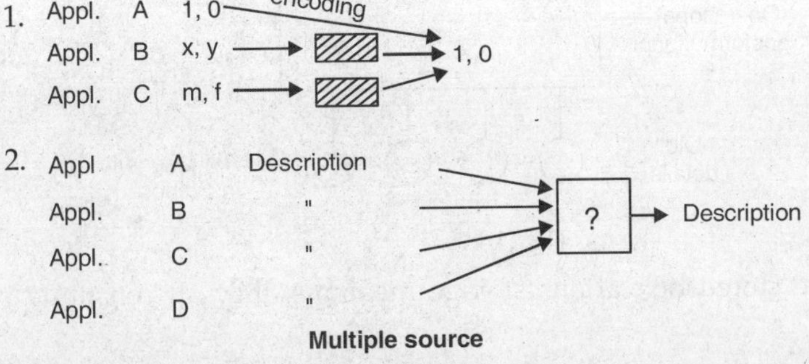

Integrated means the data is stored in a consistent format.

Time variant means the data associates with a point in time (*i.e.,* semester, fiscal year). operation data may/may not have timestamp associated with it but when it is loaded into DW, it must have a time stamp associated with the loaded data because queries are executed in D.W. for MIS/DSS purposes on the basis of time factor as major concern such as periodic reports/results.

Non volatile means the data doesn't change once it gets into the warehouse.

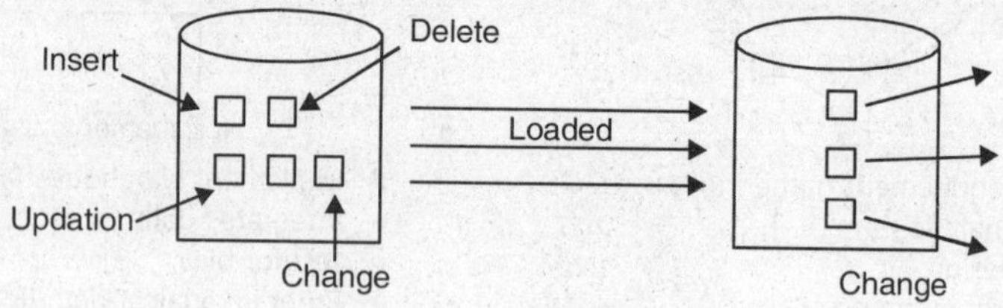

Fig. 14.8. *Operational*

Components of D.W.

The D.W is a new way to look at enterprise computing at the strategic/architectural level.

1. **DATAMART :** This is a subset of enterprise wide data warehouse. Performs the role of departmental, functional D.W.
2. **Logical D.W. :** Contains all the metadata, business rules and processing logic required to organize, package, and preprocess the data. Also it contains the information required to find and access the actual data, wherever it resides.
3. **Giant physical D.B in the sky :** This is the actual physical D.B. into which all the data for D.W is gathered, along with the metadata and the processing logic to organize, package and preprocess the data for enduser access.

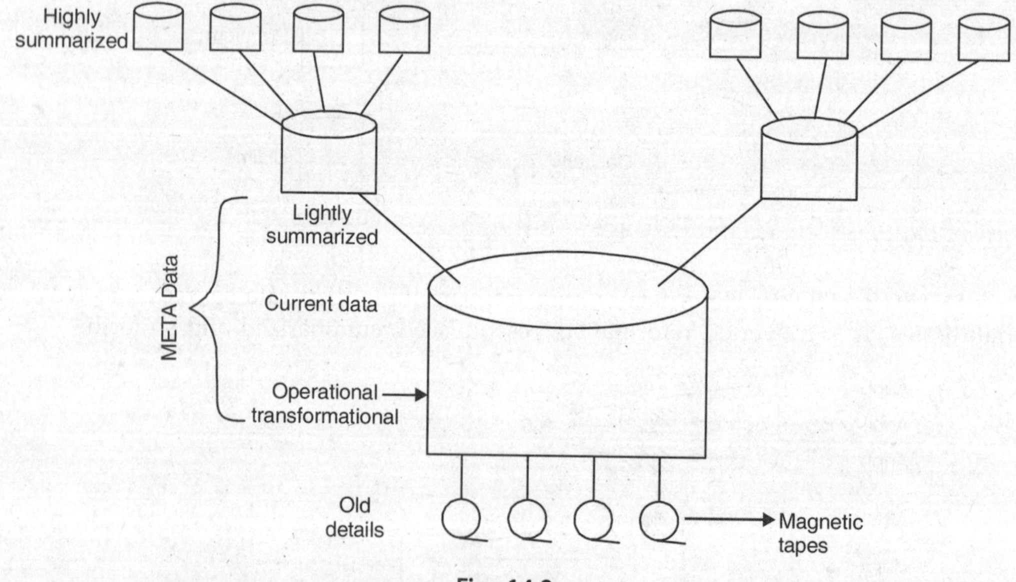

Fig. 14.9

Though details are stored on various storage mediums, they all constitute part of D.W.

SCOPE

1. DW can provide a central repository for large amounts of diverse and valuable information. They provide an excellent source for the information needed to build data marts which contain summaries and tables used to support OLAP.
2. It helps us to make insightful decisions with the use of appropriate tools to extract specific data, convert it into business information.
3. There are intelligent S/W agents which deliver not only summary information but also provide the drill-down, drill through of the information, to other decision support tools. These tools help to collect, organise, and extract current and useful information, to convert information, to insight.

Why D.W.

Operational D.B.s	D.W.
• It is designed and tuned from known tasks and work Loads, such as indening and hashing using primary keys, searching for particular records, and optimizing "canned" queries. data org., access, and implementation views.	• Here queries are quite complex. They involve the computation of large amounts of data at summarized level, and may require the use of special methods based on multidimensional.
• Supports the concurrent processing of multiple transactions, concurrency and control and recovery mechanisms, such as Locking and logging, are required to ensure the conistency and robustness of transactions.	• An OLAP query often needs read-only access of data records for summarization and aggregation. Concurrently control and recovery mechanisms, if applied for such OLAP operations, may jeopardise the execution of concurrent transactions, and they substantially reduce the throughput of an OLAP system.
• Do not maintain historical data.	• Typically maintain historical data.
• Operational DBs contain only detailed raw data, such as transactions, which need to be consolidated before analysis.	• This requires consolidation (such as aggregation and summarization) of data from heteogenous sources, resulting in high quality, clean integrated data.
• Here data is at different levels of interaction.	• Here everyone is using the same data at the same level of extraction, which eliminate after conflicting analytical results and arguments over the source.

Benefits of a D.W.

1. Improved product inventory turns.
2. Decreased costs of product information, introduction with improved selection of target markets.
3. Determination of the effectiveness of marketing programs, allowing elimination of weaker programs.
4. Helps in managing volumes of data.

Need for D.W.

- The operational systems have less of on-line historical data.

- The data here required for analysis resides in different operational systems.
- The query performance is extremely poor which in turn impacts performance of operational systems.
- The operational DBMS designs are inadequate for decision support.

Structure of a D.W.

1. **Current Data :** This data
   - Reflectss the most recent happening.
   - Voluminous as stored at low level of granularity.
   - Almost always stored on disk storage, which is fast to access.
2. **Older Data :** Features
   - Infrequently accessed.
   - Stored at a high level of detail .
   - Usually stored on removable storage medium.
3. **Summarized Data :** It is of two types :

   (*a*) ***Lightly summarized data :*** Is the data that is distilled from the current detailed level. This level of D.W is almost always stored on disk storage.

   (*b*) ***Highly summarized data :*** Is compact and easily accessible. This is found in the D.W. environment.
4. **Metadata :** This is the data about data.
   - It sits in a different dimension than other data warehouse data.
   - It contains no data directly taken from the operational environment.

Roles

- Acts as a directory that helps in locating the contents of D.W.
- Guide to mapping of data, as data is transformed from operational environment. to D.W. environment.
- Guide to alongwith used for summarization b/w current data and summarized data.
- Data interaction and transformation history.
- Data usage stastics.
- D.W. table sizes.

Functions of D.W.

Access	Transform	Distribute	Store	Find	Display and Analyze
Operational and ent. data	• Cleanse • Enhance • summarize	• Join Multiple • Populate on demand	• Reldata • Multiple platforms	• Business views and models	• Curry and Reporting • Reporting • Data miming

Flow →

1. **Data flow within the D.W.**

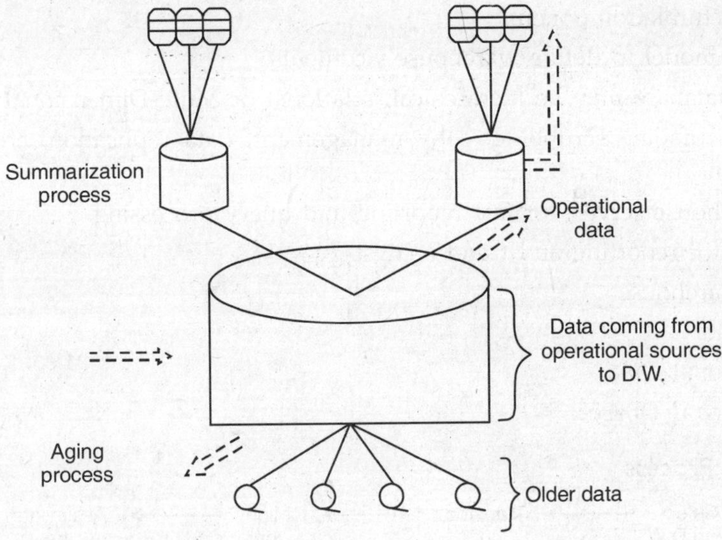

Fig. 14.10

2. **Usage :** The difference of data within the D.W receive difference levels of usage. The high level of summarization, the more the data is used.

Benefits of summarized data :

- Quicker and efficient to get to the data.
- Good Response time achieved.

Building Considerations for a D.W.

1. **Indexing :** Data at higher level of summarization can be freely indexed, so keep data at a summarized level.
    - Data at higher levels of summarization can be restructured easily.
2. **Partitioning :** Can be done in two ways :
    - ***DBMS level :*** DBMS is aware of the partitions and manages them accordingly.
    - ***Application level :*** Only the application programmer is aware of partitions and responsibility for the management, of partitions is left up to the programmer.

Why a D.W Architecture

- Data/Information, Access
- Data Access Factors
- No single view of data.
- Different user tools.
- Lock of useful Historical Capability
- Conflict b/w Application types.
  (different designs, data requirements).

- Porferation of Complex extract application.
- Architectural Components
- A data model to define warehouse's contents.
- DW's database may be hierarchical, relational or Multi-Dimensional
- Utilities of data scrubbing, copy management, data replication, cross platform common.
- A warehouse server, for fast reporting and query processing.
- A DSS for reporting and trend analysis.
- Data warehouse
- MetaData
- Operational Data
- Operational DBases.

Data Mining Process

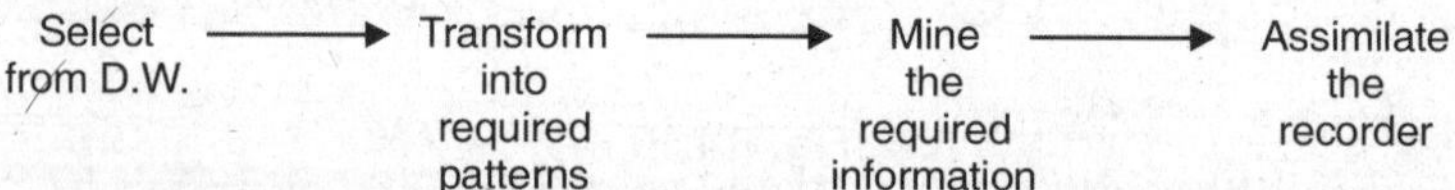

Enabling Components

1. Middleware
2. Data Source
3. Network

Data Mining Platforms

1. Massively Parallel Processing systems.
2. Symmetric Multiprocessing Systems.

Data Mining Tools

1. Improved hardware cost/ performance ratio.
2. Improved performance in parallel technology.
3. More flexible and initiative query software.
4. Greatly advanced middleware connectivity.

Real Time Data—Operational data, detailed records, history is not preserved, reluctant.

Reconciled Data—Contains detailed records from real time level, which is cleaned, adjusted or enhanced.

Derived Data—Here detailed are present in a summarized form. Low resource requirements and high application response time. It is summarized, averaged or aggregated from multiple sources of real time or reconciled data.

Changed Data—Contains a record of all change (adds, deletes and updates) to selected real time data. This data is time—stamped to document when change are made.

Meta Data—It is the data about data. Usually found in DD, DBase cataloge, programs, copy libraries.

Maintains Data : of

- How it was derived.
- What legacy environment this initially resided in.
- What alteration it went through.

Architecture of a typical D.M. System

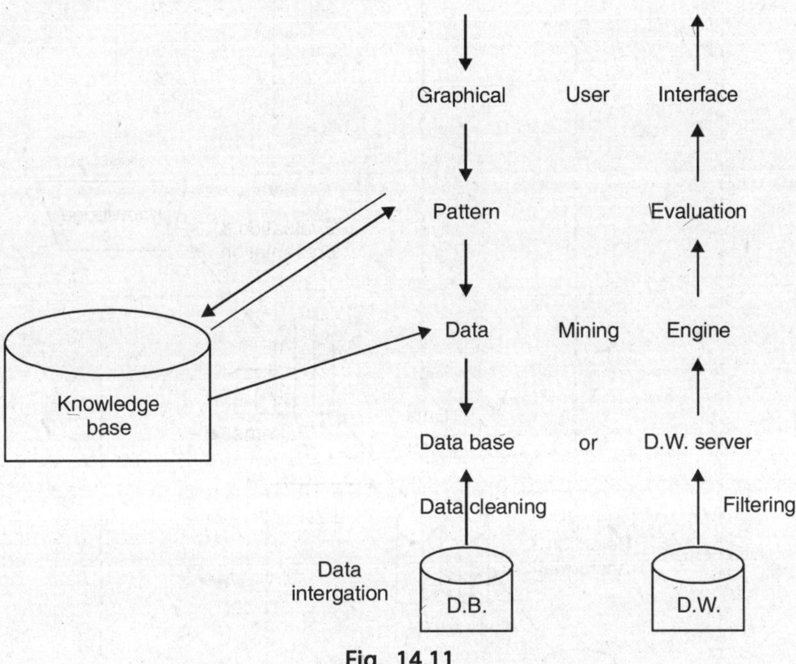

Fig. 14.11

Data Mining as a Confluence of Multiple Disciplines

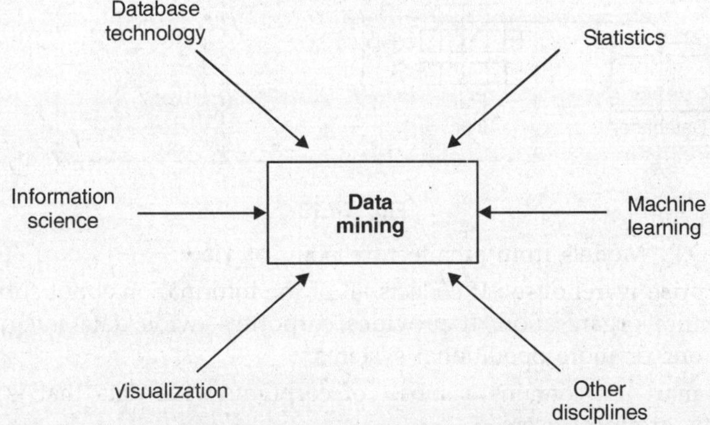

Fig. 14.12

Data Mining as a step in the process of Knowledge Discovery.

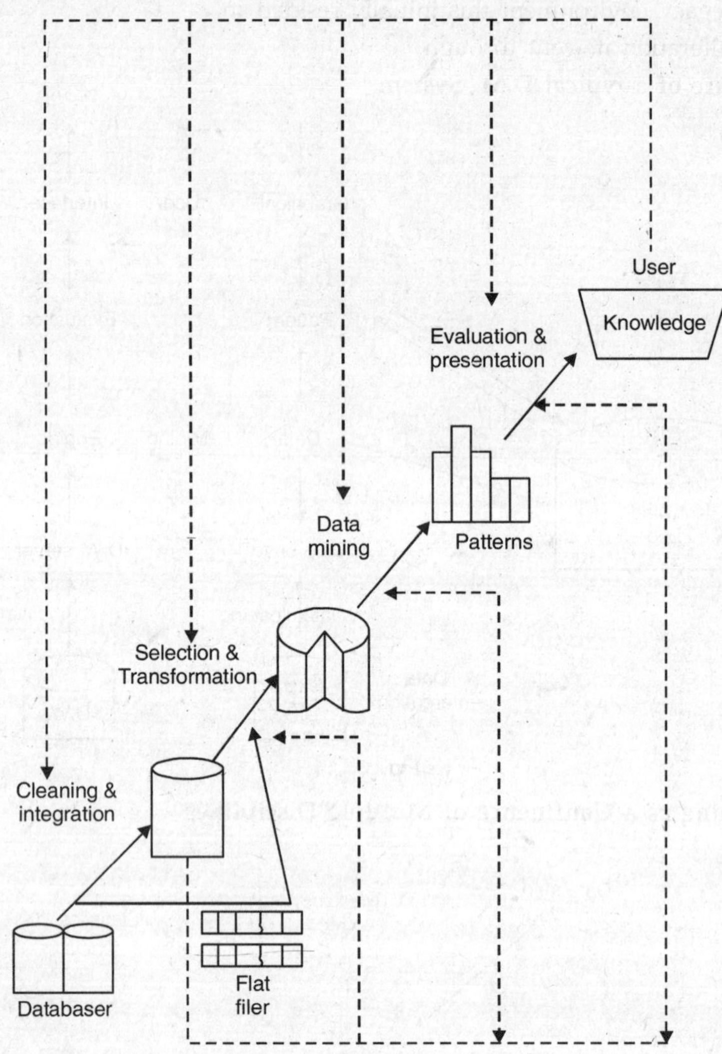

Fig. 14.13

Types of D.W Models from architecture point of view.

1. **Enterprise warehouse :** It collects all of the information about subjects spanning the entire organisation. It provides corporte – wide data integration, usually from one or more operational systems.
2. **Data mart :** It contains a subset of corporate-wide data that is of value to a specific group of users.
3. **Virtual warehouse :** It is a set of views over operational database. It is easy to build.

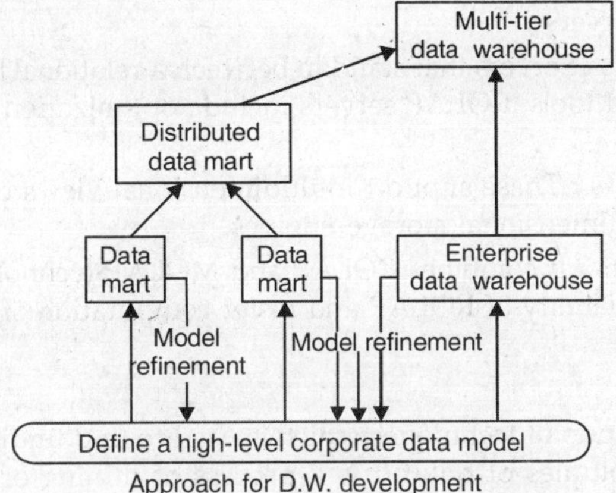

Multi-tier data warehouse
Distributed data mart
Data mart
Data mart
Enterprise data warehouse
Model refinement
Model refinement
Define a high-level corporate data model
Approach for D.W. development

Fig. 14.14

A 3 tier D.W Architecture

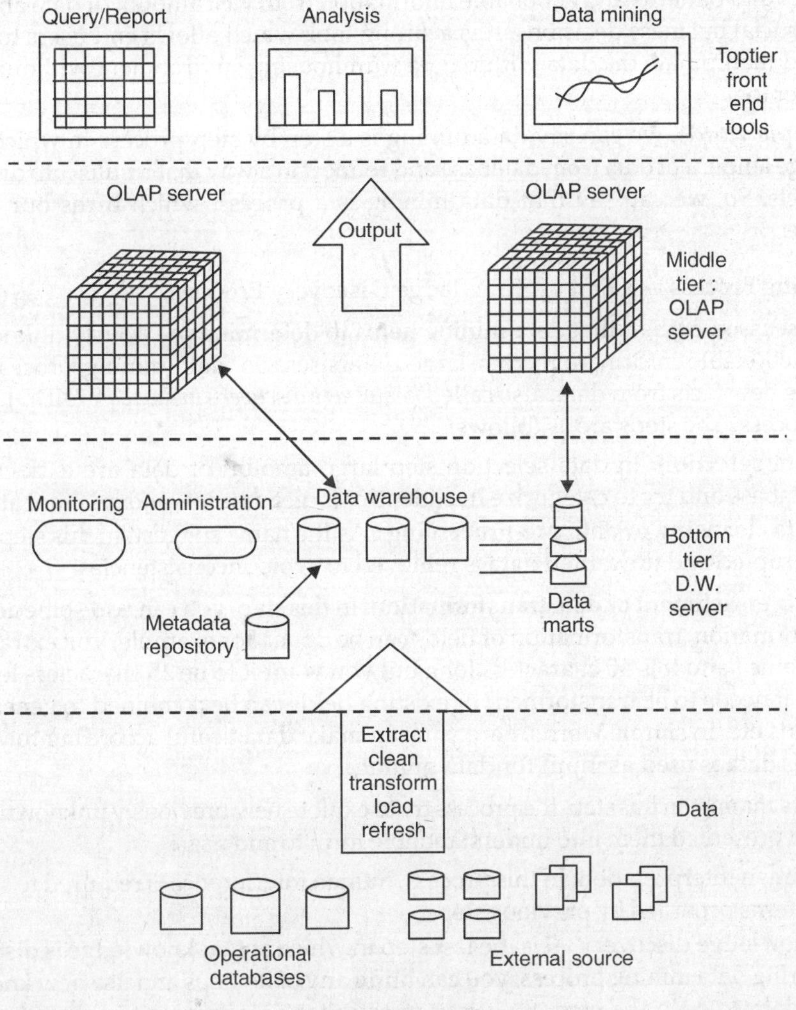

Query/Report
Analysis
Data mining
Toptier front end tools
OLAP server
Output
OLAP server
Middle tier : OLAP server
Monitoring
Administration
Data warehouse
Bottom tier D.W. server
Data marts
Metadata repository
Extract clean transform load refresh
Data
Operational databases
External source

Fig. 14.15

Types of OLAP servers :

1. **ROLAP servers :** Servers that stand in between a relational back - end server and clinet front end tools. ROLAP servers include optimization for each DBMS back end.
2. **MOLAP servers :** These support multidimensional views of data through array – based multidimensional storage engines.
3. **HOLAP servers :** It combines ROLAP and MOLAP technology; benefiting from the greater scalability of ROLAP and faster computation of MOLAP.

Data Mining

Data mining is a collection of techniques,which is used to find undiscovered patterns by manipulating large volumes of data. It is a process of mining or discovering of new information. It is used in conjunction of **data warehousing** to help in certain types of decisions. It is applied to operational database with individual transactions.

Data mining involves the use of sophisticated data analysis tools to discover previously unknown, valid patterns and actionable information from vast amount of data and using it to make crucial business decisions. It is a strong tool, which allows end users to directly) access, and manipulate the data within data warehousing environment without the need of any other tool.

In simple words, we can say data mining is a step by step process in which first we extract large amount of data from database and refine it in a way that results into discovering of new facts. So, we can say that data mining is a process, which turns our data into knowledge.

Data Mining Process as a Part of Knowledge Discovery Process

As discussed earlier, that data mining helps to determine previously unknown data patterns, actionable information from large databases. So, data mining process help in discovering new facts from data, also called *knowledge discovery in database* (KDD). KDD is a six step process. The steps are as follows:

(i) **Data selection:** In data selection step large amount of data are extracted from database and try to categorize it to identify target datasets and relevant attributes.

(ii) **Data cleansing or data pre-processing :** As the name suggest, in this step, all the corrupted and unwanted data is removed to avoid inconsistencies.

(iii) **Data enrichment or data transformation:** In this step, you can add some additional information, transformation of fields can be done (For example, you extract a field "Name" and it is 40 characters long but you want it to be 25 characters long only. So, it needs to be transformed) or existing fields can be combined to generate new fields etc. In simple words, here you can make data useful according to your use. This data is used as input for data mining.

(iv) Data mining: In this step, the process try to explore new previously unknown patterns and presented them into understandable form to end user.

(v) Human interpretation: In this process, human interference is required to study the patterns provided by previous step.

(vi) Knowledge discovery : It is the last step in which actual knowledge is discovered. During data mining process, you can **undo** any of its steps and use new knowledge or data to redo the step. So, you can say that data mining process also true to optimize the data processing. Data mining process is shown in Figure 13.2.

Goals of Data Mining

Goals of data mining falls into the following classes :

(i) **Prediction:** Data mining helps in prediction of behaviour of certain data attributes in the future. It is very helpful in complex data scenarios. Take the example of sales department, in which by analyzing buying transactions they can predict the behaviour and buying capacity of customers. By analyzing and prediction they can categorize their sales activity according to area, needs of customer, life standard of customers etc., to enhance the sales. In a scientific context, certain seismic wave patterns may predict an earthquake with high probability.

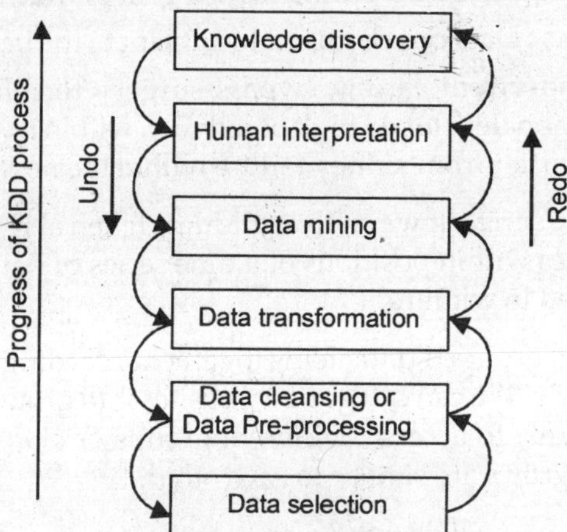

Fig. 14.16. *Data mining process (KDD)*

(ii) **Identification:** One major goal of data mining is to identify the existence of an item, an event, or an activity on the bases of analysis made on different data patterns. For example, scientists are trying to identify the life on Mars by analyzing different soil patterns. Authentication is also a form of identification.

(iii) **Classification:** Data mining is helpful in classifying the data into different categories on the basis of certain parameters. For example, in a company HR department can grade their employees on the basis of their performance parameters like their technical knowledge, functional knowledge, discipline etc.

(iv) **Optimization:** Last and the most important goal of data mining is to optimize the use of limited resources like time, cost, space, manpower and machine power in such a way that it will make a boom in output such as profits, increase in sales, cutting in expenditure etc.

Elements of Data Mining

Data mining consists of five major elements :

1. Extract, transform, and load transaction data on to the data warehouse system.
2. Store and manage the data in a multi-dimensional database system.
3. Provide data access to business analysts and information technology.
4. Analyze the data by application software.
5. Present the data in a useful format, such as graphs or tables.

Types of Knowledge Discovered during Data Mining

Data mining process results into discovery of new knowledge. The discovered knowledge can be categorized into different forms as given below :

(i) **Association rules :** Data can be mined to find relations or associations. Association rules correlate the presence of a set of items with another range of values for another set of variables **Ex.** *(a)* If a customer buys a shirt he or she also buy a matching, trouser. *(b)* If a customer buys a PC, he may also buy some CD's.

(ii) **Classification hierarchies:** The classification process is used to create different hierarchy of classes on the basis of existing set of events or transactions. **Ex.** *(a)* Customers may be divided into several ranges of credit worthiness based on the history of previous credit transactions. *(b)* Stocks may be given priority in stock market on the basis of their past performance such as growth, income, and stability. *(c)* Employees can be graded according to their past performance.

(iii) **Sequential patterns :** Data can be mixed to anticipate the behaviour of patterns.

Ex. If a patient underwent cardiac bypass surgery for blocked arteries and an aneurysm and later on developed high blood urea within a year of surgery then the patient is likely to suffer from kidney failure within the next 17 months.

(iv) **Pattern within time series:** If we analyze the data taken at regular intervals then we may find similarities within positions of a time series of data. **Ex.** Sales of woollen clothes are increased in winter.

(v) **Clustering :** We can grouped data items together according to logical relationship known as clusters. *Ex.* We can categorize websites into groups from "most likely to access" to "least likely to access". Different groups or clusters are dissimilar and records within the group are similar to each other.

Models of Data Mining

The three proposed models of data mining are as follows :

1. **CRISP (Cross-Industry Standard Process for Data mining) :** It was proposed in the mid 1990's by European consortium of companies to serve as a non-proprietary standard process model for data mining. The sequence of steps of data mining in this model is shown in Figure 14.17.

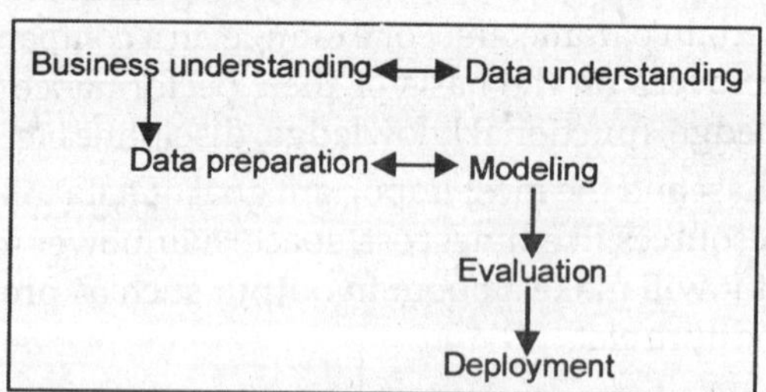

Fig. 14.17. *CRESP*

2. **Six sigma methodology :** It is a well-structured, data-driven methodology for eliminating defects, waste, quality control problem of all kinds of business activities. The sequence of steps of data mining in this model is shown in Figure 14.4.

Define ⟶ Measure ⟶ Analyze ⟶ Improve ⟶ Control

3. **SEMMA :** It is somewhat similar to six-sigma methodology. It was proposed by SAS institute. The sequence of steps of data mining in this model is shown in Figure 13.5. It focuses more on technical activities, involved in data mining.

Sample ⟶ Explore ⟶ Modify ⟶ Model ⟶ Assess

Techniques used in Data Mining

The most commonly used data mining techniques are as follows :

1. **Genetic algorithms :** Optimization techniques that use processes such as genetic mutation, combination and natural selection are design based on concepts of evolution.
2. **Artificial neural networks :** Non-linear predictive models that learn through training and resemble biological neural networks in structure.
3. **Rule induction :** THe extraction of useful if-then rules from data based on statistical significance.
4. **Decision trees :** They are tree shaped structures that represent sets of decisions. These decisions generate rules for the classification of a dataset.

Data Mining Tools

Various data mining tools are as follows:

1. Text term searching tools.
2. Sequence similarity searching tools.
3. Sequence submission tools.
4. Computer assisted passenger prescreening system (CAPPS II).
5. Terrorism information awareness program (TIA)
6. Query managers and report writers.
7. Multidimensional databases tools.
8. Exploration and discovery tools.

In the process of entracting previously unknown but singnificant information from large databases and using it to make crucial business decisions.

Data Mining leverages that data asset by transforming it into information and information into reliable decisions. Data mining has major implications across the enterprise -for productivity profitability, customer satisfaction.

D.M. analysis tend to be bottom-up, and the best techniques have been developed with an orientation towards large volumes of data.

CONCEPTUAL SHORT QUESTIONS WITH ANSWERS

Q. 1. Compare Data Mining & SQL.

Data mining	SQL
1. It is a key member in the Business Intelligence product family. Mining is analyzing data and finding hidden patterns using automatic or semiautomatic means.	1. It is a language used to retrieve and manage data in RDBMS.
2. ERP, CRM, Web logs etc form its input.	2. It requires relational database.
3. It works on algorithms.	3. No algorithms are used for queries.
4. Patterns are discovered by iteration of each subset until algorthm is applied fully like in decision making trees.	4. Queries are applied to gain a number of combinations but no definite pattern is recognized.
5. Data mining constructs models of data in question.	5. Query simply returns data that fulfills certain constraints.

Q. 2. Give differences between Database and Data Warehouse.

Thera are many differences in database and data warehouse. These differences are in the organization and data stored in both. The various differences are as follows :

Data base	Data Warehouse
1. A data base is a collection of related data. The Database system is a collection of database and DBMS.	1. A data warehouse is a collection of information as well as a supporting system.
2 The databases maintain a balance between efficiency in transaction processing and supporting query requirements i.e., they cannot be further optimized for the applications such as OLAP, DSS and data mining.	2. A data warehouse is generally optimized to access from a decision maker's needs. These are designed speicifically to support efficient extraction, processing and presentation for analytical and decision making purpose.
3. Database are generally small as compared to Data warehouses and contain data from single source.	3. Data warehouses generally contain very large amounts of data from multiple sources that may include databases from different data models and sometimes files acquired from independent systems and platforms.
4. Multidatabases provide access to disjoint and usually heterogeneous databases and are volatile.	4. Data warehouses is generally a store of integrated data from multiple sources, processed for storage in a multi-dimensional model and nonvolatile.
5. They do not support, time series and trend analysis.	5. Data warehouse support time series and trends analysis both of which require more historical data.
6. In databases, transactions are the unit and are the agent of change to the database.	6. The information in the data warehouses is much more course-grained and is refreshed according to a careful choice of incremental refresh policy.

7. Data in the databases can be changed regularly.	7. Data can only be added. Once data are stored, no change are allowed.
8. Data represent current view.	8. Data are historic in nature.
9. Same data can have different representations or meanings.	9. It provides a unified view of all data elements with a common definition and representation.
10. Data are stored with a functional or process orientation.	10. Data are stored with a subject orientation.

Q.3. Give a Comparison of Data Mining and Structured Query Language (SQL) in tabular form.

Data Mining	Structured Query Language
1. Data mining is a key member in the Business Intelligence (BI) product family, together with Online Analytical Processing (OLAP), enterprise reporting and ETL. Data mining is about analyzing data and finding hidden patterns using automatic or semiautomatic means.	1. SQL (Structured Query Language) is a database computer language designed for the retrieval and management of data in relational database management systems (RDBMS). Database schema creation and modification, and database object access control management.
2. Financial applications, Enterprise Resource Management (ERP), Customer Relationship Management (CRM), and Web logs from its input.	2. It requires relational database. It can't act on any database.
3. Discovery based approaches in which pattern-matching and other algorithms are employed to determine the key relationships in the data.	3. Verification based approach in which the user hypothesized about specific data intterrelationship and then uses the tools to verify or refute those hypothesis.
4. It is not dependent on the Analyst but Data Mining algorithms can look at numerous multidimensional data relationships concurrently, highlighting those that are dominant or exceptional.	4. It depends on the ability of the analyst to pose appropriate questions and quickly return results, manage the complexity of the attribute space.
5. Data mining works on algorithms.	5. No algorithms are used for queries.
6. Patterns are discovered by iteration of each subset until the algorithm is applied fully. For example, in making decision trees.	6. Queries are applied to gain a number of combinations, but no definite pattern is recognized.
7. Data mining constructs models of the data in question.	7. Query simply returns the data that fulfills certain constraints.

8. A data mining Query with SQL.
IF AGE > AND CAR = MINIVAN THEN
TOTAL SPENT > $100
Or
IF SEX M AND ZIP = 05566 THEN
TOTAL SPENT > $100
	8. A SQL query.
	SELECT * FROM CUSTOMER_TABLE
	WHERE TOTAL_SPENT > $100;

Q.4. Give a comparison of Data Mining and Data Warehousing.

Data Mining	Data Warehousing
1. Data mining is about analyzing data and finding hidden patterns using automatic or semiautomatic means. It is a key member in the Business Intelligence (BI), together with OLAP, enterprise reporting and ETL.	1. Data warehouse is a repository of an organization's electronically stored data. It is designed to facilitate reporting and analysis.
2. In data mining, the analyst is looking to support a hypothesis based on correlations, patterns and cause and effects relationships in statistical models.	2. Data warehousing is concerned with answering a broader question and slicing and dicing data based on experience to add value to organization.
3. Data mining is intended for user who are statistically inclined.	3. Data warehouse users tend to be data experts who analyze by business dimensions directly.
4. Data miners engage in question formulation based mainly on 'law of large numbers' to identify potentially useful relationships between data elements.	4. Data warehousing analystsare concerned with customer experience and can help the customer by improving the customer experience.
5. Data mining predicts the future.	5. Data warehouse describes the present and past.
6. Prescriptive algorithms are used in data mining.	6. Query and reporting functions are used in data warehousing.
7. Data mining rely on Historical data to derive conclusions.	7. Data warehousing also rely on historical data to derive conclusions.
8. Data mining fall short of delivering a predictive model.	8. Data warehousing also fall short of delivering a predictive model.

APPENDIX–A
EXAMINATION QUESTION PAPERS

END TERM EXAMINATION

FIFTH SEMESTER [B.TECH.] DECEMBER-2012

Paper Code: ETCS-309 **Subject: Database Management System**

Time: 3 Hours **Maximum Marks: 75**

Note: Attempt any five questions including Q. No. 1 which is compulsory. Select one question from each Unit.

Q 1. Give short answers of the following: **(2×12=24)**

(*a*) What do you understand by conceptual model of a database?

(*b*) Differentiate the terms Database user and Database administrator.

(*c*) Give example of generalization and aggregation in ER-diagram.

(*d*) Define multivalued attribute and composite attribute in ER-diagram.

(*e*) List the reasons for introducing a null value in a database.

(*f*) What is a division operator and how it is useful?

(*g*) Differentiate natural join and outer join operations.

(*h*) What is query correlation?

(*i*) Define functional dependency.

(*j*) Define atomicity, durability, isolation and concurrency in databases.

(*k*) What is the need for checkpoint?

(*l*) When is a log record written to log file?

Unit-I

Q 2. (*a*) Differentiate between Hierarchical and Network Model of a database by taking a suitable example. **(6.5)**

(*b*) What are different subsystems in DBMS Architecture and what functionalities they provide? **(6)**

Q 3. (*a*) In ER-diagram what can be different types of cardinalities? Give an example of each. **(6)**

(*b*) Draw an ER-diagram for a Book Store which maintains data of different books, customers suppliers and Publishers. Books are classified as scientific, engineering and medical. Customers can be students, faculty or Teaching Institutes. Based on category of customer appropriate discount is offered. Also, books are promoted for sale by supplier or individual publishers by contacting faculty or Institutes. (assume missing data if any) **(6.5)**

Unit-II

Q 4. Given the relational schema-

ENROLL (s#, c#, section)- s# represents student number

TEACH (prof, c#, section)- c# represents course number

ADVISE (prof,s#)-prof is thesis advisor of s#

PRE_REQ(c#, pre_c#) - pre_c# is prerequisite course

GRADES (s#, c#, grade, year)

STUDENT(s#, sname) - sname is student name

Give queries expressed in relational algebra and tuple calculus for the following queries: **(12.5)**

(*a*) List all students taking courses with Smith or Jones.

(*b*) List all students taking at least one course that their advisor teaches.

(*c*) List those professors who teach more than one section of the same courses.

(*d*) List the courses that student " John" can enroll, i.e, has passed the necessary prerequisite courses but not the course itself.

Q 5. (*a*) Explain giving example the terms integrity constraints and domain constraints. How are they enforced in Oracle? **(6)**

(*b*) Express the above queries in SQL. Give SQL commands for database modifications applying them on schema given above. **(6.5)**

Unit-III

Q 6. (*a*) Compute the closure of the following set F of functional dependencies for relation schema R= (A, B, C, D, E):

$$A \rightarrow BC$$
$$CD \rightarrow E$$
$$B \rightarrow D$$
$$E \rightarrow A$$

Fig.1

List the candidate keys for R. **(8.5)**

(*b*) "Every schema that is in BCNF must also be in 3NF". Justify this statement. **(4)**

Q 7. (*a*) Write an algorithm for calculating Canonical cover. Using the functional dependencies of Fig.1 , work out the steps to calculate canonical cover F_c. **(8.5)**

(*b*) List the physical storage media available on the computers you use routinely. Give the speed with which data can be accessed on each medium. **(4)**

Unit -IV

Q 8. Consider the following two transactions:

T_{31}: read (A) ;
read (B);
if A = 0 then B=B+1;
write (B).

T_{32}: read (B);
read (A);
if B = 0 then A= A +1;
write (A).

Add lock and unlock instructions to transaction T_{31} and T_{32}, so that they observe the two-phase locking protocol. Can the execution of these transactions result in a deadlock? **(12.5)**

Q 9. (*a*) How is database recovered after a crash using log file? **(4)**

(*b*) What is Time Stamp Protocol and when it is used? **(4)**

(*c*) Explain the Cost based query optimization. **(4.5)**

END TERM EXAMINATION

FIFTH SEMESTER [B.TECH.] DECEMBER-2013

Paper Code: ETCS-309 **Subject: Database Management Systems**

Time: 3 Hours **Maximum Marks: 75**

Note: Attempt any five questions including Q. No. 1 which is compulsory. Select one question from each Unit.

Q 1. Write short answers of **any five** of the following: **(5×5=25)**

(*a*) Represent the natural join operation of the relational algebra as a combination of Cartesian product, selection and projection operation.

(*b*) What do you mean by instance and schema? Explain the different between these.

(*c*) Explain authorization in SQL with example.

(*d*) Explain Candidate Key and Alternate Key.

(*e*) List two reasons why you may choose to define system.

(*f*) Under what circumstances multivalued dependency is known as functional dependency?

(*g*) What is the need of the normalization?

(*h*) Differentiate DML and DDL.

Unit-I

Q 2. (*a*) What are the problems with traditional file processing system? **(12.5)**

(*b*) Explain with suitable example the physical, logical and view level of database.

OR

Q 3. Draw the ER-diagram for the following problem definition:

The book club has members. The book club sells books to its members. The members place orders for books, which the book club fulfils. Each order contains one or more than one books. The books are written by author (s). The publisher publishes the book. An author can write more than one book and a book can have more than one author. A book is published by a publisher, but a publisher publishes many books. A member can place more than one order. The member also can choose not to place an order. The book club sells many books.

Unit-II

Q 4. Consider the following database schema: **(12.5)**

STUDENT (name, sroll_number, class, major)

COURSE (course_number, course_name, credit_hour, department)

SECTION (sectionid, course_number, semester, year, instructor)

GRADE REPORT (sroll_number, sectioned, grade)

PREREQUISITE (course_number, prerequisite_no)

Specify the following queries in SQL for above schema:

(*a*) Retrieve the name of students majoring in ECS (electronics)

(*b*) Name of all courses taught by professor Sharma in the year 2005 and 2006.

(*c*) For each section taught by professor Sharma, find the course number, semester, year and number of students who took the section.

(*d*) Retrieve the name and transcript of each senior student (class=4). Transcript contains course number, course name, credit hours, grade, year for each course completed.

(*e*) Retrieve the names and major department of all grade A students, i.e. students who have grade A in all courses taken by them.

OR

Q 5. Using the above database schema explains the following relational algebra operations by writing suitable queries:

(*a*) Set difference

(*b*) Set interaction

(*c*) Create view

(*d*) Natural join

(*e*) Union

Unit-III **(12.5)**

Q 6. (*a*) What do you mean by decomposition? Explain the desirable properties of decomposition.

(*b*) Discuss of role of functional dependency (FD) in Normalization. Provide an example to understand the FD.

OR

Q 7. (*a*) Explain the concepts of Object Oriented DBMS.

(*b*) What mechanism are used for (i) Database protection (ii) Accessing shared databases?

Unit -IV **(12.5)**

Q 8. (*a*) What is meant by the term Query Processing? What are the various steps involved in this process?

(*b*) Discuss the advantages of distributed system.

OR

Q 9. (*a*) Explain the process of Deadlock - Detection and Recovery.

(*b*) Why a concurrency control needed? Explain lost update, inconsistent retrievals and uncommitted dependency anomalies.

END TERM EXAMINATION

FIFTH SEMESTER [B.TECH.] DECEMBER 2014 – JANUARY 2015

Paper Code: ETCS-309 **Subject: Database Management System**

Time: 3 Hours **Maximum Marks: 75**

Note: Attempt any five questions including Q. No. 1 which is compulsory.

Q 1. Attempt **any five** questions: **(3×5 = 15)**

(*a*) Explain the purpose of database system.

(*b*) Explain Time stamp based protocols.

(*c*) Differentiate between DBMS and file systems.

(*d*) Explain the basic structure of SQL.

(*e*) What are anomalies in database design?

(*f*) Explain the advantage of object oriented databases.

(*g*) What is shadow paging? Write any two disadvantages of it.

Q 2. (*a*) What is data dependence? Explain the difference between logical and physical data dependence with example. **(7.5)**

(*b*) Discuss the basic concepts and architecture of database systems. **(7.5)**

Q 3. (*a*) Discuss the various aggregate functions in SQL with an example for each **(7.5)**

(*b*) Construct E-R diagram of the bank. It provides different kinds of bank accounts and loans. Also it operates number of branches. **(7.5)**

Q 4. (*a*) Define the terms: Ternary relationship, Weak entity set, Identity owner, Aggregation. **(7.5)**

(*b*) What is a relation? Differentiate between a Relation schema and a Relation instance. Define the terms cardinality of a relation. **(7.5)**

Q 5. (*a*) What is normalization? Why we need normalization of DBMS? **(7.5)**

(*b*) Explain about 2NF, 3NF and BCNF with an example for each. **(7.5)**

Q 6. (*a*) What is deadlock? When it is occurs and how to avoid it? **(7.5)**

(*b*) Explain measures of query cost and selection operation in query processing. **(7.5)**

Q 7. (*a*) What is meant by the file organization and indexing? Discuss the Hashbased indexing. **(7.5)**

(*b*) Discribe the concepts Serializability and Recoverability. **(7.5)**

Q 8. Write short notes on the following: **(5×3 =15)**

(*a*) Data definition in SQL

(*b*) Oracle 8 Architecture.

(*c*) Distributed DBMS.

FIRST TERM EXAMINATION

FOURTH SEMESTER [B.TECH.] Feburary-2015

Paper Code: ETCS-208 **Subject: Database Management System**

Time: 1 Hour **Maximum Marks: 30**

Note: Attempt Q.1 which is compulsory and any two more questions from remaining.

Q 1. Fill in the blanks. **(10)**

(*a*) RDBMS stands for..............

(*b*) DCL stands for................

(*c*) A special table to check any function in Oracle is..................

(*d*) An association between two or more entities is.............

(*e*) The command to eliminate a table from a database is...............table <table name>.

(*f*) Database level is closest to the users is...............

(*g*) A recursive relationship is a relationship between an entity and...........

(*h*) In a 1:N relationship, the foreign key is placed in .... table.

(*i*) A superclass/subclass hierarchy is one in which subclass has/have........... superclass.

(*j*) A..................entity related to two or more associated entities that each contains specialized attributes that apply to some but not all of the instances of the entity.

Q 2. (*a*) Describe briefly with an example: derivedattribute, multivalued attribute, composite attributes, complex attributes, descriptiveattributes. **(5)**

(*b*) What is Data Independence? Explain logical and physical data independence. **(5)**

Q 3. (*a*) Consider the two tables T1 (P, Q, R), T2 (S, T, U) as shown in Fig 1. Show the results of the following: **(5)**

Table T1		
P	Q	R
a	1	-
c	2	10
t	2	-
a	-	-

Table T2		
S	T	U
a	1	-
d	3	10
r	3	10
a	-	-

Fig.1

i. $\sigma_{p=a}(T1)$

ii. $\Pi_{P, R}(T1)$

iii. $T1 \cup T2$

iv. $T1 \cap T2$

v. $T1 - T2$

(*b*) Define the concept of aggregation. Give two examples of where this concept is useful. **(5)**

Q 4. *employee (employee-name, street, city)*
works (*employee-name, company-name, salary*)
company (company-name, city)
manages (employee-name, manager-name)
Consider the employee database and give an expression in SQL or Relational Algebra for each of the following queries **(5×2)**

(*a*) Find the names of all employees who work for SBI.

(*b*) Find the names and cities of residence of all employees who work for SBI.

(*c*) Find all employees in the database who do not work for SBI.

(*d*) Modify the database so that Hari now lives in Pune.

(*e*) Delete all tuples in the *works* relation for employees of SBI.

SECOND TERM EXAMINATION

FOURTH SEMESTER [B.TECH.] APRIL-2015

Paper Code: ETCS-208 **Subject: Database Management System**

Time: 1 Hour **Maximum Marks: 30**

Note: Attempt Q.1 which is compulsory and any two more questions from remaining.

Q 1. Fill in the blanks: **(10)**

(*a*) BCNF stands for........

(*b*) PL/SQL stands for............

(*c*) Every view serializable schedule that is not conflict serializable has.............

(*d*) Data items can be locked in...................mode where data item can be both read as well as written.

(*e*) To avoid cascading roll-back a modified protocol called............two phase locking is used, where a transaction must hold all its exclusive locks till it commits/ aborts.

(*f*) A..................schedule is one where, for each pair of transactions $\mathbf{T_i}$ and $\mathbf{T_j}$ such that $\mathbf{T_j}$ reads data previously written by $\mathbf{T_i}$, the commit operations of $\mathbf{T_i}$ appears before the commit operation of $\mathbf{T_j}$.

(*g*) **W-timestamp**(Q) is the .... time-stamp of any transaction that executed write(Q) successfully.

(*h*) An MVD $X \rightarrow Y$ in R is called a..........if (a) **Y** is a subset of **X**, or (b) $\mathbf{X \cup Y = R}$.

(*i*) ....makes use of view serializability by, in effect, deleting obsolete write operations from the transactions that issue them.

(*j*). .... always returns **FALSE** for implicit cursors, because Oracle closes the SQL cursor automatically after executing its associated SQL statement.

Q 2. (*a*) Given a relation R = (A,B,C,D,E) with the following FD's: {CE→ D,D →B,C→ A}. Find all candidate keys.

Identify the best normal form that R satisfies (1NF, 2NF, 3NF, or BCNF).

If the relation is not in BCNF, decompose it until it becomes BCNF. **(7)**

(*b*) Write down the syntax for creating a trigger and explain it. **(3)**

Q 3. (*a*) Explain the two deadlock prevention strategies. Which of the two strategies have fewer rollbacks? **(7)**

(*b*) Consider the schedule S. Draw the serializability, graph for S and state whether schedule is serializable or not. If schedule is serializable, write down the equivalent serial schedule.

S: R1(X);R2(Z);R1(Z);R3(X);R3(Y);W1(X);W3(Y);R2(Y);W2(Z);W2(Y); **(3)**

Q 4. (*a*) Given the following set of FD's for a relation R(A,B,C,D,E,F), F = {AB→C,DC→AE,E→ F}. Is the decomposition R1 (A,B,C,D) and R2 (B,C,D,E,F) a dependency preserving decomposition? Explain your answer. **(7)**

(*b*) When a transaction is rolled back under timestamp ordering, it is assigned a new timestamp. Why can it not simply keep its old timestamp? **(3)**

APPENDIX–B
SYLLABUS AND LECTURE PLAN

– GGSIPU & Other Indian Universiteis

DATABASE MANAGEMENT SYSTEMS

Paper Code: ETCS-208 **L T/P C**

Paper: Database Management systems **3 1 4**

INSTRUCTIONS TO PAPER SETTERS: **Maximum Marks: 75**

1. Question No. 1 should be compulsory and cover the entire syllabus. This question should have objective or short answer type questions. It should be of 25 marks.
2. Apart from Question No.1, rest of the paper shall consist of four units as per the syllabus. Every unit should have two questions. However, the student may be asked to attempt only 1 question from each unit. Each question should be 12.5 marks.

Objective: The concepts related to database, database techniques, SQL and database operations are introduced in this subject. This creates strong foundation for application data design.

UNIT-I

Introductory Concepts of DBMS: Introduction and application of DBMS. Data Independence, Database System Architecture - levels, Mapping, Database users and DBA, Entity - Relationship model, constraints, keys, Design issues, E-R Diagram, Extended E-R features- Generalization, Specialization, Aggregation, Translating E-R model into Relational model.

[T1,T2][No. of hrs.10]

UNIT-II

Relational Model: The relational Model, The catalog, Types, Keys, Relational Algebra, Fundamental operations, Additional Operations-, SQL fundamentals, DDL, DML, DCL PL/SQL Concepts, Cursors, Stored Procedures, Stored Functions, Database Integrity - Triggers.

[T2,R3][No. of hrs. 10]

UNIT-III

Functional Dependencies, Non-loss Decomposition, First, Second, Third Normal Forms, Dependency Preservation, Boyce/Codd Normal Form, Multi-valued Dependencies and Fourth Normal Form, Join Dependencies and Fifth Normal Form.

[T2,R1,R3][No. of hrs. 10]

UNIT- IV

Transaction Management: ACID properties, serializability of Transaction, Testing for serializability and concurrency control, Lock based concurrency control (2PL, deadlocks), time stamping methods, Database recovery management.

Implementation techniques: Overview of Physical Storage Media, File organization, Indexing and Hashing, B+ tree Index Files, Query Processing Overview, Catalog Information for Cost Estimation, Selection Operation, Sorting, Join Operation, Materialized views, Database Tuning.

[T1, T2, R2][No of Hrs 12]

DATABASE MANAGEMENT SYSTEMS LAB

Paper Code: ETCS-256 **L T/P C**

Paper: Database Management System Lab **0 2 1**

LAB BASED ON DBMS

Lab includes implementation of DDL, DCL,DML i.e., SQL in Oracle.

List of Experiments:

1. Design a Database and create required tables. For e.g., Bank, College Database
2. Apply the constraints like Primary Key, Foreign Key, NOT NULL to the tables.
3. Write a SQL statement for implementing ALTER, UPDATE and DELETE.
4. Write the queries to implement to joins.
5. Write the queries for implementing the following functions: MAX (), MIN(), AVG(), COUNT()
6. Write the queries to implement the concept of integrity constraints.
7. Write the queries to create the views.
8. Perform the queries for triggers.
9. Perform the following operation for demonstrating the insertion, updation and deletion using the referential integrity constraints.

Note:- At least 8 Experiments out of the list must be done in the semester.

APPENDIX–C

GLOSSARY OF DBMS

Glossary

INTRODUCTION : BASIC CONCEPTS

1. **Database:** Database is a collection of data.
2. **Database Management System:** Database management system is a collection of interrelated data and a set of programs to access the data.
3. **Data Independence:** Data independence is the ability to modify a schema definition in one level without affecting a schema definition in the next higher level.
4. **Data Model:** Data model is a collection of conceptual tools for describing data, data schema and consistency constraints.
5. **Data definition Language:** Database schema is specified by a set of definitions expressed by a special language called Data Definition Language.
6. **Data Storage and Definition Language:** This is a special type of Data Definition Language. The storage structure and access methods used by database system are specified by a set of definitions in data storage and definition language.
7. **Data Manipulation Language:** It enables users to access or manipulate data as organised by the appropriate data model.
8. **Database Manager or Storage Manager:** Database manager is a program module which provides the interface between low level data stored in the database and the application programs and queries submitted to the system.
9. **Database Administrator:** Database administrator is the person who has central control over the system.

E-R MODEL

1. **Entity:** Entity is an object in the real world that is distinguishable from all other objects.
2. **Entity Set:** Entity set is a set of the same type that shares the same properties attributes.
3. **Simple or Composite Attribute:** The attribute which cannot be divided into subparts called simple attribute, on the other hand, composite attributes can be divided in supports.
4. **Single-valued and Multi-valued Attribute:** Single-valued attribute has a single value for a particular attribute. Multi-valued attribute has a set of values for a specific attribute.
5. **Null Attribute:** An attribute which has no value is called a null attribute. Null value used to represent the null attribute.

6. **Derived Attribute:** The value for this type of attribute is derived from the values of other related attributes for entities.
7. **Relationship:** Relationship is an association among several entities.
8. **Relationship Set:** It is a set of relationships of the same type. Formally, it is mathematic relation on $n \geq 2$ (possible non-distinct) entity sets. if $E_1, E_2, E_3, \ldots E_n$ are entity sets, then relationship set R is a subset of $\{(e_1, e_2, \ldots e_n)\} \in e_1 \in E_1, e_2 \in E_2, e_3 \in E_3, \ldots e_n \in E_n$ where, $(e_1, e_2, \ldots e_n)$ is a relationship.
9. **Super key:** Super key is a set of one or more attributes that are taken collectively allow us to identify uniquely an entity in the entity set.
10. **Candidate Key:** Candidate key is a minimal super key. No proper subset of candidate key is super key.
11. **Primary Key:** Primary key is the candidate key chosen by the database designer as principal means of identifying entities within an entity set.
12. **Weak Entity Set:** An entity set which does not have sufficient attributes to form a primary key is called a weak entity set.
13. **Strong Entity Set:** An entity set which has a primary key is called as strong entity set.
14. **Subordinate Entity:** Member of a weak entity set is called as subordinate entity.
15. **Dominant Entity:** Member of a strong entity set is called as dominant entity.
16. **Specialization:** Specialization is the process of designating sub groupings within an entity set.
17. **Generalization:** It is a containment relationship that exists between a higher level entity set and one or more lower level entity sets.
18. **Aggregation:** Aggregation is an abstraction through which relationships are treated as higher level entities. It helps to express relationships among relationships.

RELATIONAL MODEL

1. **Domain:** Domain D is the set of values of the same type. Domain of an attribute is defined as the set of allowable values for the attribute.
2. **Tuple:** Tuple is an ordered set of attributes. It is comparable to a record in a conventional file processing system and an entity in ER model.
3. **Procedural Query Language:** In procedural query language, the user instructs the system to perform a sequence of operations on the database to compute the desired result, *i.e.* how to retrieve the data. Relational algebra is procedural query language.
4. **Non-procedural Query Language:** In non-procedural query language, the user describes the information desired without giving a specific procedure for obtaining that information. Tuple relational calculus and domain relational calculus are the Non-procedural query languages.
5. **Extension:** Extension of a relation is the set of tuples appearing in that relation at any given instant. Extension varies with time.
6. **Intension:** Intension of a given relation is independent of time. Basically, it is the permanent part of the relation. It corresponds to what is specified in relation schema. More precisely the intension is a combination of two things; a naming structure and a set of integrity constraints:

- The naming structure consists of the relation name plus the names of attributes.

- The integrity constraints can be subdivided into key constraints, referential constraints and other constraints.

7. **Key Constraints:** Key constraints are constraints implied by the existence of candidate keys.
8. **Referential Constraints:** Referential constraints are constraints implied by the existence of foreign keys.
9. **Assertions:** An assertion is a predicate expressing a condition that we wish the database would satisfy. Domain constraints and referential-integrity constraints are special forms of assertions.

   An assertion in SQL-92 takes the form:

   Create assertion < assertion_name > **check** < predicate >

   Example:

   The sum of loan amounts for each branch must be less than the sum of all account balances at the branch.

   Create assertion sum-constraint **check.**
   (not exists (select* from branch
   where (select sum (amount) from loan
   where loan branch_name = branch.branch_name)
   > = (select sum (amount) from account
   where loan.branch_name = branch.branch_name)))

   When an assertion is created, the system tests it for validity. If the assertion is valid then any future modification to the database is allowed only if it does not cause that assertion to be violated.
10. **Trigger:** A trigger is a statement that is executed automatically by the system as a side effect of a modification to the database. To design a trigger mechanism, we must meet two requirements:

    (*i*) Specify the conditions under which the trigger is to be executed.

    (*ii*) Specify the actions to be taken when the trigger executes.

    The SQL-92 standard does not include trigger. The original system *R* proposal included a limited trigger feature.

SQL

SQL Commands:

1. **CREATE Table Command:**

   Format:

   CREATE TABLE table
   ({column data type [DEFAULT expr]
   [column_constraint] | |
   table constraint}
   [, { column data type [DEFAULT expr]
   [column_constraint] | | table_constraint}]
   ....) ;

Description:

CREATE TABLE command creates the database table with specified list of attributes.

table - table name

column - name of the column (attribute)

data type - is the SQL data type

DEFAULT - specifies the value to be assigned to the column if a row is inserted without a value for this column.

Column-constraints define the restrictions placed on this column and consist of following:

[CONSTRAINT constraint]

[[NOT] NULL]:

{ {UNIQUE: PRIMARY KEY}]

[REFERENCES table [(column)]]

[CHECK (condition)]

Constraint is an optional name assigned to this constraint.

NULL permits NULL values.

NOT NULL specifies that every row must have a non-NULL value for this column.

UNIQUE forces column values to be unique.

If a column is UNIQUE it cannot be declared the PRIMARY KEY.

REFERENCES identifies this column as a foreign key from table [column].

CHECK assures that the value for this column satisfies a condition. Condition may be any valid expression that tests TRUE or false.

Table Constraint: Table constraint is identical to column-constraint except that it can reference multiple columns with a single constraint. The format of table constraint is:

[CONSTRAINT constraint]

[[NOT] NULL] |

[UNIQUE } PRIMARY (column [, column])]

[FOREIGN KEY (column [, column])

REFERENCES table [column [, column]]

CHECK (condition)]

2. **DROP Table Command:**

Format:

DROP TABLE table;

Description:

DROP TABLE drops the table and commits pending changes to the database.

To drop a table you must either own the table or have DROP ANY TABLE system privilege. Dropping a table also drops indexes and grants associated with it.

3. **ALTER Table Command:**

Format:

ALTER TABLE table

[ADD ({column_element | table constraint}

[, column_element | table constraint}] ....)]
[MODIFY (column_element [, column_element] ....)]
[DROP drop] ;

Description:

ADD allows you to add a new column to the end of an existing table or add a constraint to the table's definition. These follow the same format used in CREATE TABLE.

MODIFY changes an existing column, with some restrictions:

- You may change the type of column or decrease its size if every row for the column is NULL.
- A NOT NULL column may be added only to a table with no rows.
- An existing column can be modified to NOT NULL only if it has a non-NULL value in every row.
- Increasing the length of a NOT NULL column without specifying NULL will leave it NOT NULL.
- Views that reference a table with select from will not work after a column has been added to the table unless they are dropped and recreated.

4. **INSERT:**

Format:

INSERT INTO table [(column [, column] ...)]]
{VALUES (expression [, expression] ...) : query } ;

Description:

INSERT adds one or more new rows to the table or view. The user must have the insert authority. Table is the table into which rows are to be inserted.

If a list of columns is given an expression must be matched for each of those columns. Any columns not in the list receive the value NULL, and none of them can be defined NOT NULL or INSERT will fail. If a list of columns is not given, values must be given for all columns.

INSERT with query a adds as many rows as the query returns, with each query column being matched, with columns in the column list. If no column list is given, the tables must have the same number and type of columns.

5. **UPDATE:**

Format:

UPDATE table
SET {column = expression [, column = expression] ..... .
(column [, column] .....) = (subquery)]
[WHERE condition] ;

Description:

UPDATE updates (changes) the values in the listed columns in the specified table. Without where clause, all rows will be updated. With a where clause, only those rows it selects will be updated.

The expressions are evaluated as the command is executed, and their results replace the current values for the columns in the row (S).

6. DELETE:

Format:

DELETE FROM table
[WHERE condition] ;

Description:

DELETE deletes all rows that satisfy condition from table. The condition may include a correlated query. If where condition is not specified, it will delete all rows in the table.

7. SELECT:

Format:

```
SELECT [All ; DISTINCT
{* : { column [, column] .... } } ]
FROM {table [, table] ... }
[WHERE condition]
[GROUP By expression [, expression] ... ] [HAVING condition]
[ {UNION [ALL] : INTERSECT : MINUS } SELECT .... ]
[ORDER BY {expression : position} [ASC: DESC]
....... {expression : position } [ASC : DESC] ......
```

Description:

SELECT retrieves rows from one or more tables. All means that all rows satisfying the conditions will be returned.

DISTINCT means that only rows that are unique will be returned, any duplicates will be removed.

An * (asterisk) represent that all columns from all tables in the from clause will be displayed.

If the list of columns is given, select will select only those columns from the tables. The rows in the table which satisfy the where condition will be selected.

8. ROLLBACK:

Format:

```
ROLLBACK [WORK] { [TO [SAVE POINT] savepoint]
                  [FORCE text] }
```

Description:

ROLLBACK reverses all changes made to tables in the database since changes were last committed or rolled back and releases any locks on the table.

It discards part or all of the work you have done in the current transaction, since the last COMMIT or SAVEPOINT.

9. COMMIT:

Format:

COMMIT

Description:

To commit means to make changes to data permanently. COMMIT commits any changes made to the database since the last COMMIT was executed implicitly or explicitly.

10. DESCRIBE:

Format:

DESC [RIBE] table

Description:

DESCRIBE displays a specified table's definition. The definition includes the table and its columns, with each column's name, NULL or NOT NULL status, data type and width or precision.

11. TRUNCATE:

Format:

TRUNCATE TABLE table

Description:

TRUNCATE removes all the rows from a table. It deletes rows much faster than the DELETE statement does. TRUNCATE is not a DML statement. Therefore if you issue a TRUNCATE TABLE statement, you cannot perform roll back to recover the lost rows.

NORMALIZATION

3. **Decomposition: The decomposition of a relation schema $R = [A_1, A_2, A_3, \ldots A_n]$ is its replacement by a set of relation schemas. $\{R_1, R_2, \ldots R_n]$ such that,**
   $R_i \subseteq R$ for $1 \leq i \leq n$ and
   $R_1 \cup R_2 \ldots \cup R_n = R$
2. **Loss-less-Join Decomposition:** Let R be a relation schema and let F be a set of functional dependencies on R. Let R_1 and R_2 form a decomposition of R. This decomposition is a loss-less-join decomposition of R if at least one of the following functional dependencies are in F^+.
   - $R_1 \cap R_2 \rightarrow R_2$
   - $R_1 \cap R_2 \rightarrow R_1$

   Loss-less-join decomposition can also be defined as:

   A decomposition of a relation schema R into the relation schemas R_i $(1 \leq i \leq n)$ is said to be a loss-less join decomposition if

   $r = \pi_{R1}(x) \bowtie \pi_{R2}(r) \bowtie \ldots \pi_{Rn}(r)$

   where r is relation on relation schema R.
3. **Functional Dependency:** A functional dependency can be defined as follows: Let $\alpha \subseteq R$ and $\beta \subseteq R$. The functional dependency $\alpha \rightarrow \beta$ holds on R if in any legal relation $r(R)$, for all pairs of tuples t_1 and t_2 in r such that $t_1[\alpha] = t_2[\alpha]$ it is also the case that $t_1[\beta] = t_2[\beta]$.
4. **Canonical Cover:** A set of functional dependencies F_c is a canonical cover if every *FD* in F_c satisfies the following:

   (*i*) Each FD in F_c is simple. In a simple FD, the right - hand side has a single attribute. *i.e.* each *FD* is of the form $X \rightarrow A$.

   (*ii*) For no *FD* $X \rightarrow A$ with $Z \subset X$ is $\{(F_c - (X \rightarrow A)) \approx (Z \rightarrow A)\} = F_c$.

   In other words, the left-hand side of each FD doesn't have any extraneous attributes or the *FDs* in F_c are left reduced.

(*iii*) No *FD* $X \to A$ is redundant i.e.

$\{F_c - (X \to A)\}$ does not logically imply F_c. A canonical cover is sometimes called minimal.

5. **Full Functional Dependency:** Given a relation schema *R* and an *FD* $X \to Y$, *Y* is fully functionally dependent on X if there is no *Z*, where *Z* is a proper subset of *X*, such that $Z \to Y$. The dependency $X \to Y$ is left reduced, there being no extraneous attributes in the left hand side of the dependency.
6. **Partial Dependency:** Given a relation schema R with the functional dependencies *F* defined on the attributes of *R* and *K* as candidate key, if *X* is a proper subset of *K* and if $F = X \to A$, then *A* is said to be partially dependent on *K*.
7. **Transitive Dependency:** Given a relation schema *R* with the functional dependencies *F* defined on the attributes of *R*, let X and *Y* be subsets of *R* and let *A* be an attribute of *R* such that $X \not\subset Y$, $A \not\subset XY$. If the set of functional dependencies $\{X \to Y, Y \to A\}$ is implied by F (*i.e.* $F = X \to Y \to A$ and $F = Y \to X$) then *A* is transitively dependent on X.
8. **Prime and Non-prime Attribute:** An attribute *A* in a relation schema *R* is a prime attribute or simply prime if *A* is a part of any candidate key of the relation.

   If *A* is not part of any candidate key of *R*, *A* is called a Non-prime attribute or Simply non-prime.
9. **Unnormalized Relation:** An unnormalized relation contain non-atomic values.
10. **First Normal Form (1NF):** A relation schema is said to be in First Normal Form (1NF) if the values in the domain of each attribute of the relation are atomic.
11. **Second Normal Form:** A relation schema *R* (*S*, *F*) is in second normal form (2NF) if it is in the 1NF and if all non-prime attributes are fully functionally dependent on the relation keys. A database schema is in second normal form if every relation schema included in the batabase schema is in second normal form.

    OR

    Second Normal Form (2NF): A relation schema *R* is in second normal form (2NF if each attribute *A* in *R* meets one of the following criteria:
    - It appears in a candidate key
    - It is not partially dependent on a candidate key
12. **Boyce Codd Normal Form (BCNF):** A relation schema *R* is in BCNF with respect to a set *f* for functional dependencies if for all functional dependencies in f^+ of the form $\alpha \to \beta$ where $\alpha \subseteq R$ and $\beta \subseteq R$ at least one of the following holds.
    - $\alpha \to \beta$ is a trival functional dependency.
    - α is a super key for schema *R*.

    A database design is in BCNF if each member of the set of relation schemas that constitute the database design is in BCNF.
13. **Third Normal Form (3NF):** A relation schema is in 3NF with respect ot a set *F* of functional dependencies if for all functional dependencies in F^+ of the form $\alpha \to \beta$ where $\alpha \subseteq R$ and $\beta \subseteq R$ at least one of the following holds:
    - $\alpha \to \beta$ is trival functional dependency.
    - α is a superkey for *R*.
    - Each attribute A in $\beta - \alpha$ is contained in a candidate key for *R*.

    OR

Third Normal Form (3NF): A relation schema R is in 3NF with respect to a set F of functional dependencies if there are no non-prime attributes A in R for which A is transitively dependent on a key of R.

14. **Fourth Normal Form (4NF):** A relation schema is in fourth Normal form (4NF) with respect to a set D of functional and multivalued dependencies if, for all multivalued dependencies in D^+ of the form $\alpha \rightarrow\rightarrow \beta$ where $\alpha \subseteq R$ and $\beta \subseteq R$ at least one of the following holds:
    - $\alpha \rightarrow\rightarrow \beta$ is a trival multivalued dependency.
    - α is a super key for schema R.

    A database design is in 4NF if each member of the set of relation schema that constitutes the design is in 4NF.

15. **Project Join Normal Form (PJNF/5NF):** A relation schema is in PJNF with respect to a set D of functional, multi-valued and join dependencies if, for all join dependencies in D^+ of the form * $(R_1, R_2, \ldots R_n)$
    where each $R_i \subseteq R$ and $R = R_1 \cup R_2 \cup \ldots \cup R_n$ at least one of the following holds.
    - * $(R_1\ R_2 \ldots R_n)$ is a trival join dependency.
    - Every R_i is a super key for R.

    A database design is in PJNF if each member of the set of relation schemas that constitutes the design is in PJNF.

16. **Armstrong's Axioms:**

    Reflexivity rule. If α is a set of attributes and $\beta \subseteq \alpha$, then $\alpha \rightarrow \beta$ holds.

    Augmentation rule: if $\alpha \rightarrow \beta$ holds and γ is a set of attributes then $\alpha\gamma \rightarrow \gamma\beta$ holds.

    Transitivity rule: If $\alpha \rightarrow \beta$ holds and $\beta \rightarrow \gamma$ holds, then $\alpha \rightarrow \gamma$ holds.

    This collection of rules is called Armstrong's axioms.

    These rules are sound because they do not generate any incorrect functional dependencies.

    These rules are complete because, for a given set F of functional dependencies, they allow us to generate all F^+.

    List of Relational Algebra Operations:

Operation	Operator	Syntax
1. Select	σ	σ_{cond}(rel)
2. Project	π	$\pi_{\text{arg-list}}$(rel)
3. Rename	ρ	ρ_x (rel)
4. Cartesian-product	$\times$	$rel_1 \times rel_2$
5. Union	$\cup$	$rel_1 \cup rel_2$
6. Set difference	$-$	$rel_1 - rel_2$
7. Intersection	$\cap$	$rel_1 \cap rel_2$
8. Join	$\bowtie$	$rel_1 \bowtie rel_2$
9. Division	$\div$	$rel_1 \div rel_2$
10. Assignment	$\leftarrow$	$R \leftarrow rel_1$

Note: rel, rel_1, rel_2 represent relation names; R is a variable
Cond-condition or predicate
x-new name for relation.

TRANSATION MANAGEMENT

1. **Transaction:** A transaction is a program unit whose execution accesses and possible updates the contents of the database.
2. **Schedule:** Represent the chronological order in which instructions are executed in the system. Two types of schedule are: Serial schedule and Concurrent schedule.
3. **Serial Schedule:** It consists of a sequence of instructions from various transaction where the instructions belonging to one single transaction appear together in the schedule.
4. **Concurrent Schedule:** When several transactions are executed concurrently, the corresponding schedule is called Concurrent schedule.
5. **Serializability:** A concurrent schedule is said to be serializable if it produces the same result as some serial schedule of the transaction. There are two forms of serializability:
   (*i*) Conflict serializability
   (*ii*) View serializability
6. **Lock:** Lock is a variable associated with each data item.
   Manipulating the value of lock is called locking.
   There are two types or modes of locks.
   (*i*) Shared mode
   (*ii*) Exclusive mode
7. **Shared Mode Lock:** If a transaction T_i has obtained a shared-mode lock on item A then T_i can read A but cannot write *A*.
8. **Exclusive Mode Lock:** If a transaction T_i has obtained a shared-mode lock on item *A* then T_i can both read and write *A*.
9. **Starvation of Locks:** Suppose that transaction
   T_2 - Has a shared mode lock on data item and
   T_1 - Requests an exclusive-mode lock on same data item.
10. Hence, T_1 has to wait for T_2 to release lock on same data item.
    Mean while suppose that T_3 requests a shared mode lock on same data item. This lock request is compatible with lock granted to T_2. Hence, T_3 gets the lock. At this point T_2 may release the lock but still T_1 has to wait for T_3. But again there may be a new transaction T_4 requesting a shared mode lock on the same data item. It is possible that there is a sequence of transactions that each requests a shared mode lock on same data item and T_1 never gets the exclusive mode lock on the data item. The transaction T_1 may never make progress and is said to be starved.
11. **Cascading Rollback:** The phenomenon in which a single transaction failure leads to a series of transaction rollbacks is called cascading rollback.
12. **Deadlock:** A system is in deadlock state if there exists a set of transactions such that every transaction in the set is waiting for data item held by some other transaction in the set.
    If $\{T_0, T_1, ... T_n\}$ is a set of transactions such that T_0 is waiting for a data item that is held by T_1, T_1 is waiting for a data item that is held by T_2 ... and T_{n-1} is waiting for a data item held by T_n and T_n is waiting for a data item that is held by T_0.

13. **Failure:** The failure of a system occurs when the system does not work according to its specifications and fails to deliver the service for which it was intended.
14. **Error:** An error is the system occurs when a component of a system assumes a state that is not desirable.
15. **Fault:** A fault is detected either when an error is propagated from one component to another or failure of the component is observed.
16. **Recoverable Schedule:** A recoverable schedule is defined as a schedule where for each pair of transactions T_i and T_j such that T_j reads a data item previously written by T_{i2} the commit operation of T_i appears before the commit operation of T_j.
17. **Log:** Log is a structure used to store database modifications. It is a sequence of log records and maintains a record of all the update activities in the database. Following are the types of log records to record significant events during transaction processing.
    (*i*) **Start:** Start of transaction denoted as:
    $< T_i$ start $>$
    (*ii*) **Update log:** It describes a single database write and it is denoted as:
    $< T_i, X_j, V_1, V_2 >$
    (*iii*) **Transaction commit:** Denoted as
    $< T_i$ commit $>$
    (*iv*) **Transaction abort:** Denoted as
    $< T_1$ abort $>$
18. **Forest Protocol:** Is a variant of tree protocol. The database is organized as a forest of rooted trees. Each transaction T_j must follow the following rules:
    (*i*) The first lock in each tree may be on any data item.
    (*ii*) The second and all subsequent, locks in a tree may be requested only if the parent of the requested mode is currently locked.
    (*iii*) Data items may be unlocked at any time.
    (*iv*) A data item may not be relocked by T_i after.
    It has been unlocked by T_i. The forest protocol does not ensure serializability
19. **Lock Modes:**
    Shared Mode (S): The node and all its descendents are locked in the shared model. All these nodes, locked explicitly or implicitly, are accessible for read-only access. No transaction can update the node or any of its descendents when the node is locked in the shared mode.
    Exclusive Mode Lock (X): The node and implicitly all its descendents are exclusively locked by a single transaction. No other transaction can access these nodes. The nodes locked in exclusive mode are accessible for read and update operations.
    Intension Share Mode (IS): The node is locked in intension shared mode, which means that is descendents cannot be locked exclusively. The descendents of the node may be individually locked in shared or intension shared mode. The descendents of node that is locked in IS mode are not locked implicitly.
    Intension Exclusive Mode (IX): The node is locked in intension exclusive mode, which means that the node itself cannot be exclusively locked. However, any of the descendants, if not already locked can be locked in any of the locking modes. The descendents of the node that is locked in the IX mode are not locked immediately.

Shared and Intension Exclusive Mode (SIX): The node is locked in the shared and intension exclusive mode and all the descendants are implicitly locked in the shared mode. However, any of the descendents can be explicitly locked in the exclusive intension exclusive, or shared and intension exclusive mode.

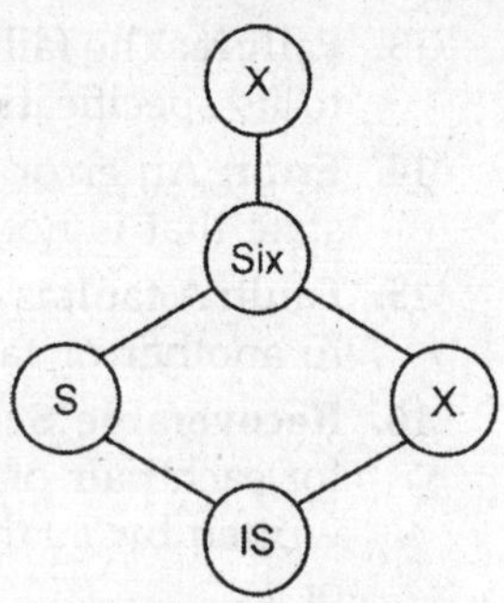

Fig. 1: Relative Privilege of the Locking Modes

Relative privilege of the various locking modes: The relative privilege of the various modes of locking can be given as follows:

- Exclusive mode has the highest privilege.
- The intension share mode has lowest privilege.
- The share mode is not comparable with the intension exclusive mode.

20. **Compatibility Matrix:** Compatibility between the current mode of locking and a request of another transaction for locking the node in a given mode is given in compatibility matrix. The entry TRUE represent that the request will be granted and transaction can continue. The entry FALSE indicates that the request cannot be granted and the requesting transaction will have to wait.

	IS	IX	S	SIX	X
IS	TRUE	TRUE	TRUE	TRUE	FALSE
IX	TRUE	TRUE	FALSE	FALSE	FALSE
S	TRUE	FALSE	TRUE	FALSE	FALSE
SIX	TRUE	FALSE	FALSE	FALSE	FALSE
X	FALSE	FALSE	FALSE	FALSE	FALSE
UNLOCK	TRUE	TRUE	TRUE	TRUE	TRUE

Storage Types: To ensure atomicity and durability properties of a transaction, we must gain a better understanding of these storage media and their access methods. There are the types of storage media. They are distinguished by their relative speed, capacity and resilience to failure.

1. **Volatile Storage:** Information residing in volatile storage does not usually survive system crashes. Access to volatile storage is extremely fast, both because of the speed of memory access itself and because it is possible to access any data item in volatile storage directly. Examples of such storage are main memory and cache memory.
2. **Non-volatile Storage:** Information residing in non-volatile storage survives system crash. Non-volatile storage is *s* lower than volatile storage by several orders of magnitude. Examples of such storage are disk and magnetic tapes. Disks are used for online storage, whereas tuples are used for archival storage. Both however are subject to failure, which may result in loss of information.

Stable Storage: Information residing in stable storage is never lost. Although stable storage is theoretically impossible to obtain, it can be closely approximated by techniques that make data loss extremely unlikely.

OBJECT ORIENTED DBMS

1. **Inheritance:** Inheritance is the process by which objects of one class acquire the properties of another class.
2. **Multiple Inheritance:** Multiple inheritance occurs when a certain subclass is a subclass two or more classes and hence inherits the functions of all super classes.
3. **Selective Inheritance:** Selective inheritance occurs when a subclass inherits only some the functions of super class. Other functions are not inherited. In this case, EXCEPT claus may be used to list the functions in a super class that are not inherited by the subclass.

DATABASE SYSTEM ARCHITECTURE

1. **Throughput:** Throughput is the number of tasks that can be completed in a given time interval.
2. **Response Time:** Response time is the amount of time it takes to complete a single task from the time it is submitted.
3. **Speed-up:** Speed-up refers to handling large number of tasks by increasing the degree of parallelism. It is defined as follows: If the execution time of a task on a large machine (with more number of processors, disks and other components) is T_L and execution time of same task on smaller machine is T_s then the speed-up due to parallelism is defined as T_S/T_L.
4. **Scale-up:** Scale-up refers to handling larger tasks by increasing the degree of parallelism. It is defined as follows: Let Q be a task and Q_N be a task that is N times larger than Q. Suppose that execution time of Q on a given machine M_S is T_S and the execution time of task Q_N on a parallel machine M_L which is N times larger than M_S is T_L. Then the scale-up is difined as T_S/T_L.

NEW APPLICATION

1. **Roll-up:** Moving from a finer granularity data to a coarser granularity data by means of aggregation is called doing a rollup.
2. **Drill-down:** Drill down is the opposite operation of rollup i.e. moving from coarser hyphen granularity to finer granularity data is called drill down.
3. **Support:** Support is a measure of what fraction of population satisfies the both the antecedent and consequent of knowledge representation rule.
4. **Confidence:** Confidence is a measure of how often the consequent is true when the antecedent is true.

APPENDIX–D

EXPERIMENTS

EXPERIMENT – 1

DATABASE MANAGEMENT SYSTEMS

Database and Tables Creation

create database Employee

create table Emp

```
(
Empno numeric (4) NOT NULL,
Ename varchar (20) NOT NULL,
Job char (10) NOT NULL,
Hiredate Datatime Not NULL,
Sal numeric (9, 2) NOT NULL,
Comm numbereric (7, 2),
Deptno numric (22) NOT NULL
)
```

Insert into Emp values (7369, 'Smith', 'Clerk', 7902, ' 17-Dec-1980', 800, NULL, 20)

Insert into Emp values (7499, 'Allen', 'Salesman', 7698, '20-Feb-1981', 1600, 300, 30)

Insert into Emp values (7521, 'Ward' 'Ward', 'Saleman', 7698, '22-Feb-1981', 1250, 500, 30

Insert into Emp values (7566, 'Jones', 'Manager', 7839, '02-Apr-1981', 2975, NULL, 20)

Insert into Emp values (7654, 'Martin', 'Salesman' , 7698, '28-Sep-1981', 1250, 1400, 30)

Insert into Emp values (7698, ;'Blake', 'Manager', 7839, '01-May-1981', 2850, NULL, 30)

Insert into Emp values (7782,, 'Clark', 'Manager', 7839, '09-Jun-1981', 2450, NULL, 10)

Insert into Emp values (7788, 'Scott', 'Analyst', 7566, '09-Dec-1982', 300, NULL, 20)

Insert into Emp values (7839, 'King', 'President', NULL, 17-Nov-1981', 5000, NULL, 10)

Insert into Emp values (7844, 'Turner', 'Salesman', 7698, '08-Sep-1981', 1500, 0, 30)

Insert into Emp values (7876, 'Adams', 'clerk', 7788, '12-Jan-1983', 1100, NULL, 20)

Insert into Emp values (7900, 'James', 'Clerk', 7698, '03-Dec-1981', 950, NULL, 30)

Insert into Emp values (7902, 'Ford', 'Analyst', 7566, '04-Dec-1981', 3000, NULL, 20)

Insert into Emp values (7934, 'Miller', 'Clerk', 7782, '23-Jan-1982', 1300, NULL, 10)

	Empno	Ename	Job	Mgr	Hiredate	Sal	Comm	Deptno
1	7369	Smith	Clerk	7902	1980-12-17 00:00:00.000	800.00	NULL	20
2.	7499	Allen	Salesman	7698	1981-02-20 00:00:00.000	1600.00	NULL	30
3.	7521	Ward	Salesman	7698	1981-02-22 00:00:00.000	1250.00	3000.00	30
4.	7566	Jones	Manager	7839	1981-04-02 00:00:00.000	2975.00	500.00	20
5.	7654	Marin	Salesman	7698	1981-09-28 00:00:00.000	1250.00	NULL	20
6.	7698	Blake	Manager	7839	1981-05-01 00:00:00.000	2850.00	1400.00	30
7.	7782	Clark	Manager	7839	1981-06-09 00:00:00.000	2450.00	NULL	10

8.	7788	Scott	Analyst	7566	1982-12-09 00:00:00.000	3000.00	NULL	20
9.	7839	King	President	NULL	1981-11-17 00:00:00.000	5000.00	NULL	10
10.	7844	Turner	Salesman	7698	1981-09-08 00:00:00.000	1500.00	0.000	30
11.	7876	Adams	Clerk	7788	1983-01-12 00:00:00.000	1100.00	NULL	20
12.	7900	James	Clerk	7698	1981-12-03 00:00:00.000	950.00	NULL	30
13.	7902	Ford	Analyst	7566	1981-12-04 00:00:00.000	3000.00	NULL	20
14.	7934	Miller	Clerk	7782	1982-01-23 00:00:00.000	1300.00	NULL	10

```
create table Dept
(
Deptno numeric (2),
Dname varchar (20),
Loc varchar (10)
)
insert into Dept valuse (10, 'Accounting', New York')
insert into Dept valuse (20, 'Research', 'Dallas')
insert into Dept valuse (30, 'Sales', chicago')
insert into Dept valuse (40, 'operations', 'Boston')
select * from Dept
```

	Deptno	Dname	Loc
1	10	Accouning	New York
2	20	Research	Dallas
3	30	Sales	Chicago
4	40	Operations	Boston

EXPERIMENT – 2

Acccess and Display Data

Use the Emp table to complete the following exercises :

1. Display each employee's name, Job, Salary and department number.

Ans. Select ename, Job, sal, deptno from Emp

	ename	Job	Sal	Deptno
1	Smith	clerk	800.00	20
2	Allen	Salesman	1600.00	30
3	Ward	Salesman	1250.00	30
4	Jones	Manager	2975.00	20
5	Martin	Salesman	1250.00	30
6	Blake	Manager	2850.00	30
7	Clark	Manager	2450.00	10
8	Scott	Analyst	3000.00	20
9	King	President	5000.00	10
10	Turner	Salesman	1500.00	30
11	Adams	Clerk	1100.00	20
12	James	Clark	950.00	30
13	Ford	Analyst	3000.00	20
14	Miler	Clark	1300.00	10

2. Display employees ame earning more than Rs.2,000. Label the column name Employee.

Ans. Select ename "Employee" from Emp where sal> 2000

	Employee
1	Jones
2	Blake
3	Clark
4	Scott
5	King
6	Ford

3. Display employees who are not clerks or salesman. Order the list by Employee name.

Ans. Select ename from Emp
Where Job not in ('clerk', ' Salesman')
order by ename

4. Display the employee name of those whose names contain the letter 'S'.

Ans. Select ename from Emp where ename like 'S'

	ename
1	Smith
2	Jones
3	Scott
4	Adams
5	James

5. Display the employee names and salaries of those having salaries less than their commission. Label the employee name 'Name' and salary column 'Salary'.

Ans. Select ename "Name", sal "Salary" from Emp
Where sal < comm

	Name	Salary
1	Martin	1250.00

6. Display employees hired in 1993.

Ans. Select ename from Emp
where hiredate between '01-Jan-1993' and '31-Dec-1993'

ename

7. Display the names and jobs of all employees in departments 10 and 20 in alphabetical order of name.

Ans. Select ename, Job from Emp
where deptno = 10 or deptno = 20
order by name

	ename	Job
1	Adams	clerk
2	clark	Manager
3	Ford	Analyst
4	Jones	Manager
5	King	President
6	Miler	Clerk
7	Scott	Analyst
8	Smith	Clerk

8. List the name, job salary for all employees who have a manager.

Ans. Select ename, Job, sal from Emp where mgr is NOT NULL

	ename	job	sal
1	Smith	Clerk	800.00
2	Allen	Salesman	1600.00
3	Wark	Salesman	1250.00
4	Jones	Manager	2975.00
5	Martin	Salesman	1250.00
6	Blake	Manager	2850.00
7	Clerk	Manager	2450.00
8	Scott	Analyst	3000.00
9	Turner	Salesman	1500.00
10	Adams	Clerk	1100.00
11	James	Clerk	950.00
12	Ford	Analyst	3000.00
13	Miller	Clerk	1300.00

9. Display name, annual salary and commission of all salespeople whose monthly salary is greater than their commission. The output should be ordered by salary, highest first.

Ans. Select ename, sal, comm from Emp
where sal > comm order by sal DESC

	ename	sal	comm
1	Allen	1600.00	3000.00
2	Turner	1500.00	0.00
3	Ward	1250.00	500.00

10. Select data as displayed :
Smith has held the position of Clerk in dept 20 since 13-Jun-83.
Smith has held the position of Manager in dept 30 since 31-Out-83.
Smith has held the position of Analyst in dept 20 since 05-Mar-84.

Ans. Select ename, 'has held the position of ' " ", Job. 'in dept ' " ", deptno, 'since ' " ", hiredate from Emp

	ename		job		deptno		hiredate
1	Smith	has held the position of	Clerk	Indept	20	since	1980-12-17 00:00:00.000
2	Allen	has held the position of	Salesman	in dept	30	since	1981-02-20 00:00:00.000
3	Ward	has held the position of	Salesman	in dept	30	since	1981-02-22 00:00:00.000
4	jones	has held the position of	Manageer	in dept	20	since	1981-04-02 00:00:00.000
5	Mertin	has held the position of	Salesman	in dept	30	since	1981-09-28 00:00:00.000
6	Blake	has held the position of	Manager	in dept	30	since	1981-05-01 00:00:00.000
7	Clerk	has held the position of	Manager	in dept	10	since	1981-06-09 00:00:00.000
8	Scott	has held the position of	Analyst	in dept	20	since	1982-12-09 00:00:00.000
9	King	has held the position of	President	in dept	10	since	1981-11-17 00:00:00.000
10	Turner	has held the position of	Salesman	in dept	30	since	1981-09-08 00:00:00.000
11	Adams	has held the position of	Clerk	in dept	20	since	1983-01-12 00:00:00.000
12	James	has held the position of	Clerk	in dept	30	since	1981-12-03 00:00:00.000
13	Ford	has held the position of	Analyst	in dept	20	since	1981-12-04 00:00:00.000
14	Miller	has held the position of	Clerk	in dept	10	since	1982-01-23 00:00:00.000

EXPERIMENT – 3

Aggregate Functions

1. List the department numbers and number of employees in each department.

Ans. Select deptno, count (*) "No. of Employees"
from Emp group by deptno

	Deptno	No. of Employees
1	10	3
2	20	5
3	30	6

2. List average salary for all the departments more than 5 perple.

Ans. Select deptno, avg (sal) "Average salary" from Emp
group by deptno
having count (*) > 5

	Deptno	Average salary
1	30	1566.666666

3. List jobs of all the employees where maximum salary is greater than or equal to 5000.

Ans. Select job from Emp
group by job having max (sal) > = 5000

	job
1	President

4. List the deptno and total salary payable in each department.

Ans. Select deptno, sum (sal) "Salary Sum" from Emp
group by deptno

	Deptno	Salary Sum
1	10	8750.00
2	20	10875.00
3	30	9400.00

5. List the jobs and the number of employees in each job. The result should be indescending order of the number of employees.

Ans. Select job, count (*) "count" from Emp
group by job
order by 2 DESC

	job	Count
1	Clerk	4
2	Salasman	4
3	Manager	3
4	Analyst	2
5	President	1

6. List the total Salary, maximum and minimum salary of employees job wise.

Ans. Select job, sum (sal) "Sum", max (sal) "Maximum",
min (sal) "Minimum", avg (sal) "Average"
from Emp group by job

	job	Sum	Maximum	Mainimum	Average
1	Analyst	6000.00	3000.00	3000.00	3000.000000
2	clerk	4150.00	1300.00	800.00	1037.000000
3	Manager	8275.00	2975.00	2450.00	2758.000000
4	President	5000.00	5000.00	5000.00	5000.000000
5	Salesman	5600.00	1600.00	1250.00	1400.000000

7. List the average salary from each job excluding managers.

Ans. select job, avg (sal) "Average" from Emp
Where Job ! = 'manager'
group by job

	job	Average
1	Analyst	3000.000000
2	Clerk	1037.000000
3	president	5000.000000
4	Salesman	1400.000000

8. List the total, maximum, minimum and the average salary of employee job wise for deptno 20 only.

Ans. Select job, sum (sal) "Sum", max (sal) "Maximum",
min (sal) "Minimum:, avg (sal) "Average" from Emp
where deptno = 20 group by job

	job	Sum	Maximum	Mainimum	Average
1	Analyst	6000.00	3000.00	3000.00	3000.000000
2	clerk	1900.00	1100.00	800.00	950.000000
3	Manager	2975.00	2975.00	2975.00	2975.000000

9. List the total, maximum minimum and the average salary of employees job wise for deptno 20 and display only those having average salary>1000.

Ans. Select job, sum (sal) "Sum", max (sal) "Maximum",
min (sal) "Minimum:, avg (sal) "Average" from Emp
Where deptno = 20
group by job
having avg (sal) > 1000

	job	Sum	Maximum	Mainimum	Average
1	Analyst	6000.00	3000.00	3000.00	3000.000000
2	Manager	2975.00	2975.00	2975.00	2975.000000

EXPERIMENT – 4

Table Modification

1. Table clien_master:

Ans.
```
create table client_master
(
client_no char (10),
name char (50),
city char (50),
Pincode numeric (6),
State char (50),
bal_due numeric
)
```

	client_no	name	city	pincode	state	bal_due
1	C00001	Gaurav	Chandigarh	160019	Punjab	15000
2	C00002	Vandana	madras	780001	Tamil Nadu	0
3	C00003	Rekha	Bombay	400057	Maharashtra	5000
4	C00004	Gagan Singh	Ludhiana	160236	Punjab	0
5	C00005	Ravi Sreedharan	Delhi	100001	Delhi	2000
6	C00006	Rukmini	Gurgaon	130002	Haryana	0

2. Table product_master:

Ans.
```
create table product_master
(
product_no char (10),
description char (50),
profit_percent char (50),
nom char (10)
qty_no_hand numeric,
reorder_level numeric,
sell_price numeric,
cost_price numeric
)
```

	product_no	description	profit_percent	nom	qty_no_hand	reorder_level	sell_price	cost_price
1	P00001	3.5 Floppies	5	Piece	100	20	525	500
2	P03453	Monitors	5	Piece	10	3	12000	11280
3	P06734	Mouse	5	Piece	20	5	1050	1000
4	P07868	Keyboards	2	Piece	10	3	3150	3050
5	P07885	CD Drive	2.5	Piece	10	3	5250	5100
6	P07965	540 HDD	4	Piece	10	3	8400	8000
7	P07975	3.5 Drive	5	Piece	10	3	1050	1000

3. Table salesman_master:

Ans. create table salesman_master

(

salesman_no char (10),

name char (50),

address1 char (50),

address2 char (50),

city char (15),

pincode numeric,

sal_amt numeric,

tgt_to_get numeric,

ytd_sales numeric,

remarks char (20)

)

	salesman-no	name	address1	address2	city	pincode	state	sal_amt	tgt_to_get	ytd_sales	remarks
1	S00001	Kiran	A/14	Worli	Mumbai	400002	maharashta	3000	100	50	good
2	S00002	Manish	65	Narinan	Mumbai	400001	maharashta	3000	200	100	good
3	S00003	Ravi	P-7	Bandra	Mumbai	400032	maharashta	3000	200	200	good
4	S00004	Ashish	A/5	Juhu	Mumbai	400044	maharashta	3500	200	150	good

4

(*a*) Change the city of client_no 'C00005' to Bombay

Ans. update client_master set city= 'Bombay where client_no='C00005'

(*b*) Change the bal_amt of client_no C0001 to Rs. 1000

Ans. update client_master set bal_due = 1000 where client_no= 'C00001'

(*c*) Change the cost priceof '3.5 Floppies' to Rs.475

Ans. update product_master set cost_price=475 where description='3.5 Floppies'

(*d*) Change the city of salesman to Bombay

Ans. update salesman_master set city='Bomday

5.

(*a*) Delete all salesman from salesman_master whose alaries are equal to Rs.3500

Ans. delete from salesman_master where sal_amt=3500

(*b*) Delete all products from product_master where the quantity on hand is equal to 100.

Ans. delete from product_master where qty_no_hand= 100

(*c*) Delete from client_master where stste is Tamil Nadu.

Ans. delete from client_master where state='Tamil Nadu'

The tables after executing queries in 4 ad 5 above are:

select * from client_master

	client_no	name	city	pincode	state	bal_due
1	C00001	Gaurav	Chandigarh	160019	Punjab	1000
3	C00003	Rekha	Bombay	400057	Maharashtra	5000
4	C00004	Gagan Singh	Ludhiana	160236	Punjab	0
5	C00005	Ravi Sreedharan	Delhi	100001	Delhi	2000
6	C00006	Rukmini	Gurgaon	130002	Haryana	0

select * from product_master

	product_no	description	profit_percent	nom	qty_no_hand	reorder_level	sell_price	cost_price
2	P03453	Monitors	6	Piece	10	3	12000	11280
3	P06734	Mouse	5	Piece	20	5	1050	1000
4	P07868	Keyboards	2	Piece	10	3	3150	3050
5	P07885	CD Drive	2.5	Piece	10	3	5250	5100
6	P07965	540 HDD	4	Piece	10	3	8400	8000
7	P07975	3.5 Drive	5	Piece	10	3	1050	1000

select * from salesman_master

	salesman-no	**name**	**address1**	**address2**	**city**	**pincode**	**state**	**sal_amt**	**tgt_to_get**	**ytd_sales**	**remarks**
1	S00001	Kiran	A/14	Worli	Mumbai	400002	maharashta	3000	100	50	good
2	S00002	Manish	65	Narinan	Mumbai	400001	maharashta	3000	200	100	good
3	S00003	Ravi	P-7	Bandra	Mumbai	400032	maharashta	3000	200	200	good

EXPERIMENT – 5

Joining Of Tables

```
create table emp
(
id int,
name varchar (20)
)
insert into emp values (1,'a')
insert into emp values (2,'b')
insert into emp values (3,'c')
insert into emp values (4,'d')
Select * from emp
```

	id	name
1	1	*a*
2	2	b
3	3	*c*
4	4	*d*

```
create table orders
(
id int,
product varchar (20),
pid int
)
insert into orders values (1,'table',10000)
insert into orders values (2,'chair',11000)
insert into orders values (3,'ac',12000)
Select * from orders
```

	id	product	pid
1	1	table	10000
2	2	chair	11000
3	3	ac	12000

Query 1

select e1. name, o1, product from emp e1, orders o 1, orders o1 where e1.id = o1.id

	name	product
1	*a*	table
2	*b*	chair
3	*c*	ac

Query 2

select e1, name, o. product from emp e1 lnner join orders o1 on e1.id=o1.id

	name	product
1	a	table
2	b	chair
3	c	ac

Query 3

select e1, name, o. product from emp e1 Left join orders o1 on e1.id=o1.id

	name	product
1	a	table
2	b	chair
3	c	ac
4	d	NULL

Query 4

select e1, name, o. product from emp e1 Right join orders o1 on e1.id=o1.id

	name	product
1	a	table
2	b	chair
3	c	ac

EXPERIMENT – 6
Data Constraints

create table sourse(
course_no char
course_name varchar(20))

insert into course values (1,'abcd')
insert into course values (2,'bcd')
insert into course values (3,'cd')
insert into course values (4,'dwe')
insert into course values (5,'oracle')
insert into course values (6,'unix')
select * from course

	course_no	course_name
1	1	abcd
2	2	bcd
3	3	cd
4	4	dwe
5	5	oracle
6	6	unix

create table course_feel(
course_no char(4) unique,.
full_part char(10 check (full_part='f' or full_part='p') unique,
fees int)
fees int)
insert into course_feel values (3,'f'11000)
insert into course_feel values (4,'p' 6000)
insert into course_feel values (5,'p' 6000)
(1 row (s) affected)
91 row (s) affected)
Msg 2627, level 14, state 1, Line 3
violation of UNIQUE KEY constraint 'UQ_course_feel_4C0144E4'.
Cannot insert duplicate key in object 'dbo, course_feel'.
The atatement has been terminated.
create table student 1(
prospectur_no int primary key,
address varchar(30),
phone_no int,
d_o_b datetime,
total_amt int,
amt_paid int,
intstallment char(1) check (installment='i' or installment='f')
)
insert into student1 values (12, 'deepak',' 12ewedd', 4131215, '12/03/99', 10000, 2000,'i')
insert into student1 values (13, 'apporv',' 12wwe', 41312, '10/28/94', 10000, 1000,'f')
insert into student1 values (14, 'apan',' gftsr56', 25413678, '11/23/07', 10000, 3000,'i')
select * from student1

	prospectur_no	name1	address	phone_no	d_o_b	total-amt	amt_paid	installment
1	12	deepak	12ewedd	4131215	1999-12-03 00.00.00.000	10000	2000	i
1	13	apporv	12wwe	41312	1994-10-28 00.00.00.000	10000	10000	f
1	14	apan	gftsr	25413678	2007-11-23 00.00.00.000	10000	3000	i

create table installment 1
(

prospectus_no int references student (prospectus_no) on delete cascale unique,
installment_amt int, due dt datetime unique,
paid char(1) check (paid='p' or paid='u')
)
insert into installment 1 values (14,2000, '03/13/99' 'u')
insert into installment 1 values (13,2500, '05/24/04' 'u')
select * from installment 1

	prospectur_no	name1	address	phone_no	d_o_b	total-amt	amt_paid	installment
1	12							

	prospectus_no	installment_amt	due_dt	paid
1	14	2000	1999-03-13 00:00:00.000	u
2	13	2500	2004-05-24 00:00:00.000	u

insert into installment values (15,4000, '12/23/97', 'p')
Msg 547, level 16, state 0, line 1
The INSERT statement conficted with the FOREIGN KEY constraint "FK_installme_prosp_54968AE5". The conflict occurred in database "master". table "dbo. student 1", column 'prospectus_no'.
The statement has to been terminated.

EXPERIMENT – 7

Indexes

create table emp1
(
EMPNO INT,
ENAME VARCHAR(20),
JOB CHAR (10),
SAL INT,
DEPTNO INT
)
insert into emp 1 values (2345, 'amit', 'analyst', 4500,20)
insert into emp 1 values (3478, 'aman', 'president', 6700,40)
insert into emp 1 values (4567, 'rohit', 'manager', 5000,10)
select * from emp1

	EMPNO	ENAME	JOB	SAL	DEPTNO
1	2345	amit	analyst	4500	20
2	3478	aman	president	6700	40
3	4567	rohit	manager	5000	10

CREATE UNIQUE INDEX empidx ON emp1 (EMPNO)
insert into emp1 values (4567,'d','f',56,65)
Msg 2601, Level 14, state 1, Line 1
Cannot insert duplicate key row in object 'dbo_emp1' with unique index 'empidx'.
The statement has been terminated.

Some Extra Queries

select DATEPART (month, GETDATE())"MONTH"

MONTH

1 11

Select DATEPART(d, GETDATE())"YEAR"

YEAR

1 2008

select DATENAME(month, GETDATE())"MONTH"

MONTH

1 November

EXPERIMENT – 8

Numeric Functions

1. select power (3,2) "Raised"

   Raised

   1 9
2. select abs(-15) 'Absolute"

   Absolute

   1 15
3. select round (15.1567,1) "Round"

   Round

   1 15.2000
4. select sqrt (49) "Square Root"

   Square Root

   1 7
5. select lower ('DATABASE SYSTEMS') "Lower"

   Lower

   1 database systems
6. select upper (database systems') "Upper"

   Upper

   1 DATABASE SYSTEMS

Questions and Answers for Viva Voce

1. **What makes SQL a non-procedural language?**

Ans. SQL determines what should be done, not how it should be done. The database must implement the SQL request. This feature is a big plus in cross-platform, cross-language development.

2. **How can you tell whether a database is truly relational?**

Ans. Apply Dr. Codd's 12 (we know there are 13) rules.

3. **What can you do with SQL?**

Ans. SQL enables you to select, insert, modify, and delete the information in a database; perform system security functions and set user permissions on tables and databases; handle online transaction processing within an application; create stored procedures and triggers to reduce application coding; and transfer data between different databases.

4. **Name the process that separates data into distinct, unique sets.**

Ans. Normalization is the process that separates data into distinct unique sets. Normalization reduces the amount of repetition and complexity of the structure of the previous level.

5. **Do the following statements return the same or different output:**

SELECT * FROM CHECKS;

select * from checks;?

Ans. Yes, the two statements return the same output. The only difference between the two statements is that one statement is in lowercase and the other uppercase. Case sensitivity is not normally a factor in the syntax of SQL. However, be aware of capitalization when dealing with data.

6. **None of the following queries work. Why not?**

Ans. (*a*) **Select ***

The FROM clause is missing. The two mandatory components of a **SELECT** statement are the **Select** and **FROM**.

(*b*) **Select * from checks**

The semicolon, which identifies the end of a SQL statement, is missing.

(*c*) **Select amount name payee FROM checks;**

You need a comma between each column name:

Select amount, name, payee

FROM checks;

7. Which of the following SQL statements will work?

(*a*) select *

from checks;

(*b*) select * from checks;

(*c*) select * from checks

Ans. All the above work.

8. Using the CHECKS table, write a query to return just the check numbers and the remarks.

SELECT CHECK #, REMARKS FROM CHECKS;

9. Rewrite the query from exercise 1 so that the remarks will appear as the first column in your query results.

SELECT REMARKS, CHECK# FROM CHECKS;

10. Using the CHECKS table, write a query to return all the unique remarks.

SELECT DISTINCT REMARKS FROM CHECKS;

Use the FRIENDS table to answer the following questions.

LASTNAME	FIRSTNAME	AREACODE	PHONE	ST	ZIP
BUNDY	AL	100	555-1111	TL	22333
MEZA	AL	200	555-2222	UK	
MERRICK	BUD	300	555-6666	CO	80212
MAST	JD	381	555-6767	LA	23456
BULHER	FERRIS	345	555-3223	IL	23332
PERKINS	ALTON	911	555-3116	CA	95633
BOSS	SIR	204	555-2345	CT	95633

11. Write a query that returns everyone in the database whoe last name begins with M.

Ans. SELECT * FROM FRIENDS WHERE LASTNAME LIKE 'M%';

12. Write a query that returns everyone who lives in Illinois with a first_name of AL.

Ans. SELECT * FROM FRIENDS

WHERE STATE = 'IL'

AND FIRST_NAME = 'AL';

13. Given two tables (PART1 and PART2) containing columns named PARTNO, how would you find out which part numbers are in both tables? Write the query. Use the INTERSECT. Remember that INTERSECT returns rows common to both queries.

Ans. SELECT PART_NO FROM PART1

INTERSECT

SELECT PART_NO FROM PART2;

14. What shorthand could you use instead of WHERE a>=10 AND a<=30?

Ans. WHERE a BETWEEN 10 AND 30;

15. What will this query return?

Ans. SELECT FIRSTNAME

FROM FRIENDS

WHERE FIRSTNAME = 'AL'
AND LASTNAME = 'BULHER';

Nothing will be returned, as both conditions are not true.

16. Using the FRIENDS table, write a query that returns the following:
NAME ST

....

AL FROM IL

Ans. SQL > SELECT (FIRSTNAME || 'FROM') NAME, STATE
2 FROM FRIENDS
3 WHERE STATE = 'IL'
4 AND
5 LASTNAME = 'BUNDY';

17. Using the FRIENDS table, write a query that returns the following:
NAME PHONE

..

MERRICK, BUD 300-555-6666
MAST, JD 381-555-6767
BULHER, FERRIS 345-555-3223

Ans. SQL > SELECT LASTNAME || ',' || FIRSTNAME NAME,
2 AREACODE || '–' || PHONE PHONE
3 FROM FRIENDS
4 WHERE AREACODE BETWEEN 300 AND 400;

18. Which function capitalizes the first letter of a character string and makes the rest lowercase?

Ans. INITCAP

19. Which functions are also known by the name?

Ans. Group functions and aggregate functions are the same thing.

20. Will this query work?
SQL > SELECT COUNT (LASTNAME) FROM CHARACTERS;

Ans. Yes, it will return the total of rows.

21. How about this one?
sql > SELECT SUM (LASTNAME) FROM CHARACTERS

Ans. No, the query won't work because **LASTNAME** is a character field.

22. Assuming that they are separate columns, which function(s) would splice together FIRSTNAME and LASTNAME?

Ans. The **CONCAT** function and the || symbol.

23. What does the answer 6 mean from the following SELECT?
INPUT:
SQL > SELECT COUNT (*) FROM TEAMSTATS;
OUTPUT:
COUNT (*)

Ans. 6 is the number of records in the table.

24. Will the following statement work?

SQL > SELECT SUBSTR LASTNAME, 1, 5 FROM NAME_TBL;

Ans. No, missing ( ) around **lastname,** 1, 5 Also, a better plan is to give the column an alias. The statement should look like this:

SQL > SELECT SUBSTR (LASTNAME, 1, 5) NAME FROM NAME_TBL;

25. Using TEAMSTATS table, write a query to determine who is batting under .25. (For the baseball-challenged reader, batting average is hits/ab.)

Ans. SQL > SELECT NAME FROM TEAMSTATS

2 WHERE (HITS/AB) < .25;

OUTPUT:

NAME

....

HAMHOCKER

CASEY

26. Using today's CHARACTERS table, write a query that will return the following:

OUTPUT:

INITIALS .... CODE

K.A.P. 32

1 row selected.

Ans. SQL > select substr (firstname, 1, 1) || '.' ||

substr (middlename, 1, 1) || '.' ||

substr (lastname, 1, 1) || '.' INITIALS, code

from characters

where code = 32;

27. Which clause works just like LIKE (<exp>%)?

Ans. STARTING WITH

28. What is the function of the GROUP BY clause, and what other clause does it acts like?

Ans. The **GROUP BY** clause groups data result sets that have been manipulated by various functions. The **GROUP BY** clause acts like the **ORDER BY** clause in that it orders the results of the query in the order the columns are listed in the **GROUP BY.**

29. Will this SELECT work?

SQL > SELECT NAME, AVG (SALARY), DEPARTMENT

FROM PAY_TBL

WHERE DEPARTMENT = 'ACCOUNTING'

ORDER BY NAME

GROUP BY DEPARTMENT, SALARY;

Ans. No, the syntax is incorrect. The GROUP BY must come before the **ORDER BY.** Also, all the selected columns must be listed in the **GROUP BY.**

30. When using the HAVING clause, do you always have to use a GROUP BY also?

Ans. Yes.

31. Cay you use ORDER BY on a column that is not one of the columns in the SELECT statement?

Ans. Yes, it is not necessary to use the **SELECT** statement on a column that you put in the **ORDER BY** clause.

32. Using the ORGCHART table from the preceding examples, find out how many people on each team have 30 or more days of sick leave. Here is your baseline that shows how many folks are on each team.

SELECT TEAM, COUNT (TEAM)

FROM ORGCHART

GROUP BY TEAM;

OUPUT:

TEAM COUNT

....

....

COLLECTIONS 2

MARKETING 3

PR 1

RESEARCH 2

Compare it to the query that solves the question:

Ans. INPUT:

SELECT TEAM, COUNT (TEAM)

FROM ORGCHART

WHERE SICKLEAVE>=30

GROUP BY TEAM;

OUTPUT:

Team Count

....

....

COLLECTIONS 1

MARKETING 1

RESEARCH 1

The output shows the number of people on each team with a **SICKLEAVE** balance of 30 days or more.

33. Using the CHECKS table, write a SELECT that will return the following:

OUTPUT:

CHECK#	**PAYEE**	**AMOUNT**
1	**MA BELL**	**150**

Ans. SQL > SELECT CHECK#, PAYEE, AMOUNT

FROM CHECKS

WHERE CHECK# = 1;

34. How many rows would a two-table join produce if one table had 50,000 rows and the other had 100,000?

Ans. 5,000,000,000 rows.

35. What type of join appears in the following select statement?

select e.name, e.employee_id, ep.salary
from employee_tbl e,
employee_pay_tbl ep
where e.employee_id = ep.employee_id;

Ans. The preceding join is an equi-join. You are matching all the employee_ids in the two tables.

36. Will the following SELECT statements work?

select name, employee_id, salary
from employee_tbl e,
employee_pay_tbl ep
where employee_id = employee_id
and name like '%MITH';

Ans. No. The columns and tables are not properly named. Remember column and table aliases.

select e.name, e.employee_id, ep.salary
from employee_tbl e,
employee_pay_tbl ep
where name like '%MITH';

No. The join command is missing in the **where** clause.

select e.name, e.employee_id, ep.salary
from employee_tbl e,
employee_pay_tbl ep
where e.employee_id = ep.employee_id
and e.name like '%MITH';

Yes. The syntax is correct.

37. In the WHERE clause, when joining the tables, should you do the join first or the conditions?

Ans. The joins should go before the conditions.

38. In joining tables are you limited to one-column joins, or can you join on more than one column?

Ans. You can join on more than one column. You may be forced to join on multiple columns depending on what makes a row of data unique or the specific conditions you want to place on the data to be retrieved.

39. Rewrite the following query to make it more readable and shorter.

INPUT:

select orders.orderedon, orders.name, part.partnum,
part.price, part.description from orders, part
where orders.partnum = part.partnum and
orders.orderedon
between '1-SEP-96' and '30-SEP-96'
order by part.partnum;

Ans. SQL > select o.orderedon ORDER_DATE, o.name NAME, p.partnum PART#, p.price PRICE, p.description DESCRIPTION
from orders o, part p
where o.partnum = p.partnum
and o.orderedon like '%SEP%'
order by ORDER_DATE;

40. From the PART table and the ORDERS table, make up a query that will return the following:

OUTPUT:

ORDEREDON NAME PARTNUM QUANTITY

...

...

2-SEP-96 TRUE WHEEL 10 1

Ans. select o.orderedon ORDEREDON, o.name NAME, p.partnum PARTNUM,
o.quanity QUANITY
from orders o,
part p
where o.partnum = p.partnum
and o.orderedon like '%SEP%';

41. Are the following statements true or false?

The aggregate functions SUM, COUNT, MIN, MAX, and AVG all return multiple values.

Ans. False.

They all return a single value.

The maximum number of sub queries that can be nested is two.

False.

The limit is a function of your implementation.

Correlated sub queries are completely self-contained.

False.

Correlated sub queries enable you to use an outside reference.

42. Will the following sub queries work using the ORDERS table and the PART table?

INPUT/OUTPUT:

SQL > SELECT *

FROM PART;

PARTNUM	DESCRIPTION	PRICE
54	PEDALS	54.25
42	SEATS	24.50
46	TIRES	15.25
23	MOUNTAIN BIKE	350.45
76	ROAD BIKE	530.00
10	TANDEM	1200.00

6 rows selected.

INPUT/OUTPUT:

SQL > SELECT *

FROM ORDERS;

ORDEREDON	NAME	PARTNUM	QUANITY	REMARKS	
15-MAY-96	TRUE	WHEEL	23	6	PAID
19-MAY-96	TRUE	WHEEL	76	3	PAID
2-SEP-96	TRUE	WHEEL	10	1	PAID
30-JUN-96	BIKE	SPEC	54	10	PAID
30-MAY-96	BIKE	SPEC	10	2	PAID
30-MAY-96	BIKE	SPEC	23	8	PAID
17-JAN-96	BIKE	SPEC	76	11	PAID
17-JAN-96	LE	SHOPPE	76	5	PAID
1-JUN-96	LE	SHOPPE	10	3	PAID
1-JUN-96	AAA	BIKE	10	1	PAID
1-JUN-96	AAA	BIKE	76	4	PAID
1-JUN-96	AAA	BIKE	46	14	PAID
11-JUL-96	JACKS	BIKE	76	14	PAID

13 rows selected.

(*a*) **SQL > SELECT * FROM ORDERS**
WHERE PARTNUM =
SELECT PARTNUM FROM PART
WHERE DESCRIPTION = 'TRUE WHEEL';

Ans. No. Missing the parenthesis around the sub query.

(*b*) SQL > SELECT PARTNUM
FROM ORDERS
WHERE PARTNUM =
(SELECT * FROM PART
WHERE DESCRIPTION = 'LE SHOPPE');

Ans. No. The SQL engine cannot correlate all the columns in the part table with the operator =

(*c*) SQL > SELECT NAME, PARTNUM
FROM ORDERS
WHERE EXISTS
(SELECT * FROM ORDERS
WHERE NAME = 'TRUE WHEEL');

Ans. Yes. This sub query is correct.

43. What is wrong with the following statement?

DELETE COLLECTION;

Ans. If you want to delete all records from the **COLLECTION** table, you must use the following syntax:

DELETE FROM COLLECTION;

Keep in mind that this statement will delete all records. You can qualify which records you want to delete by using the following syntax:

DELETE FROM COLLECTION
WHERE VALUE = 125

This statement would delete all records with a value of 125.

44. What is wrong with the following statement?

INSERT INTO COLLECTION SELECT * FROM TABLE_2

Ans. This statement was designed to insert all the records from **TABLE_2** into the **COLLECTION** table. The main problem here is using the **INTO** keyword with the **INSERT** statement. When copying data from one table into another table, you must use the following syntax:

INSERT COLLECTION
SELECT * FROM TABLE_2;

Also, remember that the data types of the fields selected from **TABLE_2** must exactly match the data types and order of the fields within the **COLLECTION** table.

45. What is wrong with the following statement?

UPDATE COLLECTION ("HONUS WAGNER CARD", 25000, "FOUND IT");

Ans. This statement confuses the **UPDATE** function with the **INSERT** function. To **UPDATE** values into the **COLLECTIONS** table, use the following syntax:

UPDATE COLLECTIONS
SET NAME = "HONUS WAGNER CARD"
VALUE = 25000,
REMARKS = "FOUND IT";

46. What would happen if you issued the following statement?

SQL > DELETE * FROM COLLECTION;

Ans. Nothing would be deleted because of incorrect syntax. The * is not required here.

47. What would happen if you issued the following statement?

SQL > DELETE FROM COLLECTION;

Ans. All rows in the **COLLECTION** table will be deleted.

48. What would happen if you issued the following statement?

SQL > UPDATE COLLECTION
SET WORTH = 555
SET REMARKS = 'UP FROM 525';

Ans. All values in the **COLLECTION** table for the worth column are now **555,** and all remarks in the **COLLECTION** table now say **UP FROM 525.** Probably not a good thing!

49. Will the following SQL statement work?

SQL > INSERT INTO COLLECTION
SET VALUES = 900
WHERE ITEM = 'STRING';

Ans. No. The syntax is not correct. The **INSERT** and the **SET** do not go together.

50. Will the following SQL statement work?

SQL > UPDATE COLLECTION
SET VALUES = 900
WHERE ITEM = 'STRING';

Ans. Yes. This syntax is correct.

51. What is wrong with the following statement?

CREATE TABLE new_table (
ID NUMBER,
FIELD1 char (40),
FIELD2 char (80),
ID char (40));

Ans. This statement has two problems. The first problem is that the name ID is repeated within the table. Even though the data types are different reusing a field name within a table is illegal. The second problem is that the closing parentheses are missing from the end of the statement. It should look like this:

CREATE TABLE new_table (
ID NUMBER,
FIELD1 char (40),
FIELD2 char (80));

52. What is wrong with the following statement?

ALTER DATABASE BILLS (
COMPANY char (80));

Ans. The command to modify a field's data type or length is the **ALTER TABLE** command, not the **ALTER DATABASE** command.

53. When a table is created, who is the owner?

Ans. The owner of the new table would be whoever created the table. If you signed on as your ID, then your ID would be the owner. If you signed on as SYSTEM, then SYSTEM would be the owner.

54. Can you have duplicate table names?

Ans. Yes. Just as long as the owner or schema is not the same.

55. When nesting transactions, does issuing a ROLLBACK TRANSACTIOI command cancel the current transaction and roll back the batch of statements into the upper-level transaction? Why or why not?

Ans. No. When nesting transactions, any rollback of a transaction cancels all the transactions currently in progress. The effect of all the transactions will not truly be saved until the outer transaction has been committed.

56. Can savepoints be used to "save off" portions of a transaction? Why or why not?

Ans. Yes. Savepoints allow the programmer to save off statements within a transaction. If desired, the transaction can then be rolled back to this savepoint instead of to the beginning of the transaction.

57. Can a COMMIT command be used by itself or must it be embedded?

Ans. A COMMIT command can be issued by itself or in the transaction.

58. If you issue the COMMIT command and then discover a mistake, can you still use the ROLLBACK command?

Ans. Yes and No. You can issue the command, but it will not roll back the changes.

59. Will using a savepoint in the middle of a transaction save all that happened before it automatically?

Ans. No. A savepoint comes into play only if a **ROLLBACK** command is issued-and then only the changes made after the savepoint will be rolled back.

60. What is wrong with the following statement?
SQL > GRANT CONNECTION TO DAVID;

Ans. There is no **CONNECTION** role. The proper syntax is
SQL > **GRANT CONNECT TO DAVID;**

61. True or False (and why): Dropping a user will cause all objects owned by that user to be dropped as well.

Ans. This statement is true only if the
DROP USER user name **CASCADE**
statement is executed.
The **CASCADE** option tells the system to drop all objects owned by the user as well as that user.

62. What would happen if you created a table and granted select privileges on the table to public?

Ans. Everyone could select from your table, even users you may not want to be able to view your data.

63. Is the following SQL statement correct?
SQL > create user RON
identified by RON;

Ans. Yes. This syntax creates a user. However, the user will acquire the default settings, which may not be desirable. Check your implementation for these settings.

64. Is the following SQL statement correct?
SQL > alter RON
identified by RON;

Ans. No. The user is missing. The correct syntax is
SQL > **alter user RON**
identified by RON;

65. Is the following SQL statement correct?
SQL > grant connect, resource to RON;

Ans. Yes. The syntax is correct.

66. If you own a table, who can select from that table?

Ans. Only users with the select privilege on your table can select form the table.

67. In Oracle, how can you find out what tables and views you own?

Ans. By selecting from **USER_CATALOG** or **CAT.** The name of the data dictionary object will vary by implementation, but all versions have basically the same information about objects such as tables and views.

68. What types of information are stored in the data dictionary?

Ans. Database design, user statistics, processes, objects, growth of objects, performance statistics, stored SQL code, database security are the types of information stored in the data dictionary.

69. How can you use performance statistics?

Ans. Performance statistics suggest ways to improve database performance by modifying database parameters and streamlining SQL, which may also include the use of indexes and an evaluation of their efficiency.

70. What are some database object?

Ans. Tables, indexes, synonyms, clusters, views are some database objects.

APPENDIX–E

DATABASE DESIGN PROJECT CYCLE

&

DBMS PROJECT

"TRAINING AND PLACEMENT INFORMATION SYSTEM"

DATABASE DESIGN PROJECT CYCLE

1. INTRODUCTION

Database design is an interactive process. Lots of tools and methods are available to design database. Database is the most important part of an organization. Growth of any organization depends upon its database. Database should be consistent. In a large organization situated in different continents with large number of users, an effective database is required to provide database independence, rights to handle database and consistent data. Database should be able to handle rapid changes, interactive queries and support distributed data handling etc. To design such kind of database a systematic procedure is required so that DBA can design an effective database.

In this chapter, we discuss database design cycle in detail.

2. DATABASE DESIGN CYCLE

To design an effective database system, a step by step procedure is required. In this procedure, different tasks are categorized to design database system. User can move forward to next phase after successfully completion of present phase and also move backward to previous phase to review it again and make necessary modifications if required. It makes a Database system design cycle. The Database system design cycle shown in Figure 1 has Seven phases as discussed below.

Phase 1—Definition of the Problem

The first step in database system design cycle is problem identification. Following processes are involved in phase 1.

(*i*) **Determine the need :** DBA draws a rough outline of the project by understanding the actual need in database designing, as database design requirements are different for different organizations.

(*ii*) **Flexibility :** This process is used to find the flexibility of rough outline of project like how much it can be enhanced in future etc.

(*iii*) **Cost estimation :** A rough overall project cost is estimated to determine the expences incur that includes, purchasing of software, hardware, development cost, conversion of existing system to proposed system and training the personnel.

(*iv*) **Risks and benefits :** All the risks and benefits are compared to determine overall benefit of using the proposed database system design.

(*v*) **Feasibility analysis :** The aim of feasibility analysis is to find out the best possible solution. In this process various alternatives are considered and evaluate them to find out the best alternative or candidate. After selecting the best candidate by DBA and other organizational personel, the design of the database system begins.

Introduction to Database Management System

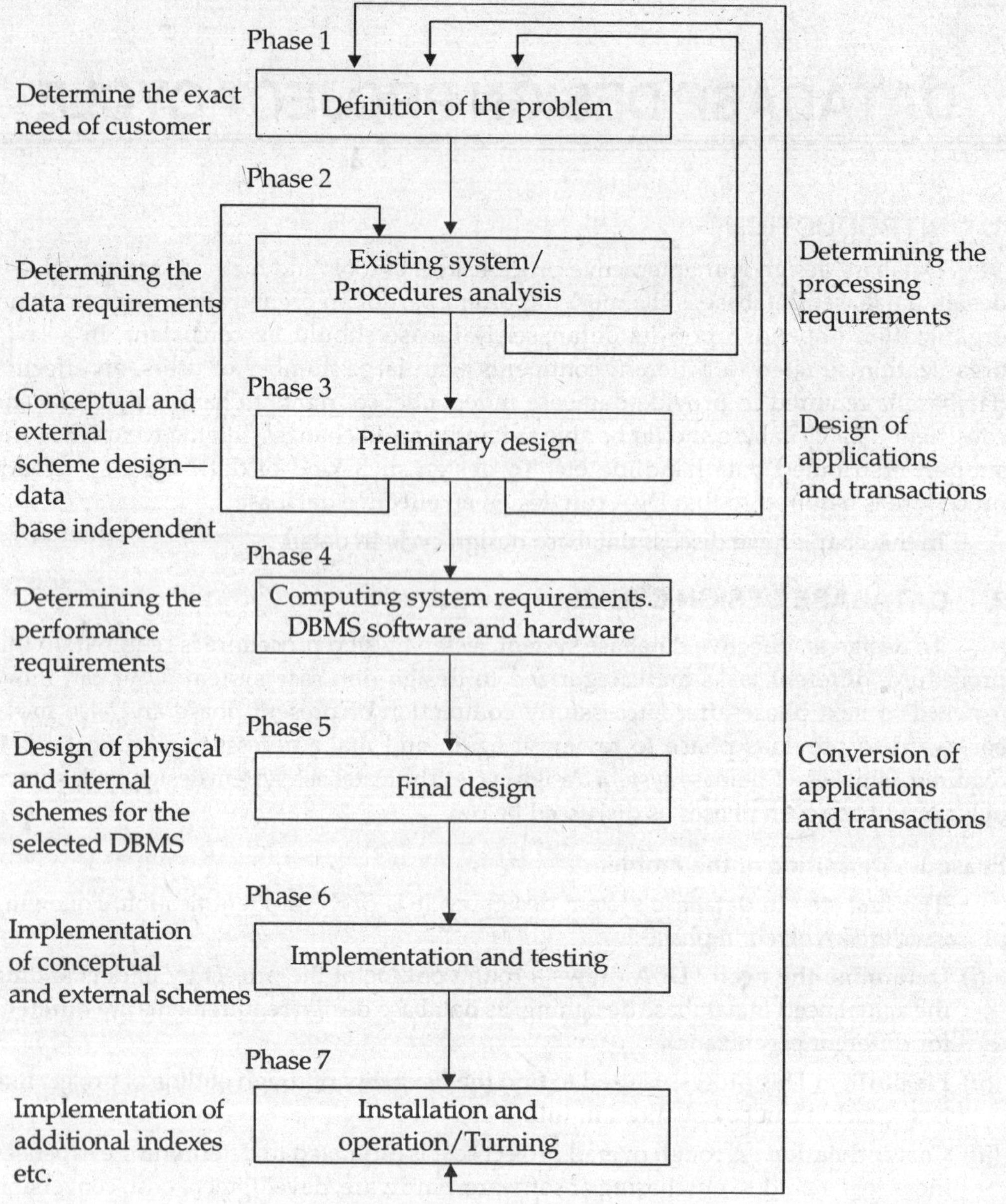

Figure 1: Database system design cycle.

Phase 2—Analysis of Existing System and Procedure

The second phase of cycle is very important in which designer study the existing system and procedures and then make a feasibility study of proposed solution in previous step. Processes involved in this phase are given below :

(*i*) **Study of existing system and procedures :** This process involves evaluating the current system by taking consideration of its capabilities, deficiencies, methods used for recording and processing data, area of improvements, basic requirements to migrate existing database system to new proposed system and current communication channels.

(*ii*) **Personal interviews :** Personal interviews are the most fruitful procedure to determine data and processing requirements. Database analyzer invites one or more key users from each group individually and then determine their requirements to determine the data and processing needs for the whole group. A formal interview may be supplemented by a questionnaire.

(*iii*) **Analysis of the procedures and information flow :** The requirements and other information gathered by different groups are analyzed together to analyze consistency and problem areas. A detailed .study of system is required to identify duplications, inefficiencies and limitations in the proposed design. This helps in determine the need of changes in procedures and its effect on the existing database system.

Analysis can be done by using some design tools like **data flow diagrams**. Data flow diagrams graphically represents the flow of data within organization. It represents data requirements and interconnection of various procedures. Designer use existing procedural documentation and information gathered from personal interviews to design these diagrams.

After designing the data flow diagrams of procedures, the proposed system is compared with the requirements that the system has to fulfill. This comparison helps in finding the need of any modification.

(*iv*) **Modification to proposed system :** Modification required in current procedures to fulfill any particular requirement, improve efficiency, newly discovered requirement and remove limitations etc., are documented. Such modifications have to be discussed with the group of concerned persons.

(*v*) **Preparing the initial proposal and requirement specifications** : After doing all modifications to the proposed system, the initial proposal and requirement specifications are prepared and discussed with the group of concerned persons for further improvement.

Throughout this phase, the major factors considered in collecting and analyzing the requirements are :

- Types of activities to be performed.
- Levels of management to be supported.
- Nature of functions to be served.

The requirement specification can be categorized into two groups :

(*a*) **Information requirements :** It specify the types of entities, their attributes and relationship among various relations that are used to store data within database.

(*b*) **Processing requirements :** It specify the data-manipulation capabilities of the system by considering usage frequency and required turn around etc.

Each process is listed with information and processing requirements. These requirements should be consistent and semantically correct. After gathering requirements, *Integrity Constraints* are defined.

The output of this phase is as follows :

- Data and its processing requirements
- Relationship between various processes
- Constraints
- Properties of data
- Operations required to improve efficiency.

Phase 3—Preliminary Design

The third step in database system design cycle is Preliminary Design. It involves the following processes :

(*i*) **Conceptual schema design :** In designing, the conceptual schema, any one of the following two approaches can be used :

(*a*) **Centralized schema design :** In centralized schema design, the different requirement specifications of different groups of users are merged together to form a single set of specifications. After merging the specifications the conceptual schema is designed from this single set. In case of any conflict during designing of schema, DBA examine each requirement specifications individually. After successful designing of conceptual schema, the views of the user groups are defined.

(*b*) **View-integration approach :** In this approach, the requirement specification of each user group is used to design their views. These views are integrated into the conceptual schema for the database. Conflicts may occur during this mapping but very easy to resolve. Conflicts that cannot be resolved by a conceptual schema to view mapping have to be examined. Example of these conflicts like one application uses unique employee number and second application named it employee ID or different applications use different data types for same attribute etc.

After resolving all the conflicts, the views are appropriately integrated to make conceptual schema. It is a step by step process, first two almost similar views are taken and merged, followed by merging of additional views one by one. There are two major approaches of integration :

(*a*) **Top-down approach :** In top-down approach, we start integration of entities, their attributes, and their relationship. Decision to split entities into number of specialized entities and add new relationships among them can also be taken.

(*b*) **Bottom-up approach :** In bottom-up approach, we start integration of a set of attributes into entities and relationships among them. The entities can be generalized and relationship is located at the higher levels.

Benefits of conceptual schema : Conceptual schema is DBMS independent and allows better understanding of information requirements and their inter-relationships. It can be easily understood by non specialist and can be easily documented.

(*ii*) **Design of applications and transactions :** Various applications and transactions are designed by analyzing processing requirements. The response requirements of applications and transactions are also determined.

(*iii*) **Determine performance requirements :** To determine performance requirements the designer need to study each operation in applications and transactions. Performance requirements plays a significant role in designing physical file structure, indexes for tables and physical devices etc.

The cycle of the steps consisting of definition of problem, existing system/procedure analysis, and preliminary design is repeated until a satisfactory design is obtained.

Phase 4—Computing System Requirements

In this phase, the designer need to choose appropriate DBMS software and the hardware equipments required. The choice of DBMS depends upon the following factors :

(*i*) **Cost :** The actual cost to design a new DBMS or to purchase a commercial DBMS and then customize it. Upgradation of existing DBMS, capital cost, initial training cost, operating cost including those for personnal, and maintenance of the hardware and software is also determined.

(*ii*) **Features provided by DBMS :** Some important features that should be considered are providing support to distribution of database, communication facilities, form based user interface, report generation facilities, reusability factor and flexibility etc.

(*iii*) **Existing DBMS :** Factors based on existing DBMS are type of existing DBMS (hierarchical, network, relational etc.), free storage space, conversion cost in case of upgradation of DBMS to different type and feasibility with new proposed DBMS etc.

(*iv*) **Actual requirements :** A major factor is the actual requirement of user that should be fulfilled by DBMS.

(*v*) **Availability :** Factors based on availability are availability of services from the vendor, experience of the personal, features available in DBMS, and hardware and soft ware availability to support DBMS etc.

(*vi*) **Flexibility of DBMS :** Now a days DBMS must be able to run on different hardware's and operating systems.

By examining all the above factors with the budget of the organisation, the designer can determine the DBMS software and hardware requirement of an organisation.

Phase 5—Final Design

In this phase of database design, designer take the preliminary design developed in Phase 3 which is in database independent form and convert the conceptual scheme into choosed DBMS specific conceptual scheme. After this conversion, views of applications are derived from it. These views are external views. The schemes are generated as programs in the DDL of the target DBMS. Following are the processes involved in final design phase :

(*i*) **Conversion of conceptual and schemes in the model of database :** As discussed earlier, that E-R model is used to design conceptual schemes in Phase 3. The designer, converts that scheme into proposed DBMS model. The conversion rule depends upon the type of selected DBMS model (Relational DBMS, Network DBMS, Hierarchical DBMS). After conversion of schemes, the designer starts work on designing the physical database.

(*ii*) **Designing of physical database :** Following are the decisions that need to be taken by the designer during designing of physical database :

(*a*) **Decision on file organization :** The choice of file organization directly affects the performance of database. The choice of file organization depends upon size of records, frequency of data manipulations and updation, distribution of storage location and size of organisation etc.

(*b*) **Decision on supporting indexes :** Indexes play a significant role in manipulation and updation oFcfatabase. DBMS uses indexes to retrive any data. If data in database is properly indexed then response time is very small and vice-versa. Indexes can be modified during database tuning and performance optimization. In database, a number of indexes are created for each record.

(*c*) **Decision on clustering of records :** Decisions should be taken regarding the partitioning of records into vertical, horizontal, or mixed fragments. **Vertical fragmentation** is appropriate if some of the record's fields are accessed more frequently than others and **horizontal fragmentation** is appropriate if some occurrences of a record are more frequently used than others.

After taking decisions on all the factors, physical database is designed and its performance is determined and compared with expected value. If the performance is not near to the expected value, then physical database is modified again.

Phase 6—Implementation and Testing

In this phase of database design, final design is implemented and tested. Following are the processes involved in this phase :

(*i*) **Implementation :** Implementation process can be categorized into following steps :

(*a*) Conversion of functional specification into technical specification.

(*b*) Writing codes using technical specifications, DDL of DBMS and compiling the code.

(*c*) Developing application programs using high level languages.

(*d*) Creating of physical database.

(*e*) Loading test data into database.

(*ii*) **Testing :** After development, system should undergo different test phases to verify its functionality, to remove bugs and to check consistency etc. It includes

(*a*) Unit testing.

(*b*) Integrated testing

(*iii*) **Documentation :** Documentation of success and failure of events are necessary to identify the actual errors. Procedure for backing up and restarting after failure of various types are outlined. Documentation is also necessary for future enhancements. After removing all the bugs, the database system is ready to install at client site.

Phase 7—Operation and Tuning

This is the final phase of database design cycle in which design is completed and ready for day-to-day operation. Following are the processes involved in this phase

(*i*) **Installation :** The database system is installed at the actual site and is ready for use.

(*ii*) **Onsite testing :** Database system is again tested at actual site and the bugs have been removed. After all necessary modification, its performance is measured.

(*iii*) **Performance Tuning :** If the measured performance is not upto mark then performance tuning is required. It may be done at **hardware level** by increasing the number of equipments, changing slow hardware etc., or at **software level** by increasing the number, of buffers, size of buffers, defining additional indexes, modifying existing indexes, and clustering of records etc.

(*iv*) **Training :** The users have been trained to use new applications throughout this phase.

ADVANTAGES OF DATABASE SYSTEM DESIGN CYCLE

1. It is the most efficient way of designing a database system.
2. Steps are categorized into different phases and work is assigned according to priority to save precious time.
3. It is a systematic approach.
4. Major modifications to database system are identified in earlier stages of the cycle.
5. Easy to take decisions on critical issues.
6. A proper documentation is done throughout the cycle that helps in understanding the flow and also helpful for future enhancements.

DISADVANTAGES OF DATABASE SYSTEM DESIGN CYCLE

Any error identified in later stages leads to start the whole cycle from the beginning.

CHAPTER 1: INTRODUCTION

1.1 INTRODUCTION

The project is aimed at developing an application for the training and placement department of the college. The system is a client server application that can be accessed throughout the organization through LAN. This system can be used as an application for the TPO of the college to manage the company and student information with regards to placement. Students logging should be able to search for various details related to company criteria, etc.

1.2 MAJOR OBJECTIVES

This project provides the facility of maintaining the details of the students and gets the requested list of candidates for the companies who would like to recruit the students based on given criteria. It also provides a way for the students to know the details of the company, package it is offering, etc.. Also data security is maintained to relatively high level by implementing it at Database level, so as to ensure that only authorized users have access to confidential client information.

1.3 TRAINING AND PLACEMENT INFORMATION SYSTEM

The whole application is having following modules:

Administrator module

In the administrator module, first administrator is asked to login A new administrator can be added only by the person who is himself an administrator by specifying his password and entering username and password of the new administrator. After successful login, the form will redirect to main menu form that contains options to add/delete/ modify student and company details, search for various inputs, etc.. Updating of database can only be done by administrator as it has one authority to do this.

Student Module

In the student, first student is asked to login. If student is a new person it must registered by the administrator. In registration page we need to provide the details to register. If student is already registered, he can login in login form. After successful login, the form will redirect to main menu form that contains links to search for various details regarding placements etc.. A student is not allowed to update as it can cause false information being updated by the student to meet company criteria.

1.4 LIST OF FORMS

Administrator Module

1. Login
2. New Registration
3. Create user
4. Delete user
5. Add company
6. View company details
7. Reports
8. Various search

Client Module

1. Login
2. View company details
3. Various Search

1.5 ADVANTAGES

Convenient

Convenient includes the overall ease of finding information through various searches thus minimizing time spent on searching in documents for any information. It also enables administrator to get details of the student qualified for a company by simply searching for a given criteria rather than looking into papers for details which can cause error.

Time Saving

It is much easier to just run a search and get result than to search all the documents and it also saves a lot of time corresponding to time involved in searching information one document at a time.

Secure Storage

Data security is maintained to relatively high level by implementing it a Database level, so as to ensure that only authorized users have access to confidential client information.

CHAPTER 2: SOFTWARE REQUIREMENT SPECIFICATION

2.1 INTRODUCTION

2.1.2 Introduction

The purpose of this document is to provide a medium to understand and provide an insight into the development of Training & Placement Information System. The document will help avoid confusion when trying to understand the relationship between technical documents, and their context within the project framework.

2.1.2 Introduction

The document described herein is limited to the research and technical aspects of the project. The focus of this document is to present the research, design, implementation and deployment view of Training & Placement Information System. Any non-technical document associated with the project is beyond the scope of this documentation.

2.2 OVERALL DESCRIPTION

2.2.1 Product Perspective

The project has been developed in replacement of normal manual paper work. While normal paper work involves creating list of company, their criteria, storing student details, searching for the eligible students according to company, etc.. This is very time consuming and involves lots paper work. Our project provides the facility to maintain details of student and companies and makes searching for various details easier. It stores the data in the database thus involving no paper work at all and also data security is maintained to relatively high level by implementing it at Database level, so as to ensure that only authorized users have access to confidential client information.

2.2.2 Product Function

It is a client server based application running on LAN enabling multiple users to access it for getting information.

The different functionalities provided by this product are as follows:

Updating informations –

The administration can update information regarding company and student in the database.

Searching–

The user can search for various information regarding student and company by means of various search criteria's being provided.

Report –

The administrator can get a printed report of all the requested details.

Login –

This authenticates the access to the software

2.2.3 User classes and Characteristics

The project may consist of user classes

Administrator - This class of people can change the information, add or remove information from the database.

Student - This class of people only searches through database.

2.24 Operating Environment

Operating System

A standard Windows PC running WINDOW VISTA/XP/98/2000/NT

Hardware platform

Pentium 4 processor and above

512 MB RAM and higher

80 GB HDD

Software specifications

Visual Studio 2005

SQL Server 2005.

2.2.5 Design and Implementation Constraints

Only authorized users should be able to access the system.

User should login before accessing application.

2.3 EXTERNAL INTERFACE REQUIREMENTS

2.3.1 User Interfaces

The user (administrator student) interacts with the system which provides user with login form of the system which prompts the user to enter the username and password.

The user (administrator) can update database with various company related and student related information.

The student can view deatails about the company search for various information through various search criteria present.

There's Help manual that enables the user to get understanding of the working of software

The About options enables the user to see the application related detail like its meaning and the owner.

2.3.2 Hardware Interfaces

Server Side

Hardware platform

pentium 4 processor and above

512 MB RAM and higher

80 GB HDD

The Software application

Visual Studio 2005

SQL Server 2005

Client Side

Hardware platform

Pentium 4 processor and above

512 MB RAM and higher

80 GB HDD
SQL Server 2005

2.3.3 Software Interfaces

Training and Placement Information System can operate with Windows XP and advanced.

2.3.4 Communication Interfaces

The security of the system is consistent through the use of password to protect the authenticity from malicious use.

2.4 OTHER NON-FUNCTIONAL REQUIREMENTS

2.4.1 Security Requirements

The security of the system is consistent through the use of password to protect the authenticity from malicious use.

CHAPTER 3: SYSTEM DESIGN

3.1 USE CASE DIAGRAM

A use case diagram is a type of behavioral diagram defined by the Unified Modeling language (UML) and created from a Use-case analysis. Its purpose is to present a graphical overview of the functionality provided by a system in terms of actors, their goals (represented as use cases), and any dependencies between those use cases.

The main purpose of a use case diagram is to show what system function are performed for which actors. Roles of the actors in the system can be depicted. Use Case diagrams are formally included in two modeling languages defined by the OMG. Both the UML and SysML standards define a graphical notation for modeling use cases with diagrams. One complaint about the standards has been that they do not define a format for describing these cases. Generally, both graphical notation and descriptions are important as they document the use case, showing the purpose for which an actor uses a system.

The use case diagram shows the position or context of the use case among other use cases. As an organizing mechanism, a set of consistent, coherent use cases promotes a useful picture of system behavior, a common understanding between the customer/owner/user and the development team. [3].

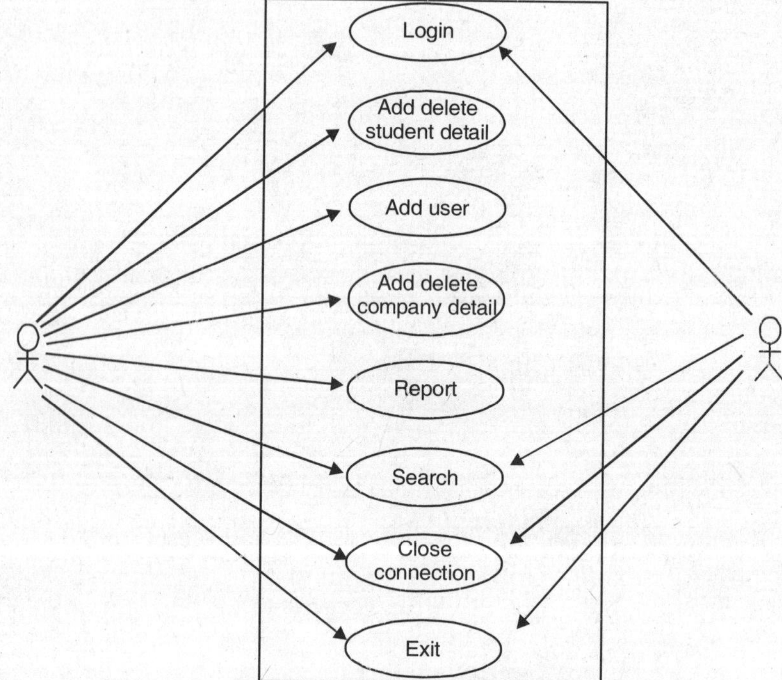

Fig. 3.1. *Use case diagram*

3.2 DATA FLOW DIAGRAM

A data-flow diagram (DFD) is a graphical representation of the "flow" of data through an information system. DFDs can also be used for the visualization of data processing (structured design).

On a DFD, data items flow from an external data source or an internal data store to an internal data store or an external data sink, via an internal process.

A DFD provides on information about the timing or ordering of processes, or about whether processes will operate in sequence or in parallel. It is therefore quite different from a flowchart, which shows the flow of control through an algorithm, allowing a reader to determine what operation will be performed, in what order, and under what circumstances, but not what kinds of data will be input to and output from the system, nor where the data will come from and go to, nor where the data will be stored (all of which are shown on a DFD). [2].

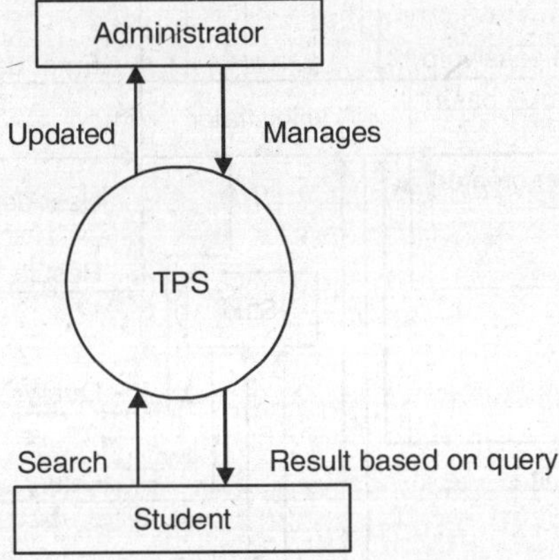

Fig. 3.2. *Level 0 DFD*

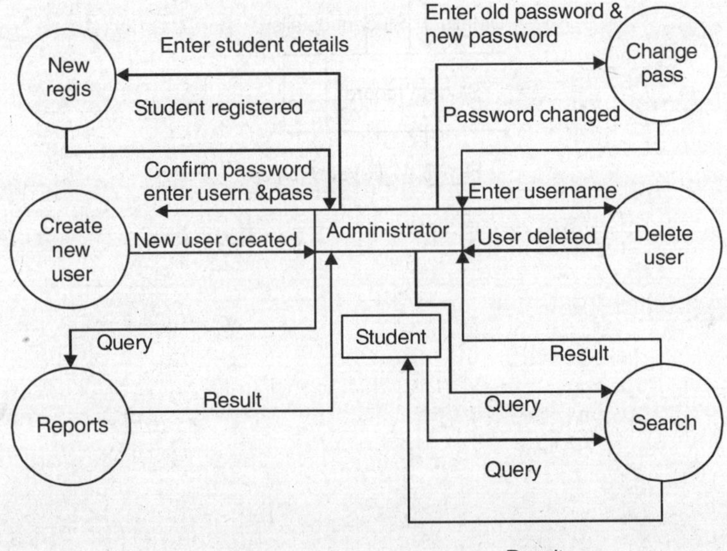

Fig. 3.3. *Level 1 DFD*

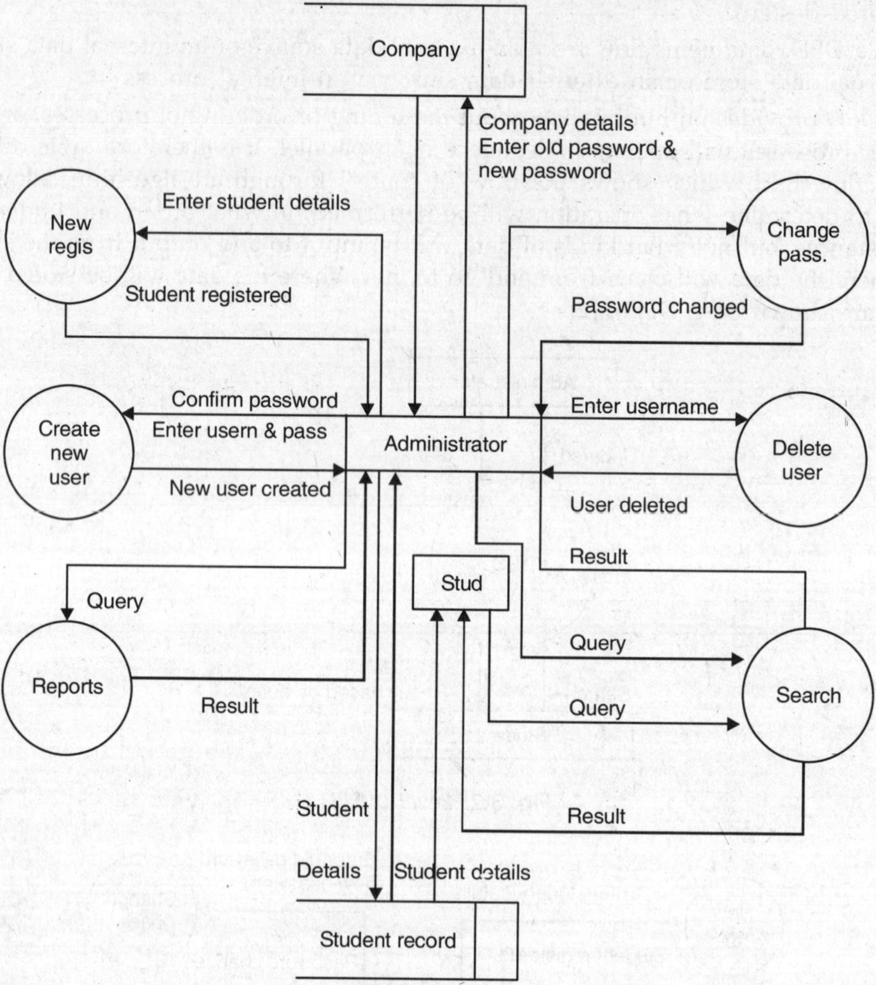

Fig. 3.4. *Level 1 DFD*

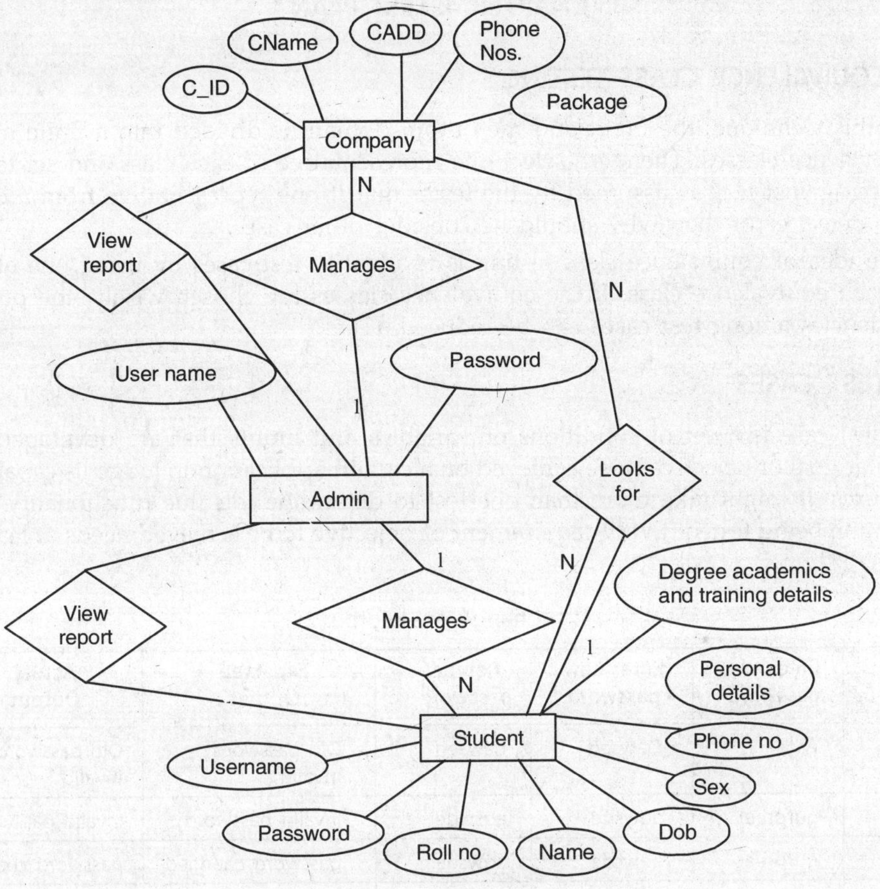

Fig. 3.5. *ER-diagram*

CHAPTER 4: TEST PLAN

4.1 EQUIVALENCE CLASS TESTING

In this technique, the input and the output domain is divided into a finite number of equivalence classes. Then, we select one representative of each class and set test our program against it. It is assumed by the tester that if one representative from a class is able to detect error then why should he consider other cases.

The idea of equivalence class testing is to identify test cases by using one element from each equivalence class. If the equivalence classes are chosen wisely, the potential dependencies among test cases can be reduced. [1].

4.2 TEST CASES

A test case is a set of conditions or variables and inputs that are developed for a particular goal or objective to be achieved on a certain application to judge its capabilities or features. It might take more than one test to determine the true functionality of the application being tested. Every requirement or objective to be achieved needs at least one test case [1].

Change Password

Case ID	Enter old password	Enter new password	Retype password	Expected Output	Actual Output
1.	Asdf	Qawsed	qawsed	Old password invalid	Old password invalid
2.	gurpreet	aqwsde	aqswde	Invalid password	Invalid password
3.	gurpreet	aqwsde	aqwsde	password changed	password changed
4.	gurpreet	asdf	asdf	Invalid password	Invalid password
5.	gurpreet	asdfa	asdfa	password changed	password changed

Create New User

Case ID	Confirm Administrator passwored	New Username	Password	Confirm password	Expected Output	Actual Output
1.	Abcd	ab1	abcde	abcde	password Invalid	password Invalid
2.	Gurpreet	abcd	abcd	abcd	Invalid password	Invalid password
3.	Gurpreet	abcd	abcde	adbce	Reenter new password	Reenter new password
4.	Gurpreet		abcde	abcde	Enter username	Enter username
5.	gurpree	abcdf	abcde	abcde	New user created	New user created

6.	Aefg	ab1	abdef	abdef	password Invalid	password Invalid
7.	gurpreet	ab1	abcde		Renter new password	Renter new password
8.	gurpreet	ab1		abcde	Renter new password	Renter new password
9.	gurpreet	ab1	abcdh	abcdh	New user created	New user created
10.	gurpreet	aswq			Renter new password	Renter new password
11.	gurpreet	aqbc11	asdfghjkl mnbv	asdfghjkl mnbv	Invalid password	Invalid password

Add Company

Case ID	C_id	C_name	Constact	Address	Email	Package	Expected	Actual
1.	1	As	25278812	Wz1,t.n.	q@gmail.com	3.5lacs	Company added	Company added
2.	1	Qw	23451234	Qw/1,vn	s@gmail.co	2lacs	compid already exit	compid already exit
3	2		2134567	Qa/123	a@d.co	3lacs	Enter comp name	Enter comp name
4.	2	We		Aq1	as@g.co	3lacs	Enter contact	Enter contact
5.	2	We	12345678	Aq/1,gk	as@g.co	5lacs	Company added	Company added
6.	3	Qa	235678	Za/12		2lacs	Enter emailied	Enter emailied

CHAPTER 5: SYSTEM FEATURES

5.1 EQUIVALENCE CLASS TESTING

The system is a client server application that can be accessed throughout the organization through LAN. It consists of two modules: - administrator and student. Administrator has all the authority of saving and updating the information in the main database. Student can only login for the purpose of searching for various information. Various form used in the application are: registration, create and delete user, add & view company details, various types of searches and reports.

5.2 TYPES OF FORMS

There are various forms in this application for feeding all the information:

5.2.1 New Registration Form

The new registration form is used for the registration of the new student. It contains 6 tabs intotal namely: profile, personal, academics, degree, training, placement. Every tab contains the fields for the respective information that is to be covered by that tab.

The student profile tab caters to or looks after the basic information about the student that makes up the profile of the student. All this information from this tab is entered into the table dbo.Profile into their corresponding columns. The end of the form's tab contains nine labels to display the name of the fields. Four text boxes, four combo boxes and one data time picker box are there in this tab. It also contains tabs which perform the functions for saving the entered details for new entries; delete to delete the corresponding record update for updating a present record.

The personal tab contains the fields which are required for gaining the personal information about the student like the parents name, student's address etc. All this information from this tab is entered into the table dbo.Personal into their corresponding columns. The front end of the form's tab contains eight labels used for the field names and corresponding four text boxes to input the value also there are two rich text boxes for taking the inputs which are longer and multiline *i.e.*, the permanent address and the correspondence address. Also the tab contains two clickable buttons one performs the function to save details entered other performs the function to update an existing record according to the entered by the admin.

The academic tab contains the fields which are required for storing the academics details of a student like tenth and twelfth diploma percentage and year of completion of tenth and twelfth diploma. All this information is entered into the table dbo.academics into their corresponding columns. It also stores the information about the number of gaps (years) between admission to college and clearance of qualifying examination.

The degree tab contains the fields which are required for gaining the information about the degree of the student like marks obtained in each sementer, percentage obtained in each semester, number of backlogs. All this degree related information gets stored into the table dbo.degree into their corresponding columns. As soon as button present degree tab is clicked, a type of marks calculator window appears which contains various fields for storing student marks in each semester along with the maximum marks of that semester. There are also fields for storing the number of backlogs of the student. When the calculate percentage button present in the marks form is pressed, total percentage is calculated and the value appears in percentage field for each semester. When calculate aggregate button is pressed, total aggregate percentage of the semesters appears in the respective column. Similarly, there is button which when pressed calculates the total backlogs of a student. All this information gets stored in the database once save button is pressed.

The training tab contains fields for getting the information regarding the training details of the student like the company name and duration of training. All the information regarding the training of the student is stored in the table dbo.training into respective columns.

The placement tab stores the information about the company in which student has been placed. It includes fields like company id, company name and package offered. All the information regarding placement of a student gets stored in the dbo.placement table once save button is pressed.

5.2.2 Create New User

This form is used to create new administrator. It requires administrator to enter his password for the purpose of confirmation. Then username is entered for the new administrator and then the password and then the password is typed again. Once the two password match, new administrator is created. The information about the new administrator is stored in the dbo.login table in the database.

It asks for the user to be deleted. Once you enter the user name and press the button, the respective user is deleted and is no longer authorized to access the system. All the information about the user in the database gets deleted.

5.2.4 Add Company

This form contains the fields for gaining the information about the company like the company id. Company name, address, telephone number, package offered, etc.. All the information about the company gets stored in the dbo.company table in the database. There are buttons for performing the functions like saving and updating the database.

5.2.5 View Company Details

It helps administrator and student to view details of various companies. It gives details of the company like the company name, company id, company's address, telephone number and package offered by the company.

5.2.6 Searches

There are various types of searches for getting required information about the student and the company like : - student information based on batch, branch, roll number, information about the placed students and about training. One can also search for company criteria for the purpose of placement.

5.2.7 Reports

There are various crystal reports for the administrator to get details about various things printed. The access to these is limited to the administrator only students don't enjoy the privilege of using these reports. Administrator can print these reports for the purpose of using the information.

CHAPTER 6: DATA DICTIONARY

6.1 ACADEMICS

Table Name : Academics

Description : This table stores the information regarding student's 10th and 12th/ diploma details.

Column Name	Data Type	Constraint	Description
rollno	Varchar(10)	NOT NULL foreign key reference table profile (rollno)	Roll number of the student
tenth	Integer	NOT NULL	Tenth percentage
ten_comp	Data	NOT NULL	Year of completion of tenth
Td	Integer	NOT NULL	Twelth/diploma percentage
td_comp	Date	NOT NULL	Year of competion of twelth/diploma
Gap	Integer	NOT NULL	Number of years between completion of twelth/diploma and admission to B.Tech.

6.2 AGGREGATE

Table Name : Aggregate

Description : This table stores the total percentage of the student in B.Tech. and number of backlogs.

Column Name	Data Type	Constraint	Description
rollno	Varchar(10)	NOT NULL foreign key reference table profile (rollno)	Roll number of the student
aggregate	Integer	NOT NULL	Total percentage in B.Tech.
t_back	Integer	NOT NULL	Total number of backlogs

6.3 LOGIN

Table Name : Login

Description : Stores username and passwrod of the administrator.

Column Name	Data Type	Constraint	Description
username	Varchar(15)	PRIMARY KEY	User name for administrator login
password	varchar(12)	NOT NULL	Password for administrator login

6.4 COMPANY

Table Name : Company

Description : Stores all the details of the company

Column Name	Data Type	Constraint	Description
c_id	Integer	PRIMARY KEY	Company id
c_name	Varchar(20)	NOT NULL	Company Name
c_add	Varchar(25)	NOT NULL	Phone number
ph1	Varchar(10)	NOT NULL	Phone number
ph2	Varchar(10)	NOT NULL	Phone number
mob1	Varchar(11)	NOT NULL	Mobile number
mob2	Varchar(11)	NOT NULL	Mobile number
email	Varchar(20)	NOT NULL	Email address of the company
package	Varchar(6)	NOT NULL	Salary per annum

6.5 DEGREE :

Table Name : Degree

Description : stores details related to degree like semester id, marks obtained in each semester, etc..

Column Name	Data Type	Constraint	Description
rollno	Varchar(10)	NOT NULL foreign key reference profile (rollno)	Roll number of the student
semestid	integer	NOT NULL	Semester id
marksobtained	integer	NOT NULL	Total marks obtained in a semester
max_marks	Integer	NOT NULL	Total marks in a semester
percentage	Integer	NOT NULL	Percentage in a semester
backlogs	Integer	NOT NULL	Number of backlogs in semester
remarks	Varchar (4)	NOT NULL	Grade

6.6 PERSONAL

Table Name : Personal

Description : It stores personal informations of the student.

Column Name	Data Type	Constraint	Description
rollno	Varchar(10)	NOT NULL foreign key reference table profile (rollno)	Roll number of the student
fname	Varchar(15)	NOT NULL	Father name of the student
mname	Varchar(15)	NOT NULL	Mother name of the student
padd	Varchar(25)	NOT NULL	Permanent address of the student

c_add	Varchar(25)	NOT NULL	Correspondence address of the student
resi	Varchar(11)	NOT NULL	Residence number of the student
mob	Varchar(11)	NOT NULL	Mobile number of the student

6.7 PLACEMENT

Table Name : Placement

Description : Stores details of the placed students.

Column Name	Data Type	Constraint	Description
rollno	Varchar(10)	NOT NULL foreign Key reference table profile (rollno)	Roll number of the student
c_id	Integer	NOT NULL foreign key reference table company (c_id)	Company id

6.8 SEMESTER

Table Name : Semester

Description : Stores semester details.

Column Name	Data Type	Constraint	Description
semesterid	integer	NOT NULL	Semester id
semester	Varchar(15)	NOT NULL	Semester name

6.9 PROFILE :

Table Name : Profile

Description : Stores student profile.

Column Name	Data Type	Constraint	Description
Roll No.	Varchar(10)	PRIMARY KEY	Roll number of the student
firstname	Varchar(15)	NOT NULL	First name of the student
lastname	Varchar(15)	NOT NULL	Last name of the student
Sex	Varchar(6)	NOT NULL	Sex of the student
Dob	Varchar(10)	NOT NULL	Date of birth of the student
Course	Varchar(10)	NOT NULL	Course of the student
Branch	Varchar(10)	NOT NULL	Branch (stream) of the student
Batch	Integer	NOT NULL	Year of admission to the institute
contact no.	Varchar(11)	NOT NULL	Student Contact number

6.10 TRAINING

Table Name : Training

Description : This table stores details about the training of the student and the duration of training.

Column Name	Data Type	Constraint	Description
Rollno	Varchar(10)	NOT NULL foreign key reference table profile (rollno)	Roll number of the student
Duration	Integer	NOT NULL	Duration of training
comp_name	Varcher(20)	NOT NULL	Name of the company where training was conducted.

6.11 USER LOGIN

Table Name : User login

Description : This table stores user name and password for student login.

Column Name	Data Type	Constraint	Description
username	Varchar(10)	NOT NULL foreign key reference table profile (rollno)	User name for student login
Password	Varchar(12)	NOT NULL	Password for student login

RESULTS

Training & Placement Information System proves to be a development in the field of maintaining details of the company and student which results in fast and easy access to various information depending up on the type of search or company criteria.

Training & Placement Information System replaces the old, bulky and unreliable methods of storing details regarding student and company as it provides a convenient way to store all information with easy access capability. While everyone may see the public data, only the registered user would be able to modify and see the details of company and student.

Here, the user is active participants throughout the process. He is the one who starts the application and does the modification in a most secure way.

SUMMARY AND CONCLUSIONS

From a proper analysis of positive points and constraints on the component, it can be safely concluded that the product is a highly efficient GUI based component. This component can be easily plugged in many other systems. Also the component is user friendly. Generally the TPO's of the Colleges has to face a lot of problems in management of the Students information. This information has to be managed manually. So, there is a need to develop a system that can solve the mentioned problem. The software comes with just that solution.

Also, it provides freedom from the paper work involved in manual operation and thus from the amount of storage required to keep them. It also provides security as data security is maintained to relatively high level by implementing it at Database level, so as to ensure that only authorized users have access confidential client information.

APPENDIX A: SCREEN SHOTS

Fig. 1. *Authenticate the user*

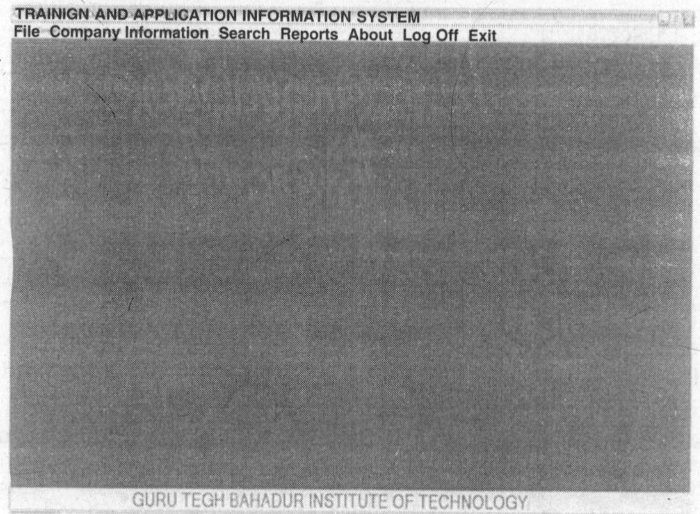

View Company Details

Company ID	Company Name	Company Address	Telephone Number	Mobile Number	Email ID	Package Offered
[illegible]	NIIT	new delhi	1	3	niit	2.5-3.0 Lakhs
2	TCS	gurgaon	1	3	tcs	3.0-3.5 Lakhs
3	Accenture	mumbai	1	3	acc	3.0-3.5 Lakhs
4	Mpahsis	bangalore	3232	45	hi@mpahsis.com	3.0-3.5 Lakhs
5	Persistant Systems	pune	43	56	hi@persistant.com	3.0-3.5 Lakhs
6	HCL	noida	2	4	hcl.com	2.0-2.5 Lakhs

Fig. 3. *Company details*

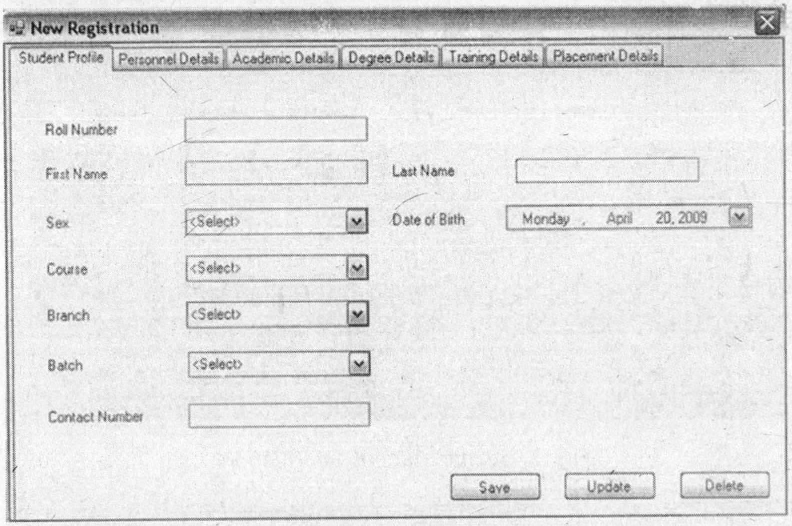

New Registration

Student Profile | Personnel Details | Academic Details | Degree Details | Training Details | Placement Details

Roll Number

First Name Last Name

Sex <Select> Date of Birth Monday , April 20, 2009

Course <Select>

Branch <Select>

Batch <Select>

Contact Number

Save Update Delete

Fig. 4. *New registration*

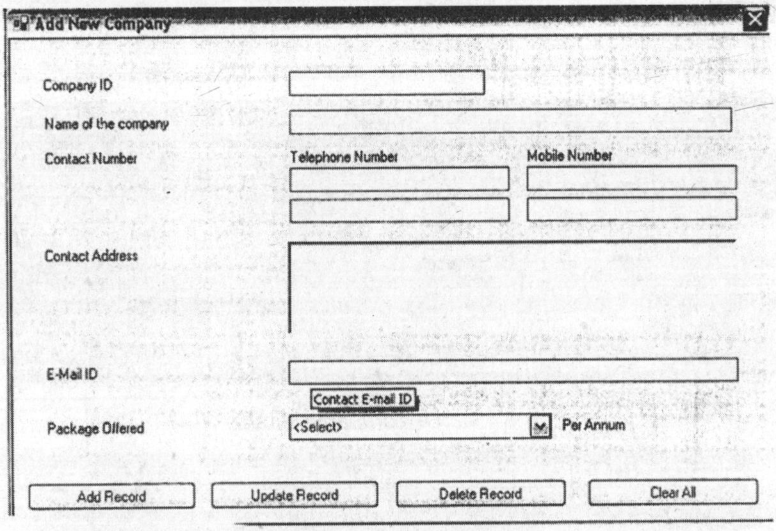

Add New Company

Company ID

Name of the company

Contact Number Telephone Number Mobile Number

Contact Address

E-Mail ID

Contact E-mail ID

Package Offered <Select> Per Annum

Add Record Update Record Delete Record Clear All

Fig. 5. *Add company*

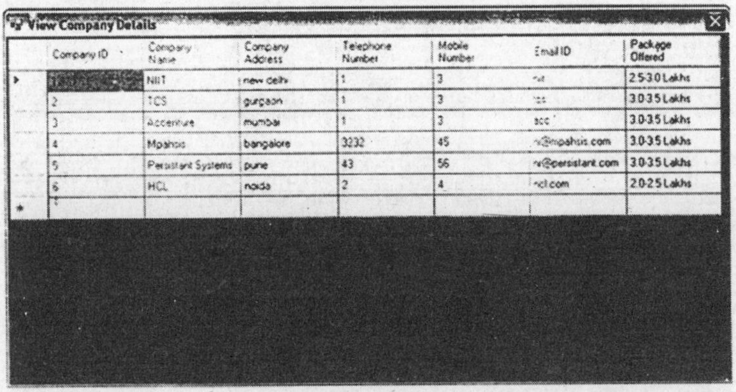

View Company Details

Company ID	Company Name	Company Address	Telephone Number	Mobile Number	Email ID	Package Offered
[illegible]	NIIT	new delhi	1	3	[illegible]	2.5-3.0 Lakhs
2	TCS	gurgaon	1	3	[illegible]	3.0-3.5 Lakhs
3	Accenture	mumbai	1	3	acc	3.0-3.5 Lakhs
4	Mpahsis	bangalore	3232	45	[illegible]@mpahsis.com	3.0-3.5 Lakhs
5	Persistant Systems	pune	43	56	[illegible]@persistant.com	3.0-3.5 Lakhs
6	HCL	noida	2	4	[illegible]cl.com	2.0-2.5 Lakhs

Fig. 6. *View Company*

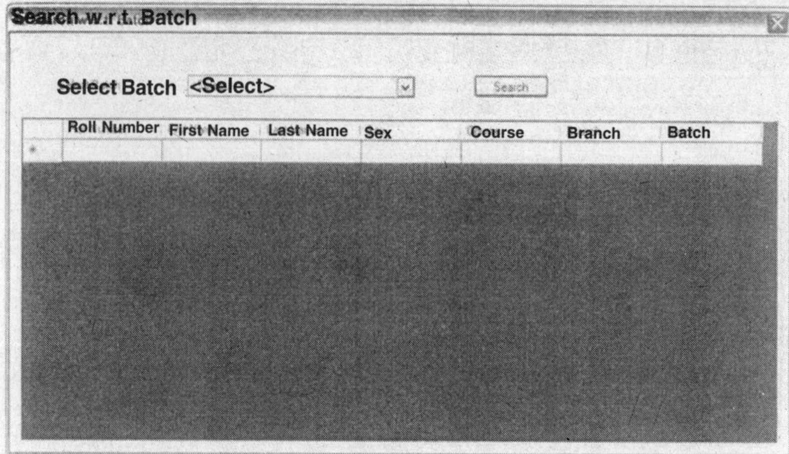

Fig. 7. *Search student information*

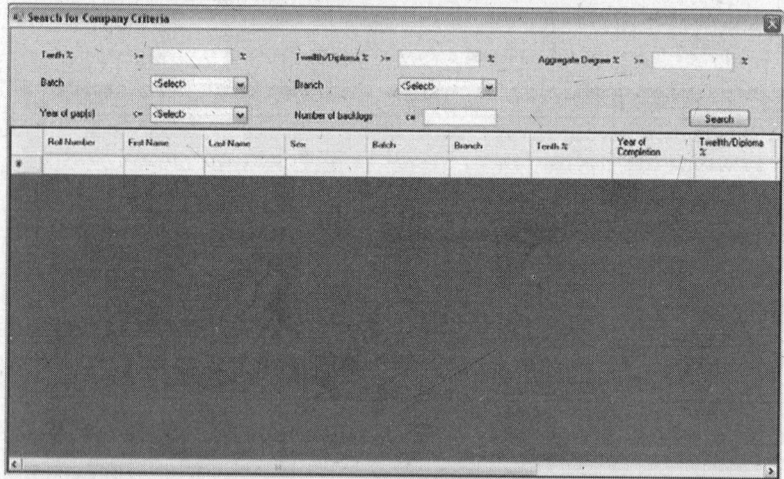

Fig. 8. *Search company criteria*

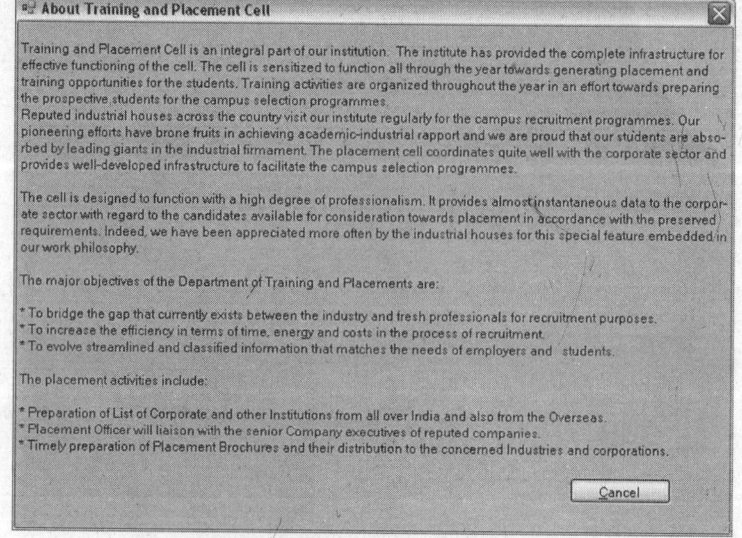

Fig. 9. *About us*

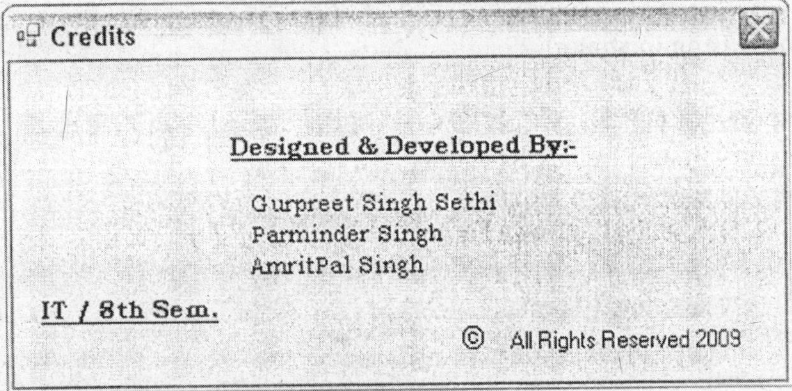

Fig. 10. *Credits*

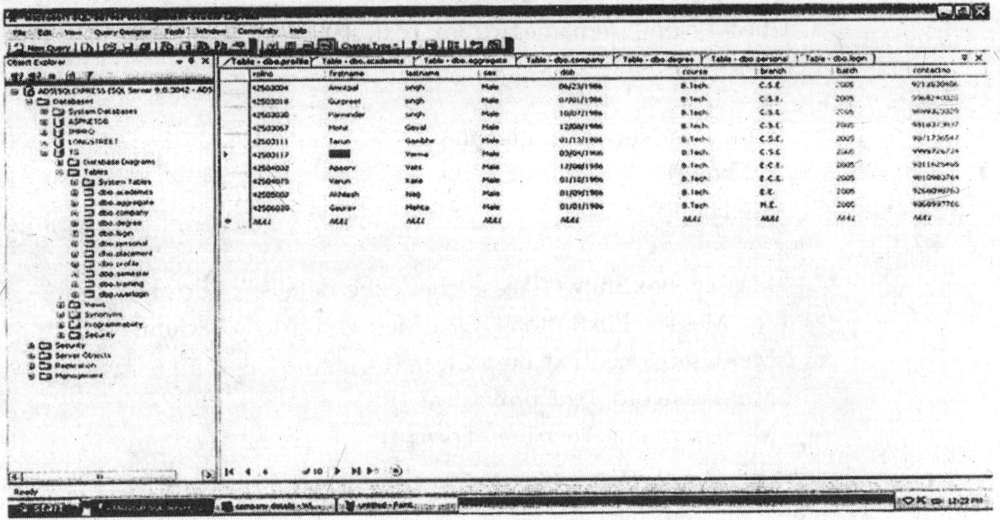

Fig. 11. *Data base*

APPENDIX B: SOURCE CODE

Login (Administrator)

```
Imports  System.Data
Imports System.Data.Sq1Client
Imports tpe.SQL.Connection
Imports System. Windows. Forms

Public Class Login Formal
    Dim a As Integer
    Private_sqlconnection As New Sq1Connection()
    Private Sub OK_click (By Val sender As System. Object, By Val e As System.
        EventArgs) Handles OK. Click
        If (CheckLogin(UsernameTextBox.Text, password TextBox.Text) = True)
            Then
            a = 1
            Dim f as New mainmenu(a)
            f. Show()
            Me.Hide()
        Else
            MessageBox.Show("Please check the details.", "Error!".,
                MessageBoxButtons. OK, MessageBoxlcon.Exclamation)
            Me. Username Text Box. Clear ()
            Me. Password Text Box. Clear ()
            Me. Username Text Box. Focus ()
        End If
    End Sub
    Private Sub Make Connection()
    Try
        Dim_clsConnection As New Make Connection()
        Dim sqlconn As New Sq1 Connection("Data Source – COMPAQ; Initial
            Catalog = TG; Integrated Security = True;uid=sa;pwd= parminder
            1987")
        'Dim sqlconn As New Sq1 Connection ("Data
Source = 169.254.231.26,1433; Network Library = DBMSSOCN; Intitial Catalog
        = TG;uid= sa; pwd=parminder1987")
        Sqlconn. Open()
        _Sqlconnection = sqlconn'_clsConnection. CreateConnection()
    Catch ex As Exception
        Message Box.Show(ex.Message.To String)
    End Try
    End Sub
```

```
Private Function CheckLogin(By Val UserName As String, By Val Password As
    Password As String) As Boolean
    MakeConnection()
Dim query As String = :select * from login where UserName = '" * userName
    & '" and Password='" & Password & ""
Dim_sqladapter As New Sq1DataAdepter(query,_sqlconnection)
dim do As New DataSet()
_sqladapter.Fill(ds)
If ds.Tables(0). Rows.Count = 0 Then
    checkLogin = False
Else
    checkLogin= True
    End If
End Function

Private Sub Cancel_Click(By Val sender As System. Object, ByVal e as
    System.EventArgs) Handles Cancel.Click
    Dim f As New logintype
    f.Show()
    Me.Hide()
End Sub

Private Sub Login Form1_FormClosing(ByVal sender As Object, ByVal As
    System.Windows. Forms. FormClosing EventArgs) Handles Me.
FormClosing
If MsgBox("Do you want to exit?", MsgBoxStyle. YesNo, "Exit") = Msg Box
    Result.No Then
    e.Cancel = True
Else
    End
End If
    End Sub
Private Sub Username TextBox_leave(ByVal sender As Object, ByVal As System.
    EventArgs) Handles Username TextBox. Leave
    If IsNumeric(Me.UsernameTextBox.Text)= True Then
MassageBox.Show("Enter character value.", "Error!", MessageBoxButtons.OK,
    MeassageBoxlcon.Error)
    Me.Username Text Box. Clear()
    Me. Username TextBox.Focus()
    End If
End Sub
Private Sub Password TestBox TextChanged(ByVal sender AS System.Object,
        ByVal e As System.EventArgs) Handles PasswordTextBox. TextChanged
    End Sub
```

End Class

Login (student)

```
Imports System.Data
Imports System.Data.Sq1Client
Imports tpe.SQL.Connection
Imports System.Windows.Forms
Public Class LoginForm2
    Dimas As Integer
    Private_sqlconnection As New SqlConnection()

Private Sub Make Connection()
    Dim_clsConnection As New MakeConnection()
    _sqlconnection=_clsConnection.CreateConnection()
End Sub

Private Sub OK_Click(ByVal sender As System.Object,ByVal e As System.
    EventArgs) Handles OK.Click
    If (CheckLogin(UsernameTextBox.Text, PasswordText. Text) = True) Then
        a = 2
        Dim f As New Mainmenu(a)
        f.Show()
        'f.MainMenuStrip.Items.RemoveAt(0)
        'f.MainMenuStrip.Items.RemoveAt(0)
        Me.Hide()
    Else
        MessageBox.Show("Please check the details", "Error!",
    MessageBoxButtons.OK, MessageBoxIcon. Exclamation)
        Me.UsernameTextBox.Clear()
        Me.PasswordTextBox.Clear()
        Me.UsernameTextBox.Focus()
    End If
    End Sub
Private Function CheckLogin(ByVal UserName As String, ByVal Password
    As String)
    As Boolean
    MakeConnection()
    Dim query As String = "select * from userlogin where UserName=" &
        UserName & ""and Password=" & Password & ""
    Dim_sqladapter As New SqlDataAdapter(Adapter(query,_sqlconnection)
    Dim ds As New DataSet()
    _sqladapter.Fill(ds)
    If ds. Tables(0).Rows.Count=0 Then
```

```
            CheckLogin = False
        Else
            CheckLogin = True
        End If
    End Function

    Private Sub Cancel_Click(ByVal sender As System.Object, ByVal e As
        System.EventArgs) Handles Cancel.Click
        Dim f As New logintype
        f.Show()
        Me.Hide()
    End Sub

    Private Sub LoginForm2_FormClosing(ByVal sender As Object, ByVal e As
        System.Windows. FormsClosingEventArgs) Handles Me.FormClosing
    If MsgBox("Do you want to exit?", MsgBoxStyle, YesNo, "Exit")= magBox
        Result.No Then
            e.Cancel = True
        Else
            End
        End If
        End Sub
    End Class
```

Mainmenu

```
    Public Class mainmenu
        Dim x As Integer

    Sub New (ByVal type As Integer)

        'This call is required by the Windows Form Designer.
        x = type
        InitializeComponent()
        'x = type
        ' Add any initialization after the InitializeComponet() call
    End Sub

    Dim a As New newregistration
    Dim b As New chagepswd
    Dim c As New addcomp
    Dim d As New viewcomp
    Dim f As New searchroll
```

```
Dim g As New searchname
Dim hAs New searchbranch
Dim i As New searchbatch
Dim j As New searchcompid
Dim k As New searchcomp
Dim l As New searchcbatch
Dim m As New searchcbranch
Dim n As New searchtbatch
Dim i As New searchtbranch
Dim p As New searchcriteria
Dim q As New introtpc
Dim r As New credits
Dim s As New newuser
Dim t As New deleteuser
Dim u As New viewusers

Private Sub Form4_FromClosing (ByVal sender As Object, ByVal e As System.
    Windows.froms.FormClosingEventArgs) Handles Me. FormClosing
If MsgBox("Do you want to exit", MsgBoxStyle.YesNo, "Exit") =
MsgBoxresult.No Then
    e.Cancel = True
Else
    End
End If
End Sub

Private Sub NewRegistration ToolStripmenultem_Click(ByVal sender As
    System.Object, ByVal e As System.EventArgs) Handles NewRegistration
    ToolStripmenultem.Click
    If x = 1 Then
        Dim gnewregistration As New newregistration
    gnewergistration.MdiParent = Me
    gnewregistration.Show()
    'a.Show()
    'a.Focus()
ElseIf x = 2 Then
    MessageBox.Show("Access Denied", "Error!", MessageBoxButtons. OK
        MessageBoxIcon.Error)
    End If
End Sub

Private Sub ChangePasswordToolStripMenultem_Click(ByVal sender As
    System.Object, ByVal e as System.EventArgs) Handles
```

```
    changepasswordToolStripMenuItem.Click
    If x = 1 Then
        Dim gchangepswd As New changepswd
        gchangepswd.MdiParent= Me
gcnangepswd.Show()
ElseIf x = 2 Then
MessageBox.Show("Access Denied", "Error!", MessageBoxButtons.OK,
    MessageBoxIcon.Error)
    End If
End Sub

Private Sub  AddCompanyToolStripMenuItem_Click(ByVal sender As
    System.Object, ByVal e As System.EventArgs) Handles
    AddCompanyToolStripMenuItem.Click
    If x = 1 Then
        Dim gaddcomp As New addcomp
    gaddcomp.MdiParent = Me
    gaddcomp.Show()
ElseIf x = 2 Then
    MessageBox.Show("Access Denid", "Error!", MessageBoxButtons.OK,
        MessageBoxIcon.Error)
    End If
End Sub,

Private Sub ViewCompanyToolStripMencuItem_Click(ByVal sender As
    System.Object, ByVal e As System.EventArgs) Handles
    ViewCompanyToolStripMenuItem.Click
    'Dim d As New viewcomp(x)
    Dim gviewcomp As New viewcomp
    gviewcomp.MdiParent = Me
    gviewcomp.Show()
End Sub
End

Private Sub RollNumber ToolStripMenuItem_Click(ByVal sender As Syste.Object,
    ByVal e As System.EventArgs) Handles RollNumberToolStripMenuItem.
        Click
    Dim gsearchroll As New searchroll
    gserachroll.MdiParent = Me
    gsearchroll.Show()
End Sub

Private Sub NameToolStripMenuItem_Click(ByVal sender/As System.n.Object,
```

```
        ByVal e As System.EvantArgs) Handles NameToolStripMenultem.Click
        Dim gsearchname As New searchname
        gsearchname.MdiParent = Me
        gsearchname.Show()
    End Sub

    Private Sub BranchToolStripMenultem_Click(ByVal sender As System.Object,
        ByVal e As System.EventArgs) Handles
BranchToolStripMenultem1.Click
        Dim gsearchbranch As New searchbranch
        gsearchbranch. MdiParent = Me
        gsearchbranch.Show()
    End Sub

    Private Sub BatchToolStripMenultem_Click(ByVal sender As System.Object,
ByVal       e As System.EventArgs) Handles BatchToolStripMenultem.Click
        Dim gsearchbatch As New searchbatch    gsearchbatch. Mdiparent = Me
        gsearchbatch.Show()
        End Sub

    Private Sub ToolStripMenulteml_Click(ByVal Sender As System.Object, ByVal e
        As System.EventArgs) Handles ToolStripMenulteml.Click
        Dimgsearchcompid As New searchcompid
        gsearchcompid.Mdiparent = Me
        gsearchcompid. Show()
    End Sub

    Private Sub CompanyNameToolStripMenulteml_Click(ByVal sender As
            System.Object, ByVal e As System.EventArgs) Handles CompanyName
            ToolStripmenulteml.Click
        Dim gsearchcomp As New searchcomp
        gsearchcomp.MdiParent= Me
        gsearchcomp.Show()
        End Sub

    Private Sub RToolStripMenultem_Click(ByVal sender As System.Object, ByVale
        As System.EventArgs) Handles RToolStripMenultem. Click
        Dim gsearchbatch As New searchbatch
        gsearchbatch.MdiParent= Me
        gserachbatch.Show()
    End Sub

    Private Sub BatchToolStripMenulteml_Click(ByVal sender As System.Object,
```

```
ByVal e As System.EventArgs) Handles BatchToolStripMenuIteml.Click
    Dim gsearchbranch As New searchbranch
    gsearchbranch.MdiParent=Me
    gsearchbranch.Show()
End Sub

Private Sub Batch ToolStripMenuItem2_Click(ByVal sender As System.Object,
        ByVal e As System.Event Args) Handles BatchToolStripMenuItem2.Click
    Dim gserarchbatch As New searchbatch
    gsearchbatch.MdiParent= Me
    gsearchbatch.Show()
End Sub

Private Sub branchToolStripMenuItem2_Click(ByVal sender As System.Object,
    ByVal e As System.EventArge) HandlesToolStripMenuItem2.Click
    Dim gsearchbranch As New searchbranch
    gsearchbranch.MdiParent = Me
    gsearchbranch.Show()
End Sub

Private Sub CompanyCriteriaToolStripMenuItem_Click(ByVal sender As
    System.Object, By Val e As System.EventArgs) Handles
        CompanyCriteriaToolStripenuItem. Click
    Dim gsearchcriteria.MdiParent = Me
    gsearchcriteria.Show()
    End Sub

Private Sub BranchToolStripmenuItem_Click_1(ByVal sender As System.Object,
    ByVal As System.EventArgs) Handles BrachToolStripMenuItem.Click
    BranchReport.Show()
End Sub

Private Sub Batch ToolStripMenuItem3_Click(ByVal sender As System.Object,
    ByVal e As System.EventArgs) Handles Batch Tool StripMenuItem3.Click
    BatchReport.Show()
En Sub

Private Sub  ToolStripMenuItem3_Click(ByVal sender As System.Object, ByVal
    e As System.EventArgs) Handles ToolStripMenuItem3.Click
    TrainingReport.Show()
End Sub

Private Sub Introduction To TPCToolStripMenuItem_Click(ByVal sender As
```

```
        System.Object, ByVal e As System.EventArgs) Handles Introduction
        ToTPCToolStripMenuItem.Click
  'Private Sub MnuAddCompany_Click(ByVal sender As System.Object, ByVal e
      As System.EventArgs)Handles mnuAddCompany.Click
      Dim gintrotpc As New introtpc
      gintrotpc. MdiParent = Me
      gintrotpc.Show()
      'End Sub
      'q.Show()
      'q.Focus()
  End Sub

  Private Sub Credits ToolStripMenuItem_Click(ByVal sender As System.Object,
      ByVal e As System.EventArgs) Handles Credits ToolStripMenuItem.Click
      Dim gcredits As New credits
      gcredits.MdiParent = Me
      gcredits.Show()
      'r.Show()\
      'r.Focus()
  End Sub

  Private Sub LogOutToolStripMenuItem_Click(ByVal sender As System.Object,
      ByVal As System.EventArgs)
      Dim s As New logintype
      s.Show()
      Me.Hide()
  End Sub

  Private Sub ExitToolStripMenuItem_Click(ByVal sender As System.Object, ByVal
      e As System.EventArgs)
  If MessageBox.Show("Do you really want to quit".,
        "Exit!",messagBoxButtons.YesN0) = Windows. Forms.DialogResult.Yes
Then
      End
  Else
      Exit Sub
  End If
  End
  End Sub

    Private Sub PlacementDetailsToolStripMenuItem_Click(ByVal sender As
        System.Object, ByVal e As System.EventArgs) Handles
        PlacementDetailsToolStripMenuItem.Click
```

```
        PlacementReport.Show()
    End Sub
Private Sub mainmenu_Load(ByVal sender As System.Object, ByVal e As
    System.EventArgs) Handles MyBase.Load
End Sub

Private Sub CompanyCriteriaDetailsToolStripMenultem_Click(By Val sender As
    System.Object, ByVal e As System.EventArgs) Handles
    CompanyCriteriaDetails ToolStripMenultem.Click
    Company Report.Show()
End Sub

Private Sub CreateNewUserToolStripMenultem_Click(ByVal sender As
    System.Object, ByVal e As System.EventArgs) Handles CreateNew
    UserStripMenultem.Click
    If x = 1 Then
If MessageBox.Show("Do you want to create new user?", "New
    User",MessageBoxButtons.You Then MessageBoxIcon.Asterisk) =
    Windows.Froms.DialogResult.Yes Then
    Dimgnewuser As Now newuser
    gnewuser.MdiParent = Me
    gnewuser.Show()
    End If
ElseIf x = 2 Then
    MessageBox.Show("Access Denied", "Error!", MessageBoxButtons.OK,
MessageBoxIcon.Error)
    End If
End Sub
```

APPENDIX–F

BIBLIOGRAPHY

BIBLIOGRAPHY

1. Korth F. Henry, Silberschatz Abraham, Sudarshan S., "Database System Concepts", McGraw-Hill International Edition, 2006.
2. Elmasri Ramez, Navathe B. Shamkant, "Fundamentals of Database Systems", Pearson Education Asia, 2006.
3. Connolly Thomas, Bregg Carolyn, "Database Systems", Pearson Education Asia. 2008.
4. Ullman D. Jeffrey, "Principles of Database Systems", Galgotia Publications, 2004.
5. Majumdar K. Arun, "Database Management Systems", TMH, 2006.
6. Panneerselvam R, "Database Management Systems", PHI, 2002.
7. Ceri Stefano, Pelagatti Giuseppe, "Distributed Database", TMH, 1985.
8. Lum Y. Vincent and Ghosh P. Sakti, "Database Management System", IBM Research Laboratory.
9. Singh S.K., "Database Systems", Pearson Education, Asia, 2006.
10. Desai, Bipin C., "An Introduction to DBMS", Galgotia Publications Pvt. Ltd., 2003.
11. Date, C.J., "An Introduction to DBMS", Addison-Wesly, 2000.
12. Bayross Ivan, "Professional Oracle Project", BPB Publications, 2004.
13. Websites: (*a*) www.google.com, (*b*) www.altavista.com.